Governing in Black Africa

PERSPECTIVES ON NEW STATES

MARION E. DORO, Connecticut College

NEWELL M. STULTZ, Brown University

Editors

PRENTICE-HALL INC., Englewood Cliffs, New Jersey

13-360586-8
13-360594-9

Library of Congress Catalog Card Number: 70-110492

Current Printing (last digit):
10 9 8 7 6 5 4 3 2 1

PRINTED IN THE UNITED STATES OF AMERICA

Prentice-Hall International, Inc., London
Prentice-Hall of Australia, Pty. Ltd., Sydney
Prentice-Hall of Canada, Ltd., Toronto
Prentice-Hall of India Private Limited, New Delhi
Prentice-Hall of Japan, Inc., Tokyo

Preface

Like Pliny some two thousand years ago, it seem possible to say *ex Africa semper aliquid novi*—out of Africa, always something new. The essence of this thought is reflected in the fact that since the end of World War II, thirty-eight states have achieved independence, and nearly half of these have subsequently experienced military coups d'etat. These new African states are also undergoing the less sensational but perhaps more significant economic and social changes that accompany their efforts to cope with the problems of economic development, poverty, and national integration. Concurrent with these important changes, an increasingly sizeable and persistent group of Africanists has conscientiously sought to record and analyze the political dimensions of the rapidly shifting African scene. The result has been an extraordinary increase in the number of published studies on Africa since 1958. Those of us who teach African politics often feel like the Red Queen in *Through the Looking Glass*—the effort to remain *au courant* requires all the running we can do just to keep in the same place.

It is often difficult to scan the dynamic changes taking place in Africa or grasp their implications for the future; nevertheless, it is possible to capture a cross section of this kaleidoscopic scene and depict the direction of these changes. The purpose of this collection is to emphasize two major trends of current research on African affairs: the shift of focus from issues of colonialism and pre-independence nationalism to the contemporary and developmental character of politics in independent states; and the application of recent advances in social science methodology to African research. Within this framework of contemporary politics and applied methodology we have attempted to create a balanced selection of the significant issues in African politics, and to offer a representative geographic coverage. Because our concern is with the newly independent black African states we have excluded the North African countries, the Republic of South Africa, and the seven dependencies which remain under colonial control. There are areas of omission, however, in terms of both the topics included and the countries represented. In some instances we plead limitations of space and refer the reader to the selected bibliography and to the footnotes in the selections for related materials. In other cases, however, what appear to be omissions are *lacunae* in research. As we culled articles from more than a decade of several dozen journals we discovered that substantial work has been done on seven or eight countries while others have been neglected. Moreover, we also found that a variety of topics have been overlooked. While there is much material on legislatures, there is relatively little on executives; political parties have been studied in depth, but voluntary associations have scarcely been touched;

similarly, local government and micro-politics have only recently become a subject of scholarly attention.

Various caveats are in order, but we limit ourselves to a cautionary theme which echoes between several of the contributors. Aristide Zolberg states this reservation for us in his disarmingly frank and concise remarks about his book *Creating Political Order:* "Very little of what has been stated here can be asserted with the degree of certainty that is required in an established area of scholarship. The data are grossly incomplete and the interpretations are tentative." Perhaps this overstates the warning and overrates the quest for certitude at a time when the need for political decisions is always imminent. We are in a field of recent vintage, in which we can count but two generations of Africanists. In view of the brief existence of this academic specialization, the literature is rich in substantive and speculative work despite the uneven topical distribution of research and the continuing paucity of information in some areas.

Our purpose is not to promote any particular view about African politics but to present evidence which is relevent to contemporary Africa as a supplement to the materials that Africanists ingeniously gather for their courses. We suspect that instructors will construct other patterns of organization with the articles in this volume—even the two of us have sometimes disagreed on the "best" selections, or the categories in which they belong. But we share a confidence that we offer a collection which partakes of a growing tradition of excellence in African studies.

We with to thank our contributors, and their publishers, for their permissions to reprint. Marion Doro gratefully acknowledges the assistance and encouragement of the Radcliffe Institute where she did much of her share of the work. Naturally, errors, omissions, and misinterpretations in our contributions as editors are our own responsibility and we take pleasure in accepting it equally.

MARION E. DORO
Connecticut College
NEWELL M. STULTZ
Brown University

Contents

TUNISIA

MOROCCO

ALGERIA

LIBYA

UNITED
ARAB
REPUBLIC

SPANISH
SAHARA

MAURITANIA

MALI

NIGER

CHAD

SUDAN

E.T.A.I.

GAMBIA
SENEGAL
PORT.
GUINEA

GUINEA

UPPER VOLTA

DAHOMEY
TOGO

ETHIOPIA

SOMALIA

SIERRA LEONE

IVORY
COAST
GHANA

NIGERIA

CENTRAL
AFRICAN REPUBLIC

LIBERIA

CAMEROON

FERNANDO PO

EQUATORIAL
GUINEA

PRÍNCIPE
(Port.)
SÃO TOMÉ
(Port.)
ANNOBÓN

RIO MUNI

CONGO

GABON

DEMOCRATIC
REPUBLIC
OF THE
CONGO

UGANDA

KENYA

RWANDA

BURUNDI

TANZANIA

PEMBA
ZANZIBAR

Old States

Independent 1951-59

Independent 1960

Independent 1961-68

Non-independent Entities

BOUNDARY REPRESENTATION IS
NOT NECESSARILY AUTHORITATIVE

0   500   1000 MILES
0   500   1000 KILOMETERS

ANGOLA
(Port.)

ZAMBIA

MALAWI

MOZAMBIQUE
(Port.)

SOUTH-WEST
AFRICA
(International
Territory)

SOUTHERN
RHODESIA
(U.K.)

BOTSWANA

WALVIS BAY
(Rep. of S. Af.)

SWAZILAND

LESOTHO

REPUBLIC
OF
SOUTH AFRICA

Introduction

In the last decade the use of the "systems approach" as a framework for political analysis has increasingly supplemented—if not supplanted —the traditional approach to the study of politics. Although the systems approach originated in the study of American politics and was later extended to comparative European studies, it has become especially important in the analysis of politics of *new* or *emerging* states. It is doubtful that a political scientist today in any branch of the discipline can afford to ignore either this method or the works of theorists now most closely identified with it—men such as David Easton, Gabriel Almond, and David Apter.[1] Indeed, reviewing Easton's *A Systems Analysis of Political Life,* Professor Bertram Gross predicted that "a scholar's ability to use Easton's ideas . . . (together with an awareness of their limitations) will probably become an 'acid test' differentiating between those engaged on the frontiers of creative political research and theory and the 'obsolescents.' "[2]

Yet, as Gross implies, the systems approach in political science is not free from criticism. Critics particularly object to what they consider an implicit and improper analogy between politics and mechanical or biological systems. Others charge that systems analysts unwar-

[1] For the best examples, see David Easton, *A Systems Analysis of Political Life* (New York: John Wiley and Sons, 1965); Gabriel A. Almond and G. Bingham Powell, Jr., *Comparative Politics: A Developmental Approach* (Boston: Little, Brown and Co., 1966); and David E. Apter, *The Politics of Modernization* (Chicago: University of Chicago Press, 1965).

[2] Bertram Gross, *The American Political Science Review,* XI, No. 1 (March 1967), 157.

rantedly assume an equilibrium or harmony among the various elements of the political system, and that this supposition is not only wrong but also produces a conservative bias in their work. These and other criticisms are serious and point to weaknesses in the technique; but even the most fervent critics of the *theoretical* utility of systems analysis in political science acknowledge that the classification schemes these theorists have established are useful in ordering comparative political data. Even if Easton, Almond, Apter, and others have not yet offered an unassailable general theory of politics—and they have not pretended to—they have at least identified an impressive number of significant variables that any such theory must take into account, and tentatively suggested some general relationships that are likely to occur among these variables.

One of the attractions of analyzing political phenomena from the standpoint of systems analysis is that the conceptual structure itself is easily understood. The existence of a *political* system is postulated distinct from the social, economic, and other systems which make up the "environment" of the political system. The distinctive feature of the political system is that it makes binding decisions for society; in Easton's words, the political system is engaged in the "authoritative allocation of values." The system itself consists of all elements that bear significantly on the function of making binding decisions. These usually include the formal and familiar institutions of government—executives, legislatures, the courts, and bureaucracies—and also the informal structures—political parties, voluntary associations, and the communications media. Ultimately, the political system includes individuals in their capacities as political actors, as, for example, citizens who vote in elections and pay their taxes, and such agencies as schools, churches, and even the family as they influence individual political behavior. Within this context, the analyst assumes that all the elements of the political system interact; thus when the properties of one element in the system are changed, all other elements are somehow affected. Indeed, the assertion of the interdependence of political variables is one of the most profound contributions of systems analysis—one that makes it exceedingly difficult to theorize about the system as a whole.

The central question for political analysis suggested by the systems approach is: How do political systems persist over time in their capacity to make binding decisions for society? Here one must distinguish between the *desire* of citizens for the survival of their political system and the *capacity* of a system to continue to perform effectively: political systems can lose their effectiveness and ultimately decline into anarchy, oblivion, or defeat. In Africa in recent years both the Mali Federation and the Central African Federation failed to persist;

numerous other examples might be cited in different parts of the world. In fact, if all political systems survived despite any form of political behavior, the question of system persistence would be irrelevant. But some systems do fail while others are capable of sustaining themselves, and systems analysis seeks an explanation for this difference in performance.

Identification of persistence as the central concern of systems analysis directs attention to the needs of the system if its survival is to be assured. Briefly, these needs are twofold: the capability of *making* binding decisions, and the capacity of *implementing* them once they are made. Implementation, the critical consideration, depends upon the supports the system can muster, specifically the material supports it can tap (e.g., through taxes and the military service of citizens), and the willingness of citizens to obey and defer to its laws and regulations. One finds that political scientists frequently examine this aspect of the system through such questions as: What are the prerequisites for stability? Investigators have employed a wide range of variables— consensus, national loyalty, economic potential, education, cultural diversity—to analyze the capacity of political systems to persist. These studies indicate clearly that the resources available to political authorities are a crucial factor in system performance.

But supports cannot be considered independent of the claims people make regarding the product of the political process. The claims are termed "demands"; they are the appeals for *particular* binding decisions. A major significance of demands lies in their implicit relationship to future supports, for the systems approach assumes that citizens are ultimately utilitarian in their political orientation. On the whole, citizens render support to the political system—agree, for example, to obey laws—because they expect a personally acceptable or advantageous outcome. While the expectations of an African tribesman and an American suburbanite are quite different, both respond to their own perceptions of their needs and ambitions. Demands (and supports) originate in the extrapolitical or cultural environment, and their character is shaped by that environment. But should the political system fail to meet these demands, the support of the demand-makers diminishes. If that particular support is critical, and if its withdrawal continues and becomes widespread, the persistence of the political system may be jeopardized.

Thus, from the systems approach, politics is viewed as the process which *converts* demands (inputs) into binding decisions (outputs) in order to ensure future supports for the political system (inputs) of the kind needed for system persistence. This formulation is highly generalized; the systems approach has been elaborated in much greater detail by a number of theorists who have added a variety of concepts that identify important subprocesses of politics. These include "feedback," the information exchanges that tie the various elements of the political system together; "gatekeeping," structural control over the volume of demands entering the political system; plus such others as system "maintenance" and "adaption." It is not necessary to explore the ramifications of these concepts here, for the point we wish to make is that the *level* at which one defines the political system—i.e., the complexity of one's definition—is dependent upon the uses to which one wishes to put that definition. Our purpose in this volume is to identify a few topic headings that provide a sensible and orderly arrangement for the presentation of the studies that follow.

While the organization of this volume has been inspired by the systems approach to political analysis, it is essential to note that there is no *African* political system, or even one *type* of political system common to all or most African states. Indeed, Aristide Zolberg has recently challenged the assumption that the modern political processes with which Africanists are generally concerned, whatever their specific character, comprise the only system engaged in the authoritative allocation of values for African societies. Zolberg suggests that alongside the modern political systems in Africa, but independent of them, traditional political processes can be seen to function.[3] This is the idea of the "dual economy" transferred to the realm of politics. We have chosen the selections that appear in this collection because we believe they illustrate political processes that are typical in contemporary Africa. In fact, the contributors often generalize for more than one African country. But while this volume serves to illuminate and identify recurring features of African politics, the existence of many exceptional instances must be acknowledged at the outset. The patterns of politics that emerge in these studies do not all appear in even one African country. We believe that they do appear sufficiently frequently in present-day Africa to justify their identification, but the individuality and unique character of each African state, even at the general level of the categories utilized here, cannot be seriously disputed.

The first three of the six units into which this volume is divided portray successive stages in the conversion process, from the formulation and articulation of demands through the production of public policies by the authoritative structures of government. But these stages not only define the flow of demands from the environment to the government, they are also distinct levels at which the development of support for the political system can likewise be considered, for in a

---

[3] Aristide R. Zolberg, *Creating Political Order: The Party-States of West Africa* (Chicago: Rand McNally and Co., 1966), pp. 128–34.

sense demand-making and support-building are reciprocal activities. It would be wrong, especially in the case of contemporary Africa, to identify the input structures of politics solely in terms of their contributions to the flow of political demands. Indeed, in many instances the support-building functions of such structures would seem to be more important.

Unit I treats the individual, the smallest element capable of political behavior, in African politics. What nonpolitical factors condition his perceptions of politics, affecting both the demands he makes upon the political system and the supports he is prepared to give to it? This unit reflects aspects of "political culture" in Africa, although clearly there is no one African political culture and no general treatment of such a topic is possible beyond the generalized sentiments of Africanism as shaped by diverse historical and contemporary forces.

Individuals seldom act alone in politics, however; they organize themselves—or are organized by others, i.e., "mobilized"—in order to maximize their influence. Functionally, groups in their political capacities "aggregate" interests, bringing together separate and individually articulated demands to create "issues" with which the structures of government can deal most effectively. In Africa the political party has been the most common and significant political organization in the recent past, and it is usually led by a single figure whom others believe to be gifted with "charisma." Parties and the charisma of their leadership mobilized Africans *against* the political system during the terminal stages of colonialism. Since independence they have less frequently been a source of demands upon the political system than an agency intended to build support *for* the regime, although increasing doubt is being cast upon the adequacy of the performance of African parties in either function. Unit II considers several means whereby Africans are mobilized for political purposes.

The agencies of government are the final destination of the flow of both demands and supports into the political system, because these are the structures that have the legal power to make binding decisions for society. Thus, the operation and comparative importance of governmental structures is treated next as the subject of Unit III.

Having sketched the processes whereby inputs to the political system are converted to political outputs, the three concluding units consider specific policy areas. As noted earlier, the importance of political outputs lies in their consequences for the maintenance and generation of support for the political system. In this regard, the needs and capacities of individual African countries vary in both degree and detail. Yet the first business of nearly all African political systems is order, stability, and national unity. Essentially, this is a matter of creating and maintaining the "integration" of African societies. Only slightly less important is the development and modernization of these societies. The role, problems, and success of government and politics in both these areas are dealt with in Units IV and V, respectively.

Finally, Unit VI offers examples of African external relations. This is both a necessary and a separable subject area, for here the potentialities for demands upon the political system and supports for it arise in part in the extrasocietal international environment, although African external relations are frequently related to attempts to meet the twin domestic needs of stability and modernization. Indeed, the foreign policies of African states often reflect the internal successes of their politics as well as the uniqueness of the combination of external pressures that influence their individual governments.

1

Determinants of Political Behavior

Politics is ultimately the political behavior—albeit frequently the collective political behavior—of individuals. The individual is not only the smallest unit of political analysis, he is, in a sense, the *only* unit. Why individuals behave as they do politically is thus a central question for political scientists, as it has been for both philosophers and pragmatists from time immemorial.

One finds a variety of methods of inquiry that link the nature of man and his political behavior. For example, the Marxist approach, based on a class analysis of politics, presumes that man is primarily concerned with material self-interest, and that people act in a manner designed to maximize their economic and social position. Another approach examines the significance of the "role" of individuals by analyzing how a person's perceptions of his place in the political process affect his role performance. How, for example, does a legislator's conception of his position affect his performance as a legislator?

A third approach turns on the relationships between personality and political behavior. It may be said that individual personality develops out of two sources: (*1*) its organic foundations, that is, reflexes, intelligence, drives, and so on; and (*2*) its cultural context. When contrasting large groups of people, or whole populations (e.g., Ghanaians and Frenchmen), one can assume that the organic foundations of personality are similar and provide no explanation of differences in political behavior. Such explanations are possible only in the analysis of the behavior of specific individuals, as attempted in Sigmund Freud and William C. Bullitt's recently published study of President Woodrow Wilson.[1] Differences of personality and political behavior between large groups of people must be attributed to cultural variables, which may also be used as an analytic tool to explore the behavior of individual leaders.

In fact, social scientists have devoted considerable energy to identifying the environmentally rooted personality traits that are relevant to political behavior. The sum of these characteristics has been conceptualized as "political culture," which Lucian Pye defines as "the set of attitudes, beliefs, and sentiments that give order and meaning to a political process and that provide the underlying assumptions and rules that govern behavior in the political system."[2] During the past decade, political scientists have given increasing attention to the question of political culture in North America and Western Europe. In large measure this work is motivated by an interest in the distinctive psychological attributes of publics in stable democracies, characteristics summarized under the rubric "civic culture."[3] By comparison, however, little work has been done on the political cultures of non-Western countries, or on the process of "political socialization" through which a political culture is created, maintained, or transformed.

According to Pye, "political culture is the product of both the collective history of a political system and the life histories of the members of that system."[4] As a major social institution throughout Africa, tribalism affects the life histories and political styles of most Africans. Tribes may differ with respect to their internal structures and values, and as David Apter has shown, these differences can be important in explaining differences in political behavior as, for example, in adapting to the modernization process.[5] On the other hand, it may also be said that tribalism in Africa tends to promote common orientations which govern the choices that individuals make. Discussed in terms of Talcott Parsons' well-known "pattern variables," these orientations may be said to include: (a) collectivism rather than individualism; (b) a concern with objects less in terms of their universal attributes than in terms of their particular relationship with self or group; (c) deference to the ascribed rather than to the objective or performance qualities

---

[1] Sigmund Freud and William C. Bullitt, *Thomas Woodrow Wilson: A Psychological Study* (Boston: Houghton Mifflin, 1967).

[2] Lucian W. Pye, *Aspects of Political Development* (Boston: Little, Brown and Co., 1966), p. 104.

[3] See Gabriel A. Almond and Sidney Verba, *The Civic Culture: Political Attitudes and Democracy in Five Nations* (Boston: Little, Brown and Co., 1965).

[4] Pye, *op. cit.,* p. 105.

[5] David E. Apter, "The Role of Traditionalism in the Political Modernization of Ghana and Uganda," *World Politics,* XIII, No. 1 (October 1960), 45–68.

of objects; and (*d*) involvement with objects that is general and diffuse rather-than limited and specific. Translated into contemporary political practices, these orientations suggest cultural explanations for nepotism and corruption in African politics, adherence to charismatic leadership, and undifferentiated political loyalties. If tradition in Africa required giving gifts to those in authority, then the processes of modernity may well entail the giving and taking of bribes; if the primordial political structure provided no device for decision-making by counting heads, the role of the loyal opposition may be difficult to establish; and if tribal authority was structurally or functionally undifferentiated, then it may not matter whether civilian or military leaders command ultimate authority.

Yet any attempt to evaluate political culture in Africa must account as well for modern influences on political life, such as tensions between intellectuals and the uneducated, urbanization and pressures for economic development, and the differential effects of colonialism. James Coleman and Carl Rosberg, for example, have identified *elitism* (the belief that in a population of illiterates the educated have a special role to play) and *statism* (acceptance of the primacy of the state in the process of modernization) as attitudes common to most of the new African leaders.[6] And similarly, Edward Shils, having reviewed both modern and traditional determinants of African political behavior, has concluded that such a combination of factors in Africa today almost inevitably results in an oligarchic form of democracy.[7]

However, these conclusions are dangerous, if they are over-generalized. The available evidence on the subjective dimensions of African politics is not only incomplete but frequently it only reflects the orientations of specific groups within the political community. J. P. Nettl has written that "a political culture may be said to exist when political authority, and the processes relating to that authority, are effectively internalized by members of the society."[8] But by this standard we are compelled to agree with Richard Dawson and Kenneth Prewitt that African states lack "a general, systematic pattern of political norms which can be adopted by the average citizen."[9] Indeed, notwithstanding those characteristics subsumed under the heading "African Personality," each African state is still in the process of *creating* its own national political culture out of its unique combination of *sub-*

6 James S. Coleman and Carl G. Rosberg, Jr. (eds.), *Political Parties and National Integration in Tropical Africa* (Berkeley and Los Angeles: University of California Press, 1964), pp. 662–63.

7 Edward Shils, *Political Development in the New States* (The Hague: Mouton and Co., 1962), pp. 86–91.

8 J. P. Nettl, *Political Mobilization* (New York: Basic Books, 1967), p. 57.

9 Richard E. Dawson and Kenneth Prewitt, *Political Socialization* (Boston: Little, Brown and Co., 1969), p. 35.

cultures, needs, and circumstances. Nevertheless, this process in itself offers insights into current political behavior in Africa, for it can be argued that the fragmented or incipient character of African political cultures is one explanation of the confusion, insecurity, and fluctuations that characterize contemporary politics in many of these new states.

Ethnicity and National Integration in West Africa

I. Wallerstein

Many writers on West Africa, whether academic or popular, assert that there is currently a conflict between tribalism and nationalism which threatens the stability of the new West African nations. In fact, the relationship between tribalism and nationalism is complex. Although ethnicity (tribalism) is in some respects dysfunctional for national integration (a prime objective of nationalist movements), it is also in some respects functional. Discussion of the presumed conflict might be clarified by discussing this hypothesis in some detail. Before doing so, it should be noted that we deliberately use the term ethnicity in preference to tribalism, and we shall preface our remarks by carefully defining our use of the term ethnicity.

In a traditional, rural setting, an individual is a member first of all of a family and then of a tribe.[1] The demands the tribe makes on him vary with the complexity of the tribal system of government,[2] as does the degree to which family and tribal loyalties are

distinct. To a large extent, however, family and tribal loyalties support each other harmoniously.

Under colonial rule, the social change brought about by European administrators and the process of urbanization has led to widespread shifts of loyalty. This process has been called "detribalization." Writers speaking of tribal loyalty often confuse three separate phenomena which it would be useful to distinguish: loyalty to the family; loyalty to the tribal community; and loyalty to the tribal government, or chief.[3] Often what a writer means by detribalization is simply a decline in chiefly authority. It does not necessarily follow that an individual who is no longer loyal to his chief has rejected as well the tribe as a community to which he owes certain

---

[1] A tribe is what Murdock calls a community, and he notes: "The community and the nuclear family are the only social groups that are genuinely universal. They occur in every known human society..." (G. Murdock, *Social Structure*, New York, Macmillan, 1949, p. 79.)

[2] Statements on the typologies of tribal organizations in Africa are to be found in: M. Fortes and E. Evans-Pritchard, ed., *African Political Systems*, Oxford, 1940;—J. Middleton and D. Tait, *Tribes without Rulers*, London, 1958;—D. Forde, "The Conditions of Social Development in West Africa," in *Civilisations*, III, No. 4, 1953, pp. 472–476.

[3] We shall not discuss further the role of the family in West Africa today. We note here that it would be an oversimplification to suggest that family ties have drastically declined in the urban areas. In any case, the strength of family ties can vary independently of the strength of tribal ties.

From *Cahiers d'Etudes Africaines*, Vol. I, No. 3 (1960), 129–139, by permission of author and journal.

duties and from which he expects a certain security.[4]

It may be objected that West Africans do not make a distinction between the tribal government and the tribal community. This is perhaps true in the rural areas but they do when they reach the city. For in the city they find that there are new sources of power and prestige which, for many persons, are more rewarding than the tribal government. Hence they tend to lose some of their respect for the authority of the chief. The tribe, however, still can play a useful, if partially new, function as an ethnic group. The *Gemeinschaft*-like community to which the individual belongs may no longer be exactly the same group as before; the methods of government are different; the role in the national social structure is different. This community, however, bears sufficient resemblance to the rural, traditional "tribe" that often the same term is used. In this discussion, however, we shall use "tribe" for the group in the rural areas, and ethnic group for the one in the towns.

Some writers have challenged the very existence of detribalization. Rouch, for example, says he finds instead "super-tribalization" among the Zabrama and other immigrants to Ghana.[5] For as Mitchell has commented of another part of Africa: "People in rural areas are apt to take their tribe for granted, but when they come to the town their tribal membership assumes new importance."[6] This is, however, a false debate. We shall see that quite often the group from which the individual is "detribalized" (that is, the tribe to whose chief he no longer pays the same fealty) is not necessarily the same group into which he is "supertribalized" (that is, the ethnic group to which he feels strong bonds of attachment in the urban context).

Membership in an ethnic group is a matter of social definition, an interplay of the self-definition of members and the definition of other groups. The ethnic group seems to need a minimum size to function effectively, and hence to achieve social definition.[7] Now it may be that an individual who defined himself as being of a certain tribe in a rural area can find no others from his village in the city. He may simply redefine himself as a member of a new and larger group.[8] This group would normally correspond to some logical geographical or linguistic unit, but it may never have existed as a social entity before this act. Indeed, this kind of redefinition is

---

[4] There are, to be sure, cases where the two loyalties decline together, and there is consequently severe anomy. Failure to distinguish this case from one in which primarily loyalty to the chief alone diminishes can result in much confusion. See this comment by Mercier in which he tries to clarify this confusion: "C'est dans cette minorité [la population saisonnière] que l'on peut parler réellement de faits de *détribalisation*, au sens de pure dégradation du rôle des anciens cadres sociaux. Au contraire, nous avons vu que, dans la population permanente, *les structures de parenté et l'appartenance ethnique* jouaient un rôle considérable." (P. Mercier, "Aspects de la société africaine dans l'agglomération dakaroise: groupes familiaux et unités de voisinage," p. 39, in P. Mercier et al., "L'Agglomération Dakaroise," in *Études sénégalaises*, No. 5, 1954.)

[5] J. Rouch, "Migrations au Ghana," in *Journal de la Société des Africanistes* XXVI, No. 1/2, 1956, pp. 163–164.

[6] J. C. Mitchell, "Africans in Industrial Towns in Northern Rhodesia," in *H.R.H. The Duke of Edinburgh's Study Conference*, No. 1, p. 5.

[7] Mercier observes: "Il faut noter également que, moins un groupe ethnique est numériquement important dans la ville, plus la simple parenté tend à jouer le rôle de liens de parenté plus proches." (*Op. cit.*, p. 22.)

[8] In Dakar, Mercier notes: "Un certain nombre de personnes qui étaient manifestement d'origine Lébou. . . se déclaraient cependant Wolof, preuve de la crise de l'ancien particularisme Lébou." (*Op. cit.*, p. 17.)

quite common. Two actions give such redefinition permanence and status. One is official government sanction, in the form of census categories,[9] or the recognition of "town chiefs"; the other is the formation of ethnic (tribal) associations which are described more accurately by the French term, *association d'originaires*. These associations are the principal form of ethnic (tribal) "government"[10] in West African towns today.

Some of these ethnic associations use clearly territorial bases of defining membership, despite the fact that they may consider their relationship with traditional chiefs as their *raison d'être*. For example, in the Ivory Coast, Amon d'Aby has described the process as follows:

L'un des phénomènes les plus curieux enregistrés en Côte d'Ivoire au lendemain de la Libération est la tendance très marquée des élites autochtones vers la création d'associations régionales. . .

Ces associations groupent tous les habitants d'un cercle ou de plusieurs cercles réunis. Leur objet est non plus le sport et les récréations de toutes sortes comme les groupements anodins d'avant-guerre, mais le progrès du territoire de leur ressort. Elles ont le but d'apporter la collaboration des jeunes générations instruites aux vieilles générations représentées par les chefs coutumiers accrochés aux conceptions périmés, à une politique surannée.[11]

It should be observed that the administrative units in question (les cercles) are the creation of the colonial government, and have no necessary relationship to traditional groupings. Such ethnic associations, formed around non-traditional administrative units, are found throughout West Africa.[12] A presumably classic example of the significance of tribalism in West African affairs is the role which traditional Yoruba-Ibo rivalry has played in Nigeria politics. Yet, Dr. S. O. Biobaku has pointed out that the very use of the term "Yoruba" to refer to various peoples in Western Nigeria resulted largely from the influence of the Anglican mission in Abeokuta in the 19th century. The standard "Yoruba" lan-

---

[9] For example, G. Lasserre writes: "L'habitude est prise à Libreville de recenser ensemble Togolais et Dahoméens sous l'appellation de 'Popo.' " (*Libreville*, Paris, Armand Colin, 1958, p. 207.)
Epstein notes a similar phenomenon in the Northern Rhodesian Copperbelt towns, where one of the major ethnic groups, sanctioned by custom and by census, is the Nyasalanders. Nyasaland is a British-created territorial unit, but people from the Henga, Tonga, Tumbuka, and other tribes are by common consent grouped together as Nyasalanders. (A.L. Epstein, *Politics in an Urban African Community*, Manchester, Manchester University Press, 1958, p. 236.)

[10] By government we mean here the mechanism whereby the norms and goals of the group are defined. There may or may not be an effective, formal structure to enforce these norms.

[11] F. Amon d'Aby, *La Côte d'Ivoire dans la cité africaine*, Paris, Larose, 1952, p. 36.

[12] Similar phenomena were reported in other areas undergoing rapid social change. Lewis reports the growth in Somalia of a "tribalism founded on territorial ties [in] place of clanship," at least among the southern groups (I. M. Lewis, "Modern Political Movements in Somaliland, I," in *Africa*, XXVIII, July 1958, p. 259). In the South Pacific, Mead observes: "Commentators on native life shook their heads, remarking that these natives were quite incapable of ever organizing beyond the narrowest tribal borders, overlooking the fact that terms like 'Solomons,' 'Sepiks' or 'Manus,' when applied in Rabaul, blanketed many tribal differences." (M. Mead, *New Lives for Old*, New York, Morrow, 1956, p. 79).
The article by Max Gluckman, which appeared since this paper was delivered, makes the same point for British Central Africa. Cf. "Tribalism in British Central Africa," in *Cahiers d'Études Africaines*, I, janv. 1960, pp. 55–70.

guage evolved by the mission was the new unifying factor. Hodgkin remarks:

Everyone recognizes that the notion of 'being a Nigerian' is a new kind of conception. But it would seem that the notion of 'being a Yoruba' is not very much older.[13]

Sometimes, the definition of the ethnic group may even be said to derive from a common occupation—indeed, even dress—rather than from a common language or traditional polity. For example, an Accra man often tends to designate all men (or at least all merchants) coming from savannah areas as "Hausamen," although many are not Hausa, as defined in traditional Hausa areas.[14] Similarly, the Abidjan resident may designate these same men as Dioula.[15] Such designations may originate in error, but many individuals from savannah areas take advantage of this confusion to merge themselves into this grouping. They go, for example to live in the *Sabon Zongo* (the Hausa residential area), and even often adopt Islam, to aid the assimilation.[16] They do so because, scorned by the dominant ethnic group of the town, they find security within a relatively stronger group (Hausa in Accra, Dioula in Abidjan, Bambara in Thiès), with whom they

feel some broad cultural affinity. Indeed, assimilation to this stronger group may represent considerable advance in the prestige-scale for the individual.[17]

Thus we see that ethnic groups are defined in terms that are not necessarily traditional but are rather a function of the urban social situation. By ethnicity, we mean the feeling of loyalty to this new ethnic group of the towns. Epstein has urged us to distinguish between two senses of what he calls "tribalism": the intratribal, which is the "persistence of, or continued attachment to, tribal custom," and tribalism within the social structure, which is the "persistence of loyalties and values, which stem from a particular form of social organization."[18] This corresponds to the distinction we made above between loyalty to tribal government and loyalty to the tribal community. In using the term ethnicity, we are referring to this latter kind of loyalty. This distinction cannot be rigid. Individuals in West Africa move back and forth between city and rural area. Different loyalties may be activated in different contexts. But more and more, with increasing urbanization, loyalty to the ethnic community is coming to supersede loyalty to the tribal community and government. It is the relationship of this new ethnic loyalty to the emergent nation-state that we intend to explore here.

* * *

---

[13] T. Hodgkin, "Letter to Dr. Biobaku," in *Odù*, No. 4, 1957, p. 42.

[14] Rouch, *op. cit.*, p. 59.

[15] A. Kobben, "Le planteur noir," *Études éburnéennes*, V, 1956, p. 154.

[16] The religious conversion is often very temporary. N'Goma observes: "L'Islam résiste mal à la transplantation des familles musulmanes de la ville à la campagne. On a remarqué que le citadin qui retourne à son groupement d'origine revient souvent au culte de la terre et des Esprits ancestraux." (A. N'Goma, "L'Islam noir," in T. Monod, ed., *Le Monde noir*, Présence africaine, No. 8–9, p. 342.) The motive for the original conversion may in part explain this rapid reconversion.

[17] G. Savonnet observes in Thiès, Sénégal: "Le nom de Bambara est employé généralement pour désigner le Soudanais (qu'il soit Khassonké, Sarakollé, ou même Mossi). Ils acceptent d'autant plus volontiers cette dénomination que le Bambara (comme tout à l'heure le Wolof) fait figure de race évoluée par rapport à la leur propre." ("La Ville de Thiès," in *Études sénégalaises*, No. 6, 1955, p. 149.)

[18] Epstein, *op. cit.*, p. 231.

There are four principal ways in which ethnicity serves to aid national integration. First, ethnic groups tend to assume some of the functions of the extended family and hence they diminish the importance of kinship roles; two, ethnic groups serve as a mechanism of resocialization; three, ethnic groups help keep the class structure fluid, and so prevent the emergence of castes; fourth, ethnic groups serve as an outlet for political tensions.

First, in a modern nation-state, loyalties to ethnic groups interfere less with national integration than loyalties to the extended family. It is obvious that particularistic loyalties run counter to the most efficient allocation of occupational and political roles in a state. Such particularistic loyalties cannot be entirely eliminated. Medium-sized groups based on such loyalties perform certain functions—of furnishing social and psychological security—which cannot yet in West Africa be performed either by the government or by the nuclear family. In the towns, the ethnic group is to some extent replacing the extended family in performing these functions.

The role of the ethnic group in providing food and shelter to the unemployed, marriage and burial expenses, assistance in locating a job has been widely noted.[19] West African governments are not yet in a position to offer a really effective network of such services, because of lack of resources and personnel. Yet if these services would not be provided, widespread social unrest could be expected.

It is perhaps even more important that ethnic associations counter the isolation and anomy that uprooted rural immigrants feel in the city. Thus Balandier has noted in Brazzaville the early emergence of ethnic associations tends to indicate a high degree of uprootedness among the ethnic group, which tends to be found particularly in small minorities.[20]

But from the point of view of national integration is the ethnic group really more functional than the extended family? In the sense that the ethnic group, by extending the extended family, dilutes it, the answer is yes. The ties are particularistic and diffuse, but less so and less strong than in the case of kinship groups. Furthermore, such a development provides a precedent for the principle of association on a non-kinship basis. It can be seen perhaps as a self-liquidating phase on the road to the emergence of the nuclear family.[21] Thus, it can be said with Parsons, that ethnic groups "constitute a focus of security beyond the family unit which is in some respects less dysfunctional for the society than community solidarity would be."[22]

The second function suggested was that of resocialization. The problem of instructing large numbers of persons in new normative patterns is a key one for

---

[19]Mercier notes: "Nombreux sont ceux qui, dans l'actuelle crise de chômage, ne peuvent se maintenir en ville que grâce à l'aide de leurs parents. Cela aboutit à une forme spontanée d'assurance contre le chômage." (*Op. cit.,* p. 26.)

See also *passim*, K. A. Busia, *Report on a Social Survey of Sekondi-Takoradi*, Accra, Government Printer, 1950; I. Acquah, *Accra Survey*, London, University of London Press, 1958; O. Dollfus, "Conakry en 1951–1952. Etude humaine et économique," en *Études guinéennes*, X-XI, 1952, pp. 3–111; J. Lombard, "Cotonou, ville africaine," in *Études dahoméennes*, X, 1953.

[20]G. Balandier, *Sociologie des Brazzavilles noires*, Paris, Armand Colin, 1955, p. 122.

[21]Forde suggests that "This multiplicity of association, which is characteristic of the Westernisation procedure, is likely to preclude the functional persistence of tribal organisations as autonomous units in the economic or political sphere." (*Op. cit.,* p. 485.)

[22]T. Parsons, *The Social System*, Glencoe, Free Press, 1951, p. 188.

nations undergoing rapid social change. There are few institutions which can perform this task. The formal educational system is limited in that it is a long-range process with small impact on the contemporary adult population. In addition, universal free education, though the objective of all West African governments at the present time, is not yet a reality in any of these countries. The occupational system only touches a small proportion of the population, and a certain amount of resocialization is a prerequisite to entry into it. The government is limited in services as well as in access to the individuals involved (short of totalitarian measures). The family is in many ways a bulwark of resistance to change.

The ethnic groups, touching almost all the urban population, can then be said to be a major means of resocialization. They aid this process in three ways. The ethnic group offers the individual a wide network of persons, often of very varying skills and positions, who are under some obligation to retrain him and guide him in the ways of urban life.

By means of ethnic contacts, the individual is recruited into many non-ethnic nationalist groupings. Apter found evidence of this in Ghana, where he observed a remarkable number of classificatory brothers end other relatives working together in the same party, kinship thus providing a "reliable organizational core in the nationalist movement."[23] Birmingham and Jahoda similarly suggest the hypothesis that kinship (read, ethnic) links mediated Ghana political affiliation.[24]

And lastly, members of the ethnic group seek to raise the status of the

whole group, which in turn makes it more possible for the individual members to have the mobility and social contact which will speed the process of resocialization.[25]

The third function is the maintenance of a fluid class system. There is in West Africa, as there has been historically in the United States, some correlation between ethnic groups and social class, particularly at the lower rungs of the social ladder. Certain occupations are often reserved for certain ethnic groups.[26] This occurs very obviously because of the use of ethnic ties to obtain jobs and learn skills.

It would seem then that ethnicity contributes to rigid stratification. But this view neglects the normative context. One of the major values of contemporary West African nations is that of equality. Individuals may feel helpless to try to achieve this goal by their own efforts. Groups are less reticent, and as we mentioned before, its members usually seek to raise the status of the group. The continued expansion of the exchange economy means continued possibility of social mobility. As long as social mobility continues, this combination of belief in equality and the existence of ethnic groups striving to achieve it for themselves works to minimize any tendency towards caste-formation. This is crucial to obtain the allocation of roles within the occupa-

---

[23]D. Apter, *The Gold Coast in Transition*, Princeton, Princeton University Press, 1955, p. 127.

[24]W. B. Birmingham and G. Jahoda, "A Pre-Election Survey in a Semi-Literate Society,"

in *Public Opinion Quarterly*, XIX, Summer, 1955, p. 152.

[25]Glick explains the role of Chinese ethnic groups in Chinese assimilation into Hawaiian society in just these terms. (C. Glick, "The Relationship between Position and Status in the Assimilation of Chinese in Hawaii," in *American Journal of Sociology*, XLVII, September, 1952, pp. 667–679.)

[26]P. Mercier, "Aspects des problèmes de stratification sociale dans l'Ouest Africain," in *Cahiers internationaux de sociologie*, XVII, 1954, pp. 47–55; Lombard, *op. cit.*, pp. 57–59.

tional system on the basis of achievement, which is necessary for a modern economy. Thus, this is a self-reinforcing system wherein occupational mobility contributes to economic expansion, which contributes to urban migration, which contributes to the formation of ethnic associations and then to group upward mobility, which makes possible individual occupational mobility.

The fourth function we suggested was the ethnic groups serve as an outlet for political tensions. The process of creating a nation and legitimating new institutions gives rise to many tensions, especially when leaders cannot fulfill promises made. Gluckman's phrase, the "frailty in authority"[27] is particularly applicable for new nations not yet secure in the loyalty of their citizens. We observed before that ethnic groups offered social security because the government could not. Perhaps we might add that this arrangement would be desirable during a transitional period, even were it not necessary. If the state is involved in too large a proportion of the social action of the individual, it will be burdened by concentrated pressure and demands which it may not be able to meet. It may not yet have the underlying diffuse confidence of the population it would need to survive the non-fulfilment of these demands.[28] It may therefore be of some benefit to divert expectations from the state to other social groups.

The existence of ethnic groups performing "an important scapegoat function as targets for displaced aggression"[29] may permit individuals to challenge persons rather than the authority of the office these persons occupy. Complaints about the nationalist party in power are transformed into complaints about the ethnic group or groups presumably in power. This is a common phenomenon of West African politics, and as Gluckman suggests:

These rebellions, so far from destroying the established social order [read, new national governments] work so that they even support this order. They resolve the conflicts which the frailty in authority creates.[30]

Thus, in rejecting the men, they implicitly accept the system. Ethnic rivalries become rivalries for political power in a non-tribal setting.

* * *

The dysfunctional aspects of ethnicity for national integration are obvious. They are basically two. The first is that ethnic groups are still particularistic in their orientation and diffuse in their obligations, even if they are less so than the extended family. The ethnic roles are insufficiently segregated from the occupational and political roles because of the extensiveness of the ethnic group. Hence we have the resulting familiar problems of nepotism and corruption.

The second problem, and one which worries African political leaders more, is separatism, which in various guises is a pervasive tendency in West Africa today.[31] Separatist moves may arise out of a dispute between élite elements over the direction of change. Or they may result from the scarcity of resources which causes the "richer" region to wish to contract out of the nation (e.g., Ashanti in Ghana, the Western Region

---

[27]M. Gluckman, *Custom and Conflict in Africa*, Oxford, Basil Blackwell, 1955, ch. 2.

[28]Unless, of course, it compensate for lack of legitimation by increase of force as a mechanism of social control, which is the method used in Communist countries.

[29]Parsons, *op. cit.*, p. 188.

[30]Gluckman, *op. cit.*, p. 28.

[31]Separatism, of course, arises as a problem only after a concept of a nation is created and at least partially internalized by a large number, of the citizens.

in Nigeria, the Ivory Coast in the ex-federation of French West Africa). In either case, but especially the latter, appeals to ethnic sentiment can be made the primary weapon of the separatists.

In assessing the seriousness of ethnicity as dysfunctional, we must remember that ethnic roles are not the only ones West Africans play. They are increasingly bound up in other institutional networks which cut across ethnic lines. Furthermore, the situation may vary according to the number and size of ethnic groupings. A multiplicity of small groups is less worrisome, as Coleman reminds us, than those situations where there is one large, culturally strong group.[32]

The most important mechanism to reduce the conflict between ethnicity and national integration is the nationalist party. Almost all of the West African countries have seen the emergence of a single party which has led the nationalist struggle, is now in power, and dominates the local political scene.[33]

In the struggle against colonial rule, these parties forged a unity of Africans as Africans. To the extent that the party structure is well articulated (as, say, in Guinea) and is effective, both in terms of large-scale program and patronage, the party does much to contain separatist tendencies.

Lingusitic integration can also contribute, and here European languages are important. It is significant that one of the Ghana government's first steps after independence was to reduce the number of years in which primary schooling would be in the vernacular. Instruction in English now begins in the second year. We might mention, too, that Islam and Christianity both play a role in reducing centrifugal tendencies.

Lastly, there is the current attempt to endow pan-Africanism with the emotional aura of anti-colonialism, the attempt to make Unity as much a slogan as Independence. Even if the objective of unity is not realized, it serves as a counterweight to ethnic separatism that may be very effective.

Thus we see that ethnicity plays a complex role in the contemporary West African scene. It illustrates the more general function of intermediate groups intercalated between the individual and the state, long ago discussed by Durkheim.[34] It points at the same time to the difficulties of maintaining both consensus and unity if these intermediate groups exist.[35]

---

[32] J. S. Coleman, "The Character and Viability of African Political Systems", in W. Goldschmidt, ed., *The United States and Africa*, New York, The American Assembly, 1958, pp. 44–46.

[33] There is normally room for only one truly nationalist party in a new nation. Other parties in West African countries, when they exist, tend to be formed on more particularistic (ethnic, religious, regional) bases.

[34] E. Durkheim, *The Division of Labor in Society*, Glencoe, Free Press, 1947, p. 28.

[35] See the discussion of this problem in S. M. Lipset, "Political Sociology", in R. K. Merton, L. Broom, L. S. Cottrell, Jr., eds., *Sociology Today*, New York, Basic Books, 1959.

The Monarchical Tendency in African Political Culture

Ali A. Mazrui

In a sense which is not intended to disparage him, Kwame Nkrumah was both a Lenin and a Czar. His secular radicalism had an important royalist theme from the start. But our interest in this article is not merely in Nkrumah himself.[1] It is in the general phenomenon of monarchical tendencies in African politics as they have manifested themselves over the years.

We define monarchical tendencies in this article to be a combination of at least four elements of political style. There is, first, *the quest for aristocratic effect*. In Africa this takes the form of social ostentation. More specifically, it means a partiality for splendid attire, for large expensive cars, for palatial accommodation, and for other forms of conspicuous consumption.[2]

Another factor which goes towards making a monarchical style of politics is *the personalization of authority*. On its own this factor could be just another type of personality cult. But when combined with the quest for aristocratic

effect, or with other elements of style, it takes a turn towards monarchism. Sometimes the personalization goes to the extent of inventing a special title for the leader—and occasionally the title is almost literally royal.

A third element in the monarchical political style is *the sacralization of authority*. This is sometimes linked to the process of personalizing authority, but it need not be. The glorification of a leader could be on non-religious terms. On the other hand, what is being sacralized need not be a person but could be an office or institution. The institutional form of sacred authority is, however, rare in new states. Indeed, the personality of the leader might be glorified precisely because the office lacks the awe of its own legitimacy.

The fourth factor in the politics of monarchism, especially in Africa, is *the quest for a royal historical identity*. This phenomenon arises out of a vague feeling that national dignity is incomplete without a splendid past. And the glory of the past is then conceived in terms of ancient kingly achievement.

TRIBAL ORIGINS OF POLITICAL STYLES

Of the elements of monarchism we have mentioned, the one that is perhaps most clearly shared by traditional conceptions of authority is the element of sacralization. A traditional chief was not always an instance of personalized power. The situation varied from tribe to tribe and from ruler to ruler. In fact, as often as not it was the *institution*

---

[1] For a discussion of Nkrumah himself and his ideological mixture, see my article 'Nkrumah: the Leninist Czar', in *Transition*, no, 26 (Kampala, 1966). Some of the points in this article are an elaboration of what I touched on in that article on Nkrumah.

[2] There have been in places vigorous attempts to control this quest for aristocratic effect. Tanzania has gone further in this attempt to control it than any other African country. See especially the Arusha Declaration in *The Nationalist* (Dar es Salaam), 6 February, 1967. But Tanzania's ethos of frugality is an experiment which faces significant difficulties internally.

From *British Journal of Sociology*, Vol. XVIII, No. 3 (September 1967), 231–250, by permission.

rather than the personality of the incumbent that commanded authority. But although the personalization of power in traditional Africa was thus by no means universal, the sacralization of authority virtually was. There was always a spiritual basis to legitimate rule in traditional Africa. The effect of this on modern African concepts of political legitimacy will emerge later in this analysis.

A related phenomenon is the place of eminence given to ancestors in most of African systems of thought. Partly out of this traditional glorification of one's forebears, and partly as a result of Western disparagement of Africa as 'a continent with no history,' African nationalists today sometimes militantly eulogize ancient African kingdoms. This, as we shall indicate more fully later, is what the African quest for a royal historical identity is all about.

Finally, there has been in Africa since independence, and sometimes for longer than that, the tendency to contrive an aristocratic effect in one's style of life. It is to this question that we must now turn in greater detail. What has led to the building of magnificent palaces in Dahomey, Nigeria, the Ivory Coast, Liberia, Ghana and other places? Why have so many African leaders since independence betrayed a weakness for a plush effect and palatial living?

Here, too, part of the explanation might lie in the general anthropological context of African political styles. Possession as a mark of status is not an entirely new development in African life. It is true that land was very rarely owned on an individual basis. In the words of Max Gluckman:

The earth, undivided, as the basis of society, ... comes to symbolize not in-
dividual prosperity, fertility, and good fortune; but the general prosperity, fertility, and good fortune on which individual life depends.[3]

Nevertheless, the *exploitation* of land, as distinct from its ownership, was not without elements of individualism and competition. To quote Gluckman again:

The secular value of the earth lies in the way it provides for the private interests of individuals and groups within the larger society. They make their living off particular gardens, pastures, and fishing pools; they build their homes, make their fires, and east their meals on their own plots of grounds. ... Men and groups dispute over particular pieces to serve these varied ends.[4]

Within the cooperative structure of kinship and common ownership, there was still room for individual effort and for *individual rewards of such effort.* And so, in addition to status based on age and custom, there was some social status accruing from material possessions. In certain societies, how many heads of cattle a person owned was part of his social standing. There was also bridewealth as a factor in stratification.

These early manifestations of possessive individualism in traditional Africa received a revolutionary stimulus with the advent of the money economy. As a Nigerian economist put it ten years ago,

New statuses arise with the emergence of a new class, the rich who have made their fortune in trade either by selling the raw produce of the land or by retailing imported articles manufactured abroad. ... The growth of this new class of rich, divorced from the land that was so important a link in the chain that bound the

---

[3] Gluckman, *Custom and Conflict in Africa*, Oxford, Basil Blackwell, 1963 (reprint), p. 16.
[4] *Ibid.*

society to the elders, has weakened the authroity of the elders. . . . The new generation that made lits money in trade has challenged the traditional basis of obedience.[5]

In many cases it was this new generation which was the vanguard of the cult of ostentation. To challenge the awesome authority of a chief sometimes required a display of alternative symbols of power. The chiefs were challenged both by those who had new educational attainments, and by those who had new material possessions. And both sets of challengers were inclined to be exhibitionist. Those who had made money had a weakness for conspicuous consumption. And those who had received some education indulged in 'the misuse or overuse of long words, in the use of pompous oratory, and in the ostentatious display of educational attainments'.[6] Both forms of exhibiting the new symbols of power helped to dilute the old legitimacy of tribal elders. Western education and the money economy had produced a form of ostentation which contributed to the corrosion of some traditional ways.

In the meantime, the tendency to regard material possessions as a sign of merit and hard work received a new impetus from the phenomenon of labour migration to the towns. An increasing number of young men left the villages for the mines or for other work in the towns—and periodically came back with symbols of success. As Philip Gulliver recounts,

In this kind of situation wage-labour become more than merely fulfilling youthful needs for clothes, bridewealth contributions and a little ready cash to establish a man as a husband, father and householder. Wage-labour is involved in obtaining goods and services which are not obtainable in the tribal areas and with standards which are not those of the home community—bicycles and radios, a wide variety of clothing, cash for luxuries, travel by bus and train, as well as a greater demand for the more traditional cloth, cattle, tools and utensils which are involved in tribal life.[7]

Gulliver goes on to add that the higher and different standard of living affected not only the migrants themselves but also the people who remained at home—'for new standards became incorporated into tribal expectations and orientations'.[8]

Prestige comes to attach itself to some of these new standards. Young men then aspire to own one day at least a few of the symbols of a 'European' way of life. In the words of Mitchell and Epstein in their analysis of social status in Northern Rhodesia,

Success in achieving this "civilized" way of life is demonstrated conspicuously by the physical appurtenances of living. The most important of these is clothes, but personal jewellery (especially wristwatches), furniture, and European-type foodstuffs are also important.[9]

These sociological tendencies have been the very basis of a new possessive individualism in Africa. The equalitarian aspects of African traditional life,

---

[5] Pius Okigbo, 'Social Consequences of Economic Development in West Africa', *Annals of the American Academy of Political and Social Science*, no. 305 (May 1956), pp. 127–8.

[6] James S. Coleman discusses this phenomenon in Nigeria in the colonial period. See his *Nigeria: Background to Nationalism*, Berkeley and Los Angeles, University of California, 1957, pp. 146–7.

[7] Philip H. Gulliver, 'Incentives in Labour Migration', *Hum. Org.*, vol. 19, no. 3 (Fall 1960), pp. 159–61.

[8] *Ibid.*

[9] J. Clyde Mitchell and A. L. Epstein, 'Occupational Prestige and Social Status Among Urban Africans in Northern Rhodesia', *Africa*, no. 29 (1959), pp. 34–9.

and the extensive social obligations of the extended family, exist side by side with an ethic which measures the individual's success by the yardstick of his material acquisitions. Kenya's Jomo Kenyatta tried to 'disgrace' a prominent Kenya leftist at a public meeting by pointing out that the leftist did not own a big house or a thriving business. The leftist, Mr. Bildad Kaggia, was present at the meeting. President Kenyatta compared Kaggia with other old colleagues of his who had since become prosperous. Addressing Kaggia directly Kenyatta said:

We were together with Paul Ngel in jail. If you go to Ngel's home, he has planted a lot of coffee and other crops. What have you done for yourself? If you go to Kubal's home, he has a big house and has a nice shamba. Kaggia, what have you done for yourself? We were together with Kungu Karumba in jail, now he is running his own buses. What have you done for yourself.[10]

What is significant here is the conviction that failure to prosper is an argument *against* a leader. As a socialist radical, Kaggia was urging a redistribution of land in Kenya to the poor. Kenyatta was suggesting that a person who had failed to prosper through his own exertions should not be 'advocating free things'.[11]

From this kind of reasoning is an casy transition to the feeling that enforced economic equality is an insult to the dignity of labour. The principle of 'to each according to his work' made sense—but it did not make sense to strive for a principle of 'to each according to his needs'. That is one reason why Kenya's Ronald Ngala felt that 'com-

munism teaches people laziness'.[12]

There is a general feeling that most of those who have become wealthy in contemporary Africa have 'come up the hard way'. They have made the money themselves and have not inherited it from a long line of wealthy ancestors. It is therefore tempting to conclude that the rich in the new countries of Africa are more deserving to be rich than some of the millionaires in the Western world. Yet even those who have *inherited* their wealth from ancestors might find grace and forgiveness among a people who like to associate their own prosperity with the blessing of their ancestors. And so Dr. Hastings Banda of Malawi could argue that behind every wealthy family in the Western world is a story of hard work somewhere down the family line. This is a defensible assertion. But Banda has sometimes gone on to the much less defensible 'corollary' that behind every poor family in the Western world is a long tradition of a lack of initiative. In his own words,

In Capitalist countries such as America or Britain, for example [when] some people are very rich and others are very poor, it is that the former have initiative and work very hard or that their ancestors or their grandfathers had initiative and worked hard, while the latter have no initiative and do not work hard or their forefathers did not have initiative and did not work hard.[13]

---

[10]See *East African Standard* (Nairobi), 12 April 1965.

[11]*Ibid.*

[12]See BBC Monitoring Service Records of African Broadcasts, Nairobi in English, ME/1892/B/2, 22 June 1965. In Lenin's terms, the principle of 'from each according to his ability, to each according to his work' is a transitional principle for the 'lower phase' of communism. The ultimate aim was, of course, 'from each according to his ability, to each according to his needs'. See *State and Revolution* (1917).

[13]'What is Communism?', speech to Zomba Debating Society, April 1964, p. 17.

But Banda is inconsistent on this latter point. In fact he retreats into saying: 'There are others, of course, who are just unfortunate and are poor through no fault of their own'.[14] Nevertheless a general admiration of the spirit of honest acquisition is a running theme in his assessment of Westernism. Banda himself manages to combine this admiration with some degree of personal frugality. But in others the admiration of acquisitiveness could include an inner compulsion to *display* one's own successful acquisitions. Such a compulsion is, of course, what leads to general social ostentation.

But what are the implications of this phenomenon for development in Africa? How much of a social ill is a quest for aristocratic effect?

When African leaders are merely acquisitive and self-seeking, certain consequences follow. But when what they acquire is *conspicuously* consumed, a different set of consequences might emerge. The point which needs to be grasped first is that an elite can be acquisitive or even corrupt without being ostentatious. Corruption in India, for example, is at least as well developed as it is anywhere in Africa. Yet there is an asceticism in the Indian style of social behaviour which affects the Indian style of politics too. Many Indian leaders have to conform to what one observer has described as 'the Gandhian image of self-sacrifice and humility which Indians demands of their politicians'.[15] Some of the leaders are sincerely ascetic in any case. But not all that refrains from glittering is necessarily Gandhian.

It is arguable that a corrupt elite which is also ostentatious is ultimately preferable to a corrupt elite which is outwardly ascetic. The problem of measuring sincerity in India is a recurrent one. The leader of Goa's Congress Party, Mr. Purshottam Kakodkar, disappeared from a Bombay hotel on 28 November 1965. A nation-wide search by the police and special investigators was carried out over a period of more than four months. In April 1966 the mystery came to an end. Mr. Kakodkar wrote to the Home Minister announcing that he had gone to a small Himalayan town for meditation.

What were his motives? J. Anthony Lukas made the following report to the *New York Times*:

Some of Mr. Kakodkar's supporters say he is only a spiritual man who wanted a few months to commune with himself before plunging into politics again. Others believe his retreat was a stunt designed to raise his political stock in Goa, where elections are to take place soon.[16]

Lukas linked this event with whole Indian phenomenon of the *sanyasi* (sadu), or spiritual recluse. The cult of withdrawing from worldly affairs can produce genuine dedication and self-sacrifice. But it can also produce some of the worst forms of hypocrisy. In the words of Lukas:

A genuine sanyasi comes to the ashram [sanctuary] to find a guru, or teacher, who he must convince of his sincerity. He must take vows of obedience, celibacy and poverty before he puts on his robes. However, many of the 'holy men' are said to be thinly disguised charlatans who make good livings as alchemists, physicians, fortune tellers, palmists or acrobats.[17]

[14] *Ibid.*
[15] See J. Anthony Lukas, 'Political Python of India', *New York Times Magazine*, 20 February 1966, p. 26.

[16] 'Goa Leader Discloses He Vanished for 4 Months to Meditate', *New York Times*, 14 April 1966.
[17] *Ibid.*

But why should the ostentatious acquisitiveness of the African kind be preferable to the ascetic accumulation of Indians? From an economic point of view, the Indian style of accumulation might be preferable, particularly if the asceticism is accompanied with an ethic of re-investment. The Indian would thus make money, continue to live humbly, and re-invest what he saves. On the other hand the African, in his ostentation, spends his money no luxurious consumer goods, often imported. He harms his country's foreign reserves and deprives the nation of potentially productive capital investment. From the point of view of economic development, ostentatious acquisitiveness tends to be dysfunctional.

But what are the political implications of the phenomenon? A major consideration is that if the consumption is conspicuous, it provides the populace with some index of how much money the leaders make. If the money is being made at the public's expense, the public is not being kept entirely ignorant of that fact. And sooner or later the public might demand an explanation. In short, ostentatious corruption is less stable than disguised corruption. Indeed, the ostentation might, in the long run, be the grave-digger of the corruption. It seems almost certain that in Nigeria part of the exultation which accompanied the overthrow of the previous regime was due to the discredit sustained by the regime for the excessive conspicuousness of its corrupt consumption.

IMPERIAL ORIGINS OF POLITICAL STYLES

But in any case it is not merely traditional Africa that has contributed to monarchical styles of political life. The imperial experience must itself also be counted as a major causal factor. It is to this that we must now turn.

The first thing which needs to be noted is that there are certain forms of humiliation which, when ended, give rise to flamboyant self-assertion. There are certain forms of deprivation which, when relieved, give rise to excessive indulgence. After the end of the American Civil War liberated Negro slaves were, for a while, in possession of money and influence. The result was often flamboyant ostentation and a swaggering way of life. Excessive indulgence had succeeded excessive indigence. Because the Negro had been too deeply humiliated in bondage, he was now too easily inebriated with power.

Something approaching a similar psychological phenomenon has been at work in Africa. In fact Nkrumah had a certain ascetic impulse in him. It is true that he spent considerable sums on the imperial structures he inherited. But his personal mode of living was not particularly indulgent. He seems to have been more extravagant on prestigious public projects than on personal forms of indulgence. He was almost certainly less self-seeking than a large number of other leaders in Africa, Asia and Latin America.

Nevertheless, Nkrumah did have a flamboyance which was, to a certain extent, comparable to that of many American Negroes at the time of the Reconstruction following the Civil War. A keenly felt sense of racial humiliation now exploded into a self-assertion which was partly exhibitionist. The monarchical tendency was part of this.

But the monarchical style of African politics has other subsidiary causes in the colonial experience. In British Africa one subsidiary cause was the British royal tradition itself. They myth of imperial splendour came to be so intimately connected with the myth of royalty that the link was conceptually inherited by the Africans themselves.

The process of political socialization in colonial schools kept on reaffirming that allegiance to the Empire was allegiance to the British monarch at the same time. This inculcation of awe towards the British royal family left some mark on even the most radical African nationalists. When the Queen appointed Nkrumah as Privy Councillor soon after Ghana's Independence, Nkrumah had the following to say of his own people following the appointment:

As you know, during my visit to Balmoral I had the honour of being made a member of the Queen's Privy Council. As the first African to be admitted into this great Council of State, I consider it an honour not only to myself, but also to the people of Ghana and to peoples of Africa and of African descent everywhere.[18]

The tendency of African nationalists to be flattered by the royal favours of the British monarch is perhaps what made Dr. John Holmes of the Canadian Institute of International Affairs come to the conclusion that 'Africans seem to have a fondness for Queens'.[19]

But what lies behind this apparent 'fondness for Queens'? One part of the answer concerns African attitudes to the British royal traditions as such. The other part of the answer is even deeper —it concerns African attitudes to the very concept of royalty itself.

The most important element in African attitudes to British royalty is, quite simply, a lingering awe. It is that awe which made Nkrumah so sincerely appreciative of being appointed a member of the Queen's Privy Council. It is

the same awe which has given the history of independent Africa four knighted Prime Ministers, one knighted regional premier, one knighted President and one knighted Vice-President—some of them are still referred to with the knightly 'Sir' by their countrymen. Many of these are now off the scene and some were regarded as conservative. But their knighthoods were seldom held against them. The Prime Ministers are Sir David Jawara of the Gambia; the late Alhaji Sir Abubaker Tafawa Balewa of Nigeria; Sir Albert Margai and the late Sir Milton Margai of Sierra Leone; the regional Premier was the late Alhaji Sir Ahmadu Bello of Northern Nigeria; the President and Vice-President were Sir Edward Mutesa and Sir Wilberforce Nadiope of Uganda. These four countries involved accounted for over sixty per cent of the population of Commonwealth Africa as a whole. At a press conference in Kampala on 23 February 1967, President Obote cracked a joke at the expense of those Ugandan regional monarchs who accepted knighthoods from the British monarch. But on the whole accepting British knighthoods has never been a point of significant political controversy in Africa.

But is all this responsiveness to British royal traditions itself part of a deeper African attachment to the concept of royalty itself? Is there such an attachment? This is what brings us back to our thesis that republicanism is, in a sense, alien to the African style of politics. The inculcation of royal awe which the British fostered in their colonies might well have reinforced the desire for monarchical glamour in the regimes which succeeded the British Raj.

But does that mean French-speaking Africans are less monarchical in their style of politics than the English-speaking ones? After all, the French speakers

[18] *I Speak of Freedom*, New York, Praeger, 1961, p. 179.
[19] See his article 'The Impact on the Comonwealth of the Emergence of Africa', *Internat. Org.*, vol. XVI, no. 2 (Spring 1962).

were ruled by a republican colonial power. This is true. However, what was gained by French republicanism was lost by the greater cultural arrogance of French colonial policy. In a sense, the French assimilationist policy and the British inculcation of royal awe had the same effect on the African—they reinforced the desire for a cultural glamour that was all African. Both the French-speakers and the English-speakers felt a need to be proud of ancient African kingdoms. And this need for a splendid past helped to create a desire for a splendid present. The very choice of the name 'Ghana' for the emergent Gold Coast was part of this phenomenon. As for the psychological quest for parity with the British royal tradition, this comes out in statements such as the following one approvingly quote by Nkrumah:

In 1066 Duke William of Normandy invaded England. In 1067 an Andalusian Arab, El Bekr, wrote an account of the West African King of Ghana. This King whenever holding audience 'sits in a pavilion around which stand his horses caparisoned in cloth of gold; behind him stand the pages holding shields and gold-mounted swords; and on his right hand are the sons of the princes of his empire, splendidly clad. . . .' Barbarous splendour, perhaps; but was the court of this African monarch so much inferior, in point of organized government, to the court of Saxon Harold? Wasn't the balance of achievement just possibly the other way round?[20]

IDENTITY AND HISTORY

This revelling in ancient glory is part of the crisis of identity in Africa. David E. Apter has argued that African nationalism has tended to include within

it a self-image of re-birth.[21] This is true. When I first visited the United Nations in 1960–1 it was fascinating to listen to some of the new African delegates revelling in the innocence of newly born nationhood. But involved in this very concept of re-birth is a paradoxical desire—the desire to be grey-haired and wrinkled as a nation; of wanting to have an antiquity. This is directly linked to the crisis of identity. In so far as nations are concerned, there is often a direct correlation between *identiy* and *age*. The desire to be old becomes part of the quest for identity. A country like Iran or Egypt would not have a longing for precisely the kind that Nkrumah's country was bound to have. The paradox of Nkrumah's ambition for his country was to *modernize* and *ancientize* at the same time. And so on emerging into independence the Gold Coast, as we have indicated, first decided to wear the ancient name of Ghana—and then embarked on an attempt to modernize the country as rapidly as possible. Mali is another case of trying to create a sense of antiquity by adopting an old name. In Central Africa we now have 'Malawi'. And when the hold of the white minority government in Rhodesia is broken we will probably have 'Zimbabwe'. In Nigeria a distinguished scholar has suggested that the name be changed to 'Songhai'.[22] The desire for a splendid past is by no means uniquely African. But it is sharpened in the African precisely because of the attempt of

[20]See *Political Thought of Dr. Kwame Nkrumah*, Accra; Guinea Press Ltd., n.d., pp. 19–20.

[21]Apter, 'Political Religion in the New Nations', in *Old Societies and New States* edited by-Clifford Geertz, New York, Free Press of Glencoe, 1963, p. 79.

[22]Reported in the *Mombasa Times*. This point is also discussed in my paper 'Nationalism, Research and the Frontiers of Significance', in *Discussion at Bellagio: The Political Alternatives of Development*, edited by Kal Silvert and published by the American Universities Field Staff, 1964.

others to deny that the African has a history worth recording.

A professor of African history in an American university has argued that:

One of the principal functions of history is to help the 'individual define his personality'. The African, as well as Western man, must see himself within a historical context ... To spring from an unhistoric cast is to be without character and without a place in the mainstream of universal history.[23]

This is an exaggeration, but one which has many converts among black nationalists, both in Africa and in the United States. Because of the nature of humiliation to which he was subjected, the Negro has often shown a passionate desire to prove that he has a past glorious enough to form part of 'the mainstream of universal history'. Occasionally, especially in the New World, the Negro has even become what a fellow Negro has called:

... the rash and rabid amateur who has glibly tried to prove half of the world's geniuses to have been Negroes and to trace the pedigree of nineteenth century Americans from the Queen of Sheba.[24]

But why the Queen of Sheba? Partly because she *was* a *Queen*. In other words, the whole concept of a 'glorious history' is too often associated with the achievements of great monarchs. Taking pride in an ancient kingdom has therefore become part of the black man's quest for a historical identity.

Sometimes, the black man's interest in some splendid phase of history in Africa is a mere cultural assertion—and does not affect policy or concrete political behavious. An example of this is the desire of nationalists like Chelkh Anta Diop of Senegal to prove that the Pharoahs were Negroes. As he put it in a talk given at the first International Conference of Negro Writers and Artists held in Paris in 1956:

... the ancient Egyptian and Pharaonic civilization was a Negro civilization ... and ... all Africans can draw the same moral advantage from it that Westerners draw from Graeco-Latin civilization.[25]

But there have been occasions when pride in an ancient kingdom has actually resulted in a significant policy decision. Such occasions include those which resulted in renaming the Gold Coast 'Ghana' and the Sudan 'Mali'. Nkrumah has even found it possible to sympathize with the pride which the British people feel for the old Empire. As he said to a British Prime Minister once:

We know that some of the older nations were willing members of the British Empire and we appreciate the historical significance of that institution, just as we look back with pride on our own African history to the Empire of Ghana.[26]

The same country which was soon to declare itself an African Republic had gone out of its way to name itself after an ancient empire. The paradox has other analogies in the history of African nationalism. The late W. E. B. Du Bois, a founding father of Pan-Africanism,

[23]See William H. Lewis's review of *Africa in Time-Perspective* by Daniel F. McCall, Boston, Boston University Press, 1964. The review was in *African Forum*, vol. 1, no. 1 (Summer 1965), pp. 158–60.

[24]See Arthur A. Shomburg, 'The Negro Digs up His Past' in Sylvestre C. Watkins (ed.), *An Anthology of American Negro Literature*, New York, The Modern Library, 1944, pp. 101–2.

[25]See Diop, 'The Cultural Contributions and Prospects of Africa', the *First International Conference of Negro Writers and Artists*, Paris, Presence Africaine, vols. XVIII–XIX, 1956, pp. 349–51.

[26]Speech in honour of Harold Macmillan on his visit to Ghana in January 1960. See 'Hands off Africa!!!', *op. cit.*, pp. 56–7.

was a Marxist; but he continued to have a proud interest in ancient African monarchs. As he once put it,

In Africa were great and powerful kingdoms. When Greek poets enumerated the kingdoms of the earth, it was not only natural but inevitable to mention Memnon, King of Ethiopia, as leader of one of the great armies that besieged Troy. When a writer like Herodotus, father of history, wanted to visit the world, he went as naturally to Egypt as Americans go to London and Paris. Now was he surprised to find the Egyptians, as he described them, 'black and curly haired'.[27]

IDENTITY AND HEROIC LEADERSHIP

But when the tasks of creating a national future and creating a national past are undertaken at the same time, there is always the danger that the present might be caught in between. The adoration of ancient monarchs might overspill and help to create modern equivalents. Ancient kingdoms and modern presidents are then foced to share royal characteristics.

Du Bois's own first visit to Africa was after the Pan-African conference in Lisbon in 1923. By the accident of a pun, the paradox of monarchical republicanism was implicit in his very mission to Africa. Du Bois tells us:

I held from President Coolidge of the United States status as Special Minister Plenipotentiary and Envoy Extraordinary to represent him at the second inaugural of the President King of Liberia.[28]

Another ideological influence on Pan-Africanism was Marcus Garvey, the West Indian who launched a militant Negro movement in the United States after World War I. In his own autobiography, Nkrumah came to admit that he was greatly impressed by the ideas of Marcus Garvey. It is not clear which Garveyite ideas left a durable mark on Nkrumah. What needs to be pointed out is that the paradox of monarchical republicanism was present in Garvey too. The International Convention of the Negro People of the World which he called in August 1920 was characterized by a kind of royal pomp and fanfare.

Gravey was elected provincial president of Africa. . . . As head of the African republic he envisaged, his official title was 'His Highness, the Potentate. . . .'[29]

Forty years later Kwame Nkrumah was President of a more modest African republic. His equivalent of a quasi-monarchical title was the *Osagyefo*, or the redeemer.

Yet this again is by no means a uniquely African phenomenon. Perhaps the need for heroic leadership of kingly dimensions is felt by most new nations. It was certainly felt by that 'first new nation', the United States of America. In the words of Seymour Martin Lipset, 'We tend to forget today that, in his time, George Washington was idolized as much as many of the contemporary leaders of new states'.[30] George Washington was the 'Osagyefo' of his America —adored with the same extravagance as that which came to be extended to his Ghanaian counterpart two hundred years later. The curious thing is that Washington was supposed to symbolize

---

[27] W. E. Burghardt Du Bois, *The World and Africa* (first published in 1946). New York, International Publishers, 1965 (enlarged edition), p. 121.

[28] See George Padmore (ed.), *History of the Pan-African Congress* (first published in 1947), London, William Morris House, 1963.

[29] See E. U. Essien-Udom, *Black Nationalism, A Search for an Identity in America*, Chicago, Chicago University Press, 1962, pp. 38–9.

[30] See Lipset, *The First New Nation: The United States in Historical and Comparative Perspective*, New York, Basic Books, 1963, pp. 20–1.

the triumph of republicanism over monarchism in his time. In the words of a former professor of Princeton University:

At that moment of history Tory ideas of royal prerogative controlled Europe; and the two Americas, with a large part of Asia, were dependent on Europe. Washington was to defend against the partisans of royal or aristocratic absolutism the cause of Republicanism merging into Democracy.[31]

Yet before long the Senate and the House of Representatives of the new United States were discussing what title their first President should bear. A majority of the Senate favoured 'His Highness, the President of the United States, Protector of their Liberties'.[32] There was strong opposition from the House of Representatives. And the Senate later agreed to the simpler title of calling him 'The President of the United States'. But the Senate gave in not because it thought 'His Highness' would be wrong, but because it did not want to set a precedent of bitterness in its relations with the House of Representatives.

As for the attitude of Washington himself, he wanted the subject dropped not because he himself was strongly opposed to 'exalted titles', but because he felt that his political opponents in the country might portray the title as a betrayal of the principles of their revolution.[33]

Yet although an actual exalted title for Washington was formally avoided, the idolization of Washington as a national hero went virtually unchecked.

When the [Revolutionary] war was won, Congress voted him an equestrian statue in bronze. 'He was to be represented in Roman dress holding a truncheon in his right hand and his head encircled with a laurel wreath'. There was a Roman amplitude about his life work, and in magnanimity of character he was as great as 'the noblest Roman of them all. . . .'[34]

The Washington cult gathered momentum. Marcus Cunliffe, the English author of what Lipset calls 'a brilliant biography of the first President', brings this out very well. He says:

In the well-worn phrase of Henry Lee, he was *first in war, first in peace and first in the hearts of his countrymen* . . . He was the prime native hero, a necessary creation for a new country. . . . Hence . . . the comment made by the European traveller Paul Svinin, as early as 1815: 'Every American considers it his sacred duty to have a likeness of Washington in his home, just as we have the images of God's saints'. For America, he was originator and vindicator, both patron *and* defender of the faith, in a curiously timeless fashion, as if he were Charlemagne, Saint Joan and Napoleon Bonaparte telescoped into one person. . . .[35]

The idea that Washington was one of the few men ever to succeed in changing the course of world history has substantially persisted to the present day. Van Dyke has argued that Washington affected the future of mankind more deeply than did Napoleon. To use his words,

---

[31]Paul Van Dyke, *George Washington, The Son of His Country, 1732–1775*, New York, Charles Scribner, 1931, pp. 3–5.

[32]See Douglas Southall Freeman, *George Washington, A Biography*, vol. XI (*Patriot and President*), New York, Charles Scribner's Sons, 1954, p. 186.

[33]*Ibid.*

[34]Van Dyke, *op. cit.*, p. 5.

[35]Cunliffe, *George Washington, Man and Monument*, New York, Mentor Books, 1960, pp. 20–1.

If young Washington had been among the hundreds scalped at Braddox's defeat, it would have had on the political development of the world a deeper and more durable effect than if the young Napoleon had been killed at the bridge of Lodi.[36]

IDENTITY AND SACRED RULERS

But admiration of secular heroes can too easily assume a sacred dimension. This tendency is again particularly marked in the political situation of a new state. In his discussion of 'political religion' in the new states, David Apter has argued that:

The 'birth' of the nation is thus a religious event, forming a fund of political grace that can be dispensed over the years. The agent of rebirth is normally an individual— an Nkrumah, a Toure who, as leader of the political movement, is midwife to the birth of the nation.[37]

Apter then cites the adulation accorded to Nkrumah, illustrating with the eulogy by Tawia Adamafio, the former Chairman of the Convention People's Party:

To us, his people, Kwame Nkrumah is our father, teacher, our brother, our friend, indeed our lives, for without him we would no doubt have existed, but we would not have lived; there would have been no hope of a cure for our sick souls, no taste of glorious victory after a lifetime of suffering. What we owe him is greater even than the air we breathe, for he made us as surely as he made Ghana.[38]

Here again the analogy with George Washington is compelling. In his

biography of Washington, Cunliffe refers to the dying Roman emperor Vespasian who is supposed to have murmured: 'Alas, I think I am about to become a god'. Cunliffe goes on to add:

George Washington . . . might with justice have thought the same thing as he lay on his deathbed at Mount Vernon in 1799. Babies were being christened after him as early as 1775, and while he was still President, his countrymen paid to see him in waxwork effigy. To his admirers he was 'godlike Washington', and his detractors complained to one another that he was looked upon as a 'demi-god' whom it was treasonable to criticize. 'O Washington!' declared Ezra Stiles of Yale (in a sermon of 1783). 'How I do love thy name! How have I often adored and blessed thy God, for creating and forming three the great ornament of human kind!'[39]

Editors of newspapers, speechmakers, and poets in early America often indulged in eulogizing Washington in godly dimensions. The editor of the *Gazettle of the United States*, an extravagant admirer of Washington, used at times the kind of epithets which were later to be echoed by the Young Pioneers of Nkrumah's Ghana. A factor which contributed to the expulsion of an archbishop from Ghana in 1962 was the spread of slogans claiming that Nkrumah would never die. Some members of the clergy in Ghana expressed reservations about the ethics of teaching such solgans—and a crisis ensued for a while for churchmen in the country.[40] Yet claims of immortality for heroes also go back at least to that 'first new nation', the

---

[36] Van Dyke, *op. cit.*, pp. 4–5.

[37] See Apter, 'Political Religion in the New Nations' in Clifford Geertz (ed.). *Old Societies and New States*, New York, Free Press of Glencoe, 1963, pp. 82–4.

[38] Adamafio, *A Portrait of the Osagyefo Dr. Kwame Nkrumah*, Accra: Government Printer, 1960, p. 95. See Apter, *op. cit.*

[39] Cunliffe, *op cit.*, pp. 14–16.

[40] For a brief discussion of some of the implications, please see Ali A. Mazrui, 'Africa and the Egyptian's Four Circles' *African Affairs*, London (April 1964).

United States. As that Editor of the *Gazette* put it in his eulogy of Washington:

Fill the bowl, fill it high,
First born son of the sky,
May he never, never die,
Heaven shout, Amen.[41]

A letter from Boston published in the same newspaper expressed similar sentiments about the first President:

So near perfection, that he stood
Upon the boundary line,
Of finite, from the infinite good,
Of human from divine.[42]

The *Gazette* was perhaps the most pro-Washington newspaper at the time. But eulogies to Washington were to be found in other newspapers as well. It was the *Daily Advertiser*, for example, which published a poem by a New York woman which said of the national leader:

The man's divine—let angels write his name
In the bright records of eternal fame.[43]

It is this extravagance of early adoration of George Washington which made him the Osagyefo of young America.

In Africa in more recent times this *degree* of adulation was by no means typical. Only Nkrumah was adored in terms which were anywhere near those used in the admiration of George Washington. Nevertheless, almost everywhere in Africa there has been a tendency to spiritualize the head of state or government in these initial years following independence.

It is this tendency towards sacred leadership which, perhaps more than any leadership which, perhaps more than any other factor, makes republicanism somewhat unsuited to the style of politics of new states. This is to assume that republicanism is usually a governmental system of secular orientation, but the assumption is more than merely defensible historically. What monarchical republics of Africa have now been out to assert is the new doctrine of the divine right of founder-Presidents. Nor is the doctrine entirely without justification in countries which have yet to establish legitimacy and consolidate the authority of the government. As Apter has put it, 'the sacred characteristic becomes essential to maintain solidarity in the community'.[44] The British Queen may be no more than a *symbol* of national unity; but the head of a new state may be an essential *basis* of such unity. He, too, might need to be accepted as 'God's annointed'—and feel 'this hot libation poured by some aged priest!'

This is where Africa's own traditional royal ways become pertinent in at least those communities which have a monarchical background. Some modern equivalent is sometimes needed for the old Stool of the Chief. As K. Macnell Steward, the West Indian poet living in Ghana, once put it,

Here, faith, religion, centres in one thing—
The Stool: take this away—the nation dies
And even colour fades out of the skies of Africa. . . .
In you mute things repose a nation's soul.[45]

Hence titles like 'osagyefo' for Presidents of Republics. Such titles help to

---

[41]Cited by Freeman, *op. cit.*, p. 212.

[42]Letter to the Editor, *Gazette of the United States*, 25 April 1789. Cited by Freeman, *op. cit.*, p. 184.

[43]The *Daily Advertiser*, 26 June 1789. Cited by Freeman, *op. cit.*, p. 212.

[44]*Op. cit.*, p. 83.

[45]See his 'Ode to Stools and Stool Worship', *African Affairs* (Journal of the Royal African Society), vol. 52, no. 208 (July 1953), pp. 185–97.

lend traditional sacredness to modernizing leadership. The words themselves have connotations that might sometimes defy the visiting student of African politics. As Ruth Schachter Morgenthau has put it,

We are accustomed to discuss the pattern of authority within parties as collective, or personal, charismatic, institutionalized but each word has a history and a set of association, mostly Western. How are we to understand references to *Fama*, roughly 'king' in Malinke, used in referring to Sekou Toure of Guinea?[46]

There have indeed been occasions when attempts to 'royalize' an African republic have been resisted by the leader himself. The most striking example of this so far has been Julius Nyerere. He has tried to discourage even such minimal ways of adulation as having streets named after him or having too many photographs of himself distributed to the public. And when, on the eve of the presidential election in Tanzania in 1965, Zanzibari newspapers were saying 'Let us elect President Nyerere as our President for life', Nyerere warned the people of Zanzibar about the dangers of excessive surrender to a leader. He said:

I might stay on until I am too old to do my job properly and then tell my son to act for me. When I died he might claim a right to the Presidency—and call himself Sultan Nyerere I; and there might be a second and a third.[47]

But in many ways Nyerere is an exception. And, in any case, the mere fact that there were public demands for his installation as President for life is an indication of the responsiveness of ordinary Africans to certain monarchical ways.

CONCLUSION

It was perhaps fitting in the history of African nationalism that the three most moving cases of exile in the colonial days should have concerned African monarchs. There was the flight and exile of Emperor Haile Selassie of Ethiopia following Mussolini's invasion of his country. This was an event which gave early African nationalists and Negro radicals in the New World a deep sense of personal humiliation.[48]

Then there was the exile of the Kabaka of Buganda in 1953—a case of an African king defying a British governor, and then being sent away from his people as punishment.

A few years earlier there had been the exile of Seretse Khama, King of the Bamangwato—kept away from his people by the British because he had married a white girl.

All three exiles during the colonial period were pregnant with powerful symbolism for African nationalists everywhere. The sense of racial humiliation was sharpened by the very fact that these were African *kings* who were suffering the indignity of expulsion from their own kingdoms.

Today exile of African rulers by colonial powers is, by and large, a thing

---

[46] Morgenthau, *Political Parties in French-Speaking West Africa*, Oxford, Clarendon Press, 1964, p. xviii.

[47] See *East Africa and Rhodesia* (London), vol, 42, no. 2138, 30 September, 1965, p. 72.

[48] Nkrumah tells us his reaction when, on arrival in London in 1935, he saw the placard of a newspaper stand 'Mussolini invades Ethiopia'. 'At that moment it was almost as if the whole of London had declared war on me personally.' He glared at the faces that passed him, wondering whether they appreciated the essential wickedness of colonialism, 'My nationalism surged to the fore.' See his *Autobiography*, Edinburgh, Thomas Nelson, 1957. p. 27.

of the past. But the royal theme in African nationalism has only found new expressions. The capital of Pan-Africanism is Addis Ababa which, of course, is also the capital of an old dynastic African empire. The President of the Ivory Coast has built himself a Palace which is almost an African equivalent of Versailles. The President of Malawi invokes witchcraft to spiritualize his absolutism. The President of Kenya has at times come near to borrowing the symbols of 'the King of Kings' himself. The highlight of the Kenyatta Day celebrations on 20 October 1965, for example, nearly became a 'Last Supper'—commemorating the last supper that President Kenyatta had before being arrested in connection with the Mau Mau uprising.[49]

Both the palaces and the political prayers are sometimes intended to create the necessary awe towards authority and make national integration possible. In a sense, the phenomenon bears comparison with the dual position of Elizabeth II—Queen of England and Head of the Anglican Church. This tie between Church and State in England is now little more than a formal legacy of British history. But in Africa the spiritualization of the head of state is part of the struggle for national cohesion. And for as long as that spiritualization continues to be deemed necessary, the secular rationalism which we normally associate with republicanism will have a touch of incongruity in an African political universe.

Yet the sacralization of authority, as well as its personalization, is a phenomenon mainly of the peak of political power in an African country. It is the head of government or the head of state who comes to symbolize 'the soul of the nation'. What is a more widespread phenomenon is the general quest for aristocratic effect. This manifests itself not merely in the paramount leader, but also further down in the pyramid of elite status. And the tendency is persisting even after the coups in those countries which have ousted their old political regimes. Not long after the Nigerian coup, one of the leading columnists in the country lamented in the following terms:

What a nice gesture it would have been if the military leaders had reciprocated [the people's call for self-imposed austerity] by leaving the official residences built by the ostentatious politicians strictly alone ... If, as it is widely believed, they were advised that their personal prestige would be enhanced by moving into these mansions be enhanced by moving into these mansions, I say it is nonsense. ... It was a mistake for them to move into the palatial edifices which had become objects of much resentment among the people.[50]

The writer allowed that Major-General Aguiyi-Ironsi might indeed have had to move into the State House 'for the sake of protocol'. After all, he was not only Supreme Commander but also head of state. 'He needs the royal environment of State House, Marina'. But what about the provincial governors? What about senior military men generally?

Nigerians would have loved to see them riding around in their official military vehicles, escorted by their troops. But not in the Rolls-Royces bought by flamboyant politicians. Not escorted by police out riders, sirens wailing and traffic brought to

---

[49]See *The Times* (London), 7 October 1965. For protest against the supper, couched in racialistic anti-African terms, see *East Africa and Rhodesia*, 14 October 1965, p. 108.

[50]Peter Pan, 'The First 100 Days: Spirit of the Revolution', *Daily Times* (Lagos), 28 April 1966.

a standstill. This nation needs a sense of urgency, a toning down of high living . . . a manifestation of that exemplary self-denial which was so lacking among the politicians . . . And the leadership must come from the Army.[51]

This was a voice of an African intellectual rebelling against the recurrent quest for aristocratic effect within the leadership of his country even after a major national shock like a violent

---

[51] *Ibid.* Some of these factors are also discussed in my book *The Anglo-African Commonwealth: Political Friction and Cultural Fusion*, Oxford, Pergamon Press, 1967.

military coup. But the aristocratic and kingly aspects of African styles of politics have deep roots, both in African traditions and in the total impact of the colonial experience. African conceptions of earned rewards, the spiritualization of ancestors, the quest for a historical identity, the assertion of cultural equality, the general desire for political glamour have all contributed their share to the monarchical tendencies in African politics. Behind it all is the newness of African politics, and the need to strengthen the legitimacy of the regimes with sacred symbols and romantic awe.

African Nationalism: Concept or Confusion?

Robert I. Rotberg

In common usage, African nationalism is descriptive shorthand for an assembly of separate and distinct phenomena, some of which have already taken on the protective colouring of popular understanding. Africans generally agree that they have experienced nationalism; they know the tree of nationalism when they see it and have tasted some, at least, of its fruits. For many of them, and for students of recent African events, its manifestations are obvious, although the quality of its spirit remains, like most spirits, capable only of inexact description. It is, in essence, pretty much what it is.

Sceptics and critics are, however, entitled to seek greater precision. Since Africa historically possessed few nations in the classical European cultural, linguistic, or religious sense, and since few now exist in such terms, how can

we write and speak of nationalism? The mere expression of anti-colonial hostility clearly does not provide sufficient proof of its existence. In a tropical African setting, the descriptive usage of nationalism dates only from the late 1940's; for hostile critics it thus seems nonsensical to assign to nationalism a long African history roughly parallel to the period of colonial intervention. Yet that is one hypothesis, the testing of which depends to a large extent upon a definition of terms.

'Nation', 'nationality', and 'nationalism' are catch-words that have been used to describe a multitude of situations, human conditions, and states of mind. I need not here rehearse the relevant literature; we all know the different uses to which 'nationalism' has been put and the inability of the various definitions adequately to depict each of

From *Journal of Modern African Studies*, Vol. IV, No. 1 (May 1966), 33–46, by permission of the journal and its publisher, the Cambridge University Press.

the particular situations.[1] Nationalism is a morass of misapplication; it describes much in general and little in particular. To add 'African' narrows the area of example but complicates the search for comparative generality. We cannot really approach the subject without knowing what it is and how it relates to similar experiences at other times and in other parts of the world.

'Nation' has historical associations. In pre-nineteenth-century western Europe, the growth of monarchical power, and the consequent establishment of centralised states, in turn brought about the creation of the nations from which nationality and nationalism flowed. Although the emergence of national cultures did not everywhere in Europe depend upon the prior establishment of political unity, such unity may almost be considered a necessary pre-condition. By the end of the seventeenth century, the monarchical quest for power had involved the bourgeoisie as well as the dynastic aristocracy; the monarchs had invoked and, in many cases, manufactured national sentiments. They had, largely in order to satisfy the designs of their own statecraft, subordinated feudal, ecclesiastical, communal, and numerous other centres of control to the overriding needs of what came to be called a 'national design'.

Monarchs hardly conjured nations from nothing. As the power of the centralised state grew, it both fed upon and nurtured the parallel growth of linguistic and cultural unity. Monarchs conscripted, taxed, and educated their subjects. Such actions assisted the spread of an often already existing vernacular while encouraging a new appreciation of the national culture. And in writing in this way, I telescope the almost imperceptible changes that took decades to achieve and longer to notice. Nevertheless, by the middle of the eighteenth century, the nation was an accepted form: it referred generally to a definite territory that was inhabited by a people who possessed a distinctive common culture and language and who felt that they constituted a nation. The concept of nationality—that is, the state or quality of belonging to a nation— naturally followed, and nationalism, if the word were used at all, continued to possess a very narrow connotation.

During the eighteenth century in Europe, populations increased, commercial and ideological intercourse intensified the relationships of hitherto isolated cities and provinces, means of communication and transport improved, and the institutional responsibilities of the state correspondingly grew more complex and important. Individuals became less self-sufficient; they depended more and more upon the efforts of others, particularly of groups of fellow nationals, and on the nation itself as the embodiment of their effort. As they depended, so they developed loyalties. Nationality acquired greater status; government conversely became, to a degree, of the people as well as by the king. 'The people' were generally properties, and, especially in Western Europe, the bourgeoisie were the principal medium for the spread of nationalistic sentiments. They thought of themselves as nationals, although some still considered themselves equally Christians and, say, Burgundians.

But these events would have comparatively little meaning for our study of African nationalism if they had not been overtaken in Western Europe by a widespread consciousness among the literate, and sometimes among the

---

[1] For an excellent study of the over-all problem, see Rupert Emerson, *From Empire to Nation: the rise to self-assertion of Asian and African peoples* (Cambridge, Mass., 1959).

masses, that the nation was a common enterprise that deserved to be run by all the nationals or their middle-class representatives. This flowed from the gradual erosion of parochial ties and the growth and acceptance of the idea (sceptics would call it the myth) of a national culture. Worship of the state became acceptable. Nationalism provided an ideology to which people (usually of the middle class) seeking an escape from the old oppressions of church or monarch, or even from foreign rule, could devote their efforts in the hope of obtaining liberty. It was the feeling of which revolutions were made.

Out of the passion of revolution and the blood of war, men espoused and spread the gospel of nationalism. This became the credo of an age when men throughout Europe and America sought to sunder the chains that deprived them of their freedom. Nationalism eclipsed previous political emotions; nationalists fought for the liberty of the oppressed everywhere. The new religion of nationhood easily gained converts. A new priesthood developed of the ambitious and the forward-looking. The fervour of the French and American revolutions stimulated others to seek the ecstasy of a nationalist religion. In this way the nation symbolised relief from oppression; the nation seemed to enshrine and to incorporate the idea of liberty. Yet the religion of nationalism had its component churches. In England, France, what became Germany, the United States, and Haiti, for example, the character and content of the devotion differed. Despite such variations, however, nationalism remained an answer to oppression, since a nation—which was far more than the sum of its individual citizens—by its very existence promised a better future to peoples possessing common cultural traits who lived within its by now well-defined borders. By extension, peoples everywhere deserved to enjoy the better future—the New Jerusalem. It is from such revolutionary roots that the notion of national self-determination stems.

The martial experience of the nineteenth century enriched the ethos of nationalism and gave birth to new nations at the same time as the older nation-states steadily made—of still somewhat disparate peoples—citizens who owed loyalties primarily to the national will. As Greeks, Germans, Italians, and others discovered their common cultural roots and rebelled and fought in order to recover their liberty, so Britons and Frenchmen (and Germans, Italians, and others) constructed the railways, roads, and canals that encouraged further unity. Telegraph and telephone lines followed. Common currencies were assumed; sometimes a customs union enhanced political attempts to achieve geographical or cultural unity. As men of ambition found their own elevation in the promotion of nationalism and national ends, so the pace of this natural process accelerated. By the end of the century, westerners assumed that nations and nationalism were the most complete embodiments of a natural human need. They could conceive of few other positive ways by which the lives of individuals might be organised.

Revolutionary nationalism diffused an ideology, and the actions of national governments unified relatively homogeneous peoples. On the basis of the European experience, states began to presuppose definite nationalities. Nationalism came to mean the consciousness on the part of individuals or groups of their membership of a nation and/or the desire to further the liberty or prosperity of a particular nation. And a 'nationalist', in the English language, generally wanted to further the interests of a particular established or submerged nation. (More narrowly, he wanted to see Ireland govern itself.)

Such definitions, abbreviated as they must be, suffice for much of Western Europe. But they blur our understanding of the older Latin American and more recent Middle Eastern and Asian revolutions, and, if we let ourselves become carried away by their seeming good sense, the definitions also obscure the meaning of the African experience. Precolonial tropical Africa had very few nations in the accepted sense, and even fewer that retained their national identity intact throughout the colonial interlude. The colonies themselves usually comprised two or more (often many more) tribal and political entities. In the ordinary sense of our definition, none of these colonies were nations. They were demonstrably not of one people. How then can we talk of the rise of African nationalism—as the self-assertion of African colonial peoples is usually described—and moreover intend that phrase to encompass a time span of four or five decades?

If we compare the African experience with that of one of the older non-European examples, many similarities are apparent. In India, Britain provided the first common, 'national', government. It defended the frontiers and gave the sub-continent its first common measure of internal security. The British Raj furthermore provided common communications, laws, and—although this is debatable—a common language. It unified India physically and, of perhaps greatest relevance, gave Indians common aspirations and a sense of a common destiny. (It is really unimportant, for our purposes, that colonial India became two independent nations; at least they both owe their existence as separate entities to the British experience.) Britain created India

of many kingdoms and principalities—we might call them proto-nations—in much the same way as, together with France, it destroyed the pan-Arabia that might have emerged from the Ottoman collapse and, in its place, substituted Iraq, Transjordan, etc.

By their very presence, the alien powers (and, conceptually, being alien is more important than western or European) made the indigenous 'nationals' more conscious than before that they were one people. They organised the states, propagated ideals that were of supposedly universal application, and, without necessarily meaning to, imposed the physical and ideological framework within which the ruled could strive against their rulers.

Without the partition and subsequent colonial rule of tropical Africa by the powers of Europe, there might have been no African nationalism. Were it not so often denied, there would be little point in stating the obvious—that the colonial powers alone created the bases of the present nations of independent Africa by arbitrarily dividing the continent into administrative entities and imposing thereupon imported legal, linguistic, and cultural concepts. This is not to say that the colonial powers completed the nation-building process; in most areas, the independent rulers must now strive to complete the unfinished national designs left to them by their previous rulers. But, in the sense of eighteenth- and nineteenth-century Europe, the colonial territories had become nations of intent; the process of unification indeed began with the conquest and continued with the 'detribalisation' of a territory like Malawi or the Congo (Léopoldville). Furthermore, for them the model of a nation existed as an absolute value.

During the colonial interlude, the populations resident within most of the various colonies admittedly possessed no common indigenous culture or language. But colonial domination gave them common experiences, a sense of common history, however brief, and, in the manner of India, a common language. They shared common grievances. They also lived within a single definite territory and, admittedly without enthusiasm, subjected themselves to the same laws and methods of administration. The Lozi of Zambia may have constituted a nation in some senses before the partition; afterwards they were in practice treated like any other member of the colonial community known as Northern Rhodesia. Although it is hard for students of European history to conceive it, the Lozi even began —in the manner of the Burgundian Christians who gradually came to think of themselves as above all French—to regard themselves as Northern Rhodesians and 'British protected persons' in addition to being Africans and Lozi from the district of, say Senanga.[2] The Ganda during the colonial interlude may have envisaged a future apart from the greater Uganda; nearly everywhere else, however, I think Africans—or least the Africans of influence who cared— sought to satisfy their aspirations within territorial boundaries. Because of the all-embracing nature of the colonial form of government, they very early accepted the idea that their fates were inextricably bound up with the new colonial nations into which they had been born. The sentiment of pan-Africanism is not new, but as the example of the National Congress of British West Africa shows, even feelings of regional unity have almost always been subordinate to 'nationalism'.

If we accept that, at some point during the colonial period, the alien-

administered territories passed into the realm of partial nationhood without losing their dominated status, then the nature of African nationalism really holds no mysteries. In its passionate form, it stems in some senses directly from the French and American revolutionary experience, and draws even more upon the sentiments that were operative in, for example, Ireland and India. The role which was played in, say, Eastern European and Irish nationalism by a ruling caste with a national consciousness differing radically from that of its subjects was to some degree played in Africa—as in Asia—by men of a strikingly different colour, religion, and cultural background, who appeared in the garb of conquerors and masters, who destroyed traditional ways of life, and promised, or appeared to promise, to turn all Africans into black Europeans.[3]

Writing of Ireland, Shaw expressed the Irish sense of common grievance against the 'intolerable abomination' of English rule:

Like Democracy, national self-government is not for the good of the people: it is for the satisfaction of the people. One Antonine emperor, one St. Louis, one Richelieu, may be worth ten democracies in point of what is called good government; but there is no satisfaction for the people in them.[4]

These sentiments have often been unconsciously echoed by Africans. Much earlier, Loewe ben Bezalel, a sixteenth-century rabbi, articulated the axioms of self-determination, particularly if we read 'submerged group' for 'people' and 'creed' for 'God'. For him, it was clear

---

[2] Cf. Emerson, *op. cit.* pp. 110, 118, and 128.

[3] E. H. Carr, in *Royal Institute of International Affairs Study Group Report on Nationalism* (London, 1939,) p. 145.

[4] G. B. Shaw, 'Perface for Politicians', in *Fohn Bull's Other Island* (New York, 1907), pp. xxxvi–xxxix.

'that every people has a might of its own and ought not to be subject to any other people, that every people has its natural habitation and a right to live there, and that it must be granted to every people to choose its own God according to its own ideas'.[5]

Africans, antagonised by the realities of colonial rule while educated in and aware of the ideals of the European national image, eventually asserted themselves with a patriotic fervour that made real the possibility of national self-determination.[6] But could they be patriots without a *patria*? Without a common culture, could they really achieve self-determination on a national basis? I submit that Africans not only could—they did. And the fact that the integrity of formerly colonial 'national' borders is everywhere so important is an indication that colonies in their latter stages were well on their way to becoming nations. Their inhabitants, led as in Europe by the ambitious, upwardly mobile, middle-class 'agitators', manned the proverbial barricades and dumped imaginary tea into the waters of disturbance. They manifested extreme anti-European attitudes, which were, in the best tradition, anti-establishment. One could label their feelings racialism, xenophobia, anti-Europeanism, Africanism, or patriotism.[7] But none is satisfactory. Only by using 'nationalism' can we place the African revolution where it belongs—squarely in the mainstream of man's long struggle to enter the New Jerusalem of liberty and equality.

If we agree that the nationalism of Africans was similar in content to the earlier Asian and European nationalisms and, broadly speaking, that virtually from the time of their conquest the African colonies all were nations in embryo, then the nationalism of Africa need not be conceptually confined—as many wish—exclusively to the 'wind-of-change' era after World War II. We can demonstrate for most of the areas a series of stages that, certainly for me, constitute the gradual but nevertheless perceptible rise of different forms of national consciousness. We can discern the three stages that I call awakening, incipient action, and triumph.

I contend that, admittedly to a greater or lesser degree, nearly all of the ex-colonies of tropical Africa experienced a gradual growth in nationalist sentiment from the time of their annexation by aliens. Yet many would say that we should not confuse the gentle murmurs of early protest with the full-blown aggressive activities of the latter-day revolution. But the hesitant early manoeuverings are just as much a part of the total process as the more obvious final phase; Africans possessed common grievances and shared the hope of common, libertarian aspirations. If we probe sufficiently deeply—as David Kimble has done for Ghana and James Coleman for Nigeria[8]—I think that almost everywhere in tropical Africa we can demonstrate a geometric continuity of African nationalism and isolate its different stages. With this generalisation in mind, let us discuss, for the sake of expository and analytical clarity, the illustrative example of Malawi.

By the time of the coming of the first

---

[5] Quoted in Boyd C. Shafer, *Nationalism: myth and reality* (New York, 1955), p. 95.

[6] See Emerson, *op. cit.* pp. 19 and 27.

[7] Lord Hailey's 'Africanism' seems particularly lacking in descriptive utility. See his *An African Survey: Revised 1956* (London, 1957), pp. 251–2.

[8] David Kimble, *A Political History of Ghana: the rise of Gold Coast nationalism, 1850–1928* (Oxford, 1963); James S. Coleman, *Nigeria: background to nationalism* (Berkeley, 1960).

European missionaries and settlers, the old area of Malawi had been disintegrated by the efforts of African invaders from the south and Arab and African slave raiders from the east. When the Europeans thus conquered what they called Nyasaland, they found it a comparatively easy task. They met resistance, but of a piecemeal, tribal, rather than a concerted, national kind. British-armed and officered African soldiers ousted recalcitrant chiefs, pacified their peoples, and, over a period of about fifteen years, subordinated Nyasaland to British administrative and legal ideas. They taxed their subjects, encouraged Africans to make roads and missionaries to open schools and hospitals, and improved the existing methods of communication. They introduced new entrepreneurial and agricultural concepts, eventually constructed a railway and, in various ways, hastened the economic development of the Protectorate. Such initiatives—particularly the collection of taxes and the consequent need to speak English for the purposes of most wage-earning employment—brought together for the first time a disparate congeries of tribal peoples. Administrative regimentation hastened the process, and the spread of educational facilities, the employment of the peoples of the Protectorate in World War I, and the steady migration of labour from the rural to the urban and plantation areas of the Protectorate quickened it still faster. By about 1920 the Nyasa nation, an artificial creation like so many other African states, could be said to exist, however embryonically. The time spans might differ, but other colonies had similar experiences.

Already the tightening grip of the administrative noose, the introduction of 'modern' codes of behavioural expectation, the hard lot of the agricultural labouring class, the spread and intensification of a colour bar, and an obvious contempt for and an attempt to transform the traditional way of life, had turned reluctantly acquiescent subjects into discontented ones. There was what we might call a nationalist awakening in various parts of the Protectorate. The self-assertive message of the millenarian preacher Elliott Kenan Kamwana received a ready response from Africans. A few years later, after the Government of Nyasaland had decisively legislated chiefs—as a group—out of existence, members of the new middle class organised the first 'native association'. Both types of responses were subsequently to provide important outlets for the expression of nationalistic feeling. Both signified that Africans were not altogether content to remain the subjects of aliens. Both had national ends in mind, but neither their leadership nor their activities were, strictly speaking, national in scope.[9]

From the stage of awakening we move to the stage of incipient action. Usually, this corresponds to the period during which associations were especially active and millenarians found ready adherents. In Malawi, however, there was an intervening stage that shared many of the characteristics of both the stages of awakening and incipient action. John Chilembwe, an American educated preacher, in 1914–15 launched a crusade in order to achieve for his fellow Nyasas the freedom that he thought they deserved. In concert with a number of chiefs and members of the emerging middle class, he viewed with dismay the way in which white employers treated their African plantation labour. He had his own dif-

---

[9] For details and references concerning much of what follows, see Robert I. Rotberg, *The Rise of Nationalism in Central Africa: the making of Malawi and Zambia, 1873–1964* (Cambridge, Mass., 1965).

ficulties with settlers and, despite his own independent financial position as the leader of the American-backed Providence Industrial Mission, Chilembwe must himself have shared the experience of racial discrimination with the mass of Africans. But what precipitated the overt expression of his dissatisfaction was the conscription of Nyasas during the opening weeks of World War I. He, like others, failed to see why Nyasas should participate in a war in which they had no stake, and from which—if Africans knew whites—Nyasas would receive little improvement in their own hard lot.

Chilembwe, at the behest of a number of other Nyasas, first adopted one of the standard means of protest—he drew up a petition in the form of an open letter to the national newspaper. In this famous letter, the admittedly westernised preacher aired national grievances and sought specifically national solutions. He wrote as a nationalist and already thought of Nyasaland as a nation and its inhabitants as fellow countrymen; but, significantly, he did not so regard the neighbouring British protected persons of Northern Rhodesia, many of whom spoke the same language as his own people. He responded to the colonial situation in a nationalistic manner that Rabbi Bezalel, Shaw, and numerous Asians and Arabs would have applauded. In part, Chilembwe's letter read:

We understand that we have been invited to shed our innocent blood in this world's war which is now in progress throughout the wide world. . . . [But] will there be any good prospects for the natives after the end of the war? Shall we be recognised as any body in the best interests of civilisation and Christianity after the great struggle is ended?
. . . we are imposed upon more than any

other nationality under the sun. [We] . . . have been loyal since the commencement of this government. . . . And no time have we been ever known to betray any trust, national or otherwise, confided to us. . . . For our part we . . . have unreservedly stepped to the firing line in every conflict and played a patriot's part with the Spirit of true gallantry. But in time of peace everything [is] for Europeans only. . . . But in time of war it has been found that we are needed to share hardships and shed our blood in equality. It is even true that there is a spot of our blood in the cross of the Nyasaland Government.[10]

This letter was signed simply, 'John Chilembwe, on behalf of his countrymen'.

Because of the actions of the official censor, few of Chilembwe's countrymen saw the letter. Even if they had, it is hardly to be supposed that it would have evoked a national response. Predictably, the Government turned it aside, and Chilembwe and the members of his cabal decided to take more positive steps to air the grievances of their fellow countrymen. Early in 1915, without having made of their own conspiracy a national movement, they rose briefly and abortively against the Government of Nyasaland.[11] The African masses—never privy to the conspiracy—remained aloof. Afterwards, there was no overt upsurge of national feeling. The government regarded the rebellion as an aberration. Its only immediate effect was to provide the administrators of the Protectorate with an excuse to regard every subsequent manifestation of discontent as

---

[10]Quoted, *ibid.* p. 82.
[11]*Ibid.* pp. 85–91. See also George Shepperson and Thomas Price, *Independent African: Fohn Chilembwe and the origins, setting and significance of the Nysasland native rising of 1915* (Edinburgh, 1958), pp. 269–319.

the dangerous sedition of revolt. None the less, the Chilembwe rising marked an extreme example of the influence on Africans—on the middle classes if no other—of the sentiments that I have been calling nationalistic. Had the rising by some fluke succeeded—and we have already shown that the nationalist prerequisites of success were lacking— Chilembwe would simply, as later nationalists did, have taken over the existing governmental apparatus and adapted it to the need of his fellows countrymen. We would probably not now question its nationalist character. Similarly, had the Thuku movement in Kenya somehow brought about the end of British rule in 1921, that too would unquestionably have found a place in the panorama of nationalism.[12] But both of these dramatic failures serve again to remind us that the rise of nationalism has had a long period of gestation.

During the years between the two world wars, politically-aroused Africans (at first only an articulate minority) almost everywhere occupied the stage of evolutionary nationalism that I have called incipient action. In a few areas, like the Gold Coast, Africans had long before begun to act politically in concert without embarking upon the third and final stage of their affair with colonialism. Elsewhere in Africa, civil servants and teachers formed associations for the first time, evangelists rebelled against European missionary supervision and established separatist sects, and millennially-minded preachers directed their quasi-political attacks against the colonial establishment.[13]

Although collectively these themes— often overlooked in the literature of and about the period—may be regarded as but a modest prelude to the triumphant march of the 1940's and 1950's, they expressed the dominant sentiment of what I have called nationalism. Africans sought a redress of common grievances within a common territorial framework. Those who thus agitated—if that is the correct word—generally accepted the particular national structure of their aspirations and spoke and acted in terms of programmes of national action. Even though few were at this time demanding self-government or even equality of representation in their respective legislative assemblies, their efforts still justify the use of the collective term nationalism.

To return to Nyasaland, associational forms of endeavour were obscured by the more immediate events of World War I, the Chilembwe rising, and its aftermath. Immediately after the European armistice, however, civil servants, teachers, evangelists, and small businessmen, with some chiefs and headmen, continued the old and organised a number of new native associations. These groups met to talk political reform and they may, in an African context, be considered proto-parties. The associations provided conventient platforms for the airing and discussion of grievances, the training of leaders, and experimentation with different techniques of protest. Since the Government controlled all the usual methods of communication, and could and did prescribe within certain narrow limits the forms of overt protest that it considered legitimate, the associations attempted to accomplish their aims by petitioning the Governor, the Secretary of State for the Colonies, and the reigning British King, by passing innumer-

---

[12]For the Thuku disturbance, see W. McGregor Ross, *Kenya From Within: a short political history* (London, 1927), pp. 225–35.

[13]Cf. Thomas Hodgkin, *Nationalism in Colonial Africa* (London, 1956), p. 114.

able resolutions in the hope that the Government would take notice, and by seeking interviews with the Governor or other administrative officials in person. But little was accomplished by such means, the Government often ignoring the very existence of the associations.

Along with separatist sects and millennial movements, rural and urban associations existed in almost every part of Nyasaland. Some operated continually, some intermittently, others occasionally. The most important were the district and provincial associations that were composed of the indigenous leaders of the Protectorate. Certain members belonged at the same time to two or more associations, others belonged to several in turn. The membership of the various associations overlapped with that of the separatist sects and millennial movements; in certain cases the leaders were identical. I doubt if any of these associations could ever have counted members or adherents in as many as four figures. But no matter how parochial and ineffectual the associations appeared, their thoughts and their actions expressed more than tribal or individual interests. They talked in terms of the Uyasa nation (few then spoke of Malawi) and accepted the integrity of its colonially-derived borders.

To name only a few of the more prominent association leaders, Charles Chinula, George Mwase, Levi Mumba, James Sangala, and Isa Macdonald Lawrence, much as they desired governmental reforms, all expressed a loyalty to the abstract nation of Nyasaland that had much in common with the feelings of nationality accepted by the middle class in, say, eighteenth-century France. Both, when the time came to feel and express their nationalism, followed the lead of the more advanced bourgeoisie. It was distinctly in the interests of the nascent bourgeoisie to keep alive and promote the cause of nationalism; and, in Nyasaland, several among their number finally realised that they could never hope to redress grievances of national concern if the voice of African protest were to continue to be expressed by many scattered sounds rather than by one united chorus that could claim and, in time, achieve a national following.

Out of this sense of the national need emerged the Nyasaland African Congress, an organisation of associations and individuals that held its inaugural meeting in 1944. Sangala, its founder, professed national aims. The speeches and resolutions of the first few meetings reflected similar ends. 'In the past grievances and other vital matters affecting the country and people have been presented to the government and/or other authorities by local organisations who were interested only in their local worries. It is considered', the Congress decided, 'that the time is ripe now for the Africans in this country to strive for unity so as to obtain the greater development of the peoples and country of Nyasaland.'[14] But, in terms of methods and accomplishments, the Congress retained an aura reminiscent of its predecessor associations. Only the attempt by white settlers to gain an overwhelming control of the destinies of the indigenous inhabitants of Central Africa, by federating Nyasaland and the two Rhodesias, provided an issue that could arouse the most apathetic tribesman and give the Congress' national aspirations the mass appeal of a full-fledged movement of nationalism.

Without taking space here to discuss the unsuccessful campaign against the Federation and the political strategies of the time, suffice it to say that Nyasa-

---

[14]Rotberg, *op. cit.* p. 183.

land entered the stage of triumphant nationalism when chiefs and members of the Congress together devoted all their energies to destroying the edifice of Federation. At first, under leaders who had gained thier experience during the politically tentative days before World War II, the Congress proved unable to take advantage of the growing anti-government sentiment in the countryside. But, from about 1955, under a group of impressively tough-minded young men and, after 1958, under the over-all direction of Dr H. Kamazu Banda, the Congress opened branches and gained paid-up adherents everywhere. They manoeuvered themselves by the end of 1958 into a sufficiently strong position to challenge the Governments of Nyasaland and the Federation openly, to defy their laws, and to precipitate a state of unrest that became a state of emergency and resulted in their own imprisonment. Nationalism in its most obvious form had achieved results of a kind that led, a few years later, to the achievement of self-government and, finally, to the independence of Malawi.

To generalise, with adjustments to the outline that I have sketched for Malawi, most of tropical Africa has exhibited this threefold time scale of nationalism.[15] Kenya, Zambia, Ghana, Nigeria, Senegal, Togo, the Congo (Brazzaville), and Gabon appear to confirm the paradigm. Depending upon how the terms are defined, Uganda and the Sudan fit. Tanzania, with a certain allowance for time lag, also meets the criteria that I have sketched. The Congo (Léopoldville) provides an example of extreme telescoping, and many other nations seem to fall in between. But we know comparatively little about tropical Africa in the years between the two world wars. A close examination of the events of those years would, I think, substantiate my contention that the rise of African nationalism is no recent phenomenon, that in most parts of tropical Africa it possesses roots that reach deep into the oldest colonial soil, and that we can conveniently divide the tree of nationalism into the three branches of awakening, incipient action, and triumph.

I would be the last to say that the mere achievement of independence by a territory concludes the working of the ethos of nationalism within it. For only a few parts of independent Africa can we say that the process of nation-building has been completed. Almost everywhere, the new rulers, inheriting the problems that colonial administrations were either unwilling or not equipped to face, are involved in a difficult struggle to finish the process of unification that began almost at the beginning of the colonial era. Despite the overwhelming support given to the nationalist movement by Africans of all classes during the final phases of the struggle and the fervour that the movement aroused in the hearts of its supporters—who thus became the relevant nationals—the present-day rulers have inherited only unconsolidated nations; as in early America, so in Africa there remain fissiparous social, economic, and psychological forces that must be overcome before we can say that the colonial nations have survived the shocks of independence.

To summarise, I see African nationalism in historical terms. For me, it has qualities reminiscent of the older nationalisms of Europe, Arabia, and Asia; despite the number of putative peoples and distinctive languages that

[15] Crawford Young, in *Politics in the Congo: decolonization and independence* (Princeton, 1965), pp. 281–98, proposes a fivefold schema that unnecessarily includes overlapping categories.

exist within each territorial boundary, I maintain that the policies and practices of the colonial powers created national entities of their arbitrarily contrived and assigned territories, and that the indigenous inhabitants not only came to accept their status as nationals, but that they began to think almost exclusively in terms of achieving their freedom from alien rule within the perimeters of their colonial existence. Within almost every territory the nationalist spirit found ready vessels. Its success owes much to the techniques and experiences of the older nationalisms; as hot wars loosened the grip of colonial control in Latin America, Eastern Europe, the Middle East, and Asia, so the cold war war assisted the progress and made possible the success of the nationalist movements of tropical Africa.

Christianity and Sociopolitical Change in Sub-Saharan Africa

Raymond F. Hopkins

Abstract. The introduction of Christianity into sub-Saharan Africa has contributed to social change and the rise of nationalism. As a product of the missionary's work, particularly during the early decades of the twentieth century, Africans learned new norms and habits and were inducted into new roles. From these, recruitment into proto-nationalist churches, mass parties, and roles in the modern sector of society has occurred. Statistical evidence from ten countries shows positive relationships between the rise of Christianity and the growth of indicators of development such as education, wage labor, electrical consumption and urbanization. Conversely, negative relationships are found with communication variables. The overall effect of Christianity, however, has been positive.

The social and political processes current in sub-Saharan Africa may be attributed to a variety of influences. Among these, one of the most important has been the impact of Christian missionaries. James Coleman, for instance, credits missionary activity as one of the three forces behind the "social mobilization"[1] of a "substantial number of Nigerians."[2] Thomas Hodgkin and Georges Balandier have shown that separatist church movements have been a source of proto-nationalist sentiment

[1] For a full discussion of this concept see Karl W. Deutsch, "Social Mobilization and Political Development," *The American Political Science Review* (September 1961), pp. 493–514.

[2] James S. Coleman, *Nigeria: Background to Nationalism* (Berkeley: University of California Press, 1958), p. 410. "Social mobilization," Coleman concludes, was the result of "a policy of determined Europeanization by Christian missionaries, a literary educational curriculum and the growth of an urbanized wage-labor force whose members were haunted by a sense of economic and psychological insecurity."

From *Social Forces*, Vol. XLIV, No. 4 (June 1966), 555–562 by permission of the journal and its publisher, The University of North Carolina Press.

and organization.[3] The Symthes and others have noted the importance missionaries in the educational process, and Thomas Okuma has found some interesting parallels between African church organization and mass party movements.[4] Our purpose in this essay is to examine the process whereby missionary activity contributed to social and political change, and then, to assess whether statistical evidence will corroborate the findings of our examination.

I

The influence of Christian missionaries in sub-Saharan Africa, we believe, has performed an equivalent function to many other aspects of social mobiliza-

tion: it has broken down adherence to traditional order and exposed Africans to some aspects of modernity. Since the beginning of the twentieth century, there has been a steady increase in the number of missionaries and African converts. Figure 1 charts this growth among Protestants. In the last 15 years, however, the relative importance of the missionary and the mission school has declined, and their influence has become increasingly ambiguous.[5] Christian proselytization rarely occurs currently among Africans unexposed to other Western cultural contact. Thus, the relationship between learning the role of a Christian and other indices of social mobilization would not be as clear-cut today as was probably the case in earlier periods. Nevertheless, it it possible to develop a fairly general and theoretical model to describe the mechanism of recruitment to Christianity and its implications for social change.

---

[3] Thomas Hodgkin, *Nationalism in Colonial Africa* (London: Muller, 1956), pp. 93–114; Georges Balandier, "Messianismes et Nationalismes en Afrique Noire," *Cahiers Internationaux de Sociologie*, 14 (1953), pp. 41–65. The political and social implications on independent church movements have also been discussed by George Shepperson and Thomas Price, *Independent African* (Edinburgh: Edinburgh University Press, 1958) and F. B. Welbourn, *East African Rebels* (London: SCM Press, 1961).

[4] Hugh H. Smythe and Mabel M. Smythe, *The New Nigerian Elite* (Stanford: Stanford University Press, 1960), pp. 49, 60. Also relevant to the study of missionary influence in education are Kenneth S. Latourette, *Christianity in a Revolutionary Age: The Twentieth Century Outside Europe*, Vol. 5 (New York: Harper & Bros., 1962), pp. 450–501; Roland A. Oliver, *How Christian is Africa?* (London: Longmans, Green & Co., 1956), and Charles W. Forman, *The Nation and the Kingdom* (New York: Friendship Press, 1964). The similarities which Okuma finds between mass parties and the Christian Church are as applicable for the rest of sub-Saharan Africa (at least below the 10° North Parallel) as for Angola. See Thomas Okuma, *Angola in Ferment: The Background and Prospects of Angolan Nationalism* (Boston: Beacon Press, 1962), pp. 54–56.

[5] John Taylor, *Christianity and Politics in Africa* (London: SCM Press, 1957), pp. 9–10, attributes this decline in influence to the fact that political functions of church leadership have largely passed to nationalists and the fact that African clergy tend to be poorly educated, far from competent and largely underpaid. Moreover, some of the new elite have been disenchanted because Christianity has been identified with white man rule and, hence, foreign to Africa, See Latourette, *op. cit.*, p. 451. Other factors which are contributing to the waning influence of missionaries and Christianity is the proportional increase in missionaries from fundamentalist sects and the expanded range of roles which now provide transit from traditional to modern society. For these points, see Bengt G. M. Sundkler, *The Christian Ministry in Africa* (Uppsala: Swedish Institute of Missionary Research, 1960), pp. 129–131; W. Stanley Rycroft and Myrtle M. Clemmer, *A Factual Study of Sub-Saharan Africa* (New York: United Presbyterian Church, USA, 1962), p. 104, and Jack Mendelsohn, *God, Allah and Juju* (New York: Thomas Nelson, 1962), pp. 1–26.

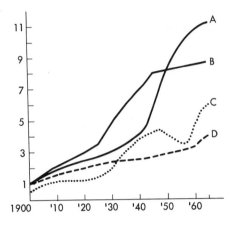

A Christian Community in millions
B Unordained Africans in 10,000's
C Ordained Africans in 1,000's
D Missionaries in 1,000's

FIGURE 1. Growth in the Protestant Church
in Sub-Saharan Africa

Figure 2 depicts the general movement or shifts in perspectives and allegiances which have taken place for many Africans (albeit over a lifetime or perhaps more than one generation). In a rather simple sense, the role of Christian is seen as an intervening variable or learning experience between that of participant in a traditional society and participant in the nascent national community.

In the initial stage, the traditional or primitive society was in a fairly stable state. Religion, as typically organized in these societies, was quite important in the successful functioning of the politi-

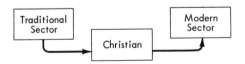

FIGURE 2. Christianity as a Step Toward
Modernity

cal processes. Religious rituals were one of the chief instruments by which power-holders maintained control over the community decision-making process, and the religious "myths" of these primitive groups (e.g., those related to tribal origin) were one of the principal means of legitimizing and also of limiting the political leadership.[6] Moreover, in these societies, the political and religious processes were closely intertwined, often in a single set of institutions and practices.

This was the scene into which Christianity entered in the form of proselytizing missionaries. These men set up missions, began raising crops, provided medical care, and offered to teach the Africans of their ways and God.[7] In spite of obvious values which missionaries offered in the form of skills, well-being and perhaps prestige the ties of traditional life prevented most Africans from accepting this new religion, at least at first.[8] Early recruits to Christianity came, therefore, largely from those already disaffected from traditional society, such as slaves and outcasts.[9]

---

[6] See Lucy Mair, *Primitive Government* (Baltimore: Penguin Books, 1962), pp. 58–60, 85–87, 216–220. Also John Beattie, *Bunyoro: An African Kingdom* (New York: Holt, Rinehart & Winston, 1960), pp. 11–16. Beattie writes, "Mythologies always embody systems of values, judgments about what is considered good and proper by the people who have the myth. Especially, myth tends to sustain some system of authority, and the distinctions of power and status this implies."

[7] The variety of activities which the missionary engaged in are detailed in Roland Oliver, *The Missionary Factor in East Africa* (London: Longmans, Green & Co., 1952), *passim.*

[8] Charles P. Groves, *The Planting of Christianity in Africa*, Vol. 4 (London: Lutterworth Press, 1958), pp. 210–237.

[9] See Chinua Achebe, *Things Fall Apart* (New York: Heinemann, 1959), pp. 147–215. Achebe's novel points out that early converts

The process whereby the new role of Christian was learned no doubt followed the classical formula of learning theory—drive, response, cue and reward.[10] Drive or motivation was supplied for early recruits by deprivations and loss of security suffered in traditional society and/or by the anticipation that rewards would be available through contact with "Europeans." Cues were generally supplied by the missionaries for responses appropriate to their conception of a Christian and the process of conversion. Rewards came both form missionaries—their presence and interest in the African, and the material possessions, skills and medicine which they provided—and from the traditional society (often in the form of increased prestige and security). Explanations of early recruitment into this new social community,[11] then, can be made in terms of the social environment and the stimulus (cues and rewards) it offers, not in terms of personality factors.

The learning of the role of Christian involved defection from the traditional society, at least in part. Moreover, it

involved a number of conflicts between the traditional roles of tribal member, father, wife, etc., and the norms prescribed by Christianity for these roles. Typical role conflicts, for instance, revolved about the paying of bride-prices or the practice of polygamy.

By World War I, the exigencies of the colonial situation had begun to undermine the authority of the chief and disrupt clientship relations in the tribal community. As the chief became a civil servant of the colonial government (or was replaced by one), and as the churches grew into large-scale institutions, the rewards and motivations leading to conversion began to undergo change. As a result, Welbourn argues, Africans were losing a sense of identity and sought to reintegrate themselves "at a more complex level."[12]

From this situation, two types of role conflict emerged. The first, conflict between Christian norms and those of traditional society, has already been mentioned as a force separating the African from traditional society. Moreover, since conversion in a number of instances was opportunistic,[13] as the perspectives of the African broadened and the attention and rewards of the missionary were spread among a much wider range of followers, the "good fortune and social status" of the role of Christian[14] tended to diminish and role

---

were largely "efulefu," that is men who were considered worthless or empty by the traditional society. Conversion of such men, along with outcasts, tended to reinforce the negative view which African traditional elites held toward the new religion. On the recruitment of slaves see Oliver, *Missionary Factor*, pp. 12–18.

[10]See Neal E. Miller and John Dollard, *Social Learning and Imitation* (New Haven: Yale University Press, 1941), pp. 1–90.

[11]Christian missions, unlike churches in present day Western countries, operated as complete social units. In addition to establishing a school and clinic to serve the community, most missions would train and employ a number of Africans to serve as "helpers, carpenters, bricklayers, cooks, houseboys, teachers and catechists." J. Merle Davis, *Modern Industry and the African* (London: The Macmillan Co., 1933), p. 283.

[12]Welbourn, *op. cit.*, pp. 203–204. In contrast to behavior typical of the more intimate traditional societies, these dissatisfied Christians sought their identity not in larger comradeship, "but in terms of status as a leader."

[13]The number of nominal conversions was certainly large as regular defections from the churches indicate. Latourette, *op. cit.*, p. 462.

[14]John Taylor and Dorothea Lehmann, *Christians of the Copperbelt* (London: SCM Press, 1961), p. 152. They find Africans commonly judge a religion by "its results" as manifested in overt events.

conflicts, as a result, became more acute. The second conflict arose from discontinuities between precept and practice on the part of white Christians. Converts who were encouraged to acquire education and to emulate their white "fathers" were frustrated and not rewarded upon discovering that they were denied both acceptance as equals and responsibilities in church affairs.[15] African Christians began discovering that compartmentalization of Christian ideals was common among whites, particularly those in the colonial service.[16] Africans came to perceive they were held in disrepute and even mild contempt by white men. Hence, the high rewards surrounding the role of Christian tended to diminish. And Africans who had internalized the norms of this role suffered frustration within the mission church.

As a consequence, defection and re-recruitment into slightly different social movements began to occur in significant numbers. Again, learning theory suggests straightforward explanations of why Africans flocked into separatist churches, beginning in the late nineteenth century, and have recently joined in mass party movements.[17] First, as rewards for playing the role of Christian diminished, extinction began. New beliefs had proved useful in the changed tribal context or in interpreting the oppressed state in which many Africans felt themselves to be (for instance,

identifying their own history with the Old Testament story of persecution and deliverance).[18] Hence, participation rather than beliefs tended to be extinguished.[19] Indeed, motivations created by social uprootedness continued, but, for many, participation in the mission church was no longer rewarding. Secondly, counter-conditioning occurred. Role conflicts which were involved in playing the role of Christian were resolved in part by the creation of similar, but substitute movements offering the same or even more rewards, but involving less avoidance situations. Motivation to participate in these independent church movements was a simple generalization of the original drive factors behind conversion. Indeed motivation to believe and participate may have increased as tribal structure continued to disintegrate.[20] But belief and participation were displaced from

---

[15]Sundkler, *op. cit.*, pp. 50–57.

[16]Oliver, *How Christian*, p. 17 ff.

[17]These separatist churches were, in many respects, the precursors of nationalist movements. Begun innocently in 1884, from the 1920's onward they became a "safety valve" for releasing antiwhite fervor. As late as 1952, for instance, there were 3,818 political prisoners (631 declared dangerous) in the Congo connected with one or another prophetic sect. Hodgkin, *op. cit.*, pp. 100, 106, 111–112.

[18]Sundkler, *op. cit.*, p. 285, finds African pastors, for instance, regularly citing the Old Testament and identifying their history with it, especially the episodes of escape and independence.

[19]Robert Frank Weiss, "Defection from Social Movements and Subsequent Recruitment to New Movements," *Sociometry* (March 1963), p. 7. Discussing differential extinction of belief and participation, Weiss states: "When reward for participation is terminated, but members continue to be rewarded for belief, they will lose the habit of participation, but retain their beliefs." We draw heavily on Weiss for our interpretation at this point.

[20]*Ibid.*, p. 12. "A continued worsening of the social conditions which motivated the commitment to the original movement could lead to ... an increase in motivation, as could deprivation of the satisfactions from ... the original movement. If the motivation underlying belief and participation increases it will be possible for increasingly dissimilar movements to attract some of the defectors." Although Weiss casts his discussion in terms of movements rather than roles, there seems to be no difficulty in applying his analysis.

the original social movement, as extinction led to a decline in the desirability of the Christian role within the setting of the mission church and counter-conditioning induced defection to the separatist church movements.[21]

This same theoretical model of behavior can also explain the defections which occurred, less dramatically but with even greater long-run consequences, into roles less similar to that of Christian. Many converts maintained nominal belief and participation in the role of Christian, while they were attracted to other roles, more "modern" ones, with a resultant neglect of their Christian duties. Thus better pay or opportunities for positions in the colonial administration or industries drew off a large number of defectors from the church.[22] While stimulus generalization as an explanation of shifts into these roles requires a loose application of the concept, nevertheless, the training provided by missionaries in efforts to convert Africans was a necessary stage in the learning process of many Africans, including the new elite, who have reached the modern sector of society.[23] Sundkler notes, for instance, the very high turnover in catechists as they have been re-recruited to higher posts more fully a part of the "modernizing" society.[24]

In summary, recruitment to these new movements and modern roles was based, at least partially, on learned responses of the earlier experience as a Christian convert. Skills, habits, symbols and goals acquired in the process of becomin a Christian were essentially able to feed into nationalist movements. In terms of the simple model in Figure 2, the body of Christians created by missionary activity presented a pool of individuals from which nationalist leadership could be recruited and with which these leaders could communicate and receive support. Oliver sums up the point this way: "During the last 50 years (since 1900) Christianity in Africa has been more than a mere religion. It has been that which has helped the African adapt himself to the new order."[25]

II

If our above analysis is correct, missionary activity should be closely related with indices of development and social mobilization. In order to assess whether this was the case, a variety of statistics have been collated and correlated. Ten sub-Saharan countries, in particular, were focused upon as convenient sources of information: Congo (Leopoldville),

---

[21]This may be explained by stimulus generalization principles, probably displacement based on inhibition by conflict. *Ibid.*, pp. 8–9.

[22]Davis, *op. cit.*, p. 284, finds that in northern Rhodesia in the 1930's "mission trained boys who could speak English and were accustomed to work with Europeans were in high demand." Moreover, as their earnings increased church contributions decreased.

[23]A background in the church, particularly a missionary education has been found to be a striking feature among modern African elite. See Forman, *op. cit.*, and Smythe, *op. cti.*, pp. 49, 60, A generation ago, according to Sundkler, "the mission was the only channel by which a gifted young man could make a career," *op. cit.*, p. 33.

[24]*Ibid.*, pp. 116–117, 157. The ladder of teacher, to pastor, to government official has been quite common in Africa, Sundkler finds.

[25]Oliver, *How Christian, op. cit.*, p. 17. Sundkler writes: "As the old ancestral order was dissolved by modern Western influences, the Christian churches grew to represent a new rallying point, a new order, a new life and a new leadership," *op. cit.*, p. 45. Latourette finds that missions were "the medium through which" Congolese (and presumably others) transition to the modern world took place, *op. cit.*, p. 479.

Ghana, Kenya, Malawi, Nigeria, Sierra Leone, Rhodesia, Tanzania, Uganda and Zambia.[26]

The validity of such data is not clearly established. Many commentators feel that all African statistics, and particularly religious statistics, must be regarded as very imprecise.[27] Indeed, examples of past errors uncovered in Christian statistics would rise doubts as to their validity with even the most uncautious of observers.[28] Nevertheless, some statistical analysis is plausible. Assuming the data probably has ordinal validity, correlation coefficients, between indicators of the amount of Christian activity in each country and indications of development or social mobilization, have been computed.[29]

---

[26]Countries formerly under French colonial rule (due to difficulty in finding historical information or statistical data) and the Union of South Africa (due to its unique characteristics) were not selected as data sources. Zanzibar is not included in the Tanzanian data.

[27]See Victor C. Ferkiss, *Religion and Politics in Independent African States: A Prolegomena* (Washington, D.C.: Georgetown University Press, 1964), unpublished draft manuscript, p. 45.

[28]Some of the more egregious errors have been noticed and eliminated from our data. Sundkler, *op. cit.*, pp. 330–332 provides some interesting examples of the sort of errors that have occurred. In 1938 one Swedish mission claimed 175 ordained men in French Equatorial Africa but really had only five; in 1957 the *World Christian Handbook* reported 1,969 missionaries in the Belgian Congo while in truth there were only 545 as the African Inland Mission had returned a figure of 1,474 compared with the actual number of pastors as in 1949 of 50. Most striking of all is the report that the Free Presbyterian Church of Scotland had 1,000 ordained men in the Union of South Africa in 1957, when, in fact, they had only one–and he was actually in Southern Rhodesia. Other corrections were found in Rycroft and Clemmer, *op. cit.*, p. 110.

[29]Use of the product-moment correlation coefficient seems completely unwarranted due both to its requirement of normality and to

The statistical evidence presented in Table 1 tends to confirm the proposition that missionary activity has influenced development. The generally high correlations on such indices as primary education and employment in nonsubsistence economy, i.e., wage-labor and nonagricultural, substantiate our argument that there has been a path of recruitment through the role of Christian to education in mission schools and jobs in the modern economy. Indeed, since missions have provided (and in some instances still do) the bulk of primary education, the relationship between primary education and Christianity would be of surprise only if it did not occur in the data. Positive and sometimes high correlations with electricity consumption and motor vehicles lend some further support to the thesis of Christian influence.

There are, however, some important reservations suggested by this set of correlations. Consistently negative correlations with communication variables: the flow of mail, radio audience, and newspaper readers, makes clear that Christian influence has not been direct or positive in all cases, and, indeed, may even have been regressive in some instances.[30] The fact that the colonial

---

the questionable validity of the data. Spearman's rank order correlation, assuming the data only has ordinal validity, also avoids the normality assumption. Problems related to the question of random samples remain unresolved. See, however, Bruce M. Russett *et al.*, *World Handbook of Political and Social Indicators* (New Haven: Yale University Press, 1964), p. 263, for a possible way of viewing this. Interpretation with respect to the significance of these correlations is difficult. As a possible guideline, however, the critical values of r_s are: r_s .44, p .10; r_s .56, p .05; r_s .74, p .01. For this statistical test and critical values see Hubert Blalock, *Social Statistics* (New York: McGraw-Hill Book Co., 1960), p. 319 ff.

[30]In the Congo, Uganda and Malawi, for

administration generally assumed responsibility for secondary school education no doubt accounts for the negative correlations it has with indicators of Christian activity. Even the associations with urbanization and gross national product do not seem consistently positive or strong, however. Thus the overall picture resulting from the figures in Table 1 is not totally consistent.

Two general tendencies are interesting to note, however. First, missionaries, pastors and, particularly African church workers (Protestant catechists and teachers) were the indices of Christian activity most closely related to the indicators of development and social mobilization. The high correlations with African church workers especially seem to support the earlier analysis since these are the individuals whose skills are being developed in a way that prepares them to assume roles in a moderizing economy or a nationalist movement. Second, higher correlations with development indicators are almost always obtained for Protestant rather than Roman Catholic measures of activity. Moreover, when Roman Catholic presence in a country is statistically accounted for or, in effect, removed from a correlation, there is little change in the magnitude of the relationship.[31]

Thus, somewhat along the lines of the Weberian thesis regarding the "Protestant ethic," the political and social impact of Catholicism in promoting change would seem to have been demonstrably less than that of Protestantism.[32]

It is interesting to compare the findings from this rather limited number of African polities to those included in a study by Russett et al., which encompasses up to 133 countries.[33] Table 2 contains a comparative summary of eight correlations on equivalent indices. The fairly high correlations between percentage Christian and all development indices in the world data are striking in comparison to the African context. These figures strongly suggest, as do the higher correlations of African missionary activity as contrasted to percentage Christian in Figure 1, that the efforts of the missionary, the representative of both Christ and Western culture, more than the mere fact that various Africans were labeled as "Christian," were the important events in effecting social and political change.

The statistical evidence presented in Tables 1 and 2 indicate that the immediate and strong effects of Christian

example, three countries with fairly high percentages of Christians, particular circumstances also may have mitigated the effects of Christianity in some areas, e.g., Belgium's colonial policies which discouraged African progress at advanced levels, the adaptability of Bagandans to Christianity such that traditional patterns remained intact to a greater extent than in other traditional societies, and the exodus of Malawi (Nyasaland) Christians to work in the copper mines and contribute to the economy of Zambia (Northern Rhodesia.)

[31] In calculations not presented here, Kendall's *tau* and partial *tau* were computed, partialing for the effects of Roman Catholics. In general the partial correlation remained about as high as the original *tau*, in some

instances it even increased (e.g., Protestant missionary averages for 1938–1962 and GDP per capita: *tau* = 38, *tau* partial = 46). This statistic is in Sidney Siegel, *Nonparametric Statistics* (New York: McGraw-Hill Book Co., 1956), pp. 219–229.

[32] Kenneth S. Latourette, *A History of the Expansion of Christianity: The Great Century*, Vol. 5 (New York: Harper & Bros., 1943), pp. 499–500, characterizes differences among missionary converts to Catholicism and Protestantism in this way: "In general, the Roman Catholic black was more docile, more dependent on the white man, and more submissive to him. The Protestant black was inclined to be more independent, think for himself, and to be more self-reliant."

[33] Russett et al., op. cit., p. 287. These figures are all based on 88 countries or less.

TABLE 1   Correlations of 17 Christian Indicators* with 15 Development Indicators* for Ten Sub-Saharan Countries

Christian indicators as % of population	Year	Primary education as % of population 1953	Secondary education as % of population 1953	Primary education as % of population 1960	Secondary education as % of population 1960	Total mail per capita 1960	Mail ratio internal/external 1960	Electricity per capita 1959	Motor vehicles per capita 1958	Wage Earners—% of econ. active males 1935	Wage Earners—% of econ. active males 1955	Nonagric. wage force as % of population 1956	Urbanization—% in towns over 20,000 1955	Gross national product—per capita 1957	Radio audience 1963	Newspaper audience 1961–1963
Roman Catholics	1933	32	−35	28				33	27	37	44	34			−46	−41
Roman Catholics	1960	22	−27	29	36	−36		47	58	35	41	22	−28	−28	−59	−56
Protestants	1938	54	−36	61		39		25	43	26	27	49		42		32
Protestants	1962	52	−38	56	21		−42	35	33	69	72	54			−38	−30
Total Christians	1935	40	−43	49				32	26	33	39	39			−32	−26
Total Christians	1948	38	−45	44			−25			40	48	39			−48	−42
Total Christians	1960	30	−29	42		−29	−26			52	56	35	−27	−22	−61	−59
Average No. Christians		38	−45	44			−25	32	26	40	48	39			−48	−42
Rom. Cath. Missionaries	1933	33	−28	26	−47		−38	33	25	38	46	36			−48	−46
Rom. Cath. Missionaries	1960	47	−32	48	−50		−50	37	30	69	76	56	20		−58	−41
Protestant Missionaries	1938	80	−54	73	−50	29	−56	62	66	87	91	86	48	44	−33	
Protestant Missionaries	1962	66	−34	47	−25	37	−41	62	59	78	83	78	47	39		
Total Missionaries	1935	74	−66	58	−38	24	−49	67	61	70	78	76	33	28	−41	−20
Total Missionaries	1950	68	−55	62	−38	21	−44	66	58	72	79	77	35	28	−38	−21
Total Missionaries	1960	58	−30	47	−38	21	−44	56	46	70	77	71	37	29	−31	−23
African Pastors	1960	58	−30	47	−38	21	−44	56	46	70	77	71	37	29	−31	−23
African Church Workers (Protestant only—average)	1938–1960	73	−63	54	43	35		81	60	26	26	64	47	51	24	24

* All correlations (r$_s$) are based on the indicator as percentage of the population. Coefficients have been multiplied by 100 for ease of reading and those below an absolute value of 20 are omitted from the table. The data upon which these correlations are based comes from the following sources: Christian data—K. G. Grubb, E. J. Bingle and R. W. Coxill, *World Christian Handbook* (London: 1949, 1962) and Rycroft and Clemmer, *op. cit.* Where Roman Catholic and Protestant figures were for different years, a middle year was chosen as representative. Development data are principally from *African Labor Survey* (Geneva: 1958) and the *United Nations Statistical Yearbook 1960 and 1962* (New York: Department of Economic Affairs, 1961, 1963). Complete sources and data are available from the author.

TABLE 2

Comparative Correlation Coefficients Between Percentage Christian and Development Indices—in the World and in Ten African Countries

	World % Christian	Africa % Christian Average 1935–1960	Africa % Christian 1960
1. Gross domestic product per capita	68	−04	−22
2. Newspaper per 1,000 population	69	−42	−59
3. Letters per capita:			
domestic	74	−14	−28
foreign	61		
4. Radios per population	68	−48	−61
5. Urbanization (towns over 20,000)	50	−16	−27
6. Education—% of population in		44	42
primary or secondary school	63	09	−15
7. Nonagricultural workers—			
% of population	50	39	35
8. Wage and salary workers—			
% of population or of working age population	50	48	56

activity seem to lie in the areas of education (notably primary education) and the labor force (i.e., wage labor and nonagricultural labor). With respect to other indices of social mobilization, such as urbanization and national income, the influence of Christianity may be more limited, at least in terms of immediate or gross effects. And the relationships between indicators of Christianity and of communication (newspapers, radios, letters) development were actually negative.[34] Before attempting to complete any picture of Christianity's influence in the African countries, however, further study will be needed. Intervening effects, such as colonial policy or tribal differences, should be investigated. Also, more precise data, possibly of a social

survey nature, will be needed.[35] On the basis of what statistical evidence we have gathered so far, the best conclusion one can draw is that the effects of Christianity are probably important, but that a good deal is left to be explained by other influences. As a single influence, Christianity can certainly serve as an independent indicator of social change.

III

This paper, in very general terms, has suggested ways in which the missionary enterprise in sub-Saharan Africa contributed to social change and the rise of national sentiment. Theories of learning and role conflict have been used to conceptualize and interpret some aspects of this change. As a product of the missionary's work, Africans

[34]It is interesting to note that the Congo, heavily Catholic, has the largest percentage of Christians and ranks eighth and ninth in newspaper and radio audience, thus heavily contributing to these negative correlations.

[35]With better data more sophisticated mathematical models could be employed, perhaps controlling for third and fourth variables.

learned new norms and habits and were inducted into new roles from which recruitment into proto-nationalist churches, mass parties, and roles in the modern sector of society has occurred. The missionary's efforts have had special significance, particularly in the early decades of this century, because the nature of his calling required the missionary to seek out and instruct Africans. Over time the effects of this learning by Africans helped foster the rise of demands and expectations for dignity, equality and independence. It was the missionary in significant measure who shaped the goals and norms manifested in the growth of nationalist movements, the development of a modern sector of life, and the ahievement of independence.

II

Agencies of Political Mobilization

In the terminology of systems analysis, political groups—associational, nonassociational, institutional, and other types—"articulate" and "aggregate" interests and political demands, and channel these into the institutions of government with the expectation that these demands will be converted into the desired official policies. Although various groups can participate in this process, in Africa political parties have been the most dominant and successful of these organizations. Others, such as trade unions, student organizations, agricultural cooperatives, and tribal associations, are most often absorbed into the political parties in much the same way that the major political parties in the United States tend to absorb the issues and sometimes even the leaders of third parties. Extraparty groups in Africa that insist on remaining independent centers of activity usually find themselves outside the orbit of effective political influence; sometimes they are labelled as subversive bodies or even are repressed. Contemporary African politics lack the social roots for the organizational pluralism one finds in the United States and Western Europe.

The brief history of African political parties—and seldom does that history span more than two decades—suggests that they have served more than the single function of demand-making. Most African parties have, in addition, been consistently involved in political recruitment, political socialization, and political communication, as well as in producing outputs such as welfare and patronage. Students of politics in the United States have long known that American parties also perform these functions. Indeed, as J. David Greenstone has observed in the case of Kampala, Uganda, many African political parties are now reminiscent of the typical American urban political "machines" of the past century both in their capacity to involve persons in a new political process and in their corruption.[1] But since independence, the ruling parties in many African states have operated less as channels for the transmission of demands to government than as agencies for broadening the front of support for the national political leadership. This is a striking about-face from the terminal colonial period when the major purpose of nearly all African parties was to mobilize their African peoples *against* the colonial regimes, and it appears that some African leaders have had difficulty abandoning what Edward Shils describes as the "oppositional mentality" they developed during the years of colonialism. Given the broad range of party functions, it is not surprising that they are the central focus of the recent literature on African politics.

Initial studies of African political parties were generally descriptive classifications of party organizations. In the 1950's such investigators as Thomas Hodgkin inquired how African parties differed in such matters as structure, membership, leadership, and goals.[2] Another early concern was to establish the dynamics of party formation and growth, and it was these studies, for example, David E. Apter's *Gold Coast in Transition* (Princeton, 1955), that rediscovered—for African studies, at least,—Max Weber's concept of "charismatic leadership" and gave it such wide-spread currency in the African politics literature. More recently, Africanists have sought to explore the effects that particular types of parties and party systems have on their respective political communities. The result is a substantial literature offering a variety of party typologies that focuses less on the structural or normative characteristics of parties than upon their presumed consequences for society. Positing the existence of cause-effect relationships is among the first steps in the construction of theory and a major task for all social sciences.

Since independence, single-party systems, or systems dominated by one party have been the rule in almost all of the new African states, and Africanists have directed much of their energy to assessing the results of such systems. In the past decade the question most frequently asked was whether single-party systems could be democratic. Although it is clear that African one-party states do not always protect democratic freedoms and public liberties, most Africanists seem to agree with

---

[1] J. David Greenstone, "Corruption and Self Interest in Kampala and Nairebi: A Comment on Local Politics in East Africa," *Comparative Studies in Society and History,* VIII, No. 2 (January 1966), 199 ff.

[2] Thomas Hodgkin, *African Political Parties* (London: Penguin Books, 1961).

Martin L. Kilson's assertion that the extent of democratic practices is not the most meaningful yardstick by which to measure or evaluate African party systems. With Kilson, most students now hold that African states are not likely to be able to tolerate opposition groups for some time to come, and that a more realistic standard of judgment is the degree to which African parties succeed in promoting stability and modernization without becoming unduly oppressive.[3] In fact, much of the current literature on African political parties is devoted to exploring the relationships between parties and party systems and the achievement of particular political "outcomes," especially economic development and national integration.[4]

Increasingly, however, many Africanists have contended that the importance of parties in the politics of independent African states has been exaggerated, not in terms of the number of functions parties are thought to perform but in terms of the quality of that performance. Bureaucracies are emerging as the more salient institutions in the political process, and some political scientists refer to the African "no-party state" to describe politics where bureaucracy apparently reigns without the need to take into account other groups in society. Indeed, the author of one of the best examples of recent "revisionist" literature has even questioned the assumed mobilizing power of the victorious nationalist movements during the colonial regime. Aristide Zolberg suggests that some scholars tend to write the political history of Africa from the point of view of the winners in the struggle for independence and, in particular, to accept uncritically the success of nationalist leaders as proof of their claims that they uniquely represented the African masses.[5] It is not surprising, therefore, that observers were little prepared for the numerous military *coups d'etat* that have followed the achievement of independence.

---

[3] Martin L. Kilson, "Authoritarian and Single Party Tendencies in African Politics," *World Politics,* XV, No. 2 (January 1963), 293.

[4] See, for example, James S. Coleman and Carl Rosberg, Jr., (eds.), *Political Parties and National Integration in Tropical Africa* (Berkeley and Los Angeles: University of California Press, 1964).

[5] Aristide R. Zolberg, *Creating Political Order: The Party-States of West Africa* (Chicago: Rand McNally, 1966), esp. Chapter 1.

For A Sociological Concept of Charisma

William H. Friedland

Abstract. Weber's concept of charisma has not been empirically useful to sociology even though it has influenced sociological thinking considerably. The reason is that Weber dealt with charisma more as a psychological than a social phenomenon. The concept can be useful, however, in the analysis of social change if the focus of attention is concentrated on the social context within which charisma develops rather than on charisma or charismatics. Utilizing the example of modern African leadership in Tanganyika, charisma appears in situations where (a) leaders formulate inchoate sentiments deeply held by masses; (b) the expression of such sentiments is seen as hazardous; (c) success—as defined by the relevant social groups—is registered.

The enormous interest of sociologists in the work of Max Weber is indicated by the popularity of his books and by the many articles dealing with Weber in recent times.[1] What has probably been most significant in Weber's work has been his typology of authority and, of the three types of authority, the bureaucratic-legal has had the most influence on present-day sociology. The literature of recent years is replete with articles dealing with bureaucracy, most of which acknowledge some debt to Weber.

However, Weber's two other types of authority—the traditional and the charismatic—have been almost totally ignored by sociologists in empirical research. Traditional authority has been bypassed largely because it has fallen within the purview of anthropology. Although this is an accident of intellectual history, sociologists have concentrated their energies on modern societies and had little involvement with traditional societies and traditional authority. Charisma, to paraphrase Mark Twain, is a subject about which much has been said but little done. In spite of Parsons' contention that "Charisma is not a metaphysical entity but a strictly empirical observable quality of men and things in relation to human acts and attitudes,"[2] remarkably little research has been *undertaken to elucidate this ostensibly empirical quality.*[3] This fact is all the more remark-

---

[1] Substantial interest in Weber began in the United States with an introduction to his work by Talcott Parsons in *The Structure of Social Action* (Glencoe: The Free Press, 1949), Chapters 14–17, the first edition of which was published in 1937. This was followed by Hans H. Gerth and C. Wright Mills, *From Max Weber: Essays in Sociology* (New York: Oxford University Press, 1946); and Max Weber, *The Theory of Social and Economic Organization* (Glencoe: The Free Press, 1947), translated by A. M. Henderson and Talcott Parsons. After this came a veritable flood of Weberian writing and commentary. Reinhard Bendix, *Max Weber: An Intellectual Portrait* (Garden City: Doubleday and Co., 1960), presents an excellent summary of Weber's ideas.

[2] *Structure . . . , op. cit.*, pp. 668–669.

[3] One needs only to examine the literature to note the dearth of empirical research on charisma. For example, the *Index to the American Sociological Review* contains no category for "charisma." A search of various indices and journals reveals, indeed, that charisma has been utilized more by political scientists than

From *Social Forces,* Vol. XLIII, No. 1 (October 1964), 18–26, by permission of the journal and its publisher, The University of North Carolina Press.

able when one considers the emphasis placed on the concept by Weber's translators and commentators.[4]

The dearth of empirical studies by sociologists can be explained, this

---

sociologists. Cf., Carl J. Freidrich, "Political Leadership and the Problem of Charismatic Power," *The Journal of Politics, 23* (February 1961), pp. 3–24; James C. Davies, "Charisma in the 1952 Campaign," *American Political Science Review, 48* (December 1954), pp. 1083–1102; John T. Marcus, "Transcendence and Charisma," *Western Political Quarterly, 14* (March 1961), pp. 236–241. Sociologists interested in charisma tend to be concerned primarily with studies of developing societies. Cf., Edward A. Shils, "The Concentration and Dispersion of Charisma: Their Bearing on Economic Policy in Underdeveloped Countries," *World Politics, 11* (October 1958), pp. 1–19; Gideon Sjoberg, "Political Structure, Ideology and Economic Development," Department of Government, Indiana University: The Carnegie Faculty Seminar on Political and Administrative Development, 1963 (reprint); W. G. Runciman, "Charismatic Legitimacy and One-Party Rule in Ghana," *Archives Européenes de Sociologie, 4* (1963), pp. 148–165; also the discussion of "heroes" by Immanual Wallerstein, *Africa: The Politics of Independence* (New York: Vintage Books, 1961), Chap. V. An application of the concept of charisma to the analysis of organizations can be found in Amitai Etzioni, *A Comparative Analysis of Complex Organizations* (New York: The Free Press of Glencoe, 1961), Chaps. 9–10. Although Weber's concept of charisma originated in his studies of religion, little empirical work on charisma in religious movements has been undertaken by sociologists. While there is an enormous literature on prophets and other charismatics, this is the work of religious scholars, Biblical students, historians, etc. An important exception is the recently published article by Peter L. Berger, "Charisma, Religious Innovation, and the Israelite Prophecy," *American Sociological Review, 28* (December 1963), pp. 940–951. Berger not only undertakes a re-evaluation of Weber's studies based upon modern knowledge of the Old Testament but suggests important refinements of Weber's ideas on the origins of charismatic figures.

[4] Cf., *Structure . . . , op. cit.,* Chap. XVII; Weber, *op. cit.,* p. 64 ff.; Bendix, *op. cit.,* Chap. X; Gerth and Mills, *op. cit.,* pp. 51–55.

writer believes, by the manner in which Weber and his successors dealt with the concept. While Weber clearly indicated a social dimension to charisma, he also stressed charisma as a *psychological attribute of a person.* Weber's successors have had similarly divided orientations toward charisma but emphasis has been, on the whole, on the idea of an individual commanding certain gifts. Sociologists have been unable to come to grips empirically with the concept because, while charisma has been interesting, as presently developed, it lies outside the purview of disciplinary interests.

This paper seeks to examine charisma and clarify the psychological preoccupations of the concept and attempts to refocus the concept in terms relevant to sociological interests. In so doing, it will be shown that Weber dealt, at least to some extent, with sociological components of charisma but that his concerns were mainly psychological. An empirical case—social change in Tanganyika—will be utilized to indicate how the concept may be dealt with in a manner consonant with sociological concerns and its importance in explaining social change.

THE CONCEPT OF CHARISMA

Charisma is crucial to Weber's system of analysis as the basis for the explanation of social change. Weber's other types of authority are stable systems within which it is conceivable that change will take place only at the micro level. The problem for Weber was to account for large-scale social change and the concept of charisma provided what Bendix calls "a sociology of innovation."[5] Though a sociology of change was necessary for Weber, it

---

[5] Bendix, *op. cit.,* pp. 272–293.

would appear that he was not at ease with it. Not only are two of his three patterns of domination concerned with stable systems but even his discussion of charisma is heavily oriented toward its stabilization and routinization.[6] Despite this orientation it is obvious from a reading of his work that the problem of change continually concerned Weber. Yet the difficulties in working with his approach to the study of social change become apparent when one examines his writings on charisma in some detail.

On the one hand, Weber's discussion of charisma sounds, all too frequently, like that of a psychologist discussing leadership. Charisma is

... applied to a certain quality of an individual personality by virtue of which he is set apart from ordinary men and treated as endowed with supernatural, superhuman, or at least specifically exceptional powers or qualities. These are such as are not accessible to the ordinary person, but are regarded as of divine origin or as exemplary, and on the basis of them the individual concerned is treated as a leader.[7]

On the other hand, Weber also recognized the existence of a social basis for its exercise: *charisma had to be socially validated.* The problem, thus, is that Weber is simultaneously concerned with psychological and sociological components: charisma is a "gift of grace" to a person and does not require external confirmation; yet, without social validation charisma does not

exist. These conflicting orientations are continually manifested.

It is recognition on the part of those subject to authority which is decisive for the validity of charisma. ... But where charisma is genuine, it is not this which is the basis of the claim to legitimacy. This basis lies rather in the conception that it is the *duty* of those who have been called to a charismatic mission to recognize its quality and act accordingly. ...
No prophet has ever regarded his quality as dependent on the attitudes of the masses toward him. ...

Yet Weber immediately continues:

If proof of his charismatic qualification fails him for long, the leader endowed with charisma tends to think his god or his magical or heroic powers have deserted him. If he is for long unsuccessful, above all if his leadership fails to benefit his followers, it is likely that his charismatic authority will disappear.[8]

Elsewhere, Weber states:

Charisma knows only inner determination and inner restraint. The holder of charisma seizes the task that is adequate for him and demands obedience and a following by virtue of his mission. His success determines whether he finds them. His charismatic claim breaks down if his mission is not recognized by those to whom he feels he has been sent.[9]

Weber's discussion of the concept of charisma, therefore, is not completely clear. On the one hand, he appears to be proposing a "great man" theory of history in which macrochange is produced by the appearance of unique persons with "gifts." This approach is essentially psychological because Weber

---

[6] Thus, in *The Theory of Social and Economic Organization,* pages 358–363 are concerned with the characteristics of charismatic authority while pages 363–373 discuss the routinization of charisma. Similarly, Bendix's material on charisma is concerned to a considerable extent with the routinization of charisma rather than with the characterization of charismatic domination. Cf., also Runciman, *op. cit.*

[7] *Theory . . . , op. cit.,* pp. 358–359.

[8] *Ibid.,* pp. 359–360.

[9] Gerth and Mills, *op. cit.,* p. 246.

argues that the charismatic figure does not require external validation of his gift but demands obedience regardless of the attitudes of others. On the other hand, Weber clearly indicates that it is not just "great men" who make history. If the charisma of unique people is not socially validated, it is insignificant.

The two-fold character of charismatic authority is reflected by many sociologists of whom only one is selected for illustrative purposes. Chinoy, for example, in discussing charismatic authority states that

> . . . men may obey simply because of the personal qualities—the charisma—of the person who commands; the appeals of the "natural leader" may transcend established institutions and challenge accepted values.[10]

Here is charisma as a psychological phenomenon. Later, however, Chinoy reflects *both* the psychological and sociological aspects:

> The emergence of a religious movement is often dependent upon the presence of a prophet, or *charismatic* leader . . . who claims moral authority for the doctrine or message he proclaims and gains support for it because of his own personal qualities. . . . Indeed, the origins of some religions are so closely identified with individuals that it almost appears as if they alone were responsible for its success. The creative role played by the charismatic leader should not be minimized; his personal qualities may make the difference between a revolution in religious doctrine and practice, and little or no change. But *no prophet can succeed unless the circumstances are propitious. He succeeds when a potential following exists because of the problems that some people face.* The importance of both the leader and the context in which he moves are

suggested in the conclusion of a historian of the Reformation that Martin Luther "found public opinion supersaturated with revolt; all that was needed to precipitate it was a pebble thrown in. . . ."[11]

Weber's formulation of the concept of charisma has not been useful to empirical analysis in sociology. This does not mean that it is without value. Indeed, it is the contention of this paper that the concept can be sociologically useful by focussing upon the analysis of social situations within which charisma develops.

It is probably true that personalities that are potentially charismatic are continually being generated.[12] Yet the "charisma" of these personalities rarely appears to be validated by social groups. The question then remains: Why does the "authority" of these potential charismatics go unrecognized? The answer to this question lies in the character of social validation. It is only when the message conveyed by charismatics to social groups is relevant and meaningful within the social context that authority emerges. Thus, while charismatics are continually being generated (or are generating themselves, in Weberian terms), their "charisma" can frequently go unrecognized or indeed be considered peculiar, deviant, or perhaps, insane. If genuine charisma is to be understood, analysis must be directed toward the social situation within which the charismatic figure

---

[10] Eli Chinoy, *Society* (New York: Random House, 1961), p. 247.

[11] *Ibid.*, pp. 279–280 (emphasis added).

[12] "Weber made it clear that charisma has been a recurrent phenomenon because persons endowed with the gift of grace—for better or worse—have asserted their leadership under all historical conditions." Bendix, *op. cit.*, p. 327. It should be added, however, that the degree to which incipient charismatics are generated may be a function, to some degree, of the cultural system which may encourage or impede the emergence of strong, innovative personalities.

operates, and the character of his message. In sum, while there are plenty of people with messages, these must be relevant to social groups before they begin to be received and become the basis for action.

In order to delineate the social context within which charisma develops, an empirical case may be useful. For this purpose, modern political and trade union leaders in Tanganyika will be utilized.

CHARISMATIC LEADERS IN TANGANYIKA

When modern political and union leaders were studied in Tanganyika, it became intuitively clear that most leaders were charismatic. Nevertheless, the problem of delineating the nature of their authority in an *objective* fashion was a major dilemma of field research. It was possible, for example, to find cases of bureaucratic-legal authority (that held by the colonial officials) and traditional authority (held by traditional clan heads in certain tribes and by chiefs in others). Yet these forms of authority obviously became less significant after 1959 than that of the African political and trade union leaders. The authority of the new leaders was unquestionable: they called on masses of people and masses responded. The political leaders could bring out thousands of people for a mass meeting; the union leaders could bring workers out on strike for lengthy periods even if they could not get them to pay their dues.[13]

What was the character of authority of the political and union leaders? If we use Weber's typology, we must reject the bureaucratic-legal and traditional systems of authority as an explanation. While it is true that the leaders had bureaucratic-legal skills—they were educated and westernized—this alone was not the source of their authority. There were, indeed, numerous Africans in the civil service and in commercial firms with better command of bureaucratic skills who did not have authority with masses of people. Accordingly, if we use Weber's categories, we are left only with charisma, which is Weber's residual category, to explain such situations. While, on the impressionistic level this observer had no doubt that the political and union leaders were charismatic, there were few useful indices for establishing the character of their authority, the strength of which was unquestionable.

AWE, SOCIAL DISTANCE AND DEFERENCE

The difference in status between leaders and followers was clearly visible on such occasions as public meetings. Leaders would assemble separately prior to meetings, entering in a ceremonial fashion. Thus, if the meeting was being held in a hall, the leaders would gather outside and wait before entering as a group whereupon followers would stand as a gesture of respect (frequently giving the nationalist salute simultaneously). The leaders were usually visible to followers while they were assembling, yet their status was secure and followers did not attempt to establish contact at such a time. Leadership was held in some degree of awe; social distance was maintained by both leaders and followers. The superior status of the leaders was marked not only by the leaders themselves (who encouraged the maintenance of social distance) but also by their followers. After a meeting, although the top-echelon leaders normally

---

[13] During 1959–60, there were two major strikes in Tanganyika. The longest, a strike of railway workers, lasted for 82 days and involved about 14,000 workers. During these strikes, the workers received little material assistance from their unions.

withdrew in ceremonial fashion, it was usual for lower-ranking leaders to come into contact with followers. These leaders were addressed by such titles as *mzee* ("elder") though the person using this mode of address might be chronologically the elder; followers would touch their right forearm with their left hand when shaking hands (a traditional form of deference), etc. Thus, both leaders and followers utilized traditionalist symbols to indicate status differences.

These indices of superordinate status only serve to demonstrate who the leaders are and how their followers acknowledge them; by themselves, they provide no indication of the character of authority. Knowing that these leaders lay no claim to traditional or bureaucratic authority, it is only by intuition that the observer designates their authority as charismatic. The need for objective indices, therefore, is one major problem in working with the concept of charisma. The dearth of such indices in the literature of the behavioral sciences is quite remarkable.

This fact elucidates a possible area for empirical research into Weber's typology of authority. If his types of authority are behaviorally meaningful, it should be possible to construct indices to distinguish them. Even though Weber's types are *ideal*, there should exist behavioral referents. In a sense Weber suggests some crude indices; thus, if a follower can explain *why* he feels compelled to obey a leader, it may be possible to categorize responses (through interviews, let us say) into the Weberian types. No attempt was made to undertake such a study during the field period because of time and other limitations, but it appears that this could be a fruitful approach to determine the character of charisma and other forms of authority.

CHANGE IN TANGANYIKA: THE BASIS FOR CHARISMA

Although it has not been possible to provide objective indices of charisma, it is feasible to (a) examine the changes in Tanganyika social structure within which incipient charismatics began to be generated and (b) analyse the specific circumstances in which charismatic leaders developed a mass following.

THE CHANGING SOCIAL STRUCTURE

Prior to the establishment of European rule in the 1880's, what later emerged as Tanganyika was a *terra incognita* which served as a slave-raiding base for Zanzibar's Arabs. With European control, a pattern of change was initiated that created a new society and, indeed, led to the eventual unseating of the Europeans.[14] European control created the need for trained native manpower and, as a result of missionary activity, there developed a small elite of westernized Africans. As the colonial powers expanded the ecnomy to pay for the cost of administration and services, a proletariat emerged. The rural peasantry was brought into the cash nexus through the introduction of taxation

---

[14] I am providing only a brief treatment of a complex process that has been described elsewhere by numerous students of Africa. For a discussion of the process in Africa generally, see Wallerstein, *op. cit.*, and Fred G. Burke, *Africa's Quest for Order* (Englewood Cliffs, N. J.: Prentice-Hall, 1964); for a discussion of the process in Tanganyika see Margaret L. Bates, "Tanganyika," in Gwendolyn Carter (ed.), *African One Party States* (Ithaca: Cornell University Press, 1962) and J. Clagett Taylor, *The Political Development of Tanganyika* (Stanford: Stanford University Press, 1963). For an excellent discussion of the early details of the process from a sociological viewpoint, see Richard C. Thurnwald, *Black and White in East Africa* (London: George Routledge, 1935).

systems and the encouragement of the growth of cash crops.

The establishment of European hegemony was not calmly accepted by the African population and a number of traditionalist revolts had to be put down by force.[15] While peace and social order were established, much of the population remained dissatisfied with the pattern of controls which had been instituted. For the bulk of the Africans, however, discontent remained largely dormant as they were affected only indirectly or lightly by European controls. For the elite which entered the European sector of the society seeking employment, however, dissatisfaction was a more active force because of the discrepancies between the ideals of western civilization (which they had learned in schools) and the realities of colonial life. Gradually, the expectations of most Africans changed as education became more widespread and as the commodities from more technologicaly-advanced societies became generally available.

The economic and social changes wrought havoc with the traditional systems. Added to the unsettling ideological influences of the second World War, the developing anti-colonial movements in Asia and elsewhere in Africa, and the sudden burgeoning of the economy be the massive infusion of capital through Great Britain's ill-conceived "groundnut scheme,"[16] a situation was created in which increas-

---

[15]The responses of the African population are examined in some detail in my paper "The Evolution of Tanganyika's Political System," in S. Diamond (ed.), *The Transformation of East Africa: Studies in Political Anthropology,* forthcoming.

[16]See Herbert Frankel, *The Economic Impact on Underdeveloped Societies* (Cambridge: Harvard University Press, 1953), pp. 141–153; also Alan Wood, *The Groundnut Affair* (London: The Bodley Head, 1950).

ing numbers of people became actively dissatisfied with existing conditions.

THE EMERGENCE OF CHARISMATIC LEADERSHIP

It was in this context that charismatic leadership could begin to emerge. It developed as genuinely charismatic for three reasons: (1) the leaders were expressing sentiments which had been inchoate in the society but which had been brought to consciousness only recently by a handful of people; (2) in expressing these sentiments, leaders were engaging in activities defined as hazardous by most people; finally, (3) Africans recognized evidence of "success" in the activities of the leaders.

The Expression of Inchoate Sentiments. The call for political change in Tanganyika made by the political leaders and the presentation of a challenge to European and Asian employers by African unionists was revolutionary. The authority of the rulers of the country and the employers until 1947 had been relatively unquestioned. Yet the political authority of the British in Tanganyika rested fundamentally upon coercion and not upon consensus.

The development of a trade union in 1947 and of a political movement in 1954 brought substantial changes. Until this time Africans had been unable to formulate their feelings about domination by foreigners. Past manifestations of discontent had taken the form of spontaneous revolts defined as "illegitimate" by the expatriate authorities and suppressed by military force. Beginning in 1947, a new challenge became manifest that was defined, in effect, as "legitimate." The legitimacy of this challenge was accepted by the British who, even though they may have detested the nationalists, recognized the right of political movements to exist. These movements began to express anti-European sentiments with impunity. As a handful of innovators began to challenge the existing social situation which has been a source of dissatisfaction for so many Africans, the basis was laid for the emergence of charismatic authority.

An illustration of this situation comes from the Congo where an American was doing research near Stanleyville. One day, the researcher saw a large number of Africans going toward the town and asked where they were going. The reply was, "We are going to Stanleyville to hear Lumumba insult the Europeans."[17] Even if the story is apocryphal, it elucidates the social situation where masses of people are unable to formulate a point of view but know what they want to hear. The western education of the new leaders enabled them to act within the bounds of legitimacy as defined by the Europeans, but, more important, they were able to formulate, for the rest of the population, challenges which were compatible with their needs.

The Hazardous Nature of the Message. That the message of the nationalist leaders crystallized a new consensus among Africans was not sufficient in itself; a second requisite for charisma lay in the hazardous nature of the message. Lumumba's insults, after all, might have landed him in a jail.

The expression of sentiments of African nationalism was seen as being dangerous precisely because it represented a challenge to European authority. In the past, European authority had been questioned only in military terms, that is, in the form of armed revolt. Europeans had utilized their superior military technology to suppress such reactions. Following the second World War, however, a different kind of chal-lenge appeared in a political and moral form. This challenged might have been presented earlier but, in the period of the establishment of the colonies, any reaction to control was considered illegitimate by Europeans. The very fact of challenging European rule on behalf of "the people" was hazardous and thus was highly regarded.

The hazardous character of the expression of such a message is illustrated in a political song current in Tanganyika in 1961. The song describes how Julius Nyerere, the leader of the nationalist movement, called the poeple to sign a petition authorizing him to go to the Governor demanding independence. The song relates how, after obtaining the signatures of the people, Nyerere went to the Governor with the people following behind:

The people with *Mheshimiwa* (an honorific term),
Seeing him produce the letter,
Some ran away, some held their hearts
Waiting and shivering with fear
To see what would happen.
They thought: surely we are going to be put in jail;
To tease a European, and he who rules us. . . .

The newly emergent proletariat also experienced an inability to express their dissatisfactions to their employers. In face-to-face contacts with employers, workers were unable to bring themselves to explain their grievances. It was left to the fulltime union leaders (who were westernized, educated clerks and not manual workers) to express these dissatisfactions.[18]

---

[17]Related in a talk by Francis X. Sutton at Cornell University in November 1961.

[18]This process is examined in detail in William H. Friedland, *Institutional Change: A Study of Trade Union Development in Tanganyika* (Berkeley: University of California, unpublished doctoral dissertation, 1963), Chap. IV.

Thus, the source of authority of this new charismatic leadership can be seen as originating in a particular social context: it consists of the ability to express sentiments which are deeply held but which are defined as being hazardous.

A qualification is necessary concerning the hazardous nature of the charismatic message. Though certainly characteristic of leaders of the African nationalist movements, I would not contend that the message must *always* be seen as hazardous for its bearer. A great many leaders characterized as charismatic have expressed messages that were not particularly hazardous to themselves. Thus, President Roosevelt's authority was charismatic, at least in part, but the expression of his various points of view hardly could be considered as dangerous to himself. Hitler's charisma grew in a period in which the expression of his message was defined as hazardous by a significant portion of society and, indeed, Hitler was jailed for a while. Yet, he retained his charismatic power after he came to dominate Germany and his charismatic messages at this stage certainly involved no hazards—at least internally within Germany. Thus, the hazardous character of the charismatic message does not always seem to be necessary and represents a condition which may be present in some circumstances but not in others.

The Need for Success. A further requisite for the emergence of charismatic authority is the validation of the message of the new leaders through the achievement of success.[19] Some victory

must be registered that validates their charisma in the eyes of their followers.

In the case of Tanganyika, it is possible to specify the character of the successes of political and trade union leaders. The political leaders were able to obtain gradual but perceivable movement toward political independence. The union leaders also could claim a series of gains. When the first union was organized in 1947 among dockworkers, a substantial wage increase was won after a major strike. Later, in 1956, when the Tanganyika unions began to grow significantly, wage increases and improvement of working conditions were obtained. All of these benefits represented success to the Africans; they were all the more significant because, in each case, Africans challenged expatriate European and Asian employers. To the bulk of the African population, the ability of the African leaders to formulate such challenges and win succssses must have almost connoted magical qualities.

Success can also be of a less material nature. In the case of the union leaders, for example, the fact that authority could be challenged with impunity was defined as success. The simple act of writing a demanding (and frequently insulting) letter to an employer of a different race might be considered to be a success even if it produced no tangible results for an aggrieved African employee.[20] Success, therefore, consisted

---

[19]"Success," i.e., social support for deviant innovations, has not been studied intensively by sociologists. This is an important element in the process of structural differentiation as discussed by Neil J. Smelser, *Social Change in the Industrial Revolution* (London: Routledge and Kegan Paul, 1960), pp. 15–16, 29, and *passim*. See also Leon Festinger, Henry W. Riecken and Stanley Schachter, *When Prophecy Fails* (Minneapolis: University of Minnesota Press, 1956), p. 5 and *passim*.

[20]Indeed, there are indications that the primary activities of some union leaders consisted more in writing obnoxious letters to employers than in obtaining the kinds of "results" that would be considered to be necessary to satisfy an aggrieved worker in the United States.

at least in part, in the ability of union leaders to challenged authority and get away with it.[21]

The initial success of an individual (still to emerge as a charismatic leader) may be very small in scale. However, if his message is meaningful to a group of people, they will provide support by expressing agreement through some form of deferential behavior. If the incipient leader continues to express similar messages which are meaningful for increasing segments of the population, additional support will be forthcoming. As the status of the emergent leader is increasingly recognized and, if the size of the following is of social significance, we can say that a leader has emerged with genuine charismatic authority.[22]

CONCLUSION

Weber's concept of charisma has raised many difficulties for sociologists because of its focus upon the psychological attributes of the heroic individual blessed with gifts. Yet, Weber saw that charismatic authority operated within a social context. By stressing the idea of the calling of the charismatic, however, Weber tended to obliterate the social context within which "genuine charisma"—i.e., charisma which is socially validated—develops. Thus, a sociological analysis of the roots of charisma should be oriented towards social situations.[23]

In any social situation, there can be found "incipient charismatics." Before incipient charismatics can emerge as genuine, the social situation must exist within which their message is relevant and meaningful to people. In some but possibly not all cases, the expression of this message may be viewed as being hazardous and some "success" as defined by the social group itself, must be registered.

This examination of the social context within which charismatic authority emerges obviously leaves much to be desired as definitions have yet to be made concerning (a) the character of social situations, (b) the content of the message which appears to be meaningful to people, and (c) the quality of success. Nevertheless, the reorientation of the study of charisma toward the analysis of social situations may provide insight into the emergence of a new system of authority and may help the sociologist to better understand the processes of social change.

Finally, it should be noted that there

---

[21] It should also be noted that in exercising the challenge to the employers, the union leaders had access to skills that were non-existent among their followers. The leaders had to know how to write their letters in a tone adequately insulting to satisfy the workers but that would remain within the libel laws. The command of these abilities—which are essentially skills characteristic of people raised in a bureaucratic-legal social system—was beyond that of the ordinary workers or farmers. Thus the modern skills of the leaders served to buttress their charismatic authority.

[22] Festinger, *et al.*, discuss a case where the size of the following remains limited to a small group. In such a case, where widespread social support is not forthcoming, the leader is considered to be non-conformist or, in extreme cases, criminal or insane.

[23] The focus on the analysis of social situations to elucidate the source of charismatic authority is similar to the discussion by behavioral scientists of leadership. Originally, leadership was studied in terms of traits of individuals. More recently, students of leadership have found a more fruitful approach in the analysis of social situations within which leaders develop. See "Introduction" in Alvin W. Gouldner (ed.), *Studies in Leadership* (New York: Harper & Brothers, 1950), pp. 3–49. Leadership studies have generally been concerned with small-scale situations and with change at the micro-level. Relatively little research has been conducted on the analysis of large-scale social change and charismatic authority.

is no intent to claim that charismatic leaders always develop in social situations similar to that illustrated here by the case of Tanganyika. Different types of charisma are probably generated by different situations. It may be necessary, therefore, to create a typology of social situations to analyse the various types of charisma that emerge.[24] This

implies that an objective typology of charismatic leadership is necessary. In particular, there is the need for a delineation of clear-cut indices of charisma.

---

[24]Sjoberg, while uncomfortable with the concept of charisma, indicates the possible value of such a typology. Contending that charisma is inadequate to sustain authority for long periods, he indicates "four principal modes of rationalizing and justifying the suzerainty of one body of persons over all others: 1) the appeal to absolutes, 2) the appeal to tradition, 3) the appeal to experts, and 4) the appeal to the governed. The first two are paramount to literate preindustrial societies and their cities; the last two dominate the industrial-urban scene." Gideon Sjoberg, *The Preindustrial City: Past and Present* (New York: The Free Press of Glencoe, 1960), p. 225. This lack of comfort with the concept does not preclude his focussing on it in his later article "Political Structure, Ideology, and Economic Development," *op. cit.*

The Ruling Party in the African One-Party State: Tanu in Tanzania

Henry Bienen

Discussion of one-party states in Africa has tended to swing from one extreme of interpretation to the other, as is common when analyses are undertaken of phenomena about which knowledge is difficult to come by and hard to organise. Studies of particular countries in depth, including politics outside the capital cities, have been rather rare. There have been some useful collections of essays which have presented material from various African countries, and there have been a number of wide-ranging and provocative articles. But we are only beginning to accumulate the necessary monographs which will allow us to formulate general propositions about African one-party systems in particular and African politics in general.

Perhaps the cart was put before the horse. In order to handle a large number of systems and to make African data meaningful for the comparative study of developing areas, typologies were devised for African politics which were neither descriptive of real systems nor of much heuristic value. At first a dichotomy was proposed between single- and multi-party systems. Observers were struck by the fact that competitive party situations seemed to survive after independence only in a few places where federal or quasi-federal arrangements provided regional strongholds of governmental power for opposition parties.

Then distinctions were made among the one-party systems themselves, as it was clear that the number of parties was far too simple a criterion upon which to decide whether or not a system was democratic or anything else about it.

From *Journal of Commonwealth Political Studies,* Vol. V, No. 3 (July 1966), 214–230, by permission of the author, the journal and its publisher, the Leicester University Press.

One of the first differentiations among one-party states was made by Ruth Schachter Morgenthau when she proposed 'mass' and 'patron' parties as categories of analysis.[1] The way that elites related to non-elites, and the ideologies of elites, were to be treated as the crucial variables. This analysis rested on the view that mass parties reached out for all the citizens in the community in order to represent, lead, and rule them. Relative to patron parties, they had an articulated organisation and institutionalised leadership. Less worked out in Schachter's analysis was the question: how successfully do mass parties represent, lead, and rule their constituents and society as a whole? In 1961 it was really not possible to say. In most of the West African states ruled by a single party independence had been only recently achieved. And in East Africa independence had come to Tanganyika alone. It was clear that some parties lost their vigour almost on attaining independence; but there was not yet much experience of *ruling* single parties.

In the first year of the 1960s the typologies constructed for African politics became more and more focused on the notion of 'dynamism'. 'Revolutionary-centralising systems',[2] 'revolutionary mass movement regimes',[3] 'mobilisation systems',[4] were all essentially defined by the characteristics of party systems. They were contrasted with 'pragmatic-pluralistic'[5] or 'consociational'[6] types. The inventors of these typologies did not insist that one kind of regime would necessarily modernise a country more than the other, but they did see the revolutionary and mobilising systems as monopolising legitimacy; demanding commitment and fulfilment from individuals; reaching people through hierarchically organised parties. And these parties were, to put it in more familiar terms, seen as tougher and more dynamic.

It soon became clear that something was wrong with the images these typologies conveyed. The dynamic parties were not getting their economic programmes across. Growth rates were not rising precipitously in Mali, Ghana, Guinea, or Tanganyika. The Ivory Coast economy was growing faster. And as research was done outside the capital cities, it also became clear that the one-party revolutionary systems were not managing affairs well at local levels either.[7] Central party organs were not exacting the responses they wanted from regional and district party bodies. Plans and commands made at the centre did not get implemented. Perhaps we should have been able to work this out deductively.[8]

In fact it should have been obvious

---

[1] R. Schachter Morgenthau, 'Single Party Systems in West Africa', 55 *The American Political Science Review* (1961), 294–307.

[2] J. S. Coleman and C. Rosberg, Jr., *Political Parties and National Integration in Tropical Africa* (Berkeley and Los Angeles, 1965), 'Introduction" and 'Conclusion'.

[3] R. Tucker, *Soviet Political Mind* (New York, 1963), 'On Revolutionary Movement Regimes', 3–19.

[4] D. E. Apter, *The Political Kingdom in Uganda* (Princeton, 1961), 22–4.

[5] Coleman and Rosberg, *op. cit.*

[6] Apter, *op. cit.*

[7] Discussions with Ernst Benjamin and Nicholas Hopkin, who worked in Ghana and Mali respectively, have corroborated my own research in Tanganyika.

[8] Aristide Zolberg has argued deductively to this conclusion using David Easton's concept of 'authoritative allocation of values' to show that 'modern' institutions deal with only a portion of total allocative activity and that the remainder must be allocated by other means, by other structures. Cf. 'The Structure of Political Conflict in the New States of Tropical Africa', paper delivered at the Annual Meeting of the American Political Science Association, 6–10 September 1966 in New

that the apparatus of modern political life, on both the 'input side' (parties, interest groups, voters, economic institutions) and the 'output side' (bureaucracies, development corporations, legislative bodies, judiciaries, parties) were not very significant for large numbers of citizens. Many Africans operated in subsistence agricultural sectors; they were producing for or buying in markets only infrequently. Many did not vote in the elections which established majority parties (and still do not). Elections that were won by the 'mobilisation' parties were often participated in by less than half the potential voters.[9] Central and local government officials tried to widen the tax base and expended tremendous energy to collect taxes; but even now the bulk of the population in many African countries pay only local taxes or cesses; many people pay no tax at all either because of exemptions, avoidance of registration, or the absence of any cash income.[10] Whether indigenous traditional institutions were comparatively weak or strong, neither personnel nor programmes always existed to replace them.

In fact, the characteristics attributed to political systems in Africa were often based on the images that African parties wished the world to see. But it cannot be taken for granted that explicit ideologies in African states have descriptive relevance, and the few people who articulate these idelogies may not even be very close to the centre of power within the party.[11] The aspirations that certain elites have to transform their societies through a single party which penetrates all communities and social structures, and which mobiliscs society's resources, may or may not be significant.

A further, though related, problem is that typologies may be based on relatively formal structures, i.e. they relate to real phenomena but they are limited to an account of how they *would* work if they worked according to the normative expectations of the elites. They are not dealing with an empirical study of processes. They do not tell us the nature of relationships within the party; nor how the party relates to society as a whole and not merely to the modern,

---

York. See also his *Creating Political Order* (Chicago, 1966).

[9] The Tanganyika African National Union (TANU) won a large majority of the votes cast in the 1960 election but the 885,000 registered voters represented about half the estimated potential voters. And since less than one-seventh of the registered voters actually voted, the voting electorate was a small percentage of the possible one. In the Presidential election Nyerere received over 1.1 million votes to his opponent's 21,276. The total vote was less than a quarter of the potential electorate. TANU claimed a membership at the time which was greater than Nyerere's vote. The more than 2.5 million votes cast in the Presidential and National Assembly elections in Tanzania in 1965 represented a marked increase. However, about 50 per cent of the possible electrorate was voting. Dennis Austin shows similar figures for Ghana in his *Politics in Ghana 1946–1960* (London, 1964), 174, where the Convention People's Party received about 15 per cent of the total potential vote in elections in 1954 and 1956. Zolberg, *op. cit.*, refers to similar phenomena in Guinca and Mali.

[10] The non-monetary sector still accounts for more than a third of Tanganyika's total Gross Domestic Product (or £200 million out of £600 million). 98 per cent of the population pay taxes only to district councils, who levy a tax of about 1 to 3 per cent on the income of all adult males. But it is estimated that 15 per cent of all males are escaping registration for taxation before official exemptions begin. See E. Lee, *Local Taxation in Tanganyika* (Dar es Salaam, 1964). Of course, taxes are hard to collect where communications are poor, means of coercion slight, and habits of this kind of payment not ingrained.

[11] For example, the ideologues of *Spark* in Ghana or *The Nationalist* in Tanzania certainly did not determine state policy nor were they often influential in the councils of the CPP or TANU.

urban, or town sectors.[12] We cannot tell from them whether or not normative expectations which may be stated in explicit ideologies at the centre are shared throughout society.

The need was therefore to focus on political structures, and parties in particularly without assuming that they operate uniformly, or with uniform effect, throughout the societies or the states in which they are found. But as soon as it began to be appreciated that national institutions, including ruling parties, were not operating in the same way in towns and countryside, or not operating everywhere in society, or being permeated by traditional patterns, assertions began to be made that the so-called African one-party states were better described as 'no-party states'.[13]

The argument for this designation can be briefly stated. Nationalist movements became parties of independence and then parties of rule in Africa. But as the victorious parties formed governments, they lost functional relevance and coherence.[14] The growth of state agencies proceeded, and party functions atrophied. 'The party became largely an agency of the governmental bureaucracy or, at the expense of its rank and file, in certain cases it became a mere extension of the personality of a strong president or prime minister. No matter what roles parties have been assigned, almost everywhere in tropical Africa—whether in single party, multiparty, or non-party states—they perform few.'[15]

One could point to a number of developments in support of this argument. Party leaders have become heads of state. They have not only formed governments but have not drawn sharp distinctions between their party, the state, and the nation. Rulers have relied on the civil service since civil servants are ordinarily better equipped for the problems of government than party cadres. Party members of influence and/or ability have entered government, not only at cabinet level but in the regular civil service. For example, TANU leaders in Tanganyika became permanent secretaries and foreign service officers; district party secretaries occasionally became civil servants in the regional administration. Across Africa, party agencies such as youth wings, student groups, and para-military wings have been transformed into adjuncts of state control. They have often been governmentalised in order to ensure their loyalty to government leaders who could not rely on party mechanisms for this. The major decisions on development policy, the drawing up of five-years plans, programmes to attract foreign investment, establishing proposed rates of growth and means of financing plans—all these decisions have more often been taken in councils of state than in party caucuses or congresses or even in national executives and central committees. Foreign advisers may have much more to say about these matters than ostensibly important party figures.

---

[12]The afore-mentioned authors are themselves conscious of these questions. In fact, their typologies are designed to seek out the data that will tell us how much tactical flexibility parties have, or how hierarchical is authority. See Apter, *op. cit*. None the less, the typologies are dependent on formal structures and political rhetoric rather than hypotheses about party function insofar as they purport to describe concrete African systems.

[13]For a discussion of this issue, see my article, 'The Party and the No-Party State: Tanganyika and the Soviet Union', 3 *Transition* (Kampala, 1964), 25–32.

[14]R. I. Rotberg, 'Modern African Studies: Problems and Prospects,' 18 *World Politics* (1966), 571. See also I. Wallerstein, 'The Decline of the Party in Single Party States' in J. LaPalombara and M. Weiner (eds.), *Political Parties and Political Development* (Princeton, 1966).

[15]*Ibid.*

And if any one could still doubt that parties no longer had primacy and centrality in African politics, the termination by the military of party rule and party existence in a number of African states could be cited.[16] Most of these states did not have so called mass or mobilisation parties. Nigeria's parties, however, were thought to have at least some of the characteristics of ruling single parties in Ghana, Guinea, Mali, and Tanganyika. They were easily overthrown by a few thousand men. Observers of the military in new states believed that strong and authoritarian ruling parties would not be so easily displaced by military intervention.[17] Yet the TANU Government had its authority successfully challenged by one battalion of the Tanganyika Rifles in 1964; less than a thousand men were able to bring the Government down, had they so wished and had the British refrained from intervening.[18] Above all, the Convention Peoples Party offered no resistance to the Ghanaian army. It is rather the disappearance of the CPP with no apparent ripples which is the striking fact of Ghanaian politics since January 1966.

When all this has been said, the idea of the 'no-party state' is not a satisfactory tool for the analysis of African politics, any more than the idea of authoritarian and dynamic mass parties.

---

[16]See H. Bienen (ed.), *The Military Intervenes: Case Studies in Political Development* (New York, 1967).

[17]W. Gutteridge, *Armed Forces in the New States* (London, 1962), 67; M. Janowitz, *The Military in the Political Development of New States* (Chicago, 1964), 29 and 103; F. Greene, 'Towards Understanding Military Coups', 2 *Africa Report* (1966), 10–14; E. Shils, 'The Military in the Political Development of New States', in J. Johnson (ed.), *The Role of the Military in Underdeveloped Countries* (Princeton, 1962).

[18]See my 'National Security in Tanzania After the Mutiny', 5 *Transition* (Kampala, 1965), 39–46.

It is based on a description of those aspects of African politics which are most visible to outside observers. This is the politics of the capital city; of the 'modern' sectors; of institutions which can be 'seen' (because they have chains of command, rosters of personnel, constitutions which define their structure and goals) and can be 'heard' (because we can more readily interview party officials and civil servants). The pendulum has swung too far away from the importance of party in African political life and from the empirically established importance of individual parties in specific polities.

I cite some examples from TANU for their own sake and because they may be suggestive of the role that African ruling parties are playing in other single-party systems.

TANU IN TANGANYIKA[19]

On the eve of Tanganyika's independence, the then Publicity Secretary of TANU (Kasela Bantu) wrote a pamphlet called *What TANU Is and How It Works*. He was trying to describe this national movement to an overseas audience and to non-Africans in Tanganyika. The aims and organisation of TANU were also being explained to its own members. The politics of Tanganyika have been marked by such attempts to define new roles for TANU and to establish the identity of the ruling party. Is it paradoxical that a national movement having become a ruling party should worry so much about its purpose and place within the nation? It is, at any rate, essential to recognise that leaders and followers alike are still asking: What is TANU and how does it work?

Posing the question in this way pre-

---

[19]I refer mainly to Tanganyika rather than Tanzania because most of my remarks pertain to pre-union Tanganyika and to mainland Tanzania only.

supposes that TANU is an integrated party, with a defined structure, and a defining ideology, and thus we must merely find out how this entity functions. However, when we begin to examine the way in which institutions that meet in Dar es Salaam and the regions and districts work and interrelate we find a number of paradoxes.

TANU is the only political party in Tanganyika *de jure* and *de facto*. TANU has been able to make sure that all organised politics takes place within the framework TANU sets. Thus political competion takes place within TANU institutions, be it elections to the National Executive Committee or elections to the heralded National Assembly of 1965. This is no small achievement. It alone would give the lie to the idea of a no-party state. The party here sets the rules for political participation. And, as we shall see, it also confers legitimacy. It faces no organised interest groups that it does not ostensibly dominate. Functional organisations are linked to it, e.g. the National Union of Tanganyika Workers. The highest-level leaders are not being challenged for their positions within the party. TANU is, indeed, hierarchically organised and led by what has come to be loosely designated a 'charismatic' leader. The President of the United Republic of Tanzania, Julius Nyerere, is the President of TANU.

And yet Tanganyika is not really dominated by a national TANU elite. That is, the central leaders who reside in the capital city—Dar es Salaam—and who fill the high Government and TANU posts, often holding both simultaneously, do not make their will felt through the pyramid structure of the party. TANU is still a party where the relationships between the centre and the organisations outside Dar es Salaam are posed as problems for the leaders. A number of interrelationships exist: be-

tween the national and the local units directly; between the centre (TANU Cabinet, Central Committee, National Headquarters staff, and the National Executive Committee which has a heavy regional and district representation) and regional and district organisations[20]; and between TANU and associated organisations (the trade union movement, the co-operative movement, the Tanganyika African Parents' Association). TANU, in practice, reflects the lack of integration in society at the same time as it must serve as an instrument for bringing about integration. No central institution exists which could possibly direct or co-ordinate the thousands of TANU elected and appointed officials who operate outside the capital. The National Headquarters staff has only a handful of full-time paid officials. There is no filing system which could allow any official to know where TANU members are located. All these illustrations are cited to show that Tanganyika is far from being ruled by a monolithic party from the capital city. It is ruled partially and intermittently by the ruling party.

This is partly a matter of the organic evolution of the party. For a number of reasons decentralised forms of party organisation inherited from the period of the anti-colonial struggle have not been overcome. TANU was the *first* national political party, formed out of the Tanganyika African Association (TAA) which began some time in the late 1920s as an association of government servants—junior officials and teachers—but which began to reach the small towns and rural areas after World

---

[20]There are seventeen regions and sixty districts in Tanganyika, excluding Zanzibar and Pemba. The districts are the old colonially demarcated administrative units. A district is often around 6,000 square miles, although it may be as small as 1,000 square miles. District capitals sometimes have less than 1,000 people. The regions have been increased in

War II.[21] TANU inherited the existing local organisations of the TAA, tribal unions, and co-operative societies.[22] However, when a new constitution was adopted and a new organisation came into existence on 7 July 1954 in Dar es Salaam, TANU inherited not only a nucleus of existing branch organisations but also a tradition of local control, poor communication between branches, domination of a political movement by town-based people, and a lack of clearly defined aims. The local TAA groups and tribal unions often expressed parochial sentiments. Some of this localism has persisted in TANU's own structure.

There was, moreover, no serious obstacle in the way of the formation of a national movement. Tanganyika did not have large, centralised chiefdoms which might have become the focus for ethnic nationalisms.[23] Most of the large tribes are recent federations. They are not historic kingdoms with strong central rulers. For example, the Sukuma, the largest tribe in Tanganyika, constituted about 12 per cent of the more than eight and a half million people in the 1957 census. This is not very much less than the 16 per cent of the population the Baganda are in Uganda. But, unlike the Baganda, the Sukuma peoples had a segmentary traditional system that did not lend itself to being made the focus of ethnic nationalism.[24]

Tanganyika has been cited as a case of extreme tribal fragmentation because over 120 tribes have been recorded in the census. But there were also positive factors making for national unity. The slave trade, besides disrupting most of the traditional social systems it encountered, spread the Swahili language inland from the coast and Swahili was fostered as a *lingua franca* by the German's use of Swahili-speaking agents. The slave trade also led to some amalgamation of peoples and thus may have facilitated the acceptance of leadership by people of differing tribes. One may even cite as a manifestation of a protean national unity the opposition to German rule which led to the Maji-Maji revolt of 1905[25]; disruption of the traditional ruling systems and weakening of chiefs by the very use of indirect rule on the part of the British colonial administration. And although Tanganyika is not urbanised, even by African standards, there did exist towns, albeit small,

number since the colonial period. Regional headquarters are towns which are usually around 10,000 in population, although Mwanza has more than 20,000 and Tanga more than 50,000. No region, and not even many districts, are homogeneous with regard to tribe, although some areas have a dominant tribal population. The towns are invariably ethnically heterogeneous.

[21] See R. A. Austen, 'Notes on the Pre-History of TANU', 9 *Makerere Journal* (1964), 1; and G. Bennett, 'An Outline History of TANU' 7 *Makerere Journal* (1963), 1.

[22] TANU's spokesmen now trace TANU's roots to the TAA and the cooperatives, denying a share in the parentage of the party to tribal unions which are described as being tribalistic and disruptive of national unity. But the tribal unions fed on reactions against the British efforts to enforce unpopular agricultural policies, just as the TAA did. And TANU was able to use the discontent organised by the tribal unions and to absorb some of their members and local bodies.

[23] See Harvey Glickman, 'Traditionalism, Pluralism and Democratic Processes in Tanganyika', paper presented at the Annual Meeting of the American Political Science Association, Chicago, 9–12 September 1964, 4.

[24] See D. E. Apter, *op. cit.* For materials on the Sukuma, see Hans Cory, *The Ntemi: The Traditional Role of a Sukuma Chief in Tanganyika* (London, 1951), and Hans Cory, *The Political Indigenous System of the Sukuma* (London, 1953).

[25] See Julius Nyerere's 'Foreword' to K. M. Stahl, *Tanganyika: Sail in the Wilderness* (The Hague, 1961), 6–7. Also Daudi Mwakawago, 'Growth of Nationalism in Tanganyika', 2 *Mbioni* (Dar es Salaam, November 1965), 5.

within many of the rural areas dominated by particular tribes. Thus TANU was able to use *wageni* or strangers who were not from the tribe of the area but who lived in the towns there.

In the towns there developed what can usefully be called a Swahili political culture. Swahili itself was important not only as a *lingua franca* which allowed TANU officials to be posted anywhere in the country, and so attain some independence of local factions. It is also an important component of a Tanzanian identity. It has become associated with TANU and with a style of life. The Swahili way of life involves having 'a conviction of one's superiority which is shown by preferring to speak Swahili . . . involvement in the affairs of a minor settlement . . . where possible, and a minimum involvement in the affairs of one's local community.'[26] It involves the possibility of being a petty official in TANU, 'with opportunities for making speeches and telling other members of the community how they must improve themselves and mend their ways.'[27] Above all, it stands for life in the towns.

TANU is both a carrier of this culture and an expression of it for all that it attempts to organise and represent rural areas. Most TANU leaders at national, regional, and district levels have lived, as adults, in the towns. The branch chairmen and secretaries aspire to be in the towns. Thus, although TANU fed on rural discontent and absorbed tribesmen in their tribal unions and was itself drawn into the countryside as an instrument for voicing that discontent, it has been appealing to antithetical cultures. Thus many real and potential tensions exist within it. TANU's scope has been its source of strength and weakness. It grew rapidly, but has co-existed with a host of traditional authorities and local leaders.

Another reason why the TANU regional and district organisations did not dominate the countryside is that success in political competition did not require it. Since TANU was never opposed by a vigorous opposition, discipline was seldom needed in order to win elections. TANU did not have to centralise to gain power over indigenous opponents. It acquired a monopoly of politics because other African political organisations either did not attempt to become national, and did not have the political bases to do so (for example, the Bahaya or Wachagga tribal unions), or were weak splinter parties from TANU (e.g. the African National Congress led by Zuberi Mtemvu and the People's Democratic Party led by C. K. Tumbo). As a result TANU has often had little direct impact upon the lives of people outside the minor towns and settlements.

The dominant single party thus became a grouping of organisations functioning under known national leaders. As it grew, it became looser, not more disciplined and monolithic. It politicised ethnic groups and embraced an increasingly heterogeneous body of individuals and associations.

It was not able either to direct internal party affairs through an institutionalised TANU centre nor to build such a centre (or strong TANU local organisations) through the use of government machinery or patronage. Moreover, periods of development which have unfolded over a more lengthy period in other ex-colonial countries have been telescoped in Tanganyika. The political movement was formed, became the ruling party, and embarked on a major *Five-Year Plan* all within ten years. Thus there was little time to confront the

---

[26] Alison Redmayne, 'Preliminary Report on a Hehe Community', East African Institute of Social Research, 1962 Conference Paper, 8.
[27] *Ibid.*

organisational deficiencies (which are after all the very crux of the matter) of the past. Furthermore, the low levels of economic development and the large share of the subsistence sector as a percentage of total output have persisted. TANU has not yet been threatened by economic interest groups, although it has had difficulties with the trade unions both before and after governmentalisation of the unions. The absence of other strong organised economic interest groups allowed TANU rulers a breathing space; but it also means that such interest groups cannot be used as instruments through which to rule.

How does such an organisation survive, then, given its own weaknesses and the context in which it operates? How can we speak of the reality of the party state?

THE PARTY STATE

In Tanganyika it is the relative weakness of structures which is striking, not their relative strengths. Yet to say that TANU is a party without a powerful centre and that it rules Tanzania partially is not to maintain that party functions are atrophying nor that power and prestige are gravitating away from the party to somewhere else—state agencies or interest groups. These are also weak, for that matter. But to put it positively, Tanzania is a party state. TANU performs important functions. Power does not reside somewhere within a polity waiting to be parcelled out to various structures. Power must be created by structures through a dynamic process and TANU is engaged in this process.

TANU's very looseness works to maintain party rule in Tanganyika. TANU's non-central bodies are oligarchical but they are internally competitive.[28] Different elected and appointed hierarchies exist within them. Party secretaries in the regions and districts who are also heads of government in regions and districts, and are called Regional and Area Commissioners, are able to prevail only through a process of compromise and consensus. They do not rule by fiat. They are not political bosses who tightly control either TANU elected official—district councillors, TANU chairmen, MPs, delegates to the National Executive Committee and the National Conference—or civil servants from central ministries who work within their jurisdiction. Functions are still very diffuse and this reflects the actual diffusion of authority among many people both in and out of TANU in the countryside.

In order to stay in touch with branch organisations, TANU regional and district secretaries must travel. Communications are poor and distances great. Thus the secretaries are constantly in motion. They are usually unwilling to delegate the running of district TANU headquarters to deputy secretaries, just as they are unwilling to leave the countryside to elected TANU officials. The solution arrived at is ingenious though not efficient in terms of utilisation of human resources. Everyone travels at once and often together. And when members of the TANU 'team' travel they do much the same things: appear on platforms together, making essentially the same

---

[28]When special TANU district electoral conferences met to select candidates to run for Parliament in 1965 the votes were often split among seven or eight candidates or more. Rarely did any one candidate win more than 50 per cent of the votes. Only 33 out of 180 final candidates polled more than 50 per cent in the selection primary among TANU district leaders.

speeches which exhort people to achieve goals set by leaders. There is a feeling of safety in numbers. Individuals reassure each other by their presence. Also, no one likes to be left out of these *safaris*. Not being on stage could be construed as a loss of status. And because there is fragmentation of authority, it is sometimes necessary for TANU chairmen, and secretaries, and civil servants to appear before people are convinced that the TANU organisation is serious about a particular matter. This is becoming less true as the party secretaries/government commissioners who have been appointed since 1961 consolidate themselves in the regional and district TANU organisations. But since there is frequent posting of commissioners from district to district, or from district to some post in Dar es Salaam, and since the elected officials have independent leases of power, few area commissioners are able really to dominate their district TANU organisation.

Many of them do not have the necessary skills to direct the activities of civil servants, and in fact they are enjoined not to try.[29] Nonetheless, the very weakness of the civil service outside the capital means that TANU officials and members perform governmental functions and legitimate the acts of the civil service. A traveller going from one district to another may find TANU members manning a road block. They may be checking for illegal movement of some commodity. Or they may be checking to see if individuals have paid their taxes. These duties devolve on TANU organisations because there are just not enough civil servants at the local level. Many districts do not have

representatives of certain ministries at the district *boma* or headquarters. At a meeting of civil servants and TANU officials the difficulty of collecting taxes comes up. Someone suggests that TANU help collect taxes. The suggestion does not always come from a TANU official; it may well come from a civil servant.

Civil servants, too, have been recruited to the post of Area and Regional Commissioners.[30] But most of these posts are still held by those who were TANU secretaries before independence. And the appointment of Commissioners in 1961 was designed to emphasise that since TANU was the Government there should be political heads of regions and districts.[31] The idea was to bring a TANU presence to government in the regions and districts. Although there was never any exclusiveness about TANU in terms of ideology or membership categories, civil servants were debarred from joining TANU under a colonial ordinance which was allowed to stand until 1964. One of the aims of opening TANU to the civil service was to strengthen TANU as well as to make civil servants politically sensitive to TANU, and to abolish distinctions between them. Nyerere had always seen the distinction between politicians and civil servants as artificial even when he was upholding the British model of a

---

[29] See the Tanganyika Government's Staff Circular No. 14 of 1962.

[30] A number of TANU leaders have had a say in the appointment of Commissioners. But President Nycrere has had to approve appointments and appointments have been made from his office at certain times.

[31] In the first batch of appointments for Regional Commissioner, six of the then ten TANU provincial scrcetaries and two provincial chairmen became Regional Commissioners. Three of the ten provincial secretaries and five of ten provincial chairmen were to become Area Commissioners. (Province was the pre-independence designation for region.)

neutral and apolitical civil service.[32] He has conceived of nation-building in Tanganyika as a unity by amalgamation, not unity by cutting out offending parts. The aim has been to create a synthesis of party and state—a synthesis which has its living embodiment in the Commissioners who became head of party and state in the districts and regions.

Where civil servants *have* had administrative and technical skills they have still relied on TANU people to 'put across' their programmes. This brings us to TANU's critical function in Tanzania. Many functions that TANU and civil service bodies together carry out are economic, and it is around economic tasks that an attempt is being made to strengthen, or build for the first time, state and party structures.

It is not true, as one of Tanganyika's expatriate planning experts appeared to think, that Tanganyika has a 'disciplined and dynamic party' whose machinery can be utilised to the maximum in achieving economic goals.[33] But whether dynamic and disciplined or not, TANU had to be used in the effort to meet pressing problems because it had local bodies, even if they were not ideally obedient nor universally close to the grass roots, which could at least try to reach ordinary people both to disseminate goals and to organise efforts.

Many people are strongly attached to TANU even if they disagree with their local TANU structures. The party still retains its legitimacy as the fighter of independence. This is a function of the still short time since independence. For many people, though not for all, of course, TANU provides an 'ought' component to an order.

There are also practical advantages to be gained from giving support to the party. Although local party organisations and the centre have not had much patronage to dispense, money and status do attach to being an office holder through TANU, and the party can also help determine who will get a salaried job, and influence the settling of old scores. Being a TANU activist or supporter gives one leverage for fighting battles over land rights or debts.

For leaders, also, TANU legitimates rule. They can justify their own orders as TANU orders. Their responsibilities are derived from TANU positions or from being given government posts by TANU. Many such posts are in fact filled by the personal appointment of the President. But he himself stresses the TANU origins of authority. Aside from the formal responsibilities that political heads of departments or regions and districts have for specific administrative and economic duties, it is often the authority of a TANU politician which enables him to get a hearing for civil servants and to support them as they explain their programmes.

We could establish without much difficulty that economic policy has been ratified rather than made by central TANU organs. A few TANU Government leaders in conjunction with expatriates in the planning and economic ministries formulated the *Five-Year Plan*.[34] Nowhere in the *Five-Year Plan* were Regional and Area Commissioners

---

[32] See Julius Nyerere, *Democracy and the Party System* (Dar es Salaam, n.d.), 26. When Nyerere told civil servants to keep out of the political arena in 1960, he was trying to insulate them from politics and from local TANU organisations as much as warning them off. Many civil servants were still expatriates who were vulnerable to attack. See Nyerere's Circular Letter No. 1, 1960, reprinted in 1 *Transition* (December 1961), 23–5.

[33] G. Karmiloff, 'Planning Machinery and its Operation in Tanganyika', Public Policy Conference No. 1, Kampala, October 1963.

[34] See my paper, 'The Role of TANU and the Five-Year Plan', presented to the East African Institute for Social Research Conference, Kampala, 1964.

mentioned. With few exceptions, neither the *Five-Year Plan* nor regional plans mentioned TANU. However, information essential for plan formulation and implementation was gathered by TANU development committees. And above all, the conditions which make civil servants depend on TANU determine the nature of TANU's own contribution to implementing development programmes.

The fact that tasks are not easily separable into component parts is related to the nature of local societies. Development does not consist in deciding to have a new well in a village and then telling technical personnel to construct the well. The deciding to have a well, getting villagers to accept the location of the well, and having villagers themselves carry out much of the construction work and co-operate with technical specialists are all a matter of political concern. Thus it is crucial to the development effort that TANU makes available numbers of men who primarily make speeches and travel around bringing people into contact with centrally or regionally established goals. Speech-making, arranging meetings, and employing persuasion not unmixed with compulsion are familiar tasks for TANU people. Local self-help and development projects provide a focus around which TANU can be organised. TANU is given something to do which it can do and which is useful. The hope is that TANU will also tighten its control over localities by popularising and implementing local development programmes.

It does not always work out in this way. Local self-help projects have more and more given way to centrally determined pilot projects and 'villagisation' schemes, and TANU-sponsored projects sometimes prove to be failures or mistakes. Still, it remains TANU's job, together with community development

personnel, to make connections for people: if you want this you must do that. Very often, Government cannot supply what is wanted and so it says: 'You must do this and then by your efforts you can get a number of valued things'. Not everyone is willing to strike this bargain. Individual perceptions of gains and effort are variable.

This applies to TANU people also. Not all TANU activists, let alone those who call themselves TANU supporters, opt for 'modernity'. It would be a mistake to conceive of a backward countryside seeded with TANU carriers of modern patterns of living. All the seminars, meetings, and exhortations that civil servants and TANU people are involved in giving are aimed, after all, at other civil servants and TANU people and not at the population at large. When individuals in a certain district are recalcitrant about doing something Government wants done it would not be unusual to find them led by someone who calls himself a TANU leader.

It remains an open question as to what and how much the TANU Government can enforce. It was reaction to enforced change against the British which swelled TANU's following. Regional and district leaders seem aware that in some places communication has already broken down between villages, district, regional, and central authorities. They are aware of the costs involved. But they cannot abandon trying to impose their will on the countryside. For without reaching the villages, Government remains essentially confined to a few urban centres and towns. This was understood by Julius Nyerere when he said: 'Others try to reach the moon. We try to reach the villages'.[35]

---

[35]Tanzania is not made up of compact villages. People live mostly in small settlements often spread out over a wide area. Thus it is physically hard to reach people.

This aim is notoriously difficult to achieve. The institutional innovations which have been constructed so that TANU can became a 'two way all-weather road between government and the people'—the development committees, party cells, TANU associated groups—can all become ritual forms without any content. But at their best, these institutional devices can become important and they are very much the manifestation of the 'party state'.

In writing of TANU's 'legitimising' function, I have tried to keep within the limits of the impressions I have formed in the course of field work in various districts of Tanganyika, but this is an aspect that needs further discussion. When it is argued by proponents of the no-party state analysis that ruling single parties are losing their functions is it sometimes acknowledged that they still have symbolic meaning. But we cannot take for granted that particular parties do in fact have 'symbolic' meaning for citizens, any more than we can accept at face value the claims of leaders that their 'ideologies' are the ideologies of party and citizens. But symbolic meanings are very important. Elites consciously try to define formulae by which they can justify their positions and through which they can bridge the gap between themselves and non-elites. If the formulae are accepted and if individuals identify with the institutions which put them forward, a reservior of legitimacy exists which can be exploited for rule. This reservoir can run dry when elites become ineffective or coercive or, as new bidders for power, make claims on the loyalties of citizens. Nonetheless, when a radical transformation of society is undertaken or desired by ruling elites, formulae must be found which not only permit development but which provide an 'ideological grease' for development.[36]

In Tanzania various leaders have begun to challenge Julius Nyerere's formulae although a battle of ideas has not been fully joined. Where Nyerere speaks of African Socialism, others refer to scientific socialism. Nyerere wants to preserve the bonds of traditional community in order to bring about modernity, and he sees TANU as the carrier of both modern and traditional values.[37] Others see a contradiction between tradition and change; for them, traditional ties must be broken by a strong party. The pages of the TANU paper, *The Nationalist*, have sometimes expressed the belief that only through social conflict will backwardness be overcome. For some ministers and TANU middle level leaders (junior ministers, commissioners, national headquarters officers) Nyerere's ideas have been too gradualist, too gentlemanly, and unsuited for rapid social and economic change, although Nyerere is not personally criticised or directly

---

[36] Alexander Gerschenkron has noted thrusts of development in Russia, Germany, and France being accompanied by specific ideas about the cause and cure of backwardness which are worked into ideologies of development. See *Economic Backwardness in Historical Perspective* (Cambridge, Mass., 1964), 22–6. See also Mary Matossian, 'Ideologies of Delayed Industrialization', 6 *Economic Development and Cultural Change* (1958), 217–28.

[37] President Nyerere's ideas have been expressed in the aforementioned *Democracy and the Party System*. See also *Ujamaa: The Basis of African Socialism* (Dar es Salaam, 1962); *TANU Na Raia* (TANU and the Citizen) published in Swahili (Dar es Salaam, 1962); and President Nyerere's Guidelines to the Presidential Commission on the One-Party State published in *Report of the Presidential Commission on the Establishment of a Democratic One-Party State* (Dar es Salaam, 1965), 1–5.

contradicted.[38] Mixed in with differing views of social change is a desire for more action and drama—and perhaps more assertion of authority—than Nyerere's formulations entail. And the political aspirations of newcomers to power, Zanzibaris and middle level leaders in particular, lead them to search for their own formulae to legitimise their aspirations and provide them with ideologies to bind their followers.

If TANU is in fact a party without strong central organs and a party which is a congeries of regional, district, and sub-district organisations which communicate with each other and with Dar es Salaam intermittently, then no single 'TANU' ideology will be likely to reflect the outlook of the whole organisation. Nor does any mechanism exist whereby an ideology could be imposed over those who call themselves TANU. There is no means for those in power within TANU to institutionalise their view of reality and to enforce this view within their own organisation. There is not even a mechanism through which all TANU members can be constantly kept in touch with a political ideology. Certainly there is no reason to believe that people either in TANU or in Tanzania at large will spontaneously embrace an ideology simply because it is promulgated by leaders. Thus it is a mistake to identify the ideas of one man, Julius Nyerere, as the belief system of a whole party which attempts to promulgate them throughout society.

Entrance into TANU becomes increasingly a *sine qua non* for being part of the nation. At the same time, the search for TANU's identity goes on. This search is inextricably linked to a definition of the 'Tanzanian way' and to the idea of a Tanzanian nation. This idea is not static. It emerges as a response to unforeseen events, like the mutiny of the Tanganyika army in 1964 which called forth an effort to incorporate the military and civil service into TANU so that they too could be 'part of the nation' and thereby become politically reliable.[39] The idea gets defined consciously in Presidential speeches and documents of state and party, e.g. the *Report of the Presidential Commission on the Establishment of a Democratic One-Party State*, the new TANU Constitution, and the Arusha Declaration. The style and content of these documents and the emergence (or failure to emerge) of an ideology of development are important, because it is through the process of defining political formulae and establishing them as legitimising doctrines that the gap between elites and non-elites begins to be closed.[40] The most recent attempt to create a frame of reference for looking at problems and for creating a political programme to deal with problems is the Arusha Declaration of January 1967. In this document the TANU National Executive Committee resolved that leaders of TANU and Government should divest themselves of shareholdings, directorships, multiple salaries, and rentals. While asserting a policy of self-reliance and self-sacrifice for the popu-

---

[38] See, for example, pieces signed 'A Critic' and 'A Contributor' in *The Nationalist*, 28.6.65, 5, 29.6.65, 6, 18.6.65, 6, and 19.6.65, 6. See also Mr. Kassim Hanga's Address to the National Assembly published in *The Nationalist*, 2.7.64, and Mr. A. M. Babu's 'Tanzania Pointing the Way to Wealthy Economy', *The Nationalist*, 4.5.65, 5.

[39] See my 'National Security in Tanzania after the Mutiny', *loc. cit.*

[40] See L. Binder, 'National Integration and Political Development', 58 *American Political Science Review* (1964).

lation at large, the NEC at the same time called for the end of privilege for leaders.

It is an empirical question as to whether or not the Arusha Declaration, or any particular doctrine, does legitimise and whether or not ideologies effectively link leaders and followers. In Tanzania there is a concern to create a working ideology and differences between various ideologies do matter. They matter not because we can understand systems in terms of ideologies propounded by leaders and publicists but because the success or failure of political formulae are crucial to the integration process.

CONCLUSIONS

It is tempting to generalise about the political systems of Africa. We can establish many 'facts of life' which are indeed common to many of them in terms of their resources, *per capita* incomes, relative shares of subsistence and monetary sectors, and so forth. And we can show that the structures of most African economies have worked against the formation of disciplined and centralised parties and have precluded totalitarian or 'revolutionary centralising' systems. But we do not have to assume that these economic factors determine political development, although we must recognise that they act as constraints on political possibilities. It is important to explore the kinds of political organisations that can and do live in various economic settings. It is also necessary to show the interaction between political organisations and the economy.

Thus it is necessary to ask: Among other things, what kinds of political leadership exist? What values and programmes are espoused? Political leaders do not sit back and wait for enough economic development to take place to change the social structure and enable them to control their organisations. They are active agents in the process of making change, even when they may be inactive leaders. It makes a difference whether or not leaders are realistic about their ability to enforce close control within the party. There are elites who try to be coercive when they can succeed only in being repressive. And it matters if the party attempts to become an agent for economic change even when the party is too weak and loose and has too few resources to tackle developmental problems effectively, because it is in the process of attempting to change the economy that the party's internal organisation evolves.

African one-party states are not bound to become more centralised, any more than economic development is bound to occur. The conditions for decentralisation or for the disappearance of parties are already at hand. The military can intervene; the parties can disintegrate in face of overwhelming social, economic, and political problems. But the remaining ruling single parties have real roles to perform. Neither military forces nor civil services are likely to make up in force and effectiveness what they lack in legitimacy and political know-how. Public order and political participation, which are pre-conditions for economic development and are the essence of political development, are not going to be guaranteed by the removal of parties.

We must now explore the remaining ruling single parties to find out how they differ in terms of political functioning and what their prospects are for continued existence. Indeed, we may have to hurry before we have no phenomenon to study. But it is too soon to proclaim the no-party state as ascendant throughout Africa, and it is very questionable whether when such regimes come about they will survive even as long as the party-states of Africa.

Beyond African Dictatorship: The Crisis of the One-Party State

W. Arthur Lewis

Since 1957 thirteen new countries have gained independence in West Africa, four former British colonies (Ghana, Nigeria, Sierra Leone and Gambia) and nine former French colonies (Mauritania, Senegal, Mali, Guinea, Upper Volta, Ivory Coast, Togo, Dahomey and Niger). A fourteenth country, Liberia, has been independent for over a century. Portuguese Guinea is now the sole remaining colony in West Africa. In 1957 each of the countries now independent had at least two substantial political parties, except Ivory Coast and Liberia. Now the situation is reversed, for they are all single-party states, whether in law or in practice, except Nigeria and Sierra Leone. My purpose here is to analyse the single-party system in the West African context, and to assess its relevance to the problems of a developing society.

We must first note that West African politicians can not all be painted with the same brush. The fourteen countries are led by men who vary widely in character, from men of the highest integrity to men who are merely self-seeking rogues. Their administrations equally run all the way from nearly the most corrupt to nearly the cleanest in the world. There are serious arguments for the single-party independently of the character of the politicians. But it would also be mistaken to forget that much of what is going on in some of these countries is fully explained in terms of the normal lust of human beings for power and wealth. The stakes are high. Office carries power, prestige and money. The power is incredible. Most West African Ministers consider themselves to be above the law, and are treated as such by the police. Decision-making is arbitrary. Decisions which more advanced countries leave to civil servants and technicians are in these countries made by Ministers, often without consulting expert advice. The prestige is also incredible. Men who claim to be democrats in fact behave like emperors. Personifying the state, they dress themselves up in uniforms, build themselves palaces, bring all other traffic to a standstill when they drive, hold fancy parades and generally demand to be treated like Egyptian Pharaohs.

Actually, only a minority of West African Presidents or Premiers have wide charismatic appeal in their own

This selection is an excerpt from *Politics in West Africa,* which appeared in *Encounter,* XXV, No. 2 (August, 1965), 3–18. It is reprinted with the permission of George Allen & Unwin Ltd., the Oxford University Press, and the author. It is abridged by the editors.

countries. The prevalence of suppression is due to the hostility which most of them arouse—indeed glory in, since the language of the West African political leader breathes hatred and violence towards political opponents, rather than the conciliatory wide appeal which is the basis of charismatic leadership. Charismatic figures do not need the oppressive tactics which so many Presidents use.

More relevant than charisma is the fact that most of the new politicians have no commitment to democracy, have never experienced democracy, and know neither its philosophy nor its history. Fifteen years ago, when politics was confined to a few people, the leading politicians were mostly highly educated men, who had been through British or French universities, had travelled in Europe, and knew something of the history and philosophy of democracy. Such men are now relatively rare in West African politics. The new politicians come mainly from the primary schools, have little acquaintance with European history, and have never been outside their country, until elected to office. For most of them independence means merely that they have succeeded to the autocracy vacated by British and French civil servants. They model themselves on the arrogant and arbitrary pattern set by Governors and district commissioners, if only because they know no better.

One can only be amused by people, including African politicians, who present the single-party state to us as a specifically African creation, emerging out of the African personality and the African social system—as if the single-party state were not one of the commonplaces of the twentieth century, to be found in nearly every continent. In my experience, the main effect of people persuading themselves that Africans are

different from other peoples is that they abandon normal standards of decent human behaviour and end by thinking that anything is good enough for Africa, even though they would not for one moment consider it for Europe or North America.

Many West Africans have resisted the single-party state, and been killed or jailed or exiled for doing so: let us not forget them. Many others, of equal courage and integrity, have accepted the single-party state because they consider it to be at present the best way of handling their country's affairs. The best way to make progress with this subject is to consider the arguments on their merits.

The Argument in Favour

Democracy means that people are willing to accept the results of fair elections; the will of the masses of the people, fairly ascertained through the ballot box, is supreme in determining who shall govern.

Now willingness to accept the results of the ballot box requires consensus. This will not be found where the contenders for power disagree so sharply on matters which they consider fundamental that they are not willing to allow their opponents to govern, whatever the ballot box may say. Labour and Conservative or Republican and Democrat accept a verdict of defeat only because they believe that the other chaps will not do anything very dreadful. If this consensus did not exist, the ballot box would not be accepted.

We are often told that strong government is needed in under-developed countries to bring about economic progress. This is true of class societies. In those parts of Asia and the Middle East where landlords take half the peasant's output as rent, land reform is necessary to create economic incentives. Equally, in parts of Latin America where large landowners hold fertile acres idle, while the peasants are driven to scrape a living in the hills, political action must lay the basis for economic progress. West Africa is different. It has no landlords, and no white settlers. The major constraints on economic development are not political.

West African governments do not need to coerce their peoples into modernisation. The key to modernisation is education, and here it is the people who embarrass the governments by sending more children to school than the schools can hold. Some governments may be tempted to try to coerce the farmers to adopt better practices: use fertilisers or better seeds; cut out diseased trees; or even to join co-operatives and collectives. They would not be wise to do so. The U.S.S.R. and China have both tried this, and have both failed. Increased agricultural productivity is absolutely essential to economic progress, but it can be achieved only by the normal means of education, example, and economic incentive.

The only important coercion which is crucial to development is taxation. West African governments need to raise 15 to 20 per cent of national income in taxes in order to provide adequate public services and contribute towards financing capital formation, but the majority now raise less than 10 per cent. If the single-party system could effect a swift increase in the share of taxes this would indeed be a powerful argument in its favour. However, swift change is not possible. Economic development depends on incentives. This means that per capita output cannot be raised much faster than per capita income, after payment of taxes; any at-

tempt to raise the share of taxation rapidly kills off incentives, and prevents growth. It is also about equally unpopular in a single-party as in a multi-party system. When tried recently in Ghana, it led to strikes and riots, and the taxes against which the workers were protesting had to be repealed.

Then there is the claim that the single-party is essential to cope with the turbulence created by economic development. Change necessarily creates tension. Farmers organise to demand higher prices; workers to demand higher wages. The primary school leavers are crowding into the towns, and the unemployed are looking for relief. There is plenty of incendiary material which unscrupulous men can use as an ambitious base for personal power. The single-party tries to contain these tensions; trade unions must belong to the party, and be subservient to its functionaries; farmers' groups, women's councils, youth organisations, and all other potential sources of tension are brought within the party framework. Thus it is hoped not merely to keep track of all dissension, but also to force dissident groups to accept what the party leaders consider to be reasonable solutions.

Success in only partial. Genuine trade unionists resent party control, and demand the right of independent action; farmers feel the same way. The party cannot prevent people from being discontented with their lot. The amount of social tension is a logarithmic function of the rate of change. At one end of the scale, as in Salazar's Portugal, one can have stagnation and peace; at the other end, as in Stalin's Russia, one has rapid change, "contained" only by imprisoning and "liquidating" millions. Given rapid change, the single-party cannot prevent tension; all it can do is to suppress open agitation. Discontent is then all directed inward upon the party, where, as we shall see in a moment, it adds to the instability of the party. This increases the effort to stamp out resistance, driving it underground, whence it breaks out from time to time in violent demonstrations.

The case for democracy is not that it prevents tensions, but that open discussion creates a healthier society than is achieved by suppression. The diffusion of responsibility diffuses conflict. Each of us belongs to several groups with different interests, and the fact that we are opposed to this man on this issue but allied to him on the next issue prevents our conflicts from running away with our emotions. Bottling up conflict, or concentrating it in and on the single-party, is undesirable. Besides, given the low quality and the inexperience of so many West African politicians, independent sources of political thought and criticism are vital to West Africa. To survive, these politicians feel that they have to destroy the independence of the farmers, the unions, the churches, the universities, and all other social institutions, by bringing them under party control. They make a desert of democracy, and then call it social peace.

In sum, much of the case for the single-party system rests on its claim to accelerate development, and to contain its tensions. The first half of this claim is bogus, and the second half is both doubtful and undesirable. The single-party system is largely irrelevant to the current economic problems of West Africa.

The fundamental political problem is neither economic policy nor foreign policy, but the creation of nations out of heterogeneous peoples. Each country contains several tribes, living at different economic levels, and tribal con-sciousness and economic difference combine to produce mutual antagonisms which menace the unity of the state.

The result of these mutual antagonisms is that every political party has a geographical base. Some tribes support it; others are hostile to it, or at best indifferent. A single-party supported equally by all the tribes is an impossible dream. Houphouet-Boigny's party comes closest to this, but even this party has not eliminated tribal divisions. The tribe is the basis of its organisation, so even in Abidjan, the capital, where live men from every tribe, the party is organised not by street or by district, but by tribe. Family, village, and tribe are West Africa's primary social units. The norm in these countries is two or three political parties, each with a different geographical and tribal base. They will not necessarily be hostile to each other, but the minimum conditions for tolerating each other are two-fold: first, they must share the central government, and secondly, the richer areas must not be taxed heavily to subsidise the poorer. The first of these conditions requires coalition government; the second requires a federal constitution.

Some kind of coalition is indicated because no numerous and politically conscious group is willing to be ruled by the others. Government involves differential taxation, jobs, and decisions where to spend money on public works, schools, hospitals, industries, and other services. To be in the opposition is to be deprived of participation in these decisions, and almost certainly to suffer economic loss. A merger of the parties is an alternative to coalition. This is feasible if the different areas are at about the same economic level. If they are not, the richer area has to maintain its political identity in order to protect itself, and is not likely to agree to a merger. It was feasible for the parties to merge "voluntarily" in Mauritania or Mali, but was not feasible in Ghana or Dahomey.

The richer group calls for a federal constitution so as to limit the extent of its contribution to the rest of the country. It can afford to spend much more per head on public services than they can. Uniform public services mean that its standards must be kept down to theirs, or that it must subsidise their services, or both. If the poorer areas have only a small minority of the population, these results may pass; but if, as is more usual, the richer area is the minority, it can be expected to resent uniformity.

When the economic differences are too great for merger of the parties, the only alternative to coalition within a federal framework is political warfare. Advocates of the single-party system do not accept this conclusion. They argue exactly the opposite case. To make a nation, they say, one must minimise tribal differences; modernisation means rising above tribe to a higher order where tribe, language, religion and geographical origin have no political significance, giving place to a common nationality as the highest loyalty. Federalism is an obstacle to this goal, because it recognises and crystallises internal differences, and the multi-party system is even worse, because each separate political party has a continuing interest in emphasising the differences on which it is based. Only a single nationwide party, operating through a central government, can ignore tribalism and emphasise national unity.

These are grand words. Their validity depends on the assumption that the single-party really can rise above tribalism. It can do this if the economic dif-ferences between the tribes are small, but not if they are large. Economic interests are, alas, more powerful than grand ideas. Even the single-party cannot persuade the richer region to carry the poorer regions on its back.

A single-party operating within a federal framework could be a logical compromise, but only if the centre of gravity were in the richer area. If the centre of gravity of the party is in the poorer areas, the temptation to increase federal at the expense of provincial resources must prove irresistible. Since the poor are more numerous than the rich (otherwise the problem would be trivial), the centre of gravity is almost certain to be in the poorer areas, so even a single-party federal system would be unstable.

The problem is more acute in some West African countries than in others; generally speaking more acute in the southern than in the northern countries. The northern countries are more homogeneous geographically, they are poor all over; whereas in the southern countries the rainfall may range from 100 inches in the south to thirty inches in the north, creating enormous economic disparities. Differences in mineral wealth also cause trouble, though less so than agricultural differences, because the mines benefit fewer people directly. Regional economic differences are an acute political factor in Nigeria, Dahomey, Togo, Ghana, Liberia and Sierra Leone, and are not without significance in the politics of Guinea, Senegal or any of the other states.

In countries like Britain and France, which have several centuries of homogeneity behind them, there is instinctive resistance to the federal solution. People protest that African countries are too small for federalism, or that they do not have enough political and administrative ability to man two levels of government, or that they need the experience of common purpose and action in a central government if they are to hang together.

It is not true that they are too small. If they were small the problem would not exist; it is only because the countries are large that there are these enormous geographical differences. However small the population may be, largeness of area creates special problems. A large country with widely differing regions cannot be governed well from one town which monopolises decision-making. Even if political considerations are excluded, good administration requires decentralisation of decisions to persons on the spot. Most West African governments are now over-centralised. Britain and France failed to develop local government because they were themselves interested in keeping power in their own hands. The tribal and village councils had no experience of the services which modern local governments have to provide, and it was easier to add these services to the machinery created by the central government. Quite apart, therefore, from any question of federalism, a redistribution of functions between central and subordinate authorities is much to be desired.

Federalism is a wide term. Outside Nigeria, formal federalism on the American pattern is not required or sought. All that is asked is a reasonable degree of provincial devolution. Countries with this kind of problem need both a strong centre and strong provincial governments; and this is not a contradiction, since government functions are now so numerous that there is plenty of room for both. It is quite true that a country needs a strong central government to hold it together, meaning by this a government which acts boldly in all spheres which are of common interest. But it is equally true that a country with sharp regional differences needs to give its provinces the opportunity to look after their own affairs, if they are to feel content with the political union. Whether one calls this federalism or provincial devolution makes no difference.

THE ARGUMENT AGAINST

The single-party fails, then, in its biggest claim—that it is the appropriate vehicle for resolving regional differences. But it would fail anyway, even if regional differences were minor. The human race has had plenty of experience of this system; there is no reason why it should bring less unhappiness to West Africa than it has brought to the other countries which have tried it.

Single-parties are not homogeneous. From the philosophical standpoint, one must make at least two distinctions: between totalitarian and limited parties; and between ideological and open parties.

By a totalitarian party we mean in this context a political party which claims to be the supreme instrument of society. In Ghana, Guinea, and Mali the party is elevated above all other institutions, which must look to it for leadership.

The ideological origins of this are thoroughly familiar; it is the basic stuff of European totalitarianism. The single party representing all the people is the Fascist branch; the single party representing only the oppressed is the Communist branch. Its adherents in West Africa picked it up during their journeys through the Communist movement. Why have they retained it, while repudiating the international Communist movement, as they have done?

Part of the answer, of course, is that it suits their authoritarian personalities; but this is not the whole answer. Equally important, in practice, is their strong hostility towards the African middle classes. A modern state cannot be run by uneducated persons. It has to be run by trained civil servants, professional men, independent businessmen, and others who live by their brains. The party is hostile to these men but has to use them. It appoints such men to be Ministers, civil servants, and managers of state enterprises, but it does not trust them. So control is kept tightly in the party executive, and party philosophy extols the party as the one source of authority.

The other philosophical distinction is between a party which is committed to a particular ideology or programme, and a party which claims to include all interests and provide a forum in which all ideas can be discussed freely. The leaders of an open party claim to recognise that opposition is inevitable, because people have different interests and attitudes, and also desirable, since this is the only way to ensure that proposals are examined properly from every angle. They, in effect, invite the opposition to join the party. To read some of these accounts, the single-party is really a grand free-for-all political seminar.

All over Africa propagandists for the single-party tend to make a good deal of its open character, but the conditions which are required for a party really to be open cannot be fulfilled. It is not enough to demonstrate, as is easily done, that two or three of these parties have a fair amount of internal democracy, good lines of communication between leaders and the rank-and-file, some members of all races, tribes, and regions, or stern codes of public morality—all this has been typical of many ideological parties: "democracy" is maintained, but only for members of the party (outside critics will find the police or party hustlers on their door-

step), and even for members of the party only if they keep within the rigid framework of the party's presuppositions. Any dissenter from these presuppositions is expelled.

The party cannot be identified with the people, and does not want to be. However popular the party leader may be, the rank-and-file of the party are something apart. The most active are the hooligans, who keep the public in line; but even the more respectable are conscious of their superiority, and their tendency to arbitrary action makes them feared. People say one thing in the presence of a party member, or even a suspect, and something quite different when they feel safe. The party is something you have to fear, and something that wants you to fear it, since this is the basis of its power. Hence when the day comes to get rid of it, few tears are shed. The funeral of the party leader who dies in office is attended by hundreds of thousands, but let that same man be put away by his colleagues, and nobody even whispers his name.

As for democracy inside the party itself, a party which expels its dissenters is not an open party, since by definition the purpose of an open party is to contain and utilise dissent. Also an open party must have no pre-determined goals, since the formulation of goals must be open to continuous argument. A socialist party or a liberal party cannot claim to be an open party. For the same reason an open party must have neutral leaders, willing to listen and be guided by dissent; and they must be easily removable, since one of the important questions which dissenters may raise is whether the particular leader is the right man to do what has to be done, A party created around a particular leader, to support his policies (as are most African parties) is not an open party.

One of the odder claims made for the single-party system is that it offers stable government; more so, for example, than coalition government. This is not so. West African single-party government is highly unstable. Where opposition is illegal, governments can be changed only by *coups d'état*. An efficient government can prevent *coups d'état* by building up an extensive secret police, which roots out opposition groups before they are ready to move, but no West African government can aspire to this degree of efficiency. Keeping an eye on the avowed opposition is fairly easy. All that then happens is that opposition builds up inside the party itself, where plots are easier to manufacture and carry through because of the prestige and freedom of movement of the high party functionaries who organise them. All the tensions and conflicts of the society come to be concentrated in the struggles of the upper hierarchy of the party, whose members become identified with conflicting interests and policies. When these tensions become too great, the leaders turn upon each other, with deadly violence.

In the course of 1962 and 1963 Ministers were arrested and imprisoned in Senegal, Ivory Coast, Mali, Ghana, Niger, and Liberia, and military *coups d'état* succeeded in Togo and Dahomey. In the early days the jails were filled by the opponents of the party; they have long been reduced to insignificance; now the violence is wreaked by one party leader upon another. This is inevitable. Opposition cannot be eliminated from any society in which men have different interests and ideas, and are affected differently by social change. The only question is whether it will have democratic outlets, through which it can express itself peacefully, or whether it will be driven to successive acts of violence, first against the party, and then within the party. Any claim that a single-party system brings political stability can be rejected outright.

The single-party thus fails in all its claims. It cannot represent all the people; or maintain free discussion; or give stable government; or, above all, reconcile the differences between various regional groups. It is not natural to West African culture, except in the sense in which cancer is natural to man, since what would be natural in these countries would be two or three parties representing different regions. It is partly the product of the hysteria of the moment of independence, when some men found it possible to seize the state and suppress their opponents. It is a sickness from which West Africa deserves to recover.

THE PLURAL SOCIETY

To say that the single-party system is inappropriate is not to say that West Africa must pattern its political institutions on those of Britain and France. Britain and France are class societies, and their institutions and conventions are designed to cope with this fact. West Africa is not a class society; its problem is that it is a plural society. What is good for a class society is bad for a plural society. Hence to create good political institutions in West Africa one has to think their problem through from the foundations up.

The word "democracy" has two meanings. Its primary meaning is that all who are affected by a decision should have the chance to participate in making that decision, either directly or through chosen representatives. Its secondary meaning is that the will of the majority shall prevail. These two meanings do not overlap, since it is normal in European Parliaments to institutionalise the minority in an opposition party or parties who are excluded from decision-making; this is justified by saying that when heads were counted in an elections one set won, and the other set lost. Europeans try as hard as they can to confine this secondary meaning of democracy to the political sphere. In all other institutions—business, sport, the family, the church, the university, and so on—committees are expected to ensure that all interests and points of view are fully represented in their membership and their deliberations, and are expected to try to reach agreement by compromise, rather than by voting. Once a committee begins to divide into factions, and to make decisions by voting, we expect its legitimate business to be neglected. The good chairman's main task is to keep his people working together as a team.

The doctrine that the majority shall have its way has become central to the political institutions of class societies. In the definition of democracy that it is "government of the people by the people for the people," the "people" does not mean all inhabitants. It means the great mass of the inhabitants—the poor and middle people—in contrast to the handful of aristocrats, landowners, and big capitalists who have hitherto monopolised political power. The doctrine asserts the right of the poor to liquidate the rich. Politics is what the mathematicians now call a zero-sum game: what I win you will lose. You have the wealth, I have the right to take it. European politics has been operating in this mould for the past three hundred years.

Translated from a class to a plural society this view of politics is not just irrelevant: it is totally immoral, inconsistent with the primary meaning of democracy, and destructive of any prospect of building a nation in which different peoples might live together in harmony. Are we, on counting heads, to conclude that the Catholics may liquidate the Protestants, the Indians of British Guiana may liquidate the Negroes, or the Negroes of some southern countries may liquidate the whites? In a plural society the approach to politics as a zero-sum game is immoral and impracticable.

Plurality is the principal political problem of most of the new states created in the twentieth century. Most of them include people who differ from each other in language or tribe or religion or race; some of these groups live side by side in a long tradition of mutual hostility, restrained in the past only by a neutral imperial power. French writers use the word "cleavage" to describe a situation where people are mutually antipathetic, not because they disagree on matters of principle, like liberals and socialists, or because they have different interests, like capitalists and workers, but simply because they are historical enemies. Cleavage cannot be overcome merely by argument and economic concessions, as in the traditional British manner, because it is not based on disputes about principles or interests. Hence it is the most difficult of all political problems.

The democratic problem in a plural society is to create political institutions which give all the various groups the opportunity to participate in decision-making, since only thus can they feel that they are full members of a nation, respected by their more numerous brethren, and owing equal respect to the national bond which holds them together. In such a society a slogan that the will of the minority should prevail would make better sense than the slogan that the will of the majority should prevail; but neither slogan is appropriate. It is necessary to get right away from the idea that somebody is to prevail over somebody else; from politics as a zero-sum game. Words like "winning" and "losing" have to be banished from the political vocabulary of a plural society. Group hostility and political warfare are precisely what must be eradicated if the political problem is to be solved; in their place we have to create an atmosphere of mutual toleration and compromise.

The better advocates of the single-party state, notably that outstanding East African statesman, Julius Nyerere, claim for it that it is superior to the multi-party wranglings inherited from European political systems, because it eliminates a kind of political warfare that could only be dangerous. In a plural society, a single-party which included representatives of all the various groups, and encouraged full discussion within the party framework, would be superior to a competition for power between parties representing different tribes or races or religions. Not all single-parties are of this type; some are totalitarian, some are ideological, and some are both. Nyerere's party is neither totalitarian nor ideological. On the other hand Nyerere's country, Tanganyika, is also one of the few new states in which cleavage is not much of a political problem. He has no powerfully organised tribes, traditionally hostile to each other, and by comparison with Ghana or Togo, not to speak of Kenya or Uganda, there are not wide economic differences, because the tribes are just about equally poor. In a society which has no economic classes, no cleavage, and small regional economic differences, there is virtually no political problem, and virtually no need for political parties, single or multiple. A good free-for-all seminar is very welcome. Once one gets away from these ideal conditions into countries where the people are divided into mutually suspicious groups, the claim of the single-party to be able to bridge the gulf fails. Each group wants to be represented by its own party, and no single-party is accepted everywhere. As we have already seen, the solution is not the single-party, but coalition and federalism. Any idea that one can make different peoples into a nation by suppressing the religious or tribal or regional or other affiliations to which they themselves attach the highest political significance is simply a non-starter. National loyalty cannot immediately supplant tribal loyalty; it has to be built on top of tribal loyalty by creating a system in which all the tribes feel that there is room for self-expression.

Anybody who has seen what a mess party politics can make of a plural society must find himself hankering after a primitive kind of democracy, in which people elect their representatives without the aid of parties, and run their affairs much as other democratic institutions are run. The single-party appeals to this longing; if everybody belonged to the same party, and could discuss issues freely, the situation would be the same as if there were no party. The main purpose of political parties is political warfare, which is tolerable in class but not in plural societies.

Trade Unionism in Tanzania[1]

William Tordoff

Berg and Butler have recently argued[2] that the usual generalisations about labour's political role in developing or colonial countries are inappropriate in tropical Africa and that these generalisations should be reversed. 'In the period before independence,' they write, 'African trade unions were rarely the instruments of political parties. To the extent that they entered the political arena their role was usually negligible. After independence they were quickly subdued by governing parties, and at least in the near future seem destined to play a subordinate role.'[3] Referring to the pre-independence period, the authors state that the links between union and party were close in Kenya, though—because of intense factionalism within both the Kenya African National Union (KANU) and the Kenya Federation of Labour (KFL)—they were less strong than in Guinea. Berg and Butler believe that 'the close union-party intimacy' in these two countries is hard to find elsewhere and did not exist (for example) in Ghana and the French Cameroons. Though the case of Tanganyika is not examined in detail, the implication is that here too there was only limited participation of the labour movement in party and political affairs. This article seeks to test this assumption and also to review the process by which the Government has 'captured' the trade unions in the post-independence period.

EARLY RELATIONS BETWEEN TANU AND TFL

The fact that trade unions in Tanganyika antedated the formation of the Tanganyika African National Union (TANU) is 1945 gave them an independent basis of power and influence. Even after 1954 the growth of new unions (as distinct from the increase in union membership) seems to have been essentially autonomous. Thus, in 1955 the initiative in establishing a national union centre, the Tanganyika Federation of Labour (TFL), was taken by local union leaders following a visit to Tanganyika of the Kenyan labour leader, Tom Mboya. Some assistance to the TFL was subsequently given by officials of the British Trade Union Congress[4] and the International Confederation of Free Trade Unions (ICFTU). External advisers, as well as local labour officers, warned trade union leaders against involvement in politics. Since the Government regarded TANU as an extremist organisation, the unionists could themselves see the danger of developing any formal

---

[1] The United Republic of Tanzania came into being in April 1964 and comprises the former independent states of Tanganyika and Zanzibar. This article does not discuss trade unionism in Zanzibar and the name Tanganyika is used throughout the pre-union period.

[2] Elliot J. Berg and Jeffrey Butler, 'Trade Unions,' in James S. Coleman and Carl G. Rosberg, Jr. (Eds.), *Political Parties and National Integration in Tropical Africa*, (Berkeley and Los Angeles, 1964), pp. 340–81.

[3] *Ibid.*, p. 341.

[4] Arthur Skeffington, *Tanganyika in Transition*, Fabian Research Series 212 (London, 1960), pp. 37–39.

From *Journal of Development Studies,* Vol. II, No. 4 (July 1966), 408–430, by permission.

attacheent to TANU. In October 1956 the first annual conference of the TFL therefore resolved that 'No Trade Union which is affiliated to the TFL should affiliate itself to TANU at the moment.'[5] For the time being, the TFL leadership was content to concentrate on strengthening union organisation by replacing the plethora of small craft unions which had sprung up in 1955 by nation-wide industrial unions affiliated to the TFL.[6] The trade union movement in Tanganyika was considerably strengthened as a result of the general strike in Dar es Salaam at the end of 1956. The fact that a number of workers were discharged and evicted from their quarters for participating in the strike, as well as the establishment of a minimum wage in the capital, convinced workers in Dar es Salaam and the other major towns that it was both necessary and worthwhile to support the unions. Thus strengthened, the TFL, working through individual unions, had by 1958 extracted from different employers substantial wage increases and other benefits (such as paid leave and sickness allowances) for more than half of Tanganyika's 400,000 workers.

This picture of a trade union movement independent of TANU and actively engaged in negotiating improvements in wages and terms of service for its members, must not however be overdrawn. Though organisationally separate, the two movements shared a common resentment of foreign rule. Union leaders were convinced that the economy was geared to foreign commercial and industrial interests and believed that they could not radically improve the

standard of living of the workers until political independence was achieved. For this reason, individual unionists joined TANU, while new union members were largely recruited from party ranks. The result was a rapid expansion in the size of the trade union movement in the second half of the 1950's. Whereas at the end of 1956 there were only 9,000 union members in Tanganyika, as compared with 25,000 in Kenya and under 2,000 in Uganda, four years later Tanganyika had 80,000 union members as against 45,000 in Kenya and 26,000 in Uganda.[7]

CLOSER UNION: PERSONAL AND
ORGANISATIONAL LINKS

In the latter half of 1957 the TFL, though still avoiding any formal link with TANU, was openly supporting the party's political programme. As Friedland suggests, probably the main reasons for this change were first the challenge being offered to TANU by the United Tanganyika Party (UTP), a multi-racial party formed in February 1956 with government encouragement; and secondly, the increasingly harsh policy which Government was adopting towards TANU.[8] Cooperation between the latter and the TFL proved mutually beneficial. The trade union movement benefited from TANU support of the boycotts—for example of the Dar es

---

[5] Quoted by Friedland, *op. cit.*

[6] Sixteen trade unions were registered during 1955, bringing the total to twenty-two. Eight of the new unions were in the Lake Province. *Tanganyika Report, 1955* (London, 1956), Col. No. 324, para. 448.

[7] Roger D. Scott, 'Labour Legislation and the Federation Issue,' *East Africa Journal* (Nairobi, November 1964), p. 23. *Cf.*, however, *Tanganyika Report 1960*, Pt. I (London, 1961), Col. No. 349, para. 406: at the end of November 1960, there were 39 trade unions, including more than 384 branches, with an estimated membership of 65,322. Seven of the unions were for African employees, while eleven others were established on a non-racial basis. Not all the unions were affiliated to the TFL.

[8] J. Clagett Taylor, *The Political Development of Tanganyika* (Stanford and London, 1963), pp. 137–63.

Salaam municipal bus system in 1957 and of beer in April 1958—organised by the trade union leaders as a prop to strike action.[9] For TANU cooperation with the trade unions in the industrial field enabled the party to hit the soft underbelly of colonial rule. The trade union movement also provided TANU —which drew its main strength from the rural areas[10]—with an organised body of support in the urban centres. This support was particularly important in the coastal port of Tanga which Stephen Emmanuel, a wealthy Greek sisal planter, was using as a base from which to capture the whole of the Tanga Province for the UTP. When, in 1957, Government closed down a number of TANU branches in that Province and took other steps to 'muzzle' the party, the trade unions were able to perform a holding operation for TANU in much the same way as the cooperative unions were to do in Sukumaland the following year.[11]

By the end of 1958 TANU and the TFL had drawn still closer together. The turning point seems to have been the success of TANU and the resounding defeat of the UTP in the first phase of the 1958–59 general election, held in September 1958. Government's attitude towards TANU changed dramatically after the election and there was no longer any danger to the TFL in forging closer links with the party. Though continuing to be organisationally separate and still concerned primarily with promoting the interests of its members, the Federation accepted formal representation on TANU committee meetings at provincial level. (It was not until February 1961 that the TFL was given two seats on the national executive committee, the main policy-making body of the party). Personal links were reinforced as TFL leaders were elected to prominent positions in the party. R. M. Kawawa, the TFL general secretary who had become a member of the TANU central committee in 1957,[12] was to become vice-president of the party three years later. In February 1959, he was returned as a TANU candidate to the Legislative Council, of which he had been a nominated member since 1957, and pressed the need for a national minimum wage.[13]

Indications were soon forthcoming of the mutual benefit to be derived from cementing the (mainly informal) alliance between TANU and the TFL. Towards the end of 1958 the party intervened in support of a major strike of plantation workers on the Mazinde sisal estate owned by David Lead, a prominent UTP supporter. Early the next year the disciplinary action taken by the TFL against E. N. N. Kanyama, general secretary of the Tanganyika Railway African Union (TRAU), showed clearly that the Federation would not tolerate any action taken by a trade unionist against TANU.[14] The Railway Union moved him from office.

---

[9] The effectiveness of strike action was reduced by the ability of Asian employees and European supervisors to maintain basic activities during strikes.

[10] L. Cliffe, 'Nationalism and the Reaction to Agricultural Improvement in Tanganyika during the Colonial Period,' paper presented to the Conference of the East African Institute of Social Research, Makerere University College, December 1964.

[11] *Ibid.*

[12] Clagett Taylor, *op. cit.*, p. 229.

[13] Unsuccessfully at this time. However, national minimum wage scales were introduced by the TANU Government a year after independence.

[14] Kanyama had given his support to an Asian parliamentary candidate not sponsored by TANU. Both incidents are discussed fully by Friedland, *op. cit.*

Kawawa's presence as general secretary (and subsequently—following a constitutional change in December 1959 —as president) of the TFL and his position within TANU helped to maintain a close working relationship between 'the two legs of the same nationalist movement.'[15] Moreover, so long as he remained at the helm, Kawawa was able to keep in check the personal rivalry between the leaders of individual unions. In September 1960, however, when a predominantly TANU Government was first formed, Kawawa became a Minister in Mr. Nyerere's Government. Unfortunately, this happened at a time when substantial issues divided the leaders of the trade union movement and the interests of the TFL and TANU began to diverge.

PRE-INDEPENDENCE DIFFERENCES

A hint of what was to follow had already been given in July and August 1960 in a heated discussion over the future of the East Africa High Commission. While TANU saw the Commission as the nucleus of a future East African federation, two of the more militant unions—the Tanganyika African Postal Union (TAPU) and TRAU —insisted that the Commission should be dissoved immediately. A declaration by the more moderate Transport and General Workers Union (TGWU) in favour of reconstructing rather than abolishing the Commission touched off a bitter internal dispute between the unions affiliated to the TFL. The dispute became personalised around C.S. Kasanga Tumbo, Kanyama's successor as general secretary of TRAU, and Michael Kamaliza, the general secretary of TGWU.[16]

'As the country moved closer to independence,' observes Friedland, 'the latent strains inherent in the differing functions of trade unions and political parties became increasingly manifest.' The key issue was that of Africanisation. Personal ambition no doubt helped to shape the attitude of several unionists. At a time when TANU leaders were becoming government ministers and African civil servants were assuming senior posts, it was natural that union leaders should look with jealous eyes at the lucrative jobs held by European managers in, for example, the East African Railways and Harbours Administration and on the sisal estates. Unionists could not see why they should be excluded from the material benefies of independence. Strong dissatisfaction with what was regarded as the TANU Government's too leisurely approach to the vital question of Africanisation was expressed by several unions—for example, by the Dar es Salaam Dock workers' Union at the end of September 1960 and again in May 1962, by the Dar es Salaam branch of the Tanganyika Union of Public Employees (TUPE) the next month, and by TRAU and the Plantation Workers' Union (PWU), both of which drew up 'master plans' for Africanisation, in the first half of 1962. Tumbo, the outspoken leader of the Railway Union, carried the unionists' cause into the National Assembly where he was joined in his criticism of government policy by several other backbenchers, some of whom had trade union connections.[17] Eventually,

---

[15]*Cf.* the speech given by Julius Nyerere, the TANU president, to the Ghana Trades Union Congress in 1961, when he said that the trade union movement in Tanganyika had become 'part and parcel of the whole Nationalist Movement.' 'The Task Ahead of Our African Trade Unions,' *Labour* (Ghana T.U.C., Accra, June 1961), p. 28.

[16]Friedland, *op. cit.*; Clagett Taylor, *op. cit.*, pp. 214–95.

[17]See (for example) speech by Mr. M. R. Kundya (Singida), *Legislative Council Debates*, 13 October 1960, cols. 143ff. The Africanisation issue is discussed fully by Friedland, *op. cit.*

early in 1962, the Government took the sting out of subsequent criticism by appointing an Africanisation Commission, which issued its report the following year.[18]

In the meantime, another clash between the Government and the trade union movement had occurred at the end of 1960, following a serious strike at the Williamson Diamond Mine at Mwadui. Certain union leaders—and especially Jacob Namfua, the recently-elected secretary-treasurer of the TFL who was to become a junior minister the next year[19]—accused the Government of supporting the management rather than the unions in the dispute. The united front which the trade union movement presented at this time dissolved a few months later when Kamaliza, who had succeeded Kawawa as president of the TFL, put foward proposals to reorganise the structure of the Federation in order to give the latter greater control over the finances of the individual unions. The government workers' unions, which represented the more vociferous wing of the trade union movement, resisted vigorously and relations between individual union leaders deteriorated sharply. This dispute, which was eventually settled by outside mediation, suggested that the TFL was incapable of setting its own house in order.[20]

In the months before independence, bitter union criticism was expressed, both outside and (especially by Tumbo) within the National Assembly, of Tanganyika's wage and salary structure and of the Government's citizenship and school integration proposals.[21] By February 1962, with TRAU threatening to paralyse the economy by staging a series of railway strikes, it had become urgent for the Government—itself the largest single employer of labour—to check the growing intransigence of the trade union movement. Moreover, Ministers found it intolerable that the country's economic progress should be jeopardised by strikes and continuing pressure for wage increases which, if granted, would benefit less than four per cent of the population. The latter point is worth underlining because, given the fact that only a relatively small number of people were involved, it might be thought that such wage claims would not in themselves constitute a serious obstacle to development. These claims covered, however, the modern sector of the economy from which the biggest increases in production were expected. They tended, moreover, to exceed the rate of productivity growth[22] and to accentuate the existing gap between the income of the organised trade unionist and the peasant majority. This fact was to be underlined later in 1962 when minimum wages legislation prescribed a basic monthly minimum wage for employees over 18 as 150/- in Dar es Salaam and Tanga, 125/- in the 18 other main towns, and 100/- in the other areas.[23] In practice (as we shall

18 *Report of the Africanisation Commission, 1962* (Dar es Salaam, 1963).

19 In October 1963 Namfua was appointed an Ag. Permanent Secretary. TUPE had already registered its strong objection to giving civil service posts to politicians. *Tanganyika Standard*, 23 September 1963. (Namfua is now an undergraduate at Balliol College, Oxford).

20 Friedland, *op. cit.* This incident was the subject of a great deal of comment in the local daily press.

21 The debate on citizenship in October 1961 was probably the most heated debate that has ever taken place in the Tanganyika legislature. See *National Assembly Debates*, 17 and 18 October 1961, cols. 303–20 and 324–74.

22 The point that the rate of wage increases exceeded the rise in productivity is undoubtely valid but never seems to have been scientifically established.

23 Statutory minimum wages were introduced with effect from 1 January 1963 by the Wages Regulation Order 1962, made under s. 10(3) of the Regulation of Wages and Terms of Employment Ordinance (Cap. 300).

see) average cash earnings by a diminishing number of African male employees exceeded these rates, and the mean wage increased about 14 per cent annyally in the three-year period 1962–64. The organised worker was in consequence some five or six times better off than the self-employed farmer who, over most of the country, continued to live at little above subsistence level.[24]

THE ESTABLISHMENT OF GOVERNMENT CONTROL

The first step taken by the Government to control the unions entailed using its power of patronage to remove the two main protagonists within the TFL. Kamaliza was made Minister for Health and Labour and Tumbo was appointed High Commissioner in London. In the second place, the Government introduced legislation into the June 1962 meeting of the National Assembly in order to 'contain' the unions and so prevent irresponsible industrial action from interfering with the development of the economy.

The Trade Unions Ordinance (Amendment) Bill sought to bring trade unions and their finances under a substantial measure of government control. It proposed that a 'designated federation' should be created to which all unions would have to affiliate in order to secure legal recognition. (There were six trade unions outside the TFL in June 1962). Secondly, the Trade Disputes (Settlement) Bill introduced conciliation and arbitration procedures which would have to be followed before strike action could be taken; its effect would be virtually to outlaw all official strikes and to remove entirely the ability of the unions to bring out their members

on short notice. A third important Bill —the Civil Service Negotiating Machinery Bill—provided for a Joint Staff Council to be established for the civil service to settle disputes and regulate relations between Government and civil servants earning less than £702 a year, who alone were eligible for trade union membership.[25]

Though several Assembly members had close connections with the trade union movement, only Victor Mkello, the general secretary of the powerful Plantation Workers' Union and who in March 1962 had been elected president of the TFL following Kamaliza's resignation, voiced the strong objection of the TFL to the first two Bills and of TUPE to the third Bill.[26] The result was that each Bill passed through all its stages on one day.[27]

The TFL (which was to be the 'designated federation') agreed, said Mkello, that all unions should be affiliated to one Federation and that trade disputes should be settled without strikes. But, he added, 'the TFL does not agree that these objects should be achieved by means of legislative compulsion.' Of the Trade Unions Ordinance (Amendment) Bill he said that the moment that

---

[24]In 1965 the average wage was nearly six times the average subsistence income—some £73 compared with £13.

[25]Subsequently however the law has been changed. The Trade Unions and Trade Disputes (Miscellaneous Provisions) Act, No. 64 of 1964, allowed all government employees except certain specified very senior officers to join a trade union, but continued the prohibition for members of the military and police forces, as well as members of the prisons and national services. See also (Tanganyika) Establishment Circular Letter No. 6 of 20 April 1965.

[26]TUPE saw the Bill as part of a move 'aimed at paralysing the struggle of civil servants to organise themselves into one powerful trade union.' *Tanganyika Standard*, 26 November 1963.

[27]The Bills become law as (in the order discussed here) Acts Nos. 51, 43 and 52 of 1962.

this Bill became law, 'there shall have been established a permanent division between the Government and the workers.' Later in the debate on this Bill, however, Mkello (who was allowed to speak twice) changed his stand to one of support for the Bill, since he understood that the Government had agreed to certain financial amendments proposed by the TFL. The debates next day on the Trade Disputes (Settlement) Bill and the Civil Service Negotiation Machinery Bill found Mkello again in a conciliatory mood. He supported both Bills but clearly liked neither of them.[28]

Many trade union leaders outside the National Assembly bitterly resented the loss of trade union autonomy and accused the TANU leadership of deception. In August 1962 Tumbo, having resigned his post as High Commissioner, returned to Tanganyika and sought to make political capital out of union discontent. He turned down the offer of his old job as general secretary of the Railway Union and entered politics directly as leader of the small People's Democratic Party. Tumbo proved a thorn in the flesh of the Government until, apparently afraid that he would be held under the recently-enacted Preventive Detention Act, he left Tanganyika and established his base at Mombasa in Kenya. Thereafter, his influence rapidly declined.

Despite Tumbo's departure, the Government was still experiencing difficulty with the trade union movement. Individual union leaders tried to assert their independence by 'freezing' their financial contributions to the TFL, thus making it unlikely that the object of building up a strong central union which had been sought by the Trade Unions

Ordinance (Amendment) Act would be achieved. Moreover, it soon became clear that strikes and the threat of strikes would continue despite the Trade Disputes (Settlement) Act. Towards the end of 1962 there was mounting unrest among sisal workers mainly over the decision to introduce a new system of payment.[29] A series of strikes led the Government to take a tough line: Mkello and the organising secretary of the PWU were detained and 'rusticated' for three months to the remote district of Sumbawanga in western Tanganyika.

This action numbed trade union opposition to the Government and over the next few months Mkello and other union leaders showed a more conciliatory attitude. None the less, rumblings of discontent continued and were given open expression in the second half of 1963. In August TUPE, backed by the TFL, alleged that there was 'brotherisation' (nepotism) in the civil service. The Government gave way to the pressure for investigation by setting up a committee, which included trade union representatives, to examine the allegations. The Committee found however that the latter were unfounded.[30] Soon afterwards—in October—the bulk of the unions affiliated to the TFL rejected proposals put forward by the Minister for Labour that the trade unions should be integrated directly into his Ministry. But two unions—the TGWU, Kamaliza's old union, and the Domestic and Hotel Workers' Union—supported integration, thus showing that the TFL was still torn apart by internal dissension.[31] In the same month spokesmen for both the Plantation Workers'

---

[28]*National Assembly Debates*, 27 June 1962, cols. 1962, cols. 1023–8 and 1052–3; 28 June 1962, cols. 1070–1 and 1079–80. (Speeches by Mkello).

[29]Discussed fully by Friedland, *op. cit.*
[30]*Sunday News* (Dar es Salaam), 11 August and 1 September 1963. The committee reported to the President on 1 December 1963, but its report has not been published.
[31]Friedland, *op. cit.*

and Railway Unions issued statements condemning the 'strike' law—the Trade Disputes (Settlement) Act, 1962; they wanted this law to be revoked so that the workers would recover their right to take strike action.[32] Then, early in January 1964 the TFL, as well as many individual unions, protested against President Nyerere's announcement that in future the civil service would be open to all citizens on equal terms, regardless of their racial origin.[33] Before trade union leaders could carry their protest any further, the Tanganyika army mutinied on 20 January.[34]

Though concrete evidence is not available, it seems possible that certain disgruntled trade unionists sought to take advantage of the unsettled conditions immediately after the mutiny when rumour-mongers raised doubts at to the stability of the country and its Government. Over 500 people were arrested and of this number probably more than half were trade unionists drawn from all parts of the country. Most detainees have subsequently been released and only a small number of civilian Tanzanians now remain in custody;[35] among them are Mkello and Tumbo, who was taken by the Kenya police to the border and arrested by the Tanganyika police early in 1964. The

mutiny brought trade union resistance to an end. Unionists who had not been detained (or who had been detained and then released) pledged their loyalty to, and expressed their confidence in, President Nyerere and his Government.

THE CREATION OF A NEW UNION

The advocates of trade union autonomy therefore lacked any spokesman when, on 21 February 1964, the Government introduced into the National Assembly the National Union of Tanganyika Workers (Establishment) Bill. Though this measure[36] passed through all its stages on one day, it altered the whole structure of the trade union movement in Tanganyika and was therefore of the utmost importance. It dissolved the TFL and its 11 member unions; established in its place one central union, comprising various industrial sections;[37] and provided for the general secretary of the Union and his deputy to be appointed by the President of the Republic. As a corollary to the new Act, provision was made in the objects of the new Union for the Union 'to be affiliated to TANU, to promote the policies of TANU, and to encourage its members to join TANU.' The Minister for Labour (who was made the first general secretary) pointed out that this was not something new, since the TFL had been affiliated to TANU since

---

[32]*Tanganyika Standard*, 24 October 1963.

[33]*Ibid.*, 8, 9, 11, and 15 January 1964. On the other hand, the Transport and General Workers' Union welcomed the President's announcement. *Sunday News*, 12 January 1964

[34]The political consequences of the mutiny have been assessed by the present writer in 'Politics in Tanzania,' *The World Today* (London, August 1965), Vol. 21, No. 8.

[35]*Parliamentary Debates*, 12 May 1964, col. 53; *The Times* (London), 12 April 1965, which reported that 25 civilian Tanzanians (including 13 Zanzibaris) remained in custody; *The Standard* (Dar es Salaam), 14 September and 1 October 1965, and *Daily Nation* (Nairobi), 26 April 1966, reporting the release of more detainees.

[36]Now Act No. 18 of 1964.

[37]Mr. Kawawa regretted that it had not been possible to form a single trade union in June 1962. See his speech on the Trade Unions Ordinance (Amendment) Bill on 27 June 1962. *Parliamentary Debates*, cols. 1054–5. The question of forming a single central union had been discussed on several former occasions— in 1956 and again in 1959–60, for example. But fear that the Government might ban the single union had led the unionists to reject the idea. (Information: Professor William H. Friedland).

1958.[38] But the TFL had slipped from under party control to the extent (according to one Assembly member) that there was 'a tug of war between the two parties, that of TANU and the TFL.'[39]

The Act provided that every person who was formerly a member of a union affiliated to the TFL automatically became a member of the National Union of Tanganyika Workers (NUTA).[40] The Minister was empowered to apply the union shop principle to an employer and his workers where more than fifty per cent of the latter belonged to the new Union and where the check-off system applied. In such cases, every employed person must become a member of NUTA within two months or have his appointment terminated.

The Union Rules provide for nine industrial sections and for the establishment, as required, of regional offices and branches.[41] Provision is also made for eight departments, including departments of eductation, accounts, and economics and research, at the Union headquarters in Dar es Salaam. The general officers of the Union are the general secretary and his deputy, the financial secretary, one assistant general secretary for each industrial section of the Union, and the departmental heads. These general officers constitute the executive council which meets monthly and is responsible to a general council for the administration of the Union and

<hr/>

[38] *Parliamentary Debates*, 21 February 1964, cols. 170–5. (Speech by Minister for Labour).

[39] *Ibid.*, col. 201 (Speech by Mr. A. P. Matsis (Arusha).

[40] The initials do not, of course, exactly correspond with the Union's title; the abbreviation purposely underlines the Union's link with TANU.

[41] *The Rules of the National Union of Tanganyika Workers* (Dar es Salaam, mimeo., n.d.), C. These Rules superseded the Provisional Rules, which were set out in the first schedule to Act No. 18 of 1964.

its affairs. In turn, the general council, which normally meets every four months, is answerable to the annual (delegates') congress, which is the policy-making organ of the Union with (probably in practice) largely confirmatory powers. Thus, the structure of NUTA is roughly parallel to that of TANU, whose corresponding national organs are the central committee, the national executive committee, and the national conference.

The Union as originally constituted had a number of defects. First, the Union structure was somewhat topheavy—probably inevitably since the Government had to accommodate within the Union the vested interests of the TFL and its member unions, each of which (with only two exceptions) was incorporated as an industrial section under a separate head. Secondly, there was not sufficient coordination between the assistant general secretaries and the directors of departments; moreover, while the former were responsible to the executive council through the general secretary, it was not clear how the directors fitted into the Union structure. Thirdly, since several of the former union leaders had been detained, some of the 'new' men who had been given positions of responsibility in the Union lacked experience at that level—though, as Friedland shows, a number of key officeholders were former senior officials of the pro-Government Transport and General Workers' Union. A fourth defect, which resulted from overcentralization in Dar es Salaam, was that regional and branch organisation was weak (though not in terms of staffing). Officials in the 10 regions and the 41 branches into which the country was (and is) divided for union purposes, lacked any precise executive functions. The chain of command, extending from national headquarters to the regions, branches and sections, was ill-defined, while the lack of co-ordination at the centre meant that regional officers might receive at the same time conflicting instructions from the different heads of departments and industrial sections. In the fifth place, accounting and financial control were inadequate for a Union which handled a great deal of money.

These defects were recognised both by Union officials and senior officers of the Ministry of Labour, and towards the end of 1964 steps were taken to remedy some of them. Thus, an accountant was appointed and an attempt was made to recruit a Director of Administration who would serve as a chief co-ordinating officer. Unfortunately, no-one with the necessary qualifications and experience could be found to fill this important post. Partly (but only partly) in consequence, many of the above-noted shortcomings remain. Above all, little has been done to streamline union organisation. Thus, in place of an integrated structure organised on a functional basis, with an effective communications system linking the headquarters official with the up-country worker, we are still (at the end of 1965) presented with a picture of an over-centralised and insufficiently co-ordinated organisation with an indifferent communications network. This last fact may account for the spate of (often misinformed) criticism which has recently been launched against NUTA by a number of readers of *The Standard*.[42] This criticism does less than justice to Mr. A. C. A. Tandau, NUTA's deputy general secretary, and many Union officials who (within the framework of an imperfect organisation) are making sincere attempts to build up a strong union movement as a means of improving the lot of the workers.

SECURITY OF EMPLOYMENT[43]

The Security of Employment Act of 1964, which was passed by the National Assembly on 3 December 1964, provides machinery for the settlement of contractual disputes between workers and employers. The Act requires workers' committees to be established in every business where ten or more trade union members are employed. Though only NUTA members may serve on a committee, the latter is to function in respect of all workers, whether or not they are Union members. The primary function of a committee is 'to consult with the employer on matters relating to the maintenance of discipline and the application of the Disciplinary Code,'[44] which is set out in considerable detail in the second schedule to the Act. Thus, discipline is no longer the sole prerogative of the employer but is made the joint responsibility of the employer and workmen. Another and important duty imposed on a workers' committee is to help in increasing productivity and efficiency at the place of work.

The Act also provides for the establishment of conciliation boards, which are complimentary to the workers' committees. These are tripartite bodies set up in the major area of employment and comprise an independent chairman, one representative of NUTA, and one

---

[42] This criticism was expressed between August and November 1965 and was answered by NUTA's Director of Publicity in *The Standard*, 30 November 1965.

[43] The section which follows is based on the Security of Employment Act, No. 62 of 1964; Michael Kamaliza, 'Tanganyika's View of Labour's Role,' *East Africa Journal* (Nairobi, November 1964), pp. 9–16; and *Parliamentary Debates*, 3 December 1964: Speech by Minister for Labour when moving the second reading of the Security of Employment Bill, 1964.

[44] Act No. 62 of 1964, s. 6 (1) (a).

representative of employers' interests. It is intended that the decision of the board on any matter referred to it will represent the agreed views of the workers and employers' representatives, but the chairman is empowered to impose his decision if agreement cannot be reached.

The Act applies to workers in the private sector of the economy earning a salary of £420 p.a. or less, as well as to certain grades of civil servants, notably members of the subordinate service and works staff and persons appointed on temporary or daily terms. Persons employed by local authorities in similar grades are also covered by the Act. It does not however apply to the more senior civil servants and local authority employees, members of the armed forces or disciplined services, a member of the Unified Teaching Service, or to workers of the East African Common Services Organisation employed in Tanzania.[45] The Labour Ministerial Committee of EACSO considered that the system of workers' committees and conciliation boards could not be established in one country alone but would require to be set up on an East African basis.

The Minister claimed that his Bill was 'significant as a practical expression of African Socialism,'[46] and would bridge the deep gulf which had previously existed between employer and worker. Given one main condition, the new legislation should go a long way towards improving the relations between workers and employers. That condition is that the workers' representatives serving on the workers' committees and concilia-

tion boards should exercise their considerable powers with responsibility and restraint. In April 1965 the Ministry of Labour organised training courses for some 10,000 members of the workers' committees. Perhaps in consequence, the new machinery outlined in the Security of Employment Act has on the whole worked remarkably well—a fact which is conceded by the Tanganyika Federation of Employers. Though it is still too early to say whether the decision to establish workers' committees in government ministries and local authorities will prove ultimately beneficial, there is at present no indication that Government's control over its own employees has been weakened. Ironically, from one point of view NUTA itself has had least direct benefit from the new machinery. The workers' committees have to some extent usurped the role of NUTA branch and section officials, and this situation will continue until the committees are fully integrated into the Union structure.

Some General Conclusions

Looking back over the ten year period from 1955, when the TFL came into being, one can see a changing pattern of relationships between TANU and the Federation. Expressed in marital terms, these were: an initial period of courtship from 1955 to 1957, followed in the latter year by engagement and, at the end of 1958, by marriage. The honeymoon period lasted until about the middle of 1960, when the first signs of a major disagreement between TANU and the TFL began to appear. The next period, one of estrangement, extended from the eve of independence to well into 1962. The TANU Government then took legislative action to repair the broken marriage, with TANU as the dominant partner. When this

---

45The orginal intention of the Ministry of Labour was to apply the Act to EACSO. Cf. *The Establishment of Workers' Committees and Conciliation Boards*, Government Paper No. 1 of 1964 (Dar es Salaam, 1964), para. 15.

46*Parliamentary Debates*, 3 December 1964.

step proved only partially successful, the Government dissolved the marital bonds and replaced the multiplicity of unions affiliated to the TFL by a single union, NUTA, firmly controlled by the Minister for Labour who was designated by the President as the Union's first general secretary. This represented marriage under duress.

The above outline has however an obvious weakness. It oversimplifies what was often an extremely complex pattern of relationships. Not only was the TFL frequently torn apart by internal disagreement among its leaders, but it was by no means always certain that the action taken by the latter—by Tumbo and Mkello, for example—had the support of the bulk of the trade union membership. Nor were individual unions particularly democratic in practice. Moreover, immediately before independence, there was even some disunity within TANU itself—Nyerere and his colleagues in the Government were badly out of touch with rank and file opinion on the issues of Africanisation and citizenship.[47] In its attitude towards the TFL, TANU in Tanganyika followed in the footsteps of the Convention People's Party in Ghana which had 'captured' the trade union movement by penetrating the central organisation, the Trades Union Congress.[48] Yet the fact remains that from 1954 onwards the great majority of trade union members were also members of TANU and the tug of war between the party and the unions was a good deal more pronounced at the

centre than in the country as a whole.[49]

Generalisations must usually be qualified and, at least as far as Tanganyika is concerned, the statement by Berg and Butler (quoted at the beginning of this article) is no exception. Though the close union of TANU and the TFL between 1957 and 1960 was not typical of the pre-independence period as a whole, during these years TANU and the TFL fused their identity to a much greater extent than occurred at any time between KANU and the KFL.[50] One can more readily accept as valid for Tanganyika Berg and Butler's assertion that after independence trade unions were 'quickly subdued by governing parties.' It was inevitable that this should happen. TANU had never ceased to regard the trade union movement as constituting the second leg of a single nationalist movement and party leaders were not prepared to tolerate indefinitely the existence of a competing centre of power, strongly entrenched in the urban areas and the sisal estates, within what (from September 1960 onwards) was a *de-facto* one-party state. 'The trade unions are the only other body than TANU which have effective access to the masses,' said Mr. A. G. Short, M.P. for Tabora, in the National Assembly on 27 June 1962. '. . . the trade union movement and the T.F.L. does represent a complex of power that the Government of Tanganyika cannot afford to ignore.'[51] Nor could the Government of a poor country, with an average *per capita* annual income of only £20, be expected to countenance strike action and ex-

---

[47]One consequence was the resignation of Julius Nyerere as Prime Minister in January 1962; he was succeeded by Rashidi Kawawa. See Colin Leys, 'Tanganyika: Realities of Independence,' *International Journal* (Toronto, 1962), Vol. XVII, No. 3.

[48]Berg and Butler, *op. cit.*, pp. 348–51 and 358.

---

[49]This is not to deny that there was some rivalry at a local level between trade union and TANU officials. *Cf.* statement by Mr. A. G. Short (Tabora), *Parliamentary Debates*, 27 June 1962, col. 1040.

[50]Scott, *op. cit.*, p. 24.

[51]*Parliamentary Debates*, cols. 1040–1.

travagant wage claims advanced on behalf of a working population which declined more or less steadily from 423,167 in 1951 to 340,344 in 1963 and 351,257 in 1964, when the workers' total cash earnings amounted to over £48 million.[52] Some indication of the dislocation to industry caused by stoppages in the period before and immediately after independence can be gauged from the following table, which also shows the substantial improvement achieved in 1963 and especially in 1964.

to which both the trade union and co-operative movements are affiliated—as subordinate, rather than as equal or parallel, organs. It is in this sense that one should read the statement in the report of the Presidential Commission on the One-Party State:

...in a newly independent country with a single national political movement, developing its economy on socialist lines, close organizational links between the Trade Union Movement, the Government and the Party are essential.[53]

Man-Days Lost Through Stoppages*

	1960	1961	1962	1963	1964
No. of disputes	203	101	152	83	24
No. of workers involved	89,000	20,000	48,000	17,000	3,500
Man-days lost	1,494,000	113,000	417,000	74,000	6,000

**Source: Budget Survey, 1965–66* (Dar es Salaam, 1965), Table 28, p. 28.

Trade union autonomy in Tanganyika can easily be justified on *a priori* grounds. It can be argued, for example, that the person who, as a worker, is a loyal member of a union can be a loyal member of TANU at the same time; that in short, no necessary conflict of ultimate loyalties is involved. The fact is, however, that political leaders in Tanganyika think increasingly in mono-institutional terms, with TANU as the core of a national political movement

Though trade union autonomy in Tanzania is certainly at an end and was symbolished by NUTA's break with the ICFTU early in 1964, it may be wrong to state that in the future the trade union movement in Tanzania is 'destined to play a subordinate role.' There is no doubt that the role to be played by NUTA, which is now closely integrated into both the government and party structure,[54] will be different from that of the TFL in the past. But that it will not necessarily be insignificant is suggested by the recently accepted report of the Presidential Commission, quoted above. The Commission stressed that

---

[52]*Statistical Abstract 1963* (Dar es Salaam, 1964) and *Employment and Earnings in Tanganyika 1964* (Dar es Salaam, 1965), p. 2. 'Working population' means the total number of persons in public and private employment, stated to be 103,801 and 247,456 respectively in 1964. The decline in total employment in 1963 by 56,684 (14.2%) was attributed by the Central Statistical Bureau (*Employment and Earnings 1964, op. cit.*, p. 2) to the minimum wages legislation.

[53]*Report of the Presidential Commission on the Establishment of a Democratic One Party State* (Dar es Salaam, 1965), p. 26, para. 79.

[54]The Presidential Commission recommended that the general secretary of NUTA should be an *ex-officio* member of the national executive committee of TANU. *Ibid.*, p. 27, para. 80.

the trade union movement has a vital part to play in eradicating mass poverty and said that 'The objectives of the 5 Year Plan can never be achieved without the active co-operation of organized labour.'[55]

Government hopes, on two main grounds, that co-operation will be forthcoming. First, because workers now enjoy security of employment and participate in a National Provident Fund scheme instituted in 1964, and secondly because—as the following table shows—average cash earnings have increased steadily over the last few years:

Average Cash Earnings for African (Male) Employees by Sector*

| | | Shs. per month | |
	Private	Public	All
1961	84	129	96
1962	104	166	124
1963	144	216	165
1964	155	222	176

*Source: Budget Survey, 1965–66, op. cit., p. 30.

Unfortunately, however, the depressed state of the world sisal market in 1965 and the fall in the prices of cotton and coffee, make it unlikely that the economy can withstand corresponding increases in wage levels in the immediate future. All the more important therefore is the attempt being made through NUTA to relate wage increases to rises in productivity.

The efforts to link wages and productivity directly together in simple agreements have met with some success. Thus, in October 1964 NUTA worked out a Wages and Productivity Agreement with the Tanganyika Sisal Growers' Association, whereby internal

improvements in the economy of the sisal industry were to be introduced in exchange for wage increases.[56] More recently, however, the Union has expressed its shock and discontent at a government announcement of new wage rates for low-grade civil servants. These rates (it has alleged) were lower than those agreed at a Joint Staff Council meeting, attended by representatives of both Government and NUTA, which was held earlier in 1965.[57] This episode, as well as the support which NUTA expressed in August 1965 for the strike of postal workers in Kenya and Uganda (who share with Tanzania a common Postal and Telecommunications Service),[58] suggest that it might not be easy for the Government to secure agreement on a national wages policy. In particular, Mr. Kamaliza has an unenviable dual role to fill. As Minister for Labour he must keep wage increases in line with productivity; indeed, President Nyerere wants him to go further and subordinate distribution (wage rate) objectives to production goals.[59] He must also have regard to the interests of the employers. Yet in his capacity as general secretary of NUTA Mr. Kamaliza must seek to promote the interests of the workers by supporting their legitimate wage claims.

---

[55]Ibid., p. 26, para., 79.

[56]Budget Survey, 1965–66 (Dar es Salaam, 1965), p. 28.

[57]The Standard, 7 September 1965. The minimum monthly wages announced for government employees were: shs. 180/- for Dar es Salaam and Tanga; shs. 150/- for prescribed towns; and shs. 120/- for other areas.

[58]Sunday News, 15 August 1965; The Nationalist (Dar es Salaam), 16 and 21 August 1965.

[59]In his address to the first annual conference of NUTA, President Nyerere said: 'Yet in Tanzania our national income is so low that every sectional interest within the community has to be more concerned with its growth than with its division. . .' The Nationalist, 25 March 1964.

NUTA has a more positive sphere in which to operate. Through the medium of the Workers' Development Corporation Limited, it has the opportunity of making a substantial contribution to the industrial development of the country. Originally established under the Companies Ordinance in April 1963 as the Tanganyika Workers' Investment Corporation Limited, it was made a subsidiary of NUTA when the Union was established in February 1964, incorporated on 28 July 1964, and adopted its present title in 1965. The general manager of the Corporation is responsible to a policy-making board of directors appointed by the executive of NUTA. The seven-member board selects its own chairman and deputy chairman who at present are the general secretary and the deputy general secretary of NUTA.[60]

The establishment of this Corporation has been made possible because the application of the check-off system to a unified labour movement assures NUTA of an income of over a quarter of a million pounds a year.[61] The Union Rules stipulate that no more than 50 per cent of Union funds shall be spent on

administration, leaving 50 per cent over for social services or investment. The executive of NUTA approves each particular project, which is required to be self-supporting, and then authorises withdrawal from the investment fund. Up to May 1965 the Corporation had obtained about £80,000 from this source.[62] This figure falls short of the annual target envisaged to be invested by NUTA in the Five-Year Development Plan, the reasons being that NUTA inherited heavy debts from the former unions and has had to furnish and equip its offices.[63]

At present the Coporation operates several canteens, a bar, and a 200-head dairy farm. It has also initiated a housing project for low-wage earners and is considering the establishment of workers' retail shops, processing industries, and a workers' hotel. The housing programme envisages the construction of some 3,000 workers' houses, but can only proceed on this scale if a substantial amount of foreign capital is forthcoming. External borrowing will tend to increase construction and rent costs which, in the limited project that has been undertaken in Dar es Salaam so far, have proved too high for low-wage earners. Ambitious —probably over-ambitious—programmes of this sort stem from a realisation on the part of NUTA officials that members are anxious 'to see that something big is being done.'[64] It just will not do for a Union housing project (for example) to be incorporated within the programme of the National Housing Corporation (which provides houses for middle-income workers). Though such co-operation would be economically

---

[60]Hadley E. Smith, 'The Government Corporation and Economic Development' (Institute of Public Administration, Dar es Salaam, mimeo. May 1965), pp. 14–15.

[61]*Cf.* Kamaliza, 'Tanganyika's View of Labour's Role,' *op. cit.*, p. 14: 'NUTA is now assured of an income approaching a quarter of a million pounds a year.' According to NUTA's Director of Publicity, the Union's membership was 232,619 at the end of November 1965. If each member pays the minimum subscription of 2/- a month (there is a sliding-scale of payment rising to 10/- a month for the highest paid workers), the Union will have an income of nearly £280,000 a year. The membership figure fluctuates however because many members are employed seasonally and redundancy was marked in 1965. Letter from J. J. Nambuta, Director of Publicity NUTA to Editor, *The Standard*, 30 November 1965.

[62]Hadley E. Smith, 'The Government Corporation,' *op. cit.*, p. 15.

[63]Letter from J. J. Nambuta, *op. cit.*, *The Standard*, 30 November 1965.

[64]*Ibid.*

beneficial, it would effectively rule out what may well become a cardinal feature of African socialism—the collective ownership control by workers of enterprises started through the direct investment of union funds.

These considerations tend to reinforce the existing trend of concentrating the Development Corporation's activities in Dar es Salaam, with as yet little material benefit for the up-country workers.[65] None the less, the Corporation has considerable potential, and leading Unionists are working hard to improve the lot of the ordinary worker. It is this potential, rather than any actual achievement to date, which encourages one to believe that the trade union movement in Tanzania may have a more important and positive role to play in the development of the country than Berg and Butler seem to assign to it.

[65] On 26 April 1966 President Nyerere announced that because of discontent among workers in Tanzania, he intended to appoint a Commission of Inquiry to look into the functioning of NUTA. *The Standard*, 27 April 1966.

III

Structures and Processes of Government

As the formal structures of the political system, governmental institutions are the concrete units that, in principle, formulate and execute official policies. To the extent that the authority and functions of executive, legislative, and judicial bodies are sanctioned and enumerated in constitutions and statutes, the nature of their powers and activities are more readily identifiable than those of unofficial agencies. Moreover, because they also operate in a routinized framework which is frequently open to public scrutiny, they are usually easier to describe and analyze. As a result, until recent decades specialists in comparative government often emphasized constitutions and formal institutions at the expense of the extralegal processes which complemented them. But institutions cannot be studied *in vacuo.* Today political scientists are equally concerned with the extralegal processes of political parties, electoral behavior, and political socialization as factors that significantly influence the operation of institutions. This is especially evident in the new states of Africa where the development and political effectiveness of extralegal processes predated, and later influenced, the independence institutions.

Because Africanists first gave their attentions to where public power lay, one finds a greater abundance of studies on the forces of nationalism and on political parties than on African executives, parliaments, and bureaucracies. Since 1960 this imbalance has been gradually redressed as evidence has accumulated on the performance of governmental structures. It should be noted, however, that the formal institutions of African governments are being defined and delineated not only by their successes, but also by negative responses to them, expressed in public unwillingness to cooperate with some executive policies and military coups.

Until the period of self-government, executive and legislative institutions in Africa were essentially adjuncts of the colonial administration, and Africans held few, if any, positions of influence within them. On the local level, as in the Native Authorities within the former British colonies, Africans participated in the regulation of community affairs; their powers, however, were limited and clearly distinguished from colony-wide policy-making. On the national level Africans were frequently admitted to legislative bodies, but on the whole such institutions were primarily advisory to the executive, rather than partners in policy-making, and the Africans' role was minimal.

Colonial policies governing African participation in legislative activities varied widely. West Africans under British jurisdiction gained access to legislative councils exceptionally early, notably in the Gold Coast (now Ghana) where the first African was appointed in 1888, and in Nigeria where four Africans were elected in 1922 to represent the towns of Calabar and Lagos. The first colony-wide elected African representation in a legislative council occurred in the Gold Coast in 1925. On the other side of the continent, however, Africans did not obtain appointive representation until 1944 when one African was admitted to the Kenya Legislative Council; other East and Central African colonies followed thereafter. The general pattern of political participation in French West Africa was somewhat different because the French assimilationist policy devolved minimal legislative authority to its colonies. Africans obtained access to the formal political structures only as *indigènes citoyens français,* but by 1936 less than one-hundred thousand qualified for this status out of a population of some twenty million.

The end of World War II marked the watershed for the development of significant political roles for Africans. As nationalist activities quickened in the early 1950's they increasingly achieved status as elected members of legislative councils and appointed members of executive councils. In the pursuit of independence Africans used legislatures as forums to publicize their grievances and their aims. The opportunities to advise and to oppose provided valuable experiences for African leaders, but less in the formulation of substantive agreements than in the areas of political organization and procedural tactics. During the usually brief period of self-government before independence Africans entered fully into policy-making, but the institutions continued to be oriented toward models fashioned by the colonizers until the post-independence period when Africans could shape their own structures in terms of their political outlook.

African governments share with other modern states the search to establish and nurture the legitimacy that gives them the public acceptability necessary for the peaceful maintenance of law and order. The uniqueness and the difficulty of this task for African states turns on the newness of their regimes and the apparent absence of firmly rooted customary responses to modern governmental institutions. Few countries in the world, however, have begun their existence with such careful arrangements for the transfer and legitimization of power. Constitutional conferences, pre-independence elections, the symbolic investiture of authority at the independence celebrations, and international recognition endowed the new African states with an aura of legitimacy and motivated Africans to accept the government's right to command ultimate authority over them.

The original intent of African constitution writers was to *create* power rather than *limit* its use, in the classical tradition of Western nations. Their purpose was to facilitate the exercise of national power in a context that had no precedent for indigenous authority to make and enforce law beyond the tribal level. This aim is especially evident in constitutions and constitutional amendments that have been adopted since independence.[1] One exception is likely to be Ghana: the first post-Nkrumah constitution promises to divide and balance power, rather than concentrate it. The experience of the rule of Kwame Nkrumah would appear to have had much the same impact upon Ghanaians as did that of King George III upon the American Founding Fathers. Still, constitutions in Africa as elsewhere do not always conform to political realities, particularly as they relate to the distribution of power. Indeed, the role of the constitution as an instrument creating authority in Africa suggests that these documents do not initially describe existing relationships.

Constitutions, however, are only one aspect of the legitimization process; the responsible and effective use of governmental institutions is the major determinant of their durability and acceptability. Africans, no less than Americans, are pragmatists, judging institutions by the results they produce. In Africa the most important institution is the executive, and it is to this office that Africans primarily attribute the successes and failures of government policies. African executives share many of the characteristics of presidents and prime ministers elsewhere in the world: they have wider powers over foreign than over domestic affairs, they tend to dominate legislatures, they must

---

[1] See, for example, J.P.W.B. McAusland and Yash P. Ghai, "Constitutional Innovation and Political Stability in Tanzania: A Preliminary Assessment," *Journal of Modern African Studies,* IV, No. 4 (December 1966) 479–515.

formulate and administer economic policy, and ultimately they must account in some manner to the general public for their administration. Yet, unlike their counterparts elsewhere, African executives operate within a political context, in Apter's terminology, of low information levels and few structures of accountability. Consequently, African executives are frequently "on their own" for the absence of powerful and organized groups lessens the public criticism which characterizes the policy-making processes in many Western states.

Executive dominance is particularly evident in its relationship with the legislature. On the whole, African legislatures are supportive rather than demand-making structures, and the national leadership frequently uses them to add legitimacy to executive policies, not as partners in policy-making and accountability. This tendency is not unique to African governments. The decline of legislative bodies generally was foreshadowed in the West by twentieth century "crises executives," coupled with such factors as party discipline in Great Britain or party confusion in succeeding French republics, and the growth of technology and specialized knowledge. Yet in many Western political systems executives still function with structures of high accountability—informed and articulate public opinion, elections, party control, pressure groups, and even occasionally the legislature itself. But in Africa executives work within a different and, historically, a more permissive framework. In the colonial era legislative activism and initiative were not notable characteristics, and when African leaders moved into executive positions during the transitional stage of internal self-government, their followers readily supported them and contributed to the pattern of concentrated power in the executive.

The power of African executives reflected in constitutions, institutions, and practices is also a product of other forces. Anthropological evidence indicates that tribal political systems rarely differentiated between political, social, and economic or executive, legislative, and judicial powers. While African legislators may look to some form of separated power, the general public is often indifferent to politicians who claim that executives usurp their legislative prerogatives. Moreover, legislators in one-party states, either through political prudence or party loyalty, tend to identify themselves with executive policy. The notion of "limited power" is a uniquely Western idea, evolved out of centuries of practice, philosophical exchange, and political expedience. Africans do not share this experience, or, for that matter, the cultural and historical context which provided the reasons for limited government. Indeed, the authority of the colonial government in no way suggested that power was limited. Even in Western societies the distinctions between differentiated structures are increasingly blurred by the need for rapid and carefully planned responses to human problems which are the product of the complexities of modern life. In much the same way, African leaders recognize the need for extensive executive powers because of the enormity of the modernization task to which they are committed.

Nevertheless, the context within which Africans are developing their political practices is distinctively their own. Few Africans today debate whether or not it is the legitimate function of government to create and regulate social and economic services; indeed, any government that failed to attempt such policies would be deemed illegitimate. Unlike Americans in the 1930's who hesitated over the question of public regulation of economic life, Africans expect their governments to initiate and promote economic measures designed to serve both the private and the public good. In some respects, African executives perform in the Bismarckian style, recognizing that in their circumstances national integration, economic growth, and the efficient use of resources are best achieved by governmental initiative. To these ends, Africans are less concerned with limiting power than with putting it to good use. The result has been a dramatic increase in the power of bureaucratic structures and a lessening in the importance of representative institutions.

Given the nature of their concentrated powers, most African executives do not utilize their position as effectively as they might. In this respect they are not Bismarckian, for they lack the efficiency and the information such an executive requires. Factors such as low literacy rates, inexperienced and uncertain bureaucrats, and inadequate channels of communication, result in faulty perceptions of what is needed by government agents, and of what is possible by citizens. In consequence, initial efforts at economic planning suffer from capriciousness and inefficiency, have minimal effectiveness, and produce public bewilderment or discontent. In many instances corruption and narrow self-interest have become instrumental in securing the unity of the political process.[2]

But executive dominance, bureaucratic inefficiency and corruption have in many cases weakened public support; indeed, the leaders of the recent military coups in Africa have consistently justified their actions in terms of the need to remedy these deficiences.[3] Even so, military leaders must establish the authority of *their* regimes, and the coercion of the military, no less than the inefficiency or corruption of civil administrations, is an inadequate foundation on which to build

---

[2] See, for example, J. David Greenstone, "Corruption and Self Interest in Kampala and Nairobi: A Comment on Local Politics in East Africa," *Comparative Studies in Society and History*, VIII, No. 2 (January, 1963), 199 ff.

[3] See "The Military Seize Power: A Summary of Recent Coups d'Etat," *Africa Report*, XI, No. 2 (February, 1966), 12.

a stable government. It is interesting to note that almost all leaders of *coups* in Africa initiate their administrations with promises of a new constitution, new elections, and a speedy return to civilian rule. The search for legitimacy may be difficult but its purposes are not forgotten even in moments of great national crisis.

The Ivory Coast Constitution: An Accelerator, not a Brake

A. S. Alexander, Jr.

The purpose of this article is not only to explain an African constitution, but also to examine, in that context, certain general ideas about constitutions and politics. The Ivory Coast, a former French West African colony, gained full independence as late as 1960. As a newly independent state, with a population of under four million, the Ivory Coast is participating in a nation-building experiment which the flood of new countries has made a widespread phenomenon of our times. The experiment is doubly meaningful for other countries. First, its results will weigh significantly in the balance of world power; secondly, as Ivorians look to the western example in pursuing their experiment, the West can see, reflected in Ivorians' words and deeds, a new and different image of itself.

There is a fundamental antithesis between the typically American notion that constitutions today serve primarily to limit government,[1] and the fact that the Ivorian constitution does not. American experience with British colo-

nial rule led to a distrust of power. The Magna Carta and Coke's view of the common law permitted the conception of a fundamental law to which the highest human powers would be subject. Social conditions in the colonies, moreover, were suited to limited government. Self-sufficient Americans expected government to protect them from enemies at home and abroad, but otherwise not to interfere. The American constitution thus serves to check power. A federal system deprives the central government of despotic strength. Separation fragments power, thus lessening the chances of abuse. Rights provisions, which are the most explicit, simply say there are certain kinds of things government may not do even if it could muster the power. Practice of these rules for over 175 years has given them greater strength to resist power.

Conditions differ sharply in the Ivory Coast. Some of the indigenous societies possessed constitutional systems,[2] yet even Ivorians have been unable to perceive how any of these could be adapted to the modern Ivory Coast. When Ivorian leaders look to France,

---

[1] See, e.g., F. A. von Hayek, *The Constitution of Liberty* (Chicago, 1960), pp. 176–92; C. E. Wyzanski, 'Constitutionalism: Limitation and Affirmation', in *Government Under Law*, ed. by A. E. Sutherland (Cambridge, Mass., 1956), pp. 473, 477–8, and 480–2.

[2] Cf. J. H. M. Beattie, 'Checks on the Abuse of Political Power in Some African States', in *Sociologus*, IX, new series no. 2 (Berlin, 1959), pp. 97, 104–8, and 111.

From *Journal of Modern African Studies*, Vol. I, No. 3 (September 1963), 293–311, by permission of the journal and its publisher, the Cambridge University Press.

whose traditions have significantly influenced them, they do not find the notion of a limiting constitution as widely accepted as in the Anglo-American world. Ivorian ideological forebears, moreover, include Marx as well as Montesquieu;[3] and Communists consider western constitutionalism a device to maintain bourgeois domination of the proletariat.

Extreme ethnic diversity is another factor which tends to make a limiting constitution inappropriate. The Ivory Coast is composed of 60 or more different ethnic groups. Its borders, determined for the convenience of French colonial administration, enclose unfriendly tribes and sever others from their brothers in Ghana, Mali, Liberia, or the Upper Volta. Little in the way of common customs and history exists to pull these groups together. This pattern makes unity with the Ivory Coast especially difficult to maintain. President Houphouët-Boigny has warned that 'an immoderate love' of liberty will not prevent him from taking measures necessary to keep his country together. He said:

I want it known here and on the borders of the Community ... that here, in the Ivory Coast, we will not put up with the licence of liberty, nor with the licence of democracy.

---

[3] See T. L. Hodgkin and R. Schachter, 'French-Speaking West Africa in Transition', *International Conciliation*, no. 528 (New York, 1960), pp. 387 and 398–9; Schachter, 'Political Leaders in French-Speaking West Africa' (unpublished MS. in Boston University Document Center), pp. 16–20. These authorities mention the close ties between French Communists and French West African leaders both before and after World War II. They also mention that the leaders took over Marxist methods which could be useful in Africa. There is no direct evidence that Ivorians borrowed constitutional notions from the Communists. But see p. 305, n. 5, below.

... Believe me, we will act as other countries do. The United States of America, a huge State of 200 million inhabitants, powerful in its financial, military and economic strength, with a stable régime which has stood the test of time, with an organized internal opposition so respected that the bipartisan principle is often applied to the conduct of foreign affairs, well! this great and powerful country proclaims before the world that the one hundred Communists on American soil endanger the American régime of 200 million people. A sanitary cordon is therefore formed around these one hundred dangerous Communists ... [At a time when the Ivory Coast is just getting started and needs outside help, when Ivorians should help preserve that political security without which no one will help us,] do you want us, out of an immoderate love of democracy and liberty, to accept that at near or distant borders instructions be given to an irresponsible minority to endanger the régime we have freely chosen? Don't count on me to do it.[4]

When the Sanwi tribe, on the Ghana border, threatened to secede and join its brothers in that country, Houphouët quickly responded by exiling some and imprisoning other Sanwi leaders without trial.

A third circumstance of major importance is the fact that, at a time when rapid change is called for, Ivorian society lacks internal dynamism. The Ivory Coast suffers from a high degree of illiteracy, a low educational level, *per capita* income around $100 a year, debilitating disease, an unfavourable climate, poor soil, and traditional elements peculiarly resistant to measures necessary for change. To this should be added the great expectations of the

---

[4] *Discours de M le Ministre d'Etat Houphouët-Boigny*, Géo. André Stadium, 7 September 1958 (Abidjan, 1958), pp. 24–5. (My translation, as with other French documents and speeches quoted, unless otherwise specified.)

Ivorian masses, which are encouraged on every side but little tempered by realism.

It can be argued—and Ivorian leaders believe it—that a stagnant society combined with desire for rapid change calls for unfettered government. The force and direction of change must come from the government, where the unusually small Ivorian élite is concentrated. The élite alone possesses the skill and understanding necessary to move society forward. Moreover, to move a stagnant society fast, some eggs have to be broken. Ivorian leaders have not hesitated to crush nongovernment unions, minimise wage increases, and institute a 'modified form of forced labour'.[5] These measures were naturally accompanied by imprisonment of labour leaders without trial and other forms of illegal coercion.[6] Yet this is the very kind of thing a limiting constitution is designed to prevent.

A final factor is the need for foreign aid. Ivorian leaders reason that suppliers of aid prefer a well-run and stable recipient. The leaders feel that stability and efficiency are possible in the present circumstances only if government is authoritarian. Dissident elements would threaten stability unless the élite could crack down on them unhampered by a limiting constitution.

When the Ivory Coast gained autonomy within the French Community a constitution became necessary, though France retained important powers, such as defence and foreign policy. The draft based on the constitution of the French Fifth Republic, which top leaders produced by the end of 1958, established a unitary state. Separation of powers was respected, but in a 'parliamentary' régime distinctly dominated by the executive. Provisions relating to fundamental rights were brief and stated vaguely in the affirmative, rather than as limitations on governmental action.

The draft assured executive dominance in a parliamentary régime primarily by three methods. First, all executive power was put in the hands of one man, the Prime Minister. Second, legislative control over the executive was strictly curtailed. In particular, the draft provided for automatic dissolution of the Assembly when it voted a motion of censure. Third, by redefining the concept of 'law', the Prime Minister gained, and the legislature lost, important law-making powers. The draft declared that the Assembly votes 'the law', which term was defined by specific enumeration of the matters with which law might deal. Many of these were traditional subjects of legislative power, such as fundamental rights and definition of crimes, but other such subjects were absent from the list. All matters other than those enumerated were for the executive.[7]

When a special committee of Assemblymen passed the draft in February 1959, they left unchanged the foregoing features. There was strong opposition to the provision for automatic dissolution, but after some extra-committee manoeuvring it received committee approval.[8] In March 1959, the Constituent

---

[5] V. Thompson, 'The Ivory Coast', in *African One-Party States*, ed. by G. M. Carter (New York, 1962), pp. 269 and 286–7.

[6] See F. Zuccarelli, *Les Chances de la démocratie dans l'ouest africain* (Paris, 1961), p. 19.

[7] *Amendements apportés au projet de constitution, par la Commission Constitutionnelle au cours de ses débats du 12 au 21 février 1959.* (Mimeographed document in the archives of the National Assembly, Abidjan.) The relevant articles are, respectively, 10–15, 49, 37, and 39.

[8] *Avant projet constitutionnel, procès-verbal des travaux de la commission spéciale* (National Assembly Archives), hereinafter referred to as *Avant projet*, 12–21 February 1959, pp. 169–70, 177, and 181.

Assembly adopted the draft—though not before Houphouët had made a special intervention to explain that the disputed provision was essential to stability, without which development would be impossible.[9]

Full independence in 1960 required a new constitution. This one, which confirmed the tendency of its predecessor to concentrate all power in the hands of the executive, was adopted by a more summary process. A government draft was submitted to the Assembly in October 1960, returned unchanged to the Government, and re-submitted to the Assembly, which adopted it unanimously at the end of the month.[10]

The major difference between the 1959 constitution and its successor is that the latter abandons the parliamentary régime. The one-man executive, now called President of the Republic, is elected by universal suffrage, not by the Assembly, for a five-year term.[11] He is no longer encumbered by the trappings of a parliamentary system, investiture, votes of confidence, censure, and dissolution. The mechanical relations between executive and legislature now resemble those in the United States.

Another important difference is that the 1960 constitution creates for the first time a Supreme Court. The Constitutional Chamber, one of four which make up the Court, may give legal advice to the executive on constitutional questions, which remains a secret between the Chamber and the executive. The Chamber may also render more

formal advisory opinions, which can be published.[12]

A third function is a kind of 'arbitration' between legislature and executive; at the request of either the President of the Republic or the President of the Assembly, the Chamber may decide whether a measure proposed by a member of the legislature is in the domain of the law.[13] The Chamber has no power, on the other hand, to decide whether a measure proposed by a minister is within the executive domain. Thus arbitration serves primarily to keep the Assembly within bounds.[14] The Chamber has no power comparable to judicial review; the executive control is assured in part because the President of the Republic appoints the President of the Supreme Court, who presides over the Constitutional Chamber, and two other members of the Chamber, for terms which expire with the executive's.[15]

The dominant President and vague affirmative statement of rights suggest in themselves an authoritarian régime. Houphouët-Boigny's nearly absolute power, entirely apart from what the constitution gives him, must also be taken into account, especially in the relations between executive and legislature. In the United States we are accustomed to think of these relations as being at arm's length. In the Ivory Coast, however, deputies and ministers take orders from Houphouët, the chief executive. The legislature does not pass

---

[9] *Procès-verbal, séance du 26 mars 1959, deuxième session extraordinaire 1959, Assemblée Constituante* (National Assembly Archives), pp. 32 ff.

[10] For an account of the stages through which the constitutions went, I have relied in part on an unpublished dissertation at the University of Chicago: A Zolberg, 'One-Party Government in the Ivory Coast' (1961).

[11] Ivory Coast Constitution, article 9.

[12] Ibid. 23 and 29. Law no. 61–201, Determining the Composition, Organisation, Powers and Functioning of the Supreme Court, 2 June 1961, articles 22 and 29. *La Réforme judiciaire en Côte d'Ivoire* (Abidjan, 1961), pp. 70–1.

[13] Ivory Coast Constitution, article 46.

[14] See Alphonse Boni, *Les Domaines de la loi et du règlement dans la constitution de la Côte d'Ivoire* (National Assembly Archives), pp. 6–7.

[15] Law no. 61–201, articles 3 and 19.

bills the executive is unwilling to carry out, nor does it refuse to pass laws which the executive proposes. But one should not exaggerate the extent to which Houphouët's power modifies the situation. The Assembly does represent a viewpoint different from the executive's. This viewpoint is manifested in debates and Houphouët himself must take it into account.

* * *

Though the Ivorian constitution does not serve primarily to limit government, it can and does exert a positive force. First, by helping to establish legitimacy, it contributes to stable and effective rule. Second, by stating authoritatively goals unattainable at present, it may hasten the realisation of those goals. Third, by providing a manual of basic organisation, it clarifies and orders the exercise of power.

THE LEGITIMATING ROLE

Legitimacy is the quality of rightful rule, and a legitimate régime is one whose subjects accept its right to govern. The value of legitimacy is that such a régime need not maintain itself primarily by force. History suggests that governments founded on force are unstable and shortlived. Their fragile equilibrium encourages increasing resort to repression, which inhibits constructive effort both by government and governed.

The basic way a government may become legitimate is by acquiring power through an accepted method. Some societies accept the notion that power should reside in succeeding generations of a family. Others believe that the people should participate more or less directly in the periodic choice of rulers. What a government does once it acquires power may also influence legitimacy. In this regard, two aspects

of governmental conduct should be distinguished. One is the form of that conduct. Society feels that certain acts should take a particular form—though form may have little effect on substance. In the Ivory Coast, for example, it is accepted that some measures should be in the form of law and therefore go through the Assembly, but this formality has little effect on the substance of the measure.

Second is the substantive aspect of governmental conduct. An issue of substance for Ivorians is whether to persecute those who dissent from governmental policy. Repeated acts which outrage society's sense of right may forfeit legitimacy. Mere errors of judgment, however, occasional violations of accepted principles, or even repeated violations that are not extreme, will normally not suffice. How far a government may go in its violations depends upon the degree to which the governed accept not only the principles of substantive conduct, but also the forms, and the method by which power was acquired. Moreover, a government which acquired power by patently legitimate means, and which faithfully follows forms, has greater latitude in violating substantive principles of conduct.

If the role of legitimacy is difficult to perceive in western countries today, it is because their governments have been established for a relatively long time, and have maintained a relatively high degree of compliance with form and substantive principles. Westerners take legitimacy for granted because it is no longer questioned. During periods of revolutionary change, however, legitimacy becomes important. Then government may lose the comfortable backlog of long acceptance. A conscious, sometimes express, effort must be made to re-establish legitimacy.

When Talleyrand decided to restore a constitutional Bourbon monarchy, during the turbulent years which followed the French Revolution, he saw clearly the importance of legitimacy. He believed that such a régime offered the most complete legitimacy by linking France's royal family to the institutions dear to the Revolution. Talleyrand felt that Napoleon's forceful rule should end, that only a legitimate régime could calm the French and strengthen their government.[16] To Ivorian leaders, steeped in French tradition, these words would be particularly meaningful.

The need for legitimacy during periods of revolutionary change explains why the perpetrator of a *coup d'état* seeks to legitimise his takeover by parliamentary investiture.[17] Likewise, in forcefully suppressing a *coup d'état*, an established government may expressly invoke its own legitimacy. A particularly significant example occurred last December in Senegal, sister republic to the Ivory Coast. Backed by police, the Prime Minister (known as President of the Council) took over the Assembly to forestall a motion of censure. President Senghor, relying on paratroopers, met force with force and, in a radio appeal to the Senegalese people, took great pains to justify his action as constitutional:

On the order of the President of the Council, the palace of the National Assembly has been surrounded by companies of police. The nation's representatives have been driven from their usual place of meeting and many of them have been arrested. Those are the facts. They are neither a part of Senegalese traditions of democracy which many envied us, nor above all are they within the

meaning of article 33 of our fundamental law [which provides that deputies are not to be arrested except in certain cases].

It is truly a deliberate violation of the Constitution of the Republic. Now article 24 of the Constitution makes it my duty to assure the regular functioning of institutions. That is why I have resorted to the armed forces, for the last word must rest with the Constitution and the law.

In the regions, the military commanders will have to submit to my orders. I give them the following order: to demand of the governors and chiefs of local subdivisions written proof of their fidelity to the Chief of State, guardian of the Constitution . . .[18]

The need for legitimacy at a time of revolutionary change is also one reason why a constitution is important to the Ivory Coast. Since colonial rule has given way to independence, and tribal authority to national, the Ivory Coast Government cannot rely on long acceptance. It must seek other ways to establish its legitimacy, and one of these is the constitution. This helps to establish legitimacy in three different ways. First, it has a symbolic function. Second, it lays down forms for governmental conduct. Third, it proclaims the principles of conduct and the accepted method of acquiring power.

As a symbol, the constitution stands for the fact that the Ivory Coast has become a member of the community of nations. Thus, when the 1959 constitution was submitted to the Assembly, Etienne Djaument urged his fellow deputies to vote for it in these words:

It is with satisfaction and serenity that we are going to vote for the monument of our political liberation. Great satisfaction, in effect, to have become adult after a difficult childhood . . . Full satisfaction to take our place among free countries . . .[19]

---

[16]Talleyrand, *Mémoires* (Paris, 1891), II, pp. 157–61.

[17]M. Duverger, *Institutions Politiques* (Paris, 5th edn., 1960), p. 39.

[18]*Le Monde*, 19 December 1962.

[19]*Procès-verbal, seance du 26 mars 1959*, *Assemblée Constituante*, pp. 44–5.

It is often said that newly independent countries adopt constitutions because everyone else does.[20] This emphasises the symbolic function of the constitution. Ivorians see that the two great powers of today, the United States and the Soviet Union, have written constitutions. Close contact with France has made Ivorians conscious of the French example. Many Ivorians believe that without a constitution they would not have a validly constituted government.

The second way the constitution contributes to legitimacy is by making fixed and certain the forms and procedures which the government is to follow. A significant example is article 41, which by defining 'law' determines whether a given measure should go through the Assembly in the form of a law, or be promulgated by the executive as a 'regulation'. In practice every measure adopted by the Ivory Coast Government is carefully compared with the list of matters set out in article 41. The Ministry of Justice and the Supreme Court advise on whether a given measure is law or regulation in every important case.

The reason for strict adherence to article 41 is obviously not because the outcome depends upon whether a measure is promulgated by the executive or goes through the Assembly. It is inconceivable that the Assembly should oppose the executive which Houphouët heads, since he also controls every deputy. The leaders were aware of this fact, moreover, as revealed in the discussions on the 1960 constitution and its predecessor.[21] The question naturally arises, therefore, why they bother to maintain such strict adherence to article 41. One reason may be that it orders governmental activity, but as far as legitimacy is concerned, the answer lies in an analogy to ritual. Like ritual, observance of the form and procedure which article 41 sets out gives a sense of regularity and formality which is associated with legitimacy.

The third way the constitution enhances legitimacy is by announcing principles of governmental conduct and proclaiming the method of acquiring power which is accepted in the Ivory Coast. The preamble declares that the 'people of the Ivory Coast proclaim their attachment to the principles of Democracy and the Rights of Man as they are defined by the declaration of the Rights of Man of 1789, by the universal declaration of 1948, and as they are guaranteed by the present Consitution.' Article 6 states: 'The Republic assures to all equality before the law without distinction of origin, race, sex, or religion. It respects all beliefs.' The first paragraph of article 62 is exceptional in that it is phrased in the negative, though it is still not stated as an express limitation on governmental action: 'No one may be arbitrarily detained.'

The framers were particularly emphatic about democracy, which is the method for acquiring power which Ivorians accept. Article 2 announces that the principle of the Ivory Coast Republic is 'government of the people, by the people and for the people', and article 3 that 'sovereignty belongs to the people' and 'no segment of the people nor any individual may exercise that sovereignty to the exclusion of others.'

[20]E.g. by H. J. Spiro, *Government by Constitution* (New York, 1959), p. 11.

[21]E.g., *Exposé général du projet constitutionnel par M Philippe Yacé, Ière session ordinaire 1960–61, Assemblée Nationale* (printed in Abidjan, and hereinafter referred to as *Exposé général*), p. 16; *Avant projet*, pp. 155 and 159–61.

The effect of announcing substantive principles and proclaiming the accepted method of acquiring power is to make them explicit and thus confirm their validity as elements of legitimacy. At the same time, the constitution sets outer limits for governmental compliance. It will be more difficult to question the government's legitimacy when principles or standards of democracy not set out in the constitution have been violated.

Compliance poses, however, a problem with regard to principles of governmental conduct which it does not pose for the other ways in which the constitution contributes to legitimacy. As far as democracy goes, the clear pre-eminence of Houphouët among Ivorian leaders would allow him to submit to periodic elections without fear of defeat. Following the forms and procedures set by the constitution may be troublesome and technically difficult, but is no threat to the present power structure. The constitution may stand as a symbol, almost entirely detached from any action the government takes. But compliance with substantive principles of conduct does affect the outcome; and yet, unless there is substantial compliance, the government may cast serious doubt on its own legitimacy.[22] The dilemma is particularly acute in the Ivory Coast, because the extreme measures which Houphouët may think Ivorian conditions require are likely to conflict with substantive principles.

The only answer is to try for substantial compliance and endeavour to give an exceptional character to violations. Ivorian leaders seem to have adopted that policy. In the first place, by phrasing most substantive principles in vague affirmative language they have increased their freedom of action. Since the constitution was adopted, moreover, the leaders' comments suggest that they intend to continue the policy of substantial compliance. Ernest Boka, President of the Supreme Court, told me in April 1961 that Houphouët would abide by the constitution, because he thought the example of leaders obeying the constitution would convince the people they too should obey the laws. Boka insisted that Houphouët really believed this, and added that he himself agreed. He further declared that this avowal by Houphouët was one of the reasons why he had accepted appointment as Supreme Court President.

More significant than the leaders' words are their actions. Violations of substantive principles have in fact been exceptional, and when they have occurred, Houphouët has sought to minimise them. Thus, as soon as the Sanwis calmed down, Houphouët released those still detained, told the exiles they could return, and re-asserted the rule against arbitrary detention by boasting that his was one of the few African régimes without improperly detained prisoners.[23]

The desirability of compliance, which Ivory Coast leaders recognise by word and deed, is one answer to those who object that the constitution is a cloak to hide the leaders' efforts to acquire purely personal power and prestige. If there is compliance, the cloak does not hide but models the shape of what is lying underneath. A further answer may be found by weighing whatever deception there may be against the advantages of legitimacy. The relevant example of the Belgian Congo is often on Ivorians'

---

[22] See G. Ferrero, *The Principles of Power* (New York, 1942), pp. 140 and 188; and R. Fisher, 'Bringing Law to Bear on Governments', in *Harvard Law Review*, LXXIV (Cambridge, Mass., 1961), pp. 1130 and 1136–7.

---

[23] *Abidjan Matin*, 4 January 1962.

lips, and they do not have to look far to see in Ghana the dictatorial excesses of an insecure leader. Internal conflict can disrupt, and divert resources from, desired development, and in such circumstances rights cannot be protected. Legitimacy helps to create a stability in which those consequences can be avoided.

A further objection to the legitimating role is that it presupposes a certain knowledge and acceptance among Ivorians not only of the constitution but also of the ideas, like democracy and human rights, through which the constitution works. It would be wrong, of course, to assume that those concepts have the same currency in the Ivory Coast of today as do comparable concepts in the United States. There are indications, however, that Ivorian knowledge and acceptance, though far from perfect, is sufficient to give reality to the legitimating role.

Knowledge among the ruling élite is more than sufficient. Among the *évolués* in general, a great many have the education, interests, and contacts which would permit them to know of and understand the constitution and the ideas through which it works. Acceptance follows close behind their knowledge. Among the masses, awareness is more limited, but real enough. Especially receptive to oral communication, the masses learn about the constitution and the ideas through which it works from leaders' speeches and from conversation with *évolués*. Moreover, Ivorian tradition has not left the masses entirely unable to understand. For example, it is precisely from an animistic, unmechanised society that one might expect understanding of the symbolic and ritual ways in which the constitution contributes to legitimacy. In addition, when violation of substantive principles brings hardship and repression, Ivorians

react like other people. This explains the singular disrepute among all Ivorians of the *indigénat*, a system which meant the arbitrary administration of criminal justice.

Even if knowledge and acceptance acceptance could be demonstrated only among *évolués*, the impact of the constitution's legitimating role would be significant. The *évolués* are a potential breeding ground for revolt; and even when there is no real threat of revolt, those holding power may be pushed to increasing acts of repression if they fear their régime is illegitimate.

The Prospective Role

The Ivory Coast constitution sets forth ideals and specific programmes for action. In doing so, it seeks to win Ivorians to accept the ideals as standards of conduct, and induce those whom it addresses to carry out the programmes. Thus, to the extent it has currency, the constitution may hasten the realisation of the ideals and programmes it sets forth.

The prospective role of the constitution complements the legitimating one. Over a period of time, the constitution can improve the imperfect knowledge and acceptance among Ivorians of democracy and the principles of governmental conduct. The legitimating role is nevertheless basically different from the prospective. In the former role, the constitution relies on ideas already to some degree accepted, and affects the present status of the government so that some compliance is essential. In the prospective role the constitution seeks to increase or create acceptance in the future; here, compliance is relatively unimportant.

Comments by Ivory Coast leaders often reflect their awareness of the fact that the constitution strives toward future perfection of ideals as yet imperfectly realised. One example is a statement made by Usher Assouan when, as reporter for the special committee of Assemblymen which examined the top leaders' draft of the 1959 constitution, he presented the draft to the Constituent Assembly. Referring to the first sentence of article 2 ('The Ivory Coast Republic is one and indivisible, lay, democratic and social'), he said that this demonstrated the Republic's strong desire 'to achieve complete democracy, not only in the political sphere, but more particularly in the social'.[24]

The recognition of the prospective role by leaders and in constitutions of other countries undergoing political rebirth confirms the importance of this role in the newly independent Ivory Coast. Madison's belief that the American Bill of Rights would play a prospective role was one of two reasons why he recommended adoption of the Bill:

The political truths declared in that solemn manner acquire by degrees the character of fundamental maxims of free Government, and as they become incorporated with the National sentiment, counteract the impulses of interest and passion.[25]

The French have relied on their various constitutions to induce acceptance of ideals or programmes;[26]

and certain provisions of the constitutions of India, North Viet Nam, and the Soviet Union are apparently designed to play a prospective role.[27] The Soviet view is suggested in the leaders' comments on the first decrees they passed. Grzybowski notes that they thought law 'offered a useful mechanism' for 'instilling new ideas on the purpose of social action in the minds of the people', among other things. 'Thus', he continues, 'the first decrees of the Soviet government were not designed to possess absolute binding force, even in the eyes of their authors. They were, according to the definition of Trotsky, "the program of the Party uttered in the language of power" and, as such, rather a means of propaganda than of administration.'[28] This Soviet view has had

Ivorian constitutions incorporate by reference:
"The Representatives of the French People . . ., considering that ignorance, neglect and scorn of the rights of man are the sole causes of public misfortune and corruption of governments, have decided to set out in a solemn declaration the natural, sacred and inalienable rights of man in order that this declaration, constantly before all members of the social body, should remind them ceaselessly of their rights and duties. . . ." The present French constitution makes the following appeal to its territories to join the Community: "In accordance with these principles [among others, the Rights of Man as defined in 1789] and the principles of the free determination of peoples, the Republic offers to those overseas territories which express the will to adhere to it new institutions based on the shared idea of liberty, equality, and fraternity and conceived with a view to their democratic evolution. . ." (French Constitution, preamble; translated by P. Campbell and B. Chapman in *The Constitution of the French Fifth Republic* (Oxford, 1958), p. I.

[27]See W. G. Andrews, *Constitutions and Constitutionalism* (Princeton, 1961), pp. 24–5 and 146; and B. Fall, 'Constitution-writing in a Communist State', in *Howard Law Journal*, vi (Harrisburg, Penn., 1960), pp. 157 and 167.

[28]K. Grzybowski, *Soviet Legal Institutions* (Ann Arbor, Michigan, 1962), pp. 3 and 42.

[24]*Rapport déposé au nom de la Commission Spéciale Constitutionnelle, deuxième session extraordinaire 1959, Assemblée Constituante* (National Assembly Archives), p. 2. Hereinafter referred to as *Rapport déposé*.

[25]J. Madison, letter of 1788 to T. Jefferson, *Letters and Other Writings* (Philadelphia, 1865), I, p. 426.

[26]An interesting example of such a statement of ideals may be found in the famous Declaration of the Rights of Man and of the Citizen in the French Consitution of 1791, which declaration the present French and

an important impact on constitutional theory and practice in the Ivory Coast as well as in other under-developed countries.[29]

Madison's reference to 'that solemn manner' and Trotsky's words, 'the language of power', suggest why the Ivorian constitution can help to gain acceptance of the ideals and programmes it sets forth. The constitution speaks with a solemnity and forcefulness lacking in speeches or written statements of policy. Unlike these, the constitution emanates not from one man, one party, or one government, but from the sovereign people. Consistent with the elevation of its source, the language of the Ivorian constitution, when setting forth ideals, has an unaccustomed breadth and nobility. These qualities also come from the fact that the constitution is hard to change. Flexibility demands broad expression, and the greater care lavished on documents intended to be lasting often produces loftier language. Difficulty of change, moreover, gives a constitution the prestige of permanence—which helps to explain why Ivorians call their constitution a 'monument'. These qualities are evident, despite translation, in the two following articles which set forth the ideals towards which Ivorians are to strive:

In setting forth programmes, the language of the Ivory Coast constitution is more specific and looks for concrete results sooner. Articles 69 and 70, for example, serve as an invitation to negotiate and an affirmation of solidarity:[31] '[The Republic of the Ivory Coast] agrees to create with [other] States intergovernmental organs of common economic management, of co-ordination and of free co-operation.' Article 70 enumerates a series of economic, financial judicial, health, customs, and other goals which the intergovernmental organs may pursue.

The historical context reveals how the framers of these articles hoped they would work. In opposing the creation of a federal executive in French West Africa, the Ivory Coast has angered leaders in neighbouring countries. The Ivory Coast wished to assuage this anger and sincerely wanted increased co-operation on a practical, non-political level. Articles 69 and 70 were designed to demonstrate the good will of the Ivory Coast and to encourage other African countries to engage in practical co-operation with her.[32] Thus, in reference to those articles, P. Yacé, President of the Assembly, said: 'Such a program corresponds perfectly to the objectives of co-operation and association which the *Conseil de l'Entente*

[The people of the Ivory Coast] assert their intention of co-operating in peace and friendship with all the people who share their ideal of justice, liberty, equality, fraternity, and human solidarity.

The Republic assures to all equality before the law without distinction of origin, race, sex, or religion. It respects all beliefs.[30]

---

[29]M. Duverger, 'La Nouvelle Constitution marocaine', in *Le Monde*, 30 November 1962.

[30]Ivory Coast Constitution, preamble and article 6.

---

[31]Stalin intended that the 1936 Constitution of the U.S.S.R. should serve a similar purpose: "Today, when the turbid wave of fascism is bespattering the Socialist movement of the working class and besmirching the democratic strivings of the best people in the civilised world, the new Constitution of the U.S.S.R. will be an indictment against fascism, declaring that socialism and democracy are invincible. The new Constitution of the U.S.S.R. will give moral assistance and real support to all those who are today fighting fascist barbarism." J. Stalin, *Problems of Leninism* (Moscow, 1947), p. 567.

[32]*Avant Projet*, p. 197; *Rapport déposé*, p. 6.

would like to promote on the African continent.'[33]

Despite the plausibility of the prospective role, it is again possible to object that the constitution is not well enough known in the Ivory Coast to have an appreciable effect. This objection has already been answered in the context of the legitimating role. But even if the constitution is sufficiently widely known, one might also object that it cannot advance Ivorians' ideals if conditions in the Ivory Coast do not permit. The objection is self-evident but does not mean there is no leeway to advance ideals. One of the conditions in the Ivory Coast is rapid change, which has caused old ideals to crumble and required a search for new ones. At such a time the constitution can serve as a fixed point where Ivorians can find some of the new ideals they are looking for.

THE ORDERING ROLE

The Ivory Coast constitution expresses solutions to vital intragovernmental problems of timing and division of labour. Agreement on the solutions may be only tentative; but the constitution can still serve as a temporary working arrangement, which tends to reduce the number and the extent of disputes over the internal functioning of government, and thus facilitates concentration on the substantive tasks with which government is supposed to deal. The way a government functions may of course affect the choice of policy or substantive measures, though perhaps less so when the government is controlled by one man as in the Ivory Coast. But even where a solution to

problems of functioning would lead to less good policy, it is usually preferable to adopt and implement that policy with reasonable efficiency rather than to pursue a better one which internal feuding would render ineffective. Moreover, a better decision on substantive issues is possible if they are not confused with procedure.

In the Ivory Coast, as elsewhere, problems of timing and the division of labour must be solved before any action can be taken. For many, the same solution may be adequate. Often, there is no real disagreement, especially where the decision has little effect on the outcome of substantive measures. Decisions on such problems each time they arise would be a waste of time and energy, and might promote harmful discord within the government. For example, if the constitution did not specify, for all to see, the length of time allowed the President of the Republic for deciding whether to accept or veto legislation,[34] then the passage of every bill could be obstructed by procedural arguments. Should Houphouët himself be allowed to decide the appropriate period for every bill, this would increase the tensions of one-man rule.

The separation of powers between the legislature and the executive is the major decision of this nature laid down in the constitution. Because of Houphouët's control of the whole governmental structure, the division is not the same as in the western system. Though the constitution gives the Assembly power to decide fundamental matters, Houphouët really makes these decisions. Scrupulous observance of the constitution's division of functions between Assembly and executive permits Houphouët to use the Assembly mainly as a sounding board, and a means of enlightening the

---

[33] *Exposé général*, p. 29. The *Conseil de l'Entente* is a loose grouping of the Ivory Coast, the Upper Volta, Niger, and Dahomey, largely under Houphouët's leadership. See, e.g., Thompson, *op. cit.* p. 297.

[34] Ivory Coast Constitution, article 13.

masses about his measures. This process is not impeded by the constitutional provision (article 41) that the Assembly should deal with such measures as civil rights, status and capacity of persons, marriage, and criminal laws. These are precisely the matters on which Houphouët needs to feel out popular reactions and encourage willing compliance of the masses. More technical and mechanical matters, such as the details of the economic management of the state and of the organisation of production, which the constitution reserves for executive action, can be more easily resolved without reference to popular reaction. A similar division of functions aids the use to which the Supreme Soviet is put by its leaders.[35]

What happens to a measure which the constitution requires that the Ivorian Assembly should pass? The Government usually proposes the measure, which is then referred to a committee composed of 23 out of the total of 70 deputies. The committee discusses the measure in secret, but a government representative participates. If there is significant opposition, the Government may agree to some changes, unless the measure would be substantially transformed. The measure is then put before the whole Assembly, which adopts it after debates that largely serve to let off steam.[36] The way the Assembly communicates these measures to the masses arises from the particular composition of the Assembly. In fact, though not in theory, each deputy represents his own ethnic group. He maintains constant contact with that group and often makes trips into the interior in order to do so; he also communicates to them the government view on measures which Houphouët proposes to pass.[37]

Two factors in particular confirm this role of the Assembly. One is the care which the framers appear to have lavished on the committee system. The other is Houphouët's tendency to let the party wither and allow the government to become the significant power structure. Normally the single party would itself act as sounding board and means of communication;[38] but it is no longer used for this purpose nor sufficiently organised to carry it out. It is logical that the Assembly, as a branch of government to which Houphouët increasingly resorts, should assume this function.

The ordering role is particularly important in the Ivory Coast because the institutional revolution preceding independence left no traditions concerning the problems of timing and the division of labour. Before 1957, the Ivory Coast was governed by a variety of institutions, both French and African: the French Parliament and executive,

---

[35] H. J. Berman, *Justice in Russia* (Cambridge, Mass., 1950), pp. 285–6.

[36] The procedure described is based on the following articles of the constitution: *Article 13.*—The President of the Republic may introduce legislation, concurrently with the members of the National Assembly. *Article 26.*—The President of the Republic communicates with the National Assembly either directly, or through messages read by the President of the National Assembly, and on these occasions there is no debate. *Article 40.*—The members of the Government have access to the committees of the National Assembly. They are heard on the demand of the committees. They [the committees] may have the help of Government officials. *Article 48.*—Discussion of proposed bills is directed to the committee's draft. The committees, on the Government's request, must inform the National Assembly of the points on which there is disagreement with the Government. The procedure has some relation to the *Règlement de l'Assemblée Nationale* (Abidjan, 1961), articles 10, 13, 17, and 23.

[37] Zolberg, *op. cit.* pp. 315–16.

[38] I. M. Wallerstein, *Africa, the Politics of Independence* (New York, 1961), pp. 96–7.

and the French West African Federal and local Territorial Assemblies. To the limited extent possible, Ivorian leaders governed through these structures. It was obvious, however, that such institutions would require radical adaptation to permit governing a single territory which had just become independent. It may be true that, in the brief period from 1957 until the 1960 adoption of the present constitution, *loi-cadre* reforms and the French constitution of 1958 granted more and more local autonomy.[39] Yet the *loi-cadre* was not designed to prepare for independence, and the changes in this brief three-year period followed so rapidly, one upon the other, that no real order was imposed. Under the 1959 Ivorian constitution, France retained power to decide such important matters as foreign policy, defence, currency, and common economic and financial policy.[40] Less than a year later, Ivorians were confronted with the problems of governing a fully independent state. At this point a new constitution was the best device to bring order out of the chaos of pre-existing institutions and newly acquired powers.

* * *

In conclusion, a few words of caution are appropriate. Ivorian leaders have not done all they could to make their constitution more meaningful and useful; nor have they amended it, except for the *ex post facto* creation of a court of dubious legitimacy to try political prisoners.[41] Article 41, which defines

---

[39]For further details see Hodgkin and Schachter, *op. cit.* pp. 388–99.

[40]French Constitution, article 78.

[41]The creation of this court is explained, and the legal texts may be found, in documents issued 12–15 January 1963 in the Ivory Coast. Copies of these documents are now at the Boston University Document Center. In addition, see *Le Monde*, 20–21 and 26 January 1963.

'the law', and article 11, which provides for a substitute when the President of the Republic dies in office, are examples of provisions which could stand improvement. It is hard to see why these improvements cannot be made when, in Senegal, several useful and ingenious amendments have been adopted.[42]

The Government has also failed in many cases to respect the constitution when it could have done so without reducing the efficacy of governmental action. An example is the failure to utilise the powers constitutionally given to the Supreme Court, and particularly the power to render formal advisory opinions. The Supreme Court has frequently given the Government legal advice on the constitutionality and other legal problems of proposed laws and decrees. Not once, however, have these opinions been published, whether favourable to the Government's position or not, though the Senegalese have published both kinds of advisory opinions. Such publicity could be most useful to the Ivorian Government. As part of constitutional ritual, and demonstrating compliance with the constitution, it would contribute to legitimacy.

Ivorian leaders are perhaps afraid that publishing advisory opinions could get out of hand. If the Supreme Court took upon itself to find constitutional obstacles to measures the Government felt essential, the conflict which might result, even though the Government is not required to follow the advisory opinions, could seriously hamper action. But this fear seems unreal, especially in view of the control the President of the Republic exerts over the process of giving advisory opinions. Further, the Government is strong enough to allow some unfavourable opinions to be

---

[42]Senegalese Constitution, articles 39 and 53.

published and publicly revise its action accordingly. The Government sometimes retreats from its position on the basis of constitutional advice, but always in secret. To make known its submission to an adverse opinion would be a lesson in abiding by the law for Ivorian citizens.

As a final word of caution, the constitution is only one element in the over-all political picture. If other elements should deteriorate radically, the constitutional foundation so far constructed could easily be demolished. The seeds of such deterioration are already apparent. While the Ivorian population increases rapidly, the contrast between cities and rural areas, between an unconsciously rich élite and a vast impoverished mass, grows stronger every day.[43]

On the whole, however, the Ivorian constitution justifies a certain optimism. Despite a failure to follow the Senegalese example of amending, and of publishing advisory opinions, the Ivorian élite have in general shown more respect for the constitution, and implemented more of its provisions, than most other African leaders. Ivorians have devised and carried through a more realistic governmental structure than in Senegal. This is shown by the recent *coup d'état* in the latter country, and by the subsequent rumours that French-speaking black Africa's maturest people will abandon their quasi-parliamentary régime for a presidential régime 'of the Ivorian type'.[44]

Finally, for those who would like to see the constitution serve increasingly to limit government, there is the striking formal resemblance to western constitutions. Although the French model is the most important, the presidential régime offers a significant parallel to the United States constitution; this is enhanced by the Ivorian framers' reliance on the committee system, although it was not intended to fulfil exactly the same function as the American.[45] It is even possible that the legitimating role, by making it desirable for the government to comply in some measure with the constitution, and the prospective role, by inducing acceptance of the ideals of fair and decent governmental conduct, may lead the Ivory Coast toward a limiting constitution.

---

[43] R. Dumont, *L'Afrique noire est mal partie* (Paris, 1962), pp. 63–8 and 221–3.

[44] *Le Monde*, 22 December 1962.
[45] *Exposé général*, pp. 13–17.

Decision-Making Among African Governments on Inter-African Affairs

I. William Zartman

One of the important, and frequently neglected, aspects of political development concerns the establishment of institutions and behavioral patterns to deal with foreign relations. New states are as much in need of development in this area as they are in regard to domestic aspects of politics. The development of foreign policy requires familiarity with the realities of national interest and national power, skill in the use of the instruments of national policy, and procedures for the formation of policy. Much work remains to be done by students of developing areas to interpret the actions of states during this phase of political evolution.[1]

African states have active ties with their former metropoles, and somewhat less active relations with two other categories of states: the leading 'Cold War' protagonists and the remaining members of the Afro-Asian area. The most important relations of any country, however, are its relations with its neighbors, since it is here that the greatest need to deal with issues on a day-to-day basis arises. If we consider only Western (North and West) Africa, at least half a decade of relations can be analysed for the whole area, while some of the states have been independent and have had relations with other parties and governments in the area for a decade.

There are two ways of examining inter-African foreign policy-making in Western Africa. One is functional based on an analysis of component processes such as stimulus, information, communication, formulation, and execution. The other is institutional, depicting the roles of the actors and the nature of the influences on the process of decision-making and execution as a whole. Although the absence of fully formed institutions and the presence of newly emerging patterns in the area might suggest that the former approach has greater relevance, the latter permits comparison with other societies, developed and underdeveloped, and brings out the evolving nature of the Western African scene. This study will therefore concentrate on the interaction of institutions in the formulation and execution of the policies of Western African states towards each other, with the functional approach used where it seems appropriate.

[1] Some work has already been done under the direction of J-B. Duroselle and Jean Meyriat by the Centre d'étude des relations internationales of the Fondation nationale des sciences politiques, Paris, in *Les nouveaux États dans les relations internationales* (Paris: Colin, 1962) and *La communauté internationale face aux jeunes États* (Paris: Colin, 1964). See also Zartman, 'Characteristics of Developing Foreign Policies', in William H. Lewis, ed., *French-Speaking Africa: The Search For Identity* (New York: Walker, 1965), and Zartman, *International Relations in the New Africa* (Englewood Cliffs: Prentice-Hall, 1966). This study draws on the latter book and on research done during 1962–1963 in nine of the sixteen North and West African states under a research grant from the Rockefeller Foundation. The assistance of the Rockefeller Foundation and the University of South Carolina is gratefully acknowledged.

From *Journal of Development Studies,* Vol. II, No. 2 (January 1966), 98–119, by permission.

Even before formal accession to sovereignty, the Western African organizations or parties established relations among themselves. Decisions were made in party councils, under the influence of or directly by a predominant nationalist leader, and were transmitted through local lieutenants to the people to be carried out or supported, with the nationalist chief and his close lieutenants filling the roles of ambassador or conference delegate in dealings with other leaders and movements. A number of nationalist movements—in Algeria, Morocco, Tunisia, Togo, Portuguese Guinea—engaged in active diplomacy before independence, making contact with other countries to win support for the political or military campaign for independence or both, gaining experience in the concerted use of negotiation and force. Some parties —in the territories of French West Africa (AOF), Gambia, and Algeria— used diplomacy in their search for regional unity, getting practice in developing and defending national points of view even before the nations existed. In some territories—Senegal, Ivory Coast, Dahomey, Nigeria—nationals took part in the activities of the French or British executive branch, serving on UN delegations, national cabinets, or the staffs of foreign ministries: all territories of AOF also sent deputies to the French National Assembly, where foreign policy was discussed, as well as having representatives in the short-lived institutions of the Community. These experiences, late and limited though they were, did much to shape the conduct as well as the content of inter-African relations.

The predominant mode of Western African political leadership is exercised through institutions built up around a 'charismatic' leader (one endowed with an exceptionally magnetic personality).

The importance of charisma as a vehicle for the transfer of loyalties and the creation of institutions has frequently been noted.[2] Attempts have been made in this way to establish a sense of legitimacy around a political leader; first in a political party and then, after independence, in the government of the state and the nation. The leader becomes the 'original ancestor' of the new nation, in a political, not a genealogical sense. This 'personalisation' may aim at creating a sense of nationhood transcending tribal and other sectional divisions within the country.[3]

Decision-making in inter-African politics derives from this situation and is usually focused on the president. The declarations of the president may become the national ideology, consecrated —where euphony permits—by 'isms' built on the leader's name. Specific, even minute, decisions may be made by the president, whose prestige in Africa and experience in dealing with other leaders gives him a special competence in inter-African relations. His anger and his ardour, his whims and his convictions, may become the mood of his country's policy, and his friendships and acquaintances mark its limits. Rare are the cases—President Houphouët-Boigny's meeting with President Kwame Nkrumah in 1957 and with President Ahmed ben Bella in 1963—when bilateral meetings between heads of state were not a prelude to rapprochement. When the chief is absent—as he frequently is for conferences, health or vacations—or is occupied with other problems, African relations may have to wait their turn, since there is no

---

[2] See especially David E. Apter, *Ghana in Transition* (New York: Atheneum, 1963), pp. 303, 323.
[3] See Jean Buchmann, *L'Afrique noire independante* (Paris: Pichon and Durand-Auzias, 1962), pp. 135–137, 355–358.

alternative figure or institution qualified to handle them. Because of the consequent necessity of dealing with problems *seriatim*, long-term or sustained action in one field, such as African relations, is not possible and projects progress slowly. On the other hand, because of the personal nature of decisions, short-term bursts of energy, rapid action, and equally rapid changes are also possible. Within this pattern of relations and decisions, the role and influence of all other groups and institutions work through the president and must be seen as modifications of the rule of centralized personalized power.

LIEUTENANTS

The president is surrounded by lieutenants, councils, advisers, and representative groups. His primary lieutenant in inter-African relations is the foreign minister. (In Ghana, Morocco, Ivory Coast, Senegal, and Niger, there has also been a ministerial position dealing with African or regional affairs, while the rest have desks or sections dealing with Africa in the foreign ministry.) The foreign minister is often either a political figure brought into the government to balance the political forces in the country—as in Dahomey, Nigeria, Mauritania—or a close friend, political *alter ego*, or relative of the president—as in Tunisia, Morocco, Senegal, Mali, Guinea, Liberia, Ghana, Algeria.[4] In such cases, diplomatic skill or experience may not be a primary criterion for selection, although capable men have occupied the post in a number

of these countries. The tenure of Western African foreign ministers has varied widely, from six years (Rudolf Grimes of Liberia) to a month (André Guillabert of Senegal), although the average is somewhat over two years. It is relatively rare that the head of state or government himself occupies the foreign ministry, but his predominant role in policy-making and even execution makes his minister above all a department head, an adviser, and an administrative assistant. The meetings of foreign ministers have thus been useful for drawing up agendas, formulating positions and defining problems, but not for bargaining, compromise and negotiation. The most ambitious mission of Western African foreign ministers was the effort of Barema Bocoum of Mali and Louis Beavogui of Guinea to solve the problems of succession in Algeria in July 1962—a pious attempt which, not surprisingly, ended in failure. However since 1962 in the Organisation of African Unity (OAU), foreign ministers have to an increasing extent taken-on a more direct decision-making role, reserving only the final signing (and the initial mandate) for their presidents.

Cabinet members other than the foreign minister can serve as presidential envoys because their political base and their method of selection is frequently similar to that of their foreign office colleagues, but their mission often has little to do with their field of competence. The Dahomeyan foreign minister was chosen to go to Togo to arrange a meeting of heads of state in 1961 because he had spent his childhood in Togo, but the Dahomeyan sent to intervene in the Togolese assassination in 1963 was the economics minister, picked because he was a fellow tribesman of the predominantly Cabre army in Togo, and the Ivoirien sent to Guinea

---

[4] The important case of Jaja Wachuku of Nigeria poses a problem of classification. As a faithful representative of Prime Minister Tafawa Balewa's views, he was a lightning rod for his prime minister, not a spokesman for his own party, the National Convention of Nigerian Citizens (NCNC).

INSTITUTIONS AND ROLES IN INTRA-AFRICAN POLICY MAKING

Number	Person	Number	Organization
1	Head of state/government	11	Presidential staff
2	African affairs minister	12	Council of ministers (cabinet)
3	Foreign minister	13	Foreign ministry
4	Other ministers	14	Other ministries
5	Party secretary general	15	Party political bureau
6	President of the legislature	16	National assembly (parliament)
7	President of comission	17	Permanent legislative commissions
8	President of auxiliary	18	National organizations
9	Para-diplomats	19	Para-diplomatic bodies
		20	Party
		21	[non-voters]
		22	External representatives
		23	Embassies

This diagram bears more of a resemblance to those of Bernard Charles ('Un parti politique africain: le Parti Democratoque de Guinée', XII *Revue française de science politique* 2: 335, 349, 352 [June 1962]) or Stephane Bernard (*Le Conflit Franco-Marocain* [Bruxelles: Institut de Sociologie de l'Université libre, 1963], III, 357) than to those of Richard Snyder et al. (*Foreign Policy Decision-Making* [Glencoe: Free Press, 1963], 63), since many of the latter's categories are inoperative in Western Africa. It can be applied to any particular state in the region more accurately, for example, by varying the vertical dimension to express role intensity and the horizontal dimension to express size. Environmental influences are omitted here.

to arrange a meeting of heads of state in 1960 was the interior minister, chosen because he was a former labour associate of President Sekou Touré. When they do serve as negotiators in their special field, however, their selection for the mission frequently indicates that the problem under discussion will be treated as a technical and not a political matter. Thus negotiations on problems outstanding between Algeria and Tunisia, Mali and Senegal, and Mali and Mauritania, involved other cabinet members than the foreign ministers, and the entire approach of the Entente has been to remove problems from politics by placing them on the level of technical co-operation among competent ministers—with partial success.

A major problem of interministerial contacts has been that of coordination, in every direction. Presidents may neglect to inform their foreign ministers, foreign ministers may keep few memoranda of their conversations for use by their staffs, other ministers may deal directly with their presidents without coordination with their foreign colleagues, and, where both a foreign and an African affairs ministry exists, the lack of coordination may lead to rivalry and undercutting, a chronic problem in Morocco and Ghana, where the offices of African affairs tend to specialise in political warfare while the foreign ministry practices diplomacy.

The other lieutenants also fill roles similar to those of ministers. The party president or secretary general (when he is not the chief of state) and the president of the national assembly are both frequently used as political envoys. Both are usually national political figures of importance, whose positions as formal leaders of the party or the nation's elected representatives gives them prestige in dealing with political matters. Particularly in Morocco, Ivory

Coast, Guinea, Senegal and Niger, presidents of national assemblies have served as special envoys; occasionally, too, other members of parliament—often presidents of permanent commissions—have performed the same ambassadorial functions.

COUNCILS

Two councils are important in the formulation of inter-African policy: the council of ministers (cabinet) and the party political bureau, two governing bodies with overlapping membership and competing functions. Rarely is the cabinet a collective organ of decision and responsibility in inter-African policy making; its members are lieutenants who act both as department heads and as presidential advisers, but who do not meet together very often as a decision-making council. In some strongly one-party states such as Guinea, Mali, and Ivory Coast, the cabinet has increased its activity since independence, at the expense of the political bureau; in other states, such as those of the Maghreb, it has tended to break down into commissions and inner circles grouped about the president's office or the palace. Nigeria, Liberia, Sierra Leone, Dahomey, and Senegal are exceptions to the general pattern of cabinet disuse; initiative for the Monrovia Group, for example, came out of a meeting of the Senegalese council of ministers, which charged Premier Mamadou Dia to consult other African states about a new conference on Congo. In general, the council of ministers by its nature may be expected to be more aware of national capabilities but less attuned to popular desires than the political bureau, and its competence in inter-African relations is likely to be greater in technical than in political matters.

More of a paradox is the role of the

party political bureau, since its importance contrasts with the same characteristic of personal, centralized decision-making that weakens the council of ministers. Throughout the area, the political bureau stands between the general ideology of the regime and the specific decisions of the president, and, more than any other organ, is responsible for formulating the principles of policy. It is also the downward channel for discussion and education within party cells and publicly on the local level. It serves as a body for making decisions on interparty relations, a cover under which inter-African relations frequently continue to be conducted. Recognition of these three general functions, however, does not imply that all parties stand in the same relation to their government or are equally effective in carrying out their functions. In some states—Guinea, Ghana, Mali, Algeria, Tunisia, Ivory Coast—the single party provides an articulated hierarchy parallel to and interlocking with government, and in several of these the party is considered to dominate the government, which then becomes simply an executory committee of the party bureau. In these states, the three functions of the political bureau are generally filled; the president predominates in the bureau but it is there that decisions on principles and occasionally details of African relations are made, and the foreign ministry is a technical organ of execution. In a number of these states, however,—Tunisia, Ivory Coast, Mali, for example —the impact of practice has forced a reversal of the roles; policy and even principles are decided in the president's office or by the council of ministers, and the party executive body becomes merely a technical organ for carrying applicable decisions down to the people and ascertaining their reactions, acting only

as a meeting of heads of departments. In a second category of states, including Senegal, Togo, and Liberia, the party occupies a more conventional position that of an electoral machine, and the political bureau is of little use as an organ either of decision or of execution. It may still perform its three functions superficially: it will issue principles of inter-African policy after hearing a periodic review of foreign relations by the responsible member; it will establish its own relations with other parties and their bureaus; and it will serve as a link between the government and local party organs.

In a third group of states, the party— in or out of power—serves to elaborate party programmes and govern party affairs, frequently without any direct governmental role in inter-African affairs. Political bureaus (whatever their local names) in Morocco, Sierra Leone, and Nigeria—all of them having multiparty systems—follow this pattern. The three functions in this case concern party activities, but often do not affect state policy towards other Western African countries; the council of ministers and the presidential or palace councils predominate over political bureaus. It should not be inferred from these categories that the political bureau is a homogeneous body. There are frequently important differences among the membership—in states as diverse as Guinea, Ghana, Senegal, Morocco, Algeria, and Tunisia—showing that party executive bodies are coalitions of several points of view, if not factions and interests.

The test of the importance of the political bureau as a decision-making organ lies not so much in its routine use, where the locus of decisions is often hard to isolate, but its role in emergencies and in important initiatives. In some states, no emergency decisions or changes in policy are possible without reference to the political bureau. Before his 1958 trip to Accra, Touré appears to have been given PDG political bureau instructions general enough to allow him to enter into a union with Ghana, and the central committee of the CPP met to approve the proposed union while Touré was still in Accra. In 1958, the executive committee of the Istiqlal formulated plans for a Maghreb unity conference, leading to the Tangier meeting in April. The CPP Central Committee again met before the Casablanca Conference to formulate general lines of policy, and before the first Lagos Conference of 1962 to decide whether to participate without Algeria. The PDG Political Bureau named and instructed its delegates to the 1959 Monrovia Conference, with subsequent approval by the Council of Ministers. The following year, the Bureau refused to continue steps toward rapprochement with the Ivory Coast, despite the initiatives of Touré.

More frequently the political bureau in western Africa sticks to principles and meets only to ratify decisions made in the presidential circle. Thus the Senegalese Progressive Union (UPS) Executive Committee met on the day following the attempted Soudanese coup in 1960, and after Dia's attempted coup in 1962, when the necessary measures had already been taken; in the latter case, Senegal's President Leopold Sedar Senghor carefully explained that foreign policy would not change, since it was made by the party, but that it would become more active in the pursuit of goals established by the third Party Congress, since inactivity was one of the defects of the previous regime. In matters of initiative, particularly in inter-African policy, the party political bureau tends to confine its activity to enunciation of principles of state policy and the ratification of decisions made elsewhere. Needless to say, the party congresses served an even more distant function, consecrating general policy lines already decided but open to reinterpretation in the light of new events. They have given their stamp of authority to change or continuity, as the occasion demands, but offer no examples of important decisions in inter-African relations.

ADVISERS

The most important of the foreign policy advisory groups, given the nature of decision-making, is the presidential cabinet or staff. Its form varies from country to country. In Accra, Flagstaff House includes a number of advisers to the president, who meet in weekly session with other foreign ministry and party officials to discuss African policy. In Abidjan, Bamako, Dakar, Lagos, Rabat, and Algiers, offices of the chief of state or head of government contain advisers whose meetings are less regular but who serve as a source of advice and information. The functioning of these bodies is little different from that of any other executive staff, and the membership contains nationals, Europeans, and exiles from other African countries. The presence of the latter frequently contributes to the distortion of information on which decisions are based and has even caused bad relations between their host and home states. Presidential advisers do broaden the base of decision-making, however, and the presidential cabinet is at least as important as the council of ministers and the political bureau as a locus of specific policy making.

Another group of advisers is the foreign ministry. In all states except Liberia, the foreign ministry started from scratch in the postwar period after independence, and in a number of states (Morocco, Algeria, Tunisia, Entente states, Guinea, Nigeria) was not created until after the other ministries had been established. Within a remarkably short time, under the pressure of necessity, the foreign ministries have developed into at least a skeletal structure along classical lines, with area and functional desks. Perhaps the most surprising aspect of this evolution has been the relative under-development of the African sections of the ministries. In most cases, one Afro-Asian desk covers the part of the world that includes the largest number of countries, the greatest population, and the majority of non-aligned states. A number of European countries, the United States, the Carnegie Endowment for International Peace, and the United Nations offer training programmes for African foreign ministry personnel, but the graduates, trained in at least the procedures of modern diplomacy, tend to be placed in European, North American, and international organization sections of their ministry.

Desk officers in the foreign ministries tend to take an active part in ministerial deliberations, but reports of these discussions frequently do not go beyond the higher levels of the ministries; the desk officer may or may not see ambassadors' reports, when they are written, and frequently has only public information media in limited supplies as his source of technical intelligence. The lack of secretarial assistance, a chronic weakness of African bureaucracies, also hampers intra-ministerial communications and record keeping. The economics affairs desk officer frequently deserves special recognition for his activity, according to personal observations in nine of sixteen western African states, perhaps because it is easier to handle economic material—even with

the limited statistical material available —than to grasp the vagaries of political matters, especially since the latter are so completely within the competence only of higher authorities. Obviously, however, detailed evaluation of specific cases depends on the personal competence of the individual.

The intermediate level in the foreign ministries tends to function best. The secretary general, permanent secretary, or secretary of state for foreign affairs, as he may be called, is a man who is both at the top of the technical 'desk' files and at the bottom of the political files. Having access to both groups, he is in the best position to bring technical information to the attention of political figures. In a number of cases where the Foreign Minister is a political figure— Guinea, Senegal, Ghana, Morocco—it has been the secretary general who has run the department. When he fails, the link between the political and the technical is broken, and policy, liberated from its informational basis, is free to flee the constraint of reality. In general, the foreign ministry has relatively little to do with the making of political decisions in inter-African affairs, which remain in the hands of the president's circle.

A third group of advisers to the president consists of his diplomatic representatives. If their job is properly performed, ambassadors and their staffs serve as a primary source of information, as spokesmen for their country's foreign policy interests, and as guardians over their country's commercial interests and expatriate populations. Unfortunately, in western Africa, ambassadors are frequently regarded more as a sign of prestige and friendship than as an institution serving a positive function. Very few states have embassies for the purpose of gathering information in countries with whom relations are not warm, an exception being the Moroccans in Ivory Coast, or for the purpose of advancing a specific foreign policy; another exception being the Moroccans in Guinea, who worked hard to keep Guinea from recognizing Mauritania.

Ironically, the criticism has frequently been made that there are too many African ambassadorial posts and that they place a costly burden on the finances of the new states. While this may be true of western African representation outside the continent, it is difficult to see its validity in inter-African relations.[5] There is a real need for small efficient embassies headed by capable and dedicated chiefs of mission who feel that their job of representation and information is as important in Ougadougou or Nouakchott as it is in Paris or Washington. Such men are hard to find. Until they are available—as they are in a few foreign services, most notably in Tunisia's—ambassadors continue to fall far short of their potential value as presidental advisers.

Instead, inter-African diplomatic representation has shown serious weaknesses. It is undermined by the practice of sending out special envoys when contacts of importance are necessary, and by the long absences of many of the ambassadors, a habit encouraged by presidential example. Some states' missions are headed by exiled politicians, whose effectiveness as either representatives or informants is seriously limited. Reports from the ambassadors to the foreign ministry tend to be few. Moreover, the language division which plagues western Africa has found many states with few diplomats

trained in the language of the country to which they are accredited. On the other hand, a few embassies have been overzealous to the point of engaging in subversion—Ghanaians have been sent home from Liberia and Ivory Coast, the Nigerian foreign minister has charged the Ghanaian High Commission in Lagos with subversive activities; both Senghor and Touré have broadcast a general warning to foreign embassy personnel; and Guinea and Liberia signed an agreement to prevent embassies in their countries from conducting subversive activities against each other.[6]

Several attempts have been made to deal with problems of representation within western Africa. One is to pool ambassadors, a solution adopted by Entente States, included in the UAM agreements, and proposed by Morocco for the Maghreb. Multiple representation poses problems of coordination and intelligence dissemination, and is effective only when there is a high degree of policy coordination among the accrediting governments or where there simply is little business to be transacted. Another method of simplifying the ambassadorial problem is by multiple accreditation. A number of non-resident ambassadors are accredited to Togo, Mauritania, and the three lesser Entente members. This solution is one merely of form, for the effectiveness of an absent ambassador is nearly nil. Only rarely is even a skeletal staff left in place

---

[5] For a good discussion of this point, see Jacques Hubert, *Les relations extérieures d'un État nouveau: le Sénégal* (Dakar: Faculté de Droit, 1963), pp. 225–232.

[6] Touré has formally charged his ambassadors to 'expound. . . the cause of Africa, to uphold this cause, to fight for its triumph, . . . to participate there [i.e., in the host country] in the struggle waged by the people of Guinea, in order to give it an international prolongation, . . . [to] constantly behave as militants'. Speech to the Third National Conference of the PDG, in Touré, *International Policy of the Democratic Party of Guinea*, vol. VII (Conakry: PDG, nd).

in the ambassador's absence. A third approach is the development of special ties. The case of the resident ministers of the Union of African States (UAS) is the most striking example, although UAM members' ambassadors to each other were also called permanent representatives. The institution of resident ministers was a farce: representatives were appointed who did not know the language of the country to which they were accredited; those who knew the language were frequently not invited to cabinet meetings as the UAS agreement provided. When they did attend cabinet meetings they were almost universally barred from party political bureau meetings where the real decisions were made, and in any case, as neither ambassadors nor cabinet ministers, they sometimes received less favorable treatment than other diplomats.

A fourth approach to the problem of representation is quite the opposite: that of non-resident ministers or no ambassador at all. Among the Entente states, there is only one ambassador (Voltaic to Abidjan) and two 'delegates' (Niger to Abidjan and Cotonou), the rest of the business being handled by frequent meetings of the cabinet ministers concerned. Such an approach is effective for the negotiation of technical problems, but is not geared to handle political problems or matters concerning expatriate nationals, topics left to the attention of the heads of state and frequently beyond their powers of solution. It is of course doubtful whether an ambassador could have prevented the anti-Dahomeyan riots in Abidjan in 1958 or in Niamey in 1963, or whether he could have solved the Ouagadougou-Abidjan dispute of 1961 or the Cotonou-Abidjan chill of 1963-1964, but he might have made a solution easier—and that, in any case, is the most that can be

expected of an ambassador. Guinea in 1964 announced that it was withdrawing its embassies from Abidjan, Accra, Bamako, and Freetown as an economy measure, but with the explanation that relations between Touré and the other four heads of state were so good that ambassadors were not needed. Such action indicates a misconception of the role both of an ambassador and of a head of state and also the disposable time of a head of state.

Finally, a number of western African states have made ample use of para-diplomatic figures and bodies. These groups and individuals perform propaganda and representational functions abroad and advisory functions at home, working with sympathetic organizations in foreign countries; their credentials, however, are more frequently personal or from their party than from their state. The African Affairs Bureau and Center of Ghana and the All-African Peoples Organization (AAPO), also in Accra but ostensibly international, are examples, as are individuals such as Kwadou Addison and Abdoulaye Diallo of the AAPO or A.K. Barden of the African Affairs Bureau. Often party and party auxiliary figures play para-diplomatic roles, as John Tettegah of the Ghana Trade Union Congress has done. In addition to serving as advisers, para-diplomatic figures are frequently the executors of policy in regard to parties, movements, and exile groups, concentrating on subversive rather than official contacts.

CONSTITUENCY GROUPS

The foreign policy decision-making process also involves certain constituency groups: parliament, 'national organizations', and parties. Parliaments are often allowed to go through the motions of a Great Debate on African (or other) foreign policy, but without effect. Although exceptionally a parliament may serve as the focus point for pressures brought to bear on relations with the non-African world—such as the debates over the Anglo-Nigerian defense pact in 1961 or the Americo-Moroccan base negotiations in 1957—inter-African relations have never aroused a western African parliament to such a degree. On the other hand, national assembly presidents, and sometimes also permanent parliamentary commission chairmen, often have an important role as presidential lieutenants and envoys.

'National organizations'—labour unions, youth and women's organizations, even farm and business groups—have a more complex role. Their strength comes from the presence of their leaders on party and government councils, from mass membership organized behind these leaders in a crucial modern sector, and also from their ability to make their own African policy and conduct their own relations with other states' national organizations if their demands are not heeded. Influence is thus derived from political position (degree of integration into the party/government hierarchy), and relations (local strength of the organization), not from economic composition.

The most important of these developing pressure groups are the labour unions. In no western African country is there a labour government, although Guinea comes closest to being an exception. There, the labour movement (National Confederation of Guinean Workers of the General Union of Black African Workers (CNTG-UGTAN) led and dominated the nationalist movement (PDG-RDA); the party, however,

did not become an auxiliary of labour, since, when labour leaders became party leaders, they left the union in the hands of secondary figures as a party auxiliary. The reverse process has led to somewhat similar results in Ghana, Ivory Coast, Tunisia, Algeria, Liberia, and Mali; there, the party moved in to control the labour union, usually by means of a deal which granted government support to one group of labour leaders in their effort to unite the unions in exchange for party and government control over the resultant single national union. Since the process was one of exchanging concessions between party and union, the result was a reciprocal pattern of influence, consecrating both labour's participation in policy decisions and the party's control over labour activities. This participation and control concerned inter-African policy as well as other matters. In a third pattern, government has controlled the conditions under which labour operates, but has been unable or unwilling to unite the unions, control their politics, or subordinate the union to the party. Such is the situation in Morocco, Nigeria, Senegal, Upper Volta. In these countries, labour's role in deciding and executing African policy can be expected to be less direct.

In the formulation of African policy, the labour unions, according to their influence within the party and government, have served to keep radical slogans before state policy-makers; in execution, they have strengthened each other's positions by participation in African labour conferences and national labour congresses. The activities of UGTAN in French West Africa, of the All-African Trade Union Federation (AATUF), founded in Casablanca in May 1961, and of the African Trade Union Confederation (ATUC), founded in Dakar in January 1962, and the repeated attempts at coordinating North African labour movements between 1956 and 1962, while ineffective from the point of view of trade union consolidation, did serve to keep policies and slogans alive and advance the prestige of Guinea, Ghana, Mali, Senegal, Algeria, Morocco and Tunisia.[7] The moderate policies and the modest approach to unity of the Entente states and Nigeria have been reflected in their unions' greater aloofness from African labour politics.

In these attempts at labour unity, did the unions act as a vanguard or as a consequence of government action, or were they the alternative to government inaction? Did they act as autonomous agents or as party or government auxiliaries? The questions are crucial to understanding the role of unions, but the answers are inconclusive.[8] Revival of AATUF in October 1963 was clearly the result of Algerian government initiative and Malian governmental support; but this is a lone example. Both AATUF and ATUC appear to be labour echoes of the Casablanca and Monrovia conferences, since they fol-

lowed on their heels; but the AATUF meeting was suggested since December 1958, in preparation since September 1959, and originally called for May 1960—all before the initial Casablanca meeting of January 1961—and the ATUC meeting was a reaction to AATUF, not a result of Monrovia. If the catalepsy of both African labour internationals can be termed existence, both of them have outlasted their political counterparts, the Casablanca and Monrovia Groups; but both have remained outside the 'spirit of Addis Ababa', their unification at the end of 1963 having fallen through on primarily ideological grounds. Labour unions in the UAS sent representatives to each other's jamborees but never took any concrete steps towards the coordination foreseen in the UAS Charter: but then neither did their heads of state. As a tentative conclusion, it may be suggested that unions operated as executory agencies of government policy only to the extent that they were effectively controlled by their governments (a situation already seen to be rare) and to the extent that such action coincided with already existing wishes of unions leaders (in Tunisia, UGTT leader Ahmed Tlili was more interested in African labour unity than was President Habib Bourguiba). In general, labour's African politics had no direct relation to state policy, but was rather an emanation of the same African unity myth (strengthened by an equally strong labour myth of proletarian unity) that lay behind government policy.

Other 'national organizations' play a role that is similar, although limited by their relative weakness within the states and their lesser influence within their governments. Youth and women's organizations have followed labour unions in their attempts to unite on the African level; particularly Guinea's

---

[7] The military constitute another group of advisers, but one whose role in inter-African relations has been minimal. A possible exception may be the role of the Algerian National People's Army (ANP) in the Algero-Moroccan border war of 1963.

[8] This study arrives at answers similar to those presented by Elliot J. Berg and Jeffrey Butler, 'Trade Unions', in James Coleman and Carl G. Rosberg, *Political Parties and National Integration in Tropical Africa* (Berkeley: University of California Press, 1964), pp. 340–381. A full study of inter-African labor politics remains to be done; the best treatment to date is found in Jean Meyriat and Anisse Salan-Bey, *Le Syndicalisme africain* (Paris: Payot, 1963), pp. 141–164. For a good treatment of North African labor, see Werner Plum, *Gewerkschaften im Maghreb* (Hannover: Verlag für Literatur und Zeitgeschehen, 1962), esp. pp. 85–100.

position has been enhanced in the process, although the influence of youth and women in African policy-making is slim. In a few countries—Ghana, Ivory Coast, Senegal, and the Maghreb states—there are socio-economic groups such as farmers' unions, industrial and commercial organizations, and cooperative associations. Although such organizations could by their nature contribute to the development of a national policy, they are in reality instruments of government control rather than organizations of socio-economic interests. Some of these groups are members of pan-African internationals, such as the Ghana-led All-African Union of Farmers, but neither the internationals nor the locals have a significant role in state policy-making or execution.[9]

Similar in position, although not usually considered among 'national organizations', are the Muslim sects, whose mass and transnational characteristics give them great potential influence in inter-African relations. Particularly the Tijani and Qadiri Sects, whose leaders are important figures in Senegalese, Malian, and Nigerian politics and in Moroccan and Algerian religious life, might be expected to create a basis for friendly relations among the countries where they have followers.[10] Because of their traditional

nature and their national orientation, however, their actual effect has been almost nil. In a few cases, leaders of the sects have been appointed ambassadors, in some instances to Muslim countries, and on a broader level the presence of Islam serves to counteract historical Sudanese antipathy to the Arabs of North Africa, but their general influence on foreign policy is even less important than, say, that of the Catholic church or the Rotarians in other parts of the world.

The final representative group in the policy-process is the party. Below the level of the political bureau, its role is largely one of education, support and mobilization rather than participation in decisions, articulation of interests, or formulation of wishes. Even officials of the PDG, whose philosophy is one of integral symbiosis between elite and mass in policy-making, admit—realistically—that this philosophical principle does not hold in foreign policy-making. They do claim, however, that regular Thursday party cell meetings are used for discussing government policy; 'the question of Kashmir and the war in Algeria are fully understood by our people', a Guinean ambassador explained in 1962.

PUBLIC OPINION AND DECISION-MAKING

The assertion that the identity of mass and elite within the party makes for a 'people's foreign policy' is not only procedurally inaccurate; given the

---

[9] A notable exception is the role of the Chambers of Commerce of Bamako and Abidjan in arranging transshipment of goods through Ivory Coast to Mali after the breakup of the Mali Federation, 'a strictly commercial operation in which the Ivory Coast government has no concern', according to the Ivory Coast government; radio Paris, 23 August 1960.

[10] For a detailed discussion of the sects, see J. Spencer Trimingham, *Islam in West Africa* (New York: Oxford University Press, 1959), esp. pp. 88–101. Note that their role is quite different in internal politics, where sects are often important factors. Allal al-Fassi, Istiqlal leader and Morocco's leading

sufi, Hajj Ibrahim Niassa, prominant Tijani figure and Senegalese politician, who is related to political figures in Ghana and Nigeria, and Amadou Hampate Ba, Malian scholar and ambassador as well as Tijani *moqaddem*, are examples of three different types of political figures whose stature is enhanced by their religious position. The effect of their religious position on foreign relations is more debatable.

understandably low level of popular aspirations, expectations, and information in western Africa, it is a meaningless proposition. Unity and disunity, regional brotherhood and narrow nationhood, sealed and open borders, even peace and armed uprisings have all been justified in the name of popular wishes. In western Africa, the people are still instruments, and the party is the means of mobilization.

Basic reasons for this situation are found in the role of public information media and public opinion in general. Because of the high illiteracy rate, the press is not yet a mass but an elite communication medium; the only exception is the Arabic press in North Africa. A number of daily African newspapers from time to time run background articles on other African countries, and some have regular and reasonably well-informed editorials on African affairs. All issues of the party press throughout the area carry lengthy hortative articles in general terms designed to mobilize support by justifying policy and channelling thought. The small daily press is also supplemented by a number of party weeklies for internal consumption (such as *al-Istiqlal* in Morocco and *Fraternité* in Ivory Coast), by three weeklies of wider circulation throughout French-speaking Africa (the two excellent reviews from Dakar and Tunis, *Afrique Nouvelle* and *Jeune Afrique*, and their highly ideological competitor from Algiers, *Revolution Africaine*), and by daily and weekly papers from London and Paris. As practice reading material for old and new literates alike, such publications help Africa to know itself and at the same time encourage perception of African events in nationally accepted terms. With few exceptions —Morocco, Nigeria—where the press is not only free but competitive, these terms follow the party or government

lead; their role in the policy-making process is therefore to keep the elite on the track it has set out for itself, not to exert influence on specific issues. Only in rare cases—Ghana, Algeria, and, to a lesser extent, Tunisia—is the press itself one of the components of the elite, in a position similar to that of the labour unions, both being controlled by and influencing the government.

Thus, public opinion on African policy in western Africa is elite opinion. The position of the mass is simply the natural corollary—both cause and consequence—of the highly centralized position of the small decision-making elite. Middle groups and figures outside the presidential circle attempt to find personal access to the council chambers of the chief, rather than force their way in by mobilizing troops among the masses. Access to the people is barred by those who got there first by winning popularity and monopolizing the popular symbols. The people in western Africa are not in the 'street', as in the Middle East, but in the courtyard of the Presidential palace, where they can move about only within very narrow limits. How narrow are the limits on the elites within the palace? Probably less restrictive than they may think. A number of states have reversed their policy in western African relations without repercussions, the reversal being accompanied by skilful justification often in the same broad terms as the previous policy. The Morocco-Tunisian rupture (1960) and rapprochement (1964), the Senegal-Mali rupture (1960) and rapprochement (1963), the Ghana-Togo rupture (1957) and rapprochement (1963), the Guinea-Ghana Union (1958) and fall-out (1963), the Guinea-Ivory Coast rupture (1958) and rapprochement (1962), the Casablanca-Monrovia split (1961) and reconciliation (1963), and many others, can all be justified as changed situations rather than changed policies, but in reality there was an element of both present, and changes in policy were made by the elite without any public protest. Yet in each phase policy was defended as that which was imposed by public opinion. Public pressure did play a role in the general drift of Tunisian policy under the impact of a radical independent Algeria, and in Morocco's relations with Mauritania, where it even forced the King's absence from his seat next to Mauritanian President Mokhtar Ould Daddah at Addis Ababa under pressure from the irredentist Istiqlal party during the first national elections. But it is doubtful, even in these two cases, whether public opinion would have been so aroused by a contrary policy that the government's position would have been endangered.

Not only is a large majority of the public outside the decision-making process; it appears not to care about the details of African relations. The already-cited shifts in policy and the lack of public reaction are eloquent testimony. Of all the leaders in the areas, only one has cited a specific case of public opinion affecting a policy change: after a concerted letter campaign of Flagstaff House, of unknown origins, Ghanaian policy favoring withdrawal of troops from the Congo was reconsidered at the end of 1960 and reversed.[11] It may be objected that mass reaction was a real element in checking Dia's attempted coup in Senegal in 1962 and in aiding the overthrow of President Hubert Maga in Dahomey in 1963 (it was not in the assassination of Olympio in 1963, nor in the takeover by Ahmed Ben Bella in Algeria in 1962). But, although these events produced changes in inter-African relations, they were not caused by issues of foreign policy. In domestic politics, public opinion—inchoate though it may be—has a role, or rather a breaking point. In inter-African policy, as a direct influence, it is still irrelevant.

Yet, western African leaders tend to be prisoners of their own tactics of popular manipulation and use of slogans. Having mobilized general public support behind them through public appeals and political machines, they assume that such support is real and meaningful in terms of particular issues, including those of inter-African relations. Unlike Europe or America, where leaders justly fear the reactions of public opinion acting indirectly through their parliaments or directly at election time, the effect of public opinion in western African relations—as on decision-making itself—is confined to the perception of the elite. Decisions are made and executed directly from the presidential palace, within the limits of communications, coordination, and political control.

---

[11] Interview with Nathan Welbeck.

Parliaments in Former British Black Africa

Newell M. Stultz

Between March 1957 and October 1966, Great Britain conferred sovereignty upon twelve of her possessions in sub-Saharan Africa.[1] The forms of government existing among these states at their independence varied in important respects. In each, however, there had been established a national legislature whose institutional structure and constitutional functions were patterned on, or adapted from, those of the British Parliament. Since their independence, a number of these countries have altered certain of the structural features of their legislatures. Furthermore, in all of these new states distinctive patterns of parliamentary performance have evolved. What, if any, structural and performance characteristics are now common to parliaments in former British Black Africa?[2]

This paper suggests eleven such characteristics. The first four items identify structural features and rest upon a review of national constitutions. The remaining items describe parliamentary performance. Here the basic sources are published commentaries upon the activities of individual parliaments.[3]

But these commentaries cover only six countries: Ghana, Kenya, Nigeria, Tanzania, Uganda, and Zambia. Moreover, these reports were prepared at different times by different authors who had, inevitably, somewhat different interests. In matters of parliamentary performance, then, we can not yet generalize for all or even most parliaments in former British Black Africa. Instead, items 5–11 identify only recurring patterns of behavior among those several parliaments for which secondary evidence is now available.

1. UNICAMERALISM

Single-house national legislatures prevail. Only four countries have had bicameral parliaments: Nigeria, Kenya, Botswana, and Lesotho. Kenya abo-

---

[1] The twelve, in order of their gaining independence, were: Ghana, Nigeria, Sierra Leone, Tanganyika, Uganda, Zanzibar, Kenya, Malawi, Zambia, Gambia, Botswana, and Lesotho. In 1964 Zanzibar and Tanganyika joined to form Tanzania.

[2] Constitutional government was replaced by military rule in Nigeria and Ghana in 1966 and in Sierra Leone in 1967. References made to these countries are for the period up to the commencement of military government.

[3] D. G. Austin, "The Ghana Parliament's First Year," *Parliamentary Affairs*, XI (Sum-

mer 1958), 350–60; J. M. Lee, "Parliament in Republican Ghana," *Parliamentary Affairs*, XVI (Autumn 1963), 376–95; Jon Kraus, "Ghana's New 'Corporate Parliament,'" *Africa Report*, X (August 1965), 6–11; G. F. Engholm, "The Westminster Model in Uganda," *International Journal*, XVIII (Autumn 1963), 468–87; B. S. Sharma, "Parliamentary Government in Uganda," *International Studies*, VII (January 1966), 448–56; William Tordoff, "Parliament in Tanzania," *Journal of Commonwealth Political Studies*, III (July 1965), 85–103; Anirundha Gupta, "The Zambian National Assembly: Study of an African Legislature," *Parliamentary Affairs*, XIX (Winter 1965–66), 48–56; John P. Mackintosh, "The Nigerian Federal Parliament," *Public Law* (Autumn 1963), 333–61; J. H. Proctor, "The Role of the Senate in the Kenya Political System," *Parliamentary Affairs*, XVIII (Autumn 1965), 389–415; and Cherry Gertzel, "Parliament in Independent Kenya," *Parliamentary Affairs*, XIX (Autumn 1966), 486–504.

From *Journal of Developing Areas*, Vol. II, No. 4 (July 1968), 479–493, by permission.

lished its upper house in 1967 and now conforms to the general pattern. Bicameralism, where it exists, is a recent phenomenon, a product of constitutional negotiations during the terminal stage of the colonial period.[4]

The role of second chambers has been to protect tribal and parochial interests. This specialized and limited function can be seen in both the composition and powers of these bodies.[5] In fact, the absence of a second chamber in most countries is one indication that most African leaders at the national level oppose the institutionalization of tribal interests and believe in strong, unitary government.

2. POPULAR ELECTION OF LEGISLATORS

Popular election from single-member constituencies is the prevailing mode of recruitment to parliamentary office. Excluding second chambers, 92 percent of all MP's in office at independence had been elected in this way.[6] The remainder, 95 members distributed among nine parliaments, had secured office variously: through direct executive appointment, 15; "special election"

by elected members of the legislature, 25; election by whites voting communally, 13; election by chiefs, 4; indirect election by lesser bodies, 33; or by ex officio appointment, 5. This latter figure does not include the attorney-general who now sits ex officio but without a vote in the parliaments of five countries.[7] The National Assembly of Zanzibar had the smallest proportion of popularly elected MP's, just 74 percent.

Since independence, five countries have altered the composition of their legislatures. In Kenya the number of elected members in the lower house was increased in 1967, at the time the Senate was abolished, in order to accommodate the former senators. This constituted no change in the principle of representation. Change in principle has been introduced in four countries and appears to manifest two desires. One is to eliminate special forms of representation that can not be controlled by the executive. In 1966 reserved seats for whites where abolished in Malawi, as they will be in Zambia also at the first dissolution of parliament. In Uganda the right of the regional assembly in Buganda (the Lukiko) to elect Buganda's representatives in the National Assembly was taken away in 1966: hereafter, MP's from Buganda will be elected directly.

The second desire, in the words of the constitution of Zambia, is "to enhance the representative character of the Assembly." The method adopted has been the appointment of MP's by the executive. At independence, Gambia, Tanganyika, Zambia, and Zanzibar provided for nominees of the executive in the assembly. In addition, Kenya, Uganda, and Botswana provided for the election of a number of MP's by the

---

[4] In Nigeria, for example, the Senate, the upper house of the Nigerian Federal Parliament, came into being less than one year before that country gained independence in 1960. A bicameral legislature had, however, functioned in the Northern Region of Nigeria from 1946 and in the Western Region from 1951.

[5] For example, the Senate in Lesotho, composed of twenty-two chiefs plus eleven other persons nominated by the paramount chief, has no power to veto ordinary legislation. Its assent is required, however, to constitutional amendments protecting the position of the paramount chief, of chieftainship in general, and of land tenure, among other matters.

[6] Figures for both Zanzibar and Tanganyika are included. A universal adult franchise for Africans was approximated everywhere except Northern Nigeria, where a universal manhood suffrage prevailed.

---

[7] The five are Uganda, Kenya, Gambia, Botswana, and Nigeria.

regularly elected members of the legislature. Because of government majorities in these assemblies, these "specially elected" members were, in fact, indirect appointees of the executive.[8] Uganda has now abolished the institution of "specially elected" members, but in 1967 the president of Uganda was empowered to appoint up to one-third of the eighty-two members of the National Assembly. The right of the executive to nominate MP's was introduced in Ghana in 1965, in Malawi in 1966, and was extended in Tanzania in 1965.[9]

Thus in seven parliaments (eight if we include Ghana) there are some MP's who owe their positions to direct or indirect executive appointment rather than to popular election. The number of

such members is commonly not more than 15 percent of all members, but it is considerably higher in Tanzania, Uganda, and formerly in Ghana, i.e., in three of the five countries that changed the composition of their legislatures after independence. The net result of all these changes has been to reduce to 80 percent the proportion of all MP's dependent upon popular election to office.

The presence of MP's directly or indirectly appointed by the executive in most parliaments is an interesting departure from the Westminster parliamentary model and deserves further comment. In part, the appointment of MP's is a carry-over of the earlier practice common during the colonial period whereby the governor nominated members to sit on the legislative council. In the contemporary period, however, there are three benefits of a system allowing for the appointment of NP's by the executive. It makes it possible for the executive to bring persons with special talents into the assembly; it allows the executive to bolster, if necessary, its legislative majority; and it makes it possible for the executive to guarantee legislative representation for certain groups in the population, e.g., women, whites, workers, farmers, trade unionists, etc. This last point is perhaps of greatest importance. G. F. Engholm has written that "candidates to Uganda's National Assembly have been drawn from the numerically very small professional elite. Agricultural interests are poorly represented measured against the industry's economic contribution."[10] Little data on the occupations of MP's in Africa exists. Such data as has been compiled sup-

---

[8] Chanan Singh notes that the idea behind the prescribed mechanism for the election of "specially elected" members in Kenya was to prevent a party capturing all such seats. But, Singh continues, the constitutional draftsmen forgot that a majority party could arrange its voting strength just so it could indeed capture all seats. Singh, "The Republican Constitution of Kenya: Historical Background and Analysis," *International and Comparative Law Quarterly*, XIV (July 1965), 935.

[9] In Ghana the manner of executive appointment was circuitous. In 1965 the National Assembly in Ghana was increased in size from 114 to 198 members. In principle, the basis of representation remained as before: Members were popularly elected from single-member constituencies. But Ghana was now a legal one-party state, and the penalties for individual political opposition were severe. In consequence, only candidates of the ruling party entered for the election, and on election day all were returned unopposed without a vote having been cast. These candidates had been selected by the party executive, which in Ghana was much the same as the national executive. Ninety-six of these candidates were holdovers from the former Assembly. The remainder, however, had been selected to give representation to a broad range of associational and institutional groups. See Kraus, "Ghana's New 'Corporate Parliament,'" *Africa Report* (August 1965), p. 8.

[10] Engholm, "The Westminster Model in Uganda," *International Journal* (Autumn 1963), p. 478.

ports the view, however, that except for such groups as teachers, civil servants, and businessmen, important occupational categories, particularly farmers, are under-represented in most African parliaments.[11] It is doubtful that *any* popularly elected assembly will closely represent the distribution of occupations (or the distribution of any demographic variable) within the electorate. The integrative needs of African politics, however, as well as the desires of some African leaders for national political cohesion, are great.

3. PRESIDENTIALISM

Except for Zambia and Botswana, which gained independence as republics, all the states at their independence were constitutional monarchies with an executive patterned on the Westminster parliamentary model. Executive authority was nominally vested in a constitutional monarch who, except in the case of Lesotho, was Queen Elizabeth II;[12] but political power rested with a prime minister and his cabinet who were responsible to a popularly (or substantially so) elected assembly.

This constitutional form has been retained only in Lesotho and Gambia, and it existed in Sierra Leone until the military takeover in 1967.[13] Elsewhere some variant of a presidential executive

has now been adopted. The changes in Nigeria and Kenya were comparatively minor. With the ending of the monarchy in Nigeria in 1963, the duties that had been exercised by the governor-general—but only those—devolved upon the new post of president.[14] In other respects, the political structure of Nigeria remained as before. In Kenya in 1964 both the posts of governor-general and prime minister were abolished, and their duties and powers were combined in the newly created office of president. The president of Kenya, who is both head of state and head of government, is thus responsible to the National Assembly for the exercise of his office. Constitutional arrangements similar to those of Kenya after 1964 were found in Botswana at independence.

In the four remaining countries—Malawi, Tanzania, Ghana, and Uganda—the presidential form of government adopted after independence broke two principles of the Westminster parliamentary model.[15] As in Kenya and Botswana, the functions of ceremonial head of state and political head of government were joined in a single office. More important, the executive (i.e., president) in these countries no longer needed the continuing support of a simple majority in the assembly; the constitutional powers of parliament were accordingly lessened. The executive in Zambia already possessed this character at independence in 1963.

Political deadlock between the executive and the legislature is thus constitu-

---

[11] See, for example, Mackintosh, "The Nigerian Federal Parliament," *Public Law* (Autumn 1963), pp. 336–37, and Guy Hunter, *The New Societies of Tropical Africa* (New York: Praeger, 1964), p. 285.

[12] In Lesotho the head of state is the paramount chief of the Mosotho, presently King Moshoeshoe II.

[13] In November 1965, a proposal that Gambia become a republic failed by 728 votes to gain the necessary two-thirds vote in a national referendum. Creation of a republic was an issue in the Sierra Leone election of March 1967 which precipitated the military takeover in that country.

[14] The president of Nigeria was elected to a fixed five-year term by an electoral college consisting of both houses of the Federal Parliament.

[15] Uganda became a republic in 1963 with an executive substantially similar to the Nigerian executive after 1963. This arrangement lasted until 1966, when the character of the Uganda executive was changed again to its present form. This is discussed below.

tionally possible in four countries, as it was also in Ghana at the time of Nkrumah's overthrow. In an era of dominant mass parties and charismatic political leadership in Africa, such conflict would seem unlikely; nevertheless, these countries have introduced certain constitutional safeguards against this possibility. Except for Tanzania, where the president is elected directly by the people independent of the election of assembly members, the mechanism for the selection of the president was designed to insure political harmony between the president and the assembly, at least at the outset of the fixed presidential term. In Uganda MP's select the president, as was to be the case in Ghana for presidents succeeding Nkrumah.[16] In Malawi the president is elected by the people, but MP's play a role in his nomination.[17] In Zambia the president is also elected by the people, but presidential elections are tied to the election of MP's in such a way as to make it likely, although not certain, that a newly elected president will have the support of a majority in the National Assembly.[18] If, however, conflict does occur despite these mechanisms, the president in all four countries (and formerly in Ghana) may dissolve parliament, although he is not required to do so.[19] In fact, a president might wish not to dissolve parliament, for if he does, he must in all cases himself stand for reelection.

4. CONSTITUTIONAL SUPREMACY

At their independence all the new states of former British Black Africa had written constitutions defining the organs, functions, and limits of government. In no country could parliament by simple majority vote amend any and all provisions of the constitution. In this sense, the constitution, to the extent that it was protected from amendment by ordinary legislation, represented a body of fundamental law. Parliament was not supreme.

Since independence new constitutions have been adopted in several countries, while in certain others the independence constitutions have been revised in important respects. Everywhere, however, the principle of the supremacy of the constitution has been retained, except, of course, in those countries where constitutional government has been overthrown by the military.

---

[16] Kwame Nkrumah was named the first president of the Republic of Ghana in the constitution of 1960.

[17] In Malawi only one candidate may be nominated for the presidency. The electorate, therefore, votes "yes" or "no." In the event a majority vote "no," no election occurs, a second candidate is nominated, and the electorate votes again, and so on until a nominated candidate is supported by a majority of those voting. The candidate is nominated by an electoral college consisting of officials of the ruling party, district council officers, MP's, and chiefs. Similar arrangements govern the nomination and election of the president of Tanzania.

[18] Before the election each candidate for election as an MP must declare a preference for one of the announced candidates for president. On election day the voter votes concurrently for MP and for president. The candidate for president receiving the greatest number of popular votes throughout the country is elected. A system only slightly different than this is found in Kenya, Botswana, Uganda, and formerly in Ghana. As in Zambia, candidates for election to parliament declare their preference for one of the announced candidates for president, but on election day the voter votes only for MP. A candidate for president is elected if a majority of those elected to parliament had previously declared their support for him.

[19] With the following exception: If the president of Zambia vetoes a bill and the National Assembly again passes it with a two-thirds majority, the president must sign the bill within twenty-one days or dissolve parliament.

"The status of the constitution as supreme law," S. A. de Smith has written, "is determined by the procedure prescribed for its amendment. Those provisions which are thought to be especially important will be protected from alteration by legislation passed in the ordinary manner and form."[20] Such provisions are commonly said to be "entrenched." The matters covered by entrenched provisions vary from country to country depending upon local circumstances, although generally the states under consideration have entrenched constitutional provisions dealing with individual rights, the basis of responsible and representative government, the independence of the judiciary, the standing of traditional authorities, and the procedure for the amendment of the constitution, among other matters. Five countries have entrenched their entire constitutions: Gambia, Zambia, Malawi, Kenya, and Tanzania.

Three methods of constitutional entrenchment are found:

(a) The simplest and most common is the requirement that bills proposing a constitutional amendment be passed by parliament with a special majority. In nine countries this is a two-thirds majority.[21] To this requirement is sometimes added a mandatory period of delay. In Sierra Leone, for example, two two-thirds votes were required with a general election intervening.

(b) A second method requires that an amendment to the constitution be approved by a body other than the legislature. Ghana has provided the only example. Under the Ghanaian constitu-

tion of 1960 power to "repeal or alter" seventeen of its fifty-five articles was "reserved to the people," that is, required the approval of a simple majority at a public referendum.

(c) A third method combines in some measure (a) the requirement that a constitutional amendment be passed by parliament, usually by a special majority, and (b) the requirement that the amendment be accepted by some other body, or bodies, usually the electorate voting in a public referendum. This is the most elaborate method of constitutional entrenchment, and in the six countries where it has existed, it has been used to protect only those provisions of the constitution that are deemed particularly sensitive. In Nigeria, however, this included some 100 of 166 sections of the constitution.[22]

5. IMPOTENCE OF SECOND CHAMBERS

Writing in 1965 on the role of the Senate in the politics of Kenya, J. H. Proctor termed the legislative contribution of the upper house "of slight value," its control over the executive "insignificant," its influence on public opinion "negligible," and its protection of the constitution "irresolute."[23] Similarly, John Mackintosh found the Senate in Nigeria to be a "negligible body."[24] In both countries the senate appears to have been virtually ignored by both the executive and the public.

The impotence of the senate in both

---

[20]S. A. de Smith, *The New Commonwealth and Its Constitution* (London: Stevens, 1964), p. 110.

[21]In Kenya a 65 percent majority is now required.

[22]Richard L. Sklar and C. S. Whitaker, Jr., "The Federal Republic of Nigeria," in *National Unity and Regionalism in Eight African States*, ed. G. M. Carter (Ithaca, N. Y.: Cornell University Press, 1966), p. 62.

[23]Proctor, "The Role of the Senate in the Kenya Political System," *Parliamentary Affairs* (Autumn 1965), p. 414.

[24]Mackintosh, "The Nigerian Federal Parliament," p. 359.

Kenya and Nigeria was to some extent intended. In the enactment of ordinary legislation neither body had more than the power of delay, on the pattern of the House of Lords. Proctor asserts, however, that after sixteen months the Senate in Kenya "had not even exercised its assigned powers in such a way as to realize fully the purposes intended by those who urged its creation."[25] That this should have been so seems due to the absence of political notables in the Kenya Senate and the fact of a safe and docile government majority. According to Mackintosh, senators in Nigeria who were elected by the regional assemblies were likewise "all loyal party men."[26] Information is lacking, but there seems little reason to expect that the upper house will be more effective in either Lesotho or Botswana, the only countries, it will be recalled, that now have a second chamber.

6. ABSENCE OR INEFFECTIVENESS OF A FORMAL PARLIAMENTARY OPPOSITION

The institution of the parliamentary opposition has been a common casualty of African independence. Except for Tanganyika and Malawi, a parliamentary opposition existed in each state at its independence. In 1964 opposition parties were formally outlawed in Ghana, a practice subsequently copied in Tanzania and Malawi. Elsewhere, oppositions have commonly experienced a marked decline in both numbers and influence. In Kenya, for example, the opposition now includes only eight MP's in the National Assembly of 170

members. A sizable opposition is now found only in Lesotho, but one existed in Sierra Leone also at the time of the 1967 military coup. Small size alone would seem to prevent most parliamentary oppositions from adequately providing alternative programs and personnel to those of the government.

Available commentaries suggest that, on the whole, oppositions have performed poorly; their criticisms of the executive have usually been ill-informed, uncoordinated, and limited to specific questions rather than general policy. I observed this myself in the National Assembly in Kenya in 1966. Mackintosh has observed that in Nigeria the opposition "never tried to organize a concerted barrage of questions on any given topic or aimed at any specific Minister."[27] (Further confirmation of this conclusion appears under item 9 below.)

In fairness, it must be added that the performance of the opposition has frequently been burdened by the failure of the executive to respect its role; indeed, many African political leaders appear to regard merely the existence of an opposition as a danger to their regimes. Anirundhal Gupta has written that a "major aim" of the executive in Zambia would seem to be "to discredit the ANC [opposition] and thus to get rid of it as soon as possible."[28] Mackintosh has asserted that had the Nigerian opposition exploited more systematically the "extremely limited" opportunities open to it, the only result would have been new restrictions imposed by the government.[29] In 1964 Prime Minister Obote of Uganda rejected the need for

---

[25]Proctor, "The Role of the Senate in the Kenya Political System," p. 413.

[26]Mackintosh, "The Nigerian Federal Parliament," p. 356.

[27]*Ibid.*, p. 342.

[28]Gupta, "The Zambian National Assembly," *Parliamentary Affairs* (Winter 1965–66), p. 52.

[29]Mackintosh, "The Nigerian Federal Parliament," p. 344.

a parliamentary opposition, calling it a "capitalist notion."[30]

7. INDEPENDENCE OF GOVERNMENT BACKBENCHERS

Government backbenchers, in their capacity as private members, have frequently assumed responsibility for airing public grievances and criticizing official policy. In 1966 Cherry Gertzel wrote that "the most significant fact about the Kenya Parliament as it entered its third session was that the [then one-party] House of Representatives had become a public forum where the representatives of the people fully exercise their right to debate critically the actions of the Government."[31] William Tordoff has pointed out that in Tanzania backbenchers "attach considerable importance to their right to question ministers,"[32] while in Uganda, according to Engholm, "in the era of independence, an M.P. feels he must assert himself and justify his position to his constituents."[33]

The independence of government backbenchers seldom extends to recorded formal divisions which, indeed, are rare, although in June 1964 government backbenchers in Kenya supported the opposition at a division to defeat the government on a question pertaining to East African federation. Backbench independence, however, is much in evidence at question time. Engholm states that in the National Assembly in Uganda, "it is now *de rigueur* to jump

to one's feet and try to embarrass the minister . . . regardless of party affiliation."[34]

The extent to which government backbenchers do assert themselves appears to vary from country to country. Tordoff found that, except during the period allowed for questions, Tanzanian backbenchers made limited use of opportunities for expressing their feelings, while Gupta has described government backbenchers in Zambia as being "more or less passive," even if they are "interested to see that certain points are raised by the Opposition so as to get information."[35] In general, it appears that the independence of government backbenchers will be greater when there is no formal parliamentary opposition, when backbenchers do not participate in the decisions that precede the preparation of parliamentary business, and when party organization at the constituency level is weak.

8. ABSENCE OF LOBBYING

Lucian Pye has written that the non-Western political process operates largely without the benefit of political "brokers" and explicitly organized interest groups.[36] This appears characteristic of the legislative process in the six countries of former British Black Africa for which we have information. Negative evidence is most obvious; still, discussing the first year of the Ghana parliament, D. G. Austin maintained that, "except for political parties, there are virtually no nationally organized societies capable of informing, persuading, moving its members and the general

---

[30]Donald Rothchild and Michael Rogin, "Uganda," in *National Unity and Regionalism*, ed. Carter, p. 399.

[31]Gertzel, "Parliament in Independent Kenya," *Parliamentary Affairs* (Autumn 1966), p. 490.

[32]Tordoff, "Parliament in Tanzania," *Journal of Commonwealth Studies* (July 1965). p. 90.

[33]Engholm. "The Westminster Model in Uganda," p. 480.

[34]*Ibid.*, p. 485.

[35]Gupta, "The Zambian National Assembly," p. 54.

[36]Lucian W. Pye, "The Non-Western Political Process," *Journal of Politics*, XX (August 1958), p.485.

public for or against a particular act of government policy."[37] Similarly, Engholm has identified the "virtual absence of pressure groups" in Uganda.[38] But even were interest groups to exist, one would suppose they would not seek to influence parliament, but would rather focus their attentions on the executive and the bureaucracy. J. M. Lee, writing also of Ghana, contended that because of executive dominance of the legislature, it would be pointless to lobby parliament. "No one," Lee stated, "who wished to promote change would think of approaching individual M.P.'s in their capacity as legislators."[39]

9. PAROCHIALISM OF DEMANDS AND INEXPERTNESS OF DEBATE

Debate in parliament for the most part is discussion carried on between members of the cabinet and assistant ministers of subcabinet rank on the one hand, and ordinary MP's on the other. The latter may be members of the opposition if one exists or, as we have seen, the government's own back-benchers. Ministers and assistant ministers have at their disposal the resources of the bureaucracy, but the ordinary MP lacks these. In the absence of external and independent sources of opinion and information such as might be provided by lobbyists, the ordinary MP in the countries for which we have data seems most often obliged, in Austin's words on Ghana, "to exercise his own judgment, supported by whatever meagre supply of facts he can discover for himself."[40] Engholm has noted similarly that the politician in Uganda "cannot be a broker of ideas; he is forced back on his own intellectual resources."[41] These are usually limited. Few MP's have specialized training, and the research libraries that are found in each parliament are inadequate and little used. Ordinary MP's necessarily must draw heavily upon their own personal knowledge and experience. As a result, demands articulated by these members are most often specific in content, unaggregated, and rooted in the local circumstances of the member's constituency. The ordinary MP performs in the role of delegate; that is, he is a person, in the words of Apter and Lystad, usually without special talents who is completely responsive to the demands of his public constituency.[42] Mackintosh has observed that the Nigerian "electorate regards representation largely as a matter of sending an emissary to put their immediate needs before the government,"[43] and Gupta writes that in Zambia MP's view it as "of utmost importance" that they bring "to the notice of the Government specific problems and grievances of their constituencies."[44] These demands may be fully aired, but broad questions of public policy are seldom adequately debated in parliament.

Parliamentary debate of national

[37]Austin, "The Ghana Parliament's First Year," *Parliamentary Affairs* (Summer 1958), p. 355.

[38]Engholm, "The Westminster Model in Uganda," p. 479.

[39]Lee, "Parliament in Republican Ghana," *Parliamentary Affairs* (Autumn 1963), p. 382.

[40]Austin, "The Ghana Parliament's First Year," p. 356.

[41]Engholm, "The Westminster Model in Uganda," p. 479.

[42]David E. Apter and Robert A. Lystad, "Bureaucracy, Party, and Constitutional Democracy: An Examination of Political Role Systems in Ghana," in *Transition in Africa: Studies in Political Adaptation*, ed. G. M. Carter and W. O. Brown (Boston, Mass.: Boston University Press, 1958), p. 29.

[43]Mackintosh, "The Nigerian Federal Parliament," p. 354.

[44]Gupta, "The Zambian National Assembly," p. 53 footnote.

issues is thus usually inexpert and of low standard. Gertzel has noted that MP's in Kenya frequently reveal "their general lack of information on a wide variety of subjects," particularly on details of financial policy.[45] And Engholm writes that in Uganda "members display little inclination to concern themselves with the minutiae of Acts, or indeed the significance of what is left out," in part because few possess legal training. "If the subject matter is at all technical," Engholm continues, "there may be no debate at all."[46] One consequence of inexpert consideration of proposed legislation is that bills are enacted speedily. Tordoff has noted that in February 1964, nineteen bills were passed by the Tanganyika National Assembly on the same day they were introduced.[47]

Greater use of standing committees of parliament might make for more expert consideration of legislation because MP's assigned to these committees would likely be encouraged to develop expertise in particular subject areas. This would be even more probable were these committees to have staff assistance. The standing orders of each parliament provide for the creation of standing and select committees, but thus far committees have been little used. Everywhere the "committee stage" is nearly always taken by a committee-of-the-whole. Engholm notes that at this point in the legislative process in Uganda, "lack of familiarity with legal jargon reduces almost the entire Chamber to silence."[48]

10. EXECUTIVE DOMINANCE

Writing of the National Assembly in Kenya, Gertzel states that backbench criticism "has not forced the Government to make any major changes in its legislative programme."[49] Likewise, Mackintosh asserts that the control exercised by the House of Representatives in Nigeria over the executive up to 1963 was "negligible."[50] In fact, executive dominance of the assembly is a recurring theme in all the published writings cited at the beginning on parliaments in Ghana, Nigeria, Kenya, Uganda, Zambia, and Tanzania. In their legislative function, parliaments in these countries have been executive rubber stamps. No important piece of legislation desired by the executive has been refused; indeed, such legislation has been enacted not infrequently with unseemly haste. Moreover, legislative initiative has rested almost entirely with the executive. There have been very few examples of private members' bills introduced in parliament, and no such bill has been enacted. Finally, conciliar control over the personnel of the executive has been virtually non-existent. Each of these countries has experienced cabinet crises; but while these have been reflected in parliament, none has resulted from the assertion of the authority of the assembly over the executive. Indeed, in Tanzania, Uganda, and Zambia the executive is not responsible constitutionally to a simple majority in the legislature, as has been mentioned. This is also true in Malawi, and was formerly true in Ghana.

Executive dominance of the legislature is clearly the result of many factors: the national political standing of those

---

[45]Gertzel, "Parliament in Independent Kenya," p. 492.

[46]Engholm, "The Westminster Model in Uganda," pp. 474, 483.

[47]Tordoff, "Parliament in Tanzania," pp. 91–92.

[48]Engholm, "The Westminster Model in Uganda," p. 484.

[49]Gertzel, "Parliament in Independent Kenya," p. 499.

[50]Mackintosh, "The Nigerian Federal Parliament," p. 352.

in top cabinet positions resulting from their leadership during the struggle for independence, the ineffectiveness of the parliamentary opposition, the gulf in expert knowledge between the cabinet and ordinary parliamentarians, and the allocation of constitutional authority, among others. Except for the first, all these factors have already been indicated. In addition, there are two other less apparent determinants of executive dominance that should be mentioned. One is the brevity of parliamentary sessions. Nowhere has the assembly sat for more than one hundred days in a year, and annual sessions of two months or less are common. The National Assembly in Tanzania sat for only twenty-six days in 1964. For this reason alone, Tordoff concluded, MP's were "quite unable to keep current events under review."[51]

The second reason is that the appointment of MP's to cabinet positions has served to neutralize the assembly in most states. Except for the Nigerian Federal House of Representatives, which had 312 members, most assemblies have small memberships. Seven parliaments, for example, have fewer than one hundred members. It has thus been possible to employ a significant proportion of the assembly in cabinet positions, reducing the number of backbenchers upon whose support the government is in principle dependent. For example, in the middle of 1966 fifty ministers and assistant ministers constituted 39 percent of the membership of the House of Representatives in Kenya.[52] The government required the support of only fifteen backbenchers to remain in office, or less than one-fifth of all backbenchers. Under these

circumstances, legislators in Kenya could scarcely hope to control the executive.

11. FUNCTIONAL AMBIGUITY

Here, while speaking generally, we again limit ourselves to those six parliaments in former British Black Africa whose activities have been described at length in the writings of specialist-observers. Among these institutions it seems clear that a decision-making role in politics has been virtually nonexistent.[53] There has been somewhat greater performance of the demand-making function. In each case, although to varying degrees, the institution has seemed to serve as a political safety valve, allowing for the ventilation of political grievances. Still, there is reason to doubt the adequacy of legislative demand-making. As has been noted, certain groups are often not represented in the assembly, and ordinary MP's are frequently poorly informed on broad questions of national policy. Thus while specific and parochial demands have been articulated in these assemblies, it seems possible to assert that these institutions have not provided their executives with adequate means, in the words of Pye, "for calculating the relative distribution of attitudes and values throughout the society."[54]

What, then is the value of parliament to these countries? Mackintosh has written that the Federal Parliament in Nigeria provided "salaries and prestige for a number of men of the second rank in political importance, while giving

---

[51]Tordoff, "Parliament in Tanzania," p. 89.

[52]The comparable figures for Tanzania and Uganda in 1964 were 37 percent and 30 percent respectively.

[53]It must be allowed, however, that in the event of a crisis of political succession, parliament in a number of countries could, in Lee's words, "acquire a brief moment of glory" (p. 392), i.e., parliament could perform an essential function of political recruitment.

[54]Pye, "The Non-Western Political Process," *Journal of Politics* (August 1958), p. 482.

Ministers an extra opportunity to . . . keep an eye on their supporters."[55] It seems likely that this is a universal parliamentary function. It might be termed the patronage function of parliament.

The supposition is that it is worthwhile to support second-rank politicians, that legislators apart from their legislative roles can perform valuable political services. In 1963 Lee noted that in Ghana MP's were regarded by the president to be "more important in their 'out-of-school' activities." The purpose of these activities was, in the words of Nkrumah, to broaden "the front or support for the leadership."[56] Other African leaders have similarly defined the work of parliamentarians to include the education and mobilization of public opinion behind the government. In 1960, for example, Julius Nyerere, then chief minister of Tanganyika, directed MP's to explain official policies to their constituents.[57]

The performance by MP's of the support-building role commonly assigned them appears, however, to have been disappointing. In 1958 Austin wrote that MP's in Ghana were taking their duties seriously, regularly visiting their constituencies on party campaigns to explain new legislation.[58] But by 1962 President Nkrumah felt it necessary to accuse MP's publicly of becoming "a new class of self-seekers and careerists,"[59] and after June 1965, MP's in Ghana received no salary for performing their parliamentary duties. They

were expected to hold full-time jobs to support themselves. Jon Kraus observed that the necessity of holding a job would inevitably diminish the extent of close contact between the MP and his constituents.[60] Tordoff asserts that since 1965 the Tanzanian government has apparently attached little importance to the work of MP's in their constituencies, while Engholm has doubted that MP's in Uganda "can translate the sophisticated categories of explanation utilized by government into vernacular languages."[61] My own view in Kenya in 1966 was that MP's were ineffectual in building support for the regime among their constituents. Indeed, few appeared to find it necessary to try.

At the least parliament does offer an additional platform from which the government can publicly articulate its policies. There is, however, some question about the extent of the audience for parliamentary debates. Gupta believes that in Zambia there has existed "great public interest" in the proceedings of the National Assembly and that these have provided "an opportunity to the people to know as to what goes on in the higher echelon of national administration."[62] In contrast, Engholm suspects that what occurs in the Ugandan National Assembly is "remote" from public opinion and information, and in a similar vein Mackintosh wrote in 1963 that victories in debate in the Nigerian parliament appeared to "count for little."[63] In 1958 Austin be-

[55]Mackintosh, "The Nigerian Federal Parliament," p. 360.

[56]Lee, "Parliament in Republican Ghana," p. 385.

[57]Tordoff, "Parliament in Tanzania," pp. 97–98.

[58]Austin, "The Ghana Parliament's First Year," p. 360.

[59]Lee, "Parliament in Republican Ghana," p. 387.

[60]Kraus, "Ghana's New 'Corporate Parliament,' " p. 10.

[61]Engholm, "The Westminster Model in Uganda," p. 476; Tordoff, "Parliament in Tanzania," pp. 98–99.

[62]Gupta, "The Zambian National Assembly," p. 53.

[63]Engholm, "The Westminster Model in Uganda," p. 476; Mackintosh, "The Nigerian Federal Parliament," p. 347.

lieved it was necessary in Ghana to "sell the idea of Parliament" to the public.[64]

Writing in 1963, Lee observed:

It is one of the principal ironies of the transplantation of the Westminster model from Britain to Ghana that it has produced almost a complete reversal from the "decorative" and "efficient" institutions of government to which Bagehot referred. The President of Ghana has inherited . . . a position which corresponds very closely to the Prerogative of the English Crown . . ., and yet remains the "efficient" part. . . . The National Assembly of Ghana, in contrast, might well be regarded as the "decorative" part.[65]

It seems possible to extent Lee's characterization to other countries for which we now have data: Parliament is primarily a decoration of the state. But decorations in politics are symbols and herein lies the most general value of parliament, for symbols confer meaning. Two specific meanings are implied in the existence of parliament. One is national political equality. After all, an assembly of some form is found in nearly every sovereign state, irrespective of its political character. A national legislature would appear to be a necessary accouterment of independence. The second meaning is popular government. No other institution seems capable of symbolizing these values as well as does parliament, especially in Africa, where the struggle against colonialism, ie., for popular government and national independence, commonly focused on the powers and composition of the legislative council. It may be asked for whom parliament is a symbol—the electorate, the national elite, foreign diplomats?

The answer to this question is not clear, although it appears to be a general supposition that parliament is a popular symbol. "It would be psychologically difficult," Lee has written, "to replace a parliament of M.P.s by a congress of party secretaries in Ghana because such an action would be contrary to the constitutional mythology of the nation's origin."[66] In 1965 in Tanzania the Presidential Commission on the Establishment of a Democratic One Party State rejected a similar proposal, holding "it as a basic principle that the supreme law-making body in the State should be directly elected by universal suffrage."[67] Despite its considerable expense,[68] the institution of parliament seems likely to endure, if only for reason of its presumed symbolic content. Even in Ghana, Nigeria, and Sierra Leone, where parliament has been abolished, the military governors have construed this as but a temporary suspension. In Africa, as elsewhere, a national political life without a parliament is unthinkable.

CONCLUSIONS

Among the six states whose parliaments we have been able to consider in some detail, the institution appears to matter little. Parliament neither structures the political process nor adds materially to the content of political decisions. Nor does it affect the distribution of political power. But if parliament in these states does not shape politics, it is itself shaped by politics. Parliament does appear to register, or

---

[64]Austin, "The Ghana Parliament's First Year," p. 360.

[65]Lee, "Parliament in Republican Ghana," p. 389.

[66]*Ibid.*

[67]*Africa Report*, X (October 1965), 22.

[68]In Kenya, for example, the cost of maintaining the National Assembly in 1965–66, while less than 1 percent of the annual budget, was greater than the cost of maintaining any one of six ministries.

mirror, many of the dominant political characteristics of its environment. It thus may be important analytically.

At the most general level, two contradictory characteristics of national political life in these African states stand out. One is the commitment of politicians in these countries to *popular government*. This can be seen in the elimination of second chambers, the predilection for presidential forms, the intention that parliament act as an agent for political socialization and popular mobilization, the place of public referenda in the constitutional amendment process, and the retention of a one-man, one-vote franchise, even while allowing the appointment of MP's by the executive to increase the "representativeness" of the assembly. The second feature is the *isolation and*

concentration of decision-making power. This is shown in the absence of lobbyists in the legislative process, the inexpertness of parliamentary debate, the ineffectiveness of oppositions, the fact of the dominance of parliament by the executive, and the independence of government backbenchers. The last named would appear to be a consequence of the isolation of decision-makers rather than its manifestation, a product of the contradiction between populist ideology and the reality of elitist rule. The future of politics in the countries we have considered will doubtless be much influenced by the working out of this contradiction. Evidence of this process certainly will be mirrored in the actions and compositions of the several parliaments.

Soldier and State in Africa

Claude E. Welch

Direct military intervention, aimed at unseating civilian governments and replacing them with ruling councils drawn largely from the army, is a relatively recent phenomenon in Africa. With the exception of the Sudan, where officers led by General Ibrahim Abboud seized control in November 1958, no supplanting of civilian authority by a military junta occurred until 19 June 1965 (Algeria). Then, in rapid succession, the Governments of Congo-Kinshasa (25 November 1965), Dahomey (22 December 1965), Central African Republic (1 January 1966), Upper Volta (4 January 1966), Nigeria (15 January 1966), Ghana (24 Feb-

ruary 1966), Nigeria once again (29 July 1966), Burundi (28 November 1966), Togo (13 January 1967), and Sierra Leone (23 March 1967) fell victims to *coups d'état*. What factors affected the timing of these coups? What salient differences can be observed between the relative quiescence of African armies before mid-1965 and the subsequent outright seizures of control? Might the forces that helped to topple civilian authority cause a subsequent downfall of military government, as occurred in the Sudan in October 1964? Should we view army intervention with alarm, as inherently detrimental to the best interests of African states, or should we

From *Journal of Modern African Studies*, Vol. V, No. 3 (November 1967), 305–322, by permission of the journal and its publishers, the Cambridge University Press.

concur with a noted authroity who suggested that 'frequent coups are a sign of change and progress'?[1]

Students of African political change almost totally neglected the role of the military until the uprisings made the omission distressingly obvious. Writings on African armies were practically nonexistent.[2] The major emphasis was placed, rather, upon 'charismatic leadership', 'institutional political transfer', 'mass parties', and similar slogans used by political scientists. Africa was the continent of the 'political kingdom' or the 'primacy of politics', not the continent of the army *caudillo* or frequent coups. Patterns of political change in Africa made knowledge of the military seem irrelevant. Two factors accounted for this lack of attention: the manner in which colonial territories gained independence, and the historical heritage of African armies.

Most African states gained independence through constitutional negotiation, through pressure exerted by party leaders against colonial powers relatively willing to withdraw. Self-government did not come through revolution. Tropical Africa (leaving aside the territories still under Portuguese control) had no Bolivar or San Martin, no Ho Chi Minh or Ben Bella. The so-called 'African revolution' thus differed from many other great political changes: hegemony was handed over without large-scale civilian uprisings, campaigns

of civil disobedience, or other techniques of political violence, in most cases.

African armies did not play a major role in nationalist movements. Standing forces were the creations of the colonial power; in the evolution toward independence, they did not participate directly, although the impact of demobilised soldiers on the growth of political awareness could not be denied.[3] But this impact was made by individuals, not by the military as a corporate group. Resentment against colonial rule was channelled through political parties, not through military uprisings.

* * *

In tracing the types of military intervention in Africa, one can distinguish three stages. The first stage, that of relative passivity and abstention from political interference, was usually confined to the immediate post-independence period. The armies remained

---

[1] Samuel P. Huntington (ed.), *Changing Patterns of Military Politics* (New York, 1962), p. 40.

[2] To take one instance, a U.S. State Department bibliography, 'Role of the Military in Less Developed Countries, January 1958–February 1964', contains references to four articles dealing with Africa, contrasted with 37 items on Latin America and 33 on the Middle East. There are no references to Africa in the bibliography in Huntington, *op. cit.*

[3] A key political event in Ghana's political history, for example, was the march on Christiansborg Castle, led by members of the Ex-Servicemen's Union on 28 February 1948. Riots broke out after the marchers were dispersed (and two killed) by police gunfire; the outbreak of violence led to the Watson Commission Report, of tremendous significance in the hastening of constitutional progress. See David E. Apter, *Ghana in Transition* (New York, 1963), pp. 169 ff., and Dennis Austin, *Politics in Ghana, 1946–1960* (London, 1964), pp. 73 ff. Demobilised veterans in Nigeria helped carry the gospel of nationalism to the 'bush': more than 100,000 Nigerians served in World War II, 30,000 of them outside their native country. See James S. Coleman, *Nigeria: background to nationalism* (Berkeley and Los Angeles, 1958), pp. 254, and Frederick A. O. Schwarz, Jr., *Nigeria: the tribes, the nation, or the race: the politics of independence* (Cambridge, Mass., 1965), pp. 57–8. Also see Donald S. Rothchild, *The Effects of Mobilization in British Africa* (Pittsburgh, Duquesne University, Institute of African Affairs), Reprint No. 2.

under substantial expatriate influence, which precluded (or certainly made more difficult) any meddling in politics. In the second stage, resentment against European officers and African political leaders exploded in mutinies. These outbursts were not intended—at least not directly—to unseat the government in control. They were aimed rather at forcing the government to adopt certain policies, notably higher pay, pension privileges, or immediate Africanisation of the officer corps. *Coups d'état* belong in the third level of military involvement. The occupants of presidential palaces were removed, possibly executed; into their offices moved the initiators of the intervention, intent on 'restoring' the country to 'normal' patterns. To be certain, this categorisation is only approximate. It is meant as a guideline for understanding and initial analysis.

MILITARY NON-INVOLVEMENT:
THE POLITICS OF DECOLONISATION

Independence brought changes in the political and administrative sectors of African governments far more rapidly than in the military sector. The pace of Africanisation differed dramatically. The replacement of European senior civil servants by Africans was a first priority for newly-independent states; this task was eased by accelerated retirement and pension schemes and by absorption into the domestic civil service of the former colonial power. In the armed services, however, the replacement of Europeans in command positions was relatively leisurely—at least until mutiny or political decision to diminish reliance on foreign officers came about.

No army in tropical Africa, apart from the Sudanese, had a significant

proportion of African officers when independence was granted.[4] In Ghana, which enjoyed perhaps the highest educational level of the sub-Saharan countries, only 10 per cent of the officers were African in 1957.[5] The *Force publique* in the former Belgian Congo had no Africans in command positions: there were but three African sergeant-majors in an army of 24,000 soldiers and non-commissioned officers, 542 officers, and 566 junior officers.[6] Not until 1959 did an African from British East Africa complete training at Sandhurst.[7] The late start in Africanisation can be attributed to the pace of political change in Africa since World War II, which far exceeded the pace envisaged by the colonial administrations.[8] Until independence was clearly recognised as the objective—in the short run, not in the distant future—of constitutional evolution, there was little value in replacing Europeans with possibly less-

---

[4] James S. Coleman and Belmont Brice, Jr., 'The Role of the Military in Sub-Saharan Africa', in John J. Johnson (ed.), *The Role of the Military in Underdeveloped Countries* (Princeton, 1962), pp. 366–7.

[5] *Ibid.* p. 370. Gutteridge notes that in January 1961, three months after Nigeria gained independence, 81 of about 300 officers in the Nigerian Army were Africans, the most senior being a Lieutenant-Colonel. William F. Gutteridge, 'Military Elites in Ghana and Nigeria', in *African Forum* (New York), II, 1, Summer 1966, p. 37.

[6] Coleman and Brice, *op. cit.* p. 379; Catherine Hoskyns, *The Congo Since Independence, January 1960–December 1961* (London, 1965), p. 59.

[7] Coleman and Brice, *op. cit.* p. 373.

[8] On the eve of World War II, the British Secretary of State for the Colonies commented, 'It may take generations or even centuries for the peoples in some parts of the Colonial Empire to achieve self-government'. Clearly he had Africa in mind. Quoted in Kenneth Robinson, 'World Opinion and Colonial Status,' in *International Organization* (Boston), VIII, 3, Summary 1954, p. 468.

experienced Africans. The supply of Africans with the requisite educational background was limited. And, at a more subtle level, the loyalty of European officers to their home country could be taken for granted. Control over the armed services was never turned over to African supervision before self-government was granted.

The armies of contemporary Africa are the direct descendants of forces created by the colonial administration. They supplemented police forces in restoring calm—often by shows of force, a reputation for rapacity, and occasionally outright brutality. Soldiers were often recruited from 'martial' tribes, then stationed far from their place of origin, often among traditional enemies. Ill-trained and ill-disciplined in many instances, colonial armies 'were often regarded by the local population with deep distrust, as hated tools of the white conqueror'.[9]

Few African leaders embarked upon drastic military reorganisation immediately after attaining self-government. The Africanisation of command positions was accelerated, but it was nearly impossible—and perhaps politically inexpedient—to remove expatriates on the spot. Although politicians supported Africanisation in principle, the uncertainties of the post-independence period gave them second thoughts about dropping experienced Europeans. President Nkrumah of Ghana, for example, retained a British chief of staff for more than four years after independence, despite pressures to name an African to the position. Even so mercurial a leader as Patrice Lumumba of the former Belgian Congo felt the need for continuity in the army—that is to say,

for the retention of European officers. 'We are not, just because the Congo is independent, going to turn a second-class soldier into a general'.[10] Even more forceful was his demand, made to the Congo Executive College two months before independence:

it is essential that the Force Publique, the only force available, stays intact. It must pass under the command of the Congolese Government exactly as it is— with its officer class, its junior officers, its traditions, its discipline, its unique hierarchy and above all its morale unshaken. This is not the moment to disorientate the Force by innovations, for an army in the process of organisation or reorganisation is not in a fit state to carry out its duties.[11]

Continuity entailed limitations on immediate promotion—a constraint many Congolese soldiers were unwilling to accept.

The contrast in the pace of Africanisation between the civil service and the officer corps was striking in many African states. As noted earlier, a mere 10 per cent of officers in the Ghanaian army were Africans in 1957. Three years earlier, however, nearly 40 per cent of senior officers in the Ghanaian civil service were Africans.[12] Analogous disproportions in the rate of advancement existed elsewhere, and helped to account for the subsequent outbreak of mutinies.

Budgets for the armies of Africa, small in the period of colonial administration, remained limited after independence. The limited size of pre-independence forces and the retention of European officers may have inhibited lobbying or pressure for increased appropriations. The conception of the

---

[9] Pierre L. van den Berghe, 'The Role of the Military in Contemporary Africa', in *Africa Report* (Washington), x, 3, March 1965, p. 17.

[10] Hoskyns, *op. cit.* p. 60.
[11] *Ibid.*
[12] Austin, *op. cit.* p. 158.

army as the former tool of colonial interests made it easy for politicians to skimp military spending. Limited resources were better spent on such popular objectives as education, health, and expansion of other public services. Even after independence, the former colonial power bore many military costs, particularly through providing equipment and training. In fact, until the officer corps was largely Africanised, until the former colonial power had disavowed its willingness to intervene in the event of insurrection, and until the aura of unity surrounding the dominant party had been broken, military pressure upon politicians—and consequently the funds devoted to military expenses —remained low.

These brief observations point inescapably to the conclusion that African armies, in the immediate post-independence period, were not 'national' armies. Their organisation and equipment depended heavily on external sources. Most of the trappings of the colonial period were simply carried over, save in states where self-government

Armed Strength and Defence Expenditures of African States *

Country	Regular armed forces†	Defence budgets ($000)	As % of total govt. expenditure	As % of estimated G.N.P.
West Africa				
Chad	900	5,835	13.5	1.8
Dahomey	1,800	4,070	12.0	2.0
Gambia	—	—	—	—
Ghana	17,000	42,000	7.4	2.5
Guinea	5,000	5,870	8.1	3.1
Ivory Coast	4,000	8,825	6.9	2.4
Liberia	3,200	3,100	6.7	1.8
Mali	3,500	8,825	21.2	3.2
Mauritania	1,000	4,060	17.9	5.1
Niger	1,200	3,650	10.8	1.2
Nigeria	11,500	54,000	9.9	0.9
Senegal	5,500	21,050	11.6	7.6
Sierra Leone	1,360	2,585	4.9	1.3
Togo	1,450	2,757	13.5	4.1
Upper Volta	1,500	2,819	14.1	6.1
Total	58,910	169,446		
North Africa and the Horn				
Algeria	48,000	101,000	11.1	4.2
Ethiopia	35,000	31,175	17.0	2.3
Libya	7,000	14,000	5.8	3.5
Morocco	44,800	62,000	10.5	4.7
Somali	9,500	6,670	18.1	4.8
Sudan	18,500	40,000	17.7	4.4
Tunisia	17,000	8,180	4.1	1.5
U.A.R.	180,000	450,000	17.4	8.6
Total	359,800	713,025		

continued

Country	Regular armed forces	Defence budgets ($000)	As % of total govt. expenditure	As % of estimated G.N.P.
Central Africa				
Burundi	950	970	6.9	0.7
Cameroun	3,500	15,800	19.5	4.2
Central Afr. Rep.	600	2,325	7.9	0.6
Congo-Brazza.	1,800	3,785	8.9	10.9
Congo-Leo.	32,000	22,500	14.5	1.7
Gabon	750	2,540	7.6	5.1
Malawi	850	1,500	3.3	1.1
Rwanda	1,500	1,300	9.7	0.7
Zambia	3,000	13,525	5.7	2.5
Total	54,950	64,245		
East Africa				
Kenya	4,775	10,200	6.9	9.8
Malagasy	4,000	9,130	8.8	1.0
Tanzania	1,800	7,225	3.8	0.3
Uganda	5,960	17,025	10.2	1.5
Total	16,535	43,580		
Southern Africa				
Rhodesia		16,900	6.6	1.9
South Africa		322,000	19.9	3.5
Total		338,900		

*Source: David Word, *The Armed Forces of African States* (London, Institute for Strategic Studies, 1966), Adelphi Papers No. 27, pp. 28–9
†These estimates exclude the police and *gendarmerie*.

brought rupture from the former administering country.[13] Defence pacts, the dominance of Europeans in the officer corps, and a relatively slow Africanisation of command positions, in contrast to the rapid Africanisation of the civil service, helped to perpetuate the image of the army as expatriate-controlled. Armies were not viewed, then, as institutions in which Africans took pride.[14] They were remnants of a time of 'national' shame, in the eyes of prominent politicians. This makes an interesting contrast with the states of Latin America, where independence came through armed struggle, and 'the leaders of the revolutionary armies moved easily and naturally into the political vacuum created by the disappearance of royal authority. Thus at the very beginning of nationhood the armed forces [of Latin America] assumed extramilitary [that is, political]

[13]Guinea is an obvious instance. After the *Non* vote in the referendum of 28 September 1958, which resulted in the country's independence, the French Government 'almost at once began to repatriate Guineans then serving in its army'. All French troops were withdrawn by 30 November 1968, and the Guinea Government eschewed any French assistance in training. For a dithyrambic view of the reorientation of the Guinean army, see Victor D. Du Bois, 'The Role of the Army in Guinea', in *Africa Report*, VIII, I, January 1963, pp. 3–5, from which the quotations were taken.

[14]Roger Murray, 'Militarism in Africa,' in *New Left Review* (London), July–August 1966, p. 36.

functions'.[15] Only in Algeria, and to a much more limited extent in Morocco, Tunisia, Cameroun, and Kenya did bands of guerrilla fighters carry forward the quest for independence.

MUTINIES AND STEPS TOWARD INVOLVEMENT

Direct military involvement in the political life of African states came initially through mutinies. Their proximate cause appears to have been dissatisfaction within the ranks over such internal issues as promotions and pay scales. Though they had a direct impact upon politics, the mutinies were not directly political.[16] In other words, these revolts primarily represented insubordination to officers, not direct rebellion seeking to displace elected officials. The causes were intrinsic to the army, not extrinsic to the political system.

Africanisation of the officer corps had barely started in most sub-Saharan states when the colonial power withdrew. The European commanders viewed their duty as being to ensure continuity in a period of profound stress. The most candid expression of this view came from General Emile Janssens, commander of the *Force publique* in the former Belgian Congo. A few days after independence, he addressed a sullen group of officers and soldiers at the Leopoldville military camp. The Congolese troops 'had the impression that independence had passed them by'—and this impression was seemingly confirmed when General Janssens wrote on a blackboard, 'Before independence = after independence'.[17] This remark infuriated the soldiers, who rebelled and dismissed all European officers. The first significant mutiny against an independent African state had started.

The self-confidence of General Janssens was more than matched by the confidence of Julius Nyerere (then Prime Minister) of Tanganyika. Shortly after the Congo mutiny, Nyerere declared, 'These things cannot happen here. First, we have a strong organization, T.A.N.U. [Tanganyika African National Union]. The Congo did not have that kind of organization . . . there is not the slightest chance that the forces of law and order in Tanganyika will mutiny'.[18] Three and a half years later, after Nyerere had devoted considerable attention to reorganising T.A.N.U. and assuring military loyalty, the First Battalion of the Tanganyika Rifles rose against their British officers and marched into Dar es Salaam, demanding higher pay and total Africanisation of the officer corps. The vaunted strength of T.A.N.U. and its respected leader seemed to crumble when confronted by a handful of mutinous troops.

MILITARY INVOLVEMENT IN POLITICS: THE SEIZURES OF CONTROL

The military seizures of control that rocked the sub-Saharan area from mid-1965 on cannot be attributed to a single factor. The complexity of events belies simple, uni-causal analysis. Many political systems were involved, each with distinct heritages and problems. To assume that 'popular discontent' or 'economic stagnation' or 'neocolonialist

---

[15]Edwin Lieuwin, *Arms and Politics in Latin America* (New York, 1961 rev. edn.), p. 19.

[16]A similar distinction is drawn by A. Mazrui and D. S. Rothchild in their article 'The Soldier and the State in East Africa: some theoretical conclusions on the army mutinies of 1964', in *Western Political Quarterly* (Salt Lake City), xx, 1, March 1967, p. 94.

[17]Hoskyns, *op. cit*. pp. 87–9.

[18]Quoted in Mazrui and Rothchild, op. cit. p. 82.

interference' brought about the *coups d'état* does not do justice to each unique combination of circumstances. Rather than search for a sole cause, we must examine a series of factors, the salience of whose components differ from one African state to another.

Significant factors that helped promote military intervention may be summarised in tabular form:

1. The declining prestige of the major political party, as exemplified by (*a*) an increased reliance upon force to achieve compliance, (*b*) a stress upon unanimity in the face of centrifugal forces, and (*c*) a consequent denial of effective political choice.
2. Schism among prominent politicians, weakening the broadly-based nationalist movement that had hastened the departure of the former colonial power.
3. The lessened likelihood of external intervention in the event of military uprising.
4. 'Contagion' from seizures of control by the military in other African countries.
5. Domestic social antagonisms, most obviously manifested in countries where a minority group exercised control (e.g. the Arabs in Zanzibar, the Watutsi in Burundi).
6. Economic malaise, leading to 'austerity' policies, which most affected articulate, urbanised sectors of the population (members of trade unions, civil servants).
7. Corruption and inefficiency among government and party officials, a corruption especially noticeable under conditions of economic decline.
8. A heightened awareness within the army of its power to influence or displace political leaders.

Let us consider these factors in greater detail.

1. DECLINING PARTY PRESTIGE

Enthusiasm for the dominant party flagged rapidly in many African states, following the initial spurt of organisational enthusiasm, and the jubilation of self-government.[19] The waning was in part psychological. Independence may have aroused unwarrantedly high expectations. The 'golden age' would be ushered in; in some remote regions, self-government was interpreted as an end to taxes, communal labour, and other unpleasant aspects of administrative control. Such hopes obviously could not be fulfilled. Economic stringency also contributed to the loss of party fervour. But the major agent of the declining prestige of political parties was internal. The tactics and organisation of parties appropriate for anti-colonial activities were not necessarily appropriate for the tasks of government after independence. Failure in the structural adaptation of political parties made them considerably less effective instruments in a self-governing African state.

Difficulties arose from the limits of the changes that political groups could effect. Loyalty to a dominant party, to its leader, and to the 'nation' it claimed to embody could not be readily accepted in the face of conflicting, ethnically-based loyalties. For most newly enfranchised Africans, an understanding of politics could not be disentangled from traditional outlooks and antagonisms. The broad, anti-colonial nationalist movements had succeeded, in varying degrees, in juxtaposing what one may call the 'sub-national nationalisms' of ethnic groups. With independence achieved and its novelty gone, the united front showed clear signs of disintegration, of a loss of vigour. Primordial attachments remained strong, despite the success of the nationalist movements in winning independence. Indeed, the extension of political awareness through party

---

[19] Aristide R. Zolberg, *Creating Political Order: the party-states of West Africa* (Chicago, 1966), pp. 37 ff.

activities may have exacerbated group tensions. The greater political awareness created by participation, C. Geertz has noted, 'does indeed tend to lead to the stimulation and maintenance of a very intense popular interest in the affairs of government. But . . . much of this interest takes the form of an obsessive concern with the relation of one's tribe, region, sect, or whatever to a center of power'.[20] To regain the apparent unity of the anti-colonial struggle was a problem with which most African leaders struggled after independence. Agreement had to be created once again—and it was to be revived through the achievement of unanimity.

Two steps are involved in this task, according to A. R. Zolberg: erasing all traces of political opposition, and modifying both dominant party and government through the creation of a new institutional order.[21] The methods by which opposition parties have been harassed and eventually removed from public attention have been analysed elsewhere in detail.[22] Essentially what was involved was civil action against politicians—legal restrictions on their activities, the manipulation of electoral machinery and regulations, rewards for 'crossing the carpet'—rather than widespread campaigns of intimidation undertaken against supporters of opposition groups. By removing the spokesmen

for 'sub-national nationalism', African political leaders hoped to eliminate detrimental parochial tendencies. However, given the deeply-rooted nature of ethnic identity and its stimulation through political participation, such measures may only have worsened the situation. It is in this context the politicians turned increasingly to the use of force, to attain goals of integration unreachable through persuasion.

The attempted elimination of political opposition by the use of force in turn affected political life in African states. The following points, drawn from Zolberg, illustrate the complexities of the shift from 'power' to 'force'.[23]

(1) Governments may fall into the snare of believing that harsh treatment will eliminate disruptive demands. However, the governments may become more vulnerable to other threats, since the limited capital of force is used up— and not readily replenished. In other words, the possibility of a 'run on the bank' within an African political system is heightened.[24]

(2) Increasing use of force enhances the significance of police, military, and other groups capable of its exercise. By contrast, the significance of political parties, civil services, or similar institutions declines.

(3) If groups, or individuals, lack the opportunity for legitimate political

---

[20]Clifford Geertz, 'The Integrative Revolution: primordial sentiments and civil politics in the new states', in Clifford Geertz (ed.), *Old Societies and New States* (New York, 1963), pp. 119–20.

[21]Zolberg, *op. cit.* p. 66.

[22]See, *inter alia*, the country studies and concluding chapter of James S. Coleman and Carl L. Rosberg, *Political Parties and National Integration in Tropical Africa* (Berkeley and Los Angeles, 1964); Martin L. Kilson, 'Authoritarian and Single-Party Tendencies in African Politics', in *World Politics* (Princeton), xv, 2, January 1963, pp. 262–94: and Zolberg, *op. cit.* p. 66.

[23]Aristide R. Zolberg, 'The Structure of Political Conflict in the New States of Tropical Africa', unpublished paper delivered at the 1966 annual meeting of the American Political Science Association, pp. 13–14. I have omitted Zolberg's point about the problem of legitimacy: he notes that the shift to force 'enhances the problem of the legitimacy of the rulers in the eyes of those to whom the implementation of force must necessarily be entrusted'.

[24]Talcott Parsons, 'Some Reflections on the Place of Force in Social Process', in Harry Eckstein (ed.), *Internal War: problems and approaches* (New York, 1964), pp. 58–61.

activity—that is, exercising power to express their demands—they are tempted to use force to press these demands.

2. POLITICAL SCHISMS

The quest for unanimity, sought by means of the dominant party, must be examined in a different context. Maintaining the cohesion of the party entailed a reformulation of party-state relations. In this reformulation, an increasing emphasis upon individual leader-ship emerged. In few African political parties has collective decision-making prevailed—if it ever existed. The reins of control have been held by a single leader. However, in states where political rivalry could not be contained within the framework of a single party, the likelihood of *coups d'état* increased. Splits between top political leaders furnished the pretext for several military incursions into African political life.

Two examples illustrate this point. General Joseph Mobutu's first intervention into Congolese politics came in September 1960. Prime Minister Patrice Lumumba and President Joseph Kasavubu had found themselves in a constitutional impasse: Kasavubu had relieved Lumumba of his duties, an action whose legality Lumumba denied. As government activity shuddered to a halt, Mobutu stepped in to neutralise all politicians and assume power, for a period of slightly over three months. He insisted that his action constituted a 'peaceful revolution', not a *coup d'état*.[25] The government would be run by *techniciens*, by which Mobutu meant Congolese university graduates and students.

Colonel Christophe Soglo attempted to heal the long-standing split in Dahomeyan politics in October 1963 by temporarily replacing President Hubert Maga.[26] However, the long-standing tensions among regionally-based politicians in Dahomey could not be effaced, and the formation of a single party (the *Parti démocratique dahoméen*) failed to resolve the unstable situation. To set the government right by eliminating the schism and regionalism encouraged by conflicting leaders was a major encouragement for military intervention. In other words, soldiers like Soglo and Mobutu were prompted to seize control to restore a political equilibrium which had been disrupted by personality conflicts. Their goal was 'caretaker' administration—not sweeping change, but minor adaptation. Minor shifts in personnel and policy would be undertaken; the status quo would be restored.

3. EXTERNAL INTERVENTION: HOW REAL A THREAT?

The plotters of *coups d'état* must always calculate the possibility of international reaction against their planned takeover.[27] In Africa, fear of external intervention to prevent military seizure of control—particularly the fear of intervention by the former colonial power—has been a significant variable in the cases under consideration.

The role of European officers has already been examined. It is reasonable to assume that the presence of ex-

---

[25]Hoskyns, *op. cit.* p. 214.

[26]The regional tensions are extensively discussed by Virginia Thompson, 'Dahomey', in Gwendolen M. Carter (ed.), *Five African States: responses to diversity* (Ithaca, 1963), pp. 207–35.

[27]A sound strategy for coups, Major Goodspeed has commented, involves assessment of the sympathies of the country's armed forces, the state of public opinion, and the international situation. D. J. Goodspeed, *The Conspirators: a study of the coup d'état* (New York, 1962), p. 210. The six seizures of control analysed in this book are European.

patriate officers moderates the willingness of African officers and soldiers to embark upon *coups d'état*, where the expatriates and the former colonial power are obviously committed to upholding the African government concerned. More important, there is the risk of large-scale intervention from the ex-administering country. British forces rapidly quelled the mutinies in Kenya and Tanganyika, upon request; French troops crushed the uprising in Gabon, once again upon request.

From the limited evidence available, it appears that the British and French Governments have been relatively circumspect. They have intervened only on the request of the duly constituted government (though how well-established Mba's Government was is an open question), where a show of force (as by disarming mutineers) would restore calm. The former colonial powers have not intervened in cases of popularly supported revolutionary upheaval (e.g. Zanzibar, the overthrow of President Fulbert Youlou in Congo-Brazzaville), in relatively popular coups in which politicians are removed from office but not executed (e.g. Central African Republic, Dahomey, Upper Volta), or in violent coups carried out with great rapidity (e.g. Togo, Nigeria).

How likely are the Belgian, British, and French Governments to become embroiled in protecting future African politicians from the ire of discontented armed forces? Not very likely, it would seem, save in cases in which very substantial investments and numerous citizens were involved, and in which international political considerations—that is to say, east–west alignments—obtrude. The use of paratroops against Stanleyville in 1964 fulfilled these criteria, but a repetition of the surrounding circumstances appears unlikely. European troop deployments in Africa have been cut dramatically. 'As far as the major powers are concerned', David Wood has commented, 'on the whole their military involvement in Africa is limited by the fact that the continent is not of prime concern for their own security. Only for France do bases in Africa constitute a major part of her strategic scheme, and she is progressively withdrawing from the area'.[28] The 16,000 French troops stationed in Africa at the start of 1966 have been considerably reduced, and bases closed down; should any of the 11 countries with which France has defence agreements call for assistance, units for intervention would come from the 11th Infantry Division, generally based in southwest France and Brittany.[29] The British Government after March 1966 maintained only 2,000 soldiers in Africa; no Belgian troops are stationed south of the Sahara, although advisers have been provided for the armies of Burundi, Congo-Kinshasa, and Rwanda; almost all American troops in Africa (5,500 out of 6,000) are stationed in Ethiopia and Libya.[30] Despite the rapid mobility offered by modern aircraft, and the retention of some French troops, the capacity of the former colonial powers to intervene has declined considerably— as well, perhaps, as their desire to become involved in what they view as domestic political crises. And, further, if a coup is rapid and the removal of politicians complete, intervention by the former colonial power would be nugatory. Leaders of coups learn quickly the value of 'Twere well it were done quickly.'

4. 'CONTAGION'

Three weeks after the assassination of President Sylvanus Olympio of Togo, Colonel David Thompson, commanding officer of Liberia's National

---

[28]Wood, *op. cit.* p. 3.
[29]*Ibid.* p. 26.
[30]*Ibid.* pp. 19, 22, and 27.

Guard, was arrested on suspicion of plotting a *coup d'état*. 'If only 250 Togolese soldiers could overthrow their government, a Liberian Army of 5,000 could seize power easily', Colonel Thompson is alleged to have argued.[31] Successful seizure of control in one state may touch off a series of coups. The Zanzibar uprising helped to trigger off the East African mutinies; similarly, the intervention of Soglo in December 1965 helped to touch off coups in the Central African Republic, Upper Volta, and Nigeria.

Contagion must be considered on two levels: the personal links among African officers in different countries, and the increasing extent of inter-state ties. Shared experiences in the French army provided the leaders of intervention in the Central African Republic, Dahomey, Togo, and Upper Volta (respectively Bokassa, Soglo, Eyadema, and Lamizana) with potentially significant individual ties. Quite likely the success of one in winning political control prompted the others to consider intervention—though no conclusive evidence can be adduced. The international connexions result from increasing interaction among African states. Since independence—especially through the periodic conferences organised by the Organisation of African Unity and its subordinate units—contacts among African leaders have multiplied. As Africa has increasingly become a sub-system in world politics, reciprocal influences among African states have multiplied. These reciprocal influences include the germ of military intervention.

5. UNSTABLE SOCIAL SITUATION

Reference has already been made to conditions of social disequilibrium affecting attempts at army seizure of con-

trol. When members of the armed forces perceive the government as dominated by members of an ethnic group hostile to the interests of another ethnic group heavily represented within the military, grievances based on tribe or region may quickly develop. Often army intervention may be given impetus by the clash of 'primordial sentiments'.

6. CORRUPTION

The puritanical tendencies of military leaders have often been commented upon. Their distaste for ostentation has served as a rationalisation—and I suspect as a reason—for intervention. To clear up the affairs of state and restore fiscal integrity and responsibility are themes frequently expounded by the leaders of *coups d'état*. General Ankrah, for example, accused President Nkrumah of bringing Ghana 'to the brink of economic disaster by mismanagement, waste and unwise spending'.[32] Attempts to reduce government spending, undertaken by all the new military leaders under review in this article, may be viewed as a response to a belief in widespread corruption. Similarly, the banning of political parties (another typical step following intervention) was partially intended to cut down opportunities for corruption.

7. STAGNATING ECONOMIC SITUATION

Rising government budgets do not indicate increasing prosperity. The dramatic increase in the expenditures of African states in the late colonial and immediate post-colonial period reflected the strong desire of political leaders to spread social benefits widely and rapidly. Universal primary education, for example, was a goal with obvious attractions—but one involving tremen-

---

[31] Helen Kitchen, 'Filling the Togo Vacuum', in *Africa Report*, VIII, 2, January 1963, p. 9.

[32] Quoted in *Africa Research Bulletin* (London), III, 2, February 1966, p. 467c. 21.

dous costs in relationship to total resources. An economic squeeze resulted, which was compounded by falls in the world prices of primary commodities such as cocoa, coffee, and cotton, on which many African countries depended for export earnings. The termination of preferential marketing agreements (especially between France and her former dependencies), as well as absolute declines in the quantity of some of the goods exported, further weakened the economic position of African states. A seemingly insatiable demand for consumer goods, manufactured items, and machinery essential for even the rudiments of industrialisation increased the need for foreign exchange. Lacking ready reserves, or a sufficiently growing revenue from exports to cover these needs, African states found themselves in an economic quandary. Few avoided inflation. Deficits were the rule, not the exception.[33] Governments became involved with 'suppliers' credits', loans of dubious economic validity, and stopgap schemes for economic betterment.

Yet the demands could not be stilled. The economically most privileged parts of contemporary African society—the civil servants, the trade unionists, and above all the politicians—benefited to the greatest extent from government pay rises. Even so, their inflated aspirations could not always be satisfied. Discontent with salaries in Dahomey and Upper Volta helped to ignite the civil disturbances that preceded the *coups d'état*; the precarious economic position of Ghana before the anti-Nkrumah coup has been well documented.[34]

Revolutions are made by the relatively privileged, not the downtrodden.[35] The privileged of modern Africa are the educated. They gained most from independence, especially through the expansion of benefits brought by Africanisation and salary increases. When the flow of these perquisites was interrupted through financial necessity, however, the discontent of the educated could not be easily contained.

8. MILITARY SELF-IDENTIFICATION

The seizure of control by military juntas normally does not occur when officers recognise civilian control of the armed forces as legitimate. For intervention to take place, members of the military must distinguish between the 'national interest' of the country and the policies espoused by the government in power. The denial of the legitimacy of the duly constituted civilian government is the first—and probably the most important—step in the military seizure of power. The 'disposition to intervene', as S. E. Finer has suggested, is based on a distinction between 'national interest' and the practices followed by the government.[36] If the armed forces are to remain in their barracks and not attempt to displace the political leader-

---

[33]In the Congo, to take an admittedly extreme example, the central government in 1962 estimated it would receive approximately 4,000,000,000 francs, while expenditures totalled more than 19,000,000,000 francs. Edouard Bustin, 'The Congo', in Carter (ed.), *Five African States*, p. 138n.

[34]See reports of hearings of 15 commissions of enquiry established by the Ankrah Govern-

ment, and the rescheduling of Ghana's external debt of £280 million, in *West Africa* (London).

[35]Brinton's observations on revolutions seem apposite here. In his comparative analysis, he suggests that revolutions occurred in societies 'on the whole on the upgrade economically before the revolution came, and the revolutionary movements seem to originate in the discontents of not unprosperous people who feel restraint, cramp, annoyance, rather than downright crushing oppression. Certainly these revolutions are not started by down-and-outers, by starving, miserable people'. Crane Brinton, *The Anatomy of Revolution* (New York, 1965), p. 250.

[36]S. E. Finer, *The Man on Horseback: the role of the military in politics* (London, 1962), pp. 23–60.

ship, they must accept civilian supremacy.

The 'disposition to intervene' arises in part from the unique technological and organisational position of the armed forces. The military pride themselves on their efficiency and *esprit de corps*. Their centralisation, hierarchy, discipline, and intercommunication—quite apart from their control of modern weapons—set them apart from most institutions within a given society. Recruits into the armed forces generally receive intensive training, instilling in them a sense of the unique heritage and duty of the army. As many analysts of the role of the military in new states have observed, this indoctrination may prove extremely beneficial in implanting 'a sense of citizenship and an appreciation of political action'.[37] Yet this indoctrination may serve just as well to implant loyalty to the army as an institution set apart from its political system. There may be the emergence of a strong sense of the honour and duty of the military, including the duty to intervene to correct the misdeeds of politicians. When the military seizure of control is rationalised by coup leaders, in the words of a main plotter against Nkrumah, as 'necessary to save our country and our people', the 'disposition to intervene' is clearly present.[38]

* * *

The preceding analysis has been aimed at presenting the complexities of the 'causes' of military intervention. To pick out a single factor as 'The Cause' of a *coup d'état* is nearly impossible. Military intervention resulted from the combination of many factors. In the coups surveyed in this article, economic, cultural, and political reasons were intertwined; the declining prestige of political parties and the growing consciousness among the military of their power obviously played significant roles. The diminished likelihood of external intervention, and the effects of contagion, must be added to a sense of grievance within the army as part of the background. When and how the coups occurred differed greatly. There seem to be no uniform circumstances under which the military seized control—save that the popularity of the government had noticeably declined among the politically relevant strata of the population, and that army officers seemed to become aware of a unique duty to protect the 'national interest'. To change personnel and policies was the major objective of *coups d'état*; accordingly, they grew out of a background analytically distinguishable from the conditions that promoted the mutinies, discussed previously. By early 1966, it was clear that the armies of Africa had emerged as perhaps the most significant shapers of policy. No longer can our understanding of postcolonial Africa leave aside the political role of the military.

---

[37] Lucian W. Pye, 'Armies in the Process of Political Modernization', in Johnson (ed.), *The Role of the Military*, p. 83.

[38] Colonel A. A. Afrifa, *The Ghana Coup, 24th February 1966* (New York, 1966), p. 37.

IV

National Integration

As a political factor, integration represents the cumulative effect of individual allegiance to and identification with society and its goals. When these sentiments are shared widely by individuals in a country they foster a high degree of national unity and sense of national purpose, thus providing a basis for concerted action and justifying whatever sacrifices national leaders may call on citizens to make. The extent to which individuals feel they belong to their society and contribute to its intrinsic merit can be the measure of a country's quality or level of integration. Indeed, political integration is a crucial factor in any society, irrespective of the stage of its national development.

The concept of integration is a comparatively old idea in the literature of the social sciences, and one finds a variety of definitions, with subtle—even semantic—differences. Myron Weiner, for example, has listed five common uses of "integration," but concedes that they do not exhaust the possibilities, for "since there are many ways in which systems fall apart, there are many ways of defining 'integration'."[1] Perhaps the single most utilitarian definition is provided by Lucian W. Pye who posits the problem of integration as the extent "to which the entire polity is organized as a system of interacting relationships, first among the offices and agencies of government, and then among

[1] Myron Weiner, "Political Integration and Political Development," *The Annals*, CCCLVIII (March 1965), 54.

the various groups and interests seeking to make demands upon the system, and finally in the relationships between officials and articulating citizens."[2]

Such a definition offers the possibility of at least two different dimensions of integration: (1) territorial or horizontal, and (2) political or vertical. The first is concerned with bridging the social distances between groups by subsuming the parochial loyalties of culture, region, language, and ethnic and tribal groups to the over-riding interests of the national community. This process reconciles local interests with each other at the same time that it creates a common denominator of national interest. The second form relates primarily to the political distance between the masses of the people and their national leaders; political integration minimizes this distance and establishes a participant political community.

National integration in Africa usually refers to the process of achieving territorial integration; the question of political integration remains as a problem for the future. Not every African president has alienated himself from the masses by becoming a dictator, nor has every ruling party become a self-serving, coercive political machine. An elite-mass gap exists in varying degrees in many African countries, but in most it has not yet been politicized and is likely to remain relatively less important than the difficulties produced by cultural and ethnic diversity on the territorial level.

The importance of national integration for politics is its significance and relevance for system performance. The problem may be examined in terms of the question: Why do citizens accept the decisions of their government? Apart from the state's power to coerce, why do people pay taxes, obey unpopular laws, and otherwise perform onerous duties? Citizens sometimes do these things because they anticipate that government policy ultimately serves their own individual self-interests. At a more general level, however, public obedience to government rests on the presumption of citizens that governmental decisions are inherently proper because the power of the authorities has been legitimately acquired and legitimately exercised. Public acceptance of the legitimacy of government confers on the authorities political power which transcends the limitations of public self-interest.

What are the sources of this sense of legitimacy? Consent and consensus are vital factors, but these are in part the products of national longevity and the existence of shared traditions and values which Africans do not yet fully enjoy. The spirit of *negritude*, Africanity or Pan-Africanism as an expression of the sense that "We are all Afri-

---

[2] Lucian W. Pye, *Aspects of Political Development* (Boston: Little, Brown and Co., 1966), p. 65.

cans" provides intellectual and emotional appeals for many Africans, but such claims ignore the centrifugal tendencies of traditional diversity and do not themselves produce a modern national sentiment. Africans in the mass are not yet deeply attached to their particular structures and processes of national government, even though they may not be hostile to them. Thus popular support for African goverments must necessarily rest heavily on the quality of official policies and evidence of their effectiveness. Yet unlike in the older states of the West where demands on government remained limited while the processes of integration developed gradually, African citizens expect their governments to provide greater security, higher standards of living, employment, and educational and medical facilities. Indeed, these expectations appear to have increased in the post-independence period as African citizens await implementation of the generalized promises of the independence movements. Given the meager reserves of legitimacy upon which these governments can draw, and the undeveloped human and material resources with which they can work, the potential for political instability is obvious. African governments have had to concern themselves with actively promoting national integration to an extent far greater than did Western governments at comparable stages in their national histories when governments were expected to do little except provide for the general security.

New states with low levels of territorial integration encounter special problems as they seek to produce outputs that are specifically responsive to political demands. Social cleavages tend to be parallel and coincide; persons who differ over one set of social criterion— religion, means of livelihood, language, or regional identification—are also likely to differ on other values. In consequence, political differences tend to involve the whole personality of political actors and relate to what are termed the "fundamentals" of politics, i.e., the basic questions of the organization and goals of society. The effect, as analyzed by James S. Coleman, is detrimental to the political process: "In the community which does not create in its members the potential for cross-pressures, individuals are consistent; groups of friends are of one mind; and the organizations are unified—all the conflict is shifted to the level of the community itself."[3] But differences on "fundamentals" are usually regarded as so important that defeat on such a question is intolerable, or at least not easily compensated for by victories on other issues. Moreover, such differences are not usually negotiable and are especially difficult to resolve through reconciliation, particularly as the grounds for compromise under the new, nontraditional political processes are unfamiliar. The parties to a dispute on "fundamentals"

[3] James S. Coleman, *Community Conflict* (Glencoe: The Free Press, 1957), p. 22.

expect to gain total victory and to leave their opponents in total defeat; there is no acceptable half-way house and there are few, if any, honorable grounds for political bargaining. This situation is especially unbearable for talented minorities who consistently find themselves politically out-flanked by a "permanent majority" and are unable to find a role for themselves in shifting coalitions on the national scene. As African leaders at the national level experience the effects of few public cross-pressures, the escalation of local issues to the level of their various subcommunities, and persisting differences on "fundamentals," they necessarily increase their efforts to foster the territorial integration of their states, to build a "nation" and create a "people." Given the difficulties of their task it is to be expected that they should develop ideologies to promote the legitimacy of their political systems or resort to coercive measures that discourage opposition, or do both concurrently.

Patterns of National Integration

*Aristide R. Zolberg**

The concept 'integration', which came into general usage in the social sciences by way of nineteenth-century evolutionary thought, was eagerly seized upon as an heuristic device for the study of new states because it evoked the fundamental notion of making whole or entire by addition or combination. But the concept wears better as a signal of topical concern than as a building block in a rigorous theoretical edifice. The most obvious problem is that the very richness of suggestion embodied in the word 'integration' generates promiscuity. As Myron Weiner has indicated, although most observers generally view the achievement of 'integration' as the most pressing problem of the new nations, 'The term . . . is now widely used to cover an extraordinary range of political phenomena.'[1] Yet the present article

[1] Myron Weiner, 'Political Integration and Political Development', in *The Annals of the American Academy of Political and Social Science* (Philadelphia), 358, March 1965, p. 53. He singles out five distinct current usages: (1) the process of bringing together culturally and socially discrete groups into a single territorial unit and the establishment of a national identity in the context of some sort of plural society or the prior existence of distinct independent political units; in this sense, 'integration' refers to subjective feelings; (2) the establishment of national central authority over subordinate political units or regions; 'integration' here refers to objective control

*Associate Professor of Political Science, University of Chicago. An earlier version of this article was presented at the seventh world congress of the International Political Science Association in Brussels, September 1967. Field work in the Ivory Coast and Mali was supported by grants from the Ford Foundation and the Social Science Research Council.

From *Journal of Modern African Studies,* Vol. V, No. 4 (December 1967), 449–467, by permission of the journal and its publisher, the Cambridge University Press.

will not attempt to provide a strict definition of national integration. This decision is based on the belief that, at the present stage of development of the subject matter, the advantages of a certain degree of promiscuity outweigh the costs of premature monogamy.

It is possible, nevertheless, to clarify several other matters. Having distinguished five current usages, Weiner concludes that they do not exhaust the list and that 'Since there are many ways in which systems may fall apart, there are as many ways of defining "integration".'[2] The latter remark points to a second problematic aspect of the concept. While it is usually assumed that when a system falls apart there is an absence of integration and that persistence is due to successful integration, this only indicates that integration is often equated with persistence. In order to be meaningful, integration must incorporate the notion of a system's capability to deal with a limited range of internally and externally generated stresses. From this point of view, it is possible to account for the demise of a highly integrated system as the result of drastic changes in its environment, as well as for the persistence of a weakly integrated system as the result of inertia, of coercion, or of the operations of exogenous factors—stemming from the international system—which in some parts of the world, and at some points in time, tend to support the integrity of weak political communities.

Thirdly, integration is often treated as an all-or-nothing state of affairs and tends to be equated with the absence of conflict as well as with persistence. But we know from Georg Simmel and others that conflict is not necessarily an index to the instability of a relationship, but often an index of stability. For example, the political manifestations of antagonism stemming from primordial attachments may thus be indications of an incipient political community in which integration has emerged as an issue (or set of issues), while the absence of conflict (as in some of the least developed African states before independence or in the United States several decades ago) may merely indicate that a non-participant political culture prevails.

The fourth and fifth problems concern the contents to which the processes subsumed under 'integration' refer. What is being integrated, and into what wholes? In contemporary new nations, national integration refers to 'the aggregation of independently defined, specifically outlined traditional primordial groups into larger, more diffuse units, whose implicit frame of reference is not the local scene but the "nation"—in the sense of the whole society encompassed by the new civil state'.[3] Not only do the referents of these traditional attachments vary widely from one part of the world to another, but in any particular situation they are far from being fixed features in the social landscape. As Clifford Geertz has pointed out, 'By a primordial attachment is meant one that stems from the "givens"—or, more precisely, as culture is inevitably involved in such

---

by a central authority; (3) the problem of linking government with the governed, with special stress on the 'élite-mass gap'; (4) the growth of minimal value consensus assumed to be required for the maintenance of a system; and (5) the capacity of people in a society to organise for some common purpose'

[2] *Ibid.* p. 54.

[3] Clifford Geertz, 'The Integrative Revolution: primordial sentiments and civil politics in the new states', in Geertz (ed.), *Old Societies and New States* (New York, 1963), p. 163.

matters, the assumed "givens"—of social existence.'[4]

The social scientist concerned with the process of integration cannot hope therefore to treat the 'givens' of his problem as a set of independent variables with information secured from ethnographic handbooks. He must ascertain what sorts of identities are relevant, especially in relation to politics, at a given point in time; he must somehow detect within the general culture of a particular area what sorts of identities, though not immediately obvious, are potentially relevant. Primordial ties constitute a moving rather than a static pattern of identities; interaction between various identities does not occur once and for all when 'tradition' encounters 'modernity', but goes on throughout the process of change.

If it is dangerous to start from a clear baseline, it is fatal to anticipate a neat outcome. Our notion of what makes an integrated whole is by no means affectively neutral, but reflects what we hold to be a desirable whole from the point of view of specific political values. Hence, we exclude systems in which coercion is an important feature, or which involve a more or less hierarchical relationship between two complementary communities defined in reference to one another, as in the 'plural society' discussed by M. G. Smith.[5] But, within the generally accepted limits of contemporary usage, social science tends to reflect two models of national integration only: a pluralist version derived from an idealisation of the American experience, which involves the creation of cross-cutting affiliations by superim-

posing non-coincidental cleavages over primordial ones, culminating in hyphenated identities; and an assimilationist version, derived from an idealisation of French experience, which assumes that primordial and civil ties are mutually exclusive and that integration takes the form of a sort of zero-sum game culminating in the emergence of a homogeneous nation. Models derived from the institutionalisation of arrangements which assume the persistence of distinct sub-national identities tend to be dismissed as quaint sports if they are relatively stable and do not conflict with salient contemporary values (as with the religious communities of the Netherlands and linguistic communities of Switzerland), or as pathological cases if they appear to be a source of recurrent conflict (as with language groups in Belgium and Canada, or racial communities in the United States). This is unfortunate from a theoretical point of view and also because it deprives the contemporary new nations of knowledge of the political experiences perhaps most relevant to their needs.

Some progress toward the resolution of these difficulties can be made if the concept 'national integration' is used in an open-ended way, to encompass the notion that wholes can consist of different types of parts related in many possible ways. In this sense, it does not refer to the attainment of a known, permanent end-state, but to a shifting relationship between various changing identities within the framework of a variety of possible political arrangements capable of coping with a specifiable range of stresses. This alerts us to the fundamental fact that the definition of 'national integration' within a given society at a particular time is the most important starting point for an understanding of the phenomenon itself. The remainder of

---

[4] Ibid. p. 109.
[5] M. G. Smith, *The Plural Society in the British West Indies* (Berkeley and Los Angeles, 1965), especially preface and ch. IV.

this article illustrates a preliminary attempt to implement the approach outlined in the introduction by comparing two cases from West Africa.

1. THE PRIMORDIAL GIVENS IN THE IVORY COAST AND MALI

In spite of the efforts of several generations of observers and officials, all Africans cannot be assigned to mutually exclusive classificatory sets of similar character called tribes or ethnic groups. Immanuel Wallerstein, concerned specifically with the relationship between ethnicity and national integration, sought to correct simple notions of 'tribalism' by distinguishing between a 'tribe'—defined as a community with government, usually in a rural setting—and an 'ethnic group'—a community dissociated from government, usually in an urban setting—and observed that 'Membership in an ethnic group is a matter of social definition and interplay of the self-definition of members and the definition of other groups.'[6] But this distinction helps us understand the contemporary urban setting at the expense of our grasp of rural areas and of the past. Paul Mercier has pointed out that, although an ethnic group ('tribe' in the Wallerstein sense) usually suggests a closed group, descendants of a common ancestor, he agrees with S. F. Nadel that in fact an ethnic group is the theory its members make of it and hence that ethnic reality in Africa has a relative character.[7] Furthermore,

Jean Gallais has observed that in the Western Sudan, for example, traditional ethnic identity involves not only the 'given' of descent, but also techniques of exploitation of nature, history, religion, and spatial organisation, and that some of these components were based on achievement as well as ascription.[8] Units of government and primordial groups did not necessarily coincide in traditional Africa.

Taking Mali and the Ivory Coast, and using general compendia such as Baumann and Westermann, Murdock, or colonial handbooks, one could come up with equally long lists of distinct tribes and ethnic groups for the two countries and hence reach the conclusion that both are ethnically fragmented.[9] But even a passing familiarity with these two countries tells us that this would be an erroneous conclusion. How then do we get at the more significant features of their respective ethnic landscapes? A first approximation can be achieved by analysing the two countries with the aid of that questionable, but nevertheless indispensable construct, the ethnographic or culture circle.

The net cast by the French over the area now known as the Ivory Coast caught parts of four distinct circles.[10] Roughly speaking, the Atlantic East

---

[6] Immanuel Wallerstein, 'Ethnicity and National Integration in West Africa', reprinted in H. Eckstein and D. Apter (eds.), *Comparative Politics* (New York, 1963), p. 666.

[7] Paul Mercier, 'Remarques sur la signification du "tribalisme" actuel en Afrique noire', in *Cahiers internationaux de sociologie* (Paris), July–December 1961, pp. 61–80—my translation.

[8] Jean Gallais, 'Signification du groupe ethnique au Mali', in *L'Homme* (Paris), II, 2, May–August 1962, pp. 106–29.

[9] Unless otherwise specified, the ethnographic discussion which follows is based on H. Baumann and D. Westermann, *Les Peuples et les civilisations de l'Afrique* (Paris, Payot, 1957), and George P. Murdock, *Africa, its peoples and their culture history* (New York, 1959).

[10] Both the Ivory Coast and Mali are taken as they existed when their territory was defined after the reconstitution of Upper Volta in 1947. For details concerning the Ivory Coast, see Aristide R. Zolberg, *One-Party Government in the Ivory Coast* (Princeton, 1964), pp. 11–18.

(mostly Akans and peoples who constitute the 'lagoon cluster') accounts for one-third of the population; the Atlantic West (Kru and peripheral Mande) accounts for another third; and the remainder of the population, in the north, is divided approximately evenly between the Upper Niger (Mande) and Voltaic circles (Senufo, Lobi). Using the same sort of classification for Mali, we come up with a very different distribution into three circles: the Upper Niger, in which Baumann and Westermann include the Mande and all their relations as well as the Peul (Fulani), with approximately 70 per cent of the country's population; the Voltaic circle, in which they include both Senufo and Songhai, about 20 per cent; and the remainder, 10 per cent or less, falling into the category of Sahara nomads. If we modify this to overcome the uncomfortable association of very different groups in two of these categories, we come up with: Mande and related peoples, at least half the population; Peul, approximately one-fifth; and about 10 per cent each for the Songhai, the Senufo and their relations, and the 'North Africans'.

More important than these raw data are some factors which stem from the broader context from which they are derived. The four culture circles of the Ivory Coast not only divide the country more evenly, but none of them constitutes any sort of cultural core with a centre in the Ivory Coast itself: the Malinke are oriented towards Mali and Guinea; the Senufo towards Mali and Upper Volta; the Akan are segmented offshoots from the core culture located in Ghana; and the various peoples contained in the Atlantic West circle are fairly isolated forest peoples whose cultural affinities seem to have been discovered only very

recently when some of them found themselves sharing the oddity of patrilineage and a diet based on rice, in the midst of matrilineal Akan who eat yam and plantain in the new towns of the south-eastern Ivory Coast. Although our present knowledge of Ivory Coast history is thoroughly inadequate, it is probably accurate to suggest that there was in the past relatively little interaction between these circles towards the 'middle'. The self-image of the Ivory Coast, fostered by early explorers, later administrators, and internalised by educated Africans with the acquisition of basic knowledge of their own country, is one of very great fragmentation; 'une poussière de peuples', 'un morcellement'. Perhaps because of this very lack of core, the tendency within each of these circles, which might otherwise serve as referents for larger identities, has been towards further fragmentation as well. The only merger into a larger identity which comes to mind is that of the various 'lagoon peoples' and some of the Akan in and around the older town of Grand-Bassam, the country's first point of large-scale European contact. This 'Bassamois' identity, similar to that of the 'Cape Coaster' in Ghana, is in a sense the exception which confirms the rule.

The situation in Mali is fundamentally different. The Mande not only constitute approximately half the population, but their unity is defined with reference to the historical tradition of Mali. These traditions, as Gallais points out, also provide important links between the Mande of the region and emigrants, such as the itinerant Dioula, and certain 'assimilated' groups, in particular the Peul, Marka (Sarakolle), Bambara, Bozo, Somono, and perhaps even the Dogon. This does not mean, of course, that conflicts did not prevail within the Mande core, or between it and the other groups mentioned; but the sense of a 'global belonging' to historical Mali has persisted. It has made, according to Gallais, for a 'permeability' of the ethnic groups, which in turn facilitates a process of 'ethnic mutation' observed throughout the area, which I shall discuss below.[11]

The second major state-building tradition in the area is that of Songhai, which is eccentric both from the point of view of its own culture (with the centre located in Niger) and from that of historic Mali. But although Songhai provides an important alternative identity, which remains problematic from the contemporary point of view, it is linked with Mali by means of the bond of Islam. The Voltaic peoples and the Saharan nomads are more clearly eccentric from the point of view of the Malian core than the Songhai. Hence, Mali contains a very important ethnic core, in which ethnicity consists of more than a mere 'peace area'; but, since it is associated with a tradition of state-building, it approximates to the notion of a 'people'. All other groups must be defined in relation to this Malian people.

2. CULTURAL ASSIMILATION IN MALI AND SUPERTRIBALISM IN THE IVORY COAST

Although the data needed for a serious discussion of different patterns of social change in the Ivory Coast and Mali are not available, some of the contrasts are evident. In the Ivory Coast the major effect of cash-crop agriculture (cocoa, coffee) and its accompanying economic nexus was to make for fairly sharp divisions between different parts of the country, which coincided with distinct culture circles because these cash crops were spatially localised. In the mid-1950's, for example, *per capita* cash income derived from agriculture varied in the ratio of 6 to 1 between the richest and the poorest region of the country; in 1957, the average proportion of children of school age attending school varied in the ratio of nearly 9 to 1 between the highest and lowest ranking *cercles*.[12] There tended to develop, in a sense, poorer and richer tribes, differentiations which coincided with earlier distinctions between Northerners and Southerners, Easterners and Westerners. This pattern of modernisation also led to a great deal of migration by certain vanguard groups into rural areas outside their own ethnic region in search of land; a coincidence of cleavages, stemming from an economic situation (traditional landowners vs. renters; owners vs. hired labour) accompanied by ethnic differentiation, thus set the stage for deep antagonisms uninhibited by cross-cutting affiliations.

There is no equivalent of this situation in Mali. The absence of cash crops as valuable as cocoa and coffee, which foster the rapid growth of a distinction between 'planter' or 'farmer' and agricultural worker, together with the more general absence of dramatic economic development, has meant that a much larger proportion of the population is still primarily involved either in subsistence farming or animal

---

[11]Gallais, op. cit. p. 214. For the contributions of language to the reinforcement of this process, see Maurice Houis, 'Mouvements historiques et communautés linguistiques dans l'ouest africain', in *L'Homme*, I, 3, September–December 1961, pp. 72–92.

[12]See Zolberg, *op. cit.* pp. 23–48. On educational recruitment, see Rémi Clignet and Philip Foster, *The Fortunate Few* (Evanston, 1966).

husbandry—or, more accurately, in a very complex network of well-established agricultural and animal markets which are not orientated toward Europe. The general poverty of the country is also reflected in the low level of school attendance everywhere. Hence, the factors in the Ivory Coast which have made for additional differentiations stemming from modernisation are simply absent from the Malian scene. There are far fewer opportunities for the sort of sudden ethnic confrontation that is typical in many parts of the Ivory Coast. This means that there are at the same time fewer opportunities for the growth of the sort of 'transactional integration', discussed by Karl Deutsch, which is assumed to accompany modernisation, and less interference with pre-existing tendencies toward historic trends of integration into the Malian cultural core.[13]

The clearest locus for the observation of these divergent patterns is in the towns. In the Ivory Coast, they are on the whole very recent agglomerations which have been growing in a particular way by the constant accretion of individuals, from very diverse groups, who have come a fairly long distance, almost like the metropolitan immigrants of the United States. For example, the population of Abidjan in 1955 included only approximately 7 per cent of ethnic 'natives' (i.e. people belonging to the group in whose area the city had grown); approximately 11 per cent came from groups located in nearby areas (i.e. the *cercle* of which the city is a part), while 36 per cent came from areas in the Ivory Coast outside the *cercle*, and 46 per cent

from foreign countries. Bamako, in 1960, was about as large as Abidjan had been in 1955; but the descendants of the Bambara founding families and the later immigrants who shared their language and culture constituted 25.5 per cent of the population.[14] Although this was a substantial drop from the 47.5 per cent of Bambara noted in 1948, it is significant that the Bambara, together with the other groups associated with the founding of Bamako—the Malinke, the Fula, and the Sarakole—constituted about two-thirds of the population in 1960, approximately the same proportion of the total as in 1948. Hence Bamako remains a locus for the meeting of ethnic groups with a long tradition of association, while Abidjan is a place of abrupt confrontation between strangers. From these different situations have emerged divergent patterns of integration.

Every observer of the Ivory Coast scene has singled out the proliferation of urban voluntary associations based on ethnic links as a major phenomenon.[15] In the capital city in particular, where neighbourhoods are not ethnically homogeneous (possibly as the result of colonial controls over the process of settlement in the city), these organisations began to rise possibly as far back as the 1920's to provide substitutes for contiguity, and they continue to operate as the effective foci of social life. While it is true, as Wallerstein has observed, that many scattered ethnic identities were modified in the direction

---

[13] See especially Karl W. Deutsch, 'Social Mobilization and Political Development', reprinted in Eckstein and Apter, *op. cit.* pp. 582–603.

[14] The discussion of Bamako is based on data presented by Claude Meillassoux, 'The Social Structure of Modern Bamako', in *Africa* (London), 2 April 1965, pp. 125–42.

[15] The great significance of this phenomenon, which is of course not unique to the Ivory Coast, was first stressed for that country by an African observer. See F. Amon d'Aby, *La Côte d'Ivoire dans la cité africaine* (Paris, Larose, 1952), p. 36.

of amalgamation, as with the westerners referred to above, it is also true that the sheer enlargement of the population has facilitated the process of particularisation of some identities. In other words, people from diverse villages might find themselves to be 'Bété' in Abidjan; but as the number of Bété increases, it becomes possible to differentiate between different kinds of Bété. In the Ivory Coast, opportunities to move in the latter direction are usually seized upon. The 'tribe', which usually started out as a spatially contiguous group, is not dissolved by population movement; it is transformed into an ethnic group with rural and urban components, following a process which Jean Rouch has dubbed 'supertribalism'.[16]

In the older towns of Mali, which grew up over a long period as centres of African trade, craftsmanship, and regional political organisation, within the historic tradition discussed earlier, there is often a dominant ethnic group (or several groups viewed as co-founders) which sets the tone of the urban culture to which later immigrants and less prestigious groups are drawn. Immigrants often begin by living in a new, ethnically homogeneous neighbourhood; they sometimes have specialised occupations and are relatively endogamous. They are integrated into the town society by embracing certain habits of the more prestigious group,

such as dress, occupation, and the Islamic faith. If they already belong to one of the components of the Malian tradition, they tend to retain their ethnic identity; but it becomes overshadowed by a new one derived from the urban culture. If they belong to one of the peripheral, less prestigious groups they may abandon their original identity altogether by adopting a lineage name (*diamou*) from the dominant group, following a process which Gallais has called 'ethnic mutation'.[17] These phenomena are not limited to the towns. In rural areas, it has been observed that non-Muslim Voltaic peoples, for example, can 'become Marka' by adopting Islam. The town itself constitutes a focus of civilisation for the surrounding area. Hence, the tendency has been towards the amalgamation of diverse groups into regional societies centred on towns, in which ethnic ties becomes a subidentity and cultural assimilation occurs.

3. Pre-Independence Political Experiences

Both countries were subjected to a common colonial administrative system for about 75 years. Whether practices varied significantly between the two, or within either, has not yet been ascertained. Since the available studies of political change in the Ivory Coast and Mali have looked upon colonial institutions almost exclusively as sources of discontent within the framework of the study of nationalism, the role of these institutions from the point of view of national integration cannot be discussed, except for the obvious statement that they provided the new territorial focus that defines the very subject with which we are concerned.[18]

---

[16] J. Rouch, 'Migrations au Ghana', in *Journal de la société des africanistes* (Paris), XXVI, 1–2, 1956, pp. 163–4. Wallerstein has correctly pointed out the misleading implications of this term, since the group from which the individual is 'detribalised' is not necessarily the same as the one into which he is 'supertribalised'. But the term does have the advantage of pointing to a more specific phenomenon than 'ethnicity' and its usefulness should emerge from the discussion of Mali that follows.

[17] Gallais, *op. cit.*

[18] This statement is intended to be self-critical. Future studies might indicate that the

Political life in the Ivory Coast after World War II was dominated from the very beginning by the *Parti démocratique de la Côte d'Ivoire's* efforts to form a vast ethnic coalition on the basis of pre-existing ethnic associations reflecting the 'supertribalism' discussed in the preceding section.[19] Much of the post-war political history can be understood in terms of the process of fragmentation and recombination of this coalition. Benefiting initially from its advantage as the first political organiser, the P.D.C.I. faltered once the extension of political participation, together with the natural interests of competing political entrepreneurs, often acting with the encouragement and support of the French colonial administration, led to the appearance of new political organisations which challenged the P.D.-C.I. by appealing to separate ethnic identities. But this very process of ethnic reaction-formation prevented the P.D.C.I.'s opponents from coalescing into a stable alternative ethnic coalition, thus ultimately facilitating the P.D.-

---

colonial system, based on notions of territoriality, was more congruent with pre-existing modes of governmental organisation in Mali than in the Ivory Coast, and hence constituted less of a stress upon the former system than upon the latter. This may account in part for the sense of political continuity one encounters in Mali, and the greater ability of Malians to give an indigenous flavour to an imported administrative system. In the Ivory Coast, the administration appears much more artificial and contrived, French rather than African, even after recruitment was Africanised.

[19] The main sources for Ivory Coast politics are Ruth Schachter Morgenthau, *Political Parties in French-Speaking West Africa* (Oxford, 1964), I. Wallerstein, *The Road to Independence: Ghana and the Ivory Coast* (The Hague, 1964), and Zolberg, *op. cit.* For details of the ethnic coalition, see Aristide R. Zolberg, 'Mass Parties and National Integration: the case of the Ivory Coast', in *The Journal of Politics* (Gainesville), xxv, 1, February 1963, pp. 36–48.

C.I.'s recovery. Therefore, the construction of a monopolistic political organisation between 1952 and 1959 was based on the techniques of machine politics. The P.D.C.I. secured support by co-opting ethnic leaders into the organisation by means of a major distributive effort, itself made possible by the sheer accident of prosperity stemming from high prices for tropical commodities during and immediately after the Korean War, a prosperity which was later bolstered by protectionist props extended by France towards its show-case colony. More often than not, these techniques enabled the leadership group to overcome the permanent ethnic tensions which sometimes erupted into violent, but necessarily localised, conflagrations in certain parts of the country. As the centre grew stronger, it was able to solve remaining problems by repression when co-option failed, as in the case of the Agni of Sanwi. Although there was little stress on formal party organisation, partly in order to create a businesslike image attractive to foreign investors, the party remained very effective from the point of view of its own organisational needs. The entire system of political communication between the centre and the localities took the form of ethnic channels, through official representatives such as members of the Territorial (later National) Assembly, or other forms of ethnic clientship. The territorial system was replicated, in a microcosm, at the local level. The manner in which the system worked may perhaps be symbolised by the fact that a few years ago, for example, the Bété concerned with school problems in their region went to Abidjan to see, not the Minister of Education, who was from the Southeast, but the Minister of Agriculture, who was a Bété.

In Mali, during the equivalent period, there developed a significantly different process.[20] For 10 years from 1945, there were two main poles of organisation, led by men of typically ambiguous ethnic status. Initially, the *Union soudanaise* (U.S.) built around Mamadou Konaté obtained considerable support among Malinké residents of Bamako as well as in the Malinké heartland and in Sikasso. The *Parti progressiste soudanais* (oddly referred to as P.S.P.), seemed to grow especially in the Marka (Sarakollé) communities of Bamako and elsewhere, as well as among animist populations such as the Bambara and the Minianka. The U.S. soon lined up its more purely Malian base with Songhai by making an alliance with politicians in Timbuktu and Gao, while the P.S.P., perhaps in an effort to build a sort of anti-Mali coalition, linked up with the Fulani of Macina. Smaller groups, such as the Dogon and the group constituted by the regional society of Kayes, were courted by both parties and changed their allegiances repeatedly, while the Sahara nomads never really became involved in the mainstream of political life.

Although the later success of the U.S. must be attributed in part to its better sense of organisation, the dominant factor appears to have been the congruence of its efforts with the integrative tradition of statebuilding by means of cultural assimilation that prevails in the core area of the Western Sudan. Although the party also relied on machine-like techniques such as distribution of offices to supporters, the absence of economic prosperity necessarily limited the organisation's capability in this respect. And although one can detect a concern with 'ethnic arithmetic' in Mali as well as in the Ivory Coast, the integers differ from the ones typical of the Ivory Coast. They refer to regional factions which are themselves not supertribal associations in the Ivory Coast sense, but rather segments of communities which have already undergone the processes of assimilation referred to earlier.[21] It is significant, in this respect, that the political crises which occurred in the later 1950's, when it become clear that the game of politics was being played for keeps, usually involved not whole ethnic groups, but rather conflicts such as the one between the ethnically heterogeneous supporters of two successive Bambara dynasties, the Coulibaly and the Diarra, for control of Segou and its surrounding region. The clearest example of political conflict based on ethnic identity more narrowly defined is the protracted struggle between Negro Malians, as a whole, and the 'White' Saharan nomads. But this is the exception which confirms the rule, and it is based on the eccentric position of the nomads in relation to the Malian culture.

Because in Mali the historical region, usually centred on a town such as Segou, Timbuktu, Mopti, or Kita, is at least as significant for the purpose of

---

[20]The main sources currently available on Malian politics are Morgenthau, *op. cit.*; Thomas Hodgkin and Morgenthau, 'Mali', in James S. Coleman and Carl Rosberg, Jr. (eds.), *Political Parties and National Integration in Tropical Africa* (Berkeley and Los Angeles, 1964), pp. 216–58; and Frank Snyder, *One Party Government in Mali* (New Haven, 1965). See also Aristide R. Zolberg, 'Political Revival in Mali', in *Africa Report* (Washington), x, 7, July 1965, pp. 15–20.

[21]A careful examination of this process is presented in Nicholas Hopkins, 'Government in Kita: structure and process in a Malian town', unpublished dissertation, Department of Anthropology, University of Chicago (1967). I am grateful to Dr Hopkins for his useful analytic suggestions concerning Mali.

secondary identification beyond the primary kinship link as the ethnic group in its general sense, the growth of the one-party state has tended to take on the appearance of a confederacy of regions represented by ambassadors at the centre. In the Ivory Coast —where regions do not have the same character and the relevant secondary identification is the tribe, extended through the phenomenon of super-tribalism—the ethnic group, in the urban sense discussed by Wallerstein, is the most important mediating link between the centre and the parts.

In both cases this is symbolised by the nature of party organisation in the capital city. In Bamako the *Union soudanaise* is organised into 11 branches, based on wards which were once but are no longer ethnically homogeneous: the city constitutes a microcosm of regions, and most political life is conducted on a territorial basis in these neighbourhoods. In Abidjan, the activities of the P.D.C.I. are based on over 100 ethnic committees and sub-committees. Despite repeated resolutions to modify this system because it is viewed as unmodern and incongruous, the committees not only continue to exist, but the process of constant discovery of hitherto submerged ethnic identities goes on as well.[22] As a microcosm, the city reflects the fact that political life in the Ivory Coast is not really based on territory, since the individuals who participate in the life of the committees live all over the city and are brought together not as neighbours but as tribesmen. Since these capitals are not only microcosms in the figurative sense, but account for a large part of the total political activity of the country and are the places where models of integration are most visible to leaders and followers, the contrast is fundamental.

4. CONTEMPORARY APPROACHES TO NATIONAL INTEGRATION

Although nationalist movements view themselves as 'the nation in a state of becoming' and derive their claim to legitimacy from this view, it is really only after independence that the problem of national integration comes to be posed in its most acute form. It is not by accident that almost every African political leader has exclaimed in dismay, on the morning after independence, that the nation now appears to be less united that it was when the first wave of political action was launched during the colonial period. The very words used, 'nation-building', 'la construction nationale', suggest a prevalent feeling that the edifice is far from completed, but also that the new rulers have a particular attitude to the problem: a nation does not merely happen as the result of historical forces; it does not merely entail a liberation from oppression or from the cocoon of a false identity. It must be designed and the plan must be executed. This takes precedence over all other tasks, including economic development. Although the latter goal has usually been assigned a very high priority, typical economic policies often do not make sense except as economic means to political integration.[23] The search for a plan, programme, map, or political formula requires analysis at the cultural or ideological level; its execution

---

[22] See, for example, the incident reported in Zolberg, 'Mass Parties and National Integration'.

[23] See Aristide R. Zolberg, 'The Political Use of Economic Planning in Mali', in Harry Johnson (ed.), *Economic Nationalism in Old and New States* (Chicago, 1967).

in the face of a given situation requires analysis at the structural level.[24] It is out of the interplay between these two levels of action that the crucial problems of integration emerge and that our analysis can best grasp its essence.

The Ivory Coast and Mali share with other party-states of West Africa a characteristic approach to national integration, which involves, at the ideological level, a Jacobin-like definition of national unity as 'political oneness', i.e. the elimination of the political manifestations of social cleavages. Much of this is already so familiar to social scientists dealing with Africa that there is little need to repeat it in detail here.[25] Concerning ideology, however, it may be useful to note that, despite the vast amount of scholarly activity devoted to analysing the political thought of the new African leaders, our understanding is incomplete because the tendency has been to use the concept in its narrower sense, i.e. in reference to manifest statements of political thought expressing a fairly high level of complexity in the European tradition. One of the consequences of this approach has been that observers have sometimes concluded that a country like the Ivory Coast has no ideology. Since this is tantamount to saying that its leaders have no idea (literally) of where they are going, the absurdity of such statements is fairly

obvious. True, there are differences in the style of presentation of political ideas between the Ivory Coast and Mali, and these stylistic differences may have important consequences; but 'ideology' cannot be an all-or-nothing category of analysis.

Furthermore, because it may be assumed that the most significant ideological statements made in Africa are addressed to African audiences and because very few leaders are inclined toward the more reflective life, our reconstruction of the ideology of a given country must proceed from the analysis of many occasional statements delivered verbally at meetings or over the radio rather than from organised treatises. Finally, 'ideology' must be reconstructed from acts themselves; for example, both Mali and the Ivory Coast have formally eliminated from their National Assemblies the geographical basis of representation, thus modifying a political tradition stemming from several centuries of western experience and maintained even in the Soviet Union, without the sort of extended debate on representation which would accompany such a move elsewhere. At one level, this can be taken merely as a clever device to undermine the opposition; but at another, it represents a fundamental statement of the image which the present-day rulers are trying to create of 'the Nation'. It is a symbolic manipulation of reality which tells us more than many speeches.

At the structural level, both countries have attempted to transform the party and the governmental apparatus into reliable instruments of the rulers' ideological purpose. Here also there is a fundamental similarity of approach but with some important differences of emphasis due in part to contingencies encountered at the crucial time of

---

[24] The significance of the ideological level is stressed by Clifford Geertz, 'Ideology as a Cultural System', in David E. Apter (ed.), *Ideology and Discontent* (New York, 1964), pp. 47–76; and by Leonard Binder, 'National Integration and Political Development', in *The American Political Science Review* (Washington, D.C.), LVIII, 3, September 1964, pp. 614–31.

[25] See, for example, Aristide R. Zolberg, *Creating Political Order: the party states of West Africa* (Chicago, 1966), ch. II, and the literature cited therein.

political take-over. Mali and the Ivory Coast have retained the 'mass party' design which characterised the nationalist phase, and the prefectorial administrative hierarchy, which stresses representation of the state at all levels, inherited from the colonial period. Initially, the relationship between these two instruments was weighted in favour of the party in Mali and in favour of the administration in the Ivory Coast; but the modifications that have occurred in both countries in recent years suggest a movement toward a common middle. Since 1962, the Malians have made a great effort to improve the quality of their administrative cadre and to endow this bureaucracy with a legitimacy from which effective authority will stem; after a deep crisis of the party between 1959 and 1963, the Ivory Coast leadership devoted much to a revival of the party as a controlling mechanism.

To what extent these respective parties and governmental bureaucracies function as effective integrative structures, it is difficult to say. Briefly, it is likely that the functions of parties in this respect have been overestimated, while the functions of the state apparatus have been underestimated. The parties have not transformed society, but rather, by incorporating existing structures such as ethnic associations in the Ivory Coast and regional coalitions in Mali into their own organisation, they have reinforced these patterns, endowed them with a renewed legitimacy, and provided a broader frame of reference for their operations. On the other hand, the state apparatus constitutes a field of operation for an occupational group which has internalised to a greater extent than any other a sense of territorial community. It is quite evident from recent events in

Ghana and elsewhere that state bureaucracies have greater resilience than even the most spectacular mass parties.

In both cases, the two institutions have been formally equalised by means of the creation of a sort of national super-parliament convened at the request of the President—who himself stands at the pinnacle of both hierarchies—whenever necessary. The creation of a sort of Estates-General of Mali or of the Ivory Coast, to which are called not only all party officials and members of the government cadre, but also leaders of recognised associations (labour unions, women, youth, veterans) other notabilities (such as religious or community leaders in Mali, and businessmen as well as leaders of ethnic associations and even some chiefs in the Ivory Coast), is significant at both levels of analysis discussed earlier. It provides some valuable clues to the categories of differentiation that are approved as part of 'the Nation'; and it also tells us something about the structural mechanisms that are in the process of being institutionalised to promote nation-building.

It is possible, however, that the similarities discussed above mask the emergence of profound differences of purpose and of ultimate orientation. These differences stem from all the factors discussed earlier in this essay, with the addition of the very disparate means available to the respective ruling groups for the pursuit of their national goals.

In the Ivory Coast, where economic development and its concomitants, including education, are progressing at a remarkable rate partly as the result of colonial circumstances but also because of choices made by the rulers, one senses that the founders are gambling on the beneficial effects of transactional integration, in the Deutschian sense, i.e. the social mobilisation of the population into a national community as the result of predominantly non-political factors. The one-party state enables the founders to hold politics in abeyance, almost in a Gaullist sense, while these processes are allowed to develop. Ivoriens continue to have little faith in their ability to derive integrative ideas and mechanisms from the givens of their own traditions; hence, super-tribalism continues to be the basis of political management, approaching a form of non-territorial federalism of ethnic segments, while the search for integration is oriented towards the creation of a new Franco-African culture, into which the population must be assimilated as rapidly as possible. References to African traditions are rare; when symbols of this sort are used, they are often of European invention and strike the observer as artificial. This orientation helps to explain the peculiar sense that many observers have of the Ivory Coast as a *nouveau-riche*, upwardly mobile, other-directed, brazenly modern country, with little ideological romanticism.

The contrast is very great in Mali, a country initially so poor from the point of view of a modern economy and so unlikely to make much economic progress that non-political factors cannot be relied upon to bring about the great integrative transformation. Here, the integrative culture stresses a territorial federalism combining the great regional traditions of the ancient Sudanic states, Mali and Songhai, as well as the lesser urban traditions of the old cities, all connected by Islam, and reinterpreted to fit into a Marxist-Leninist linguistic mould. This cultural identity, symbolised by the very choice of the country's name and by

the slogans about the rebirth of Mali which were created during the crisis of independence, is fully compatible and continuous with the process of assimilation of eccentric peoples into the core culture of the area and its regional sub-cultures.

Although French is taught in Mali's schools and the country is developing a modern apparatus of training institutions, through which a new occupational stratification is being institutionalised, the process of assimilation into a sort of generalised urban African culture takes place at the uppermost levels of the new stratification system as well. For most civil servants in Mali, from the highest to the lowest levels, Islam is becoming a civic religion and 'Bambara' a national language. The Malian party-state is the contemporary avatar of an older polity which defines the very order of society itself. Not being able to modernise, Mali may well be striving for a form of integration that is not western, on the basis of an ideology which places faith and righteousness above material welfare. Paradoxically, the Ivory Coast, which is often viewed as a 'conservative' country, justifies the present in terms of the future; Mali, the 'revolutionary' country, justifies it in terms of continuity with the past.[26]

---

[26]In mid-1967, the Political Bureau of the *Union soudanaise* was disbanded and the National Committee for the Defence of the Revolution, created in 1966 and headed by President Keita, asserted its authority over both party and Government. Similar changes appear to have been implemented at the local level. A tentative interpretation of these events is that they constitute a response to 'leftist' pressures, themselves stimulated by a 'rightist' reorientation of economic policy at the beginning of the year. More fundamentally, however, this constitutes another step in the direction of undifferentiated authority structures inherited from the colonial period.

CONCLUSIONS

Although the view persists that national integration consists of a zero-sum game between fixed and mutually exclusive 'traditional' and 'modern' identities, whose content can be easily defined, social scientists have begun to develop a more mature view of the subject. In the African context, for example, Mercier has pointed out that in most countries 'tribal nationalisms' are usually less concerned with the rejection of the political framework constituted by the territory than with searching for equilibrium inside the system.[27] Wallerstein has stressed even more forcefully that competition among ethnic groups (i.e. the urban phenomenon) is not necessarily dysfunctional from the point of view of national integration, since 'in rejecting the men they implicitly accept the system. Ethnic rivalries become rivalries for political power in a non-tribal setting.'[28] Crawford Young, writing on the Congo, has reminded us that there is nothing inherently 'backward' about cultural self-assertion and that 'ethnic loyalty in itself is a natural and indeed a necessary phenomenon; psychological liberation requires pride in one's antecedents and the Congolese has an ethnic identity as well as a Congolese and African self.'[29] The new level of understanding of the complex relationships between ethnicity and national integration is denoted by Geertz's remark that 'The integrative revolution does not do away with ethnocentrism; it merely modernizes it.'[30]

The brief overview of Mali and the Ivory Coast presented in this article has indicated how the primordial 'givens'—social and economic changes stimulated by various factors during the colonial period, as well as the ideologies and organisational activities of the new ruling élites and the resources available to them—are elements which contribute to the formation of distinct incipient patterns of national integration. These patterns do not exhaust the range of possibilities, even within the African continent, but merely illustrate the manner in which maps might be drawn. As we learn more about which features of the landscape must be included in our maps, we shall also be able to achieve much greater precision about those features that are relevant.

Whether the processes that are occurring in the two countries discussed or elsewhere on the continent will result in the relatively near future in a kind of societal and political wholeness, which we can recognise as a form of 'national integration', cannot seriously be foretold. The Ivory Coast and Mali have already moved farther along this difficult path than many African countries which have encountered insuperable obstacles in the processes of integration, or than others—much less dramatic cases—where the obstacles are not even visible because the processes have barely been launched. In pursuing our efforts to understand the problems of national integration, however, we must remember that the path on which most new states travel is so narrow and arduoos that progress can be interrupted or even reversed. The processes that are occurring need not

[27] Mercier, *op. cit.*
[28] Wallerstein, in Eckstein and Apter, *op. cit.* p. 668.
[29] Crawford Young, *Politics in the Congo* (Princeton, 1965), p. 271.
[30] Geertz, 'The Integrative Revolution', p. 154. See also Suzanne Bouzon, 'Modernisation et conflits tribaux en Afrique noir', in *Revue francaise de science politique* (Paris), XVII, 5, October 1967, pp. 862–88.

necessarily lead to successful outcomes; and it is perfectly possible in the contemporary world for countries to persist as political units even though they are poorly integrated.[31]

Finally, we must also free ourselves from the fixed point of view provided by our own recent historical experience of the 'nation' as the avatar of the integrated society. It is true that the nation provides a universal model employed by the politically conscious strata of almost all countries of Asia and Africa. But it is equally true that this model is a very general one, much like the other leading components of the definition of modernity they use, democracy and socialism. The concept of the nation today encompasses a range of meanings even broader than that which emerged in the course of European history, as traced by numerous historians. Furthermore, whatever the model of the nation may be when it is first translated into an ideology designed to guide a new country's faltering steps toward the future, it must necessarily undergo many modifications as the future becomes the present. When and if the word becomes

flesh, it may differ so much from any previously existing political entities that we shall have to stretch the referents of our definition of the nation as a set of political arrangements, or invent a new word altogether.

All these uncertainties about the past, the present, and the future, which are at the root of out discomfort with the concept 'national integration', also ultimately give the utmost relevance to our concern with the subject to which the concept refers. Many current analytic schemes attempt to overcome these uncertainties by rising to a very high level of generalisation, from whence the past, the present, and the future appear to be clearly visible. The largely inductive comparative strategy illustrated here, which moves from the identification of patterns to the construction of more elaborate typologies, takes these uncertainties in its stride. As Geertz has put it, 'It is by watching the integrative revolution happen that we shall understand it. This may seem like a mere wait-and-see policy, inappropriate to the predictive ambitions of science. But such a policy is at least preferable, and more scientific, to waiting and not seeing, which has been largely the case to date'.[32]

---

[31]I have discussed these issues in greater detail in 'A View from the Congo', in *World Politics* (Princeton), October 1966; and in 'The Structure of Political Conflict in Tropical Africa', in *The American Political Science Review*, forthcoming, 1968.

---

[32]Geertz, 'The Integrative Revolution', p. 167.

Potential Elites in Ghana and the Ivory Coast: A Preliminary Comparison

Remi P. Clignet and Philip Foster

Abstract. This study examines patterns of social recruitment in two highly selective systems of secondary education in two adjoining African states with differing colonial and educational traditions. Marked differentials occur between two groups of sampled students of roughly equivalent academic status in the two areas. Ghanaian students are uniformly drawn from higher socio-economic groups than their Ivory Coast counterparts. However, in relation to population characteristics the two systems appear to function in a similar manner. Furthermore, both groups are characterized by a considerable degree of uniformity concerning career aspirations, expectations, and perceptions of future roles.

In spite of a growing body of literature dealing with the emergent elites of the new African states, it must be confessed that we know very little about them. There is sometimes a tendency to speak of them as if they were homogeneous in character; yet much material concerning their social origins, their aspirations, and their value orientations remains extraordinarily impressionistic.

Further, the term "elite," although frequently used, is very ambiguous. An elite may be defined in terms of its common possession of a single attribute or set of objective attributes. Thus, in the African context, we could regard as members of an elite all individuals who have achieved a given minimal level of education or income or who are engaged in particular occupations. This definition has shortcomings if we are concerned with elites in terms of their decision-making abilities (political or otherwise) or their capacity to act as generalized reference groups for the remainder of the population.[1] Thus, in the following pages, when we examine the characteristics of two samples of secondary-school students in the Ivory Coast and Ghana, we shall treat them as "potential elites." Their schooling provides a necessary, but not sufficient, qualification for them to assume key positions in their societies.

In most contemporary African states, employment opportunities within the modern economic sector are dominated by the demands of government and other public agencies. This bureaucratization of the employment structure confers a high premium upon educational qualifications (usually as mea-

[1] For example, if education is used as the criterion of elite membership, it is clear that the two groups of students we compare below constitute part of the national elite. They certainly fall well within the top 1 per cent of the population in level of schooling. However, we do know that a substantial proportion of these groups will enter primary-school teaching or low-grade clerical work. Neither of these two occupations enjoys very high prestige or status within either country.

From *American Journal of Sociology,* Vol. LXX, No. 3 (November 1964), 349–362, by permission of the authors and the publisher, The University of Chicago Press. (Copyright 1964 by the University of Chicago Press.)

sured by examination success) for access to elite roles. Recruitment policies of the larger firms in the private sector also present the same characteristics.

Furthermore, in many areas, explosive rates of growth in the output of the schools are associated with a very sluggish development of job opportunities in this modern sector. This has very rapidly raised the minimal educational qualifications necessary to enter most occupations. Thus, a post-primary education becomes a critical factor in occupational success, and in no country in Africa south of the Sahara do more than 2 per cent of any age cohort enter any form of secondary institution.[2] We therefore feel justified in regarding African secondary schools as "elite reservoirs" whose graduates will fill most positions of power and authority in the next few decades. A crucial problem of research is, therefore, to examine the social composition of secondary-school populations and to ascertain to what extent recruitment patterns are fluid or constricted.

A second step is to analyze how this recruitment function is affected by the residue of colonial experience. For example, although a great deal has been written about differences between French and British colonial policies, no empirical evidence exists with respect to contrasts in processes of elite selection within areas formerly governed by the two colonial powers. We have, therefore, attempted to compare the characteristics of a sample of secondary-school students in Ghana, an ex-British territory, with those of a similar group of students in the formerly French Ivory Coast. These countries

provide a good opportunity for controlled comparison insofar as they are largely similar in terms of a whole range of characteristics but differ with respect to certain key variables.[3]

SOME COMPARISONS BETWEEN GHANA AND THE IVORY COAST

First, there are substantial similarities in the economies of Ghana and the Ivory Coast.[4] Although the latter is rather the less developed of the two, both countries rank highest in income per capita among the nations of West Africa, with a level of between $150 and $200 per annum. The comparative prosperity of the two states is, in large measure, attributable to an extensive development of profitable cash crops in the southern and central portions of the respective territories. The occupational structure of both countries is relatively more complex than those of other West African states (with the possible exception of Senegal).

These over-all economic similarities are reinforced by the fact that the pattern of sociocultural change in both areas has followed similar lines. European penetration was initially effected from the coastal zone with the gradual incorporation of other traditional groupings in the central and northern areas at a later date. Thus maximal change has occurred in the southern

[2] Clearly, we refer here to the African population only and exclude the Union of South Africa, where levels of education among Africans are considerably higher than for the rest of the continent.

[3] The particular appropriateness of Ghana and the Ivory Coast for a comparison of this type has already been noted by R. J. Harrison Church, *West Africa: A Study of the Environment and of Man's Use of It* (3d ed.; London: Longmans, Green, & Co., 1961), p. 344.

[4] The best general sources for the background of the two areas are, for Ghana: D. E. Apter, *The Gold Coast in Transition* (Princeton, N.J.: Princeton University Press, 1955); and for the Ivory Coast: Ministère des Finances des Affaires Economiques et du Plan Service de la Statistique, *Inventaire économique et social de la Côte d'Ivoire* (Abidjan: 1960).

and central areas of both nations; and it is in these that the exchange economy is most developed, processes of urbanization most advanced, and formal education most in evidence. In contrast, the populous northern areas are, in both cases, far less developed, with a greater emphasis on subsistence farming, lower levels of urbanization, and a more limited diffusion of formal education. Both territories are divided into a largely Christian south and a predominantly Islamic north.

There are equally striking similarities in terms of ethnic composition. Since these nations are adjacent to each other, the Akan peoples of southern and central Ghana are closely related to the Anyi and Baoule groups of the southeastern and central Ivory Coast. Further, the Ewe of Ghana and the Kru groups of the Ivory Coast, though belonging to different ethnic clusters, do manifest substantial similarities in their pattern of social organization and stand in similar relationship to the Akan peoples of both areas. Last, some of the Voltaic peoples of northern Ghana are represented in the Ivory Coast, and there are parallels between their culture and that of the nuclear and peripheral Mande of the latter nation.

Given these substantial similarities between the two countries, we must now indicate in what respects they diverge. Clearly, their patterns of administration were and are rather different. Traditionally, the French tended to develop a system of direct and internally centralized administration which was, in turn, closely integrated with their West African Federation and the metropole itself. Conversely, the British relied to a greater extent on indirect rule (particularly in Ashanti and the northern areas) and developed a less centralized pattern of administration which also deemphasized

the direct links between Ghana, the other areas of British West Africa, and the metropole.

More important, although the pattern of French penetration in the Ivory Coast substantially paralleled British expansion in Ghana, it always lagged behind it. Thus, by the end of the nineteenth century, the British had effectively incorporated most of the territories that now constitute contemporary Ghana, and in the southern zone, in particular, the European impact was already considerable. By contrast, the French were not able to establish effective administration in some areas until after the close of the first World War.

THE SCHOOL SYSTEMS

Since educational diffusion is a corollary of European overrule, it is clear that this "staggered" development of the two areas had considerable implications for the growth of their educational systems. By 1950, Ghana, with a population of roughly 5 million, had 281,000 individuals enrolled in formal schools at all levels, while the Ivory Coast, with an estimated population of 3.2 million, could point to only 35,000 persons enrolled. During the last decade the difference at the primary-school level has been closing, owing to massive investment by the government of the Ivory Coast in primary education.[5] However, at the secondary-school stage the contrast between the countries remains formidable and needs further examination.

The school system in the Ivory Coast

---

[5] This is not to suggest that primary-school expansion in Ghana has been negligible. On the contrary, it has been substantial, but the maximum growth rate has now been passed and the system continues to grow at a slower pace.

consists of a six-year primary sequence followed by a highly differentiated system of secondary studies. In 1963 there were a little under 300,000 students in primary schools compared with less than 20,000 in all kinds of post-primary institutions. These post-primary schools vary greatly in prestige, ranging from Centres d'Apprentissage offering a four-year terminal program of vocational training to the academic and technical Lycées which provide access to university studies. It is the latter group of institutions which concerns us here, since they are the crucial segment of the whole system so far as processes of elite formation are concerned.

The Ghanaian system is much larger. By 1960, there were already 512,000 pupils in the six-year primary schools and, most strikingly, no less than 225,000 in all types of post-primary education. The vast majority of the latter were in so-called middle schools: these provided a terminal four-year sequence for most pupils but also acted as feeder institutions to a small group of highly selective public secondary schools which offered a five-year course.[6] In 1960 there were over 14,000 students in these latter institutions which are, in fact, generally comparable to the Lycées and Collèges of the Ivory Coast. It is clear, therefore, that a comparison of potential elites in the two nations can be most effectively made by contrasting Ghanaian secondary-school students with their

counterparts in the Lycées of the Ivory Coast.

However, this ignores the crucial problem of obtaining comparable groups when the cycle of secondary studies is so different. With this in mind, it was decided to compare Ghanaian pupils in the final year of their five-year basic secondary course with Ivory Coast Lycée students preparing the first part of their *Baccalauréat* examination.[7] This constitutes a crucial cutoff point in both systems. In Ghana, approximately 60 per cent of the students successfully pass the General School Certificate examination at the end of five years, but of these successful candidates, only about one-third enter the sixth forms which prepare directly for the university. In the Ivory Coast, just under 40 per cent of the candidates pass the first *Baccalauréat* successfully at the first attempt and enter for the one-year course preparing for the second *Baccalauréat*, which is preparatory to university study and is thus roughly similar to the Ghanaian sixth form.

The two samples discussed in the following pages are, therefore, very comparable in terms of level of study and type of school and were drawn as follows.[8] The Ghanaian sample, con-

---

[6] This figure excludes some 6,000 pupils enrolled in private secondary schools in Ghana. However, these institutions are, for the most part, at such a low level that they are usually more comparable to middle schools. It is noteworthy, also, that public secondary schools in Ghana are not, for the most part, "government" schools but are institutions often founded by voluntary agencies but now overwhelmingly aided from government funds.

[7] Generally, the curriculum at this level in both systems is not highly specialized, though there is more "streaming" by subject groups in the Ivory Coast.

[8] In 1961, Ghana had forty-six secondary schools with fifth-form classes. The twenty-three schools selected for investigation were randomly drawn from this list stratified by region, type, and size. In the case of the Ivory Coast, the smaller size of the system made it possible to attempt a total coverage at the *Baccalauréat* level. However, 18 per cent of students were not reached, owing to temporary absence from classes. Girls were excluded from this comparison in view of their small number at this level in the Ivory Coast. Also, since their backgrounds are very different

sisting of 775 fifth-form boys drawn in 1961 from twenty-three secondary institutions, constituted just over 45 per cent of the entire male fifth-form population in the secondary schools at that time. Correspondingly, the Ivory Coast sample of male students sitting for the first part of the *Baccalauréat* was drawn in 1963 from the eight institutions which prepare for this examination. The sample comprised 259 cases or 82 per cent of all pupils at this educational level in the Ivory Coast.[9] At this stage the Ghanaian system contains over five times as many students as that of the Ivory Coast.

This suggests that the two systems can only be contrasted not in terms of two colonial prototypes but also in terms of their relative level of growth and "maturity."

Social Background of Potential Elites

We must first consider the ethnic characteristics of these two groups of students. This is no idle academic problem in the context of contemporary African politics. With the advent of

---

from those of boys, they certainly would have distorted the picture as far as Ghana is concerned.

[9] In practice, Ghanaian students have completed anywhere between thirteen and fifteen years of education before reaching the fifth-form level. This is because selection for secondary school can be from any one of the middle-school years. Conversely, the Ivory Coast students have theoretically completed twelve years of education. Therefore, we might expect the latter group to be younger than the Ghanaians. In fact, the reverse is the case. Ivory Coast students average 20.3 years of age and Ghanaian students, 19.2. This is due to the far greater incidence of doubling classes in the Ivory Coast system (47 per cent of the sample had doubled one or several previous classes) and the fact that children probably start schooling later than in Ghana.

independence, ethnic minorities increasingly demand equal access to key institutions in the new states. In particular, they claim that they have obtained less than their "fair share" of crucial roles, owing to their lack of opportunities to obtain school places.[10] In both Ghana and the Ivory Coast, such inequalities in educational provision have been very evident.

Table 1 illustrates the pattern of differential ethnic recruitment into secondary schools in the two areas. To simplify the picture, we have divided both nations into three general ethnic zones (southern, central, and northern) and classified the numerous groups into one or the other of these categories. Further, to facilitate comparison, we have provided crude selectivity indexes by computing the ratio between a group's representation in the general population and its representation in the sample.

It might have been expected that in the smaller and less-established system of the Ivory Coast, inequalities in ethnic access between north and south would be more marked. In fact, this is only partially true. To be sure, in Ghana, the variations between the southern and central groupings which were substantial at all levels of education up to 1945 seem to have been largely eradicated, while in the Ivory Coast they are still very apparent. In this context it is important to note that the central portion of Ghana includes the major cocoa-producing areas and constitutes the economic heartland of the nation. The gap between economic development of southern and central Ghana is proportionally less than that

---

[10] For Ghana, this point is discussed more fully in Philip Foster, "Ethnicity and the Schools in Ghana," *Comparative Education Review*, VI (October, 1962), 127–35.

TABLE 1

Ethnic Background of Sampled Students in Relation to Ethnic Characteristics of Populations of Ivory Coast and Ghana

Ethnic Groups	Ivory Coast			Ghana		
	% of Population*	% of Sample	Selectivity Ratio	% of Population†	% of Sample	Selectivity Ratio
Southern	31.2	50.5 (131)	1.6	47.0	64.2 (498)	1.4
Central	30.2	21.3 (55)	0.7	20.7	28.2 (218)	1.4
Northern	34.2	20.5 (53)	0.6	30.7	6.3 (49)	0.2
Other	4.4	6.2 (16)	1.4	1.6	1.2 (9)	0.8
No answer		1.5 (4)			0.1 (1)	
total	100.0	100.0 (259)		100.0	100.0 (775)	

*Computed from Ivory Coast, Ministère du Plan, *Inventaire économique de la Côte d'Ivoire, 1947–1956* (Abidjan, 1958), p. 26.
†Computed from Gold Coast, *Census of Population, 1948* (Accra, 1950), pp. 367–69. These figures are not entirely reliable and no data are yet available from the 1960 census concerning the present ethnic composition of the population.

between the corresponding zones of the Ivory Coast. Though the northern areas of both countries are very similar in their level of development, northern Ghanaians are far less successful in getting into post-primary education of this type than are their Ivory Coast counterparts. This is in spite of the fact that the far greater size and maturity of the Ghanaian educational system might have led us to expect a greater access of northern groups into the secondary schools. Not only are there proportionally more places available in Ghanaian secondary institutions but these places are geographically more diffused throughout the country. This suggests that the growth of an educational system does not quickly even up ethnic inequalities.

There has historically been a close relationship in Africa between the growth of the schools and the development of towns; it was usually within urban centers that a demand for formal schooling was first manifest. The growth of an exchange economy and the development of new Western-type occupations, access to which was often dependent on formal educational qualifications, stimulated an early desire for education. Moreover, urban children tended to adjust more rapidly to the requirements of the schools. Both Ghana and the Ivory Coast have, therefore, long been faced by persistent and sharp differentials between urban and rural levels of primary schooling. It is interesting to examine these differentials at the secondary-school level (Table 2). This table indicates the nature of this relationship in the two

TABLE 2

Background of Sampled Students in Relation to Size of Birthplace and Present Residence

Population of Town or Village	Distribution of Ivory Coast Population*	Birthplace of Sampled Students	Selectivity Ratio	Present Residence of Sampled Students	Selectivity Ratio	Distribution of Ghanaian Population†	Birthplace of Sampled Students	Selectivity Ratio	Present Residence of Sampled Students	Selectivity Ratio
Below 5,000	82.3	62.5	0.8	48.6	0.6	77.0	38.1	0.5	26.8	0.3
5,000–9,999	4.3	11.6	2.7	12.4	2.9	6.0	14.3	2.4	12.1	2.0
10,000–49,999	3.7	10.8	2.9	13.9	3.8	9.3	24.4	2.6	26.7	2.9
Above 50,000	9.7	7.3	0.8	20.8	2.1	7.7	19.4	2.5	33.3	4.3
Not born in or not resident in Ivory Coast or Ghana		6.9		3.1			3.5		0.6	
No answer		0.8		1.2			0.3		0.5	
total	100.0	99.9		100.0		100.0	100.0		100.0	

*Computed from Ivory Coast, Ministère du Plan, *Inventaire économique de la Côte d'Ivoire, 1947–58* (Abidjan, 1960), p. 37.
†Computed from Ghana, *Population Census, 1960*, Advance Report of Vols. III and IV.

territories, using the rather crude measure of community size as an index of urbanization. We also have attempted to show an almost identical degree of drift of the students in both samples from the smaller villages to the very largest towns.[11]

It is clear that Ghanaian students come from a more urban background in terms of both birth and residence than do their Ivory Coast counterparts. This is understandable enough in view of the rather higher levels of urbanization in Ghana as a whole. However, this tells us very little about how the two educational systems function in terms of selection when the residential characteristics of the population as a whole are taken into account. In spite of the fact that Ghanaian students are more urban in background, it could still be concluded a priori that the relationship between secondary-school selection and urban origin is looser in Ghana than in the Ivory Coast; such a pattern would not be surprising since the Ghanaian secondary-school system offers far more places in relation to population. Conversely, it could be suggested that the smaller the system, the sharper the differentials are likely to be—a pattern found in so many Western countries. However, these two assumptions seem hardly tenable in this instance. If anything, the urban/rural differentials are rather more marked in Ghana than in the Ivory Coast, particularly if we look at the pattern of recruitment from the very

smallest and the very largest communities. Ivory Coast enrolments from the smallest centers are proportionally larger than in Ghana. Also, there is in Ghana a linear relationship between size of birthplace or place of residence and secondary-school access—the larger the town, the greater the proportional representation of students from these centers. This is not duplicated in the Ivory Coast; students born or resident in the very largest towns (Abidjan and Bouaké) are actually less well represented in the system than those from medium-sized communities.

We are somewhat puzzled by these unexpected disparities. Very tentatively we suggest that they may be due to differences in the geographical dispersion of towns and secondary schools in the two countries. Thus Abidjan is the only highly urbanized center in the Ivory Coast, and the overwhelming bulk of secondary schools are concentrated there. These are essentially national institutions recruiting from the whole country. Since, however, the rate of growth of the population of Abidjan has expanded faster than the school system, students coming from this city are proportionally disadvantaged as compared with individuals from other areas.

In Ghana, conversely, there is a more even dispersion of both schools and urban centers. Although secondary institutions theoretically draw upon a national population, they tend to recruit on a far more regional basis.[12] It could have been hypothesized that, under such conditions, rural boys would be proportionally more favored

---

[11]Actually, this movement is very complex and involves not only direct migration from the very smallest to the very largest centers, but also a multiplicity of small-scale movements to towns slightly larger than the place of birth. It also correlates in some measure with a migration from the northern and central areas to the coastal zone, though this is more marked in the Ivory Coast.

[12]For example, within the investigated schools located in Abidjan, only 18 per cent of the sampled students actually lived in that city. By contrast, in the investigated schools of Accra and Kumasi, no less than 40 per cent of sampled students were permanent residents.

than their Ivory Coast counterparts. Yet this is clearly not the case—far from evening up urban/rural contrasts, the geographic diffusion of educational facilities and towns has tended to sharpen differentials.

Thus we can see that, with respect to both ethnicity and urbanization, the growth of an educational system does not necessarily, in the short run, lead to a lessening of differentials in recruitment. When, however, we examine the family backgrounds of the two groups of students in terms of paternal occupation, the picture seems to conform more closely to our expectations (Table 3). First, it is evident that although Ghana and the Ivory Coast are alike in so many other respects, their occupational structures are very different. To be sure, both are peaked and constricted at the summit, but there is in Ghana a much greater level of growth and differentiation at the higher occupational levels. The greater maturity of the economic structure of Ghana is reflected in the fact that the proportion of students from "white-collar" backgrounds is about double that in the Ivory Coast and the offspring of skilled workers and artisans are relatively more numerous in the Ghanaian group. Conversely, the children of farmers and fishermen form a larger proportion of the enrolment in the Ivory Coast sample.

However, if we relate these figures to the population base, it is apparent that the Ivory Coast system tends to favor the selection of children of professional and clerical workers to a far greater degree than does the Ghanaian system. In terms of this variable, the expansion of the Ghanaian system has tended to produce a more open pattern of recruitment than that prevailing in the Ivory Coast.

Let us finally take a look at the educational backgrounds of the fathers of our two groups of students (Table 4). As we might expect, it shows a pattern very similar to that in the preceding table and reflects the much more substantial development of formal education in Ghana. Well over half of the fathers of the Ghanaian pupils have gone beyond primary school as against just over 10 per cent of the Ivory Coast fathers. In fact, 4 per cent of Ghanaian fathers have completed a university education, while there is not one example of this in the Ivory Coast sample. Indeed, nearly all Ivory Coast fathers in the "above-primary" category only went as far as the "École Primaire Supérieure," while almost half of the Ghana fathers in this category had gone even beyond middle school.[13]

Unfortunately, the selectivity ratios for the two systems cannot be computed for parental education, since no data exist concerning the educational level of adult males in the Ivory Coast. We do know that, in Ghana, the education of the fathers of our students is very much higher than that prevailing among the adult male population. Indeed, the gradient among selectivity ratios is far steeper than it is for either urban/rural or occupational characteristics, indicating the rather greater importance of paternal education in influencing secondary-school access.[14] We have little doubt that the situation is

---

[13] In the Ivory Coast, the structure of the educational system did not allow Africans to pursue regular secondary studies of the metropolitan type before 1928. Correspondingly, although it was difficult for Africans to undertake such studies in the Gold Coast before 1928, opportunities did exist; by that time there was a very small but highly significant group of second- or third-generation university graduates.

[14] The Ghanaian selectivity ratios vary from 0.4 for students with uneducated fathers to 13.0 for students whose fathers had attended university or its equivalent.

TABLE 3

Paternal Occupations of Sampled Students Compared with Occupations of Adult Male Population in Ghana and Ivory Coast

Occupational Group	Ivory Coast			Ghana		
	% Adult Male Population*	% Sampled Students	Selectivity Ratio	% Adult Male Population†	% Sampled Students	Selectivity Ratio
Professional, higher technical and administrative	0.3	7.7 (20)	25.7	1.5	20.8 (161)	13.9
Clerical and allied (including teachers)	1.7	10.0 (26)	5.9	5.4	15.6 (121)	2.9
Private traders and businessmen	3.3	6.9 (18)	2.1	3.8	11.0 (85)	2.9
Skilled workers and artisans	0.9	3.1 (8)	3.4	11.8	10.6 (82)	0.9
Semiskilled and unskilled workers	7.0	1.2 (3)	0.2	13.4	1.5 (12)	0.1
Farmers and fishermen	86.3	67.9 (176)	0.8	62.8	37.4 (290)	0.6
Other (including police and uniformed services)	0.5	2.3 (6)	4.6	1.3	0.6 (5)	0.5
No answer		0.8 (2)			2.5 (19)	
total	100.0	99.9 (259)		100.0	100.0 (775)	

*Computed from UNESCO, *Première mission du groupe de planification de l'education en Côte d'Ivoire* (Paris: UNESCO, 1963), p. 19; and from UNESCO, *Situation et perspectives de l'emploi dans le cadre du plan décennal de développement, 1963*, Table IIH.

†Computed from Ghana, *Population Census, 1960*, Advance Report of Vols. III and IV.

much the same in the Ivory Coast. We do know that the fathers of our students are more highly educated than the adult males of Abidjan for whom data do exist, and it is certain that this latter group is far better educated than the bulk of the Ivory Coast male population.[15] We would hazard that the selectivity gradients by level of paternal education are probably

even steeper than those for Ghana.

Let us now draw together our previous discussion. It is clear enough that there are considerable differences in the social backgrounds of these two very significant groups of students. Ghanaian pupils, in general, are more "acculturated" than their Ivory Coast counterparts in terms of certain background characteristics. They are much more likely to be drawn from the larger urban centers and to come from families with higher occupational and educational backgrounds. Further, in

[15]See République de la Côte d'Ivoire, *Recensement d'Abidjan, 1955* (Abidjan, 1960), p. 37.

terms of religious affiliation, Ghanaian students are overwhelmingly Christian (less than 5 per cent are Moslem) while over 15 per cent of the Ivory Coast group are Moslems.

However, if we compare the characteristics of pupils with those of the general population, it seems clear enough that both systems function in a similar manner. To be sure, certain differences are apparent; the French schools are much more selective in terms of occupational background, though urban/rural differentials are a little less marked. Indeed, what is surprising about the Ivory Coast system is that it seems to be about as fluid in its recruitment patterns as is the Ghanaian system, in spite of its very limited size. We suspect that part of the explanation may lie in the fact that Ivory Coast secondary schools are normally free while even in the public schools of Ghana, substantial tuition and boarding fees are still charged.[16]

TABLE 4

Comparison Between Paternal Levels of Education of Sampled Students in Ivory Coast and Ghana

Level of Education	% Ivory Coast	% Ghana
None	65.3	32.4
	(169)	(251)
Some primary school	14.6	7.3
	(38)	(57)
Completed primary school	4.6	2.1
	(12)	(16)
Above primary school	12.4	52.9
	(32)	(410)
No answer	3.1	5.3
	(8)	(41)
total	100.0	100.0
	(259)	(775)

[16]About 50 per cent of the Ghanaian students had bursaries and scholarships, but in

However, what is outstanding about these systems is that both recruit from very broad segments of the population. Selection is undeniably skewed in favor of particular groups, but it is noteworthy that almost 70 per cent of Ivory Coast students and nearly 40 per cent of Ghanaian students come from farming families in which parents are overwhelmingly illiterate. A great deal has been made about the "exclusive" and "aristocratic" nature of elite academic institutions of the French or British type in Africa. The plain fact is that they are by no means exclusive in their clientele and draw upon able individuals from most ethnic and socioeconomic groups. This suggests that the elites of the two territories are likely to be extraordinarily heterogeneous in terms of social origin for some time to come.[17] In this sense, the functional differences between British- or French-type educational systems are minimal. Such differences as do occur are largely explainable in terms of the absolute size of the educational systems and the different socioeconomic profiles of the two nations.

Of course, it is interesting to speculate whether existing fluidity in access to secondary schooling will continue to increase or will diminish in the future. It is possible to argue that, as the number of educated elites increases, they will be able to command differen-

most cases these only covered a part of tuition and subsistence costs.

[17]It is possible that patterns of recruitment may become more constricted in the future. However, we do not believe that this will be the case in Ghana (see Philip Foster, "Secondary Schooling and Social Mobility in a West African Nation," *Sociology of Education*, XXXVII [Winter, 1963], 165–71). Correspondingly, in the Ivory Coast, two recent administrative decisions have limited access to the second cycle of studies and imposed subsistence costs on students. It will be interesting to see what effect these regulations will have.

tial access into the schools for their children, with the result that patterns of recruitment will become more restricted. This argument has considerable force, but we would suggest, however, that elites will not be able to effectively monopolize access to secondary schooling since they are not in a position to resist or even control mass demand for education. Indeed, they themselves are ideologically committed to the provision of mass schooling at all levels.

SOME COMPARISONS CONCERNING ACADEMIC AND OCCUPATIONAL ASPIRATIONS

We may now examine how these two groups of students differ in their perceptions of their academic prospects and future occupations. This is a crucial area for research, for within the context of these slowly developing economies the possibility always arises of blocked educational and occupational mobility for later cohorts of students.

First, it is quite evident that many students in both samples tend to hold quite unrealistic expectations concerning their educational prospects. The chances of a Ghanaian fifth-form student's entering the pre-university sixth form are about one in five; in the Ivory Coast, two out of five move from the first to the second *Baccalauréat* level. However, 49 per cent of the Ivory Coast students and 37 per cent of the Ghanaians felt "certain" that they would be able to continue their full-time studies; a further 40 and 48 per cent, respectively, felt that they had an extremely good chance of so doing. Virtually no student in either sample wished voluntarily to discontinue his schooling. This is a remarkable level of commitment to a continuing education, a commitment, it must be added, which

is closely linked to the occupational and status benefits supposedly imparted to schooling. However, the fact is that the educational structures of both nations are sufficiently constricted to make these hopes unrealistic; and, unless educational expansion at lower levels of the system is paralleled by an increase in the number of places available at the more advanced stage, the number of frustrated pupils is likely to increase.

Given the fact that students consistently overestimate their educational chances, what can we say about their career aspirations? Students were asked to state the job they would most like to enter if they were entirely free to choose. Table 5, therefore, really represents a profile of those jobs believed to be the most desirable within the contemporary occupational structure of the two countries.

Clearly, student aspirations are virtually identical in both samples. Most individuals aspire to professional or semiprofessional careers, as one might expect in the light of their progress so far in the educational system. Even more informative is the high proportion of students in both countries who are oriented to scientific and technological occupations. There is a persistent myth that academic secondary schools in West Africa have been busy producing a non-technologically oriented, literary elite who are committed to careers in the administration.[18] This is clearly not the case, for individuals attracted to essentially administrative functions comprise well under a fifth of the sample in both cases. It is also apparent that these students do not want to become clerks, as we are so often informed.

---

[18] For a typical view see Judson T. Shaplin, "A Sea of Faces," *Bulletin of the Harvard Graduate School of Education*, VI (Summer, 1961), 4.

There are some interesting additional features. A high level of choices for medicine reflects the very high status traditionally accorded this occupation in both nations, and, indeed, this has historically been one of the only professional jobs available to Africans. Conversely, the other professional occupation that has been traditionally held in such esteem in West Africa, that of law, is chosen by very few contemporary students. Only 4 per cent of the Ghanaian and less than 2 per cent of Ivory Coast pupils are interested in legal careers, whether in the administration or in private practice. One may speculate whether disinterest in this occupation, which is still very highly rated in terms of prestige and income in both countries, largely reflects the para-political position of the legal profession. Law may be remunerative; it also carries with it certain "occupational hazards."[19] This judgment would tend to be supported by the fact that very few students envisage a career in politics. In fact, less than 1 per cent of Ivory Coast pupils and only 1.5 per cent of Ghanaians even remotely contemplate political careers. This casts doubt upon some contemporary observations by political scientists concerned with Africa who argue that a high degree of political orientation characterizes potential elites. To be sure, up to the independence period, fluidity in political developments did make a political career attractive to a large number of individuals in the educated and semi-

educated cadres. However, at present, in both areas the stabilization of the existing regimes has led to the virtual monopolization of higher and intermediate political positions by cohorts educated in the previous period. Furthermore, careers in opposition politics are, for very obvious reasons, not attractive under present conditions.

TABLE 5

Occupational Aspirations of Sampled Students

Occupation*	Ivory Coast	Ghana
Medicine	20.5	17.3
	(53)	(134)
Other professional	15.1	18.5
	(39)	(143)
Higher administrative	15.8	19.4
	(41)	(150)
Science and technology	39.4	28.7
	(102)	(222)
Clerical	1.5	4.4
	(4)	(34)
Primary-school teaching	1.5	5.0
	(4)	(39)
Uniformed services	2.3	4.5
	(6)	(36)
Other and no answer	3.9	2.2
	(10)	(17)
total	100.0	100.0
	(259)	(775)

*Occupational categories which are not self-explanatory are as follows: *Other professional:* university professors and secondary-school teachers (in both the Ivory Coast and Ghana the latter group is accorded professional ranking), economist, statistician, etc. *Higher administrative:* Executive posts within the public administration or larger commercial enterprises. For convenience, we have also included politics and law within this category. *Science and technology:* This includes a wide spectrum of occupations. Typical are pharmacy, engineering, surveying, agricultural research, veterinary work, etc. *Primary-school teaching:* In Ghana, this also includes middle school teaching, which is ranked almost identically with primary-school teaching in occupational ratings made by students. *Uniformed services:* Police and military.

[19]The marked "legalism" of both metropolitan powers toward the end of the colonial period insured both high income and occupational security for members of the legal profession. The politicization of bureaucratic structures since independence has greatly limited the legal practitioner's autonomous role.

Both groups, but especially students in the Ivory Coast, have therefore shifted their career aspirations to professional occupations very often of a scientific or technological variety, but with a very heavy emphasis on occupational security. Thus, in both samples, when students were asked what constituted the most crucial factor in determining their occupational choice, security was ranked far higher than prestige, congenial conditions of employment, pay, or promotion opportunities. Further, students were asked what type of job they could *expect* to get if they were unable to continue with their studies beyond their present class. Their answers evidence characteristics very different from their occupational aspirations (Table 6).

Very few students actually anticipate entering professional or semiprofessional occupations, while the few who expect to pursue scientific and technological careers can envisage only

TABLE 6

Occupational Expectations of Sampled Students

Occupation	Ivory Coast	Ghana
Medicine	0.0	0.0
Other professional	0.3	1.6
	(1)	(12)
Higher administrative	1.9	0.1
	(5)	(1)
Scientific and technological	6.7	8.2
	(17)	(63)
Clerical	25.5	49.8
	(66)	(386)
Primary-school teaching	51.4	34.5
	(133)	(267)
Uniformed services	4.6	4.5
	(12)	(35)
Other and no answer	9.6	1.3
	(25)	(11)
total	100.0	100.0
	(259)	(775)

low-level employment as laboratory assistants or agricultural demonstrators. Overwhelmingly, both groups expect to enter only two types of occupation: clerical work and primary-school teaching, both of which are accorded only moderate ratings in terms of prestige and perceived income.[20] There is, however, an interesting reversal between the two samples regarding these two occupations. We suspect that greater Ivory Coast emphasis on primary teaching reflects the rather recently higher rate of expansion in the primary system and the subsequent increase in job openings.

The table shows one thing very clearly; these students have no illusions as to the occupational currency of their education. They have attended school for anywhere between eleven and fifteen years and lie within the top 1 per cent of the population so far as educational experience is concerned. Yet, given their present level of schooling, they expect no more than clerical work or primary-school teaching. The unfortunate thing is that they are probably right.

A great deal is made of the so-called insatiable need for educated personnel in these developing areas. However, it

---

[20]Students in both samples were asked to rank an identical list of twenty-five occupations ranging from professional to unskilled jobs. In the Ivory Coast, "primary-school teacher" was ranked ninth in terms of prestige and thirteenth in terms of perceived income. The corresponding Ghanaian rankings were nineteenth in both cases. In Ghana, in particular, the primary-school teacher is ranked only at about the level of a motor-car mechanic or petty trader. "Government clerk" was ranked fifteenth in terms of prestige and fourteenth in terms of perceived income in the Ivory Coast. By contrast, the Ghanaian group ranked this occupation eleventh in both cases. It is interesting to note that the reversed nature of the rankings corresponds to the differential job expectations of the two samples.

is quite evident that the definition of "need" often depends upon an implicit comparison being made between the educational and occupational profiles of developed areas and those of Africa. However, to use Western profiles as "templates" for African development is quite unjustifiable, since in terms of the market situation in many African states the demand for educated personnel is quantitatively and qualitatively very limited. Thus in both the Ivory Coast and Ghana the bulk of new employment opportunities generated over the last few years have been in low-level teaching and clerical jobs. The paradoxical situation arises that, in spite of the limited diffusion of education in both countries, even a relatively long schooling does not guarantee high-status employment. To put it another way, the combination of limited job opportunities and a growing educational system leads to a sharp drop in the occupational returns for a given level of schooling.

These students therefore display a mixture of optimism and hardheadedness as regards their occupational future. They certainly overrate their chances of continuing their education and tend to aspire to a cluster of occupations, entry into which is essentially determined by their ability to obtain access to further studies. However, they are extraordinarily realistic in estimating what kinds of occupation their *present* level of education will enable them to enter.

In these respects the two samples are very much alike, and they also tend to give similar responses concerning employer preferences and location of work. The traditional domination of job opportunities by government in both areas is reflected in a substantial preference for occupations within the public sector: over 69 per cent of Ivory Coast and 84 per cent of Ghanaian students would prefer to work for the government. However, significant differences do occur. More of the Ivory Coast sample would prefer to be self-employed (11 per cent as against 4 per cent), while only 12 per cent of Ghanaians would choose to work for a private employer, as against 18 per cent of the Ivory Coasters. At present, Ghana is rather more committed to the development of the economy along socialist lines, and openings in the public service are proportionately more numerous and more differentiated than in the Ivory Coast.[21]

Furthermore, both groups express a strong preference for employment in the largest urban centers within which the elites are overwhelmingly concentrated; almost 70 per cent of the students in both countries wish to reside in such major towns as Abidjan, Accra, and Kumasi. However, a markedly higher proportion of Ghanaians express a preference for working in rural areas (29 per cent as against 8 per cent). This is surprising in view of the more urban background of Ghanaian students.

SOME CONCLUDING
OBSERVATIONS

Our initial problem in this paper was to indicate the part played by secondary schools in processes of elite recruitment in two new African nations. There are certainly distinct differences in the social background of secondary-school pupils as between Ghana and

---

[21] Probably about 60 per cent of employment within the modern sector of the Ghanaian economy is with some form of public agency, while in the Ivory Coast this figure is approximately 25 per cent.

the Ivory Coast, and certain contrasts are apparent in some aspects of recruitment. Yet the evidence demonstrates that both systems tend to operate in a rather similar manner. In spite of a very limited number of places and formidable academic barriers to entry, the secondary schools of both nations draw upon very broad segments of the national populations. To be sure, the chances of achieving secondary-school access vary considerably as between subgroups but this does not imply that the majority of students come from privileged socioeconomic or ethnic minorities.

There has been some recent speculation regarding the political implications of the widening gap between African elites and the masses. In the case of these two countries, this concern is not justified. Post-primary education, insofar as it plays a critical role in elite formation, is still available to young people from the most "humble" circumstances and is not the prerogative of a predetermined group. In this sense, the contact between the potential elite and the masses is very marked. However, in another respect, the prolonged educational experience of this minority does set it apart from the rest of the population. How effectively secondary schooling generates a feeling of common identity among its beneficiaries is beyond the scope of this paper. It could well be that formal education creates patterns of affiliation that transcend other social and ethnic loyalties. It is only in that kind of context that we can talk meaningfully of a "gap" between the elite and the mass.

Furthermore, both groups of students are remarkably similar with respect to the nature and level of their aspirations and expectations. Moreover, both face a very restricted range of occupational opportunities. In effect, secondary education up to this level no longer allows automatic access to high-status occupations and roles. Its importance has come to lie in the degree to which it feeds into higher education. Completion of the fifth form or the first *Baccalauréat* now only enables individuals to enter occupations that up to a decade ago were filled mainly by primary- or middle-school leavers. Preoccupation with job security among students may well reflect their difficulties with respect to employment.

Most of the new African states share a primary commitment to economic development plus a belief in the key role to be played in this respect by the educated cadres. Yet we have seen that both samples are oriented toward government employment in the largest urban centers and attach overwhelming importance to occupational stability. Such individuals, we suggest, are not highly likely to emerge as potential innovators in the field of economic development. At the present time, indeed, African entrepreneurs are usually far less educated than members of the bureaucracy. Insofar as the latter group tends usually to limit the autonomy of economic activities, it will be interesting to see to what extent effective communication can be maintained between bureaucratic and entrepreneurial elites with very different levels of formal education.[22]

---

[22]For an interesting discussion of the relationships between bureaucratic and entrepreneurial elites in the new nations, see S. N. Eisenstadt, "Problems of Emerging Bureaucracies in Developing Areas and New States," in Bert F. Hoselitz and Wilbert E. Moore (eds.), *Industrialization and Society* (The Hague: UNESCO and Mouton, 1963), pp. 167–68.

The Limits of Federalism: an Examination of Political Institutional Transfer in Africa

Donald Rothchild

While Africa was in the throes of the decolonisation process, many of its leaders considered classical federalism an effective way of reconciling unity and diversity.[1] Along with their counterparts in Europe, they reasoned that federalism would compensate for the nation-state's inability to meet modern political, economic, and strategic demands without at the same time threatening the special interests of the constituent parts. Federalism would avoid the extreme of overcentralisation seemingly implicit in unitary government as well as the risks of disintegration which continually threaten multilateral economic and military communities. Such a system had worked for political craftsmen in earlier times; now it was to be extended to the needs of Africa.

By the mid-1960's, however, Africans were less enamoured of the Dicey-Wheare model of federalism—doubting both the prospects of its adoption and its usefulness if adopted. Clearly their attitude diverged somewhat from that of their peers in Europe. Whereas many Europeans continued to regard political federation as a practical and realisable

goal in the not-too-distant future, Africans came more and more to question the system's capacity to create lasting unity and to solve the basic challenges of development. Federalism thus became suspect on utilitarian grounds: it had failed in both East and West Africa to provide an easy formula for enlargement or stability. Consequently, despite similar aspirations for unity, Africans and westerners viewed differently the question of federalism's utility under modern conditions.

Even so, one point must be emphasised at the outset: Africa has indeed made enormous strides toward unity. If integration is analysed at four levels —the traditional unit, the nation-state, supranational arrangements, and continental unity—rather than at a single level alone, it is evident that Africa has shown impressive results in the traditional and national categories and substantial successes at balancing 'integration loads and integration capabilities' at the supranational and continental levels.[2] Significant accomplishments have occurred in the past, and new experiments are likely in the future.

Yet what is striking about successful integration efforts thus far is that they have not been along conventional (one might almost say orthodox) federal

---

[1] Throughout this article, federalism is used in A. V. Dicey's sense of a constitutional system which distributes 'the force of the state among a number of co-ordinate bodies each orginating in and controlled by the constitution'. *Introduction to the Study of the Law of the Constitution* (London, 9th ed., 1952), p. 157. See also K. C. Wheare, *Federal Government* (London, 4th ed., 1963), pt. 1.

[2] See Karl W. Deutsch, *Political Community at the International Level* (Garden City, 1954), pp. 43–4, and Karl W. Deutsch *et al.*, *Political Community and the North Atlantic Area* (Princeton, 1957), pp. 41–3.

From *Journal of Modern African Studies*, Vol. IV, No. 3 (November 1966), 275–93, by permission of the journal and its publisher, the Cambridge University Press.

lines. Thus, despite efforts to devise federal systems in Nigeria, Mali, East Africa, Ethiopia, the Congo Republic, and the very special case of Central Africa, the results have not been notable for their enduring qualities. Federal systems have remained operative for relatively brief periods of time, followed by fissure into separate, sovereign parts or movement towards unitary systems. Federalism has proved brittle; it has disintegrated in the face of pressures beyond its capacity for reconciliation, making way for more centralised forms of government— either within the existing state framework or within the parts that composed the federal state.

What accounts for the fragility of federalism under African circumstances? Africa's aspirations for regional and continental unification are genuine; yet its attempts to apply traditional federal formulae towards this oft-proclaimed goal of unity have met with repeated failures. Why is federalism unable to rise to the African challenge at this time? An understanding of the reasons for this failure may help to avert dysfunctional attempts at nation and region-building in the future as well as to provide important insights into the nature of the African political process generally.

Federalism's Lack
of Appeal

In analysing the difficulty of applying federalism under present-day conditions, two main factors must be examined: the attitude of the leaders and the impact of prevailing political, economic, and social conditions.

As might be anticipated, federalism had less appeal for the ideologue than for the pragmatist. Its overlaps, duplications, compromises, excessive legalism, and lack of symmetry offended the ideologue, who seemed to recoil almost instinctively from proposals for federalism, except, perhaps, at the pan-African level. The outstanding example of this is Dr Kwame Nkrumah, whose avowed hostility to federalism stemmed in large measure from his bitter battle against Ashanti federalist aspirations at the time of Ghana's independence. Nkrumah successfully headed off all attempts to place subregional restraints on his power within his own country and went on to raise grave doubts about the utility of federalism elsewhere. In a famous statement that provoked the ire of East African leaders, he observed:

In order to improve effectively and quickly the serious damage done to Africa as a result of imperialism and colonialism, the emergent African States need strong, unitary States capable of exercising a central authority for the mobilization of the national effort and the co-ordination of reconstruction and progress. For this reason, I consider that even the idea of regional federations in Africa is fraught with many dangers. There is the danger of the development of regional loyalties, fighting against each other. In effect, regional federations are a form of balkanization on a grand scale. These may give rise to the dangerous interplay not only of power politics among African States and the regions, but can also create conditions which will enable the imperialists and neo-colonialists to fish in such troubled waters.[3]

In line with this disinclination to experiment with federalism at the nation-state and regional levels, Nkrumah advised his Congolese counterpart,

---

[3] Kwame Nkrumah, *Africa Must Unite* (London, 1963), pp. 214–15.

Patrice Lumumba, against the use of the federal form in the Congo.[4] For Nkrumah, federalism was anathema because it inhibited economic development and was tainted with 'tribalism' and 'neo-colonialism'. 'Once one starts laying down in the constitution what powers the federal government should have', he argued pragmatically in support of his general ideological position,

a vast area of doubt is created. It is not clear whether this or that particular matter is within the power of the federal government or of the regional government. Nothing can be done by either in regard to the matter until the courts have pronounced one way or another as to where power lies.

In consequence just at a time when a strong government is necessary, federalism introduces an element of paralysis into the machinery of State, and slows down the process of governmental action . . .[5]

But if the ideologue rejected federalism in no uncertain terms, the pragmatists proved themselves to be less than dedicated to the federal principle. For some of the pragmatists, federalism was no more than a transitional step on the path toward a unitary structure; for others it was, much as Nkrumah alleged, a disguised form of 'balkanisation'. In Nigeria, for example, the politicians linked most intimately with the federal system were quick to raise questions about the long-range desirability of this type of polity. The Federal Prime Minister, Alhaji Sir Abubakar Tafawa Balewa, not only made a point of commenting on the imperfections inherent the in Nigerian system of

federalism;[6] but he also expressed a wish to see a more centralised system evolve. 'The time may come', he declared in a lecture at University College, Ibadan, 'after understanding one another better, and without one tribe dominating the other, when we can hope for a unitary form of government, but not now.'[7] Federalism was a response to Nigerian circumstances—in particular, the nature of Nigerian fears and the configuration of power within the state[8]—not a desired end in itself. It was preferable to disunity, but intrinsically a second best.[9] This being the case, what a paradox that such political leaders as Prime Minister Balewa should have paid with their lives for attempting to operate a system with which they had limited sympathy!

Pragmatism was also evident in Milton Obote's acceptance of a federal relationship in Uganda. Throughout most of this century, the British developed Uganda along essentially unitary lines—an approach which awakened very real apprehensions within the

---

[4] On Lumumba's hostility to federalism, see J. Gérard-Libois and Benoit Verhaegen, *Congo 1960* (Brussels, 1961), vol. 1, pp. 36–7.

[5] *Evening News* (Accra), 19 April 1961.

[6] *Daily Times* (Lagos), 30 September 1961; and Lionel Brett (ed.), *Constitutional Problems of Federalism in Nigeria* (Lagos, 1961), p. 1.

[7] *West Africa* (London), 3 March 1962, p. 243.

[8] On the circumstances involved in the adoption of Nigeria's federal system, see my *Toward Unity in Africa: a study of federalism in British Africa* (Washington, D.C., 1960), pp. 151–77.

[9] Dr M. I. Okpara, the Premier of the Eastern Region, expressed these feelings in 1960 when he described the federal system as having many drawbacks (i.e. expense and lack of strength). At the same time he observed that it was 'better to have a united country with a federal system of government than to disintegrate. We as a party have not found favour with the federal system of government. We prefer the unitary system where the little tribalist will be eliminated.' *Daily Times*, 25 March 1960.

kingdom (and province) of Buganda.[10] Baganda leaders, citing West African precedents, expressed deep fears of a strong central government supported by an unsympathetic majority party in parliament. As independence neared, the Buganda Lukiiko seized the initiative and, despairing of the kingdom's position within the new state, declared Buganda's independence as of 31 December 1960. Baganda leaders were clearly bargaining for guarantees of autonomy. They were seeking to reverse the long-standing trend towards unitary government and to create negotiating capital for an agreement on a decentralised political structure. In this, their efforts were soon rewarded.

Obote, as opposition leader, recognising that a *détente* with the powerful and united Baganda was essential if stability were to be achieved, subsequently conceded their main demands —a federal relationship and indirect election by the Lukiiko of Buganda's representatives to the National Assembly. Obote's diplomatic coup brought him to power as Prime Minister of a reunited Uganda, presiding over a coalition cabinet of his own Uganda People's Congress (U.P.C.) and the Buganda-based Kabaka Yekka (K.Y.)[11] Obote himself was quite clear that both the state and the government were marriages of convenience. As he told a reporter on the first anniversary of independence:

I am proud of the fact that we have delivered Uganda to the first anniversary of her independence in one whole piece. We took it over from the British in one piece and we have delivered it in one piece.[12]

Then, as independence wore on and the challenge of national integrity receded, Obote applied a strict interpretation of central government rights under the constitution. Because the basic law was ambiguous with respect to the distribution and transfer of powers, central authorities were in effect left with wide discretion to determine the nature of the federal relationship.[13] Controversy soon arose over the transfer of forestry and police services within Buganda as well as fiscal and juridical relations between governments. When, with one exception, each controversy was resolved in favour of the central government, it became obvious to all that the dynamics of politics under African conditions placed heretofore unrecognised powers in the hands of central leaders. Obote could stress, for example, that the transfer of services to the federal states was not obligatory under the constitution;[14] and there was little Buganda authorities could do to force his hand.

This show of strength in intergovernmental relations was not without its spillover effects in the political arena. The drift of Kabaka Yekka members into the ranks of Obote's U.P.C. soon permitted him to thrust K. Y. out of the government coalition.

[10]For the purposes of this article, the Bantu nomenclature is used throughout. Thus the place is Buganda and the people are the Baganda.

[11]For a more detailed description of Obote's relations with Kabaka Yekka, see Donald Rothchild and Michael Rogin, 'Uganda', in Gwendolen M. Carter (ed.), *National Unity and Regionalism in Eight African States* (Ithaca, N.Y., 1966), pp. 359–60 and 400–2.

[12]*Uganda Argus* (Kampala), 9 October 1963.

[13]With the publication of the Western Kingdoms and Busoga Act soon after independence, the quasi-federal nature of Kingdoms other than Buganda became apparent to all. See my 'Majimbo Schemes in East Africa', in *Boston University Papers in African Politics* (Boston, 1967).

[14]*Uganda Argus*, 20 February 1963.

Moreover, as the U.P.C. gained a firmer and firmer place in the Buganda political scene, the kingdom's ability to exercise a meaningful autonomy declined. Thus the pragmatism which led to Obote's initial agreement to a federal relationship was a poor guarantee for the system's maintenance once the internal distribution of power was altered significantly. The same Obote, who had described the 1961 report proposing a federal relationship as an admirable piece of work, by 1965 was dwelling on the difficulties and drawbacks involved in federal systems.[15] In the following year, he seized power and suspended the 1962 constitution. Parliament subsequently adopted a new constitution, which abrogated Buganda's entrenched privileges and treated the country as a unitary state. Consequently, as power relations changed within a country whose leaders seemed less than keen on the workings of federalism, a basic adjustment in the system—if not its collapse—seemed virtually inevitable.

Nigerian and Ugandan leaders thus sought federalism mainly to ease the transition to unitary rule;[16] on the other hand, certain Congo (Leopoldville) leaders advocated federal government in order to ensure a dispersal of power on a long-term basis. Of course a distinction must be drawn here between the federalism of Leopoldville's Joseph Kasavubu and that of Katanga's Moise Tshombe. Whereas Kasavubu espoused federalism as a means of securing cultural autonomy

for his Bakongo people, Tshombe was motivated by parochial political considerations within Katanga as well as a desire to minimise Katanga's fiscal contributions to the Congo as a whole.[17] The distinction is significant; yet it by no means ruled out an overlapping of outlooks and interests—as indicated by the Tananarive conference of Congolese leaders in March 1961 which proposed a constitutional arrangement for their country essentially confederal in nature.[18] Kasavubu's 'sentimental' political vision and Tshombe's tough-minded realism led temporarily to a meeting of minds.[19]

In the case of Tshombe at least, there is much evidence to support Nkrumah's contention that federalism amounted to balkanisation in disguise. As early as December 1959, Tshombe outlined his party's position on the future Congo constitution when he called for the creation of 'sovereign' states which would surrender 'a determined part of their sovereignty to a Federal State'. How much power were the states to surrender? Obviously very little, as Tshombe specified that the competency of the central government 'would be limited to questions of general interest to the Congo'. In addition, he proposed that central authorities be prohibited from inter-

---

[15] *Uganda Argus*, 17 July 1961, and 12 May 1965.

[16] The same preference for unitary government was evident among Soudanese leaders of the Mali Federation. See William J. Foltz, *From French West Africa to the Mali Federation* (New Haven, 1965), p. 179; and see p. 183 for subsequent Senegalese disillusionment.

[17] Crawford Young, *Politics in the Congo: decolonization and independence* (Princeton, 1965), pp. 504 and 511. Also see René Lemarchand, 'The Limits of Self-Determination: the case of the Katanga secession', in *The American Political Science Review* (Menasha), LVI, 2, June 1962, pp. 412–6.

[18] It is significant that Article 1 of Resolution 3 agreed upon by the Tananarive round-table conference described the future constitutional structure of the Congo as 'a confederation of states'. Benoit Verhaegen, *Congo 1961* (Brussels, 1962), p. 37.

[19] A. A. J. Van Bilsen, *L'indépendance du Congo* (Brussels, 1962), p. 164.

vening in 'interior matters' or in economic affairs, 'except within the limits of co-ordination at the national level'.[20] The trend of separatist thinking was already set, which led ultimately to Tananarive and a subsequent demand (in Tshombe's negotiations on the Plan of National Reconciliation) for 'a fully decentralised federation'.[21] As Prime Minister Cyrille Adoula indicated, such an emphasis on separatism ran counter to the spirit of co-operation and co-ordination essential to true federalism. 'If Mr Tshombe really wants a federal régime', Adoula wrote, 'he must accept all its consequences, including the renunciation of privileges in the division of foreign currency. To fix a definite percentage beforehand is out of the question'.[22] Tshombe, in brief, was no more committed to a lasting and genuine federalism than were Balewa and Obote. Consequently the federal principle lacked crucial support from the key leaders of Africa—

making its application in the decolonisation era perilously difficult.

INSUFFICIENT OR OVERBEARING CENTRES OF POWER

If the leaders were less than convinced about the efficacy of the federal principle, what can one say about the conditions under which they operated? In the final hours of colonial rule, the political élite of a number of African countries hammered out federal constitutional arrangements. Many of these arrangements were expedients aimed at achieving unity on a wide territorial basis, while at the same time accommodating racial, tribal, and regional demands. Local nationalists recognised the need to establish viable units for political, economic, and strategic purposes; yet they feared highly centralised state structures, which they felt would place them at the mercy of powerful central governments. In Ghana, Ashanti expectations of regional safeguards proved vain;[23] and this early experience led other groups, such as the Baganda, to insist on firm guarantees under a federal-type constitution before independence.

In essence, the African proponents of federalism (frequently spokesmen for tribal and other ethnic groups) hoped that the conjunction of large size and competition between the regionally-based parties would result in a diffusion of power which, through constitutional means, would protect their interests. James Madison's diversity hypothesis was to be applied to African circumstances! 'Extend the sphere', Madison commented,

---

[20]Informations et Documentation Africaines, 'The Federalist Vocation' (Brussels, INDAF, n.d.), pp. 2–3.
In a letter to the Prime Minister of Belgium of 14 October 1959, Tshombe and J. B. Kibwe had written: 'The position of our association on CONAKAT which groups 905 of the autochton population of the Katanga, has always firmly approved an integral federal structure for the Congo, which would grant to each of the federate regions the most extensive powers, especially in budgetary, social (including education) and economic matters, as well as in respect of administrative services, the total devolution of which would relieve the administrative machinery which weighs too heavily upon the federal capital.' Ibid. pp. 1–2.
[21]'Report to the Secretary-General from the Officer-in-charge of the United Nations Operation in the Congo on Developments relating to the Application of the Security Council Resolutions of 21 February and 24 November 1961'; U.N. Doc. s/5053/Add. 13, 26 November 1962, Annex IX, p. 2.
[22]*Ibid.* Annex III, p. 3.

[23]See Donald Rothchild, 'On the Application of the Westminster Model to Ghana', in *Centennial Review* (East Lansing), IV, 4, Fall 1960, pp. 465–83.

and you take in a greater variety of parties and interests; you make it less probable that a majority of the whole will have a common motive to invade the rights of other citizens; or if such a common motive exists, it will be more difficult for all who feel it to discover their own strength, and to act in unison with each other.[24]

Madison's fear of the tyranny of the majority is applicable to the African situation, where tribal and minority ethnic groups are apprehensive about placing unlimited power in the hands of central authorities, legitimised in their actions by majority support. But did size and an increased social diversity in fact lead to a meaningful diffusion of political power? The period immediately following independence substantiated this contention to a limited extent only.

For the diversity hypothesis to be meaningful under African circumstances, two prerequisites seemed essential—that there be a sufficient number of politically effective groups within the system to ensure a diffusion of power and that there be adequate linkage between these groups to enable co-ordinated activities to take place as well as to keep disruptive elements from seceding.

Certainly new social and economic interest groups such as trade unions, teachers' organisations, youth societies, and the army could not be relied upon to bring about a dispersal of power along geographical lines in Africa, because of their thoroughgoing commitment to modernisation and their participation on a large scale in centrally administered activities. Therefore, if there were to be a dispersion of power

on an areal basis, it had to come either from the powerful regional interests (i.e. such great tribal nations as the Ashanti, Buganda, Yoruba, and Bakongo) or from territorial interests grouped as constituent units in a new supranational state.

But could ethnic and nation-state units be effective regional centres of power while at the same time imposing curbs upon the 'secession potential' inherent in such power?[25] The momentum of politics in the decolonisation era soon revealed centripetal forces too strong for a balance to take place between energetic regional and national governments at one and the same time. In Ghana, for example, despite Ashanti appeals for federalism both before and immediately after independence, an insufficient diffusion of power existed for federalism to become a meaningful proposition. Not only did Nkrumah's Convention People's Party (C. P.P.) draw electoral support from the various ethnic groups of the south, but what is often overlooked is that he also received some support in Ashanti and the north. The federalist-minded Ashanti were therefore too divided in their political loyalties as well as being too inflexible in their attitudes toward modernisation to offer an effective alternative to C.P.P. leadership. Ghana was not lacking in ethnic diversity as such; it was lacking, however, in the kind of political pluralism which could withstand the pressures for what is variously described as 'undiluted', 'centralised' or 'one man, one vote' democracy.

To all intents and purposes the same over-all pattern could be observed in

---

[24]*The Federalist* (New York, n.d.), no. 10, p. 61. Some of the material in this part is the result of collaboration with Professor J. David Greenstone of the University of Chicago.

[25]See Charles D. Tarlton, 'Symmetry and Asymmetry as Elements of Federalism: a theoretical speculation', in *The Journal of Politics* (Gainesville), xxvii, 4, November 1965, p. 873.

Uganda, for the powerful, progressive, internally united, and strategically located kingdom of Buganda was not, standing by itself, able to create the conditions for lasting political pluralism in the country. But when the Buganda-based Kabaka Yekka lost its position as a partner in the coalition cabinet at the centre and proved unable to compensate for defections from its ranks by spreading its power base into other regions, the federal relationship seemed less and less effective as a protection against national authority. The Buganda experience demonstrated once again the difficulties involved in establishing federalism in situations where only one powerful ethnic group was dedicated to the federal principle.

Where the conditions were modified, and two or more major regional or territorial groups were determined to safeguard their interests, the situation still did not lend itself to stable government along federal lines. Such political pluralism generated structural instability, tending either toward revision along unitary lines or toward greater autonomy—even secession.

The revision of existing federal structures along unitary lines may have taken longer to effect where two or more regional centres of power were involved, but the end result was roughly similar to those of Ghana and Uganda. Thus centripetal forces eroded the importance of federalism in Camerounian experience;[26] they also undermined the ten-year federal experiment between Ethiopia and Eritrea, and, for a temporary period under Major General Aguiyi-Ironsi's régime, gained the upper hand in the struggle against disruptive forces in the federation of Nigeria.[27] In the latter two cases, national leaders bitterly denounced the federal form of government after applying unitary solutions. His Imperial Majesty Haile Selassie I endorsed 'reunion' as a fulfilment of the people's aspirations and criticised federalism as alien to the people's traditions and their desire for modernisation.[28]

The revamping of federal structures to allow for a loosening of links or the complete disruption of existing federal systems also illustrates the instability inherent in situations where two or more powerful traditional or territorial groups are present. In Nigeria, ethnic intransigence was largely responsible for the cabinet crisis which brought about the downfall of the 1953 constitution; it is significant that the 1954 constitution which followed this crisis consciously strove to bring harmony between the various constituent parts by greatly increasing regional competence.[29] This increase in regional

[26]See Willard R. Johnson, 'The Cameroon Federation: political union between English- and French-speaking Africa', in William H. Lewis (ed.), *French-speaking Africa: the search for identity* (New York, 1965), pp. 206–11.

[27]In February 1966, the military régime appointed Francis Nwokedi as Commissioner on Special Duties, charged with establishing an administrative machinery for a united Nigeria. *Sunday Times* (Lagos), 13 February 1966. The possibility of some new type of federalism was not precluded for, some weeks after Nwokedi's appointment, General Ironsi appointed a nine-man study group to make proposals on a new constitution. This study group included Dr T. O. Elias, Chief F. Rotimi Williams, Professor E. U. Essien-Udom, and other well known scholars and administrators. *Daily Times*, 1 March 1966.

[28]*Ethiopian Herald* (Addis Ababa), 16 November 1962.

[29]As B. J. Dudley notes, other factors accounting for the decentralisation of constitutional responsibilities included a positive attraction on the part of Nigerian leaders to the 'Wheare model', and fiscal self-sufficiency arising from the boom in commodity prices. See his 'Federalism and the Balance of Political Power in Nigeria', in *Journal of Commonwealth Political Studies* (Leicester), IV, 1, March 1966, pp. 16–17.

autonomy—and the consequent weakening in central authority—complicated the task of central leadership. Prime Minister Balewa subsequently felt that he lacked the necessary power to deal swiftly and decisively with successive crises in the Western Region in accordance with the norms prescribed by the system; he therefore watched from the sidelines while violence held sway in the Region. The central government's *'immobilisme'*, encouraged by a system which burdened federal authorities beyond their capabilities, led to an impasse in which intervention by the most powerful interest group not identified with the system became inevitable.

The same disruptive tendencies are implicit in territorial (or what President Julius Nyerere calls 'anachronistic') nationalism.[30] If nationalism is a force for integration on a continent subdivided by hundreds of traditional allegiances, it is also a disintegrative force with respect to supranational groupings. Conflicting nationalist aspirations were responsible for the break-up of the nineteen-month-old Mali Federation linking Senegal and the former Soudan. The strains resulting from national jealousies, ideological differences, varying cultural attachments, and economic policies were such as to tear the two-unit federation apart as soon as national leaders became pitted against one another in an open struggle for power.[31]

Nationalism also proved an impor-

tant factor in delaying hopes for the creation of both an East African federation and a Senegambian union. Although in June 1963 the East African leaders pledged themselves to political federation, the following year brought little in the way of concrete steps toward that unity—and in fact some hurried consultations aimed at maintaining existing organisational links.[32] Uganda withdrew from the interterritorial travel agency, seemed for a time to be contemplating withdrawal from the University of East Africa, and insisted in the federal negotiations on a loose association of states.[33] Kenyans and Tanzanians perceived their interests in terms of a tightly-knit federation (i.e. central control over foreign affairs, citizenship, external borrowing, agriculture, marketing boards, and so forth); at the same time, Tanzanian leaders, disappointed at the failure to make rapid strides toward supranational unity, made moves which increased control over their own domestic situation, but at the expense of East African unification. Such decisions as those enacting a one-party state by law, following separate defence policies, demanding special protections for Tanzanian industries in order to equalise the disadvantages in the common market carried over from colonial experience, and, finally, setting up

---

[30]Colin Legum, 'The Changing Ideas of Pan-Africanism', in *African Forum* (New York), 1, 2, Fall 1965. p. 52.

[31]See my article, 'The Politics of African Separatism', in *Journal of International Affairs* (New York), xv, 1, 1960, pp. 595–606; also Foltz, op. cit., and I William Zartman, *International Relations in the New Africa* (Englewood Cliffs, 1966), p. 121.

[32]See Joseph S. Nye, Jr., *Pan-Africanism and East African Integration* (Cambridge, Mass., 1965); Donald Rothchild, 'A Hope Deferred: East African Federation, 1963–64', in Gwendolen M. Carter (ed.), *Politics in Africa: seven cases* (New York, 1966); and Ali A. Mazrui, 'Tanzania Versus East Africa: a case of unwitting federal sabotage', in *Journal of Commonwealth Political Studies*, III, 3, November 1965, pp. 209–25.

[33]A statement of the working party disagreements on the nature of federal structure was published by the *East African Standard* (Nairobi), 3 June 1964.

separate currencies and banking institutions all increased national power while weakening inter-unit links. For the time being the East African Common Services Organisation ensures a continuance of administrative ties; nevertheless it remains to be seen whether these links can survive the fissiparous counterpulls of 'anachronistic nationalism'.

Similarly in Senegambia, territorial political and economic interests have thus far thwarted all attempts to merge tiny Gambia into neighbouring Senegal. The split is a tragedy resulting from the colonial partition of Africa and makes little sense in economic, geographical, ethnic, or political terms. To overcome this unfortunate situation, a United Nations commission of experts recommended that a loose form of federalism be considered as a possible solution. 'Clearly, this formula', reasoned the commission of experts,

would make it possible to reconcile respect for the Gambia's identity with the needs inherent in its geographical and economic position; moreover, it is difficult to see what serious disadvantages this formula could involve, so long as the stages are carefully planned, or what grounds there might be for not regarding it as the solution most consistent with the interests of both countries.[34]

Federation may have made sense for the experts, but it stood little chance against contrary nationalist aspirations in Senegal and Gambia. Defence and diplomatic pacts were successfully negotiated immediately after Gambia's independence;[35] but federation involved a greater integration load than the political conditions would permit.

In addition to the need for a sufficient number of politically effective groups within the system, the second prerequisite for the diversity hypothesis was that considerable linkage should exist between the politically powerful actors on the scene. Because the above discussion has shown the diffusion of power to have been either inadequate or so great that it threatened the continuance of federal ties, little discussion of the role of linkage is needed. Some mention of the extent to which linkage must overcome the impact of tribal compartmentalisation is pertinent none the less.

Traditional loyalties not only tend to challenge the educated élite's ability to speed modernisation, but also tend to inhibit the growth of trans-tribal activities. Tribalism, by dint of its exclusivism and separatist potential, complicates consensus politics under the best of circumstances in Africa; with the introduction of federal government, consensus becomes a problem of manifold proportions. In both Uganda and Nigeria, the ethnic factor made coalition government a prerequisite of stability in the period immediately after independence. However, coalition government under such circumstances proved difficult to manage over an extended time; so much effort was consumed in maintaining stability that valuable energy was diverted away from the central problems involved in modernisation.[36] And in the political field, ethnic-based parties had a difficult time finding new support outside their home base.

In Uganda, non-Baganda local of-

---

[34]United Nations, *Report on the Alternatives for Association between the Gambia and Senegal*, TAO/Gambia/Senegal/1 (New York, 1964), p. 26.

[35]*West Africa*, 18 July 1964, p. 791.

[36]For a statement of the advantages of coalition government in Africa, see W. A. Lewis, 'Beyond African Dictatorship', in *Encounter* (London), xxv, 2, August 1965.

ficials have strongly resisted Kabaka Yekka's attempts to open offices and campaign outside its regions of origin; in Nigeria the story was much the same, for the Hausa-Fulani leaders of the north treated Action Group efforts to win support in their areas with open hostility and suspicion. 'It is doubtful ...', observes K. W. J. Post, 'if the late Sardauna of Sokoto ever forgave the Action Group for the onslaught it launched on his Northern "fief" in the 1959 election.'[37] As such feelings were carried over into the sphere of inter-governmental relations, they created an inflexible situation which was ultimately to contribute to the downfall of the system itself. It is paradoxical that tribalism—the *raison d'être* for the adoption of federal government in these countries—should come full circle and turn out to be partly responsible for the system's undoing.

But if federalism was agreed upon as an expedient means of reconciling the need for unity with the desire for local autonomy, constitution makers must have worked on the assumption that linkage would occur as the system gained legitimacy. Co-ordinated activities of an economic and social nature within a single state structure necessitated such a development. The evidence now available indicates, however, that tribal differences tend to be too fundamental for such ties to come about easily. Thus the Congo's size and ethnic diversity proved no guarantee of group security within a stable constitutional structure, as ethnic fears and ambitions could not be harmonised sufficiently within the political order.

Linkage did occur to some extent in Nigeria, where representatives of the country's major ethnic groups partici-

pated in federal politics while still retaining positions of influence in their home regions. Consequently a significant degree of integration took place at the centre, among the spokesmen of the various ethnic groups, ensuring that the aspirations of the leading peoples would be given a sympathetic hearing at the highest levels. Nevertheless, precisely because a number of important interests (particularly the Yorubas) felt alienated from the mainsprings of power at the centre, the linkage was inadequate to the requirements of the system.[38] By leaving major ethnic interests on the outside, the imperfections of Nigerian linkage left the system weak and exposed. In the end the pressures of the Western Region crisis proved too great for linkage to endure intact, and a new linkage of questionable durability, based on the nationalism of a modernist interest group (the military), replaced the old, unstable order. Clearly the conjunction of large size and competition between regionally-based parties had not proved a stable foundation for African federalism.

OTHER UNFAVOURABLE CONDITIONS

In addition to noting the difficulty of adapting James Madison's diversity principle to African circumstances, mention must be made of a number of other conditions militating against the application of classical federalism to this continent. These conditions relate to the nature of the political process, the nature of interterritorial links, and

---

[37]'The Crisis in Nigeria', in *The World Today* (London), XXII, 2, February 1966, p. 44.

[38]In April 1965, Prime Minister Balewa did include five members of Chief S. L. Akintola's Nigerian National Democratic Party in his cabinet. However, because the Action Group was excluded from the federal government, a significant proportion of Yoruba opinion remained outside the system.

the nature of interest group activities and aspirations.

With respect to the political process, it is important to keep in mind that federalism is but one element of western liberal values.[39] Wrenched away from an environment that accepts the unquestioned worth of political pluralism, constitutionalism, legalism, and compromise, it tends to operate against an alien and inhospitable background. This alienation becomes more poignant when complicated by third-world conditions of poverty, illiteracy, and ethnic separatism.

The implications of this are enormous. The facts of political life in the developing lands necessarily run counter to the kind of environment in which a stable, co-operative federalism could be established at this time. Political pluralism is considered a virtue in many western countries, for differences between groups are less than fundamental and a consensus exists as to goals and values; in Africa, however, such a consensus is lacking and pluralism is deemed essentially a threat to the system.[40] Constitutionalism and legalism at the modern state level, broadly accepted as means of reconciling interests in the west, are frequently looked upon by Africans with widespread indifference and even fear as imported systems dangerous to their countries' unity and therefore to their modernisation.

The political process during and after decolonisation, highlighted by a remorseless struggle for power between local élites, complicates the emergence of conciliatory intergroup relations on a multi-dimensional basis. More often than not the parliamentary system hurriedly thrust upon African states by the departing colonial régimes is superseded by a single-party or no-party system, which looks most critically at the kind of diffusion of responsibilities between constitutionally entrenched authorities required by federalism. Consequently these new leaders, convinced that western-style constitutionalism hampers the tasks of order-building and modernisation, play down the values of western liberalism, thereby creating a climate basically unhealthy for federalism.

The effect of these background conditions on federalism can be seen in the difficulties involved in creating and working federal relationships. The heavy political load factor in Africa is a consequence of the two major challenges confronting the governing élite—the need to secure order and to modernise the society. Tribal and racial cleavages impede the growth of consensus in new states, causing politicians to shun reconciliational systems wherever possible, as well as to look inward to the nation-state, rather than to attempt to solve basic economic and political questions within a broader geographical perspective. Concentration upon order-building leaves little time and energy for federation, whether by aggregation or disaggregation.

The needs of modernisation also impose heavy burdens on federal government. In earlier times, when federal schemes were effected in the west, state systems were comparatively stable and citizens made minimal demands upon their governments; the present-day welfare state era, however, places great strains on federalism, both in the level of services required and in

---

[39] See the discussion by A. H. Birch, 'Opportunities and Problems of Federation', in C. Leys and P. Robson (eds.), *Federation in East Africa: opportunities and problems* (Nairobi, 1965), pp. 6–9.

[40] Ruth Schachter, 'Single-Party Systems in West Africa', in *The American Political Science Review*, LV, 2, June 1961, p. 305.

the nature and extent of state participation. As the Soviet Union has shown, economic planning and administrative decentralisation can be complementary. But analogies to Africa drawn from this experience may be misleading, for the African states have by no means approached the U.S.S.R.'s level of sophistication in the planning sphere; with their limited manpower reserves and capital resources, and fragile governmental structures, they must concentrate their main planning efforts at the centre. This high priority on central planning and control, coming at a time when the centripetal forces of the nation-building process are already intense, makes the application of such a reconciliational system as federalism a complicated process in the postcolonial era.

The tensions inherent in the political process also run counter to the evolution of complementary élites. The artificiality and newness of African states as well as the evolution of integral nationalism thwart the emergence of the kind of value framework in which tolerance and diversity flourish. Consequently, political conflicts are too fundamental in nature, with elections becoming something akin to 'win all, lose all' battles between adversaries. Because these conflicts are so basic and the stakes so high, single-party or no-party control along centralised lines becomes an accepted feature of political life.

This situation obviously has grave implications for federalism. The crucial actors on the political scene tend to be alike in the manner in which they chafe at institutional or interest group restraints upon their freedom of action as well as in their perception of politics as something approximating a 'zero-sum' game;[41] therefore little flexibility

is left for such essential requisites of federalism as compromise and tolerance. Thus Senegalese fears of eclipse in a Mali Federation dominated by Modibo Keita and his militant, unitary-minded *Union soudanaise* led to a hasty retreat from commitments no longer to their liking. Similar apprehensions were evident among Action Group politicians in Nigeria; it was precisely because these representatives of Yoruba and minority interests were anxious about their place in a Nigeria run by other peoples that they went to such great lengths to protect their interests from what they considered implacable Northern Peoples' Congress hostility. They failed to secure entrance into the federal coalition or to split the country into many regions;[42] so they sought other means (alliance with the National Council of Nigerian Citizens, and, finally, in desperation, violence). Their apprehensions made stable federalism unworkable and led directly to the collapse of the system.[43]

---

more players must be equal to the loss of one or more rivals'. Karl W. Deutsch, *The Nerves of Government* (New York, 1963), p. 66.

[42] See Donald Rothchild, *Safeguarding Nigeria's Minorities* (Pittsburgh, Duquesne University Institute of African Affairs, reprint no. 17, 1964); and Frederick A. O. Schwarz, Jr., *Nigeria: The Tribes, the Nation, or the Race* (Cambridge, Mass., 1965), pp. 82–100.

[43] The same anxieties were evident in the discussions over the proposed East African federation, not only among the spokesmen for traditionalist Buganda or the moderately conservative Kenya African Democratic Union but also, more significantly, among such leaders as Prime Minister Obote of Uganda. A comment on this might be the statement of the Kenya Minister of State, Joseph Murumbi, at the height of the federation debates: 'I feel that in Uganda, we have this difficulty of the leadership there fearing they will be absorbed into an East African Federation. Some of the Uganda leaders feel they might become non-entities overnight.' *Uganda Argus*, 25 October 1963.

---

[41] A situation 'where any gain by one or

The nature of inter-unit linkage also inhibited the easy transfer of federalism to Africa. A combination of the colonial heritage and low levels of economic development has limited transactions between contiguous sovereign states in East and West Africa as well as between regions within such large states as Nigeria, the Congo (Leopoldville), and the former Mali Federation. The effects of the colonial heritage are evident in many respects: the arbitrary linguistic divisions of West Africa, the existence of competing and poorly connected road and rail services, the inadequacy of airline and telecommunications ties, and the special subsidy, tariff, and commodity agreements between the former metropolitan powers and their African associates. Also, trade flows between these African countries are relatively small;[44] as a result, the co-ordination of the continent's economic efforts is now accorded a lower priority than the maintenance of access into existing high-priced markets in Europe and North America.

Of course, where a strong sense of community preceded the establishment of common political institutions, the chances of these joint institutions surviving separatist pulls in an area of low social and economic exchange are enhanced. The importance of such a sense of community is illustrated by the cases of Somalia and Cameroun, where irredentist sentiments proved sufficiently strong to unify peoples artificially separated by the chance factors of colonial occupation. But subsequent events have underlined the great extent to which these acts of integration by impulse are special cases indeed.

Precisely because there is nothing natural about most of Africa's multi-tribal states, the building of a sense of community is one of the main challenges that face Africa's new leadership. For reasons already discussed, African leaders fear reconciliational devices such as federalism and, spurred on by the urgency of the problem that confronts them, seek to foster the building of a sense of community by the most direct means at hand. The unitary, one-party, or no-party system fosters élite linkage in particular and social linkage in general, thereby bridging both the tribal divisions inherited from the past as well as the conditions arising from a low rate of communications and transactions in the present.

Finally, the nature of interest group activities in Africa, as compared to those in Europe, gives little impetus to federal integration. Whereas expectations of rising prosperity lead European interest groups to seek increased transnational co-ordination, their African counterparts often lack this 'myth of utilitarian benefits' which Europeans assume would arise from wide geographical unification.[45] In the industrial societies of Europe 'supranationality and a lively spillover process are able to flourish'[46] because pluralism, free enterprise, and a broad economic interdependence create a trans-national

---

[44]In 1964, Tanganyika, which had domestic exports totalling £70,111,861, sold £4,109,794 worth of goods to Kenya and £1,020,935 worth to Uganda. Such trade patterns are likely to foster a sense of national self-interest rather than trans-national community, a tendency apparent in recent Tanganyikan trade restrictions and quotas. *Reporter* (Nairobi), 9 April 1965, p. 37.

[45]Amitai Etzioni, *Political Unification: a comparative study of leaders and forces* (New York, 1965), p. 252.

[46]See Ernst B. Haas and Philippe Schmitter, 'Economics and Differential Patterns of Political Integration: projections about unity in Latin America', in *International Organization* (Boston), XVIII, 4, Autumn 1964, p. 726. See also Ernst B. Haas, *The Uniting of Europe* (Stanford, 1958), pp. 291–9.

framework in which the political actors must operate to a very significant extent. By comparison, African leaders are much freer to determine whether or not to enter into federation arrangements because interest groups in Africa are neither as powerful nor as transnationally oriented as their European counterparts. In this sense, Uganda's Obote has greater manoeuvrability than France's de Gaulle, in that he can more easily refrain from committing his country to a political federation if the risks seem to him to outweigh the anticipated rewards.

CONCLUSION

In consequence, Africa is faced with a situation of little flexibility regarding constitutional systems. It continues to need a formula which will reconcile the requirements of central leadership with the demands of regional autonomy. At the same time, classical federalism is ideologically suspect and the political, economic, and social conditions of the continent are such as virtually to preclude the adoption of the Dicey-Wheare model at this time.

If the federal compromise proved unable to survive the politics which ensued after independence, it logically followed that constitutional changes would have to avoid the reconciliational middle and move towards one of the polar extremes—unitary government or loose inter-unit arrangements. The ruling élite's preference for unitary systems is a response to two essential challenges to successful administration: the maintenance of national stability and unity, and the achievement of modernisation. Strong central leadership is viewed by civilian and military élites alike as a prerequisite for modernisation. These men chafe impatiently at regional limitations upon

their authority and reject the conflicts and compromises of federalism as wasteful, disconcerting, and even corrupting. They seek order and symmetry, national integrity, and rapid strides toward modernisation. Quite naturally, then, concessions to tribal or ethnic autonomy are feared as divisive manoeuvres. And wherever the leaders of the independence period made expedient moves to include regional guarantees in order to speed decolonisation, the men in power of a few years later felt no compunction about breaking colonialist-inspired constitutions, which they saw as inhibiting the achievement of their primary responsibilities.

But the obverse of this drive for unitary forms is the fear of centralised power they engender. As indicated above, the most powerful of traditional groups fell one by one as they came into conflict with a determined central government. The protections of federalism proved unavailing even in Nigeria, despite that country's great size and diversity of effective interest groups. None of this was lost upon the leaders of Africa's sovereign new nations, who genuinely aspired for interterritorial unity but sought to avoid the price such unification would entail. Therefore, they shunned both unitary and federal formulas in their trans-national relations, and experimented instead with a wide range of multilateral economic and administrative arrangements—such as the East African Common Market and Common Services Organisation, the Central African Customs Union, the Council of the Entente, and the Afro-Malagasy Common Organisation.

Nevertheless, if federalism, the middle way, seems alien to the special conditions of Africa, the need for reconciliational political forms remains too basic to disappear in the years to come. As indicated by the decree issued by Nigeria's Colonel Gowan restoring the regions and confirming the regional nature of the civil services, some recon- ciliational elements are essential within the new African states if now submerged regional or sub-regional interests are to be mollified in the future. At the supranational level, reconciliational systems may also prove valuable in facilitating the development of present loose arrangements.

In fact, a hesitant and tentative movement away from the polar ex- tremes can now be perceived. Within Nigeria, some type of federal arrange- ment seems the best hope of averting disaster, and it is significant that conferences of 'Leaders of Thought' in two regions have urged the adoption of 'a loose federation with autonomous regions'.[47] Some such trend might also

---

[47] *West Africa*, 3 September 1966, p. 992.

occur in the Congo, as the leaders of that country search for an enduring system which could hold its diverse peoples together. Among the multilat- eral arrangements, on the other hand, the movement towards a tightening of bonds between constituent units has been slow and tedious. Some progress is evident within the ranks of the franco- phone states, but even here the success- es remain too scattered to be described as a trend. Nevertheless it is possible that if these arrangements could secure the kind of long-term political com- mitments which would ensure their survival, a 'spillover' of responsibilities might occur into related fields. Such an expansion of activities could lead to the emergence of neo-federal constitu- tional systems which owe their life and vitality to African rather than Euro- pean initiatives. Reconciliational con- stitutional systems are not dead in Africa; they have yet to find their African expression.

Military Coups and Political Development:
Some Lessons From Ghana and Nigeria

Edward Feit

I

Are the military coups that have shak- en Africa recently simply a working- out of personal animosities, are they due to chance, or are they the result of something inherent in the very nature of present-day African political systems? It is to questions such as these that this article is addressed, and to which it seeks to provide tentative answers. Further, if, as will be argued here, the African coups result from something inherently systemic, what conclusions

can be drawn at present about Africa's future political development?

Before the coups, students of armies in the "third world" did not rate the political potential of African armies very highly.[1] The reasons varied from

---

[1] James S. Coleman and Belmont Price, Jr., "The Role of the Military in Sub-Saharan Africa," in John J. Johnson, ed., *The Role of the Military in Underdeveloped Countries* (Princeton 1962), 359; William F. Gutteridge, *Military Institutions and Power in the New States* (New York 1965), 141–44; S. E. Finer, *The Man on Horseback* (London 1962), 228.

From *World Politics,* Vol. XX, No. 2 (January 1968), 179–93, by permission.

the small size of the armies to such matters as the politicization (or lack of politicization) of the officer corps. The military revolts in former French Africa and in the Congo did not seriously shake expert opinion because the revolts took place in countries barely viable and of little political importance or, in the case of the Congo, in a country ravaged by rebellions. The coups in Ghana and Nigeria have given the problem different dimensions; they have, in fact, necessitated fresh thinking about African politics as a whole.

Ghana had been built up by Ghanaian "agitprop," by foreign publicists, and by some academics who should have known better as the epitome of the thrusting "single-party state." With a "party of mobilization" headed by a "charismatic" leader, Kwame Nkrumah, it was setting the pace in creating entirely new "African" forms of government based on African socialism. Its teething troubles over, it was said, Ghana would be the model for much of Africa. Nigeria too lacked neither publicists nor academic supporters. It was represented as Africa's showcase democracy and as an alternative to the "single-party state." Because of its size and potential resources it was pointed out as a potential African world power.

Myths such as these were rudely exploded, first, by the Nigerian coup of January 15, 1966, and then by the Ghanaian coup that followed some six weeks later when, on February 24, 1966, the Ghanaian army toppled the Nkrumah regime while Nkrumah was out of the country on a fatuous mission to end the Vietnam war. Both coups, the Ghanaian and the Nigerian, swept aside the civilian governments and all instruments by which those governments had been conducted without meeting serious resistance or protest. That small armies were able, with so little difficulty, to set aside the regimes that had ruled their countries must indicate that these regimes had little substance to them, that they were little more than shadows. But if this is indeed so, then where were the substantive institutions? What are, in truth, the political *institutions* of Africa?

With the question put in this way, a pause to examine the meaning of the term "institutions" is surely called for. Institutions are defined by Samuel P. Huntington as "stable, valued, recurring patterns of behavior," and this definition is accepted here. Huntington goes on to say that the extent to which an institution is established can be measured by its complexity, adaptability, autonomy, and the coherence of its organizations and procedures.[2] Institutions thus embrace a continuum of codes and practices that, as Lucian Pye has suggested, fit together as parts of a meaningful web of relations.[3]

The only institutions in Africa that meet this definition are the traditional African systems, the tribes, and the administrative institutions introduced by the colonial powers. The significance of the coups can therefore be made clear only if institutional interaction with other forms of political organizations, both before and after independence, are outlined.

Thus the most significant political fact in present-day Africa could well be the way in which traditional African institutions complemented the institutions of colonial administrations. The significance of this institutional relationship has often been lost sight of because of the attractive power of the myth of "African nationalism."

---

[2] "Political Development and Political Decay," *World Politics*, XVII (April 1965), 394.

[3] Lucian W. Pye and Sidney Verba, eds., *Political Culture and Political Development* (Princeton 1965), 7.

The successful working together of colonial officers and tribal rulers was facilitated by their mutual commitment to order and stability. Colonial officers and tribal rulers alike wanted to preserve what was, for different reasons, a mutually beneficial status quo. In this joint effort each could provide something that the other could not—always an ideal basis for cooperation.

By the grid they imposed which held the tribes together without integrating them, the colonial power ensured intertribal peace. Once the fear of external attack was removed, tribal rulers could concentrate on building power and influence within the tribes. Fear that their own followers might overthrow them was alleviated for chiefs who satisfied the colonial officers, for they could count on the full weight of colonial authority behind them. Canny politicians then as now, the chiefs realized that it was best to join a system that they could not beat. They could preserve a fair measure of tribal authority, providing that they stuck to the sphere that the colonial power assigned them. Colonial officers, always thin on the ground, could do little more than divide their labors with the chiefs. Detailed supervision was, in any case, out of the question. Local administration thus remained with the traditional ruler who, like most of his people, considered little other than local affairs important. As a result there was little friction between colonial rulers and their African subjects.

So by their common working the administrative and the traditional system served to legitimize each other. The administrators protected traditional systems from change and made their preservation acceptable to the governments at home. The traditional rulers, in turn, helped to make colonial practices institutional among their followers.

The political system so made institutional was a combination of administrative and traditional rule, and we shall therefore term it an administrative-traditional system. Given its objectives, the system succeeded quite well. It was generally accepted and understood. There was, in any case, little to oppose it. Nationalism and democracy were not African conceptions, although to those Africans who assimilated them, there was much in the working of the colonial system to cause them distress. But the opposite must also be borne in mind. Conor Cruise O'Brien, hardly a friend of colonialism, wrote in the fall of 1965 of the almost mawkish sentiment for Britain he found among Ghanaians to whom he spoke.[4] But in speaking of the administrative-traditional system of the colonial period, it is important not to romanticize. The colonial system fell far short of the Western ideals. It was not democratic and was intended to benefit mainly the colonial power. Emphasizing the status quo as it did, it tended to ossify African society at the Iron Age. Perpetual backwardness is, perhaps, too high a price even for peace and stability, but this point will not be debated here. What matters for the moment is that the colonial system worked well, that it was understood, and that it secured the objectives of its sponsors at low cost in life and treasure.

Although the European powers came to Africa to promote their own benefit, ironically in seeking this benefit they brought into being the very classes who were to challenge their rule. New classes were the result of encouraging Africans to leave their villages and come to the workplaces in the towns, in the

---

[4] "Contemporary Forms of Imperialism," *Studies on the Left* (Fall 1965), quoted in *Current*, LXIX (March 1966), 15.

factories, in the mines, and in the offices. But it was these very men who could be accommodated only with greatest difficulty in the colonial system, if they could be accommodated at all. The colonial system was based on the working of an administrative-traditional regime, a regime poorly adapted to integrating Africans outside their own tribal environments. The colonial system, although complex and coherent, was not flexible enough to provide places that would satisfy large numbers of Africans neither sufficiently "Westernized" to fit the one set of institutions nor sufficiently traditional to fit the other. The colonial officers were, again to borrow a phrase of Huntington's, "the victims of their past successes." The successes of the system of "indirect rule" led to its hardening into dogma. Resting as it did on the continued authority of tribal rulers, the system was to be confronted with the need for increasing participation of men among whom this authority was eroding. This was the basic contradiction of colonialism.

Under the impetus of expanding the "modern" sector in their African colonies, the colonial governments created "available masses," to use William Kornhauser's terms, who were soon to find "accessible elites" to lead them in the persons of the post-World War II political entrepreneurs.[5]

In bridging the years before and after the Second World War, it is important to distinguish the earlier politicos from the new and different group that came to the fore after the war. The earlier politicos will be called the "old politicals" to distinguish them from the later leaders, already referred to as political entrepreneurs. The old politicals were a congeries of notables or relatives of traditional rulers. They had received some education, often higher education in the colonial country. Although they claimed to speak for all Africans they represented little more than themselves, a fact that colonial administrators were never loath to put before them. Their political activity was marginal, if not trivial, and concerned either grandiose schemes for "West African union" or the role of some chiefly house, such as the controversy over the House of Docemo in Lagos. Committed to legality and to constitutional change, they represented no danger to the colonial power. They could be satisfied with seats in the legislative and executive councils, which, having only advisory functions, did not interfere much in the running of the administrative-traditional system. Those for whom such places could not be found could be committed to the system by incorporation in the administration itself. Indeed the Gold Coast, as Ghana was then called, was the first to have such appointments made and had the largest proportion of African civil servants when the recruitment of Africans was extended elsewhere.[6]

Thus the British gave the old politicals, whose numbers were anyway small, a sense of participation in politics without relinquishing much control. In fact, the assignment of seats in the councils to old politicals was a useful lever in forcing their accommodation to the administrative-traditional regime. The richest prizes fell to the parties that gave preference to the traditional and conservative elements, ensuring that these and other parties were soon under traditional control.

---

[5] *The Politics of Mass Society* (London 1960), 51–68.

[6] Dennis Austin, *Politics in Ghana, 1946–1960* (London 1964), 8 n.

In fine, against the background of an expanding class of people who could not be easily fitted into the system, the administrative-traditional regime seemed to be working well before the Second World War. It was only in the aftermath of the war that problems that had been in the background moved to the forefront.

II

After the Second World War, Britain, like all of Europe, was exhausted and impoverished. The center of world power had shifted away from Europe and the mantle of world leadership had fallen on the United States and the Soviet Union—powers traditionally hostile to colonialism. Within the colonies themselves large numbers of Africans had been mobilized and had seen and learned much of the outside world. Even in colonies untouched directly by war a new spirit seemed abroad. Colonial powers were made aware that restoration of the status quo that had existed before the war could be reestablished and maintained only at enormous cost, a cost few were willing, let alone able, to pay. Rebuilding Europe itself would involve massive assistance from the United States whose goodwill was therefore essential. Handing over power to what seemed to be "popular rule" in the colonies might win this goodwill, and as the so-called popular parties had extremely narrow bases, their leaders would in turn, it was thought, be forced to maintain the administrative-traditional system by the simple logic of circumstances. The only popular support would be that obtainable through the tribes, and lack of training among the entrepreneurs and their following would ensure the retention of expatriate administrators, in whose hands would rest all crucial decision-making powers. Hostility between the new entrepreneurs and the traditional rulers would assure the British government of an arbitrative role, and this, together with expatriate administration, would mean that the trappings of power, rather than its substance, would be handed over to the new rulers. Their weakness would entrap the political entrepreneurs in the administrative-traditional system just as their old political predecessors had been.

The new political entrepreneurs were supported not, as believed abroad, by "mass parties" but, as Henry Bretton and others have convincingly demonstrated, by political machines.[7] The distinction is that a political party aggregates demands and converts them into legislative policy, whereas a political machine exists almost exclusively to stay in power. To this end its main concern is to offer rewards and bribes to anyone who can contribute to keeping it in power. Office alone is its reason for existence, and with office comes the opportunity of enrichment at public expense. But the personal political machine was, in Africa, subject to pressure from the African institutions. To many of the traditional rulers, the parties being created by the new politicals were another vehicle for carrying on tribal conflict at a new level. So, as political entrepreneurs competed in building their machines, they had to decide between two alternatives: whether to tie the machine closely to a tribe or whether to "go it alone" without specific tribal support. The Nigerian parties were, in general, personal-tribal machines, and the Ghanaian opposition parties were simi-

---

[7] Bretton, *Power and Stability in Nigeria* (New York 1962) and *The Rise and Fall of Kwame Nkrumah* (New York 1966).

lar. Largely preempted from obtaining the support of the main Ghanaian tribes, Nkrumah's machine was of the second type.

The first attempt at a political machine in Nigeria was Nnamdi Azikiwe's NCNC.[8] It sought to represent itself as encompassing all Nigerians, but this machine splintered as independence neared and other entrepreneurs combined with ethnic interests to bring into being political machines based on Nigeria's core tribes. The NCNC itself became an Ibo party backed by the Ibo Union. The political machine of Obafemi Awolowo and the Yoruba tribe, the Action Group, was founded largely on the initiative of the Egbe Omo Oduduwe, a powerful tribal association in Western Nigeria. Surely not much needs to be added about the connection between the political machine of Sir Ahmadu Bello, the late Sardauna of Sokoto, which, as the Northern People's Congress, drew support largely from the Hausa-Fulani peoples. Nigeria became independent with a combination of personal-tribal machines heavily infused with traditional elements dominating each of her regions. Because such "parties" would from the outset be committed to the status quo, the power structure in Nigeria, the British believed, would be kept intact after independence.

In Ghana, smaller and relatively more homogeneous, a clash of ambitions among the old and new politicals turned events in a different direction. Nkrumah, brought into Gold Coast politics to convert the United Gold Coast Convention (UGCC) into a machine, split it instead and, taking most of its activists with him, began

to construct a machine of his own, the Convention People's party (CPP). The old politicals were, as indicated earlier, closely tied to the Ashanti chiefdoms, and so Nkrumah was preempted from forming a tribal party even if he had wished to do so, which is in itself doubtful. But the wealth of Ashanti and the importance of its cocoa production in Ghana's economy posed a threat to the power Nkrumah sought to secure for himself. He met this threat by cutting down the legal powers of the chiefs and also by financial pressure and by destooling the chiefs who were recalcitrant. These actions, and the replacement of traditional rulers by others of his own choice after the legitimate chiefs had been destooled, antagonized not only the chiefs themselves but also many of their followers.

By placing their supporters in lucrative administrative posts the political machines of both Ghana and Nigeria burdened the administration and antagonized the administrators who patterned themselves after British models. But the machines were, nevertheless, compelled to make such appointments, as the "parties" they represented had virtually no base of support in the country, unless, as in Nigeria, this support came from tribal chiefs or political organizers who could deliver the votes. The chiefs and the organizers had to be rewarded by bribes, among which were appointment to administrative boards. A recent paper of the Northern Nigerian government, for instance, points out that the Northern Nigerian Marketing Board, which handled about $180 million worth of produce per annum, did not have one qualified person in charge.[9] The multiplication of useless office holders not only burdened

---

[8] The NCNC was formed in 1944 as the National Council of Nigeria and the Cameroons; the name was changed in 1961 to the National Convention of Nigerian Citizens.

[9] "60m Without Safeguards," *West Africa* (March 4, 1967), 305.

the budget and opened the path of corruption but also was frustrating to administrators who had gone the painful path of training and who found themselves under political appointees who were illiterate or semiliterate.

There was, in addition, friction between the machine politicians and administrators similar to that which Lucian Pye describes in Burma.[10] In Africa, as in Asia, administrators had come to politics with clear models of their careers and a view of government taken over from the days of British rule. Government, to them, was government by administration without political interference. The administrators felt themselves competent and believed that they could run the country as well as the British administrators had done. The politicians, on the other hand, had come to politics without any clear conception of what it is that a politician does, other than to wield power. Lacking knowledge of how power was to be wielded, the politicians tried to make up for lack of role conception by constant aggression and to blame failures on "sabotage" by the civil service. The administrators, on the other hand, were immobilized by the political appointees and by their own lack of security. In addition, they resented those slurs on their prized competence which often were made by politicians for whom the African administrator had nothing more than contempt.

The results of such "nation-building" are not hard to trace. In Nigeria they led to fresh entrepreneurial attempts at party-building, as each region sought to erect such structures in the other regions as to gain control of the country as a whole. The more populous, albeit more backward, North, for instance, sought to perpetuate its rule and protect itself against the more advanced South by sponsoring political entrepreneurs who would build "parties" that would be entirely dependent on the North for their financing and continuance in office. The most notable and, in a sense, successful of these machines was the Nigerian National Democratic party (NNDP) of Chief Samuel Akintola who, in a complex political play, split the Action Group when its leader, Chief Awolowo, was arrested on various charges of treason and peculation. In a patently rigged election the NNDP was able to secure "victory," but could not reap its fruits as the announcement of its having won the election sparked violent rioting in the West, rioting that threatened the stability of the region and indeed of the entire federation. The situation was worsened by rumors that another political machine was to be established in the Middle Western region as well. Instead of each remaining in its own region, therefore, the Nigerian machines tried to extend themselves to the other regions, endangering the entire federal balance.

What happened in Ghana can best be described, in Chalmers Johnson's term, as a "power deflation," a loss of power accompanied by an attempt to use increased force to retain control.[11] In his effort to keep his machine in power Nkrumah sought, on the one hand, to play different factions in the country against one another and, on the other hand, to build his own sources of support, an army and police of his own. It was undoubtedly this threat to their arms monopoly that prodded

[10] *Politics, Personality and Nation Building: Burma's Search for Identity* (New Haven 1962), chap. 7.

[11] *Revolutionary Change* (Boston 1962), 27–33.

the regular army into action against Nkrumah, rather than objections to "one-party rule," which African officers have sometimes represented as the cause of their revolt.[12]

In short, the political machines, whether in combination with a tribal core or just on their own, were unable to replace the British government at the head of an administrative-traditional system or to offer anything else that could take its place. The result was not only the decay of the organizations that the British had left behind, accompanied by instability, but also the "fissiparous tendencies" so much described by British political scientists. With the disappearance of the central administrative grid that had created a nonintegrative unity among the tribes, the African states were showing signs of coming apart. An analogy drawn from political theory may make matters plainer, although like all analogies it is not perfect. The British government acted as Hobbes's Leviathan. The social compact was that of the chiefs and the British government and had secured protection in exchange for independence. Once this compact was dissolved and no new Leviathan appeared, the tribes began to revert to a "state of nature" with each against the other.

III

If the African states were not to dissolve into their component tribes a new Leviathan would have to be created, and this was to be the role, whether foreseen or not, of the new military governments. It is this aspect of the coups, and not the coups themselves, that will occupy attention.

As the apotheosis of administration,

armies would appear to have obvious advantages in reconstructing an administrative-traditional order. With their chains of command, allocation of functions, specification of rank, and unity of purpose, everything is structured to ensure centralized control and coordinated action. In Africa this has even greater significance, for the army is often the *only* well-organized and coherent arm of government—the only arm that can make its writ run throughout the country. However poorly it may compare with the armies of developed countries by objective military standards, its organization is superior to any other that the government commands. Then, again, armies enjoy certain moral advantages over civilian branches of government: the moral force associated with self-sacrifice, discipline, and courage; freedom from the taint of corruption; and the conception of representing something over and above the passing regimes. Lastly, and perhaps most significant, armies have a monopoly of the most modern and lethal arms.[13]

But because countries are so much more complex than armies, administration of countries is more difficult than administration of armies, and soldiers make poor governors of countries. When, in addition, the country has been brought to a sorry pass by a corrupt civilian government that has preceded the military, the problems are compounded. Officers who assume power under these conditions have to make good on at least some of the politicians' promises while repairing the damage done to the body politic, and they have to do this while preserving the impression of a more just rule. In these matters their military experience is a poor guide. In each country

---

[12] A. A. Africa, *The Ghana Coup, 24 February 1966* (London 1966), 85–86.

[13] Finer, 228–29.

where a military putsch has taken place the officers find a similar solution. In Ghana and Nigeria the officers seem to have chosen the same alternative as was chosen by the British in their time: to abrogate all political activity, to rule by administrative fiat on the central level, and to reconstruct the alliance with the chiefs on the local level—in other words, to rebuild the administrative-traditional system with the officers assuming the role of the British government. The pattern seems, by the logic of the situation, to involve much the same institutions in much the same way.

The military leaders of Ghana and Nigeria, in their attempts at reconstituting the administrative-traditional alliance, followed similar courses. The military commanders made themselves the equivalent of the colonial governors and lieutenant-governors. They appointed themselves and some of the administrators from the civil sector to posts on the virtual equivalent of the executive councils, although the new organizations had obviously greater powers than the old councils had had. Thus the alliance with the civil servants was rebuilt. As part of the compact, it seems, civil servants may have obtained immunity for acts committed under the old dispensation, for in both Ghana and Nigeria administrators were notably absent from the inquisitions that followed the coups. Although it would be too much to hope that administrators had been the incorruptible servants of the public in the face of so much corruption, it is only the politicians' records that have been scrutinized.

Another factor has, however, entered the picture. Although administrators now have greater freedom of decision than they had in the past, freedom from the political interference that they so resented, they do not seem to know how to use this newfound freedom yet. Indecision rather than administrative firmness seems the rule. Again one could turn to Pye's Burma study, which describes a similar phenomenon there.[14] Basing their claims to power on competence but lacking confidence, administrators, by remaining inactive, avoid putting their competence to the test.

Some similarities between Ghana and Nigeria have been pointed up, yet the Ghanaian coup seems successful so far, whereas the Nigerian coup failed. In Nigeria, the initial military takeover of January 1966 was followed by another in July, leading to consequences that cannot even now be assessed. Some reasons for these different outcomes can, however, be suggested.

Both administrators and traditional rulers were strongly regional in sentiment in Nigeria, a fact that must always be borne in mind. Before the coup the regional governments had tended to overshadow the federal government in importance. Holding Nigeria together —given the complex arrangements of core tribes and minority tribes, central and regional administrations, as well as conflicts of personality—might have been possible for a disinterested outsider whose disinterest was generally recognized by all. Such had, in fact, been the position of the British in colonial times. The army officers, however genuine their dedication to Nigeria, clearly did not fit this description. Whatever their protestations, tribal and regional interests were of overwhelming importance to them. The military coup itself could, indeed, be described in tribal and regional terms. It has been argued that it was either a Southern attempt to preempt a planned Northern

---

[14]Chap. 7.

takeover of the country as a whole or a direct attempt by Southern officers to take over the entire country. Those who perished in the coup in January, officers and politicians alike, were both Northerners and Southerners who had supported the puppet NNDP. The July coup, on the other hand, seems to have claimed the lives mainly of Southern officers.

Events were apparently set in train by a meeting of the Northern People's Congress leaders, who ruled at the federal level, and a group of army officers who agreed to use the military to put down the rioting in the West. Southern fears were aroused that the North would invoke military power to keep its puppets in office. If the South feared a Northern takeover before the coup, the shoe was on the other foot after it, and the military government tried, by concessions to the sensibilities of other regions, to set at rest fears that the coups presaged a Southern takeover, particularly by the Ibo of the East. To that end, for instance, Major (later Lieutenant-Colonel) Hassan Katsina, a scion of the Northern ruling elite, was made military governor of the North, similar steps being taken to appoint military governors in other regions from the same core tribes as dominated the regions. Actions such as these may have softened the effects of the coup, especially in the North, but did not allay suspicions.

The military regime in Nigeria won over the administrative cadres by favoring them over the traditional elites who had been involved in machine politics. Attached as the administrators may have been to the institution of tribalism, they were not necessarily equally well disposed toward the administrative interference of tribal political machines or of their appointees to administrative posts. As it was, the traditional rulers were reduced in power. Customary courts were stripped of judicial functions, tribal appointees were dismissed from various specialized boards, and the "elected" members of the local councils were dismissed. In every case civil servants replaced the former incumbents. But in doing these things the officers revealed the fatal flaw in their arrangements. Even with administrative support, the military were in no position to administer the country without traditional support any more than the British had been. Although the administration was the main base of military support, this support was also alienated when General Agyui-Ironsi, the supreme commander, tried to centralize the country.

The reasons for General Ironsi's decision are obscure and, as the General himself has been killed, may never be brought to light. One can speculate that, having only administrative support and, as an officer, favoring central control, Ironsi may have believed that centralizing the country and creating a unified civil service would consolidate both administrative support and administrative control. But, whatever his motive, General Ironsi put himself and his supporters into the same position as the CPP had in Ghana—as a "party of unification" alienated from the primary institutions of the country.

The decree to centralize the civil service and do away with the regions crystallized out all the suspicions about the military regime. The threat to abandon regional division set off immediate rioting in the North. Attempts by Colonel Katsina to placate the traditional rulers by promises that the "people"—a euphemism for the rulers themselves—would be consulted before any step was taken seem to have satisfied them only partly. Even though the most violent response was that of the North, other regions were equally apprehensive. The administrators, on the other hand, on whom the military government relied, were also opposed to unification. Once again it was the North that was the principal source of this opposition. Because of its educational backwardness, a backwardness that had suited the Northern rulers for a time, the North had the smallest cadre of trained administrators. Thus, if qualification were the only basis for civil service appointments, which Ironsi had stated would be the case, the North would fall under the control of the other regions in an administrative system of rule. Northern fears were further reinforced by such provisions as the dropping of Hausa as a language requirement for civil service officers. In other regions, administrators felt that tribal affiliation secured their more rapid promotion, a matter of importance of them. Even deeper ran the fear that, should a central civil service be set up, the tribe with the most men at the top would be able to give continuous preference to fellow tribesmen and make the civil service its preserve. For these and doubtless for other reasons, the administrators wanted the existing system to remain.

Beset on all sides by troubles, the military government could do little. The Northern riots, directed mainly against Ibos in the towns, riots in which troops participated, showed that the officers had lost control of their men. Food shortages, which, it was bruited about, were caused by tribal associations, added to the problems confronting the military government. The shortages were met mainly by exhortations by the military governors against hoarding. The actions of the military

were becoming as futile as had been those of the Nkrumah political machine.

The July coup, in a tragic manner, settled the problem of unification, if it settled little else. Southern, mainly Eastern, officers were killed in the coup, which was, it seems, the Northern revenge for the January coup. The July coup and the violence that preceded and followed it have brought the continued existence of the Nigerian state into question. Each region is, as far as can be ascertained, becoming more like a tribal state. Whether anything can be saved of unity or whether a traditional and administrative system as had existed before can be rebuilt remains a moot question.

That the Ghanaian coup succeeded better is perhaps because the Ghanaian officers not only had ready-made allies to hand, but also because they have so far been astute enough not to lose them. The National Liberation Council, as the military government was styled, could count on the intelligentsia and on the traditional rulers, both of which groups had been alienated from the Nkrumah regime. The intelligentsia had been driven into exile, sent to prison, or reduced to silence. Administrators had been confused by the maze of organizations the political machine had conjured up, to which more were constantly being added. The traditional rulers had been displaced and now looked to the National Liberation Council for a restoration of their positions. The military government acted promptly to set up councils that would engage the energies of the intelligentsia and promised to displace chiefs wrongly enstooled by Nkrumah. The military government was, it therefore seems, taking realistic steps to restore the administrative-traditional system that had succeeded in the past.

The broader question of the survival of the National Liberation Council is, however, still problematic. The administrators are not, as mentioned earlier, proving equal to the task of decision-making without strong direction from a political sector, and the Council does not seem able to give such directly political leads. Already rumors of plots are in the air, and these usually precede trouble. The lives of the members of the National Liberation Council have been threatened, and even a comic opera plot was mounted by some former supporters of Dr. Nkrumah and two junior officers. As in Africa the comic has only too often become deadly serious, even these manifestations cannot be taken lightly. There is evidence that the army officers are not off their guard. Yet in spite of such threats to its position the Council has released from prison many of the major cogs of Nkrumah's political machine, and the fact that it can do so at a time like this indicates the absence of any real support for the machine itself.

IV

"Men," a cynic once wrote, "make their mistakes in order to repeat them." If this *mot* be applied to political development, men can be said to knock down their political structures just to replace them with ones essentially similar. And it is this tendency of political forms to reappear that has been a major theme of this article. The reason why structures keep emerging is, it has been suggested, the absence of change in the institutions that underlie the structures. Given certain institutions, one could argue, only certain structures are appropriate. If the most

appropriate structures are removed and replaced by others less appropriate, men will seek to change back to the most appropriate. Such efforts need not, of course, succeed. Nor is it likely that the original structures, the organizations and procedures, will be reestablished as they were. But the efforts to return to what was most appropriate will be persisted in.

The arrangements made in the colonial era were, it now seems, the most appropriate for Africa given its stage of development. So appropriate were they that much of what has happened in Ghana and Nigeria can be interpreted as an attempt to return to these institutions after the failure of the newer forms, dominated by political machines, became manifest. The political machines could not replace the British government at the head of the existing institutional structure and could not offer an alternative of their own.

Although nothing is more dangerous than prophecy in African politics, it may well be that the African governments of tomorrow will be neither democratic nor Communist. Nor, let it be added, will these take on any especially "African" form of either. The system that will prevail will, most likely, be an adaptation of administrative and traditional rule along the lines of former colonial government with legislative and executive councils providing the forums for a largely empty political activity. The system will, thus, divide political labors much as they were divided before. Systems of this sort are likely in Ghana and in the regions of Nigeria, whether the latter remain federated or not. Events alone can, in the last resort, give the final answer.

V

Development

Pressures for government action to promote national development are a major source of stress on all African political systems. Fundamentally, Africans see "development" as *economic* development—the creation and growth of the material capabilities of their societies. In a continent in which most countries have annual per capita incomes under $100 and population increases during the past decade have consistently outstripped national economic growth rates, economic development is clearly a necessary precondition to satisfaction of the desires for higher standards of living and an improved quality of life that are at the heart of the "revolution of rising expectations" created during the nationalist era. Further, Africans see economic change as the central feature of the more general goal of social modernization, for many of the more obvious features of modern societies, such as urbanization and industrialization, are initially economic in character. Economic development may not insure a society's advance to modernization, but without it modernization will be difficult if not impossible. But how should an African country promote its own development most efficiently? Since the achievement of independence, political leaders in Africa have sought both the technical means to develop their economies rapidly and the ideological supports necessary to justify the public sacrifices that may be required for economic growth.

Programmatically, nearly all of the new states of tropical Africa profess adherence to "African Socialism" as the theoretical framework for their development strategy. Various leaders, such as Leopold Senghor and Julius Nyerere, have tried to codify this doctrine in the process of developing their own national economic policies. But as yet there is little continental agreement on the specific content of African Socialism, despite attempts to establish such agreement as that at Dakar in 1962. To date Africa has not produced a dominant theoretician of development, although several African leaders have aspired to fill this role. Each national leadership has devised its own action-program for development, and these programs have differed on such questions as the importance of formal Marxism-Leninism, the relevance of Soviet and Chinese experiences, and the necessity for total state control of the economy.

Nevertheless, there are recurring themes in the policy statements of African leaders on the problems of development which suggest that they share a general orientation.[1] One of these is to explain the poverty of African countries in the terminology of colonial exploitation. Such an explanation, however, is historical in character and offers no remedy for poverty, although it provides African leaders with a moral basis to make requests for economic and technical assistance from the former colonial powers. A second theme is the social obligation of all citizens to work for the improvement and benefit of their community; this has been explicitly spelled out in numerous instances, such as Julius Nyerere's pronouncements on the concept of *Ujamaa* and Kenya's 1965 policy paper on African Socialism.[2] The obligation of all to work is a positive assertion directed at increasing the productivity of those engaged in subsistence agriculture, converting subsistence activities into cash enterprises, and urging labor unions to change their goals from consumption to production. In this view, increased productivity is seen as the key to African development.

A third theme is related to the foregoing. African Socialists scorn the relevance of the notion of the "class struggle" to contemporary Africa. In their view African societies are not divided into mutually antagonistic classes based on the institution of private property. Emphasis is placed, rather, on the cohesion of traditional African communities. Indeed, African Socialists see it as the special task of African governments to prevent the emergence of class differences and economic exploitation in the process of development and to maintain the unity of African society. One finds this expressed, for example, in

---

[1] The discussion following is adapted from William H. Friedland, "Four Sociological Trends in African Socialism," *Africa Report,* VIII, No. 5 (May 1963), 7–10.

[2] See Julius K. Nyerere, "Ujamaa: The Basis of African Socialism," reprinted in William H. Friedland and Carl G. Rosberg, Jr. (eds.), *African Socialism* (Stanford University Press, 1964), pp. 238–47; *African Socialism and Its Application to Planning* (Nairobi: The Government Printer, 1965), pp. 4–5.

Nyerere's Arusha Declaration of 1967 which condemned conspicuous consumption by various African politicians and urged socialist self-reliance for all citizens.[3] It is this belief that the social cohesion of tribal Africa can be transposed directly to the level of the new nation-state that provides the distinctively "African" content of African Socialism.

Most common, however, is the assumption that political and state action is an adequate and efficient means to produce economic advance. "Seek ye first the political kingdom," Nkrumah said, "and all things will be added unto it." Indeed, several writers on Africa have suggested that political commitment is a necessary precondition to rapid economic change.[4] Yet clearly, economic development is both the cause and effect of a wide range of changes in society, and it has been a major task of social theorists to identify and interrelate these manifold variables. The goal has been greater understanding of the broad process of social modernization and the manner in which that process occurs.

With some exceptions, the literature on modernization has projected a linear and "rhythmic" process of interrelated social, political, psychological, economic and other changes, and this view has commended the study of modernization from the standpoint of the history of countries that are already modern. In effect, the process of modernization is frequently defined in terms of case histories of the countries of the West. A.F.K. Organski, for example, posits four "stages" through which all countries move as they modernize: primitive unification, industrialization, national welfare, and abundance.[5] The case of England would seem to support Organski's view. In England the problems of industrialization were confronted *after* the English people had come to be a recognized and accepted political community but *before* the development of wide-spread public expectations regarding the performance of government in the field of social welfare.

Most of the new states in Africa, however, are compelled to cope with the problems of political unification, economic industrialization, and national welfare simultaneously and in a very brief period of time. In particular, they must respond to public demands for a broad range of social services before they have the economic capacity to do so, and in the absence of a deeply rooted political framework within which to

---

[3] *The Arusha Declaration and TANU'S Policy on Socialism and Self-Reliance,* (Dar es Salaam: Publicity Section of TANU) 1967.

[4] See, for example, George Dalton, "History, Politics and Economic Development in Liberia," *Journal of Economic History,* XXV, No. 4 (December 1965), 569–91; and Robert L. Hess and Gerhard Loewenberg, "The Ethiopian No-Party State," *American Political Science Review,* LVIII, No. 4 (December 1964), 947–50.

[5] A. F. K. Organski, *The Stages of Political Development* (New York: Alfred A. Knopf, Inc., 1965).

balance these demands while finding solutions to them. Indeed, Karl Deutsch suggests that "social mobilization," i.e., the variety of rapid social changes which accompany economic development, tends to increase the government's burdens more quickly than it can develop the capabilities to cope with them.[6] And, Samuel Huntington, extending this point, argues that the short-run political product of rapid "social mobilization" in the new states will likely be instability, or "political decay," rather than "political development."[7]

[6] Karl W. Deutsch, "Social Mobilization and Political Development," *American Political Science Review,* LV, No. 3 (September 1961), 493.

[7] Samuel P. Huntington, "Political Development and Political Decay," *World Politics,* XVII, No. 3 (April 1965), 386–430.

Social Change and Modernization in African Societies South of the Sahara

S. N. Eisenstadt

I

Social change in Africa has been studied from a variety of points of view by different social science disciplines—anthropology, sociology, political science, and economics. The first impetus has come from anthropologists, and they have quite naturally focused at first on the processes of change and disorganization of the various traditional social and cultural patterns and organizations and then on the possible recrystallization of some such traditional elements within the more modern and differentiated societies. Thus, studies of different aspects of detribalization, of the changing status of chiefs or of women, or of the undermining of the older traditional frameworks were made side by side with studies of the development of urban voluntary organizations in which many traditional elements and orientations tended to subsist, or with studies of the new religious cults and movements in which too the confrontation of old and new often served as the main focus of research.

These studies have gradually come close to some of the first major concerns of sociologists who became interested in these areas and who focused first on the study of various aspects of urbanization, with its major and varied social problems such as delinquency or family disorganization, or incipient forms of industrialization, and secondly on the emergence of various modern-time types of organizations—schools, trade unions—or of new "educated", professional and semi-professional élites.[1]

Lastly, political scientists have come in, studying first the various forms of

[1] See for good collections of such materials: D. Forde (ed.), *Social Implication of Industrialization and Urbanization in Africa South of the Sahara,* Unesco, 1956; A Southall (ed.), *Social Change in Modern Africa,* London, 1961.

From *Cahiers D'Etudes Africaines,* Vol. V, No. 3 (1965), 453–71, by permission of author and journal.

nationalistic movements that developed in most African countries and later on—after the establishment of independence —the various new forms of political organization—especially the basic political institutions on the one hand, and political parties and other types of political organizations on the other.[2]

The original emphasis of most of these studies—with perhaps the partial exception of the political ones—was the study of social change and disorganization, of the emergence of new types of social organization which were drifting, as it were, into new directions—but directions which were not readily discernible, and whose new overall contours were not fully perceived. At most, there could be found in most of these studies an implicit assumption that these changes are going into some direction not dissimilar from that of other modern, industrial societies, even if such developments in African societies were weak and intermittent, and even if disorganization and the establishment of colonial frameworks were more easily to be found than the development of more stable social forms. Some such assumptions could also be discerned in many of the first studies dealing with political movements and parties.

But with the establishment of new states and political structures, there took place a very important shift in this whole area of research. It has created the possibility, even the necessity, of studying these various phenomena together, in their mutual interrelationship, in what was often called their "global" or "total" setting.[3]

The very establishment of these new

political frameworks pointed out to the importance of new integration problems, to the emergence and crystallization of new overall, integrative frameworks which tended, as it were, to bring together the various processes of change into some common focus. It was the development of these new societal centers which gave a new meaning to the various processes of change which were studied by the diverse social science disciplines and which were now necessarily brought together into some sort of common framework. The emergence of these centers has necessarily changed the perception and analysis of the processes of change: they had to be evaluated from the point of view of structural recrystallizations which could be interwoven into the new center and upon which the new center was greatly dependent.

These new centers had very specific characteristics. They were conceived in their ideological and institutional forms as an attempt at modernity, at the establishment of a new modern order, of new modern societies, which were to take their proper place among other modern societies.

Hence the study of the varied processes of change became, in a way, part of the broader study of modernization, and the basic problem which confronts them today is to find out the specific problem and fashion of modernization as they appear in African societies.

II

The first natural step towards such an analysis would be to find out to what extent African societies do develop in the direction of modern societies, to what extent they develop the major social features and problems of modernity.[4]

[2] See for instance: D. E. Apter, "Ghana in Transition", *Athenaeum*, New York, 1963.

[3] See for instance: G. Balandier, «Phénomènes sociaux totaux et dynamique sociale», *Cahiers Internationaux de Sociologie*, vol. XXX, 1961, pp. 23–24.

[4] For a further exposition of these points of view see: S. N. Eisenstadt, "Modernisation,

The broad socio-demographic and structural corollaries of modernization as they develop in the major institutional spheres have by now been well studied in the literature. Perhaps the best overall summary of the socio-demographic indices of modernization has been coined by Karl Deutsch[5] in the term of "social mobilization." He has defined it as the "process in which major clusters of old social, economic and psychological commitments are eroded and broken and people become available for new patterns of socialization and behaviour" and has indicated that some of its main indices are exposure to aspects of modern life through demonstrations of machinery, buildings, consumers' goods, etc., response to mass media, change of residence, urbanization, change from agricultural occupations, literacy, growth of *per capita* income.

Similarly, the major structural characteristics of modernization have been identified as the development of a high extent of differentiation, of free resources which are not committed to any fixed, ascriptive (kinship, territorial, etc.) groups, the development of specialized and diversified types of social organization, the development of wide nontraditional "national," or even supra-national group identifications, and the concomitant development in all major institutional spheres of specialized roles and of special wider regulative and

allocative mechanism and organizations such as market mechanisms in economic life, voting and party activities in politics and of diverse bureaucratic organizations and mechanisms in most institutional spheres.

But beyond these varied socio-demographic or structural characteristics of modernity or modernization there looms a somewhat larger, in a way more crucial, problem. Modernization implies not only the development of the various aspects of growing structural differentiation, but also the development of a social system which not only generates continuous change, but also, unlike many other types of social systems, is capable as well of absorbing changes beyond its own initial institutional premises.

Hence, the central problem of modernization can be seen as the ability of any system to adapt itself to these changing demands, to absorb them in terms of policy-making and to ensure its own continuity in the face of continuous new demands and new forms of political organization.

In other words, modernization creates in its wake problems of sustained social, economic and political growth as its central problem. The ability to deal with continuous changes of political demands is the crucial test of such sustained growth, of development or modernization.

Research on development and modernization has been guided by assumptions—often implicit—about the conditions of such sustained growth. These assumptions are now being undermined and the examination of the African case may be of special interest or importance for their critical evaluation.

The first such assumption was that of the primacy of the economic sphere in development and modernization, of the central importance of the economic

Growth and Diversity", *The Carnegie Faculty Seminar on Political and Administrative Development*, Indiana University, Bloomington, 1963; S. N. Eisenstadt, "Modernisation and the Conditions of Sustained Growth", *World Politics*, XVI, No. 4, July 1964, pp. 576–595, where further bibliographical references are given.

[5] "Social Mobilization and Political Development", *The American Pol. Sc. Review*, LV, Sept. 1961, pp. 463–515.

solvent for the development of viable modern societies and political régimes.

Second was the assumption of the relative assurance of the continuity of modernization, of "sustained growth," of continuous development in any institutional sphere—be it economics, politics or social organization—after the initial "take-off."

The third basic assumption was that of the very close interrelatedness of almost all the major aspects of "development," or of modernization, in all these major institutional spheres of any society.

It may, of course, be claimed that the first assumption—that of the primacy of the economic sphere in development —was discarded relatively early in the game, when some at least of the economists discovered that the conditions of development and effective functioning of a modern economic system could not be understood in economic terms alone, and when the analysis of the non-economic preconditions of economic development became one of the major problems of research in this field. However, the very concern with the preconditions of economic growth tended to reinforce the implicit assumption that once such initial economic take-off is attained development and modernization are more or less assured also in other spheres. Thus, interestingly enough, while the literature about the *preconditions* of economic growth is, and continues to be, very abundant, that on the political or social *consequences* of economic growth is only beginning now to emerge.

The second assumption, about the assurance of continuous development, or modernization, once the initial "take-off" stages have been attained, can be found with different degrees of explicitness in many economic and political analyses—whether in Rostow's *Stages of Economic Growth* or in the first analyses on the development of political institutions in the so-called New Nations. Most of these first analyses were oriented towards the elucidation of the conditions under which parliamentary-constitutional régimes can successfully operate in non-Western societies. While it was usually fully acknowledged that such conditions may not be ripe in many of these nations, it still was often implicitly assumed that if such political institutions can be *implanted* in these countries in the first stages of their *independence* their continuity and working can perhaps be assured. It was only later that, for instance, Emerson, one of the first students of nationalism and politics in Asia, wrote about the "Erosion of Democracy" in Asian countries[6] and even this remained for a relatively long time an isolated attempt. Hence until lately we find but few systematic analyses of the crises and breakdowns of political modernization or economic development after the initial "take-off."

The third assumption, that of the interconnectedness of the various institutional aspects of modernization, predicted that the process of modernization in the different institutional spheres —be they economic, political or in the field of social organization—are closely interrelated, so that they tend necessarily to go together and to coalesce in relatively similar patterns. It unwittingly brought over a relative neglect of the study of the structural and organizational variety attendant on modernization. Although almost everybody who dealt with these problems did stress that the concrete social and political forms which will develop in the New States will somehow differ from the Western

---

[6] See: R. Emerson, "The Erosion of Democracy in the New States", in H. Eckstein and D. E. Apter (eds.), *Comparative Politics*, New York, 1963, pp. 625–644.

ones, yet the assumption of the close interrelationship between the various institutional aspects of modernization was conducive to the neglect of systematic studies of these structural varieties and to a continuous implicit "Western-centricity" of many of these studies—and to the search for conditions under which institutions of the western type can successfully develop and function in the developing societies or New Nations.

Many analyses of processes of modernization which took off from some of the preceding assumptions often lead to or were based on the—usually implicit—assumption that the conditions for sustained growth can be found in the continuous extension of these various socio-demographic and/or structural indices.

Thus, for instance, one possible and very often propounded view has been that the more a society exhibits or develops the basic characteristics of structural specialization and the higher it is on various indices of social mobilization, the more modern it would be, i.e., by implication, the better it would be able to sustain continuous growth and absorb continuous changes.

According to this view, the traditionalism or modernity of a society could be measured by the extent of development of social mobilization within it and by the extent to which its basic principles of allocation and organization were particularistic, diffuse and ascriptive as against universalistic, achievement and specificity oriented. Thus, for instance, according to one of such studies, traditional society tends to be a familistic one while the modern one tends to divest the family unit from most of its functions, and the family itself develops more into the direction of the small nuclear family.

Needless to say, such an approach has a very great extent of plausibility. However, it is not fully borne out by the available evidence. Many researches—analyzed elsewhere—indicate that the picture is not so simple or clear-cut. In many cases, we find that the extension of the socio-demographic or structural indices of modernization may give rise to what may be called "breakdowns" of modernization. In general, it can perhaps be said that certain levels of "social mobilization" and of structural differentiation constitute a necessary condition of the modernization, but that the continuous development of these processes does not constitute a sufficient condition of the continuity of modernization in the sense of the creation of an institutional framework capable of continuous absorption of change.

III

Of special interest here are the implications of the non-tenability of the third basic assumption, namely the assurance of continuity of growth after the "take-off."[7]

In both the economic and the political spheres it has become quite obvious that there does not exist any assurance about such continuity. The case of Argentina in the economic sphere, of Burma or Indonesia in the political sphere, are among the most pertinent examples of the possibility of breakdowns after some initial—or even sometimes relatively advanced—stages of modernization.

A great part of the contemporary history in general and of the contemporary international relations in particular is, in a way, the history of

---

[7] S. N. Eisenstadt, "Breakdowns of Modernisation", *Economic Development and Cultural Change*, Vol. XII, No. 4, July 1964, pp. 345–367.

breakdowns or of stagnation of political régimes or economic systems which had seemingly "taken-off" into modernity—and yet could not continue to fly at all or to attain higher altitudes.

But the more paradoxical—and more significant—outcome of these processes was that such breakdowns or stagnations did not necessarily lead up to the total collapse of these new régimes or to their return to some traditional social and political form.

These régimes, which evince different degrees of development or modernization in the economic, political or social sphere, and different types of stagnation, tend to coalesce together into some new forms of viable ongoing social and political systems.

Such new polities and societies certainly differ in many ways from the "older" (Western) modern ones nor do they necessarily develop into the direction of these "older" societies, and yet they by no means remain any longer simply traditional societies.

Moreover however stagnating or unstable these régimes are, they evince some capability of reorganization and continuity, and they develop various internal and external policies which aim at assuring for themselves the conditions of such continuity.

The conditions which gave rise to such régimes varied and should constitute foci of research. But one such general condition should perhaps be indicated here—namely the contemporary international setting.

This setting, and especially the situation of "cold-war" on the one hand, and the growing drawing together of almost all régimes of the world into one common international setting, on the other hand, are of no small importance in contributing to the possibility of crystallization of such tendencies in relatively stagnating régimes.

The competition between the great powers for influence in the major areas of the world on the one hand, and the ideological legitimation for any "independent" régimes on the other hand, may easily provide some very crucial resources both for the development of some initial modernization and for the stabilization of relatively regressive régimes.

IV

The preceding analysis poses two basic problems before the student of processes of modernization in Africa south of the Sahara. One is the identification of the specific structural characteristics of the processes of modernization as they develop in African society, as distinct from those of other modern societies, and of the conditions which explain their development.

The other major problem is the identification of those forces which—within these structural frameworks—facilitate or impede the development of this ability for sustained growth, of the continuous absorption of changes and new problems.

From this point of view it is very significant that within most African states the emphasis on change, progress, and economic development is one of the main tenets of their political and ideological orientations. But at the same time, their institutional capacity to absorb changes may be small compared to their aspirations for change although it necessarily greatly varies among the different new states according to various conditions.

The ability of the élites of the new states to implement the manifold changes as they would like to is often limited and very often they are barely able to maintain their own continuity and stability. It is this contradiction which constitutes perhaps the major problem or focus of investigation in the study of modernization in African societies.

In order to be able to analyze this problem, we first have to go back to the analysis of some of the most important features of modernization as they have developed under the colonial régimes in Africa south of the Sahara.[8]

Perhaps the major characteristic of the process of modernization in colonial societies is that it has been unbalanced, especially in the relations of the processes of change and transition between the "central" and the local level. Most changes introduced either directly or indirectly by the colonial powers (or by the "traditional" authorities of the independent societies which cooperated with the European powers) have been focused on the central institutions of the society. The most obvious changes were in the broad frameworks of political and economic institutions. In the political field, the introduction of unitary systems of administration, the unification or regularization of taxation, the establishment of modern court procedures, and, at later stages, the introduction of limited types of representation, have greatly changed overall political structures and orientations. These changes have introduced certain universalistic criteria and orientations toward general rules and modern procedures. Even where various forms of indirect rule were practiced some change necessarily took place in political organization, though this change was much slower than in cases of direct rule.

Similarly, many changes have been

effected in the economy, notably the change to a market economy, and in the educational field by endeavoring to provide new types of modern education for selected local élites.

At the same time, however, the colonial powers saw it as part of their task to effect these changes only within the limits set by institutions existing at the local level, i.e., the level of the village, community, or tribal unit. Here the colonial powers attempted to contain most changes within the limits of traditional groups and/or to limit, as much as possible, the extent of any change. Although many changes did develop within the local communities, as the literature on detribalization of the family indicates, the rulers tried, so far as possible, to contain these changes within traditional system; and most of their administrative efforts on the local level were aimed at strengthening the existing organizations and relations, at maintaining peace and order, and at reorganizing the systems of taxation. Thus, while the administration attempted to introduce innovations—particularly new taxes and improved methods of revenue administration—it tried to accomplish this within a relatively unchanging social setting, with the implicit goal of limiting changes to technical matters. Thus there tended to develop here a basic contradiction: on the one hand, attempts were made to establish broad, modern, administrative, political, and economic settings while, on the other hand, these changes were to be limited and based on relatively unchanged sub-groups and on traditional attitudes and loyalties.

This situation created a process of disequilibrium or of unbalanced change, continuously spiralled by the very processes of colonization and its international setting. In all colonial societies it gave rise to some Westernized groups

---

[8] S. N. Eisenstadt, *Essays on Sociological Aspects of Political and Economic Development*, The Hague, 1961; T. Hodgkin, *Nationalism in Colonial Africa*, London, 1956.

and élites which usually became the spearheads of nationalistic movements, and it did also greatly influence some of the basic characteristics and orientations of these movements.

The modernizing orientations of these movements were focused mostly on the political and much less on the cultural sphere in the sense of reformation of the basic internal value-orientations of these groups. Consequently the relations between the rising nationalistic élites and the wider strata of their societies were usually concentrated in the political sphere and to a much smaller degree in the economic and cultural spheres. In most of the non-political spheres there tended to develop—albeit with great differences between different countries —relatively fewer active modernizing groups in the economic and cultural spheres.

Even more problematic was sometimes the extent to which the major social groups or strata in these societies were able to develop from within themselves active orientations and resources for modernization and were able to become integrated into wider frameworks. While all of them did undergo processes of social disorganization in various spheres of social life—especially in the economic and social ones—, the extent to which they were able to develop new autonomous orientations towards modern frameworks and goals, and to create the resources for the implementation of such goals was not very great—although, of course, it differed greatly from place to place.

V

These problems became more acute with the attainment of independence, when the leaders of the nationalistic groups became ruling élites, officially bent on overall modernization of their countries and faced with the double problem of establishing new political centers, frameworks, institutions and consensus and of keeping themselves in power.

It is within the framework of these new political centers that the potential discrepancy between the great emphasis on change and the frequent inability of the institutional framework to implement such change tended to develop. This potential discrepancy can perhaps be best understood through an analysis of the basic structural characteristics of modernization as they tend to develop in contemporary African societies.

Several such characteristics can be discerned. Let us start first with some of the characteristics of the new emerging modern centers.

First comes the development, within the political sphere, of a tendency towards a strong emphasis on the executive on the one hand and toward single or dominant parties, which encompass most types of political aspirations on the other. The strong emphasis on the executive can be easily discerned in most of the constitutions of the new African states which invest the head of State or of Government with very far-reaching constitutional and institutional powers.[9]

The tendency towards a dominant or single party system has by now become so widespread in African societies as not to need any special further comment. It is however important to stress that it is connected with (or to some extent explained by) the differential sequence of modernization in the different institutional spheres which will be analyzed later on. Closely related with it is the great importance of the

---

[9] See for instance: G. M. Carter (ed.), *African One-Party States*, Ithaca, 1962; and R. Schachter, "Single Party Systems in West Africa", *The American Pol. Sc. Review*, June 1961, pp. 294–307.

governmental and political sector in the modern sectors of economy. While the concrete contours of this sector do greatly differ as between various African countries, yet some common features can be discerned. Government corporations, centrally controlled large-scale cooperatives and various enterprises run directly by the government or the party can be found in varied degrees as very important—if not the most important— parts of the African (as distinct from the foreign) modern economic sectors.

The tendency to maintain single or dominant party systems is also closely connected with the development within the modern sectors of African societies of relatively large-scale, highly bureaucratic organization and with the attempts to subsume many "smaller groups like trade unions or various types of voluntary associations, within the framework of unified political party units."[10]

As against these characteristics of the center there stand out some of the structural characteristics of the broader groups. The first such characteristic is the relatively low level of "social mobilization" as measured either by socio-demographic indices or by the extent and scope of social differentiation. The predominance of "primary occupations" in general, of farming in particular, the continuing persistence, even if in changed forms, of various traditional frameworks, all of them attend to this fact, the exact extent of which has, however, yet to be more fully explored.[11]

A second important aspect of the process of modernization of the broader social groups in Africa is the relative

---

[10]See for instance: United Nations, 1963, *Report on the World Social Situation*, XIV; and J. Meynaud et A. Selah-Bey, *Le Syndicalisme africain*, Paris, 1963.

[11]*Report on the World Social Situation*, 1963.

sequence of modernization in different institutional spheres—the relatively quick development of the political aspirations of the wider social groups and their overall political modernization before a concomitant extent of economic, professional and often even educational development. The high level of political modernization gave usually rise, in its turn, to a quicker development of educational facilities and aspiration—especially of the more generalized and "humanistic" ones—which often outstripped the economic facilities. Closely related to these characteristics is the tendency to profusion of relatively small scale often ephemeral types of social grouping which are to no small degree connected with the processes of change and with the breakdown of various traditional units.

A third basic characteristic of the modernization of the broader social strata in African societies is the continuous persistence, transformation and structural recrystallization of various traditional forms and frameworks.

Tribal associations or groups within the framework of the more broader political parties, trade unions or various voluntary associations are one important indication of this trend. The continuous recrystallization of traditional symbols, relations and groupings within the more religious frameworks—be they various autochthonous or Islamic and Christian religious organizations— constitutes another such indication.

VI

The synchronization of these different characteristics, of the special temporal sequence of modernization in different spheres, of the relatively low united level of differentiation coupled together with the tendency to large-scale and monolithic organizations point out the great importance of the processes and structures which bring together the traditional and more modern sectors.

Of special importance here are some characteristics of the new emerging system of social stratification, especially as it bears on processes of transition from more traditional to modern sectors. It has already been pointed out above that the range or scope of the modern sector is relatively small although it is continually expanding. But this very expansion displays certain specific characteristics.

First, it is, on the whole, more heavily concentrated in the administrative and political than in the business or purely economic areas. This is closely connected with the predominance of the government on the economy on which we have already commented above. Second, the characteristics of mobility to the modern sector and especially to its more predominant or upper positions are of interest here. Usually two channels of mobility—often overlapping—seem to be of special importance. One is the education, the other is the political party.[12]

Although there is as yet but little adequate evidence, some of the available data seem to indicate that the importance of the educational channel is continuously on the rise and that the more it becomes an important avenue of mobility, the greater becomes the pressure on educational facilities on the one hand and the smaller the return on investment in education on the other—especially insofar as the modern occupational sector does not expand to the same degree as the educational system and the access to it.

There are also but few adequate data on the differential access to educational facilities but the existing data seem to indicate that while there develops here, as in most other modern countries, a tendency for sons of well-to-do (urban and educated) people to have greater chances of educational advancement yet, on the whole, there is a relatively large extent of openness and accessibility of the educational positions to sons of other (i.e. especially farming) groups.[13]

Thus there tends to develop here a combination of the relatively restricted scope and nature or type of the upper positions in the modern sector (here of special interest is the relatively smaller importance of economic or professional positions) as against the relatively broader base from which the recruitment to these positions takes place.

The process of crystallization of new frameworks or mechanisms which could serve as bridges between the new centers and the broader periphery has also been evident in the search for new symbols of common cultural identity.

Several dimensions of this search stand out. One is that of "traditional-modernity" and the search for those elements of the specific historical heritage which may best contribute to the crystallization of new, more flexible, specifically African symbols of modernity.

A second dimension is focused on the possible crystallization of a meaningful personal and collective identity transcending any given particularistic collectivity. Perhaps the quest for "African Personality" is the best illustration—if not necessarily solution—of this search.

---

[12]See: «Éducation et Développement», *Tiers-Monde, Problèmes des pays sous-développés*, t. V, n° 17, janvier-mars 1964.

[13]J. Foster, "Ethnicity and the School in Ghana", *Comparative Education Review*, Vol. 6, No. 2, October 1962, p. 127.

Third and last, there is the possible incorporation and interpretation of several different historical, religious and ideological traditions—the specific historical heritage of these societies, the broad religious orientations brought by Christianity, Islam and resistance to them and the new, modern national, international and social ideologies. It is around these varied dimensions and confrontations that the attempts to forge out new symbols of collective identity are being centered.[14]

VII

The preceding analysis indicates that the process of modernization will, in African societies, necessarily develop structural forms which are in many respects different from those of other modern or modernizing societies.

But beyond this, it poses also the problem of the extent to which there will develop, within these societies, conditions for sustained growth and modernization. This problem is of crucial importance in African societies; and their very process of modernization may intensify some of its aspects.

On the one hand, the crystallization of the various structural characteristics of modernization analyzed above points out some potential weaknesses of the new emerging centers. Among them the most important are the possibilities of the crystallization of close oligarchic élites oriented mainly towards self-aggrandizement and the maintenance of

[14]See among the many works dealing with "The African Personality": Ezekiel Mphahlele, *The African Image*, 1962; The First International Conference of Negro Writers, *Présence Africaine*, Nlle Série, Nos. 8–9–10, Paris, June-Nov. 1956; *The West African Intellectual Community*, published for the Congress for Cultural Freedom, by Ibadan University Press, 1962; also G. Balandier, *Afrique ambiguë*, Paris, 1957.

their own position of power and prestige and the erosion of commitments to collective and developmental goals.

On the other hand, these élites face already now the problems of development and absorption, within the new central institutional settings, of new social forces which were not initially fully represented by them or which are being created by the very impetus of modernization.

The most important of these forces are, first, the possible persistence or opposition of older (even if transformed) tribal or traditional forces. Second, within the urban sector there exist the possibilities of the development of a discontented, usually small middle class of workers and Trade Union leaders, as well as of soldiers, veterans and the possibility of alienation among younger elements who become discontent with what, for them, is already an Establishment.

It is out of these varied elements that new orientations of protest and different structural possibilities, breakdowns, stagnation, or transformation, tend to develop. They create, through their demands, potential splits within the élite and strains on the working of the central institutions—and pose the question or the problem of the conditions under which the new centers with their specific structural characteristics will be able to facilitate continuous and sustained growth and development. Truly enough time and experience have been too short to enable any conclusive analysis, but, taking into account the experience of other areas, we may perhaps attempt to point out some of the problem areas which should be analyzed from this point of view.

Perhaps the most crucial problem here is the extent of compatibility or affinity between the modernizing élites and the major social strata. Of great importance here is, first, the general level of development, of "internal modernization" of the different strata which take part in the process of modernization, and the general level of resources which are generated by them in this process.

Second is the interrelationship among different élite groups and especially the extent of harmony or dissociation between the more technical, professional and administrative élite on the one hand and the more generalized, "solidarity-making" political and cultural élites on the other.

Comparative research on modernization has indicated that, insofar as there exists some affinity of this kind, even if it is a rather passive one, between the modernizing élite or élites and the major groups and strata, and among the major modernizing élites, then the process of political modernization is relatively smooth. Similarly, the stronger and more cohesive internally are the major strata, and the more they are able to participate in the process of modernization in various institutional spheres, the greater becomes the extent of resources which they are able to put at the disposal of various modern institutions and organizations, as well as their ability to regulate through some autonomous mechanism some of the problems attendant on the growing differentiation and modernization so as to articulate realistic political demands and influence the formulation of major political goals and policies by the élites.

In more general terms it can be stated that relatively continuous progress and institutionalization of modernization in general and of political modernization in particular tends to be greater insofar as the modernizing élites are relatively strong and cohesive, and can mobilize adequate support from different strata without giving rise, by this very process, to new cleavages within the society and

undermining the cohesion of its major strata.[15]

VIII

On the basis of the preceding analysis it might perhaps be possible to indicate some of the aspects of the African scene which may be of crucial importance from the point of view of the development of conditions facilitating sustained growth.

In this attempt we must go beyond the description of the structural characteristics of modernization as they develop in African societies and look for those forces which may impede or facilitate the development of that type of interrelation between the modernizing élites and the broader strata which is so crucial for the process of sustained growth.

It is as yet very difficult to delineate and analyze these forces on the African scene, but it might be worthwhile to indicate some areas which should, I think, constitute fields of research concerning these problems. It is, of course, very important to analyze at first the various possible sources of economic resources and activities which may help to provide the necessary frameworks for economic and socio-political development. As this problem would probably be taken up by the economists, I will not dwell on it here. Instead I would like to emphasize the importance of identifying those aspects within the internal structure of African societies which may serve as important starting points for recrystallization in the direction of new, flexible modern frameworks, and the extent to which they may bring about the cohesiveness of the élite, its dedication to collective goals of develop-

---

[15]S. N. Eisenstadt, "Modernisation and Conditions of Sustained Growth", *World Politics, loc. cit.*

ment and modernization as well as the maintenance of affinity and solidarity among the various élites and between them and the broader strata on the other.

Four broad areas seem to be of very great importance from this point of view and may constitute the focal points of fruitful research. The first is the examination of possible points of recrystallization within the traditional "tribal" frameworks. In this context it is necessary to recognize the assumption that all traditional or tribal frameworks are necessarily the most important determinants of the degree of adjustment or adaptation to modern conditions. The important characteristics seem to be the degree of solidarity of the family and of the community, of flexibility of élites and of systems of stratification, and probably other factors, which are not always directly related, in a one-to-one way, to the basic structural "typological" characteristics of traditional societies. They seem to exist both in the more and the less "traditional" societies, and to be more closely related to the cultural differentiation and interrelations between different sub-groups which exist within the common framework of these different types than to their overall structural characteristics.

The processes of religious and ideological transformation which have been taking place are a second important area for such potential recrystallization. These processes of religious reorganization and recrystallization contain on the one hand important possibilities of development of orientation to wider, more flexible and differentiated activities and goals, while on the other hand they may also contribute for the crystallization of some more flexible and cohesive symbols of collective identity.[16]

---

[16] Georges Balandier, *Sociologie actuelle de l'Afrique Noire*, Paris, 1963 (2ᵉ éd.).

Third, the process of political transformation itself, with the strong drive to the center which it implies, embodies similar possibilities of transformation, although it may at the same time—just like the other spheres mentioned above —contain many possibilities of rigidity and breakdowns.

A fourth area, the development of which is crucial for sustained growth, is that of education. We have already seen above that education provides one of the most important channels of transition from the traditional to the modern sectors in African societies; it is henceforth but natural that its structure and organization can greatly affect the whole process of modernization.

Two aspects of the developing educational systems seem to be of greatest importance from this point of view. The first is the extent of heterogeneity and variety of the educational system, the lack of rigid adherence to a narrow "academic" or legalistic schooling system, the development of varied educational programs, and the resultant facilitation of creation of a more flexible and dynamic status order. The other important aspect is the nature of the interrelation between educational expansion and the general direction and tempo of economic and social development and modernization.

Educational systems and educational planners are faced here with two basic and, to some extent, contradictory possibilities. One is the development of a relatively "conservative," stagnative educational system, geared mostly to the needs and self-image of a relatively small, restricted élite and loosing most of its dynamic innovative and change-oriented potentialities. The other is that of a rigid, undifferentiated expansion of the educational system outstripping the realistic possibilities of absorption of the new educated cadres in the developing economy, thus creating situations of intensive cleavages, conflicts and potential breakdowns.[17]

The extent to which the developing educational systems of African societies will be able to overcome this dilemma may be of crucial importance for their process of modernization; and the investigation of the conditions facilitating such developments certainly constitutes one of the major areas of research in this field.

IX

But it is not only the developments within each of these spheres which are important as indications of possible recrystallization.

Of no lesser importance is the extent to which the processes in these four areas coalesce together at the center and create within it either a flexible or a "frozen" and "rigid" status and political and ideological or value system.

The extent of the flexibility of the political and status system, of the mutual openness of various élites and social groups, the extent of interchangeability of different élite tasks (e.g., economic, political, cultural), the extent to which the original "traditional" élites are ready to accept new subgroups, and the extent of common solidarity between the different and especially the various modern élites and groups in a society are crucial for the

development of institutional frameworks capable of growth. Insofar as such flexibility tends to develop, it may greatly facilitate the creation of an institutional framework capable of absorbing continuous changes because it facilitates the development of new élites willing to learn new modern roles in the economic organizational and political spheres.

Such new élites (or the members of the old élite who have learned new tasks and patterns of behavior) can often acquire an established place in the structure of the communities, and find some sort of *modus vivendi* with the older élites. The new criteria of status (i.e., of economic achievement and specialization, of participation in a political party or youth movement) may then overlap with many of the older "traditional" ones and with each other without creating closed groups constituted according to only one type of criterion, and in this way enable relatively continuous development of varied organizations within a relatively common structure.

Such flexibility of the status system may enable the development of some new status criteria and groups without great disruption of the cohesion of the older groups.

In such cases not only have the new groups access to existing social positions but new types of centers of wealth, power and prestige and of criteria of access to them can develop, and the relative position of different groups with regard to all of them may change continuously.

Both such status flexibility and the opposite tendencies to ascriptive freezing of structural arrangements can be found in all spheres of social organizations—in political parties, in labour organizations, in different areas and channels of mobility—and are not neces-

---

[17]See for instance: A. Callaway, "School Leavers and the Developing Economy of Nigeria", *in* R. O. Tilman and T. Cole (eds.), *The Nigerian Political Science*, Durham, N.C., 1962, pp. 220–238; L. Gray Cowan, "British and French Education in Africa: A Critical Appraisal", in Don C. Piper and T. Cole (eds.), *Post Primary Education and Economic Development*, Durham, N.C., 1964, pp. 178–200; and S. N. Eisenstadt, "Education and Political Development", in Piper and Cole, *op. cit.*, pp. 27–48.

sarily tied to any specific structural form of level of development.

The development of such status flexibility or rigidity is closely related to what may be called value and ideological transformation of the society. The major problem here is the extent to which, out of the varied searches for new religious and ideological contents and symbols, there may indeed develop what may be called a value and ideological transformation.

In this context, it is very important to distinguish on the one hand between those modernized—nationalistic, political or social—élites which while creating new symbols and political frameworks are not able to effect within their respective societies any structural transformation which would facilitate continuous growth, and on the other hand those élites which are relatively more successful in this sphere.

Although it is as yet too early to indicate the exact types of value and ideological orientation which facilitate such transformation, still some of their characteristics—as derived from comparative research—can perhaps be tentatively indicated.

The élites which are to some extent successful in effecting such transformation aim, in the ideological and value spheres, at the development of a new, more flexible set of symbols and collective identity which without negating the traditions can incorporate them into these new symbolic frameworks. They aim at the transformation of the internal values of wider social groups and strata and at the development, among these groups, of new, more flexible orientations. They tend to develop simultaneous orientations to collective ideological transformation and to concrete tasks and problems in different institutional spheres in terms of wider changes and not only in terms of providing various immediate benefits to different social groups—although they hope that ultimately the new political system will also bring marked improvements in the standard of living of the broader groups and strata of the population.

It is therefore very important to attempt to analyze the developments in this field in African societies not only from the point of view of the manifest content of the different new ideologies, and religious movements, but also from the point of view of the development of these broader orientations and of the possibilities for value and ideological transformations that they may imply.

All these formulations are necessarily very preliminary ones—but they attempt to indicate some of the areas and processes, the investigation of which seems to be of great importance for the understanding of problems of modernization in African societies. The investigations of the exact ways in which these various processes develop within the new structural frameworks emerging in African societies are still very much before us but might perhaps constitute one of the major foci of research in this area.

African Explanations of Underdevelopment:
The Theoretical Basis for Political Action

Kenneth W. Grundy

I. INTRODUCTION

Scholars, theoreticians, and statesmen in the West and in the Communist world have propounded numerous explanations of the political, economic and social underdevelopment of Africa and Asia. But few have sought to determine exactly what the leaders of the underdeveloped countries themselves think about the problems of underdevelopment. To what do they attribute their retarded status? Answers to this question are important for at least three reasons. First, their views serve as basic theoretical and empirical foundations for domestic measures designed to ameliorate the relatively backward conditions. Second, their answers also temper and condition their attitudes and policies toward the West and the Communist world. Third, a comprehension of their views gives us an opportunity to assess their current ideological tendencies and thus it provides an added dimension in which to discuss future Western policy alternatives. This paper, therefore, attempts to describe and analyze the various explanations for underdevelopment advanced by the leaders of six West African states—Ghana, Guinea, Ivory Coast, Mali, Nigeria, and Senegal.

African theories of underdevelopment are inextricably linked with the concepts of imperialism and colonialism. Consequently, a clarification of these elusive terms would be in order. African nationalists use the terms colonialism and imperialism loosely and frequently interchangeably. In most cases, however, it is the modern colonialism of the European powers to which they refer. By generally equating European colonialism with imperialism they have adopted, perhaps unwittingly, the Leninist nomenclature.

Lenin's application of the term imperialism is somewhat different from that generally used in the West. Imperialism ordinarily applies to any attempt by a state or group of states to exercise control over another people or territory. In other words, imperialism is simply expansion into additional territory and domination of subject peoples for the advantage of alien rulers. As a general phenomenon, imperialism is as old as recorded history and is not associated with any particular ideology, belief, or economic system. Modern colonialism, however, is a particular form of imperialism.[1] The two are related but distinct concepts, and must not be confused or used imprecisely. What Lenin was referring to in his classic pamphlet, *Imperialism: The Highest Stage of Capitalism*, was not imperialism as a general phenomenon, but colonial imperialism or colonialism. In its modern context, colonialism is the establishment and maintenance by one nation-state of political domination

---

[1] For a similar, although more detailed categorization of different varieties of imperialism see: Hans Kohn, "Reflections on Colonialism," in Robert Strausz-Hupé and Harry W. Hazard (eds.), *The Idea of Colonialism* (New York, 1958), pp. 2–16.

From *Review of Politics,* Vol. XXVIII, No. 1 (January 1966), 62–75, by permission.

over a geographically separate territory, and the subsequent social, cultural, and economic subordination of its indigenous population. The criterion which distinguishes modern colonialism from other kinds of imperialism is that the former is marked by significant racial, cultural, and/or religious differences implying a superior-inferior relationship between rulers and ruled, all of which is reinforced by a political and legal system designed to maintain, if not perpetuate, this definite supremacy and subordination.

II. AFRICAN EXPLANATIONS OF UNDERDEVELOPMENT

The leaders of Ghana, Guinea, and Mali openly state that their backwardness is a direct product of European colonialist exploitation. In their view, colonial rule has prevented the socioeconomic development of Africa in the interests of the indigenous masses. Quite accurately they contend that the Europeans regarded the African economy as an appendage of the metropolitan economy, to be exploited for enhancing the national power, profit, and prestige. The Europeans took slaves, profits, and raw materials out of the continent, the argument continues, and left virtually nothing in return. The resulting conclusion is that in order to foster development in their own interests, Africans must terminate colonial political control.

President Sékou Touré of Guinea, in particular, assumes a most intransigent position on this question. Rejecting traditional Western explanations (racial inequality, intellectual retardation, and ethical or social inferiority, among others), he asserts that Africa's level of development is a product of the economic conditions brought about by foreign intervention and domination.[2]

Touré attacks the entire foundation of the colonial political and economic system. He maintains that imperialist domination brought about the fragmentation and destruction of the precolonial African economy.[3] The reconstituted economy was then integrated as a subordinate part of the economies of the metropolitan countries. All colonial policies, notwithstanding philanthropic and altruistic justifications and rationalizations, were instituted on the basis of just one criterion: did it benefit the metropolitan interests? Funds were denied potential African entrepreneurs. Technical training was limited to those select individuals who could bolster the colonial system and help it function. Social welfare schemes were developed to keep African workers healthy and therefore productive. Traditional institutions were either destroyed or retained on the basis of their utility to the colonial regime. According to Touré, this was the real nature of European colonialism.

After destroying the indigenous African economy, the imperialists replaced it with capitalism—not competitive capitalism as a rule but monopoly capitalism in its most odious form. The commercial system which evolved, the *economie de traite*, sought to exploit in a systematic way Africa's resources and raw materials at the expense of the native population. In Touré's words: "The colonial system took our goods at a very paltry price and sold them at a very high price. The profits . . . did not go to the producers who were the real creators, the true

---

[2] Sékou Touré, "Africa's Future and the World," *Foreign Affairs*, XLI (October, 1962), 145–146.

[3] Sékou Touré, *Toward Full Re-Africanisation: Policy and Principles of the Guinean Democratic Party* (Paris, 1959), p. 39.

owners of the products; they went through many middlemen . . . into the cash boxes of the colonialists."[4] It was this "mercantile circle"—from the commission-agent to the importer, to the wholesale dealer, to the retailer, to the African peddlers and hawkers, and finally to the keepers of the market stalls —which made the colonial commercial system so distasteful. Caustically he told the United Nations General Assembly: "This is why . . . no colonized country has yet attained a social level comparable with what are considered the lowest levels in Europe."[5]

Touré's views are shared by the radical wing of Mali's governing *Union Soudanaise*.[6] It spokesman, Minister of State for Justice Madeira Keita, once asserted that aside from the *Office du Niger*, a gigantic cooperative agricultural project, French colonialism contributed nothing to Mali. In public works, health, power, transportation,

education, and the general economic infrastructure, he continued, Mali made almost no progress under French control.[7] The officials of the militant *Union Nationale des Travailleurs Maliens*, Mali's only labor union, concur in fixing responsibility for underdevelopment on the colonialist powers.[8] The dominant moderate faction of the *Union Soudanaise*, still relatively revolutionary in the overall spectrum of African political thought, is only slightly less inclined to censure colonial rule *in toto*. Although President Modibo Keita sees foreign oppression as the prime reason for African backwardness, he is less hostile in his condemnation of colonialism, and implies that in some respects it might have been beneficial. Ghana's Kwame Nkrumah joins the Guineans and the Malians in branding underdevelopment a product of colonial rule.[9]

Far less denunciatory criticisms of colonial rule have been expressed by the leaders of Nigeria and Senegal. The most effective nationalist in preindependent Nigeria, Nnamdi Azikiwe, was uncompromising in his appraisal of British rule. As scathing as Touré and Nkrumah, Azikiwe's earlier views by no

---

[4] *Ibid.*

[5] United Nations, General Assembly, Fifteenth Session, Plenary, *Official Records*, A/PV. 896 (October 10, 1960), p. 564. Perhaps the prime, indeed the only relevant example of an Afro-Asian state that managed to avoid colonialism or external domination of one sort or another was Japan. The Japanese were able to retain control over their islands, and thus stand as an embarrassing example of an underdeveloped country that reached higher levels of economic development without being subjected to, or blessed by, European political and economic control. Japan demonstrates that it was possible to modernize and industrialize through imitation and emulation rather than through subjugation. While too much reliance cannot be placed on this lone example, it does serve in a small way to strengthen Touré's argument.

[6] Discussions of Malian political theory appear in Kenneth W. Grundy, "Marxism-Leninism and African Underdevelopment: The Mali Approach," *International Journal*, XVII (Summer, 1962), 300–304; and in my chapter, "Mali: The Prospects of 'Planned Socialism,' " in William H. Friedland and Carl G. Rosberg, Jr. (eds.), *African Socialism* (Stanford, 1964), pp. 175–193.

[7] Madeira Keita, "Le Mali et la Recherche d'un Socialisme Africain," (carbon typescript, Embassy of the Republic of Mali, Washington, D.C., n.d.), pp. 1–2.

[8] See, for example: République du Mali, *Congrés Extraordinaire de l'U.S. R.D.A., 22 Septembre 1960, Le Mali continue . . .* (n.p.: Imprimerie du Gouvernement du Mali, n.d.), p. 30.

[9] Nkrumah's interpretation of how underdevelopment was brought to Africa is most completely and concisely stated in *Towards Colonial Freedom* (London: 2nd ed., 1957), originally published in 1947 and one of his first political essays as a nationalist organizer. A more comprehensive analysis of his views appears in my article, "Nkrumah's Theory of Underdevelopment: An Analysis of Recurrent Themes," *World Politics*, XV (April, 1963) esp. pp. 440–444.

means resemble his current moderate position on other matters relating to underdevelopment such as trade policies and economic planning. An ardent anticolonialist, the colonial theme dominated almost all of Azikiwe's pre-1960 writings and speeches. Colonialism, he felt, interrupted normal African development, and forced backwardness on the technologically less advanced natives.[10] In a postindependence speech he told a London audience: "Slavery played its shameful role in depopulating Africa; capitalism denuded it of its wealth; colonialism deprived it of its birthright, and imperialism emasculated its will to live as a human being [sic] and to enjoy its fair share of the bounties of the good earth."[11] To Azikiwe, the white man has cause to be ashamed of the way in which he carried his "burden" or his *mission civilisatrice*. To many Africans, the "white man's burden" was more often a bag of plundered gold than an altruistic mission to improve the Africans' lot.

Chief Obafemi Awolowo, inspirational leader of the opposition Action Group, is also implacably opposed to foreign political and economic domination. But before his ideological about-face he was a good deal less impassioned in his evaluation of the British presence in Africa. In 1957, for example, he praised the British for giving the Nigerians a "common nationality" and for leaving behind a heritage of "order, good government and parliamentary democracy."[12] For him imperialism

took on a tripartite meaning. He once said that there were three imperialisms reigning side by side and in concert. They were, first of all, the "imperialism of ignorance, disease and want," second, British colonialism, and third, the "imperialism of local caesars who flourished under the aegis of British imperialism."[13] He warned his compatriots that it would be naive and dangerous to imagine that the only enemy to be destroyed was British colonialism. On the contrary, unless Nigerians worked hard and in the right direction, "when Britain abdicates sovereignty in Nigeria, she would leave behind the other two imperialisms, whose reigns would be poignantly grinding and oppressive."[14] This was a time when most nationalist leaders insisted that the surest and most rapid path toward self-government lay in focusing unified mass pressures on the alien power. In their speeches, as has been illustrated, there was just one cause for underdevelopment—colonialism. In choosing to scatter the blame for backwardness in three directions, Awolowo was risking political suicide. Indeed, a case might be made that this was the result, for his Action Group soon came to be regarded as a special interest, regional, and ethnic party whose electoral appeal was severely limited. Subsequent elections have, in large measure, demonstrated this.

On one occasion Awolowo even dared to criticize anticolonialism *per se* as a political strategy. In his eyes, it thwarted the interests of the Nigerian people. He asserted that anticolonialism was coterminous with "negative nationalism," which sees nothing good in

---

[10]Cf. Nnamdi Azikiwe, "Ethics of Colonial Imperialism," *Journal of Negro History*, XVI (July, 1931), 287–308. He wrote this article while a student at Lincoln University.

[11]Nnamdi Azikiwe, "The Future of Pan-Africanism," *Présence Africaine*, XII (First Quarter, 1962), 7.

[12]Obafemi Awolowo, *Forward to a New Nigeria* (London, 1957), p. 21.

[13]Obafemi Awolowo, *Awo: The Autobiography of Chief Obafemi Awolowo* (Cambridge, 1960), p. 269.

[14]*Ibid.*

foreign rule. Thus any cooperation with the colonial powers was regarded as an act of treachery. This "negative national-ism," he argued, would simply result in the prolongation of African enslave-ment.[15]

Since his Action Group became the Opposition in the Federal Legislature, Awolowo has substantially altered his pronouncements. In the past Awolowo admitted that in some respects colonial-ism was beneficial to Nigeria. But his postcolonial approach, largely a tactical shift, may be illustrated by the follow-ing passages from a speech delivered in June, 1961.

The scramble for Africa as well as the permanent settlement of Europeans in certain parts of Africa was motivated wholly and solely, and without any re-deeming feature, by the political, economic and military self-interests of the European powers which engaged in that unholy adventure.

* * *

For more than sixty years thereafter [since 1885], Black Africa suffered under the grinding heels of alien conquerors and settlers.

Today, for most parts of Black Africa, the inhuman, humiliating and degrading position delineated above remains more or less the same . . . barring a handful of countries on the Continent, Africa is still as ever under Western imperialist bond-age.[16]

Without attempting to explain this ideological change of heart, it should be noted that the Action Group is an almost wholly Yoruba-based party securing its electoral support primarily from the Western Region and in the Yoruba areas of the Eastern and Northern Regions. Since no broadly

based revolutionary political movement has taken root in Nigeria, perhaps Awolowo and his partisans sense a gap in the country's political spectrum. Should the moderate policies of the government coalition fail to satisfy popular expectations, the left-moving Action Group could conceivably be the logical successor, perhaps in concert with other parties or movements. In many respects, therefore, the doctrinal evolution of the Action Group is primarily a function of political ex-pediency in its struggle to expand its political influence.

Senegalese leaders attribute under-development to a variety of factors, not the least of which is colonialism. Presi-dent Léopold Sédar Senghor explains that European conquest and colonialism have brought profit not only to the capitalist bourgeoisie but also to the European middle classes and pro-letariat.[17] In linking colonialism to capitalism he feels that "European monopoly capitalism," by buying raw materials at extremely low prices and selling manufactured goods at artificially high prices in the colonies, was the "economics of slavery."[18] Colonialism thus contributed to the industrial devel-opment of Europe and raised the living standards of the European masses, to the detriment of Africa and Africans. Nonetheless, it should be borne in mind that to the Senegalese officials colonial-ism is not the only reason for African backwardness.

Senghor places colonialism in a

---

[15]*Ibid.*, pp. 294–295.
[16]Obafemi Awolowo, *African Unity* (Iba-dan, 1961), pp. 1–2, 2–4.

[17]Léopold Sédar Senghor, *Nation et Voie Africaine du Socialisme* (Paris, 1961), p. 95. Senghor's views are shared by his former Prime Minister, Mamadou Dia. See his book, *The African Nations and World Solidarity*, trans. by Mercer Cook (New York, 1961).
[18]Léopold Sédar Senghor, "A Community of Free and Equal Peoples with the Mother Country," *Western World*, No. 18 (October, 1958), 40.

broad historical perspective. As he sees it, colonialism is a "transitory stage" of history, like feudalism and capitalism. But like other stages of history, it had its "moments of light" as well as its "dark moments." He employs a Marxist historical interpretation in which successive stages of history are considered to be at once progressive and yet, in their dying years, regressive. Thus colonialism had both negative and positive features. "If it destroyed some of the values of our civilization," he has said, "Europe sometimes brought us substitutes, almost always fertile ones: complementary ones."[19]

In this framework, the clash between two civilizations is always tortuous for the weaker of the two. But as Senghor optimistically observes: "What matters is that from this encounter, inhuman though it may be at first, a new civilization should arise, grafting the skills of the colonizers on to the living stock of the colonized."[20] Europe brought destruction to Africa, but unintentionally she also brought values that were lacking in African life—technical skills and methods. Placed in this context, colonialism would appear to be for Senghor a necessary evil—a historical necessity.

In many of his writings and speeches Senghor implies that those very same processes which enrich European life materially could and should have been used to Africa's benefit, had the Europeans desired it. This is central to Senghor's critique of European colonialism. There is an important distinction here between the ethical and the objective or practical consequences of colonialism. Ethically colonialism is evil. The object is to dominate alien

peoples for a multitude of economic and political reasons. But objectively, colonialism is progressive—that is, it has a modernizing and generally beneficial effect on Africa's history. This is what Senghor speaks of when he regards colonialism as a necessary evil. It could have been more progressive had the Europeans chosen to give the Africans a greater share of the fruits of the African economy. If the "white man's burden" had been taken seriously, and its spiritual and moral components given play, then Africa would have gained a good deal more than it actually did from its contact with Europe. But the benefits of colonialism, its objective consequences, were largely residual or fortuitous in character. They came as by-products of policies undertaken to bring political, strategic, or economic advantage to the metropolis and its people. They were not the primary intention or objective of the colonial powers, but rather unintentional, often accidental, by-products of European contact and exploitation. Similarly, there are both positive and negative facets of Communism in Eastern Europe, Nazism in Germany, and Japanese expansion into Southeastern Asia, for example. The questions to be raised in cultural contacts of this sort are: what price must be paid for positive achievements? Could Westernization and modernization have been introduced with less exploitation and less psychological damage?

If Senghor seems a bit reluctant to attack the colonial powers for their African activities, President Félix Houphouet-Boigny of the Ivory Coast is even more restrained. Indeed, since his *Rassemblement Démocratique Africain* (R.D.A.) severed its parliamentary alliance with the French Communist Party in October, 1950, Houphouet might well be considered on the surface an African apologist for French colonial

---

[19]Léopold Sédar Senghor, "Some Thoughts on Africa: A Continent in Development," *International Affairs*, XXXVIII (April, 1962), 189.

[20]*Ibid.*

policies. His ruling party has conspicuously refrained from using colonialism as a scapegoat for all domestic or African ills or for excoriating France. Since 1950 he has seldom directly blamed the French for African underdevelopment. On the contrary, he has sought to identify his interests with those of France and has repeatedly referred to the "Franco-African community," "Frenchmen of Africa," and "the mother country" in laudatory terms. He once even hinted that underdevelopment might, to some degree, be the result of natural handicaps of tropical countries.[21] Praising France's colonial policies as being "liberal" and beneficial to the African masses, he asserted that "France's accomplishments are even more praiseworthy if it is remembered that she has borne the impact of two wars. . . ."[22]

While the French presence in Africa is "the result of military conquests" or of "peaceful penetrations," France has, to her credit, suppressed slavery, halted interethnic quarrels, educated the masses, and instituted sanitary and medical improvements without precedent, and has given her culture to an African elite.[23] Thus French rule, far from the cause of underdevelopment, is regarded by Houphouet as the motive force behind Africa's economic, political, and social development and maturity. This, argues the former French cabinet minister, is the real legacy of colonialism.

---

[21]Félix Houphouet-Boigny, "Black Africa and the French Union," *Foreign Affairs,* XXXV (July, 1957), 594.

[22]*Ibid.,* 595.

[23]*Ibid.,* 598–599. In another instance he has stated: "Despite certain mistakes made by the colonizers, we have profited from the progress of their colonization, and they have left us in the best possible condition." *Afrique Nouvelle* (Dakar), No. 711 (March 22, 1961), 5.

For as long as Houphouet can make his pro-French posture pay, in terms of satisfying his countrymen's desires or in terms of blunting their expectations, and thus minimizing dissatisfaction and solidifying his own ruling elite in power, he will no doubt maintain his present ideological orientation. One thing seems certain: Houphouet is a clever and pragmatic political opportunist whose rise to power and retention of it are due to his willingness to abandon one doctrinal stance for another, if it proves expedient. His shrewd ability to assess popular currents and to manipulate and ride them obviates the necessity for theoretical consistency.

Despite Houphouet's theoretical flexibility, he appears most sympathetic and most intent in defending the interests of the indigenous cocoa and coffee farmers. Houphouet himself is a member of a prominent Baoulé family, and his father was a prosperous coffee planter. In 1940 Houphouet became Chief of his home district and a planter in his own right. Since that time his personal landholdings have been steadily augmented. In 1944, largely because European planters enjoyed privileges and advantages at the expense of Africans, Houphouet helped organize and became president of the *Syndicat Agricole Africain,* an African planters' trade union. This body defended the interests of the small African farmers who were being squeezed by the big French planters and lumbermen, and the large commercial enterprises. The P.D.C.I. grew out of the *Syndicat,* and since that time the Party has reflected the interests of the indigenous planters. The economic power of the *Ivoirien* coffee and cocoa planters is substantial. Coffee production, accounting for over 45 percent of her exports by value, is central to the country's economy. Cocoa contributes another one-third of her exports. African farmers control some 95 percent of the production of each commodity. Thus, through all subsequent ideological (which in fact were largely tactical) transmutations, the interests of this increasingly prosperous landed group have been upheld.

III. A COMPARATIVE ANALYSIS OF AFRICAN VIEWS

From the foregoing description it appears that there exist in West Africa diverse shades of opinion on the etiology of underdevelopment. Nevertheless, those Africans who blame colonial rule and colonialism are the dominant voice. This suggests that such a thing as an "African" explanation of underdevelopment is discernible. With the obvious exception of Houphouet, the leaders of the six states examined here, to one degree or another, fix responsibility for their status on European colonial regimes.

It is understandable that the politically conscious, Western-educated, bureaucratic African ruling elites should direct their antagonisms at the colonial system. The Europeans had brought with them alien political domination, racial tension and conflict, and economic exploitation; although, to be sure, they were not the first to impose such relationships on Africans. Although Africa's leaders were trained and made politically aware by Western contacts, it was the colonial system that imprisoned them. The system had whetted their appetites, raised their expectations, and cultivated their aspirations, but simultaneously denied and frustrated their advancement beyond fixed limits. They had been socially, politically, and economically thwarted by an order imposed from without for the benefit of foreign interests. Feeding on an inflated self-image of their societal importance, they soon realized that the colonial order was the only barrier between them and total political power.

Despite their underlying anticolonialism, West African leaders differ in the degree to which they link colonialism and European capitalism. Some conform to what might be called a crude Leninist interpretation of underdevelopment. The most extreme—Touré and the Malian radicals—accept Lenin's explanation that colonialism is an inevitable structural outgrowth of capitalistic society. This view stigmatizes capitalism at the same time that it attacks colonialism, for the latter, it is believed, arises out of the necessity of capitalist countries to find outlets for investment or "finance capital." The officials of Mali's labor union actually usurp the Hilferding-Lenin nomenclature. The term "finance capital" was also used at the Sixth Pan-African Congress in 1945. Nkrumah, Touré, Awolowo, George Padmore, and Senghor all have expressed the opinion that colonialism is a product of capitalist "economic necessity." The first four maintain that this is a normal characteristic of highly developed capitalist societies. Senghor indicates that this was a normal characteristic of all technically advanced peoples. But in accepting certain aspects of Leninist analysis, it must be emphasized that African nationalists reject the Leninist prognosis of the eventual construction of a socialist (Communist) state by violence, if necessary.

Kwame Nkrumah adheres to a position, only slightly less Leninist, between the doctrine that colonialism is an inevitable stage of capitalism, and the view that colonies and colonialism are not necessarily "the highest stage of capitalism," but rather the result of policy choices made by imperialist governments.

Perhaps the most widely shared position on this question holds that colonialism is a policy which might be undertaken by *any* state or group of states—not uniquely by capitalist states in a certain stage of development. In this camp can be found President Azikiwe, President Senghor, former Prime Minister Dia, President Houphouet-Boigny, and others. Senghor, Dia, and Houphouet, in particular, are especially wary of Communist imperialism. They emphasize that Communist regimes are no less capable of imperialism than are the European powers. At other times, they stress the possibilities of "micro-nationalism" and "micro-imperialism"—that is, the danger that African states might attempt to "colonize" or dominate other African states.

This diversity of views corresponds rather closely to the Marxist spectrum, for even within Marxist ranks different notions of the causes of colonial imperialism have arisen. These range from the views of Lenin and Rosa Luxemburg to those of Rudolph Hilferding, Karl Kautsky, and Karl Renner. Renner went so far as to suggest that imperialism was no longer an exclusively capitalist impulse.[24] The current Soviet and Chinese Communist doctrines accept Lenin's explanation. In this regard, most West Africans are not followers of contemporary Marxist-Leninist doctrine. Nevertheless, their attitudes toward this issue do resemble Lenin's and spring from the Marxist womb.

In attributing their underdevelopment to colonialism, from whatever sources, Africans, excepting Houphouet, stand in direct opposition to traditional Western views of underdevelopment. Western statesmen, in the past, have

---

[24]A brief discussion of various Marxist positions can be found in: E. M. Winslow, *The Pattern of Imperialism: A Study in the Theories of Power* (New York, 1948), esp. chap. vii.

fallen back on several different explanations. For example, notions of tropical climate and health conditions, cultural stagnation, racial inferiority, geographical isolation, the "Negro personality," psychological resignation to environment, absence of challenge, or the presence of overly demanding challenge have enjoyed currency from time to time. More recently, impersonal forces such as lack of investment capital, scarcity of technical training and skills, and other economic determinants are designated. But too few Western politicians go deeper in their search for the underlying reasons. Few are willing to ask the sometimes embarrassing question, why is there so little capital, technical skill, education, or economic incentive? Few are willing to fix even partial responsibility on Western colonialism.

Consequently most West Africans regard official Western explanations as inadequate and incorrect. In the African view, Western theories do not get to the heart of the problem. Since Western theories of underdevelopment in large part are rationalizations and justifications for Western colonialism, it is understandable that they should ignore or fail to recognize the essentially political barriers by which the colonial powers have hindered any development in the interests of the indigenous masses. Western ideas are also rejected because they are largely static rather than dynamic theories of underdevelopment. In other words, there is a built-in yet often unrecognized pessimism in official Western views which the African is forced to disregard if he is to see any possibility for future advancement. Explanations for backwardness based on geographical, climatic, racial, and psychological factors are largely deterministic—they admit of little or no immediate possibilities for change.

Politicians in underdeveloped countries can never accept what they regard as an unfavorable *status quo*. To adopt such Western views would be to resign themselves to a perpetually underdeveloped or relatively less developed status. Quite naturally they are not so inclined.

But there is still another, more obvious and understandable, reason why Africans subscribe in varying degrees to Marxist-Leninist rather than Western explanations of underdevelopment. In large measure Marxism-Leninism absolves the peoples of underdeveloped areas of all responsibility for their backwardness. Objectively, this makes a great deal of sense. Colonial rule offered Africans and Asians little opportunity to exercise a real option to develop or not to develop. Although Africa may not have developed in the absence of colonialism, at least it would have been the Africans' choice and their clear responsibility. Thus, it is easy for nationalist leaders to affirm views which place responsibility for unhappy circumstances on outsiders. Lenin's theory supplies a simple explanation readily acceptable to the underdeveloped peoples.

To blame the colonialist powers for Africa's underdevelopment suffers, objectively, from the weaknesses of most monocausal theories. A multiplicity of causal factors is thereby reduced to a single-factor explanation. But although this oversimplification may be empirically inadequate, it is politically expedient and fruitful. To comprehend such a theory, one must return to the nature of

political ideology. Its *raison d'être* is successful political action, and historically, simplified theories yield results in mobilizing mass action. Sophistication of theory may be possible and indeed useful in influencing potential elites. But the masses are generally moved and persuaded by monocausal theories.

Too often Westerners are content to sit back and "destroy" Marxism-Leninism in an abstract way, or "prove" its logical or theoretical unsoundness. But it must be pointed out that political theory does not attain validity simply in an abstract way. How does Marxism-Leninism measure up against the effectiveness of complex analytical systems employed by Western decision makers, particularly in regard to underdeveloped areas? As far as the Africans are concerned, Leninist theory appears more in tune with their life experiences, than are Western theories. But it must also be understood that Africa's leaders accept merely the essentials of Lenin's doctrine of imperialism—that underdevelopment arises from colonialism. Only a small number adhere to the argument that there is a direct causal relationship between "monopoly capitalism" and modern colonialism. Even fewer accept in its entirety the orthodox Leninist account which marks the genesis of colonialism as stemming from internal pressure from the interests of "finance capital." None accepts the direction of the Communist parties of the Soviet Union or the Chinese People's Republic, the earthly interpreters of orthodox Marxist-Leninist dogma.

African Socialism: Declaration of Ideological Independence

Ruth Schachter Morgenthau

In this period of "decolonization," Africans are evolving their own political ideology to meet several needs. It must fill the gap left by the achievement of independence and set post-independence goals, limits, and guides for national action. It must also help define the identity of new nations, most of which have questionable borders, fluctuating institutions, and ethnic communities with little sense of nationhood.

It is at the domestic level that African socialism has widest discussion. The phrase is convenient, because it allows Africans a certain degree of ideological neutrality. In most of Africa, the term capitalism is unacceptable because most African capital is foreign-owned, and therefore even African businessmen associate capitalism with the worst of colonialism. Communism is unacceptable because most Africans see it as yet another foreign attempt to undercut their independence. Although the Communists have claimed until recently that there is only one road to socialism, the various spokesmen of African socialism flatly deny this. Indeed, some of the colonial postwar reforms which Africans welcomed were inspired by British and French socialist traditions.

Socialism has the further advantage of being connected with two basic ideas that provided the impetus to the African independence movements and remain post-independence goals: equality and a better future. Socialist literature has much to say about economic development, the chief preoccupation of the newly independent governments,

when the transition is being made from *uhuru* to *uhuru na kazi* (in Swahili, from *freedom* to *freedom with toil*). Most African leaders recall their own first experience of loneliness in an industrialized city, and compare this with the sense of belonging that the extended kinship group provides most individuals in Africa, where people may be poor but help each other. They want an ideology which can help protect their people against the pressures and dislocations of economic change: "We do not want to or need to repeat your mistakes," they say. They hope, also, to escape the class struggle which accompanied European industrialization.

African socialism does have an international dimension in the call for African unity and pan-African association. This rests upon the recognition that many of the new African states are small, most are weak, and all are among the poorer nations in an international system which is tending to make the rich richer and the poor poorer. Unity among the poorer nations might help bring about faster acceptance of the need for "welfare world" rather than simply "welfare state" measures.

THE AFRICAN FEATURE

What is the specifically African feature of this socialism? On this most spokesmen agree. It is the solidarity of the kinship group, most evident at the local level. President Julius Nyerere of Tanganyika has explained, "[The Afri-

From *Africa Report,* Vol. VIII, No. 5 (May 1963), 3–6, by permission of author and journal.

can] is not a member of a 'commune'—some artificial unit of human beings—he is of a genuine community, or brotherhood." ("Will Democracy Work in Africa?" by Julius Nyerere, *Africa Report*, February 1960, p. 4). This solidarity was very important to the nationalist political parties which achieved independence. Most Africans still live at least in part within the subsistence economy, and from this sector came the bulk of the contributions to party finances in the form of free transport, gasoline, housing, food, work, and other volunteer services. These contributions did the job done by hired professionals in political parties in industrialized countries.

The post-independence task, as most African leaders see it, is to preserve the sense of community found in the extended family, spread it throughout the whole society, and harness it to development. To describe this task, Julius Nyerere and Sekou Toure, on opposite sides of the continent and educated respectively in the use of Catholic and Marxist political vocabularies, nevertheless coined similar words. Nyerere spoke of the "communitary" society; Toure, of the "*communaucratique*" society. (Nyerere, *op. cit.*, p. 4; "*L'Expérience guinéene et l'unité africaine*," by Sekou Toure, *Présence Africaine*, Paris, 1959, p. 394.)

Extending this "sense of community" to the national level poses serious problems. The solidarity of a village is based on kinship; so are the communal claims to the land. In contrast, cooperatives must be based on contract and employees must be selected on merit. In a modern system, recruitment based on kinship is nepotism. Here lies one of the main points of controversy. Are the actual institutions of kinship or only its spirit to be preserved? Can anything more than the spirit of village solidarity be infused into the new economic institutions?

In most French-speaking countries, the new governments encouraged *investissement humain* programs, in which villagers gave their time to build or improve roads, bridges, meeting halls, schools, infirmaries, and mosques. They planted communal fields to produce agricultural crops and to replace food being imported in return for precious foreign exchange. The initial enthusiasm for *investissement humain* wore off, however, as it became increasingly clear that more planning would be needed to produce effective results. Many governments have tried to encourage producer cooperatives at the village level, some along the lines of Israeli *kibbutzim*.

SENGHOR INTRODUCES PHRASE

Perhaps the first time the phrase "African socialism" was used was in French, as *socialisme africain*. It was coined by the Senegalese poet and politician, Leopold Senghor, in the late 1940's when he, with Mamadou Dia and others representing the rural areas of Senegal, broke from what was then the only Senegalese party, an organic branch of the French Socialist Party, *Section Française de l'International Ouvrier* (SFIO). Senghor used several arguments to distinguish his new party: it was to be based on African, rather than French, socialism; and it would not share the anti-clerical orientation of the SFIO, but would be based on a socialism of "believers," Christian and Moslem. Senghor was himself a Catholic, and for a decade he and his associates allied their party with the French Catholic *Mouvement Republicain Populaire* (MRP).

In the late 1950's, with independence imminent, Senegalese thinking about African socialism changed, due in part to the contributions to the first development plan of a team of economic specialists close to Pere Lebret and the White Fathers of Dakar. By then, Senghor had been deeply impressed by the writings of the Jesuit scientist Teilhard de Chardin, and, as a result, his own ideas blended with the general body of Latin Catholic political thought seeking a reconciliation with socialism. The first postwar generation of Senegalese trained in French universities studied these ideas. Cheikh Amidou Kane, former Commissioner of the Senegalese development plan, a Moslem, was among those influenced.

Discussion and the phrase itself spread via Catholic intellectual circles in both France and West Africa. It was also widely used throughout the Catholic-inspired trade movement, the West African section of the *Confédération Française des Travailleurs Chrétiens* (CFTC). Senghor used the phrase more than did Mamadou Dia. During the lifetime of the Mali Federation, an essay on African socialism delivered by Senghor in 1959 provided the framework for its dominant federal party, the *Parti de la Fédération Africaine*. Use of the phrase spread with Catholic political ideas to the Congo, the Central African Republic, and Tanganyika, where the White Fathers were active participants in political dialogues.

Partly because of these origins, the phrase "African socialism" is not welcome everywhere. Some Africans, who associate socialism with a universal Marxist tradition, call it *"le socialisme de Go-go"* (loosely translated, "the puppet's socialism"). Members of the younger generation of university graduates who constitute the bulk of the opposition in Senegal, and leaders of governments in Mali and Guinea have on varying occasions said *"socialisme en Afrique oui,"* but *"socialisme africain non."* They attack Senghor's version of African socialism for similar reasons that they attack his ideas on negritude. They believe both concepts have racist and provincial overtones and that Senghor is not sufficiently concerned with universals. They accuse him of theorizing for French audiences rather than from African experience. They differ with Senghor's political practice, claiming that a socialism used to explain its policies by a government that backed the French position in Algeria and continues to have French bases and a majority of French technicians in top civil service posts cannot be a socialism acceptable to true African patriots.

Some of Senghor's opponents find the term African socialism too convenient to ignore. The Republic of Mali, whose leaders avoided all contact with Senegal for some time after the breakup of the Federation, nevertheless uses the term in a favorable context in *l'Essor*, the official organ of the *Union Soudanaise*, the dominant party. When the leaders of Mali and Guinea speak of the need to develop a specifically African form of socialism and deny the existence of a class struggle, they are using language similar to that of the Senegalese leaders but applying it to very different economic and social conditions.

Mali and Guinea are as yet little developed and little urbanized; relatively few people earn money who are not employed by the government, and individual property is relatively unknown; no social group can yet be called a middle class. The social base in Senegal and Ghana is different; their leaders are speaking of a different reality when they deny the existence of a class struggle in African society. Both in Senegal and in Ghana, if the leaders wanted to avoid the emergence of an African entrepreneurial class they would have to wipe out an already existing group—and neither government is prepared to take such a measure. Ghana has a middle class growing up around cocoa farmers and traders; this group does not dominate the governing Convention People's Party. Senegal, too, has a growing middle class profiting from the export of peanuts, including neo-traditional Moslem *marabouts* (Koranic teachers) who profit from the labor of their disciples. Unlike Ghana, these groups dominate the Senegalese mass party. Senegalese opposition leaders have this in mind when they attack Senghor's ideas of African socialism. With varying emphases, they argue that African society is not classless and demand that the extremes of wealth and poverty be reduced in Senegal. In general agreement on this point are Abdoulaye Ly's *Parti du Regroupement Africain-Sénégal* (PRA-Senegal), Cheikh Anta Diop's *Bloc des Masses Sénégalaises*, and Majhemout Diop's banned *Parti Africain de l'Indépendence* (PAI).

POINTS OF DISAGREEMENT

African spokesmen of socialism disagree on many points. To some, like Senghor, the village is the source from which African society will be transformed; it is almost a mystical entity whose institutions must be preserved. Others believe that, while the spirit of communal cooperation found in some villages and most kinship groups must be the inspiration for the new African society, the traditional institutions are doomed.

There is a difference, too, in the role assigned to the individual within the state. Senghor, and those who share his debt to Emmanuel Mounier's *personnalisme*, developed in the immediate postwar period in the French Catholic review *Esprit*, emphasize that society exists for the individual and not the reverse. At the same time, they claim the individual can fulfill himself only through service to society. This is a difference at the level of theory, since, in practice, the Senegalese Government, like those of Mali, Guinea, Ghana, and most other African states, uses repressive techniques readily: jails opposition party leaders or potential ones, discovers plots against the security of the state, compels papers to print only favorable comments, and demands uncritical loyalty from civil servants and others who enjoy state patronage.

Guinean and Malian leaders couple the ideas of individualism and selfishness. Sekou Toure warns his followers against *"aventures personnelles."* In both states, intellectuals are warned not to think they count more than anyone else in the party; all are urged to be vigilant lest there emerge a privileged class. Nkrumah has something similar in mind when he attacks "a new ruling class of self-seekers and careerists." (Kwame Nkrumah, "Dawn Broadcast," April 8, 1961.)

There are differences also in the use of Marxist ideas and vocabulary. Senghor and Dia do this but little. But steadily in Guinea and Mali, and increasingly in Ghana's CPP, the principles of democratic centralism are emphasized and Marxist language is employed. At the same time, the dominant party leaders of these three nations differ quite sharply with orthodox Leninist principles of party organization. Recruiting is not limited, the party is open to all who want to join, thus building mass-based rather than class-based parties. They show no interest in any eventual fading away of the state; strong states are what all the governing parties call for. None is interested in having a workers' vanguard organization; all use pressure to force trade unions to conform. All government parties deny the existence of a class struggle; only some younger generation radical opposition leaders accept it.

Another difference among the spokesmen of African socialism is in their ideas about the party system. All lead single-party systems; there is one dominant party, and opposition groups, if allowed to exist at all, are certainly not allowed conditions for growth; but the ideas justifying this practice differ. Nyerere has said that a multi-party system might emerge eventually, probably through a split in the party organized by the "founding fathers" of the new state, but this is not yet the moment for it. Senghor also holds that a *parti unifié* is necessary under the emergency conditions following independence. Keita and Toure, on the other hand, advocate a single-party system, a *parti unique*, as a good in itself, as best under African conditions.

There is disagreement also on the role the state should have in economic development. Where individual land ownership does not exist, as in most of Guinea and Mali, the governments are taking steps to maintain the communal bases of land ownership. But where individual African landholders emerged under colonial rule, there are no signs governments intend to eliminate them. All proponents of African socialism say that the government must have a considerable part in economic planning and that there must be state enterprises, but there is disagreement about the extent. Ghana and Senegal do not discourage the growth of their existing indigenous entrepreneurial classes; but Mali and Guinea, where such groups do not exist, discourage their formation and assume that the government will take on most of the risks and responsibilities for development. At the same time, all

welcome foreign capital from government or private sources, although there are variations in controls and conditions.

IDEAS AND REALITY

The terms of discussion of African socialism change with experiment, experience, and testing. Ghana, for example, started from relatively little official emphasis on socialism; there were only a few references to it in Nkrumah's autobiography (published in 1957) and in the early CPP literature. When the international price of cocoa fell after the late 1950's, the Ghana Government had to ask people to pull in belts and pay more direct and indirect taxes, and discussion of socialism became more widespread. Guinea, on the other hand, started with the clear objective of building a socialist economy and set about doing it with some Soviet help. It set up a government monopoly to handle export and import trade and sharply curtailed the role of African middlemen. These measures, and several other factors, had disastrous results for Guinea's economy, however, and Guinean leaders have now reversed their policy. Controls over export and import trade have been reduced and traders have been freed to compete.

The African setting gives content to the discussions of African socialism. This is what Sekou Toure meant when he said:

To understand both the language of Africa and its true content we must seek to find in its words, expressions, formulations, not the abstract character of a dialectic, but the substance and reality of the life they express." ("Africa's Future and the World," by Sekou Toure, *Foreign Affairs*, October 1962, p. 142.)

The Political Survival of Traditional Leadership in East Africa

Norman N. Miller

Viewed from the higher echelons of government in the new nations, the rural leader is an insignificant individual who goes about managing his local affairs and carrying out—with varying degrees of success—the policies and hopes of the government. Viewed from below, from the inner recesses of the village, the leader is a man of authority; a man who has used wealth, heredity, or personal magnetism to gain a position of influence. As seen by nation builders and development experts, the rural leader is tacitly pointed to as the key to success. It is he who can mobilise the people. It is through him that more energy will be expended, more muscles used, and more attitudes changed. Conversely, it is the leader's lack of initiative that will entrench the *status quo* and doom the modernisation schemes before they begin.

An important group of these rural leaders comprises the former traditional authorities—chiefs, sub-chiefs, and headmen—who occupied bureaucratic positions within the indirect rule systems of colonial régimes. Although legally deposed by many independent African governments, such leaders continue to exercise substantial influence, particularly in the building of local institutions in the rural areas. Some have been able to move into party or administrative positions; others have been so strong that the local authorities have been forced to deal with them directly as spokesmen for their area. Other traditional rulers have no formal leadership position but, through manip-

ulation of their past legitimacy, have continued to dictate local policies and shape major decisions. Whatever the basis, the political survival of traditional leaders is significant because they provide the vital linkage between the government and the people. They influence the success of specific modernisation schemes by serving as translators, interpreters, and mediators of government goals. This form of leadership is basically syncretistic, a leadership pattern among chiefs and headmen which is a synthesis and reconciliation of the opposing forces of traditionalism and modernism.[1] The result is form of leadership which is neither modern nor traditional but an incorporation of both. The process is one of accommodation and compromise. It is a reconciliation of demands from (*a*) the traditional, custom-bound elements of rural society, and (*b*) the modernising bureaucratic groups made up of local administrators and political party leaders.

A key characteristic of syncretistic political behaviour is constant change. The political system is one in which values and guidelines for action come from two competing subsystems—a fluid situation, which allows a great

---

[1] The term 'syncretistic' is occasionally applied to prophets' movements and separatist church movements in the sense that they derive a part of their doctrines and ritual from traditional religion. It can also have broader meaning, as Hodgkin points out, in the search for some form of synthesis between European culture and traditional values. See Thomas Hodgkin, *Nationalism in Colonial Africa* (London, 1956), pp. 99 and 171.

From *Journal of Modern African Studies,* Vol. VI, No. 2 (August 1968), 183–98, by permission of the journal and its publisher, the Cambridge University Press.

deal of personal jousting and bargaining on the part of the traditional leaders. The individual leader can respond to a peasant in one way on a given topic and answer a bureaucratic administrator on the same topic in another manner. This phenomenon promotes the speaking to two worlds in different tongues, a duality of response. For the villager, the situation is often in flux. New syncretistic guidelines, principles, and practices are mixed and are not fully understood. The leader himself is unpredictable; he will often vacillate between extremes of what is traditional and what is modern. Specific examples of syncretistic behaviour include speeches which mix the names of national leaders and tribal heroes; the use of amulets, charms, and protective medicines to ensure victory in a difficult political test; the use of diviners, practitioners, and religious technicians to aid the leader in solving modern problems; the constant mixing of slogans that refer to heroic tribal myths alongside national modernising propaganda; and the employment of vernacular proverbs to gain support for bureaucratic demands.

From the administration's point of view, such syncretistic leaders cause difficulty and delay. Each new project or procedure usually needs a new bureaucratic overture. Most syncretistic leaders view each innovation as something that must be reconciled with both traditional and modern values; there are no precedents and no procedures that can be easily repeated. The leader must weigh his position in the new situation and mark his course carefully to gain the needed synthesis. A project can take on extreme political overtones for the entire rural area, and be negotiated *ad infinitum*. The delay often continues until the leader can find his footing among other rural influentials. Like politicians in any society, his continuing goal is to maximise his future bargaining potential and to safeguard his current leadership position.

Modern syncretistic leadership is based on the very real need of both peasants and government to have a rural intermediary. The fundamental issue at stake is *the application of coercive force*. Alien bureaucratic leaders, administrators, and even party officials have the ability and the authority to use coercive force in the rural areas. What they do not have is the necessary degree of consensus to obtain the needed co-operation on bureaucratic projects. Conversely, the traditional leaders still hold some authority and are accepted as legitimate in the eyes of the peasant. This is in spite of the fact that they lack the legal ability to use coercive force. The result is that each system of leaders needs the support of the other. The marriage between the two systems tends to produce forms of syncretistic leadership behaviour, which may be distinguished as either *alliance* or *coercion*. A third distinction is made when syncretistic leadership breaks down and disappears, and a situation of *mutual hostility* exists.

Alliance. This form occurs when communication between the traditional leader and the modernising agent (administrator or party official) is established, and the traditional leader translates the desires of the modernising agent to the people. The main elements in the relationship are that (*a*) the traditional leader's authority has been bent to serve the ends of the modernising agent, probably by some type of persuasion, (*b*) articulation to the people has been favourable and activating, and (*c*) the task, programme, or campaign will be undertaken. The alliance situation closely resembles the relationship between chiefs and the colonial administration under indirect rule. Communications between the two groups tend to be good on specific issues, and co-operation is forthcoming. Consensus has been established on an *ad hoc* basis, and there is agreement on the bureaucratic norms to be used. The interest groups that exist in the rural areas tend to be sympathetic to co-operation between the two positions and support syncretistic behaviour. Group allegiance remains unchanged and common interests are articulated by the reconciling leader.

Coercion. This form occurs when overt bureaucratic coercion is applied to the traditional leader and partial co-operation is gained. The traditional leader, however, goes only as far as he is forced to go in activating the people. From the administrator's point of view, plans and projects are delayed, barriers are encountered, and obstructionism and inaction are commonplace. Communication between the two groups is distorted through the various selective processes. Consensus is tenuous and there is often disagreement on the bureaucratic norms to be applied. Traditional interest groups are somewhat hostile to the modernising pressures, and the syncretistic leader has difficulty holding support for the issues at stake. Group allegiance can shift rapidly, and there is no clear-cut common interest. Traditional leaders become increasingly wary of decrees and written words; they tend to demand the familiar face-to-face methods of doing business as a prerequisite to co-operation.

Mutual Hostility. This situation occurs when the relationship between the two leadership groups has broken down and syncretistic leadership is non-existent. Traditional leaders withdraw and attempt to avoid contact with bureaucratic agents. Entrenchment takes place and the *status quo* is idealised. Projects, plans, and campaigns flounder; as a result, incriminations and reprisals are aimed at the 'unco-operative' traditional leaders. Communications are ruptured. Little or no consensus exists, and there is blatant disagreement on norms and bureaucratic rules. In this situation, interest groups lack cohesion and members may shift allegiances rapidly. Government attempts at gaining public participation meet with failure and there tends to be an entrenchment of the leaders in each camp. Structures that do exist become binding, in that the bureaucratic leaders are increasingly formalistic, petty, impersonal, and critical of the 'backward' traditional leadership. Both types of leaders are inclined to articulate their built-in biases. Attitudes and opinions bind the individual to the system of which he is a part. Modernisation attempts are usually abortive.

The alliance and coercion forms of syncretistic leadership promote one or more forms of neo-traditionalism. Because traditional leaders are constantly reconciling traditional values, it is understandable that many of these values may be brought forward in slightly altered form and embraced as significant and important. This may be termed revivalism, in that the people's current beliefs need 'to embody the moral prescriptions of the past and apply them to modern conditions'.[2] This is not necessarily a resurgence of historic interest in the past, as has occurred in Ghana and Buganda, but a

---

[2] David Apter, *The Political Kingdom in Uganda* (Princeton, 1961), p. 27. Also see Apter's 'The Role of Traditionalism in the Political Modernization of Ghana and Uganda', in *World Politics* (Princeton), xiii, October 1960, pp. 45–68.

revival of past guidelines for application to modern behaviour. Because most Africans are not very far from the land-based, practical problems of rural life, the solutions to contemporary problems could be expected to be land-based, and familiar in terms of past symbols and ritual. Syncretistic leadership exists because of this traditionalism and the ability of rural leaders to capitalise on traditional habits.

In summary, the fundamental argument is this: rural traditional authorities survive in modern times as local political leaders. They do so by serving as intermediaries between modernising bureaucratic authorities and the custom-bound populace. When they fail to serve as intermediaries, a condition of mutual hostility between themselves and modernising authorities develops, and there is a failure to reach bureaucratic goals. When some accord is reached, the situation is in essence syncretistic, that is, the traditional leader serves to balance the demands of the populace and the bureaucratic groups. Snycretism can take the form of alliance or coercion. Under either situation traditional leaders must capitalise on certain culture-bound factors that support traditionalism, and also specifically manipulate such things as local myth, ritual, symbol, and customary law. If this balance is maintained, a tendency toward neo-traditionalism can be expected. When neo-traditionalism persists, the modernising bureaucratic authorities will attempt to check such tendencies as threats to bureaucratic goals. Conflict may be expected because the syncretistic leader tends to rely on the more traditional basis of influence, and in essence to tip the balance in favour of the customary values. This, in turn, causes modernising agents to exert pressure on the syncretistic leader to re-align with bureaucratic goals. The

result is either a re-balance under alliance or coercion conditions, or a rupture in relations causing mutual hostility. This over-all thesis may best be illustrated and expanded upon by focusing on a particular nation and a specific ethnic group.

A CASE FOR ANALYSIS: THE NYAMWEZI OF TANZANIA

The political organisation of an ethnic group such as the Nyamwezi includes, in the broadest sense, the traditional institutions by which law and order are maintained, the organisation of authority in sub-systems—the chiefdom, village, or family—and those institutions which safeguard the integrity of the political units.[3] As used here, the political organisation is the widest effective social group which creates and maintains order, forces compliance with the norms of that social order, and socialises and maintains support for the authority figures who are in positions of leadership.[4] In a study of a non-western, multi-centred, traditional society, leadership and authority are functionally diffuse. Leaders perform political activities from a position which may be attained through a combination of religious, economic, and familial legitimacy. Kin relations and ritual activities take the place of the more specific functions in western societies associated with political office and binding contracts.

---

[3] The writer is indebted to Mary Eaton Read Nicholson and Richard Simpson for helpful comment and criticism on this portion of the manuscript.

[4] See discussion of the political organisation of the related Sukuma people in J. Gus Liebenow, 'Responses to Planned Political Change in a Tanganyika Tribal Group', in *The American Political Science Review* (Menasha, Wisconsin), L, 2, 1956, pp. 442–61.

THE BACKGROUND: NYAMWEZI POLITICAL ORGANISATION[5]

Three key factors characterise the Nyamwezi traditional political system. First, there has never been a paramount chief who has unified all the Nyamwezi. Each chiefdom was autonomous and, except for a few periods of consolidation, chiefs were always wary of attempts at unification. Political cohesion among the Nyamwezi does not lie in an over-all centralised political authority, but is based on similarity in customs, laws, language, and political and economic structures. Second, the political organisation of each chiefdom has been a pyramidal hierarchy; below the chief are headmen with territorial jurisdiction, and below the headmen are sub-headmen with village or neighbourhood jurisdiction. Third, in the person of the chief was found the main decision-making authority affecting the individual peasant.

Basically, political life in each chiefdom centred around the chief, whose sources of authority were his magical-religious functions, his administrative position, his role as the military commander, and his position as supreme judge. Specifically, he was believed by his people to be the earthly representative of the founder of the chiefdom. He was thought to be able to influence the fate of the land and was generally believed to be able to enlist ancestral spirits to aid the community. Most chiefs were thought able to call on the ancestors to control the elements—to bring rain or to stop floods.[6] When functioning as judges, chiefs traditionally had the power of life and death.[7]

The specific sources of chiefly power may be briefly summarised: (a) the chief was the sole proprietor of land and controlled the allocation of such land to the cultivators; (b) in time of famine the chief controlled the dispensing of food from chiefdom granaries; and (c) his accumulated wealth from fees, fines, booty, tools, and unused property enabled him to purchase the loyalty of key subjects, including warriors.

Conversely, the traditional restrictions on a chief's power came from several sources: (a) subjects could demand a chief's removal if his supernatural powers were believed to have failed; (b) the delegation of chiefly authority for war, adjudication, religious ceremony, and ritual performance effectively reduced the over-all authority of a chief and often made him dependent on functionaries in the chiefdom; (c) the fear of ancestral vengeance in a vanquished area kept most chiefs from occupying conquered lands and expanding their territorial holdings; (d) the ability of families to 'hive off' from an abusive chief and to join another

---

[5] The Nyamwezi number some 363,252 (1957 census) and are the second largest of Tanzania's 120 ethnic groups. They mainly inhabit Tabora, Nzega, and Kahama districts in the central plateau region. Tabora district is the focus of the present study. The most important background literature includes Rev. Fr. Boesch, *Les Banyamwezi, peuple de l'Afrique orientale* (Münster, 1930), and R. G. Abrahams, *The Political Organization of Unyamwezi* (Cambridge, 1967).

[6] Some of the ritualistic functions of the chief included magical preparation of seed, control of rain, village cleansing after twins were born, and control of epidemics and calamities such as famine, rinderpest, hail, or man-eating lions. The responsibility of each chief was to find the cause of the problem and to initiate measures against it, usually with the aid of a diviner.

[7] Within the memory of living elders, death sentences were given for treason, cattle theft by a stranger, adultery with a chief's wife, and occasionally for witchcraft. Murder, arson, and assault generally received less severe penalties. Execution in the Unyanyembe chiefdom, for example, was by mutilation and leaving the condemned to the hyena.

chiefdom restricted a chief for fear of losing manpower and tribute; and (e) collective action by peasants to remove an abusive chief was possible as a last resort, and meant complete loss of property, wives, and livestock for the chief.

In the years of British colonial administration, 1915–61, the consolidation of many chiefdoms took place and chiefs were given local administrative and court responsibilities.[8] Politically, however, few chiefs gained influence outside their districts, and most were only involved with parochial events within their chiefdoms. Important administrative functions stayed primarily in the hands of the British district officer, and political participation and intra-district integration were not attained. In positive terms, however, some consensus was undoubtedly achieved, and a degree of inter-area co-operation reached. Certainly the underpinnings of the post-independence structure of local government were established—such as the district councils and village development committees—and some experience gained in governmental procedures and parliamentary rules.

In the final years of the British administration, when nationalistic forces began to gather strength (1945–61), the institution of chieftaincy came under the greatest stress. Throughout the country chiefs faced a classic dilemma: whether to support the demands of the Tanganyika African National Union (T.A.N.U.) that colonial rule be abolished, or to support the British administration in attempting to contain the nationalistic protest. Fear of losing their paid positions as government adminis-

trators kept most Nyamwezi chiefs from joining the party. In the late 1950s, however, as independence became more probable, a few chiefs secretly joined the political movement and allowed their personal membership cards to be used to aid local recruitment.

Because the chiefs were generally apathetic in the nationalistic movement and because they represented the *status quo*, they were repeatedly accused by the party of being lackeys of the colonial government. This conflict between the traditional and party leaders is a significant legacy in Tanzania's attempt at economic and political modernisation. In hundreds of individual cases T.A.N.U. officials so harassed traditional leaders that a major impasse was created between the two groups. Differences arose between peasants who supported chiefs and headmen and those, generally younger individuals, who supported the party leadership.

Chieftainship has remained particularly strong in the remote hinterland where urban influences have not penetrated. It is in the same remote areas that the party is attempting to gain the support of the people and to provide the interpretation and guidance originally gained from traditional leaders. As could be expected, the old disputes between chiefs and party leaders often militate against the party overtures. Party statements are no longer nationalistic protests designed to end colonialism, but are attempts to mobilise the people for modernisation schemes. Often new goals are espoused by old T.A.N.U. personalities. For traditional leaders, this in itself is reason enough for non-co-operation. The upshot is often a destructive whispering campaign against any modernisation project backed by the party.

In essence, a major source of the chief's difficulties was the necessity of

---

[8] Tabora had 12 chiefdoms in 1961. The other Nyamwezi districts of Nzega and Kahama had a total of 20 chiefdoms.

having government support and popular support at the same time. Simultaneously withstanding accusations from the party, maintaining popularity with the peasants, and being a government agent caused the institution of chieftaincy to rest on a tenuous balance.

THE MODERN SURVIVAL OF TRADITIONAL LEADERS

The long-established institution of chieftainship, around which so much of Tanzania's political history had evolved, was dramatically abolished by the independent African Government on

end. As the Government moved to fill the administrative void with civil servants, the chiefs and headmen moved to consolidate their remaining influence. Throughout the nation examples of chiefs retaining power in a local area and gaining some governmental recognition were common. In these cases the government reaction was to appoint the chief a local government official; and, where the situation demanded more administrative expertise, to appoint a deputy with the chief.

The village headmen who served under the chiefs in the colonial admin-

Traditional Leaders in Tabora District, 1963 and 1966 *

	Chiefs	Headmen
Traditional leaders in power when chieftaincy was abolished, 1963	11	97
In governmental positions, 1966	2	88
Employed by political party or co-operative society, 1966	1	2
Detained by government for political activity, 1966	1	0
Under arrest for peculation, 1966	0	2
Deceased, 1966	1	2
Others: local councillor, retired farmer, other work, 1966	6	3

*Source: author's research. A survey of other Tanzania districts, including Nzega, Mpanda, and Rungwe, indicates that 25–35 per cent of the chiefs were able to remain in governmental positions of power.

1 January 1963.[9] Chiefs were legally dethroned, but their influence did not

---

[9] By the African Chiefs Ordinance (Repeal) Act of 1963 (Act no. 13 of 1963, effective on 1 January 1963). The Act states that the African Chiefs Ordinance, Cap. 331 of the Revised Laws, is repealed (section 1) but that if any Chief is an ex-officio member of a Council or Board he may continue to be a member if the Minister concerned concurs (section 2). Earlier, in 1957, the powers of the chiefs had been curtailed by the African Chiefs (Special Powers) Ordinance, which laid down that any chief whose chiefdom was in a district where a District Council was being formed remained the authority for the chiefdom, but 'must not... encroach on the jurisdiction of the new district council in any way'.

istration have also been able to remain in power as paid officials. These individuals are basically traditional leaders, in that they generally came from families who historically retained the headmanship. Many also had kinship links with the local chief. Others gained their position because they served some magical-religious functions or because they were acceptable to the people, to their chief, and to the British administration. In modern times headmen usually hold posts as village executive officers in the local government structure or serve as village representatives on district councils.

Specific evidence of the contemporary political survival of traditional chiefs and headmen may be seen in data concerning the Nyamwezi leaders of Tabora District (table p. 271). The chiefs who gained some official position were those who had enjoyed widespread popular support in their chiefdoms and had also had strong ties with party and administrative leaders. The chiefs who survived politically were those who had attained the highest education and, significantly, the shortest tenure of office. Chiefs who were reduced to the status of local councillors or retired farmers had been in office the longest and were the more closely identified with colonial rule. Most had smaller chiefdoms and a more localised base of support, and thus faced a greater possibility that local antagonisms weighed against them. Chiefs with longer tenure were also more conservative and more out of touch with changes in the nationalistic period. Undoubtedly they had few contacts with African party and government leaders; a fact that limited their opportunities when the new governing élite abolished chieftaincy in 1963.

Traditional headmen had an even greater political survival rate than did the chiefs, largely due to the headmen's appointment as village executive officers in the local government system. It is in this situation that an impasse for the administration has occurred. The headman deals directly with the people; it is through him that effective administration, adjudication, and modernisation must come. He has continued to hold village administrative posts, although often uneducated and uninterested in the efficient administration which the government desires. To replace him with an 'enlightened' headman is to remove the most acceptable leader and to incur the distrust and objection of the people.

To leave him in his crucial position is to jeopardise the modernisation goals of the central government. Although most central government officials recognise this problem, chiefs and headmen have not been eased out of power. The fundamental reason is that a number of complex attitudinal and environmental factors favour their retention.

ATTITUDINAL FACTORS IN TRADITIONAL SURVIVAL

Modern support for the institution of chieftaincy is so ingrained in the behaviour of most rural cultivators that, in spite of legal changes, a chief's influence continues. Habit, fear of rapid change, and the nonacceptance of local government administrators who have replaced traditional authorities underlie local attitudes. Other reasons persist. The peasants' widespread insecurity about the future promotes the survival of traditional leaders; for example, a former chief may hold power because his followers are sure neither of what the future will bring nor that the old chief will not be reinstated. Administrative changes are rapid enough to keep most peasants confused. The knowledge that other chiefs are still in authoritative governmental positions promotes the idea that the old chiefs may eventually regain influence. Caution and the desire not to burn bridges allow an atmosphere of tolerance toward traditional leaders to exist.

If a chief's tenure reaches back through two generations, his position as a respected leader may be confused with his position as a former chief and a general aura of authority accorded him. For many conservative peasants the deposed traditional chief is the closest and most trusted leader. For others, the fear of an ex-chief on the basis of his magical-religious power is enough to sustain his authority. Moreover, since the Government has legally withdrawn support from the chief, he can now define his relationship with peasants on a more intimate basis than before and join vehemently with them in criticism of the Government. Criticism of the administration on the basis that it does not do enough for the people is a common bond among cultivators. Since the new African Government cost the chief his livelihood and official position, there is every reason for him to join the people in the criticism of Government.

Basic Nyamwezi attitudes toward authority are also important. First, there is no tradition of questioning an authority figure unless he has flagrantly abused his powers. A chief's or headman's early authority would carry over to the present because he was originally in power. Such an individual would be far more acceptable than the imposed authority who is alien to the village.

Secondly, attitudes towards generosity are important. Authority figures have always been expected to be generous and to look after the needy. Europeans seldom recognised this custom, often with the result that the peasant was confused and annoyed and the administration's goals frustrated. This was basically a failure to realise that, as authorities, Europeans were expected to be generous with their food, drink, transport, medicine, and the like. Modern African local government officials share the European attitudes and seldom fulfil the peasants' expectations of generous leaders. Consequently it is more natural for a peasant to support the familiar leader who at least pays lip service to the old custom. A similar belief that the chief will look after the people in time of calamity is not transferred to the local government authority. Such authority is too far removed from the individual, there usually cannot

be a face-to-face request for help, and there is little assurance that the administration would help an individual even if it could.

Considering over-all village behaviour, support for traditional leaders comes mainly from five village groups whose members rely on the chiefs and headmen as councillors, ritualists, confessors, or interpreters of modern events. These groups are: (a) the generally conservative elders over 50, (b) men between 15 and 50 who are uneducated, untravelled, and generally apolitical, (c) nearly all uneducated women over 30, (d) children under 15, and (e) the practising group of diviners, healers, medicine men, and soothsayers. Groups that tend not to support the traditional leaders are: (a) educated or semi-educated men between 15 and 50, (b) village dissidents, agitators, rebels, (c) enterprising or innovating local-level educators, administrators, politicians, and (d) the few semi-educated women between 15 and 30.

THE USE OF SPECIFIC TECHNIQUES

In analysing how traditional leaders remain in power, however, a distinction should be made between the more general attitudes operating in Nyamwezi society and the specific customary practices which provide traditional leaders with a basis for political action. A further distinction may then be made concerning how leaders manipulate myth, ritual, symbols, customary law, and the like, for their own ends. First, the following customary practices persist and lend credence to the traditional system:

(a) *Use of Political Assassination.* The ultimate control of a Nyamwezi chief has been assassination by the royal family or headmen, usually by suffocation or poison. Occasional reports of headmen being assassinated occur today, and the deaths of two chiefs in the last ten years have led to trials and imprisonment under accusations of poisoning.

(*b*) *Use of Traditional Medical Practices.* Various types of practitioners exist today to promote cures, dispense herbs and medicines, and in some areas to act as diviners and soothsayers. Some practitioners aid traditional leaders in ritualistic activity and help them gain success in specific undertakings. A traditional leader's dispensing of amulets, protective devices, and special medicines to ensure success in political undertakings is commonplace.

(*c*) *Continuance of Dance Groups.* Societies composed of specific groups (old men, young men, women, etc.) carry on the traditional dances, often for modern occasions such as celebrations marking independence day or the founding of the party. Vestiges of the past that tend to support traditional leaders are seen at such times when dancers clad in modern dress shout the names of honoured warriors of Nyamwezi history and refer to the heroic deeds of past chiefs.

(*d*) *Continuance of Tribute.* Although the filling of chiefs' private granaries ceased officially in 1927, some chiefdom granaries continued to be kept as an administrative guard against famine; and small homages and gifts are still presented to traditional leaders in return for their favour.

(*e*) *Use of Honorific Greetings.* Honorific titles and the clapped-hand greeting to honour a chief are widely used.

(*f*) *Use of Traditional Elders' Councils.* The newly constituted village development committees for most Nyamwezi villages are composed largely of elders who have previously served on the village councils. More progressive individuals such as the local teacher or dispenser are occasionally on the committees, but former chiefs and headmen often dominate such meetings.

(*g*) *Use of Traditional Boundaries.* The boundaries of traditional chiefdoms are used today in delineating local government, court, and village development committee jurisdictions. Tax rolls are kept on the basis of chiefdom boundaries, and traditional headquarters are often used for modern offices. The result is a tendency for farmers to think of the new administrative units in terms of the old chiefdom, and to think of the new administrators in terms of chiefs and headmen.

A major reason why the above practices persist—and thus allow an environment which promotes traditional leadership—is that the chiefdom itself has remained the broadest political unit with which a rural African is directly concerned. The individual is first and foremost a member of a chiefdom whose geographical borders are known, whose leaders are dealt with on a personal basis, and whose authority system the farmer still understands most completely. Within the context of the chiefdom the traditional leader can use specific techniques to promote his own survival. Such techniques include the manipulation of ritual, the use of symbols, the reliance on a semi-judicial position in customary law, and the use of a position in a secret society.

Most ritualistic ceremonies carried out by chiefs and headmen in modern times are either those connected with the agricultural cycle or those employed to prevent disease and natural calamity. The ceremonies take the form of appeasing ancestral spirits, visiting the graves of former chiefs, protecting against witchcraft, controlling rainfall, ensuring fertility, and the like. For the more conservative elements of Nyamwezi rural society, these practices are important. The more educated chiefs and headmen who carry out limited ceremonies usually do so to appease their followers. Other chiefs use the ritual function for self-aggrandisement and as a basis of authority.

The importance of symbols and regalia lies in their actual possession. The physical holding of the regalia meant the holding of office. A modern transposition of these symbols has occurred; the possession now of the symbols of an administrative chief, such as records, files, books, pencils, and the like, has come to be equated with a position of authority. Most deposed chiefs and working headmen have these trappings of office and rely on them to give an official air. Other symbols of chieftaincy are still maintained by retainers and guardians of the chief's quarters. When worn by the chiefs and headmen, such regalia remind the peasants of the customary power of the office and, in fact, give modern authority to the traditional leader.

With reference to customary law, the traditional leader had a dual judicial role in the colonial period. He was the most important informal interpreter of customary law, and he had the full legal and administrative powers of a court magistrate. When chieftaincy was abolished in 1963, it became illegal for chiefs to hold court. In fact, however, many chiefs continued to act as unofficial judges in such matters as bridewealth, marriage, divorce, guardianship, land tenure, and rights regarding property, claims, and wills. Headmen, moreover, continued to have the legal right to hear local disputes and are, in fact, semi-judicial. Under Nyamwezi customary law the headman is particularly prominent in the allocation of land and the settlement of land disputes. Other conflicts, such as those over cattle, bridewealth, or inheritance, usually reach the headman when a family or families find themselves deadlocked. If the headman fails to reconcile the problem, the village development committee is the next step.

For both chiefs and headmen, the adjudication of customary law has remained an important function, and a continuing basis of authority. The removal of a case to the primary court, with an alien magistrate who is not from the local area and who probably is not a Nyamwezi, represents either a serious breach in the processes by which internal conflicts are resolved in the community, or a case between individuals who fall under different headmen or chiefs. In terms of political survival, any traditional leader who holds a position as a judge and mediator is in a strong position to continue his authority.

Secret societies are also used to give a former chief a claim to authority. Those that exist today are basically voluntary, and operate for such reasons as the curing of sickness, divining, spirit possession, ancestor worship, totemism, rain-making and the hunting of specific animals. Although these societies have diminished in popularity and have not in recent years been overtly political, they do exist in most places. The significant point is that chiefs and headmen occupy the higher ranks of the organisations. Because the societies cut across village and chiefdom boundaries, the officers have a potentially wide scope for political activity. Contemporary evidence suggests that traditional leaders use their positions in secret societies to reach influential elderly audiences, or as one of several claims to legitimacy.

SYNCRETISM AND NEO-TRADITIONALISM

Syncretistic, reconciling behaviour depends in part on the persistence of some form of neo-traditionalism—a revival of past values. Traditional leaders must selectively use the past to ensure their position in the decisions of the future. Periodically, old values must be re-embraced and new conditions must be interpreted in light of earlier values. A movement of this nature occurs within an ethnic group and is in response to the encroachment of unacceptable modernistic values.

Such a neo-traditional movement occurred among the Nyamwezi between 1958 and 1964. The leaders of the movement, who were mainly chiefs, religious leaders, and trade-union officials, preached the long-term support of chiefly rule, the use of Swahili as the official language, and a re-emphasis on African dress and culture. Prior to independence in 1961 the movement was anti-administration, anti-European, and against the multi-racial local government ideas then under consideration. Following independence, the neo-traditional leaders continued to be against the African administration and against limiting chiefly powers. Criticism was also levelled at African government leaders because they were allegedly pro-Christian and discriminated against Muslims. The Government's reaction has been to negate the movements by emphasising the modernising, nation-building values that citizens should embrace and, in specific Nyamwezi areas, by forcing a few powerful chiefs to recant publicly.

Moderate neo-traditionalism, however, continues because the Government is not yet in a position to withdraw totally the powers of headmen and a few chiefs. The syncretistic leader is still the intermediary. Four main reasons exist for the persistence of these neo-traditionalists. First, to obtain literate, competent, and acceptable leadership at the village level requires higher pay and more rewards than the local government can afford. Secondly, to recruit competent village leaders entails persuading the individual that he should live in a remote village far from the more interesting urban areas. This constitutes a hardship that most educated leaders find difficult to accept.

Thirdly, potential rural leaders often do not come forward from within the local area because they fail to understand what the new positions entail, or because they fear responsibility. Such reluctance is based on not wishing to incur the jealousy of neighbours, not wanting to appear prosperous or grasping, and not wishing to supersede a more traditionally qualified person. Fourthly, the ostracism of unpopular local officials is common enough to be a major restraint on over-ambitious individuals. The social position of anyone who is ostracised is, in Nyamwezi terminology (*bubiti*), equated with a hyena-like condition—all that is anti-social, dirty, nocturnal, and scavenging. In summary, neo-traditionalism is condoned and inadvertently promoted by the Government simply because only traditional leaders can be found to fill the rural leadership vacuum.

* * *

Syncretism in political leadership is promoted by the persistence of traditional values and attitudes, and the counter-demands of the modernising bureaucratic state. The necessary environment for syncretism is perpetuated by the specific culture-bound revival of customary values, and the manipulation by leaders of symbols, ritual, customary laws, and the like. The syncretic phenomena will continue as long as traditional value systems are in conflict with intruding modernising systems. Predictably, the traditional system will be changed by the implanting of new rural institutions, such as cells, co-operatives, parties, and administrative structures, which demand mass participation, which require new behaviour patterns, and which establish new goals for rural peoples. The success of the rural institutions will depend on the extent to which rural people manipulate these structures merely to create new forms of old organisations. In some places this will happen; gradualism will hold sway, traditional leaders will refuse to be influenced by administrators, and the organisational goals will not be reached. In other areas, innovative local leaders will accommodate the new rural institutions and the government's goals will be attained.

In general, there is a paradoxical coexistence of action and inaction in the rural areas. The situation is one of constant stimulation, reaction, and reformation. It is an ongoing process of change set upon a seemingly static society. The irony is that the human and the bureaucratic systems are experiencing constant upheaval, and yet the ebb and flow of rural life seems to be that of a dull monotony, unaltered and unchanging.

Representative Government, Bureaucracy, and Political Development: The African Case

Michael F. Lofchie

Political scientists are beginning to focus renewed attention on the relationship between bureaucracy[1] and the development of viable representative government in Africa.[2] The reasons for this resurgence are many and varied, but most derive from the changing character of the African political environment. The era of nationalism has ended and has been replaced by a period of extreme turbulence and instability. In a political context in which institutional forms shift abruptly, and in which representative structures of government have an evanescent quality, bureaucracy seems to offer at least one stable and persisting sector in the political arena. Moreover, there can be little doubt that as conciliar structures decline or disappear, bureaucracies—both military and civil—take on a dramatically heightened political role.

The uncertainties of contemporary African politics have caused social scientists to reexamine the implicit premises of their research. A succession of military coups, recurrent crises of national unity, and the high incidence of

[1] As used in this paper, the term "bureaucracy" refers only to the civil administration of a society and does not include the military unless so specified.

[2] This concern is not a new one and has roots which extend to the earliest political literature in African studies, Raymond Buell's *The Native Problem in Africa* and Lord Hailey's monumental *African Survey*. One of the most important preoccupations in this early literature was the extent to which the diverse administrative practices of the various colonial powers could be viewed as "training grounds" for eventual democratic government.

From *Journal of Developing Areas,* Vol. II, No. 1 (October 1967), 37–55, by permission.

anomic and violent behavior have generated a basic challenge to the early assumption that the survival of civil institutions per se could be taken for granted. A long-standing debate over whether single-party systems could be "democratic" has been replaced by a dialogue over whether such terms as "decay" and "breakdown" are more appropriate than "development" and "modernization" as generic, encompassing descriptions of the process of political change in newly independent nations.[3]

The same sense of uncertainty has manifested itself in the treatment of the relationship between bureaucracy and political development. Joseph LaPalombara's edited volume, *Bureaucracy and Political Development*,[4] for example, sustains a running debate among the contributors over whether bureaucracy plays an essentially positive role, facilitating political development and socioeconomic modernization, or has a negative impact, restricting the growth of representative institutions and hampering the emergence of groups and classes characteristic of a modernizing society. Summarizing several of the authors, LaPalombara notes that "the presence of a strong bureaucracy in many of the new states tends to inhibit the growth of strong executives, voluntary associations and other political institutions essential to viable democratic government,"[5] and "the bureaucracies of the developing areas will often hamper the growth of a private entre-preneurial class. Merchants and others who might work to transform the economy are incessantly harassed."[6] S. N. Eisenstadt, whose essay contains echoes of both sides of the debate, argues on the positive side that if structural differentiation, functional specificity, and the acquisition of new and enhanced governmental capabilities are the central attributes of political modernization, these qualities are to be found in bureaucracy far more than in other institutional sectors of the society. Moreover, he argues, bureaucracies have historically performed a variety of functions critical for the modernization of their societies. These include unification and centralization, socialization, and the regulation and aggregation of group demands.[7]

Much of this debate revolves around the meaning and significance to be attached to a single idea, one which is shared by a host of authors writing about the relationship between bureaucracy and political development. The idea, stated as a proposition, is that there is a grave developmental imbalance between bureaucracy and the representative institutional sectors of the polity and that bureaucracy is far more developed and powerful than the conciliar structures of government—parties, legislatures, and associational interest groups. Some authors even assert that the "overdeveloped" character of bureaucracy is at least partly responsible for the weakness and fragility of the representative elements of the system.

To illustrate the broadly diffused and central importance of this concept in the literature on bureaucracy and political development, several quotations are

---

[3] See, for example, S. N. Eisenstadt, "Breakdowns of Modernization," *Economic Development and Cultural Change*, XII (July 1964), 345–67, and Samuel P. Huntington, "Political Development and Political Decay," *World Politics*, XVII (January 1965), 386–430.

[4] (Princeton, N. J.: Princeton University Press, 1963).

[5] *Ibid.*, pp. 22–23.

[6] *Ibid.*, pp. 24–25.

[7] S. N. Eisenstadt, "Bureaucracy and Political Development," in *Bureaucracy and Political Development*, pp. 96–110.

offered. Fred W. Riggs has stated the concept in the following terms:

A phenomenon of utmost significance in transitional societies is the lack of balance between the political policy-making institutions and bureaucratic policy-implementing institutions. The relative weakness of political organs means that the political function tends to be appropriated, in considerable measure, by bureaucrats. Intrabureaucratic struggles become a primary form of politics.[8]

Ferrel Heady speaks of "an imbalance in the growth of political institutions [in the developing nations] with the bureaucracy among those in the more mature category." He expands on this viewpoint as follows:

Imbalanced political development is another characteristic of past events in the developing countries. Traditional cultural patterns, colonialism and the telescoping of change have produced political systems that are askew as judged by experience in the more developed polities, particularly those with a representative democratic political framework. Means for interest articulation and aggregation, through such instrumentalities as an informed electorate, organized associational groups, competing political parties and representative legislative bodies are either weak or absent except in the most rudimentary form. On the other hand, the executive agencies of government are dominant under an elitist leadership.[9]

A similar theme can be found in the writings of S. N. Eisenstadt:

In the formal structures of government, some parallel tendencies can also be discerned [uneven change]. . . . The first is the obvious preponderance of the executive over all other branches of government. This development flows from the need to take over and operate the governmental machinery smoothly. It is connected with a strong emphasis on governmental activity. . . . The legislature is usually passive and subservient or so unruly as to minimize the effects of its own influence and power. This does not mean that the different legislative bodies in all new countries are totally ineffective, though in some they may be non-existent. It does indicate that their effective function as mediators between the executive and the population at large is rather weak.[10]

Because the idea of institutional imbalance is of such central and pervasive importance in the literature on bureaucracy in developing countries, it forms a useful point of departure for this essay.

The concept actually consists of two quite distinguishable propositions. First, in a large number of new states, representative institutional structures— legislatures, parties, and electoral processes —are characterized by extreme weakness and fragility. Second, the bureaucratic sector, possessing high functional capability and high relevance to economic development, has gained an overwhelming degree of influence over government policy. The purpose of this article is to explore these two propositions and to attempt to identify some of the possible relationships between them. It thus seeks to achieve two distinct objectives: to identify the basic causes of weakness in the representative structures of government and to examine the sources of and limitations on bureaucratic power. In so doing, it may be possible to assess the extent to which

---

[8] Fred W. Riggs, "Bureaucrats and Political Development: A Paradoxical View," in *Bureaucracy and Political Development*, p. 120.

[9] Ferrel Heady, *Public Administration: A Comparative Perspective* (Englewood Cliffs, N. J.: Prentice-Hall, 1966), pp. 61, 64–65.

[10] S. N. Eisenstadt, "Political Development," in *Social Change*, ed. Amitai and Eva Etzione (New York: Basic Books, 1964), pp. 321–22.

bureaucratic overdevelopment contributes to representative weakness.

REPRESENTATIVE STRUCTURES OF GOVERNMENT— THE CAUSES OF WEAKNESS

The almost universal decline or disappearance of political parties, the ineffectuality of legislative bodies, widespread tendencies towards executive dominance and personalistic authority, and the ease and rapidity with which constitutional arrangements are altered are the most conspicuous symptoms of fragility in the representative structures of government. These phenomena have been accompanied by a series of military take-overs, an increasing incidence of political violence, and a growing preference for strong presidential constitutions. In many African countries, elected local governments have been deprived of power and authority by the transfer of their functions to the central government administration.

Some of the major reasons for the deterioration of representative government in Africa can be revealed by contrasting the African pattern of political development with that which occurred historically in those Western states which have successfully evolved viable systems of representation. Lucien Pye has identified the effective institutionalization of representative government in Western societies with the resolution of a set of historical crises.[11] Of the six crises distinguished by Pye, four are especially relevant for comparative purposes; these are identity, legitimacy, participation, and distribution. It can be argued that the major historical condition which enabled England and

the United States, for example, to handle these crises was that in the Anglo-American experience, the crises were confronted sequentially and in the order stated.

The purest case of this phenomenon is the United States. The creation of a strong sense of national identity, facilitated by a high degree of linguistic and cultural homogeneity, was ensured by the common experience of revolutionary war, after which elements of the society opposed to the creation of an independent American national identity either emigrated or remained silent. The formulation of a constitutional framework, legitimatized by the agreement of the former colonies, took place during a period of relative tranquility when no other major crises had to be dealt with and, more importantly, occurred only after the completion of the war. One highly relevant feature of the American constitution was that it did not provide for a high degree of direct popular participation. The president, for example, was to be chosen by the electoral college as a means of insulating that office from popular involvement in the system. The Senate, as well, was to be indirectly elected by nomination of the separate state legislatures. Perhaps most importantly, universal suffrage was not established and each state was to set the franchise requirements for its own citizens. Property and other restrictive qualifications were common. Only gradually, during the nineteenth century, were limitations on the right to vote eliminated—thus allowing universal suffrage to become a reality. Distribution or, more specifically, governmental activity to affect the social distribution of national income did not become an issue until the New Deal. At that time, the society moved abruptly away from the classical liberalism of the nineteenth century and into full acceptance of the

---

[11]Lucien Pye, *Aspects of Political Development* (Boston, Mass.: Little, Brown, 1966), chap. 1.

idea that providing minimal standards for impoverished and deprived social groups was a state responsibility.

In England, the crises of identity and legitimacy were intertwined. The gradual creation of a centralized constitutional monarchy and the establishment of a sense of national identity were both completed (at least for England, Scotland, and Wales) by the end of the eighteenth century. At that time, however, popular participation was seriously restricted by property and other requirements which limited suffrage. The gradual enfranchisement of the working class and their incorporation into the political system required more than a century to complete. Despite the social dislocation created by the industrial revolution, state welfare activity did not become a vital issue until the post-World War II Labour government. As in the United States, it remains the principal domestic issue to this day.

The sequential pattern of crisis confrontation distinguishes Western historical experience markedly from that in Africa and other developing areas. One common feature of newly independent African states is that they must confront all these crises at once; that is, they must establish a unified sense of national identity, work out mutually agreeable constitutional arrangements, incorporate culturally diverse elements into the political system, and conduct extensive welfare programs simultaneously. In a political context in which the "rules of the game" lack widespread consensual validity but universal suffrage encourages maximum popular involvement in the political process, the difficulties of formulating widely agreeable welfare policies are greater than representative systems can easily endure.

This difference in the historical phasing of the development process contributes directly to the enormous burden on Africa's political systems and hence to the weakness of their representative structures. In Western democracies, the early stages of the industrial revolution preceded the creation of fully participant democratic institutions. In both Western society and in the developing areas, socioeconomic transformation from relatively simple agrarian life to an industrial, commercial, and urban pattern has involved massive problems of human dislocation and deprivation: overcrowding, low wages, inadequate standards of health and sanitation, and generally degrading conditions of existence. The restricted character of participation in Western societies, however, meant that impoverished urban and rural masses were usually structurally unable to translate their socioeconomic grievances into demands on the polity. In Africa, universal suffrage and a political culture stressing norms of equality and participation have stimulated deprived groups to transmit their grievances directly to the state and to demand ameliorative welfare measures.

The time differential in the historical evolution of political culture is itself highly significant. When the lower and working classes were enfranchised and thus became participants in the Western polity, the prevalent political values were largely derived from classical laissez-faire liberalism. Despite structural access to the political system, groups advocating distributive measures by government encountered a pervasive economic ethos which stressed that the "greatest good of the greatest number" could be achieved only if the state remained aloof from the economy. Only the free competition of economic forces, so the theory went, would result in true human progress. This ethic discouraged distributive claims and generally enabled the state to neglect or ignore the socioeconomic grievances of substantial segments of the population. An important consequence of the extended period of laissez-faire was that claimant political groups were inducted into the system and largely socialized to *its* rules, procedures, and norms before they were able to make significant economic demands.

By the time distributive claims acquired legitimacy, industrialization and commercialization had provided substantial resources for the polity to undertake ameliorative welfare activity. It is important to note, however, that this economic growth had taken place partly because the state was not diverting resources from capital reinvestment and accumulation into immediate spheres of consumption (health, education, welfare). The Western polity faced powerful distributive demands only at a time in its development when resources were available to meet them. Its ability to respond positively to claims for welfare activity reinforced and solidified its legitimacy.

In Africa, participation has been combined with a political culture stressing the need for extensive state welfare activity far earlier in the development process than was the case in the West, at a time when most economies are not yet sufficiently productive to make substantial resources available for distributive purposes. Virtually all African countries, even those which do not profess "African socialism," have fostered high public expectations in such areas as health, education, and allied social fields. Because of economic scarcity, however, many governments cannot but fail to meet their own articulated goals. Such failures lower popular confidence in government and weaken the legitimacy of its representative structures.

The social crisis of urbanization, partly due to economic change, is probably far greater in Africa today than it was in the West at a corresponding period in its development. The reason for this is to be found in the relationship between technology and modernization. When Western nations were being transformed from rural-agrarian societies into an urban-commercial pattern, technology was simple and labor intensive. No matter how many migrants flocked to the cities and no matter how limited their skills, jobs could nearly always be found in the emergent industrial complex—in coal mines, textile factories, or building roads and railroads. In the United States, the widespread utilization of child and female labor and the absorption of massive immigration from Europe indicate that urban labor was a scarce commodity. Although human conditions were extremely poor, some form of employment and therefore some personal income was available. Furthermore, the regular availability of jobs for relatively unskilled laborers was a major vehicle for the socialization of culturally and linguistically differentiated ethnic groups.[12]

The availability of employment also meant that for a long period social pressure on the government took a special form. The major demand was for legislation to regulate and improve work conditions rather than for massive welfare expenditures. Since this legislation could be implemented at relatively little governmental cost, it was fairly easy and inexpensive for the state to satisfy the public demands. Some limited welfare activity was undertaken by political parties, and this led to the creation of large, stable, and deeply

---

[12]Oscar Handlin, *The Uprooted* (New York: Grosset and Dunlap, 1951), chaps. 3–6.

loyal bodies of party supporters. These loyalties were often strongest among new ethnic groups being absorbed into the polity, moreover, they have frequently persisted long after welfare became a state responsibility. Party-sponsored welfare activity was thus not only important for the promotion of a broad sense of national identity, but has been a critical factor in enabling political parties to remain dynamic and autonomous.

African nations are experiencing industrialization during an era of automation and complexity. New plants and industries do not guarantee the expansion of employment opportunities because industrial capacity can be radically increased at marginal cost in added labor. Cities attract large numbers of rural migrants because they represent opportunity for upward mobility, but since almost invariably new industries are highly automated from their inception, the number of additional jobs is small and expectations go largely unfulfilled. Moreover, the new jobs usually require a relatively high degree of training and skill. This aggravates an already critical gap between elite and mass since cities tend to become increasingly divided between a small number of well-paid workers and a vast majority of unemployed. Despite much concealed unemployment, the elite-mass gap remains one of the most visible and salient features of urban life in Africa and contributes to a widespread sense of social deprivation and frustration. Not only does the economy fail to function as an agency of socialization, but it in fact generates additional pressures on the polity. The highly volatile character of urban crowds in such Asian countries as India, Pakistan, Burma, and Indonesia has already become a major source of political instability. The same is increasingly true of numerous African countries, and several of the recent military coups can be traced directly to the inability of representative institutions to handle the problem of anomic behavior in the cities.

Of the African countries where military coups have not yet occurred, Kenya faces perhaps the most potentially explosive problem of urban discontent. The long period of white settler domination led to the emergence of a substantial population of landless Africans. Most of the landless had little choice but to move into Nairobi to seek employment and to settle in sprawling African slums. Government land resettlement programs have alleviated but have not solved the problem of population pressure on the land, and migration from rural areas continues to oversupply urban labor needs. Rural migrants and school leavers unable to find jobs form a vast community of unemployed. The vivid contrast between the poverty and squalor of the African slums and the affluence of the former European suburbs (now partially occupied by the new African elite) and the economic discrepancies between the unemployed and those with positions in Nairobi's emergent industrial complex are serious political irritants and have strengthened support for the radical opposition party, the Kenya People's Union. The government has attempted to minimize the political expression of discontent by fostering rapid industrial growth, but the opposition charges that this has been at the expense of socialist policies which would provide immediate relief. Many observers believe that present stability is based upon the personal magnetism of President Jomo Kenyatta and upon the government's ability to maintain a low-key political atmosphere. Some fear, however, that if a major succession crisis occurs, an outburst of radical protest could force the regime to rely heavily upon the military for political control.

With regard to the direct relationship between bureaucracy and representative institutions, the contrast between Western and African experience is particularly striking. Fred Riggs has pointed out that the spoils system, as a mode of bureaucratic recruitment, was extremely important in encouraging the development of strong political parties in Western society.[13] He argues that spoils provided an attractive material incentive to the formation of effective party organization and as such stimulated party activity during the formative period of national politics. At times when ideological commitment waned, spoils furnished an important substitute focus for partisan competition. Of perhaps greater importance is the fact that spoils made civil service personnel entirely dependent for their positions upon political leadership and thus encouraged the complete subordination of the administrator to the politician. Limited spoils recruitment remains an important party activity even today in the United States, but the important point is that by the time merit replaced spoils as the basic method of recruitment, parties had acquired a high degree of functional and organizational autonomy.

Political parties in most post-colonial African societies confront a well organized and long established pattern of merit recruitment to the civil service. As a political practice, the principle of achievement has the opposite consequence from spoils. It deprives party organizations of an important material incentive to partisan activity, and it stresses the autonomy and independence of the administrator from the

politician. The essence of achievement recruitment is that civil service positions are awarded because of personal skills and training, not for loyalty or service to partisan causes. This notion is deeply engrained in the minds of many African civil servants and can easily become the basis for resistance to demands or pressures for greater political responsiveness. One of the most critical difficulties faced by African parties has been to find a basis for maintaining their members' commitment. Without spoils to reward party activists, and without partisan welfare activities to ensure the stable loyalty of supporters, most parties have experienced a steady erosion of membership and leadership after independence.

One important reason for the weakness and decline of representative organs of African governments and for the critical imbalance between the representative and bureaucratic sectors of the polity deserves special attention. This is the tendency of intellectual elites to gravitate towards administrative rather than political careers. Political parties have thereby been particularly affected. The achievement of independence deprived African parties of their basic appeal—the moral fervor of the nationalist cause—and left them vulnerable to a loss of both mass following and key personnel. With the assumption of power, strong pressures compel political leaders to become bureaucrats. Such tasks as operating the governmental machinery and achieving economic development are, or seem to many to be, administrative in character. The highest party officials often assume ministerial positions and, in most cases, have little time or energy to spare for maintaining party organization. As Africanization of the civil service is pursued, skilled leaders at all levels of the party hierarchy begin to assume

---

[13]Fred Riggs, in *Bureaucracy and Political Development*, p. 127.

civil service reponsibilities. The movement of party personnel into administration is so deleterious to party organizations that it has been cited as the basic cause for the decline of political parties throughout Africa.[14]

The greater prestige, security, and often material rewards of an administrative position are also a powerful factor, and in many African countries tend to divert emergent elites from political to bureaucratic careers. Of ominous long-range significance is the tendency of African university students to ignore elective office and seek instead lifetime employment in their respective civil services.[15] The ultimate consequence of this may well be a significant talent gap between bureaucratic and representative structures which would certainly worsen the discrepancy in power and authority between these two sectors of government. This condition is increasingly evident in the four West African states of Guinea, Mali, Senegal, and Ivory Coast where, according to Aristide Zolberg, "within a short time, . . . it is likely that these regimes will be composed of a senescent party and of a young vigorous governmental bureaucracy which will not hesitate to take its place in the sun."[16] James Coleman and Carl Rosberg have suggested that in a few extreme cases this could lead to "the emergence of a purely administrative state (not unlike the preindependence situation) with the party being kept alive by the governing elite for purely symbolic, legitimating and community development purposes."[17] In describing such cases, some scholars have used the term "no-party state."

* * *

Some of the basic conditions which cause the weakness and fragility of representative government in Africa may be summarized as follows:

1. African states need to confront simultaneously a set of complex "crises of development" that in Western societies were dealt with one at a time. Because a sense of common national identity and consensual validity for political institutions are only marginally established when universal opportunities for political participation are established, representative structures must absorb the demands of social groups which neither identify with the nation-state nor accept its institutional setting.

2. Because a political culture stressing welfare norms tends to precede even the early phases of industrialization in Africa, widespread demands for social services arise before the economy has generated sufficient resources to meet these demands. Since the publicly declared values of political leadership frequently reflect welfare aspects of the political culture, the polity is placed in a position of failing to achieve its own goals. In Western societies, the comparatively late intrusion of strong welfare expectations into the polity meant that, by and large, adequate resources have been available to carry out social policy. This has been an important factor in reinforcing legitimacy and institutionalization.

[14]Immanuel Wallerstein, "The Decline of the Party in Single-Party African States," in *Political Parties and Political Development*, ed. Joseph LaPalombara and Myron Weiner (Princeton, N.J.: Princeton University Press, 1966), pp. 201–14.

[15]See, for example, Dwaine Marvick, "African University Students: A Presumptive Elite," in *Education and Political Development*, ed. James S. Coleman (Princeton, N. J.: Princeton University Press, 1965), pp. 463–97.

[16]Aristide R. Zolberg, *Creating Political Order* (Chicago, Ill.: Rand McNally, 1966), p. 125.

[17]James S. Coleman and Carl G. Rosberg, Jr. (eds.), *Political Parties and National Integration in Tropical Africa* (Berkeley and Los Angeles: University of California Press, 1964), p. 676.

3. The tendency for African states to enter the process of industrialization at a technologically automated level generally means that their economies create insufficient added employment to absorb rural-urban migration and population growth. Since new types of employment usually require a high degree of skill and training, the societies become increasingly divided between a skilled industrial elite and a mass of unemployed. Extreme social deprivation and political frustration result, while the consequent anomic behavior in the cities has become a major source of political instability.

4. Certain aspects of bureaucracy contribute to the weakness of representative institutions. The greater attractiveness of administrative careers siphons some of the most able and talented political leaders. The result is a visible discrepancy in intellectual competence between political parties and national bureaucracies, which critically impairs the viability of both parties and national assemblies. The political parties' ability to control and manipulate administration is also reduced by the universal practice of achievement recruitment to civil service positions. The basic concept of merit recruitment is that civil servants hold their positions by virtue of personal skill and training, not political loyalty. In Western society, spoils recruitment and the parties' (not the administrations') important welfare functions during the formative period of political institutions were fundamental to the creation of strong party organizations.

BUREAUCRATIC POWER—ITS SOURCES AND LIMITATIONS

The proposition that bureaucracy has gained radically enhanced power and authority by performing political functions left undone due to the weakness of representative structures (the second half of the concept of institutional imbalance) can best be assessed by examining the sources of bureaucratic influence and the limitations on its exercise. At least four separate factors contributing to a growth of administrative influence can be identified: (1) the increasingly scientific and technical character of government policy; (2) the widening gap in specialized training and intellectual skills between the administrative and representative sectors of government; (3) a tendency to designate administrative areas in broad terms; and (4) the absence of mechanisms for exercising political control over administrative activity.

1. A growing role for bureaucracy seems to be an inherent feature of our age, for the formulation and implementation of any dimension of national policy requires highly specialized technical skills. Bureaucracy is a sector of government where these qualities are almost invariably found in considerable disproportion to other sectors, and several eminent political scientists have noted that the intricate nature of government programming in a technological era has resulted in a dramatic growth in the administrators' influence even in societies with viable and dynamic representative structures.

   That the role of specially qualified administrators should be particularly great in developing countries is not surprising. Since the promotion of overall economic growth is a state responsibility, civil servants with competence in this field gain a special position in government circles. Administrative experts in such areas as development economics, international trade, agricultural marketing, and cooperative organization have influence which far exceeds that of most Western administrators. However, to the extent that political leadership retains power and authority to set basic national goals and to make fundamental decisions regarding domestic and foreign policy priorities, growing bureaucratic influence need not impair the essential character of representative government.

2. In many African countries, the influence of administrative cadres is further heightened by a marked discrepancy in technical skills between the bureaucracy and the representative structures, indeed, by the intellectually impoverished character of most party organizations. This gap can easily lead to the complete administrative domination of internal decision-making processes. Moreover, due to the weakness and fragility of their representative institutions, many African political elites are deeply absorbed with problems of stability and sheer political survival. These pressures compel them to devote their efforts to symbolic functions—to the legitimization of the regime and to the consensual validation of their own leadership status. In this way, pervasive instability reinforces the tendency to leave the running of the country in administrative hands. Unless political leadership is relatively free of day-to-day political crises, its role will be limited to the articulation of broad, diffuse, and non-controversial goals. In this context, the area of administrative discretion and flexibility becomes highly political since fundamental questions such as policy priorities and differential resource allocation become subject to bureaucratic decision.

3. Most governments operate daily on the basis of regular assumptions about what is "political" and what is "administrative." In recently independent African states, these assumptions tend to reflect former colonial attitudes and practices and, since colonial governments were largely administrative in orientation, the sphere of what is political is frequently conceptualized in narrow terms. In addition, the older notion of "politics" was frequently somewhat invidious or pejorative in connotation. The validity of any rigid distinction between politics and administration is dubious, particularly in developing areas where the range of state activity is extraordinarily wide.

The distinction is even more unrealistic when "administrative" tends to be defined broadly—with the result that certain phases of policy are construed as administrative although, in fact, they are highly political. One important example of this is the implementation of rural development projects. The methods for organizing a cooperative movement, a self-help project, or an agricultural improvement scheme can significantly affect the social and political relationships of a rural area, hence the power structure of a country. Project implementation, however, is nearly always identified as administrative and, except in cases where a politician has a personal interest in a project, is left in the hands of administrative officials.

4. Closely related to the wide range of governmental activities defined as administrative is the fact that few African countries have developed effective mechanisms for the political control and supervision of administrative activity. There is virtually no African equivalent to the Congressional Committee of Inquiry or the Swedish Ombudsman. Although the press can sometimes offer an outlet for the grievances of individual citizens against administrative abuse, the fact is that parties, legislatures, and individual political leaders do not possess an institutionalized mechanism for exercising political control of administrative behavior. This elaborately interrelated set of factors has led to the emergence of a powerful and influential role for the administrative class in Africa and in other developing areas.

* * *

There are also, however, a number of inherent limitations on the degree of influence that civil bureaucracies can exercise. Perhaps the greatest of these is the indirect nature of administrative power which depends almost exclusively on the capacity to influence the political structures of government. Civil bureaucracies do not possess internal mechanisms of authoritative decision-making and are, for this reason, unable to react to crises of decay in the political sector. This may help explain two significant aspects of administrative behavior in states now under military governments. When the representative structures of government were exhibiting symptoms of a breakdown in authority, civil officialdom was unable to provide even an interim form of national leadership. The tendency for civil bureaucracies to exert power by influencing political leadership may also explain why administrators in Africa have adapted so quickly and easily to the military leaders who assumed control after the deterioration of party regimes.

Lack of legitimacy is an additional constraint on the power of civil administrators. Whatever legitimacy they do acquire is usually derived from the political system as a whole and its terms extend only to the implementation of authorized governmental programs. Such officials as permanent secretaries or ministerial executive officers do not possess a constituency and cannot appeal to the public on behalf of policies they favor. Moreover, African bureaucracies have not acquired an associational clientele. Social modernization has not yet fostered an array of politically autonomous and functionally specific interest groups. In industrial societies, such groups are often a powerful source of influence and support for government agencies and departments. One potentially powerful set of voluntary associations is the trade unions. These could, for example, strongly support government bureaus sponsoring social welfare legislation. In many African countries, however, trade unions have been denied independent political action by restrictive legislation.

A final cause of weakness is, quite simply, that civil bureaucracies are not intrinsically unified structures. Bureaucracy is inherently segmented along functional lines, therefore the generalization that intrabureaucratic politics are often a miniature replica of national politics is basically untrue. National politics involves complex patterns of conflict and cleavage among an array of ethnic, regional, class, and functionally organized groups. Intrabureaucratic politics almost invariably involves functional fragmentation, one policy area contending against another for a larger portion of scarce governmental resources. The tendency towards intersectoral conflict seems so ubiquitous and so engrained a feature of administrative behavior that it is doubtful whether the civilian sector of any African bureaucracy can, on its own, generate an authoritative, centralized source of leadership.

Possession of these basic qualities—legitimacy, a centralized mechanism of decision making, and an ability to employ force—is not only the basic prerequisite for the effective operation of any political system but is also the basic difference between military and civil bureaucracies. When representative structures have become so weakened or ineffectual that they no longer exhibit these qualities, a political vacuum is created which must be filled by an alternative source of leadership. The fact that civil bureaucracies are virtually incapable of acquiring these attributes constitutes a fundamental limitation on their capacity to provide leadership. The military can. Almost all African armies possess both a centralized and articulated system of command and the capability of using force. In addition, their access to the public limelight provides a propitious means of achieving popular support, which largely explains why it has been fairly simple for army officers to assume control of so many African countries.

The military's near monopoly of the means of compulsion, its ability to restore order by force, and its capacity to impose discipline on a chaotic society have most frequently been cited as the principal reasons for a military assumption of power. These are certainly the basic preconditions for a military coup and the means by which successful take-over is accomplished. The unique quality which military leadership offers to a politically turbulent developing country is its capacity to furnish an authoritative source of command and to mobilize a popular consensus. The military can, by ceremonial display, by appeals to national pride, and by stressing the need to purify the political arena of corruption and conflict, arouse a level of popular support which often exceeds that available to party leadership. If this support is not legitimacy, it often seems to serve the same function in creating a widespread willingness to accept the new regime.

The availability of a unified extra-bureaucratic source of authority is so important and so independent a variable that it seems to determine whether or not civil bureaucracy plays a positive role for development. Where a source of firm political guidance is present, bureaucracy ordinarily performs a range of functions critical for economic growth, social modernization, and political stability. Some of these, described by S. N. Eisenstadt, include maintenance of a unified political framework, regulation of the political struggle, provision of essential services, and political socialization.[18] Where administration has performed these roles for development, an effective, extra-

bureaucratic center of authority has almost always been operative. Where an extra-bureaucratic center of authority is absent, or weak due to a crisis of legitimacy, civil bureaucracy seems prone to varied forms of internal breakdown rather than to an expansion of its power. Three separate types of administrative malfunction may be distinguished: corruption, alienation, and sectoral fragmentation.

Corruption is the most widely discussed form of bureaucratic deterioration, perhaps because it is the most visible and dramatic. Two types of administrative corruption are particularly relevant to the prospects of viable representative government—pervasive bribe-taking and the protection of expedient bureaucratic interests. There is a heated dialogue among political scientists about the consequences of large-scale bribery for political development.[19] Some argue that it may have positive developmental benefits. It may, for example, facilitate capital accumulation and the emergence of an indigenous entrepreneurial class since civil servants who gain wealth through bribery may reinvest it in the local economy. To the extent that the consequent economic growth helps satisfy rising popular expectations and thus strengthens popular approval of elected political leaders, corruption can, albeit indirectly, contribute to the institutionalization of representative civilian regimes. Similarly, in situations where the existing entrepreneurial group is of alien origin and is thus often subjected to harassment or intimidation, corruption may introduce a note of pragmatism and rationality into the system and

[18] S. N. Eisenstadt, in *Bureaucracy and Political Development*, p. 110.

[19] For an excellent discussion of this topic and of the literature surrounding it, see J. S. Nye, "Corruption and Political Development: A Cost-Benefit Analysis," *American Political Science Review*, LXI (June 1967), 417–27.

thereby may encourage the entrepreneurs to continue their economic activities. Other scholars point to the integrative potential of corruption or to the possibility that it may help humanize a regime which, in the eyes of an illiterate and tradition-oriented population, must appear to be distant and unresponsive.

Most of these arguments seem highly dubious. Much of the money gained through corruption tends to be expended on conspicuous consumption, or placed in a numbered Swiss bank account, or converted to easily redeemable assets in a hard currency country. In the case of alien entrepreneurial groups, the insecurity engendered by official or semiofficial harassment is rarely compensated for by benefits derived from administrative dishonesty. The position of the Asian minority in East Africa is ample evidence of this. One of the most critical economic difficulties faced by the three East African states has been the flight of capital precipitated by Asians' fears of economic and social discrimination. Even if the arguments seeking to validate corruption have a ring of truth, there is serious question as to whether the general atmosphere of inequality, elitism, and political cynicism which seem to accompany extensive bureaucratic dishonesty is worth whatever benefits are derived.

The exact manner in which corruption contributes to parliamentary decline is not clear—partly because the true extent of corruption in any given country is difficult to measure and partly because corruption tends to operate as one factor among several in contributing to political decay. Ghana and Nigeria illustrate this. In Ghana, administrative and political corruption, combined with blatant mismanagement of the economy and extravagant foreign expenditures, led to a reduction in the standard of living and to unpopular conditions of economic austerity before the military seized power. The first Nigerian coup was also a product of multiple causes which included electoral violence, governmental paralysis, and ethnic fears—but corruption was an important additional ingredient. The "dash" system had become so extensive and so engrained that it hindered the implementation of needed development programs. In both cases, however, the real relationship between corruption and parliamentary collapse was probably far more subtle and indirect. During the final months of civilian rule corruption provided political mood music. It created an atmosphere of cynicism and even scorn for representative institutional structures and led to a general association of civilian rule with dishonest government. In this way, corruption helped to break down whatever residual legitimacy the old regime possessed and ensured that the military leaders would assume power in an environment of civilian compliance.

A second form of corruption is the collective protection of narrowly defined bureaucratic interests such as tenure, seniority rights, fringe benefits, and the concealment of poor performance. The tendency for bureaucrats to band together in mutual self-protection is a natural by-product of the radical elite-mass gap in many African states. Since few if any opportunities for horizontal mobility are present, the personal consequences of losing a civil service position are disastrous. One possible consequence of this situation is an extreme degree of compartmentalization and specialization with corresponding overemployment in government agencies and services. The end result is that overall performance levels decline since strong internal pressures develop against individuals who seek to excel.

Without firm political direction, administrators may easily become alienated from the human problems of their societies. There are several structural reasons for this phenomenon. Unless political goals are continuously redefined for administrative personnel, there is a tendency for the rules and procedures of bureaucratic operation to be treated as ends in themselves. The highly specialized and compartmentalized character of most bureaucratic work is such as to obscure the broad objectives of public policy. This situation, often termed "ritualism," has considerable relevance to numerous African bureaucracies. The principal reason for this is that as Africanization of the civil service occurred in many countries, recruitment tended to be unevenly distributed among the ethnic groups of the society because of differential access to higher educational opportunities. In many countries, the leadership and mass base of dominant governing parties do not come from the same ethnic group which furnishes a large proportion of the higher civil service. When this is the case, the tendency is for these political structures to regard one another with suspicion and apprehension, attitudes that are scarcely compatible with the mutual cooperation requisite for achieving national goals.

Uganda is an excellent example of an African country where the governing party and the public service have, to a considerable degree, been recruited from different ethnic sources. A large proportion of Uganda's higher civil servants are members of the interlacustrine Bantu kingdom of Buganda in the southern part of the country. This condition resulted primarily because Buganda became the most developed region in Uganda, both economically and in higher educational facilities. In addition, the center of government and administration has always been located within Buganda, a factor which encouraged educated Baganda to enter government service. Throughout the colonial period, the British authorities regularly utilized the Baganda as civil servants, even making extensive use of them as local administrators in non-Baganda areas of the country; and there was never a serious effort to broaden the colonial bureaucracy's ethnic base. Uganda's governing party, the Uganda People's Congress (UPC), while possessing nationwide organization and membership, is based largely in the northern part of the country among Nilotic tribes such as the Lango. These ethnic groups furnish the UPC not only with its most fervent supporters but with virtually all of its top leadership.

Party-bureaucracy relations in Uganda, subject to strain since independence, have been severely complicated by political events of recent years. A long-standing power struggle between northern and southern elements of the UPC was decisively won by the northern group in early 1966. One of the central issues in this power struggle was the extent to which the central government of Uganda would allow the southern Bantu kingdoms, including Buganda, to control their own affairs. The northern victory meant, in effect, that the government would pursue a policy of centralization and would reduce the degree of autonomy hitherto enjoyed by the Baganda, Ankole, and Toro tribes. In terms of development policy, the northerners who control the UPC are determined to bring about concentrated growth in the north. Rising tensions between the Baganda and the central government led to a military confrontation in the late spring of 1966. The Uganda army invaded the palace of the Baganda king, causing him to flee the country, and established a military occupation of the Baganda area. Army brutality during these events brought personal tragedy to the families of many Baganda officials of the central government. Today, many Baganda officials are deeply antagonistic towards the UPC regime and basically unsympathetic with its constitutional and economic objectives. While few go so far as to resist the government openly, there is little willingness to support or implement its policies. There can be little doubt that ethnic tensions between government and civil service are among the major causes of the generally ritualistic and inefficient character of the Uganda bureaucracy.

Bureaucratic in-fighting and fragmentation along functional lines are also highly dysfunctional to national development. The internal power relationships of government ministries and departments rarely correspond with the order of priorities that is best for national growth. Since the most common bureaucratic posture in these struggles is a defensive one (an effort to guard an established budgetary position) the typical result of intra-administrative battling is budgetary inertia and stalemate. Patterns of expenditure with no rationale other than historical precedent may be continued year after year in disregard of developmental criteria. More important, the antagonisms generated in heated budgetary struggles tend to make cooperation and communication between government organs difficult. Since numerous development programs require collaborative efforts among agencies or ministeries, entire projects are thereby jeopardized.

Effective development planning can, in large measure, overcome these dysfunctional administrative tendencies. Planning is the major sector of government bureaucracy, with the possible exception of finance, which does not have a specific functional or sectoral commitment. To the extent that planners have an "interest" to pursue within the bureaucracy, it can be identified as the rational pursuit of economic growth. For this reason, planners can perform a valuable function in helping to overcome centrifugal administrative tendencies. Their support in a budgetary disagreement carries the weight of representing the economically sound choice. Planners can use this influence to achieve a gradual but substantial shift in the overall distribution of governmental expenditures. Planners also perform yeoman service in galvanizing other administrative sectors into developmental activity. By their continual barrage of requests for suggested development projects, development estimates, and growth statistics, planners do much to help overcome the tendencies towards alienation and routinization among the sectoral ministries.

Unfortunately, few governments appreciate the extent to which planning is a fundamentally political, not economic process. The most important functions of planning—resolving bureaucratic conflict, generating development consciousness, and modifying the priority patterns of government policy—require political means (influence, authority, and bargaining) and have immensely political consequences (the success or failure of socioeconomic modernization). Despite these conspicuously political characteristics, planning is almost invariably conceptualized as an economic enterprise and little thought is given to increasing the power of planners in the decision-making process. As a result, planners are normally compelled to operate with insufficient power to accomplish their objectives.

Regardless of how much administrative power planners are given, however, their role cannot be effective unless there is an extra-bureaucratic source of power to sanction and enforce their decisions. Planners can buttress and supplement political authority by performing certain politically sensitive functions—selection of economic priorities, coordination of the bureaucracy, and mobilization of administrative resources for development—but if the polity lacks an independent source of authority, planners will become impotent despite administrative measures to enhance their position. When the absence of political authority leads to dysfunctional bureaucratic tendencies, planners will be no more immune than anyone else. They are, in the last analysis, one group of civil servants among others and as such are politically unequipped to acquire the necessary degree of legitimacy and support to function as an autonomous political force.

From the standpoint of representative government, the most disturbing tendency in African politics today is not the increasing role or importance of bureaucracies, but the decline of national parties as an institutional source of political authority. Where this has occurred, the most common leadership pattern is a personalistic cabinet autocracy, with a more or less fictional party organization performing a weak legitimization function. The characteristic symptoms of this stiuation are that national politics deteriorates into little more than a power struggle among top leaders (though the struggles may exhibit vague ethnic or ideological connotations), subordinate echelons of party organization become apathetic, and formal legislative organs of government recede in importance and visibility.

Personalistic regimes of this type seem highly susceptible both to the practice of corruption and to widespread popular equation of politics with corruption. Why this is the case is not altogether clear. The reason may be that institutional regimes are more adept at concealing or disguising pervasive administrative malpractice. Conversely, since the essence of personalistic autocracy is the absence of institutionalized responsibilities between leadership and society, the greater autonomy of leaders may facilitate corrupt behavior. Whatever the cause, there seems to be a direct and positive relationship between governmental personalism and political corruption. In this situation, the very concept of representative government becomes discredited, and the regime loses the necessary support and legitimacy to remain in power. When this occurs, the military is likely to seize control and as an instrument of national purification will usually be able to attract popular support for a period of military rule.

International Affairs

In terms of systems analysis, a State's foreign relations are viewed in the same way as its domestic politics. The State (the political system) receives inputs of both demands and supports from the international environment, i.e., from other States, and produces foreign policy outputs that affect the persistence of the system. Indeed, the systems approach makes it impossible to delineate sharply between a State's domestic politics and its foreign relations. The positions all countries take in foreign relations often have important domestic as well as international ramifications; and many of the new nations employ the supports they receive from other States—e.g., economic aid and technical assistance—to meet internal demands. Even if this were not the case, the critical relationships for systems persistence between political inputs and outputs are *aggregate* relationships, and they are not separable into independent calculation for either domestic or foreign affairs.

On the whole, the foreign policy goals of African states are to preserve their independence and protect themselves against foreign aggression, to gain respect and influence in world affairs, and to establish friendly and productive relations with other countries. Because of their limited resources and political fragility, they are particularly vulnerable to international pressures as they seek to realize these goals. In order to compensate for their individual national weaknesses, African countries have sought self-consciously to create a framework of continental unity that concurrently shields Africa from external demands and maximizes its importance in world affairs. The theoretical foundation of this unity is the doctrine of Pan-Africanism, and although African leaders differ on its application, this doctrine serves as a symbol of African unity abroad and as a reference point for inter-African affairs on the continent.

The origins of Pan-Africanism are most obvious in the Black Diaspora and subsequent subjection of the African slave in the New World, but within Africa the gradual erosion of traditional life under the effects of colonialism produced similar, if initially more localized results. Both the slave and the African under colonialism were thrust into the bottom of a stratified social order that disrupted their traditional cultural patterns while denying them full access to the modern society in which they labored. As a result both were alienated from their own culture as well as from the social and political structures in which they found themselves. This ultimately gave rise to a sentiment of shared deprivation and humiliation on the part of all black people and to a sacrosanct code of universal black brotherhood. Although the alienation of black men has never been intellectually systematized in the way Marxism defines the degradation and eventual release of the oppressed and exploited proletariat, it produced wide-spread anticolonial and anti-racial attitudes among black men on a world-wide basis. In due course, what began as a negative expression of grievance became a positive movement of cultural and political restoration that creates a sense of dignity for black men everywhere.

Until 1945, when Kwame Nkrumah and Jomo Kenyatta asserted their leadership at the Sixth Pan-African Congress in Manchester, England, Pan-Africanism was primarily a cult of New World Negroes and exiles from Africa. Although none of their activities produced immediate or concrete results, they gradually communicated the black man's growing indignation about his condition. Pan-Africanist sentiments within Africa were expressed initially in direct attempts to preserve local traditions and tribal identity through agencies such as separatist churches and irredentist activities. After World War II, during the flowering of African nationalism, the sense of "Africanness" took on continental importance as nationalist leaders sought to support and encourage each other. It is only in the past decade, however, that Pan-Africanists have had access to the resources of government to help them convert their ideal into reality.

Pan-Africanism has provided a crucial support for the entry of African states into the international system. Because of its historical evolution, it provides a counterforce to the international image of African poverty and underdevelopment. Pan-Africanism establishes another image of Africa, one which suggests that despite its poverty Africa is rich in brotherhood, human dignity, and cultural values. Moreover, this image makes the implicit claim that Africa's material poverty is due to imperialist exploitation, a past the West can expiate only by economic aid and political nonintervention. A concomitant claim is that African states should be free to choose their own allies and make their own foreign commitments. These views can be set in either a militant and radical context of hostile challenges and bitter denouncements, or in moderate and reasoned statements of purpose and principle. Nevertheless, while African states differ in their methods of realizing their national goals, all employ the Pan-Africanist themes of anticolonialism, antiracism, and African unity to support themselves against foreign pressures and to make demands on the international system.

Although it is difficult to gauge the present effectiveness of Pan-Africanism as a basis for the foreign relations of African states, its currency is validated by the continuing competition for its leadership. In 1958 Nkrumah effectively Africanized increasingly militant Pan-Africanist sentiment by organizing the All African Peoples' Conference in Accra. This meeting politicized Pan-Africanist sentiment at the same time that it sparked a rivalry for continental leadership between radicals, who expressed their anticolonialism in antiimperialistic policies, and moderates, who were less inclined to sharply negative reactions to the past. This contest for leadership offered rewards of prestige on both the international and national scene and ultimately materialized in radical and moderate regional groupings, all of which were organized in the name of African unity.

Initially, Nkrumah's more militant outlook had a special appeal for nationalist leaders who were still engaged in independence struggles. When the former French colonies and Nigeria achieved independence in 1960, however, they were inclined to a functionalist and gradualist approach to African unity, and also favored retaining economic ties with the former colonial powers as a reasonable means of promoting national economic development. Subsequently, African countries have been divided on whether Pan-Africanism should be applied as an acceptable substitute for hard-won national sovereignties, or merely as one weapon to be used in the protection of Africa's political integrity. Nevertheless, recognizing the dangers of divisiveness and the importance of inter-African cooperation, the African states joined together in the Organization of African Unity (OAU) in 1963 in Addis Ababa, and pledged to disband their initial groupings. This organizational amalgamation of the militants and the moderates has not ended African tendencies to adopt divergent foreign policies or to operate in competing blocs. It has served, however, to restrain public differences among them and to transform some apparently irreconcilable conflicts of national interest—for example, over borders—into politically negotiable issues.

Several factors account for the persistence of radical and moderate clusters of African states in matters of foreign policy. Doubtless one of these is that the doctrine of Pan-Africanism tends to underestimate the influence of diverse historical experiences, the multiplicity of tribal cultures, and residual orientations towards the former colonial powers in government policies, administrative practice, and trading patterns. Moreover, the applicability of the themes of anticolonialism and antiracialism is lessened by independence, although African states are unanimous in the view that their own independence and dignity is unfulfilled so long as Africans in Southern Rhodesia, Angola, Mozambique, and the Republic of South Africa are not free. Most of all, however, differences in the foreign policy orientations of individual African states reflect differences in the calculations of African leaders as to how they can best promote their national interests. The moderates have foreseen a net gain for their countries in continuing associations with their former colonial rulers, while the radicals, emphasizing the psychic rewards of demonstrating their independence even at the expense of favorable trade relationships, have deliberately sought new allies and commitments outside the West.

The militancy of foreign policies that rejected alignment with former colonial powers, sought relationships with Communist China, and motivated the economic boycott of South Africa has been tempered by international political and economic realities. China's invasion of India in 1962 indicated that nonalignment afforded little protection against Cold War protagonists, and the 1964 Zanzibar revolution translated the theoretical image of communism into a material threat. Moreover, the boycott of South African goods resulted in relatively serious damage to the national economies of some African states but had no effect on the Republic's *apartheid* policy.

But if militancy has had little enduring relevance for African claims on the international system, it nevertheless provides continuing support for inter-African affairs. Few issues unite African states or validate Pan-Africanist sentiment more than their reactions to the South African and Portuguese regimes and to foreign intervention in African disputes. Consequently these states support liberation movements and revolutionary tactics against Angola, Mozambique, Southern Rhodesia, and South Africa but oppose the use of white mercenaries, as in the Congo. In pursuing these ends, African leaders utilize whatever international support they can muster; some accept aid from the Eastern communist bloc, and all exert political influence through the Liberation Committee of the OAU and seek legal remedy through the Special Committee on Colonialism in the United Nations.

On the international level Pan-Africanism also structures the expression of African policies, organizes the voting strength of African states in the United Nations General Assembly, and directs their participation in UN agencies such as the Economic Commission for Africa. Nevertheless, African states are increasingly aware that fulfillment of the major Pan-Africanist ideal—that all of Africa shall be free—will be difficult. Lacking national power and observing that the international community no longer actively supports freedom movements, as it once did in the nineteen fifties and sixties, they conclude that the goal of a free Africa depends largely on their own capacities. In the first decade of their international policy experience, African leaders have operated in a context of inadequate information, uncertainty, and political innocence. Pan-Africanism has therefore provided a useful cornerstone for their international relationships while containing their disputes and disappointments and establishing a political framework for future action.

Colonial Rule in West Africa: Factor for Division or Unity

Michael Crowder

Nowadays it has become almost a platitude to say that the Channel divides West Africa. Nevertheless it is true that when the traveller crosses from Nigeria to Dahomey or from Gambia to Senegal, even at points where the same ethnic group is to be found either side of the border, he feels that he has crossed those twenty miles of water that separate England and France. It may only be an impression formed from seemingly irrelevant details: the long sticks of French bread offered him instead of the oblong blocks of wrapped bread; the change from one side of the road to the other, the uniform and equipment of the policeman, particularly the gun he carries in his holster; the cut of the young dandy's clothes; the type of cloth used by the women. Yet so marked are these differences in detail that the Senegalese driver in Lagos will have "Frenchboy" shouted after him, and conversely the Senegalese student will talk of his Nigerian fellow as "l'Anglais". These differences, of course, are not only superficial. Anyone who has attended conferences in which both French and English-speaking Africans have participated, will know the tendency for the two groups to separate out either into hostile groups as was the case at a Conference on the Press held at the University of Dakar in 1960 or at least into mutually indifferent groups. And the barrier between them is not only one of language, but of outlook on basic matters such as law, politics, and culture. The educated Yoruba from Dahomey, in his Parisian-cut suit, may have a language and social heritage in common with his cousin from Nigeria, probably wearing *agbada;* but when it comes to talking in terms of their respective present-day judicial systems and their ideas about democracy and local government, then the

From *Civilisations*, Vol. XIV, No. 3 (1964), 167–78, by permission of author and journal.

real gulf between them becomes apparent. The gulf is one of which modern African leaders are aware and which they are attempting to bridge as rapidly as possible,[1] whether it is through demonstrations of political solidarity such as the Ghana-Guinea-Mali Union, or the introduction of French or English into the curriculum of secondary schools where in the colonial era they were never taught at all. Whilst this gulf is one of the greatest barriers to African unity at present, it is necessary to defer further discussion as to its character until certain other questions have been asked, the answers to which will help give some understanding of the nature of this division:

1. To what extent did the French and British bring internal unity to the new political entities they created in West Africa?
2. To what extent did each colonial power try to encourage inter-territorial contact within its own group of colonies in West Africa?
3. To what extent did the colonial powers encourage contact between their two respective groups of colonies?

To take the first question, we may put the problem bluntly: how much has colonialism contributed to the internal unity of the now independent states of West Africa? Clearly the greatest unifying factor brought by the colonial powers to their colonies was the introduction of a lingua franca, though this was of course less important in an area like Northern Nigeria, where they already had a lingua franca in Hausa, than in areas like Ivory Coast where there was a multiplicity of tribal groups and consequently of languages. But the spread of the new lingua franca was dependent largely on the amount of education the colonial power was prepared to make available. In the case of most of the former French African colonies, though the quality of education was nearly always higher than in the British West African colonies, it was nevertheless thinly spread. In Guinea, for instance, just before independence the proportion of children of school age attending primary school was less than 10%.[2] There was a much better record in British West Africa, with the notable exception of Northern Nigeria, where English education was scant and Hausa remained dominant; Northern Nigeria is, for instance, the only political unit in West Africa which has a bilingual legislature. The French on the other hand, even in schools for Muslim chiefs where Koranic law and Arabic were taught, used French as the language of instruction.

The second major contribution to the unity of these new political units was the introduction of common legal, political and administrative institutions. Here clearly the French did much more, not only for unity at the level of the individual colony but also for unity within the bloc of French colonies, for with the exception of Senegal, where the Four Communes had special status, each territory was administered in the same way under the same law and, after 1946, under the same representative institutions. The French system of administration, though based on chiefs like the British system, used them in such a way as to destroy their traditional political authority almost completely. The chief became a mere agent of the administration, a sort of

---

[1] Only recently, on April 9th, 1964, President Senghor of Senegal delivered a marathon lecture in English to the University of Ibadan on "Democracy and Socialism".

[2] *A. O. F. 1957* published by the Haut Commissariat de la République en Afrique Occidentale Française, Dakar 1957.

civil servant, appointed on grounds of his potential efficiency rather than with regard to his traditional claim to chieftaincy. Insofar as chiefs are the repositories of tradition and therefore major continuing factors for ethnic differentiation in the state, the French may be said to have done the modern African nation a great service in thus reducing their powers. The British, however, under their system of indirect rule, did much to preserve traditional political institutions, so that the system of native administration in Nigeria differed greatly in its application not only from one region to another, but within regions. In French Africa, the only aspects of traditional law to survive after 1944 were those affecting inheritance, property, marriage and divorce. In some parts of what was British West Africa, customary penal law, involving even the death-sentence, is still practised. The French-speaking states inherited a uniform pattern of administration, with emphasis on the powers of the central government, whilst the former British states inherited patterns of administration whose original emphasis was primarily on local government institutions, sharply differentiated according to ethnic origin, and resulting in many cases in strong centrifugal tendencies. This does not of course mean that the French states have escaped problems of regionalism and tribalism, as recent events in Dahomey and Chad have shown. However traditional political institutions and ethnic differences are not nearly such great barriers to national unity in the French-speaking African states as in the former British Colonies. Indeed the French were on the whole much less conscious of the tribal origin of their colonial peoples than the British seemed to be. An African to the Frenchman was a Dahomeyan rather than a Gun, a Senegalese rather than a Wollof. This was certainly not the case with the British, who invariably asked which tribe a man came from. The army in the colonial period in Nigeria, for instance, had definite preferences for particular ethnic groups as sources of recruitment. An interesting result of this attitude is the frequency with which Nigerians filling in application forms for jobs write down their tribal origin in answer to the question as to their nationality.

The new sense of nationality was further aided by the demarcation of rigid boundaries between the political units created by the colonial powers. These frontiers, often cutting across traditional political divisions,[3] may have been of marginal significance to the Fulani herdsman, except as far as tax evasion was concerned, but for the trader carrying his goods from one colony to another, particularly if it was from a French to a British colony or vice versa, the frontier further promoted the process of national self-identification. At school, children were taught to recognize on a map the shape of the colony to which they belonged. Boundaries, then, had two important functions in the fostering of a sense of national unity: first they provided a physical barrier albeit weak, between one colony and another, second they aided in the conceptualization of the state, separating it off clearly from other colonies.

Another major factor creating conditions for national unity was of course economic development.[4] This cut across traditional divisions in the country;

[3] The concept of a boundary as a line drawn on a map was of course unknown in pre-colonial Africa.
[4] See L. P. Mair "Social change in Africa" *International Affairs*, vol. 36, No. 4, October 1960 for an interesting discussion of this topic.

and, through the building of railways and roads, opened up trade between groups that had previously had little contact with each other bringing them into vast new areas of exchange. Economic development has led to a noticeable redistribution of population through labour migration and through the growth of major cities. Whilst ethnic groups may have tried to maintain their identity in cities through tribal unions, it is there that tribal barriers are beginning to break down. For instance in Dakar it is now increasingly common for Lebou and Toucouleur, Wollof and Serer to intermarry.[5] Economic development has led to the creation of new classes, with new social goals, in which ethnic differentiation is increasingly less important as a factor. It has provided a new social structure in which educational attainments are more important than status in the tribe, and in which, with the exception perhaps of Nigeria, where preoccupation with the obtaining of chiefly titles (particularly in the Western Region) seems all-absorbing, keeping up with the Jones in the matter of cars, refrigerators and radiograms is becoming much more important than the achievement of traditional status. The emergence of a new Westernized elite was actively encouraged by the French but was to a considerable extent frustrated by the British especially before the second world war. The British hoped to direct its educated elite into service in the native administrations rather than the Central Government, at least in Nigeria, whilst the French (though somewhat halfheartedly in the interwar period) had as their goal the creation of an educated elite that could work in the central administration.

[5] Michael Crowder, *Senegal-A Study in French Assimilation Policy*. London 1962.

We come now to that thorny question of "divide and rule". To what extent did the colonial powers deliberately adopt a policy of divide and rule in their African colonies so as to avert or delay independence? This is of course very difficult to assess. One could insist that the British, through their system of indirect rule, tried to emphasize and prolong existing differences, and with their concomitant reluctance to allow, for instance in Nigeria, Africans to participate in the central administration, were doing this to maintain their position as overlords. On the other hand a French administrator like Delavignette is full of admiration for the fact that Lugard brought Northern and Southern Nigeria together, and in view of the fact that none of the great Sudanese kingdoms managed to extend its hegemony over both savanna and forest,[6] he may be justified in calling this Lugard's greatest achievement. In the political history of both Ghana and Nigeria, it seemed to nationalist leaders that Britain had an almost obsessive preoccupation with the rights of minorities immediately before independence. And in the case of Ghana there was certainly strong feeling that the British were behind the opposition moves for a regional constitution in the days immediately before independence. It is safe to say that there was among the British a tendency to emphasize potential differences rather than similarities; and their concern with safeguarding the position of minorities involved in some cases years of constitution-mongering before they would agree to set the seal on independence. This contrasts radical-

[6] A point emphasized by Professor J. F. Ade Ajayi in his paper to the seminar on the Problems of Pan Africanism held at Ibadan University entitled "The Relevance of Pre-colonial Africa", 22nd January 1964.

ly with French willingness to give overnight, as in the case of the *Loi Cadre*, a standard constitution for each of its territories from Mauretania to Gabon. Nevertheless as will shortly be seen, it is France against whom the accusation that she deliberately divided in order to rule is more justified. It is difficult to maintain an argument that Britain had, at least after 1948, any ambitions to perpetuate her rule in West Africa. Her preoccupation with the position of minorities and the resultant delaying tactics were inspired by a concern which may have been misguided, that it was her duty to provide for the differences in the country to which she was giving independence—differences which of course her policy of indirect rule was not a little responsible for consolidating.

We now come to the second major question: how far was colonial rule responsible for bringing together territories under the same administration? In the first place it must be remembered that France was in a better position than Britain for doing this in West Africa since all her possessions were geographically contiguous. But, in addition, the underlying philosophy of France in matters concerning her colonial empire militated in favour of close contact between her various colonial possessions in Africa. First her logical approach to all questions pertaining to government, whether at home or abroad, insisted that the African empire must be administered in the same way throughout. Despite the fact that men like Lyautey and Harmand advocated a colonial policy for France similar to Lugardian indirect rule, in practice France at no time in Black Africa paid much attention to traditional institutions, so that the only reality for the administrator was French law, French institutions and

French culture. Nor did France attribute to any of her territories, with the exception of Senegal, a particular character. Whereas the British administrator served most of his career in the same territory, or in the case of Northern Nigeria in the same region, the French administrator rotated between colonies as different as Guinea and Chad. The African civil servant also did tours of duty in territories other than the one from which he originated. The French African colonies were organised into two federations with a large number of common services, such as higher and secondary education, health, transport and communications. The budget of the federation was always more important than that of the constituent territories which, after the second world war, were heavily subsidized from Paris through the Federal Budget. The existence of a single monetary system, a single customs system, an interregional civil service, and federal schools like the William Ponty School in Dakar where a great number of the present-day elite of French-speaking Africa received its training, created a background for African unity. These prospects were further improved by the establishment of a Great Council in each federation, composed of representatives of the territorial assemblies, which were brought into being by the Constitution of 1946. Not surprisingly, then, African politics developed on a pan-French-African scale, with men like Leon Mba of Gabon and Modibo Keita of Sudan both working together as members of the same political party—in this case the RDA (*Rassemblement Démocratique Africain*). For further example, Gabriel d'Arboussier, a Mulatto born in Mali, has served as a politician in the following countries because of his connection with R.D.A.:

French Equatorial Africa, Ivory Coast, Niger, Federation of Mali and Senegal. Thus at all levels in French West Africa the situation was ideal for the development of pan-African or at least pan-West African politics.

It was therefore a serious reversal of policy when in 1956 as a result of increasing pressure on France to extend democratic self-government in some form or other to her Black African territories, she passed the *Loi Cadre* (or Outline Law) which gave autonomy to the individual territories, but gave no executive power to them at the federal level. Hitherto, at both the territorial and federal level, Africans had had only legislative powers. The executive still lay in the hands of the administration. This law elicited from the Senegalese Senghor[7] angry outbursts against this allegedly deliberate attempt at balkanization of Africa, and later at the 1957 Congress of the R.D.A. at Bamako from Sekou Touré of Guinea also. The French could of course reply with some justification that they were merely acting in response to the known wishes of the leader of the most powerful political party in French Black Africa, Felix Houphouet-Boigny, leader of R.D.A. He had been insistent that Ivory Coast be taken out of any federation that would involve her, as the richest territory in the federation, subsidizing the others, that is, supporting the budget of a political federal executive as she had hitherto the administrative federal executive.[8]

Behind this dispute there lay the growing rivalry between Ivory Coast and Senegal, and more specifically between Abidjan, prosperous territorial capital of Ivory Coast and Dakar, the federal capital of French West Africa: The latter was being developed not only as a political but also as an industrial centre, a destiny for which Ivory Coast could legitimately feel Abidjan was more suited in view of the great industrial development that has in fact taken place there since independence. It was thus clearly in the interest of Senegal to stand as champion of federation, and for Ivory Coast to

---

Blanchet *op. cit.* pp. 71–72 quotes M. Ouezzin Coulibaly, late Premier of Upper Volta, and Secretary of the R. D. A. at the Bamako Congress of 1957 as blaming politicians for dividing Africans against themselves. M. Blanchet himself suggests that much of the division in French African politics of that period was fostered by the fissiparous nature of French politics:-

"Mais, en mettant en relief la part que prennent dans la vie africaine ces considérations purement partisanes, elles amènent l'observateur à se demander si le système parlementaire français, si les préoccupations électorales des partis politiques et leur transposition sur le plan local, ne sont pas responsables d'une grande partie des divisions constatées dans chaque territoire. Sans qu'il y ait nécessairement, de la part des factions politiques françaises, volonté systématique de désunir les Africains, l'association de leurs pays à un régime aussi politisé que le nôtre n'aurait-elle pas contaminé les élites africaines au point de leur faire prendre aux jeux purement politiques un plaisir immodéré et—il faut bien le dire—merveilleusement accordé à leur tempérament? On peut se poser la question avec quelque remords. M. Ouezzin Coulibaly avait beau ne pas incriminer spécialement la métropole, on ne pouvait pas ne pas se sentir un peu honteux à l'entendre déclarer au congrès constitutif de la Convention auquel il apportait le salut du R.D.A. "Les Africains ne sont pas divisés, voyez-les au village. Ce sont les hommes politiques qui les divisent par le mensonge, la surenchère et la démagogie."

---

[7] Senghor's bitterness is well brought out in his intervention in the debate in the French National Assembly 1 February 1957 cited in *Présence Africaine*, No. 17–18 of 1958 "Nous ne sommes plus les grands enfants qu'on s'est plu à voir en nous, et c'est pourquoi les joujoux et sucettes ne nous intéressent pas".

[8] André Blanchet *L'Itinéraire des Partis Africains depuis Bamako*, Paris 1958, also Gil Dugué *Les Etats-Unis d'Afrique*, Dakar 1959.

oppose it. This jealousy in retrospect can also be seen as symptomatic of the growth of local nationalism within the administrative units that made up French West Africa.

However in 1957 as far as French West Africa was concerned Houphouet-Boigny was alone in his stand of loyalty to his territory as against a wider loyalty to the Federation, as the Congress of his party at Bamako so clearly showed. Leon Mba, the R.D.A. leader from Gabon, in French Equatorial Africa, took up a similar stand on the grounds that he did not want his small but rich territory to subsidise the other three members of the Equatorial federation. In the *Grand Conseil* of French West Africa too, unanimous resolutions in favor of the creation of a federal executive were passed. Did France then deliberately break up the federation? Clearly, to give self-government at the territorial level with no executive authority at the federal level diverted the attention of politicians from federal to regional politics. It is known that the High Commissioner for French West Africa, Gaston Cusin, was against the creation of a federal executive, whilst his counterpart in French Equatorial Africa was in favour of it. It was further whispered in the corridors at the Bamako Congress that the then Premier of France, M. Bourgès-Monoury, of whose cabinet Houphouet-Boigny was a member, was hostile to a federal executive.[9] It

was said in some quarters in France that the projected Franco-African Community would have a greater chance of survival if it consisted of a series of small economically unviable states rather than of the two large federations, which Senghor had always insisted were the only media through which Africa could negotiate with France on anything like terms of equality. Certainly France was right in thinking that a balkanised Africa would be more dependent on her in the post-independence era, as subsequent events have proved. In the light of her scarcely-veiled hostility to the creation of the Mali Federation two years later, the evidence seems to favour the view that France conceived the *Loi Cadre* largely as a means of prolonging her domination over her African territories and was not motivated by any concern for acknowledging existing differences within these federations. As Dr. Nkrumah has asked in a wider context "Can we seriously believe that the colonial powers meant these countries to be independent viable states?"[10] On the other hand at the meeting of the Monrovia powers' experts in Dakar in 1961 the Senegalese Foreign Minister

---

[9] Blanchet (*op. cit.*, pp. 88–89) makes the following points concerning Ivory Coast's economic reasons for rejecting federation. She considered herself the "*vache à lait*" of the Federation. With 1/7th of the population she had in 1956 (the year before the R.D.A. Bamako Congress) accounted for 38/100 of the exports and accounted for 88/100 of its revenue in dollars. It did not have its cocoa and coffee prices buttressed against the fluctuations of the world market as Senegal

and other members of the Federation did for their ground-nuts and palm-oil. Ivory Coast therefore felt itself justified in considering itself different from the other territories of the federation. The Ivory Coast did of course enjoy some of the fruits of French price stabilisation policy, but it was economically of less advantage to her than to Senegal. See *Commodity Stabilisation Funds* published by F.A.O. E/CN/13/51. C.C.P. 62/22 of 6th April 1962 for details of subsidies to crops in French-speaking Africa. There is an excellent discussion of Ivory Coast's economic position in the former A.O.F. in Elliot J. Berg's "Economic Basis of Political Choice in French West Africa" *American Political Science Review*, June 1960, pp. 391–405.

[10] Kwame Nkrumah *I Speak of Freedom*, Preface, p.xi, New York 1961.

Doudou Thiam blamed African politicians for failing to maintain the federation that France had created: "But here, we must admit, we have not yet made much progress; in some cases, we have indeed fallen behind. To take, as but one example, the countries of the former French West Africa, we are surprised to note how, since our accession to autonomy, and then to independence, our internal legislations have become diversified, how indeed our economic systems have sometimes taken opposite directions. Before, we had the same economic legislation, the same labour legislation, the same laws concerning rent, housing and commercial rents, the same fiscal legislation, the same customs legislation and the same judicial organization, the same system of public freedoms. Today we consider all that with nostalgic feelings somewhat tempered by our accession to independence."[11]

President Azikiwe had made similar complaint with respect to the lack of cooperation between the former colonies of British West Africa and their dismantling of such common services as Britain did set up. Here, of course, Dr. Nkrumah must bear much responsibility. Ghana, as the first of the British West African colonies to gain independence, could have seized the initiative in retaining these common services. Instead Nkrumah quite deliberately withdrew Ghana from them on the grounds that regional groupings would prove a stumbling block to the achievement of continental unity. Even if Britain abandoned any attempts at common administration once her colonies ceased to be mere coastal footholds, she did at least maintain a common currency service and encouraged co-

operation through a number of interterritorial institutions such as research organizations, or the West African Airways Corporation. Fourah Bay and Achimota College served as meeting grounds for the young members of the elite of West Africa. But it is difficult to see how any serious attempt at a Pakistan-type administration between even two of the four states, such as Gambia and Sierra Leone, as was frequently advocated, could have been effective in the long run. Even if the problems of lack of continuity had been overcome, there was still the imbalance of size, with the giant Nigeria at one extreme and the geographically and economically absurd Gambia at the other. Even so, had Britain given the African politicians in the post-war period the opportunity of frequent meetings such as the French Africans had, not only in the *Grand Conseil* but also in the corridors of the metropolitan assemblies in Paris, perhaps there would have been a possibility of the development of a pan-British West African party. However there are those who believe African unity as represented by the R.D.A. and other pan-French African parties was an artificial unity, Paris-bred. Thus André Blanchet has described the R.D.A. as a gift of Paris to Africa.

We come now to the third question: how far did France and Britain try to encourage cooperation between their respective sets of colonies? The answer is they made almost no effort at all. There were almost no institutions for common consultation over colonial problems whether these were political, cultural or economic—with the exception of the Anglo-French Standing Consultative Commission for Togo which was forced on both powers by the United Nations. As R. J. Harrison Church complained in 1957 "many

---

[11]Only the rather poor English translation of this speech was available to me.

problems result from the quite incredible ignorance of what is going on across the artificial boundaries. Despite the work of the Trusteeship Council, of Anglo-French cooperation, of the Scientific Council for Africa, and many other bodies, much research is pursued in ignorance of similar work across the boundary."[12]

Economically there was a marginal amount of interterritorial trade, and most of what did take place was of a pre-colonial pattern such as the export of cattle from Niger to Nigeria or of kola-nuts from Nigeria to Niger. One of the obvious exceptions to this was labour migration, particularly of Mossi to the mines and cocoa farms of Southern Ghana. A glance at the map will show how communications were developed by each power as though the other's territories did not exist. Roads stop short of the international boundaries; railways run parallel to each other. The most fantastic examples are the Gambia river, one of the finest waterways in Africa but denied its natural hinterland by the French, and the so-called "Operation Hirondelle" in Niger and Dahomey. In order to prevent groundnuts and other produce in Niger from being exported through Nigeria, Niger's natural outlet to the sea, the French built a superb road up through Dahomey, bridged the Niger at Gaya-Malanville, to join up with a road that ran across Niger parallel to the Nigerian border. All this to export groundnuts through the port of Cotonou rather than down the Kano railhead. The excuse for this at the time of the plan's conception was the frequency of hold-ups at the Kano railhead, but by the time the scheme got into operation, the Nigerian railways were in fact capable of dealing with Niger's produce.

In the field of education, the situation was the same. The schools of Nigeria and Ghana, with very rare exceptions, never included French in their curricula.[13] The French lycées did teach English, but not with a view to increasing possibilities of contact with English-speaking neighbours, only because the schools were based directly on the French system of education, and for the *baccalauréat* the student had to take a second language to French, and this could be English or German or Spanish. Indeed such was the isolation between the two groups, that one can say without much exaggeration that contact between them was at the level of the Fulani herdsman and the Hausa trader. The French tried to bring their colonies into the orbit of a greater France in which naturally the British colonies could play no part. As Thomas Hodgkin wrote in 1954: "In British West Africa everyone who is politically conscious is a nationalist of some kind. In French West Africa there are Catholics and anti-clericals, Communists and Gaullists, Socialists, Syndicalists and Existentialists."[14] Even Sekou Touré, for all his political revolt against France, is leader of a country that is still culturally very much dependent on her. And it is this heavy French orientation, with Paris still a glittering Metropole even after independence, that has led to considerable suspicion of the French-speaking

---

[13]It was however easier for a Yoruba child from Dahomey, for instance, to transfer to a primary school in the Yoruba West of Nigeria, where the first years of education were conducted in the vernacular, than vice versa, since all primary education in French territories was in French; and no concession was made either to teaching of or in the vernacular.

[14]Thomas Hodgkin *West Africa*, pp. 5–6, January 9, 1954.

---

[12]R. J. Harrison Church *West Africa*, London 1957.

African on the part of his English-speaking brother.

This orientation is given further emphasis by the economic dependence of the former French African colonies on France. Whilst it is true that the former British colonies were heavily oriented in their trade patterns towards Britain and the Commonwealth, Britain never adopted a policy of protection of her West African colonial market against other European countries, such as France did. This means that consumer habits in post-independence French-speaking Africa are still heavily biased towards French goods, and the membership of France in the E.E.C. has as yet not made much inroad into the preponderance of French goods in the shops of Dakar and Abidjan. Such dependence is further emphasized by the heavy reliance on French aid by nearly all the French-speaking states, including Mali which has attempted in the international field to follow as far as possible a policy of positive neutralism, but is still an associate member of the E.E.C. and has remained in the franc zone. Indeed it is almost impossible to assess French aid to her former African colonies as a report by a French Senatorial Commission, charged with this task, has emphasized. Aid is given in many different forms, one of which is through individual French Ministries![15]

* * *

We come finally to the most difficult question of all: how deep are the differences that were engendered by

colonial rule and how easily will they be overcome? There is a tendency on the part of the pessimistic outsider to exaggerate these differences and a reverse tendency on the part of the pan-Africanist to try and dismiss them on the grounds that "we are all Africans after all". Most people will agree that the colonial experience, though it covered such a short period in Africa's history, was one in which the changes and innovations brought about by its subjection to European colonial rule have been disproportionate in their importance to the length of time in which they took place. And the cynic will point to the difference in the impact of the French and British experience as one of the basic causes of the break-up of the Ghana-Guinea-Mali union; though close to hand is the failure of the Mali Federation, which from many points of view—the shared colonial experience of the two component states, their contiguity, their common adherence to Islam—should have succeeded. And the only example in West Africa today of two political units created by the two different colonial powers coming together in political union is that of the Southern Cameroons and the Cameroun Republic, respectively English and French-speaking, to form the Cameroun Federation. In this experiment we may be able to see some of the sort of difficulties that will be faced in any future attempts to bring English and French-speaking Africa together.[16]

---

[15]Senate paper no. 53, 1re Session Ordinaire de 1961–1962 "Rapport Général etc. sur le projet de loi des finances pour 1962" . . . by Senator Marcel Pellenc, Tome III, Examen des Crédits et des Dispositions Spéciales, Annexe No 8, *Coopération* (Rapporteur-spécial: M. André Armengaud).

[16]It has been objected that the Cameroun experiment in bringing together French and English-speaking Africa will not be very instructive for other such experiments since the common German experience of the two participating members of the Federation makes this a "special case". But this argument can be reduced to absurdity for we can argue that the proposed union of Gambia and Senegal will be a special case, since they have identical

But before attempting to diagnose these, I would like to point to two major problems that are general rather than particular ones. The first is the language barrier, which can of course be broken down if there are sufficient funds and teachers available. But behind any language, it must be remembered, lies a whole philosophy of life, a system of thinking, particular attitudes to such basic questions as liberty, democracy, justice, and the place and nature of culture, understanding of which comes only after really intensive study of the language. The second problem is the continued dependence of the French-speaking territories on France, not only economically but also culturally. This has led to a certain clannishness among the French African states in the contemporary African scene. The Brazzaville group is an obvious example of this, having apart from its explicit economic and political aims, something of the atmosphere of an old boy's club about it.

Unfortunately it is too early yet to draw satisfactory conclusions about the Cameroun experiment. In two years' time it may give us a better idea of the real problems involved in joining former French-speaking and English-speaking states. Claude Welch, Junior,[17] in a recent series of articles in *West Africa*, seems to me to have been more optimistic about the federal experiment than the reports of other recent visitors, both European and Camerounian, would justify. He considers that "Because of the flexible policy of the federal and state governments, most problems of reunification have been solved satisfactorily". In this he can point, as he does, to the successful changeover of the side of the road on which people drive in the West Cameroun, and further examples such as the introduction of uniform currency, and changeover of weights and measures. But it still remains a fact that there are customs posts and checkpoints between the West and East; that the contact over the state border is infrequent; that the federal radio has only one hour of English a day; that economically the West Cameroun has been hard hit by the changeover to the franc zone, particularly as far the sale of her banana crop is concerned. There are still the immense problems of legal and administrative harmonisation to be overcome.[18] But then these were to be expected.

---

[18]Victor T. Le Vine in his chapter on "Cameroun" in Gwendolen Carter (ed.) *Five African States-Responses to Diversity*, New York 1963, is much less optimistic than Welch about the federal experiment and writes: "There is even some question whether in some respects the Camerouns had not moved farther apart rather than closer together". Le Vine cites the lack of institutional unity as provided by the constitution, the lack of political unity in the federation, where "political activity remains primarily state activity", and the lack of progress towards economic integration though this is one field in which the prospects for integration seemed initially favourable. He also refers to the quite understandable reluctance of the West Cameroun to change over its educational system. He concludes: "Thus national unity is still rather far away. The complexity and magnitude of the problems facing the states considered both individually and together must temper the most qualified optimism about the Camerounian future". For an interesting discussion of the ideology of unification see Mr Le Vine's recent paper "The Politics of Partition in Africa: The Cameroons and the Myth of Unification" *Journal of International Affairs*. XVIII, 2, 1964, pp. 198–210.

---

ethnic composition; or should Niger and Northern Nigeria wish to federate they have not only many ethnic groups in common, but both formed part of the Fulani Empire, etc. . .

[17]Claude Welch Jr., "Cameroon since Reunification" *West Africa*, October 19, 26, November 2, 9, 1963.

What I would like to suggest in conclusion is that a superficial impression indicates that most of the difficulties that the Cameroun federation is experiencing today (many of which will be the experience of Gambia if it unites with Senegal) are the legacy of colonial rule, rather than what one might call African differences.[19]

---

[19] A striking illustration of this is the rivalry that will ensue between the river ports of Kaolack and Ziguinchor in Senegal and Bathurst in the Gambia, if the two countries federate. Had Senegambia been created in the first place it is likely that Bathurst would have become the most important city rather than Dakar. As it is, Bathurst, at the head of the Gambia river, but cut off from its natural hitherland, is only a small port of 20,000 population. The ports of Kaolack and Ziguinchor have been developed in order to handle the trade which but for the colonial boundary would have flowed down the Gambia river to Bathurst. If the two countries federate and adjust their economies to the same scale

In this sense colonial rule has been a very definite factor for division in Africa. But on the other hand I do not think we should underestimate the factor for unity that colonial rule has been at the national level, in this case overcoming many of these African differences. It could also have been a factor for unity in the case of former French West and Equatorial Africa at the inter-territorial level, if France had not chosen to rend asunder federations she had built up in order to perpetuate if not her rule, at least her political influence and cultural and economic domination in Africa.

(many goods on sale in Bathurst cost twice as much in Dakar at present!) then the natural tendency will be for trade to be directed towards the Gambia river again to the profit of Bathurst and to the detriment of Kaolack and to a lesser extent Ziguinchor, both important political centres.

Pan-Africanism

Rupert Emerson

The African scramble for independence has led to two major political trends which have at least the superficial look of being contradictory but which may still turn out to be complementary. One is the consolidation of states, and, it may be, of nations, within the frontiers traced on the map of Africa with an imperial flourish by the colonial powers. The other is the unceasing agitation and conferring to secure some sort of African unity which would bring together within a common framework either all the African peoples or such more limited groupings of them

as are now prepared to join forces for general or particular purposes. The unanswered, and still unanswerable, question is whether the states which have been emerging in such quantities, with more still to come—29 African Members of the UN at the end of 1961 as against five in 1955—will serve as the building blocks for a greater African union or whether they will jealously guard the separate identity which they have now achieved.

The realist is likely to be tempted to dismiss Pan-Africanism as an idle and romantic dream, unable to make a

From *International Organization,* Vol. XVI, No. 2 (Spring 1962), 275–90, by permission of author and journal.

significant breach in the solid walls of state sovereignty which Africans are in process of erecting. The turn of events may well prove him to be correct, but in the interim the devotion to Pan-Africanism is both widespread and charged with emotion. Nkrumah is far from being alone in his repeated insistence that the independence of particular African states takes on its full meaning only if all of Africa is free and if African unity is achieved. This sense of a mutuality of interest in freedom among all African peoples and countries found virtually no counterpart in the corresponding anticolonial drive of the Asian peoples, each of which pursued and enjoyed its independence without significant regard for the others. In the eyes of the believers the case for African unity rests not only on such utilitarian grounds as the need to collaborate and to establish a common front against Africa's enemies but also on the *mystique* of the conviction that Africans are born to share a common destiny. To the special circumstances of Africa which press toward unity the contention is often added that this is an era of global interdependence in which particularist nationalisms have become anachronistic.

I. SELF-DETERMINATION AND TERRITORIAL INTEGRITY

The present consolidation of African states within the former colonial frontiers runs counter to much of what had been both predicted and desired during the colonial era. It was widely assumed that as soon as Africans came to freedom they would sweep aside the arbitrary boundaries imposed by the imperialists which cut across tribes and overrode the dictates of geography and economics. The continent had been partitioned to meet colonial convenience, but it would now be reshaped to realize its "natural" contours and return to its African essence. The accusation that the colonial powers had arbitrarily divided Africa among themselves rested on indisputable historical evidence; the further accusation, however, that they had broken up pre-existing African unity could be established only by a reconstruction of history. The balkanization of Africa is an old-established matter to which European colonialism only added new dimensions. Furthermore, the fact was normally neglected that while the job might on a number of counts have been much better done, the creation of states of a sensible size to live in the modern world could only be accomplished by a lumping together of tribal peoples who had no heritage of common identity.

The characteristic problem confronting anyone who seeks to establish the political shape of Africa south of the Sahara is that there are no "natural" communities or political entities between the smallest and the most typical expression of African community, the tribe, at one extreme, and the whole of the African continent at the other. A number of African kingdoms and empires which reached beyond a single tribe existed in the past, but they appear to have left only a slight imprint, if any, as far as a continuing sense of community is concerned, although the names of Ghana, Mali, and the like still command respect. Such regional groupings as West or East or Central Africa are not infrequently spoken of, but they generally lack clear definition, could be constituted in a number of different guises, and have no identifiable African past. This is not to deny that unions built on such regional foundations may come into being, but, only that, if they do, they will either be new creations or adaptations of cooperative arrangements established under colonial auspices.

The political vehicle to which the Africans south of the Sahara have everywhere entrusted their new found independence is the colonial state, despite the fact that none of these states had any existence prior to their invention by the colonial regimes responsible for them. (This includes Liberia if the Americo-Liberians are substituted for the colonial regime.) In all or most of the countries a great number of the people still have no effective awareness of their "national" stature, as defined by the colonial boundaries, but the political life of the leaders and their followers in the nationalistic movements was led at the level of the colonial territory. As soon as they got down to serious business parties and movements were organized on the basis of the several territories, and the immediate enemy to be overcome was the colonial government, even though at a remote distance behind it there stood the imperial power. During the search for independence each territory had its own party or parties, each concentrating on the political situation of that particular territory and paying relatively little attention to the activities of its neighbors. The one notable exception was in the two big French federations of West and Equatorial Africa, where parties—most notably the *Rassemblement Démocratique Africain* (RDA)—overflowed the lesser territorial boundaries and operated at a federal level in a number of the countries which have since come separately to sovereign independence. In the postwar years when the RDA flourished it was no doubt a relevant item not only that the federations were in existence but also that much of the political life of the territories centered in Paris and in the National Assembly where they were all represented, thus bringing the African leaders into intimate contact with each other. It seems reasonable to assume that the federal and Parisian ties which were thus built up among the leaders were largely responsible for the fact that since independence the former French colonies have made move after move to regain at least some of the unity which was sacrificed as the individual territories began to exercise the autonomy granted them under the *loi cadre* of 1956. In Lockean terms it might be said that the territorial units with which the leaders had mixed their political labor were the ones which retained political existence as colonialism came to an end; and in the French case this concerned both the twelve separate territories and the two federations they had constituted.

In most instances the transition from colonial status to independence was made in amicable agreement with the controlling power, which meant that the new African regimes could take over intact the going concerns, as they have been called, of the colonial administrations. Except for the lack of a foreign office and perhaps of a military establishment, the instrumentalities of government were already in operation and needed only to be nudged over to a new posture. The leading African political figures were often already substantially in charge of the affairs of their countries in the last phase of colonialism, and the africanization of the government services was in varying degrees under way. If new constitutions were generally written, they tended to build on the inherited institutions. The more painful transition in the case of

Guinea, where France resented the assertion of independence, and the speedy disintegration of the Congo, where no preparation had been made for independence, only underlined the good fortune of the rest.

The universal African acceptance of the practice of concentrating on the going concerns of the inherited colonial territories had worked to undermine the earlier conviction that major realignments of the political boundaries would be necessary. This earlier version found expression in one of the resolutions of the first All-African People's Conference which met in Accra in December 1958. Speaking up for the unity of Africa and a Commonwealth of Free African States, this resolution

denounces artificial frontiers drawn by imperialist powers to divide the peoples of Africa, particularly those which cut across ethnic groups and divide people of the same stock; calls for the abolition or adjustment of such frontiers at an early date; calls upon the independent states of Africa to support a permanent solution to this problem founded upon the wishes of the people.

This doctrine appears to find continued expression in some of the statements and policies of President Nkrumah, in part no doubt as justification for his claim that because of tribal affiliation Togo and parts of the Ivory Coast should be joined to Ghana. Their "liberation" would be a part of the process of doing away with colonialism's evils—although Sylvanus Olympio of Togo and Félix Houphouet-Boigny of the Ivory Coast fail to see it in that light.

A significant reaffirmation of Nkrumah's position appeared in the communiqué which he and President Abdulla Osman of Somalia issued at the conclusion of the latter's visit to Ghana in October 1961. It will be remembered that Somalia has extensive territorial claims against Ethiopia, Kenya, and French Somaliland, based on the Somalis on the wrong side of the frontiers. The communiqué sees a union of African states as the step which would automatically make obsolete the frontier problems inherited from the colonial regimes, but also recognizes the imperative need to call upon the principle of self-determination as a means of removing the artificial colonial frontiers which were drawn without respect for ethnic, cultural, or economic links.[1]

This is not a doctrine which has found favor as the years have gone by. Indeed, as early as April 1958, the Conference of Independent African States, also meeting at Accra, in demanding respect for the independence, sovereignty, and territorial integrity of African states, took a conservative

---

[1] *The Party* (Accra), October 1961 (No. 14), p. 13. When it was reported that Sylvanus Olympio, then Prime Minister of Togoland, was opposed to the integration of his country with Ghana, the Ghanaian Ministry of Foreign Affairs issued the following statement: "The arbitrary carving out of the African Continent by the imperialist powers during the 'scramble for Africa' in the 19th century resulted in an unnatural and unsatisfactory situation. People of the same ethnic group, indeed sometimes members of the same family, came to be ruled by different powers and were compelled to regard their brothers across the border as foreigners. The Ewes along the Ghana/Togoland border are not the only such victims. The Sanwi, Aowin and Nzema peoples on the Western borders of Ghana are in a similar plight.

"The Prime Minister's suggestion is therefore no bid for expansionism. It represents the natural urge of these peoples to achieve the basic ethnic regrouping of the communities which had been violated by the plans of the imperialist powers for domination and exploitation." *Ghana Today* (London), November 25, 1959.

position very difficult to reconcile with the revolutionary implications of self-determination. Be it noted that this was a conference of *states*, and not of *peoples*, the latter term meaning parties, movements, and other nongovernmental organizations. I have been able to find in the records of the several succeeding African conferences of either states or peoples no repetition of the plea that self-determination should be relied upon to restore Africa to its proper dimensions. The more left-inclined gathering of African states at Casablanca in January 1961 seems to have made no pronouncement on these subjects, except, of course, its call for African unity, but the larger meeting of twenty African states at Monrovia in May 1961 came out firmly for the absolute equality of states, noninterference in internal affairs, respect for sovereignty, and unqualified condemnation of outside subversive action by neighboring states. In this setting self-determination is acceptable only for territories as a whole and not for ethnic pieces of them.

Responsible political leaders everywhere are wary of the principle of self-determination, and African political leaders have good reason to be warier than most. For the reasons which have been suggested above, the African state system as a whole and in its parts is fragile. It has neither the sanction of old-established political entities nor well-knit communities to lend stability to its states. The effective units of community are the tribes, but to open the door to African tribal self-determination would be to move toward a balkanization which would verge on anarchy, if it did not wholly achieve it. Furthermore, it is generally true that the present leaders seek a modernization of their societies in which the tribal past would play at best only a

ceremonial role. To allow the tribes to take over as the dominant elements in the shaping of Africa would be to expose to ruin much of what these leaders have accomplished and seek to accomplish in the immediate future. The tragic affairs of the Congo, where tribalism partially reasserted itself when the central authority collapsed, stand as a warning as to what may happen.

Given the circumstances of Africa it is eminently comprehensible that there should be a determination on the part of many African statesmen to stand by the existing political structure of the continent even though any one can with ease poke his fingers through the loopholes with which it is riddled. The consolidation and utilization of what presently exists seems a far sounder procedure than an effort to reconstruct the political map of Africa which would run the immediate risk of creating a far worse situation than the one which now exists.

Considerations of this sort led President Olympio to look with a skeptical eye on the pretensions of Pan-Africanism and to plead the cause of the present African countries:

In their struggle against the colonial powers the new African states, arbitrary and unrealistic as their original boundaries may have been, managed at last to mobilize the will of their citizens toward the attainment of national independence. Achieved at great sacrifice, such a reward is not to be cast away lightly; nor should the national will, once unified, be diluted by the formation of nebulous political units.[2]

It is a fair summary of his contention to say that he warned against pursuing a shadowy vision of African unity and

[2] Sylvanus E. Olympio, "African Problems and the Cold War," *Foreign Affairs*, October 1961 (Vol. 40, No. 1), p. 51.

counseled instead the use of the tools at hand to tackle "the central task to which we are committed—the earliest possible economic and ˌsocial betterment of our people." For this purpose, he held, the principle of national sovereignty should be retained, combined with an active policy of cooperation with other African states.

In similar vein the Abbé Fulbert Youlou, President of the Congo (Brazzaville), is cited as having remarked concerning Pan-Africanism that "those who talk about it should start by sweeping up in front of their own hut, before thinking of sweeping up before that of their neighbor."[3]

II. THE SOURCES OF
PAN-AFRICANISM

The Pan-Africanism which is being pursued simultaneously with the internal consolidation of the new states has many faces and can take on many guises. The simplest and, all in all, perhaps the most satisfactory version of it is the sense that all Africans have a spiritual affinity with each other and that, having suffered together in the past, they must march together into a new and brighter future. In its fullest realization this would involve the creation of "an African leviathan in the form of a political organisation or association of states," as Nnamdi Azikiwe, Governor-General of Nigeria and one of the pioneer leaders of African nationalism, recently put it in a speech in which he expressed his conviction that such a leviathan was bound to arise.[4] At lesser levels it

might involve an almost infinite variety of regional groupings and collaborative arrangements, all partial embodiments of the continent-embracing unity which is the dream of the true Pan-Africanist.[5]

The sources from which Pan-Africanism derives are in part obscure and debatable and in part reasonably clearly written on the record.

How much of the claimed sense of common identity is to be attributed to the feeling that all Africans, despite the unmistakable physical differences among them, are members of the same race? Here, as in most other social-political manifestations of the idea of race, what is important is not the unascertainable biological fact of common physical heritage but the belief that there is such a heritage, at least in the sense of distinguishing Africans from the other peoples of the world.

One complication raised by the racial approach is the question as to whether North Africa, Arab and Berber in composition as against the *Afrique noire* south of the Sahara, forms a part of a single continental Pan-Africa. If blackness of skin be taken as the principal outward criterion of Africanness, the North African peoples evidently belong in a different category, but the general assumption and practice have been to include North Africa in in Pan-African family, despite the fact that it has attachments to the Arab world of the Middle East not shared by sub-Saharan Africans as well as attachments to the broader world of Islam which are shared by only some of the peoples to the south. My own crystal ball suggests that while for some purposes the North African countries

---

[3] Cited by E. Milcent, "Forces et idées-forces en Afrique Occidentale," *Afrique Documents*, Mai 1960 (No. 51), p. 63.

[4] Nnamdi Azikiwe, "The Future of Pan-Africanism," a speech made in London on August 12, 1961, published by the Nigerian High Commission, London.

[5] The article by Erasmus H. Kloman, Jr., which appears elsewhere in this issue, gives an account of many of the more recent African groupings.

will be drawn into continental African groupings, they will continue to have Arabic, Mediterranean, and Muslim affiliations which will keep them from anything approaching total absorption into a conceivable Pan-African union.

Even though Africans generally, having been the principal victims of a prior racialism, repudiate a new racialism asserting itself in a Pan-African guise, it seems very difficult to escape racial conceptions as one of the basic elements in Pan-Africanism. The concept of *Négritude*, expounded by Aimé Césaire, Léopold Senghor, and others, bases itself explicitly on the people of "Negro race" (incidentally leading into the further demographic question as to the relation of African-descended people through the world to a Pan-African or Pan-Negro movement). Nkrumah's conception of the African Personality is less obviously tied to racial moorings but it cannot evade the racialist implications which are inherent in any such idea. Senghor overtly brings these implications to the fore in his assertion that

Négritude is the whole complex of civilised values—cultural, economic, social, and political—which characterize the black peoples, or, more precisely the Negro-African world. . . . the sense of communion, the gift of myth-making, the gift of rhythm, such are the essential elements of Négritude, which you will find indelibly stamped on all the works and activities of the black man.[6]

It is both fruitless and unwise to seek to give to either *Négritude* or African Personality a precise and specific content. Both, like Americanism and other similar concepts, stand as proud symbols of the accomplishments and

virtues of a people, to be phrased in large and generous terms. Any effort to define them more closely runs the risk of starting arguments which divide those whom it is sought to unite rather than to bring them together. One key feature of these concepts and of the general trend of African thinking in recent years is that black has become a color to admire and be proud of. The earlier assumption, convenient for the slave owner and white ruler, had been that white represented the superior beings endowed with a high and advanced civilization whereas black stood for the properly servile inferiors who had not progressed beyond the primitive stages of mankind. African nationalism has brought about a transvaluation of values which establishes the African as a person of consequence and the heir of a history and culture, still in process of rediscovery, which have made their contribution to the world. To be black is itself a distinctive bond of unity.

Running through this range of thought and emotion is the conviction that the Africans as a people have been oppressed, exploited, and degraded to a greater extent than any other great mass of mankind in history. No elaborate exposition of the centuries of the slave trade, slavery, and colonialism is needed to point the moral of the African belief that they have been collectively mistreated and that their common identity has been forged in the flames of their common suffering. If all hands have been against them in the past, it is all the more neccessary for them now to join forces to ensure that their weakness does not again invite disaster.

In the creation of the conception that the continent forms a single Pan-African whole a large role has been played by the Negroes overseas and

---

[6] Léopold Sédar Senghor, *West Africa*, November 4, 1961, p. 1211.

particularly those in the West Indies and the United States. Having lost the memory of the particular tribes and regions from which they came and being aware of the anonymous unity which slavery had thrust upon them, it was natural that they should look across the Atlantic and see Africa and their fellow Negro brethren as a whole. Many Negro religious figures, teachers, professional men, and others contributed to the stream which flowed toward Pan-Africanism, but four names can be singled out as peculiarly significant: E. W. Blyden, who was the distiguished nineteenth century precursor of later developments; W. E. B. Du Bois, who fathered a series of Pan-African Congresses; Marcus Garvey, who sought to establish a "universal confraternity" and a "central nation" for the Negro race; and George Padmore, who served as a crystallizing center for Pan-Africanism in London, influencing many Africans, including Kwame Nkrumah.

The considerable number of African leaders who have been educated or have lived abroad must have experienced a similar inclination toward a Pan-African outlook as they were thrown into contact with Africans from many countries and were forced to look at the affairs of their continent through other eyes and from afar.

It seems eminently probable that not only Africa's elements of unity but, perversely, its diversity and heterogeneity as well have had an influence in promoting Pan-Africanism. Precisely the instability of African states within their arbitrary frontiers and the lack of any "natural" stopping points between the tribe and continental Africa in the large lend an attraction to the broader view which it might not otherwise have—and which it may cease to have if and when African states achieve the internal consolidation which they are now seeking. The depth and breadth of an exclusive attachment to the new states is inevitably open to question, and it is reasonable to think that some of the ills from which Africa suffers or which potentially threaten it can be better handled on a collective basis than by some forty separate political entities. Thus Gabriel d'Arboussier, Senegalese Minister of Justice, predicting a Union of West African States by 1965, sees as the decisive weapon in the present evolution of Africa the unity which it has not yet achieved but which is imposed on it by its multiple diversities and internal divisions whether they be tribal, religious, ethnic, or territorial.[7]

In particular, the threat of contingent anarchy contained in the fact that Africa's tribal structure only accidentally coincides with state frontiers might be greatly eased if larger unions of states could be brought into being, thus making possible arrangements by which tribes that straddle boundaries within the union could reestablish some measure of unity. It is, of course, true that in many parts of Africa boundaries are sufficiently porous to enable people to move easily back and forth across them in the interior, but the more states assert their sovereignty the more the boundaries will seal them off from each other, making formal agreements necessary if tribal and other customary links are to be maintained. Thus an East African union, for example, of the kind which has been much discussed recently, could lay the groundwork for a solution or at least an amelioration of the three-way political

7 Gabriel d'Arboussier, "La coopération des Etats africains et les problèmes internationaux," *Afrique Documents*, Mars-Avril 1961 (No. 56), p. 68.

partition which has been imposed on the Somalis and the Masai and perhaps of the problem of the Kenya coastal strip as well.

III. THE VARIETIES OF PAN-AFRICANISM

To identify the sources of Pan-Africanism is a far easier task than to predict what practical results it is likely to achieve.

The first goal which the Pan-Africanists have always set for themselves—the liberation of all of Africa from alien rule—should be reached shortly with the one great exception of South Africa where the end of white domination in the peculiarly objectionable form of *apartheid* is still not in sight. The two other major areas of difficulty are the Rhodesias with their strong white minorities and the Portuguese territories of Angola and Mozambique where no effective move has been made to prepare the Africans to manage their own affairs. Failure to achieve speedy independence and self-government for the African majorities in the great southern reaches of the continent would be a blow to African aspirations, but it is arguable that nothing could better promote the practical advance of Pan-Africanism than its confrontation by a continued unyielding colonialism, perhaps involving new Sharpevilles in the form of violent suppression of nationalist agitation. The result of such a situation might well be that Africa's independent states would band more closely together to furnish aid to their oppressed brethren than they would otherwise be ready to do.

The first step is to win independence; the second is to knit together the newly freed peoples. On the face of it, there is a ring of gross improbability about the dream that within the foreseeable future a great leviathan might be created which would embrace all the African states within a single political structure. Although some sort of collaborative functional arrangements may conceivably be worked out on an Africa-wide basis, it is likely that any close political union will be limited to regions such as West or East Africa, and that even at the regional level functional collaboration, as, for example, in relation to transport and communications, health and sanitary provisions, and certain economic matters, is much more probable than a merging of sovereignties. Furthermore, any strong regional movement or organization would be likely to impair the possibility of realizing a full Pan-Africanism. Thus, the meeting of the Pan-African Freedom Movement of East and Central Africa (PAFMECA) in Addis Ababa in February 1962, which seems to have broadened and strengthened the ties among East and Central African countries and to have added some South African connections as well, was viewed with dismay by Ghanaian observers who saw it as threat to all-African solutions.

One important federation which seems sure to break up is the Federation of Rhodesia and Nyasaland which has been bitterly fought by the African communities, particularly in Northern Rhodesia and Nyasaland, since its origin in 1953. As African majorities take over in these countries the hostility to the links which bind them to Southern Rhodesia will presumably make the maintenance of the existing federal structure impossible although a new scheme of African-inspired organization may emerge, perhaps within the broader framework offered by PAFMECA. The Commission for Technical Co-operation in Africa South of the Sahara (CCTA) is also running into difficulty because of the continued membership of the colonial powers, and most notably of the Portuguese.

To the regionalism of geography may be added two other categories of regionalism: one of language and the other of ideology.

A regionalism of language finds its principal expression in the efforts of the former French dependencies to regain some of the advantages which came to them as members of the West and Equatorial African federations and to build even more extensive joint enterprises within the ranks of the African peoples *d'expression française*. The most elaborate of these is the so-called Brazzaville group, or, more formally, the Union of African and Malagasy States, which has a membership of a round dozen of the former French colonies and trusteeships, only Guinea, Mali, and Togo having held aloof from it. After several earlier meetings, at one of which the subsidiary Organization for Economic Cooperation was created, the conference at Tananarive in September 1961 further elaborated the structure of the union, adopting an over-all charter, establishing a Post and Telecommunications Union, and drawing up a defense pact which requires ratification by the parliaments of the members. Two lesser groupings embrace four of the states formerly in French West Africa and the four which made up Equatorial Africa.[8]

The continued existence of these organizations within the Union is specifically provided for, as is the participation of the Union in the arrangements deriving from the Monrovia conference.

No corresponding links have been formed among the former British African territories, although those which have come to independence have remained within the Commonwealth—and remained all the more happily with the departure of South Africa from it. It is, of course, also true that in maintaining the Federation of Nigeria the British held within a single political unit approximately as many people as were contained in the whole of French Africa south of the Sahara.

At least until very recently English-speaking Africans and Negroes tended to monopolize both the term "Pan-Africanism" and the movements and congresses associated with it.[9] In part, perhaps, this arose from the fact that many of the outstanding French African leaders were for a time drawn to France and to Paris, with the result that they somewhat lost sight of their African heritage. It has also been suggested that France frowned upon Pan-African conceptions because their advocates were likely to be precisely those radical

---

[8] The multiplicity of the groupings which can appear was well illustrated by the speech made by President Youlou in welcoming the heads of state of former French Equatorial Africa to a conference in Brazzaville in November 1960. Asserting that this was the hour of communities, he ended with a *vive* for each of the four republics, the Equatorial Community, the African Community, and the Community of States *d'expression française*. No grouping having an African language as its base has yet been seriously proposed.

[9] "As a movement which was conceived in America and which blossomed in West Africa, pan-Africanism remains essentially an English-speaking movement, a delayed boomerang from the era of slavery as practiced on the West African coast two centuries ago. It is significant that, linguistically and ethnically, most of the American Negroes in North America came from the coastal areas on the Gulf of Guinea, and only a few from the interior areas of Senegal and Niger." Paul-Marc Henry, "Pan-Africanism: A Dream Come True," *Foreign Affairs*, April 1959, p. 445. See also T. Hodgkin and R. Schachter, "French-speaking West Africa in Transition," *International Conciliation*, May 1960, p. 432; Philippe Decraene, *Le Panafricanisme*, Paris, 1959.

nationalists who were pressing most vigorously for modernization and equality: "French repudiation of the goal of independence led to deep suspicion of the goal of unity."[10] Whether or not the French are to be held directly responsible for the breaking up of the federations of West and Equatorial Africa, it is clear that they did nothing to encourage their maintenance or re-establishment after 1956.

As independence came in sight, however, French-speaking Africans have demonstrated an increasing interest in associating themselves with the Pan-African movements from which they have at all events never been wholly divorced. Particularly for those who, like Senghor, stressed the anachronistic parochialism of nationalism in the contemporary world, the broader horizons of Pan-Africa were inevitably appealing, and even the union of Africa was seen as only a steppingstone to the union of mankind.

Another side of the coin is the accusation which has been leveled by Nkrumah and others against the ex-French states that they are tools of neocolonialism both in allowing the language barriers imposed by imperialism to determine their alignments and in the degree to which they have remained tied to France financially and otherwise. Certainly a number of the territories left behind in the collapse of the two federations seem hopeless experiments in endowing with life artificial political entities which have no prospect of economic and political viability. Their dependence on France for the barest minimum of survival cannot help but raise questions as to the reality of their independence; and for the entire Brazzaville group it is a

---

[10]Immanuel Wallerstein, *Africa: The Politics of Independence*, New York, Vintage Books, 1961, p. 111.

plausible speculation that a large share of such coordination as they have achieved between themselves has been the product of activities which have taken place in Paris rather than in one or another African capital.

IV. CASABLANCA AND MONROVIA

The two major ideological groupings, which go under the names of the cities in which they originated in 1961, Casablanca and Monrovia, both cut across the linguistic boundaries and thus help to prevent a permanent freezing of the lines dividing the former British and French territories. On a larger scale these two groupings carry on the attack on linguistic solidarity which was initiated with the Ghana-Guinea union in 1958, later extended by the addition of Mali (the ex-French Soudan) after the breakup of the Mali Federation in 1960.

Although it is tempting to read a deep and long-lasting ideological conflict into the split between these two major groups, many observers are inclined to be skeptical of the solidarity of each of the groups within itself and of the depth and sticking power of the ideological divergence. Certainly it is premature to assume that any political situation in Africa has as yet had time to achieve real stability. Both within each of the states and in the relations between them forces are at work which sharply challenge the existing order and may end by overthrowing it. The series of apparently cordial state visits which the heads of countries in the opposing blocs pay each other, with the consequent communiqués endorsing friendship and African unity, indicate that the ideological lines are far from representing any total separation.

When these cautionary remarks have been made, however, it is essential to recognize that as of now serious cleavages divide the members of the two groups which tend to head in different directions in outlook and policy. Undoubtedly the Casablanca group, of which Guinea, Ghana, and Mali constitute the sub-Saharan members, is more activist, radical, and left-oriented, taking its anticolonialism, its socialism, and its Pan-Africanism a good deal more seriously than does the larger and more conservative Monrovia grouping in which Nigeria and Liberia play leading roles and which includes the entire Brazzaville community as well as Ethiopia and Somalia from the other side of the continent. Relations between Guinea, Ghana, and Mali on one side and the Soviet bloc on the other tend to be considerably more intimate than those between the latter and the Monrovia contingent.

As a matter of principle it is possible to find a sharp differentiation in the Monrovian tendency to look to a series of agreements on functional collaboration as contrasted with Nkrumah's constant insistence, laid out for example in his opening address to the first All-African People's Conference in 1958, that the primary aim must be the attainment of the Political Kingdom, after which all else will follow.[11] In practice, however, neither the Guinea-Ghana-Mali union nor the Casablanca group as a whole has made any significant move toward an actual political merger, although the constitutions of the first three countries provide that sovereignty can be surrendered in

---

[11]John Marcum distinguishes between the Casablanca and the Monrovia groupings on the basis of their representing monolithic and pluralist unity respectively. "How Wide is the Gap between Casablanca and Monrovia?" *Africa Report*, January 1962 (Vol. 7, No. 1). This article contains (p. 4) a useful table showing the membership of African countries in the different groupings.

whole or in part in the interests of African unity. One concrete success which Nkrumah has achieved was the agreement with President Yameogo of Upper Volta in mid-1961 to remove the customs barriers between the two states, a step which Nkrumah hailed as wiping out the artificial territorial barriers imposed by the imperialists. On its side, the Monrovia group, in its meeting at Lagos in January 1962, adopted in principle a charter for African unity which would bring an elaborately structured organization of African states into being.

The Nkrumah doctrine that African unity must be sought through a merger of sovereignties in a new Political Kingdom has not found many takers among the African leaders. The reasons for this rejection are not hard to find, among them being the manifest disinclination to accept the proffered headship of Nkrumah himself in a potential African union. This is a difficulty which must be a recurrent one: where strong one-man leadership has established itself, as is so often the case in Africa, it will be a painful process to select from among the leaders of the states which are uniting one to stand out in splendor while the others sink back to subordinate positions. The surrender of the trappings and the more substantial perquisites of sovereignty is not a step which is lightly taken, even for the attainment of African unity. Several of the African leaders have indicated plainly enough that they have not fought the battles for independence in order to abandon it again in favor of someone else's rule. Thus the Prime Minister of Nigeria, with an icy side reference to Nkrumah, remarked that his country had waited one hundred years for freedom and did not propose to throw it away on gaining independence, and Houphouet-Boigny similarly protested that his Ivory Coast had not come to independence in order to be subjected to a backward African country.[12]

V. AFRICAN HARMONY AND DISCORD

Deep in the heart of every true believer is the conviction that the principle of the natural harmony of interests applies in his domain. For the Pan-Africanist this implies belief in the assumption that, once the affairs of the continent cease to be distorted by the machinations of the colonialist and neocolonialist, African states and peoples will live in harmony with each other. Such a view rests upon the faith that the apparent differences and difficulties between states can be overcome by goodwill since all Africans have common outlooks and desire the unity of their peoples. In actuality the potentialities for conflict among African states are as great as those in other parts of the world; and several of them center on Ghana either because of its ethnic-territorial claims on Togo and the Ivory Coast or because of plots which it is alleged to have concocted against

the regimes in other African countries. Three other disputes may be mentioned which seem symptomatic of the kind of troubles which may be coming along as the African states work out their relationships among themselves and establish their own continental balance of power: Morocco's claim to take over Mauritania, the demand of Somalia that the Somali-inhabited portions of Ethiopia and Kenya should be joined to it, and the controversy between Cameroun and Nigeria as to the status of the northern portion of the former British Cameroons. To these must of course be added any number of possible disputes arising from cross-frontier tribal claims, not to mention all the usual subjects which offer fertile fields for disagreement among states.

The suspicions which divide the African states came out clearly in the opening address of Governor-General Azikiwe to the conference of the twenty Monrovia group countries at Lagos on January 25, 1962. Referring with regret to the absence of the Casablanca contingent (it was, incidentally, rumored that Guinea and Mali would have liked to attend), he warned about an ideological difference between the two groups which stemmed from "the conspicuous absence of specific declaration" by the Casablanca states of belief in the fundamental principles enunciated at Monrovia. These were the inalienable right of African states, as at present constituted, to legal equality, to self-determination, to inviolability of their territories from external aggression, and "to safety from internal interference in their internal affairs through subversive activities engineered by supposedly friendly states." He recalled that the United Nations Charter provides such safeguards in general terms, but asked for overt adherence to the Monrovia principles.

---

[12]For Nkrumah, see *The New York Times*, January 14, 1960. For Houphouet-Boigny see "Les Chances de l'Afrique," *Revue Politique et Parlementaire*, Juillet 1961, pp. 3–11. Nnamdi Azikiwe in 1959 affirmed his confidence in the creation of a United States of Africa, but warned that:

It would be capital folly to assume that hard-bargaining politicians who passed through the ordeal of victimization and the crucible of persecution to win their independence will easily surrender their newly-won power in the interest of a political leviathan which is populated by people who are alien to one another in their social and economic relations. It has not been possible in Europe or America, and unless Africa can show herself different from other continents, the verdict of history on this score will remain unchallenged and unaltered.

Zik, A Selection from the Speeches of Nnamdi Azikiwe, Cambridge, University Press, 1961, p. 72.

Otherwise it can be a matter for speculation whether these principles are capable of becoming spectres to haunt the conscience of those who would rather pay lip service to the Charter of the United Nations, whilst secretly they nurse expansionist ambitions against their smaller and perhaps weaker neighbors.

Another variant of difference between the African states, this time coming from the Casablanca side, was contained in a speech delivered by President Modibo Keita of Mali in June 1961.[13] Here he spoke of his continuing conviction that the countries of Africa can never achieve full independence as long as they remain small and each concentrates on itself alone. Although, he pointed out, the constitution of Mali provides for total or partial abandonment of sovereignty on behalf of a grouping of African states, actual political unification with other states could be undertaken only if there were an identity of views on both international policy and domestic economic policy. Even without such an identity of views, cooperation would be possible with all African states, whatever their political or economic position, but the conditions for a political merger were much more stringent. President Keita had, of course, been one of the central figures in the collapse of the Mali Federation, whose demise could in good part be attributed to sharp disagreements on both foreign and domestic policy between Senegal and Soudan. It might be added that the more recent divorce of Syria from Egypt, shattering the United Arab Republic, was in part attributable to similar differences in outlook and policy between the two countries.

_____

[13] Modibo Keita, "The Foreign Policy of Mali," *International Affairs*, October 1961, p. 435–36.

Which way the African future will turn is still a matter for wide-open speculation. It is evident that strong forces are pulling in a number of different directions, that African states are frequently divided among themselves, and that all African leaders express their devotion to the cause of African unity although with varying interpretations and varying degrees of intensity. Most of them would undoubtedly concur in the verdict of Julius Nyerere, principal architect of Tanganyika's independence, that African nationalism is different from other nationalisms of the past in that "the African national State is an instrument for the unification of Africa, and not for dividing Africa, that African nationalism is meaningless, is dangerous, is anachronistic if it is not at the same time pan-Africansim."[14]

How different African nationalism is remains to be seen. Insofar as precedents are relevant it is clear on the historical record that elsewhere the more parochial nationalist forces have almost always won out over the more broadly integrating supernational forces. It remains the fact that the rediscovery of Africa by the Africans is still only in its opening stages. It is a vast continent which has always been internally divided, and the superimposed colonial divisions worked to prevent the different peoples from eatablishing any real contact with each other. Pan-African gatherings, United Nations caucuses, and a host of other meetings and interstate visits are bringing at least an upper crust of the African peoples in touch with each

_____

[14] *World Assembly of Youth Forum*, No. 40, September 1961, p. 14. Most of the leaders would presumably also agree with Nyerere's further contention that only African unity can save the continent from the rival imperialisms of capitalism and communism.

other, but it will be long before the colonially-determined lines of transport and communications can be so reconstructed as to open up easy intercourse between the countries.

But perhaps the precedents are not relevant. Times have changed and African nations still have an insub-stantiality about them which distinguishes them from their fellows around the globe. Of all the questions which may be asked the most significant is as to the depth and universality of the belief that Africans are born to a common destiny.

Africa as a Subordinate State System in International Relations

I. William Zartman

Interpretations of patterns and trends in postwar international relations have frequently noted the outmoded position of the nation-state, the shrinking nature of the world, the extension of a single international relations system to global limits, and the rising importance of superpowers and regional organizations. It was then often concluded that the coming unit of international politics was likely to be not the territorial state, as in the past, but new regional groupings of states, where the component members would collectively acquire greater power by individually giving up some of their sovereignty to a bloc or group.[1]

If events in Europe, the North Atlantic, and the Soviet bloc have tended to give temporary supporting evidence to this view, the actions of the rest of the world have scarcely followed suit.[2] Logical as this preview of world politics may be, it seems to have been disavowed by actual happenings. Yet the divorce between analysis and reality is not total. Many characterizations of the bloc-actor concept appear simply to have gone too far in the right direction. Instead of a global system of interacting regional blocs there has appeared instead a dominant system of bipolar configurations, covering a number of autonomous, subordinate state systems, each limited to a geographic identification area and reflected in a regional organization. A pioneer analysis has already been made of the subordinate system in the Middle East, and attempts have been made to apply

[1] See the discussions in Roger D. Masters, "A Multi-Bloc Model of the International System," *American Political Science Review*, December 1961 (Vol. 10, No. 4), pp. 780–789; Stanley Hoffmann, *Organisations Internationales et Pouvoirs Politiques des Etats* (Paris: Colin, 1954), especially pp. 416–417; John Herz, *International Relations in the Atomic Age* (New York: Columbia University Press, 1959), pp. 96–108; John Herz, "The Rise and Demise of the Territorial State," in James N. Rosenau (ed.), *International Politics and Foreign Policy* (New York: Free Press, 1961), pp. 80–86; and Kurt London, *The Making of*

Foreign Policy: East and West (New York: J. B. Lippincott, 1965). For commentary see Arnold Wolfers, *Discord and Collaboration: Essays on International Politics* (Baltimore, Md: Johns Hopkins Press, 1962), especially pp. 19–24.

[2] Latin America, or the western hemisphere, is a borderline case that deserves examination as a subsystem.

From *International Organization,* Vol. XXI, No. 3 (Summer 1967), 545–64, by permission of author and journal.

the same concept to southern Asia.[3] This study deals with the subordinate state system of Africa.

As frequently occurs in social sciences there is some confusion about the basic concept: Is the subordinate system—indeed, any international relations system—a fact, a goal, or a tool of analysis? Is it to be discovered, created, or invented? Does it have objective existence independent of volition, is it a quality to be attained, or is it a way of ordering and interpreting observable qualities and quantities?[4] Although different, these three

aspects of the concept are not necessarily mutually incompatible. A "team" can be at the same time an existing situation of relationships between co-workers, a goal of a group leader, and a yardstick for evaluating relations. Like a team, a subordinate system may be both a conscious creation of some statesmen and the unintended result of other statesmen's actions for other purposes. As in the case of a team—or of a state, a government, or many other subjects of political science—it is easier to identify a system than to ascertain when it was born or when it disappeared. The purpose of this study will be to describe and analyze the subordinate state system of Africa as a fact in contemporary world politics, showing the actions that have expressly or involuntarily tended to perpetuate it.

I

To do this it will first be necessary to establish the *components* of a subordinate state system and ascertain their relevance to African relations.[5] The first component is a *geographic region* that serves both as a territorial base and as an identification area. The use of "Africa" and "African" as a reference symbol by outsiders and an identity symbol by Africans makes the geographic region appear obvious.[6] Even

---

[3] Leonard Binder, *The Ideological Revolution in the Middle East* (New York: John Wiley & Sons, 1964), pp. 254–278; Michael Brecher, *The New States of Asia* (New York: Oxford University Press, 1963); and George Modelski, "International Relations and Area Studies: The Case of South-East Asia," *International Relations* (London), April 1961 (Vol. 2, No. 2), pp. 143–155. See also Thomas Hodgkin, "The New West Africa State System," *University of Toronto Quarterly*, October 1961 (Vol. 31, No. 1), pp: 74–82; and Stanley Hoffmann, "Discord in Community: The North Atlantic Area as a Partial International System," *International Organization*, Summer 1963 (Vol. 17, No. 3), pp. 521–549.

This article uses the most valuable of the above works—the original article by Michael Brecher which appeared in XV *World Politics*, Vol. 2: 213–235—as its starting point. Brecher's article was the first attempt to deal precisely and conceptually with the concept.

[4] More specifically, what is to prevent an analyst from describing a subregion as a system, as in Hodgkin, *University of Toronto Quarterly*, Vol. 31, No. 1, pp. 74–82 (although Hodgkin was writing before the continentality of the system was totally apparent)? Essentially nothing, except the ineffectiveness of the argument, suggesting that a subordinate system may be more a tool of analysis than a reality. However, it seems difficult to avoid key elements of autonomy and limits of the system; yet these are underemphasized in Brecher. In fact, subregions such as West or North or East Africa are relatively autonomous on some levels of relations and will be referred to here as subregional constellations (see below). Their integral membership in the African subordinate system, however, seems undeniable.

[5] The phrase "regional system" may be less likely to raise political connotations to people sensitive of a colonial past, but "subordinate system" is retained here because of its established use; see Binder, and Brecher. Binder calls his system an "international system" and Brecher a "state system"; both terms are adequate.

[6] See the excellent discussion by Ali A. Mazrui, "On the Concept of 'We Are All Africans,'" *American Political Science Review*, March 1963 (Vol. 57, No. 1), pp. 88–97, reprinted in Ali A. Mazrui, *Towards a Pax Africana: A Study of Ideology and Ambition* (Chicago: University of Chicago Press, 1967), pp. 42–58.

if there has been some racial antagonism between Africans north and south of the Sahara, negritude has never been adopted as a basis for identification in international relations; by the same token the ethnic distinctness of the Malagasy population has not prevented it from being part of the African system.

Nevertheless, the limits of the geographic region are less obvious than the insularity of the continent might imply. On the one hand, the close relations between independent African party-governments and nationalist movements in still dependent territories suggest a continental area of interaction. On the other hand, the fact that African leaders aspire to the extension of the system to the entire continent by the liberation of Africans from white rule indicates that the subordinate international system has not yet attained its maximum geographic limits. The way out of these conflicting criteria is to identify the inner limits of the system as containing the independent, anticolonialist states of Africa. The remaining, white-ruled territories then form a fringe area, in a position similar to that of Israel in the Middle Eastern system. The antagonistic relations between the system and the fringe area are one of the elements that help keep the system together.[7]

The very term "Mother Africa" suggests that the identification area is highly sentimentalized, reinforcing the outer limits of the region. This view is clearest in the Pan-African school of African nationalism that considers itself and its national parties as merely territorial representatives of a continental movement and regards state independence as incomplete, if not insecure, until all the continent has been liberated. Thus, sentimentalization of the area serves as the basis for political action to bring "colonialist" territories within the system. Even "moderates" and "state nationalists" think of themselves as Africans although they may differ over the policy consequences to be drawn from this identity. In both cases the "macronationalistic" or continental identification supports and holds in place—as well as rivals—the "micronationalistic" or state-nation identification in the same way as a man (and his wife and children) distinguishes himself from brothers and cousins without destroying the sense of family or clan.[8]

To the African this continental self-consciousness is first of all negative, the rejection of European control and European-defined identification. Thereafter it becomes positive, both the assertion of and the search for distinguishing characteristics. Shared experiences—such as the colonial struggle, denigration by colonialists, confrontation with modernization, similarity of aspirations—form the basis of a sentimentalized continental identity.

The inner limits of the system coincide with an organizational definition of the area. The Organization of African Unity (OAU), which will receive more attention below, is open to "each independent sovereign African State," members pledging themselves "to observe scrupulously the principles . . .

---

[7] Dependent territories such as the Spanish Sahara and Portuguese Guinea play an important buffer role in intra-African relations, an indication that fringe areas—particularly those outside of the southern redoubt—may have some of the characteristics of membership in the system.

[8] On the two types of nationalisms see Doudou Thiam, *The Foreign Policy of African States* (New York: Frederick A. Praeger, 1965); on the state-nation see I. William Zartman, "Characteristics of Developing Foreign Policies," in William H. Lewis (ed.), *French-Speaking Africa: The Search for Identity* (New York: Walker and Co., 1965), pp. 179–193.

of the present Charter."[9] An *international organization* may be considered a second component of a subordinate system, although not as necessary to its existence as the other components—any more than an organization is necessary to the existence of a world system of international relations. The African organization serves a double purpose. In its inward focus it serves as a framework for relations between its members, replacing their former patterns of relations with a forum for problem solving and an arena for competition. In its outward focus it becomes an alliance avowedly directed against the colonialist governments of the nonliberated territories with the purpose of defending and extending the system.

The third characteristic is intrarelatedness or *autonomy*, a condition wherein a change at one point in the system affects other points and where intrasystem actions and responses predominate over external influences. Despite the continuing influence of France and, to a lesser extent, the United Kingdom and the effects of the Cold War on African foreign policies relations between African states are primarily governed by intra-African stimuli; in fact, the independence movement has the primary purpose of making this so, and African solidarity and support behind the struggle for independence in various countries have had the dual effect of breaking ties with the metropole and strengthening relations between African states. The formation of African groups and alliances has been the result of African events—the African independence movement, the Congo breakdown, internal government changes. After major internal events—Algeria's 1965 coup, Ghana's 1966

coup, Morocco's Ben Barka affair, Nigeria's military takeovers—diplomatic missions have been sent to other African states to explain the official position. Moroccan and Somali irredentism, Tanganyikan appeals for an African force to replace the British after the 1964 mutinies, the OAU provision for solution of African problems by African states, and African conferences on the Togolese assassination, the Algerian-Moroccan and Somali-Ethiopian wars, the Congo rebellions,[10] and the Rhodesian problem have all been evidences of autonomy or intrarelatedness.

Obviously, the subordinate system is autonomous but not independent; that is, it is not free of influences and relations involving outside areas. One problem in this context arises from overlapping systems. Both the African and Mideastern subordinate systems include the Sudan, the Maghreb, and the United Arab Republic (Egypt). The oft-discussed question, "Is Northern Africa Arab or African?," is not answerable in yes-or-no terms; all of Arab Africa is in both areas. The Maghreb has used its membership in the African system to counterbalance Egyptian dominance in the Arab system and to give itself the greater independence that comes from choice. Egypt has used its membership in both systems to give it greater influence in foreign relations; Nasser's "three circles"—the Arab, African, and Muslim "worlds"—all include African states.[11] The recognition of overlapping systems

---

[9] Articles IV and VI of the Charter of the Organization of African Unity. The text of the Charter can be found in Mazrui, *Towards a Pax Africana*, Appendix I, pp. 219–229.

[10] On the Congo conflict as an "attempt to keep the Cold War out of Africa" see Robert C. Good, "The Congo Crisis: A Study of Postcolonial Politics," in Laurence W. Martin (ed.), *Neutralism and Nonalignment: The New States in World Affairs* (New York: Frederick A. Praeger, 1962), pp. 34–63.

[11] Gamal Abdel Nasser, *The Philosophy of the Revolution* (Cairo: Government Printing Office, 1958), pp. 66–67.

in interpreting foreign policy alternatives and possibilities for states with dual membership is both a more helpful and a more realistic way of looking at foreign policies than is the attempt to force such states exclusively into one area or the other.

In sum, an autonomous, subordinate, African system with certain identifiable characteristics does seem to exist and to be capable of performing limited functions under certain conditions. These functions fall into two broad categories: problem solving and self-maintenance. Where the capabilities of the system are overburdened and the system can no longer perform its functions, the door is opened to external influences. The most readily available are France and Britain, former metropoles, and the Union of Soviet Socialist Republics and the United States, cold-war protagonists. Africa's lack of sufficient resources to achieve its own economic development causes it to turn to outside sources of aid, for example, opening the system to foreign penetration and threatening its autonomy. Its low capability of controlling the use of violence has led to similar outside appeals. Thus, Tanganyika called on Britain to control its mutinous army, the Democratic Republic of the Congo called on the UN and on mercenaries to turn chaos and rebellion into order, the OAU called on Britain to intervene militarily in Rhodesia, and Gabon (and allegedly some other states) appears to have called on France to put down internal revolt.

The system can handle its functions only when problem solving and autonomy are the subject of consensus and are higher values than political advantage, ideological commitment, or a *particular* outcome of a dispute. When the latter values predominate (when consensus is absent) and Africa is split,

African states scramble for outside allies and the system fails. Thus, the autonomous African system which replaced the Eurafrican colonial system is no more perfect than it is totally independent of outside influence; when burdens exceed capabilities, postcolonial or cold-war influences enter, often by African invitation. Many of Africa's foreign policy troubles are found in the dilemma posed by the two functions: The desire to solve problems, which often exceeds system capabilities and requires outside help, clashes with the desire to maintain the autonomy of the system.[12]

II

The description of the system's internal operations begins with the *configuration of power*. Power is a relative situational consideration and may be defined as the capability of achieving a goal. The items to be considered under the configuration of power include its level, distribution, basis, and use. The *level* of power in Africa is low, both within the system and toward outside states. This means simply that African states have little capability of influencing the decisions of other African and non-African states. The reasons for this situation are found in the other components of power configuration. The second component is the *distribution of power*, which is highly diffused within the system rather than being hierarchically

---

[12]The conflict between these two functions also has important ideological ramifications in internal politics. See Herbert Feith, *The Decline of Constitutional Democracy in Indonesia* (Ithaca, N.Y: Cornell, University Press, 1962), on problem solvers and solidarity makers; see also I. William Zartman, "Ideology and National Interest," in Vernon McKay (ed.), *African Diplomacy: Studies in the Determinants of Foreign Policy* (New :Frederick A. Praeger, 1966).

structured. This characteristic is highly important to the nature of the system, for it means that there is little chance for a polar pattern of relations, with power concentrated in one or two states, and that even within camps, groups, or alliances, relations will be between relative equals rather than centered about single states. The distribution of power brings the legal fiction of states' equality—so important in the world view of the new nations—closer to reality in Africa than in many other areas of the world.

There are, however, a number of present and future qualifications to this general description of African power. Although the distribution is relatively egalitarian on a continental level, there are important differences within certain regions. Among its Conseil de l'Entente partners Ivory Coast has a dominant position. Algeria, Egypt, and Ghana have enough power to be seen as a threat by some other African states, giving rise among the latter to policies designed to reduce the three states' influence. Other states appear to be destined for a more powerful position in the future because of their size or development potential, and in some cases they are already cashing in on this potential with increased influence in the present. Such states include Nigeria, Kenya, the Congo, and, again, Algeria. Finally, there are states whose poverty in resources, smallness of population and territory, and/or general underdevelopment are characteristics of long-term weakness. Libya, Mauritania, Togo, Niger, the Central African Republic, Chad, Rwanda, Burundi, and Somalia may be in this category although situational peculiarities may from time to time suddenly give them a position of importance.

The *basis* of power is found in the classical elements of national power although an examination of the African system may suggest that there are some new elements to be considered. Size alone is no direct index to power; in Africa it is especially illusory since many of the largest states include large areas of desert and jungle, and even in those which do not the effectiveness of territory as a power base is reduced by the inadequacy of transportation and communication systems. Population is a relevant element of national power; but a closer examination of the reasons for its importance—a source of military strength, a consuming market, productive and exportable skills—suggests that raw figures must be tempered by considerations of illiteracy, heterogeneity, underemployment, ruralism, poor integration, and apathy. Again, the only valid generalization that can be made is that states with the smallest territories and populations tend to be the weakest.

Military size, preparedness, and armaments also form one of the important elements of national power, and armies in Africa range from fewer than 1,000 men (Burundi, the Central African Republic, Gabon, Malawi, Chad, and Gambia) to 100,000 or more (Egypt). Yet there are important inhibitions to the use of African armies, including their inadequacy for the local terrain, their primary utilization for internal security, the general disapproval of military means as contrary to African unity, and the danger of inviting cold-war intervention. On their own, African armies are unable to face each other in decisive combat for a long time. More important to the military power of African states is the whole range of paramilitary means available, ranging from the more or less uncontrolled marauding bands that are a fact of African frontiers

(Shiftas, Somalis, Reqeibat, Tuareg) to the actual training and arming of insurgent movements inside another country (from Egypt to Eritreans and Libyans, from Algeria to Moroccans, from Algeria and the Sudan to Congolese, from Mali to Senegalese, from Guinea to Camerounians, from Ghana to Nigerois).

Diverse economic elements form a variable basis for power in Africa. Energy and mineral resources—oil, gas, aluminum and iron ore, and electricity—all provide some African states with a means of influence over others, particularly in the supply of needed energy or the location of industries. Agriculture is less significant since there is not a great deal of intra-African trade and even less interdependence on food supplies. Economic development is a matter of growing importance, and differences in development are bound to increase in the future. At present the difference in development (as measured, for example, by the continental range of per capita incomes from $40 in Chad, the Congo [Brazzaville], Niger, Rwanda, Somalia, Upper Volta, and the Central African Republic to about $200 in Algeria, Gabon, Ghana, and Ivory Coast) is not enough by itself to give one state a decisive advantage over another, largely because development has not concentrated on items of leverage over other states and because African states have not had the occasion to bring their development to use in foreign policy.

A final element of national power—geographical position—has had more importance. Coastal states which control inland neighbors' access to the sea and states which lie astride river, rail, or pipeline routes enjoy a certain amount of influence. States whose geographical position favors a buffer policy, such as Libya, Mauritania, Togo, and occasionally Dahomey, are also able to "borrow power" from their stronger neighbors. It should be noted, at the end of this listing of power elements, that the relation between the basis of power and the actual power a state possesses in a particular situation is neither direct nor constant nor as simple as standard enumerations of the elements of national power might imply.

With some of the more tangible elements of national power in Africa suffering from underdevelopment power within the system appears to rest on more elusive bases. One is each state's vote in international organizations: the United Nations, the Organization for African Unity, and subregional groups and alliances. Here, at least, individual members possess an item in demand by other states and can bargain over its use within limits imposed by their own interests, policies, and ideologies. It is the latter element, ideology, which also acts as a basis for power as states attempt to become centers of authority for others which are susceptible to appeals to "correct," or "truly African," or "revolutionary" action.[13] If a state can monopolize popular symbols without destroying their universality, it can create rules of conduct for fellow believers. African states have often been very effective both inside and outside the system in "decreeing the unthinkable" in matters of neocolonialism, foreign bases, and external alliances, thus exercising power over other states' policies. A related element of power, intangible but important, is the prestige of African leaders which has given Kwame Nkrumah, Gamal Abdel Nasser, Modibo

---

[13]See Zartman in McKay; and Joseph S. Nye, Jr., *Pan-Africanism and East African Integration* (Cambridge, Mass: Harvard University Press, 1965).

Keita, Félix Houphouët-Boigny, Haile Selassie, and others a sympathetic audience among their peers. Finally, Africa also has its share of persuasive diplomats who can appeal to principles, reason, and interest in order to influence others.

On the basis of these elements what is the *use* of power within the African system? Power can be exercised in many ways, involving the use of real or implied gratifications or deprivations. In Africa the means—other than psychological—for gratifying or depriving other states are slim. Except for a restricted list of items—ideological approval, a few ores, ports, and transportation lines, and limited skills, monies, and trade items—African states have few items that other African states want or need. The same is true in regard to their weight in the dominant cold-war system where their political neutrality and their openness to foreign economic interests are about all they can offer.

The situation is somewhat different in regard to the territories between the inner and outer limits of the system.[14] Here independent African states have financial resources, bases, arms supplies, and military or paramilitary forces to exert their power, as well as port and airfield rights, votes in international organizations, and diplomatic means of persuasion. All of these items are in short supply but are available. Portugal, Rhodesia, and the Republic of South Africa, on the other side, have larger military and economic resources but smaller voices on the world stage; they also have trade items which African states want or need. The simple balance sheet indicates why independent Africa has concentrated on nonmilitary sources of power. The inherent difficulty in this situation is also evident: Africa's greatest strength is in those elements that are slowest in producing results.

The characteristic, egalitarian weakness in the different components of the African subordinate system's power configuration has had an important effect on the dominant world view within the system. Globally revisionist, African attitudes frequently reject power as a basis for international relations, both in its past manifestation —the colonial system—and in the present—the Cold War. The African world view regards recent history as a struggle between power and justice, with Africa on the losing side of justice both under colonialism and within the present great-power confrontation.[15] Since Africa is deficient in the current coin of world politics, it rejects relations on a power basis (often including parts of current international law, which appears only to consecrate *de facto* power dominance). Since nationalist movements generally benefited from colonial withdrawal by the powerful European states with relatively little direct pressure (deprivation) or reward (gratification) and without resorting to the ultimate use of power, force, the possibility of creating a new

---

[14]See Waldemar Neilsen, *African Battleline* (New York: Harper & Row, 1965); Amelia C. Leiss (ed.), *Apartheid and United Nations Collective Measures: An Analysis* (New York: Carnegie Endowment for International Peace, 1965); and Ronald Segal (ed.), *Sanctions Against South Africa* (Baltimore, Md: Penguin Books, 1965).

[15]Some examples to substantiate this gross generalization, "the African world view," are found in Thiam; Sékou Touré, *The International Policy and Diplomatic Action of the Democratic Party of Guinea* (Conakry: P.D.G., n.d. [1962]); Kwame Nkrumah, *Consciencism* (New York: Frederick A. Praeger, 1963); Mamadou Dia, *The African Nations and World Solidarity* (New York: Frederick A. Praeger, 1961).

world order without power and based on justice seems real to them. This aspiration also appears to be necessary since to the African neutralists the cold-war protagonists seem irresponsible and dangerous in their handling of overwhelming power, threatening to destroy the world for conflicting goals that are not worth the cost. In sum, in a world where Africa does not have the power to protect itself and promote its own goals, it proposes a new system of international relations that emphasizes its rights and deemphasizes the classical means to attain them. The inherent contradiction, sharpened by the fact that the faster developing states in Africa do in fact seek to increase their power and use it in classical ways, is typical of an idealistic view of international relations.

III

The second element in the description of a subordinate system concerns the *nature of relations*, including quantity, quality, intensity, and patterns. The first three components are related but are extremely difficult to analyze, particularly on the political level. Some indication can be made by studying commercial relations between African states.[16] Two significant charac-

teristics are visible: the existence of distinct subregional trading groups (West, Central, East-Horn, and Northern Africa) and the existence of certain "hinge" states which are members of two groups (Senegal and Nigeria trading with both West and Central Africa, the Democratic Republic of the Congo in both East-Horn and Central Africa, Egypt in both East-Horn and Northern Africa, and Morocco-Algeria-Tunisia in Northern Africa but trading with the Central

---

Ghana and Nigeria; Egypt corresponds first with Northeast Africa and second with Northwest Africa (Maghreb), far more than with Black Africa but far less than with the Middle East; Morocco corresponds with the Maghreb, Egypt, Mali, Senegal, and the Entente, in that order, while Nigeria shows an equally broad scattering, with its coastal neighbors, Sierra Leone, South Africa, Liberia, and the Democratic Republic of the Congo. Further information would be instructive, for mail exchange in the countries noted does tend to confirm some political patterns. (Data taken from *Statistiques des Expeditions dans le Service Postal International, 1961* [Berne: Universal Postal Union, 1963].) A chart of commercial relations on which the following conclusions are based was made from data given in the *Yearbook of International Trade Statistics 1963* (New York: United Nations, 1965). The expression "East-Horn" is used because the region is composed of two subgroups: East (three East African Common Services Organization [EASCO] states plus three ex-Belgian states) and Northeast (Egypt, the Sudan, Ethiopia, and Somalia) Africa. Northern Africa comprises the five Mediterranean states; Central Africa refers to the five ex-French equatorial states plus the Democratic Republic of the Congo and Nigeria. Separate data is not available for the states of the former Central African Federation; the Republic of South Africa and colonial territories are not included in the conclusions. For analytical use of transaction flows in intra-African relations see William J. Foltz, *From French West Africa to the Mali Federation* (New Haven, Conn: Yale University Press, 1965); and L. P. Green and T. J. D. Fair, *Development in Africa* (Johannesburg: Witwatersrand University Press, 1962).

---

16 Postal and telecommunications would also tell something of intra-African relations, were the raw data available. See Karl Deutsch, *Nationalism and Social Communication* (New York: John Wiley & Sons, 1953). The few independent African countries for which statistics are reported (five plus South Africa) provide a basis only for observations, not conclusions. Generally, correspondence within Africa is numerically inferior to correspondence with the former metropole and is largely shaped by linguistic lines. Specifically, Senegal has frequent exchanges with the Entente and only secondarily with its four neighbors; Togo shows frequent exchanges with the Entente and Senegal and only secondarily with

and Western subregions). These same characteristics also appear in political relations.

When applied directly to political matters, *quantity*, *quality*, and *intensity* are valuable concepts but difficult to reduce to any summary appreciation. Quantity refers to the number of contacts, including visits by delegations and meetings at international conferences; quality refers to a range of feelings from amity to enmity; and intensity refers to the emotional level of these feelings. However, since bilateral relations tend to change rapidly in Africa, a new political "weather map" for the continent would be necessary every six months. Although quality and intensity could easily be estimated, a sounder way of measuring these components would be through a quantitative analysis of each country's newspaper or leaders' speeches.[17] Such a task is beyond the scope of this article, but a qualitative evaluation of relations shows several characteristics.

One is the presence of subregional constellations within the continental pattern, in the Maghreb, West Africa, and East Africa, with less of a subregional pattern in Central and Equatorial Africa. Another characteristic is the creation of "bridges" between regions, for example, by conflict between Morocco and Mauritania, attraction between Mali and Algeria, friendship between Nigeria and the Congo, influence of Ghana in East Africa, and varied reactions to Egyptian policy. The first and second Con-

golese crises have had the visible effect of creating a continental pattern of interactions; the problems of the Portuguese territories and, to a growing extent, the Rhodesian affair work in a similar direction. A third characteristic is the kaleidoscopic nature of African relations where a slight turn of events brings dramatic new patterns; until firmer patterns of friendship and rivalry are established, yesterday's friends can become today's enemies—as relations between Rabat, Algiers, Tunis, and Cairo, between Dakar and Bamako, between Brazzaville and Leopoldville, or between Conakry and Accra have shown—and then become tomorrow's friends—in many of the same cases. A last characteristic is that while enemies usually have different close friends (with some notable exceptions), the converse is not necessarily true: Close friends usually do have different enemies. In addition, few friendships and enmities are of such serious nature that they involve the entire continent. Thus, African disputes have never separated all states in the system into two opposing camps; there have always been some uninvolved or unaligned states to serve a mediatory function. This characteristic corroborates some aspects noted in the configuration of power.

The final component in the nature of relations refers to multilateral *patterns*.[18] In a sense Africa's search for a definition of unity, which has been the dominant theme of intra-African relations, has been an attempt to find

---

[17] See Ithiel de Sola Pool, *Symbols of Internationalism* (Stanford, Calif.: Stanford University Press, 1951); Kenneth Boulding, "National Images and International Systems," in Rosenau, pp. 391–398. On the need for such "maps" see Charles A. McClelland, *Theory and the International System* (New York: Macmillan, 1966), p. 106.

[18] "Pattern" is used here where most analyses have used "system." The change in term seems necessary; a pattern is only one element in the operation of a system, and a system can continue to exist in transition between two patterns of relations. Masters (*American Political Science Review*, Vol. 10, No. 4, pp. 780–789) uses the term "structures."

satisfying patterns of relations as states balance the demands that unity places on their policy against those imposed by other ideological imperatives. Since the period leading to the formation of the OAU—and only to a lesser extent the subsequent period, still not ended—was a time of search, patterns could be discarded one after another until some satisfying definition of unity was found. What is even more significant is that the new African states apparently stumbled on some of the classical patterns of international relations, suggesting that theoretical concepts used in the West do have relevance in other areas.

The simplest pattern of relations is a multilateral extension of bad-neighbor relations. Although it is usual, if not normal, that a state has more difficulties with its neighbors than with other states, such a situation only becomes a pattern when the state takes the next logical step and forms an alliance with its neighbor's neighbor because they both have the same enemy (the state in the middle). The result may be called a *checkerboard* pattern or a Kautilyan pattern after the Indian statesman who so well described it.[19] It has frequently appeared in Africa. The interlocked alliances of Guinea, Ghana, and Mali (Union of African States [UAS]) and of Ivory Coast, Upper Volta, Niger, and Dahomey (Conseil de l'Entente) are one example of this pattern. In the horn of Africa a similar pattern began when two objects of Somali irredentism, Kenya and Ethiopia, signed a mutual

defense pact in late 1963, but the pattern did not extend as far as in North and West Africa; that is, Somalia did not then ally with Uganda or the Sudan although it did tighten relations with Egypt. Why did the pattern stop in East Africa instead of spreading as it did in North and West Africa? The simplest answer is that the Somalia conflict has had no interest for the second ring of states around Somalia; whereas relations within West Africa were so intertwined that, once begun, a pattern spread to other states in the subregion, Somalia's subregion included few members and Somalia could not find other states to share its goals or its enemies.[20]

The primitive checkerboard of West Africa soon turned into a more sophisticated pattern of relations, the *balance of power*, and in the process turned the pattern from a subregional to a continental complex of relations. The balance of power is a mobile pattern of alliances whereby any state or group of states is prevented from achieving hegemony; it can be ended by failure (one side achieving dominance), breakdown (both alliances falling apart), or resolution (alliance members forgetting the conflict or the hegemony issue and moving on to another pattern). The African balance-of-power pattern grew out of the Western

---

[19] Kautilya, *Arthasastra*, trans. R. Shamasastry (Mysore: Mysore Printing and Publishing House, 1960), especially pp. 289–293; and George Modelski, "Kautilya: Foreign Policy and International System in the Ancient Hindu World," in *American Political Science Review*, September 1964 (Vol. 58, No. 3), pp. 549–560.

[20] It is remarkable that a checkerboard pattern did not appear in North Africa, i.e., that Morocco and Tunisia never united against the Algerian revolution and sporadic interference. To the contrary, the period between 1958 and 1962 was filled with alternate Tunisian and Moroccan attempts to win the National Liberation Front (FLN) to *their* side, to the exclusion of the other neighbor. The only checkerboard that has appeared was the Algerian-Egyptian "entente" under Ahmed Ben Bella, with Morocco, Tunisia, and Libya in various positions of enmity but never allied in a counterentente.

African checkerboard.[21] The first step was the formation of the Brazzaville Group of moderate states (including the Entente) in 1960 for the purpose of 1) checking the Moroccan campaign for hegemony over Mauritania, 2) checking the radical states' efforts in the Congo, and 3) seeking an agreeable definition of African unity. The counter-alliance was the Casablanca Group (including the UAS), formed in 1961 to promote its activist members' policies in the same three areas. Both alliances then sought to expand, but only the Brazzaville Group was successful; it gained new members and formed the Monrovia-Lagos Group. However, by this time (1962) the first two issues had died away, another issue which had kept the alliances apart—recognition of the Algerian Provisional Government (a member of the Casablanca Group)—was obviated by Algerian independence, and the African unity issue was the only problem left. In this situation the balance of power was no longer relevant, and it disappeared in the process described above as resolution as African states sought another pattern of relations centered about the remaining issue of unity. Because the expanded moderate alliance in the last stage was stronger than the radical counter-alliance, however, its ideas on the new pattern would be expected to predominate, as in fact happened at Addis Ababa with the founding of the OAU.

A third pattern of relations came into effect in 1963 with the formation of the OAU, which at the same time serves as the organizational framework for the system. The new pattern of relations bears many similarities to the *concert* as practiced in other parts of the world.[22] In a concert pattern states meet regularly to handle common problems on the basis of some common ideals (including agreement that problems should be handled by members of the system); the formation of firm alliances is excluded although differences of opinion are not. The OAU has served such a purpose, sometimes inconclusively but with enough prestige derived from its nature as the embodiment of the African unity mystique to be effective in its role. The principal organ of the OAU, the Assembly of Heads of State and Government, was busy enough setting up institutions during its first two sessions (Addis Ababa in May 1963, Cairo in July 1964) to keep this prestige. Council of Ministers' meetings precede and prepare the work of the annual summit although the Council's other meetings have been less successful in dealing with concrete problems, such as support of nationalist movements in dependent territories, solution of disputes between members, or resolution of the Congo problem. The Commission of Mediation, Conciliation, and Arbitration has never functioned, and the Defense Commission and the Liberation Coordination Committee have been ineffectual. The Secretariat, under Diallo Telli, has been caught between the need for vigorous efforts to keep the Organization going and criticisms coming from member states jealous of their sovereignty; it has, however, been prevented from becoming a supranational power

---

[21] For a more detailed analysis of these events see the author's *International Relations in the New Africa* (Englewood Cliffs, N.J.: Prentice-Hall, 1966).

[22] The concert system (pattern) is described in Richard Rosecrance, *Action and Reaction in World Politics* (Boston: Little, Brown, 1963), pp. 156–159.

center in its own right, thus keeping the pattern of relations on a concert level.

During 1965 some of these specific weaknesses caused member states to complain of the ineffectiveness of the Organization and to search about for new patterns of relations. In general, the radical members, seeking to strengthen the Organization and use it to impose their concept of orthodoxy on the policies of member states, tried to organize relations on a hierarchical pattern. Many of the moderate states reacted to this pressure by reinforcing the only remnant of the balance-of-power pattern that had continued to exist, the Brazzaville Group, reconstituted and enlarged as the Afro-Malagasy Common Organisation (OCAM). At one point, in March 1965, it appeared as if the radicals would take up the challenge and return to a balance-of-power pattern, but preliminary meetings at Bamako and Conakry did not result in the formation of a new counteralliance. At the same time the radicals for a second time failed in their attempt to change the Congolese government and the concert pattern was preserved. Boycotts and walkouts during the OAU Council of Ministers and third Assembly of Heads of State meetings in the latter months of 1965, followed by bitter fights over the size and use of the budget and the ineffectiveness of liberation policies at the Councils of Ministers and fourth Assembly in 1966 have all contributed to increased disenchantment with the Organization. Nothing, however, indicated a return to a balance of power since the OCAM group remains quiescent and no counteralliance appears to be forming. A continuation of the present concert-like pattern, despite its troubled record, seems best to fit other characteristics of the system, particularly the configuration of power.

IV

The third element in the description of the African subordinate system may be called the *normative characteristics* of the system. These "rules" are *de facto* guidelines of policy, established by consensus through the development of the subordinate system and resulting from its power configuration. Like any laws, they are not universally accepted and have been broken in the past. Each time that they are used as a basis of a state's policy decision, their effectiveness is reinforced; conversely, if they are broken too frequently or in particularly important cases, such action creates pressure for normative readjustment. Thus, the conflict between the radical, intervention school and the moderate, sovereignty school in the second Congo case was a basic conflict over rules to govern relations in the system as well as a conflict between camps and ideologies. Consensus on normative behavior is particularly important to the existence of a true concert pattern of relations.[23]

Rule One is that intrasystem solutions are to be preferred over extrasystem solutions to African problems whenever possible. The effect of this rule is to maintain the autonomy of the system. Examples have already been given in the discussion of autonomy; others include the whole African independence movement which seeks to put problems of government into the hands of national elites, the Ghanaian (1960) and Congolese (1964)

---

[23]On norm making at Addis Ababa see T. O. Elias, "The Charter of the Organization of African Unity," *American Journal of International Law*, April 1965 (Vol. 59, No. 2), pp. 243–264.

appeals for African troops in the Congo, the Zambian negotiations (1965–1966) to circumvent the Mozambique outlet to the sea, the Moroccan-Algerian rejection (1963) of the Arab League good offices in their border dispute, to name a few. A less tangible but more striking example is the frequently successful attempt of African states to change the rules governing postcolonial bases, neocolonialism, colonial return, nuclear armament, and indeed general foreign intervention, putting them outside the realm of "thinkable" actions of foreign states in Africa.

It is worth pausing a moment to notice the relation between this attempt to change external rules and the characteristics of the system already noted. In a world context Africa's security problems are largely out of its hands; the absence of effective modern armies, atomic weapons, and industrial power (including a self-sufficient armaments industry) all put Africa at the mercy of the outside, should power be reduced to its raw terms of force. Even if the chances of military intervention are in fact slight, such a situation of basic insecurity is difficult for any state to live with, and especially so for a new one that is sensitive about its sovereignty and independence. Thus, it becomes imperative for African states to minimize the chances of military intervention—one of the basic functions of a neutralist policy—and to create psychological barriers (in the absence of military barriers) to intervention. Restated, this means that African leaders are deeply aware of the existence of a power vacuum;[24] since they are aware that it is caused by their inability to fill it, they at-

tempt to strengthen the walls that contain it. If African states can make intervention "unthinkable" and can also make it unwarranted by handling their own problems, insecurity is reduced.

Rule Two establishes a hierarchy among the three primary goals of African states: independence, development, and unity, in that order. The fate of the North African Tangier Conference (1958), of the Mali Federation (1960), of plans to consolidate the East African Common Services Organization (1963) and former French Equatorial Africa (1959) as federal or confederal units, and more broadly of the "Africa Must Unite" school all show the priority of independence over unity. Decidedly, despite the contrary pressure of Pan-Africanism, the state as the African political unit seems here to stay. By the same token, examples such as the West Africans' problems in locating a common steel mill, the North Africans' emphasis on an economic approach to Maghreb unity, and the East Africans' attachment to a common market, among others, show that national development is preferred to regional development but that if regional "unity" is to take place, it will probably do so first on economic grounds. This hierarchy simply brings out the continuing reasons why political unity is so difficult to accomplish, despite its mystique in Africa, and shows that under the present rules unification is not a foreign policy alternative among African states. The only exception is the case of Zanzibar, which falls only slightly short of joining the other cases of

---

[24]See the discussion in Cecil V. Crabb, Jr., *The Elephants and the Grass: A Study of Nonalignment* (New York: Frederick A.

Praeger, 1965), especially pp. 96–99. On neutralism see also Francis Low-Beer, "The Concept of Neutralism," *American Political Science Review*, June 1964 (Vol. 58, No. 2), pp. 383–391; and Martin (ed.), *Op. cit.*

unification (Morocco, Ethiopia, Somalia, Cameroun, and Ghana), all of which took place before or with independence.

Rule Three states that wars of conquest are not policy alternatives. This rule derives from military weaknesses of African states, from their fear of foreign intervention, and from the inhibitory effect of such values as legitimacy (independence) and unity. Morocco's restraint in the Moroccan-Algerian war and in its irredentist compaign against Mauritania, Ghanaian restraint against Togo, Somali reluctance to engage its army in its irredentist campaign, and the Egyptian withdrawal in the 1958 border dispute with the Sudan are all cases in point. This rule has even been codified in the OAU Charter provisions against use of force and against intervention in internal affairs.[25]

The combined effects of Rules Two and Three are important.[26] With unification and military conquest ruled out as policy alternatives the strongest form of good and bad relations becomes economic cooperation and political warfare, respectively. The OAU nonintervention clause and political actions such as the OCAM stand on the Congo and against Ghanaian subversion in neighboring countries are attempts to further reduce policy alternatives by removing the possibility of political warfare, but without complete

success. Lesser forms of intervention, such as propaganda, conspiracy, subversion, terrorism, and guerrilla warfare,[27] still are used. Lessons of experience, such as the Sudan's decision to stop arms supplies to the Congolese rebels when it found out that the arms were actually going to the Sudanese rebels, may help to accomplish what appeals to virtue have failed to attain. Another attempt to enforce the antisubversive extension of Rule Three through the use of one available element of power was OCAM's threat not to attend the third OAU summit at Accra, and thus weaken Ghana's prestige, if subversion did not stop. This attempt was successful in suspending political warfare in early 1965 and in weakening Nkrumah's regime internationally.

Rule Four is that all available means will be used to extend the boundaries of the inner system to its outer limits. This is a restatement of the emphasis on independence for the entire continent, but Rule Two also indicates the limitations on the means. For power will be applied only to the extent that it does not jeopardize the independence of the existing states, either by sapping their resources or by opening them to serious retaliation. This rule was already in formation during the Algerian war, when it created dilemmas for Tunisia and Morocco in their support of the Algerian nationalists, and it has severely limited support for nationalist movements "south of the battle line," including intervention in Rhodesia. In fact, it was not just Moïse Tshombe's political views that limited Congolese support for Angolan nationalism but a realistic evaluation—visible in Zambia and Malawi as well—of an exposed

---

[25]See Article III of the OAU Charter and, more specifically, the resolutions of the first Assembly of Heads of State, Cairo, July 1964, reprinted in Colin Legum, *Pan-Africanism* (2nd ed.; New York: Frederick A. Praeger, 1965), pp. 303–304.

[26]In other language, what is in formation is an integrated security community which rejects attempts at amalgamation. See Karl W. Deutsch and others, *Political Community and the North Atlantic Area* (Princeton, N.J.: Princeton University Press, 1957), pp. 5–6.

[27]See Zartman, *International Relations in the New Africa*, p. 88.

position (indeed, the latter fact may be viewed as instrumental in producing the former). So long as the interests of the states north of the battle line are not brought seriously into question by the Southern African regimes, Rule Two—independence over unity, state over revolution—will undermine the active solidarity behind liberation.

V

The enumeration of characteristics of the African system enables a tentative concluding analysis of possible future changes and their effect on intra-African relations. The most likely change in a component of the system, capable of causing its breakdown, is the destruction of its seemingly fragile autonomy. If African events become of direct and primary interest to outside—particularly cold-war—states to the point where outside stimuli outweigh African sources in triggering African responses, the very existence of the system is in danger. This would take place, as seen, if African states gave up their neutralism to take active part in an outside conflict or if an African conflict was beyond the continent's ability to contain and drew in major participation of outside powers. While the former is unlikely, the entire southern African conflict is a possible case of the latter and could mean an even more serious dislocation of the African system than the first Congo crisis which arose during its early formative years. Direct involvement by cold-war protagonists in a prolonged Rhodesian war, a South West African invasion, a South African revolution, or a guerrilla campaign in Portuguese territories would take the control of African relations out of African hands. Yet foreign involvement may, from the African's point of view, be the only way to accomplish a desirable policy objective. The dilemma is evident: Is liberation worth the price of the loss of autonomy and nonalignment? The answer to the same question concerning development has been negative, the Africans rejecting increased aid when it involves political strings and alignment. In both cases, however, the dilemma has been tempered by the disinclination of outside powers to threaten autonomy, either through active participation in the liberation campaign or through major increases of aid to aligned states.

Another source of change in the system concerns the level and distribution of power. At the present time power is so highly diffused that increases or decreases foreseeable in the short run are unlikely to affect the nature of intra-African relations. Nor is the advent of new states, through either the further breakup of present units (e.g., Nigeria) or the independence of present territories (e.g., Portuguese Guinea or Rhodesia), likely to alter the configuration of power in the continent, particularly since any new states can be expected to have their power reduced by problems of domestic consolidation after independence. The formation of new states through the integration of present units into a larger regional complex would certainly change the power configuration although such an event seems unlikely to take place, as has been seen.

A very few countries, however, could increase their power significantly enough to alter at least regional and perhaps eventually continental relations. The most notable example is Algeria, which already has a sizable army and a substantial economic infrastructure; politically, it has a strong attachment to African liberation and revolution, derived from its own experiences. If domestic political stability can be added, Algeria will have united basic conditions for a role of increased activity in African relations. The result could be predominance in the region (Maghreb), leadership of a radical policy in the continent, and/or catalyzation of alliances and counteralliances. It is difficult to see any states south of the Sahara and north of the battle line capable of a similar short-run power increase, Ghana being the only state with the beginnings of a heavy industrial base but handicapped by unstable politics, a small population, and an unclear foreign policy direction.

One possible change in the nature of relations would be the reinforcement of the present regional constellations to the point where several autonomous systems of interaction would come into being. This would depend on African states turning their attention to conflict and cooperation with their neighbors, losing their interest in African events in other parts of the continent and in the OAU, and following the lead of the regional committees of the Economic Commission for Africa (ECA) in focusing on regional economics; it would also suppose a decrease in the importance of the "hinge states," a disenchantment with the liberation struggle, and a disappearance of "bridging" issues. There is no reason to infer that such a change would necessarily bring about either harmony or conflict although, whatever the quality of relations, the increased quantity in a regional context would probably also involve increased intensity as other focuses of relations fell in importance.

Another likely change in the nature of relations would be a return to a balance-of-power pattern of ideological alliances and counteralliances. OCAM has concentrated on economic and cultural harmonization and has not reassumed the politically active role it played as the Afro-Malagasy Union (UAM). Meetings of the radical states —Algeria, Egypt, Mali, Guinea, the Congo (Brazzaville), and Tanzania— were to have been held in Cairo in February 1967 and in Algiers in May but were postponed. It is this group, however, which has the greatest potential for introducing a new alliance pattern since it is minority, activist, and generally dissatisfied with the content of African policies, including those in the OAU. The likelihood of such a turn of events would be enhanced by the development of new African issues of the magnitude of the Algerian or Congolese issues in 1960–1961; again Rhodesia affords the most explosive possibility although Djibouti or Spanish Sahara would be more divisive in their effects. Prolonged internal unrest in an African state involving outside assistance could also act as a catalyst for the formation of rival alliances although the events of Nigeria and Ghana show that, to the present, African states have been unwilling or unable, respectively, to intervene directly in internal unrest, and the second Congo crisis shows that, to the present, even when undertaken such intervention is ineffective.

In this light the attempts to establish norms ruling out guerrilla warfare for purposes of intervention in internal affairs have been more effective than might initially be suspected. Indeed, even terrorism, subversion, and conspiracy, while not eliminated, have been relatively ineffective as policy alternatives, and their ineffectiveness reinforces the norm. However, next to Rule One, discussed above, Rule Three is the most likely of the four present normative characteristics to undergo change. Two types of wars of conquest are possible: the border war that culminates a period of bad blood and the Goa-type incident, often involving competing African armies. There are numerous occasions for the former, particularly where nomadic forays along a permeable frontier are followed by a military riposte; they are likely to be as inconclusive in terms of territorial conquest as they have been in the recent African past.[28] The Goa-type incident has greater potential for disturbance, particularly in colonies claimed by two African states, such as Djibouti (Ethiopia and Somalia) and Spanish Sahara (Morocco and Mauritania supported by Algeria) although the colonial power in both cases presently is in a stronger position than Portugal was in Goa. The foreseeable limits of military strength in the near future suggest that Rule One would be broken along with Rule Three, for prolonged military measures cannot be sustained by African armies without concurrent outside help.

The preceding review is an attempt to indicate areas where the nature of the current system could change. If such changes now appear unlikely, this is only to say that certain presently identifiable characteristics of intra-African relations exist, not that they are immutable. Nor is it to predict that such

---

[28]See Zartman, *International Relations in the New Africa*, pp. 87–119, 165–166; and Ravi L. Kapil, "On the Conflict Potential of Inherited Boundaries in Africa," *World Politics*, July 1966 (Vol. 18, No. 4), pp. 656–673.

changes are imminent, a task beyond the capabilities of political science. If it has been able to indicate areas where changes might take place and to isolate characteristics useful for analyzing present relations and future changes, it will have been useful.

It will also be of value if it can be used to indicate further areas where research is necessary and relevant to a coordinated study of international relations. The need for detailed research in quantity, quality, and intensity of relations has already been cited, together with some suggestions on methodology. More conceptual and empirical work is required on the types and tactics of international organization, including the dynamics of alliance formation and the behavior of states in a concert organization such as the OAU. Africa is also a particularly apt area to study two other major problems in dealing with international relations: the choice and use of policy alternatives when power is consistently low, and the formation and enforcement of norms. Finally, the concept of the subordinate state system suggests further investigation of the question of systems overlap, partially analyzed above. How do states use dual membership? What types of relations are handled in which system and at what level? When and for what types of problems does a state have recourse to a universal organization (UN), a continental organization (OAU), a regional organization (e.g., Entente), and/or its own individual resources?

Africa and the World: Nonalignment Reconsidered

Fred L. Hadsel

Abstract. African nonalignment developed between 1955, when its Asian counterpart flowered at the Bandung Conference, and 1965, when it was shaken by the failure of Afro-Asians to hold their conference at Algiers. Articulated by a number of leaders but never adopted by them all, African nonalignment usually involved efforts to assure independence, resist external "neocolonial" intervention, avoid entanglement in great-power conflict, emphasize economic development, seek "aid without strings," proclaim confidence in the moral rightness of the underdeveloped nations, and exert influence in certain international issues. Toward the end of this decade, and especially in 1965–1966, many African countries reconsidered their views on nonalignment. The Soviet-Chinese split was disillusioning. The change in African leadership through military take-overs caused a turning toward national problems of political stability. Continental questions, especially those of southern Africa, grew in importance, as did the pragmatic emphasis on economic development. Nonalignment in its old form has been transformed, but since many of the reasons for its first growth continue, it may well reappear in a modified form.

African nonalignment was initially formulated and first flourished during the decade between the holding of the Afro-Asian conference at Bandung in 1955 and the failure to hold the "Second Bandung" at Algiers in 1965. Two streams of thought and action contributed principally to African nonalignment—the Asian conferences in the immediate postwar period, where nonalignment, as a term, received general currency, and the African independence movement of the 1950's, which within a few years transformed a largely colonial domain into a generally independent continent. These two streams were like the White and Blue Niles at their confluence at Khartoum. At first, they retained a separate identity, although traveling along the same direction, but fairly soon they largely intermixed, even though they never quite lost the qualities of their separate sources.

The several Asian conferences between 1947 and 1954 were a search for identity on the part of new independent nations and a reaction against colonialism as they had known it during their dependent years. This movement came to a heady fruition in the Bandung Conference of 1955. Thereafter it involved itself more and more with African and other nations—eventually reaching as far west as Cuba and, in due course, becoming entangled with the Sino-Soviet dispute. In the course of this development, it lost whatever Asian cohesiveness it ever had and became a battleground for other powers and other movements.[1]

_____
[1] See especially G. H. Jansen, *Nonalignment and the Afro-Asian States* (New York: Frederick A. Praeger, 1966); Cecil V. Crabb, *The Elephant and the Grass: A Study in Nonalignment* (New York: Frederick A. Praeger, 1965); John W. Burton (ed.), *Nonalignment* (London, 1966); *Nonalignment in Foreign*

From *The Annals*, Vol. CCCLXXI, (July 1967), 93–103, by permission of the author and the publisher, The American Academy of Political and Social Sciences.

GROWTH OF POLITICAL
NONALIGNMENT IN AFRICA

During the formative period of Asian nonalignment, the activators of independence in Africa were so deeply enmeshed in their struggle both to achieve leadership within their potential area of authority and to obtain independence from their colonial metropoles, that they initially had neither the time nor the inclination to branch out beyond these immediate goals. However, as the independence movement gained momentum, its leaders instinctively sought cooperation from each other, and out of this pan-Africanism of the 1950's came the desire for still wider association that led to a marriage of the newer African with the older Asian movement. A measure of this expanding association is found in the number of Africans attending such meetings at the beginning and the end of the first decade of African involvement in nonalignment. At Bandung in 1955, four African countries took part while, after the floodtide of independence, twenty-eight African countries were represented at the Cairo Conference in 1964.[2]

Thus, the independence movement of this decade was what in economic jargon is called a "precondition" for the development of African nonalignment. The pan-African movement, then, gave African nonalignment its initial formulation and, in fact, was an important conditioning element throughout this period.[3] For example, Ghana's independence in March 1957 provided its leader Kwame Nkrumah the sovereign political base from which to launch the first Conference of Independent African Nations, April 1958, and the first All African Peoples Conference, December 1958. Thereafter, conference followed conference in the continent until the meeting at Addis Ababa in May 1963, which established the Organization of African Unity (OAU). The charter was an amalgam of these various movements. It dedicated the member nations (1) to safeguard their national sovereignty, (2) to eradicate colonialism from the remaining dependent territories of Africa, (3) to support unity among member nations, and (4) to uphold nonalignment in Africa's relations with the rest of the world.

It is impossible for any observer to measure the strength of African devotion to these various principles, which, in any case, merged one into another. It would be logical to assume that the intensity of feeling was probably greatest with respect to national sovereignty and most diffuse with respect to political nonalignment. The problems of national development, continued colonial control, and all-African co-operation were certainly of more immediate interest. Whatever the difference might be with respect to these questions, there was a generally held feeling of mutual endeavor, even brotherhood, in the OAU, which was more tangible than the sentiments recorded at the more infrequent meetings of Africans and Asians. For one thing, the OAU was more active. It held three full Assemblies, ten Foreign Minister meetings, and a number of commission and special meetings

---

Affairs, THE ANNALS, The American Academy of Political and Social Science, Vol. 362 (November 1965).

[2] African delegations were in the following ratio: Bandung, 1955: 4 of 29; Belgrade, 1961: 10 of 24; and Cairo, 1964: 28 of 47.

[3] See especially Colin Legum, *Pan-Africanism: A Short Political Guide* (rev. ed.; New York: Frederick A. Praeger, 1965); S. Okechukwu Mezu (ed.), *The Philosophy of Pan-*

Africanism (Washington, D.C.: Georgetown University Press, 1965); and Immanuel Wallerstein, *Africa: The Politics of Unity: An Analysis of a Contemporary Social Movement* (New York: Vintage, 1967).

in the period 1963–1965, while during the same years the larger Afro-Asian nonaligned group held only two conferences and foundered in two preparatory meetings for the third. For another thing, the OAU soon turned to national and colonial questions. Resolutions dealing with these issues were widely discussed and generally accepted, even though differences on such matters as the pace of African unity were sometimes sharply drawn. After the first meeting, the OAU did not deal with nonalignment as such, and while certain of its resolutions were concerned with issues which related to nonalignment, it tended to concentrate on problems within the continent.

Nevertheless, a number of African leaders developed an extensive interest in nonalignment. President Nasser had taken part in the Bandung Conference, and the other three African heads of state sent senior ministers. Presidents Nkrumah, Touré, Keita, Nyerere, Obote, Ben Bella, and others were increasingly active in nonaligned conferences after their countries achieved independence. At the same time, nonalignment obtained less explicit adherence from other African leaders. In these cases, endorsement ranged from support of particular goals to lip-service for political purposes. Finally, a fairly small group of African leaders made it clear to their colleagues that they did not subscribe at all to this point of view, even though their countries were members of the OAU.

It is difficult, even impossible, to try to make an exact count of the views of African leaders on nonalignment during this decade. Governments changed; new problems emerged; attendance at particular meetings was sometimes incomplete. Rather, the events of this first decade of African involvement in the movement showed a wide variation in the degree of acceptance of the ideas making up the doctrine and a similar diversity in the extent of participation in formulating such views in the nonaligned conferences. This is hardly surprising when one considers the range of ideas which, in accumulation, made up the political content of African nonalignment of this period.

Principal Themes of Political Nonalignment

Although the number of African leaders who devoted themselves actively to the propagation of nonalignment was relatively small, no single person was recognized as the high priest of the movement, and many of them were concerned with one or a few of its tenets. While, therefore, it is possible in very general ways to identify the principal themes of nonalignment, it is also necessary to pave any formulation with caveats as to the universality, cohesiveness, and application of these ideas. In short, it is hard to be more than impressionistic or to achieve more than an approximate consensus as to the recurring elements.

First, nonalignment was one formulation of an overriding aspiration, that of preserving the independence of the African nation. By no means the only way this desire could be articulated, nonalignment was nevertheless a call to judge foreign policy primarily on the basis of new-found freedom.

Second, nonalignment performed two very important tasks in the internal politics of African nations whose independence and political stability was not always secure. In states made up of disparate peoples and divergent traditions, nonalignment helped secure the support of these various elements in the body politic by reinforcing the goal of independence in foreign policy. In states where either the anticolonialist or pro-Communist groups were at odds with the government—or with each other—nonalignment became a means of neutralizing these critics of the established leadership.

Third, nonalignment, which was viewed by the skeptics as wishful thinking, was in another sense a supremely realistic assessment of the weakness of small nations in a world of more powerful nations. Proponents of nonalignment in this context argued that the only way for a small nation to maintain its identity was to stay out of the struggle among the giants. In a similar sense, advocates of nonalignment declared that military alliances with the powerful caused small countries to forfeit their independence, and abstention from such alliances was therefore considered the hallmark of the nonaligned.

Fourth, nonalignment could not escape the historical circumstances from which it emerged. Being part of the independence movement and intensely anticolonial in background, nonalignment sometimes emphasized primarily *not* aligning with the former colonial powers or their Western allies. Even after independence, since many colonial administrators, institutions, and connections remained intact, African leaders under pressure to seek further attributes of sovereignty attacked those nationals and nations closest at hand. Hence, Western critics of nonalignment claimed that it, in fact, leaned toward the East. This charge seemed reinforced when one observed the active participation of either the Soviet Union or Communist China, or both, in conferences which were ostensibly nonaligned. Such a climate of controversy not only made "real" nonalignment next to impossible to define, but made a real consensus on the term impossible, even at conferences of the nonaligned.

Fifth, nonalignment provided a welcome basis for co-operation among nations which were otherwise distant from each other in geography, people, or history. In that sense, it was an umbrella under which widely different nations could find a communion of views, such as anticolonialism or disarmament; a common cause, such as economic development or eradication of disease; or confirmation of their fears, especially concerning great-power pressures.

Sixth, nonalignment became a means of co-operation among nations with a view to exercising influence in world affairs which individually or in small groups they could not otherwise achieve. Inherent in this co-operative effort was often a judgment as to the moral right of the nonaligned as against the immorality of power politics as exercised by the great powers of the world. To some observers this appeared to be little more than moralizing based on weakness and was a point of view quickly forgotten when it came to issues closer at home. But to others, this point of view stemmed from an urgent search for human values and a desperate fear that they would be destroyed before they could be achieved.

Other elements were to be found in nonalignment, such as the condemnation of nuclear weapons, the instinctive aversion to military bases, and the danger of external involvement jeopardizing domestic economic growth. Specific situations or particular problems called forth variations in these themes. But like the abstraction of the composite "average man" in public opinion surveys, these six elements were the most common attributes of nonalignment during this decade.

Evolution of Economic Nonalignment in Africa

During the same decade between Bandung and Algiers, African leaders also developed their views with respect to economic nonalignment. More diffuse than its political counterpart, and neither as fully formulated nor as generally endorsed, economic nonalignment became increasingly important in African thinking as this period moved to a close.

Three general reasons account for the different state of economic nonalignment. In the initial surge of independence, the emphasis was more generally placed on political action and political effect. Most African leaders appeared to accept President Nkrumah's admonition of seeking first the political keys to the kingdom of full independence. Moreover, the various conferences dealing with nonalignment tended to emphasize the political more than economic.

Equally important, moreover, was the fact that African nations were already in a special economic relationship with European countries, both individually and with the Commonwealth and European Economic Community. All of them were heavily dependent upon external assistance from the West. It might be within the realm of the practical for many of the African nations to eschew military alliances, but it was obviously impossible for any government to avoid economic agreements with the former metropoles.

PRINCIPAL THEMES OF ECONOMIC NONALIGNMENT

Under these circumstances, it is understandable that the themes of economic nonalignment developed during the decade between Bandung and Algiers were neither clear-cut nor universally supported. Moreover, they developed more slowly in an era where political considerations predominated.

First—aside from the overriding desire to obtain as much economic assistance as possible—there developed a desire on the part of many African leaders to decrease dependence on a single foreign country. Stimulated in part by criticism from within the country, these leaders tended to equate a greater degree of independence with a larger number of nations giving them assistance. In the first instance this usually meant turning to the United States, whose technical assistance and developmental aid increased to a high point in 1963.

Second, for political reasons as much as economic, there developed a tendency to balance the West against the East. There then began dialogues with the Soviet Union, East European countries, and finally with Communist China. This trend was also attractive to a number of Africans as a direct means of increasing their total help, and it was attractive to some because they hoped to play off one power bloc against the other.

Third, the slogan of "aid without strings" became a part of the doctrine of economic nonalignment. In some cases, this became an emotional reaction against even efforts to make assistance more efficient; in others, this attitude was part of the negotiating process that took place as African countries sought to minimize the burden inherent to obtaining funds for economic development. Whatever the exact rationale, it is clear that some leaders exaggerated the strength of any alleged strings, and a number were certainly fearful lest their independence of political action be compromised by such agreements.[4]

Further, there developed among some spokesmen, especially of Sub-Saharan Africa, the point of view that the West had an obligation to assist their economic growth. The colonial powers

---

[4] This view reached an extreme point in Kwame Nkrumah, *Neo-Colonialism: The Last Stage of Imperialism* (New York: International Publishers, 1965; London, 1965).

(including the United States) had taken their manpower during the years of slave trade; they had exported their resources, both mineral and agricultural; and as developed nations they had a duty to help the less developed.

Finally, the preference increased in certain African quarters for multilateral assistance rather than bilateral. These proponents stated that since the United Nations, the International Bank for Reconstruction and Development (IBRD), the International Monetary Fund (IMF), and other specialized agencies were not controlled by any single power, it was better to obtain assistance in that form if at all possible.

THE PERIOD OF TRANSITION

Toward the end of the decade between Bandung and Algiers, African nonalignment began a transformation which is still under way. This transitional period, however, is too much with us to permit a satisfactory sorting out of the interaction which affected African nonalignment. What we can discuss, instead, are several probable causes of the change we are living through, and certain directions along which African thought seems to be moving. Infallibility in this analysis is clearly impossible.

In the first place, the change was certainly a product of the split between the Soviet Union and Communist China. This split destroyed one of the assumptions of the Third or Nonaligned World—that these countries of Africa and Asia were standing between two giant blocs. In fact this situation recently stimulated the editor of *Jeune Afrique*, the most widely read of francophone journals, to declare that the Third World had become the Second, since the Communist world, which had been the Second, had fallen apart. As the split widened and the competition intensified, the Chinese in particular became more militant in pressing nonaligned countries to join them in attacking the West and the Soviet Union. This not only revealed the hypocrisy of Communist co-operation with nonaligned countries, but it highlighted the futility of trying to get agreement on a nonaligned position in particular problems in which Communist China had a stake, such as its border dispute with India.

The history of the Afro-Asian People's Solidarity Organization (AAPSO) just before and during this transitional period illustrates some of these points. Originally an organization receiving considerable support from African nationalist movements and governments, AAPSO had become a battleground of the Chinese and Soviets by the time it held its conference at Moshi, Tanganyika, in February 1963. It had also been receiving less support from African governments, who found that, while the secretariat was located in Africa, it was, in fact, dominated by the two major Communist powers. As AAPSO became more and more a transparent front organization, it became less attractive to many African leaders. Moreover, when AAPSO sponsored the Havana Tri-Continental Conference which was finally held in January 1966, it became clear to the overwhelming number of African countries that AAPSO's interest in their continent was incidental to its interest in expanding communism.

The greater awareness in Africa of Communist China's militancy during 1965 was another element in the disillusionment with China as a colleague in nonalignment. For example, Chou En-lai's statement in Dar es Salaam in June 1965 that Africa was ripe for revolution implied a point of view and an apparent willingness to intervene in African affairs that was not appreciated by many African leaders. Equally sobering as an indication of general Chinese Communist philosophy and tactics was the long statement by Marshal Lin Piao in September of the same year. This statement, which was repeatedly broadcast by the Peking radio, placed the underdeveloped world, that is, Africa, within a plan of Communist conquest which, to say the least, contradicted African aspirations for nonalignment.

A dramatic change in the fortunes of nonalignment also occurred in 1965, during the two unsuccessful efforts in June and October to hold the Afro-Asian Conference at Algiers. The issues and maneuvers which accompanied the preliminary meetings of the Standing Committee and the preparatory meetings of the Foreign Ministers involved Sino-Soviet rivalry and Asian politics more than they did issues of African nonalignment. A number of African states had throughout been skeptical concerning the usefulness of the conference; the African Commonwealth nations came out in favor of postponement on the eve of the first attempt in June; and the cross-currents of debate divided even those African countries who attended the October meeting, when postponement was finally accepted by the participants.

It has been argued with some cogency that the failure to hold the Afro-Asian conference in Algiers did not finish off nonalignment, but it did bring to the end the cycle of Afro-Asian conferences, in which the rationale of nonalignment had been developed. It meant the end, for the time being at least, of international meetings such as those in Belgrade (1961) and Cairo (1964) whose *raison d'être* had been the value and influence which might be derived from international association of nonaligned nations.

In the meantime, there had begun a series of political changes in Africa which within a year would have considerable effect upon the personalities of the continent's leadership. The first occurred in Algeria in June 1965. During the following winter and spring, leadership changed in the Congo (K), Dahomey, Central African Republic, Upper Volta, Nigeria, and Ghana. These developments had two principal effects on African nonalignment. First, the changes removed two of the activists among nonaligned leaders, Ben Bella and Nkrumah. Second, as the pattern of leadership changed, there was a perceptible turning of attention away from distant foreign issues to problems of politics in Africa and at home.

Along with the series of political changes in the leadership of Africa, there also developed a new pattern in the issues which preoccupied the African nations. The Congo problem, which had long been a barometer of conflicting African attitudes on the United Nations, the role of metropoles, and the orientation of newly independent African nations, slowly became less acute as an international issue as the rebellion within the country was brought under control and the government at Kinshasa gained acceptability within Africa. Meanwhile, the issues in southern Africa were increasingly concerning the leadership elsewhere in the continent. The most dramatic of these emerging issues was Southern Rhodesia, whose unilateral declaration of independence on November 11, 1965, opened a new phase in the problems of southern Africa. Rhodesia occasioned a special meeting of the OAU Foreign Ministers in December 1965 and became a principal concern of the organization thereafter. At the same time, it became apparent to most observers that other issues in this part of Africa—the Portuguese territories, Southwest Africa, and South Africa itself—were occupying a larger amount of attention than matters outside the continent.

It would be a serious exaggeration to suggest that after 1965 a clear-cut swing away from political nonalignment took place. Circumstances were too complex to be neatly described, and the responses of the various leaders were inevitably in terms of the problems which were of particular concern to their particular country. One of the most articulate of African leaders, President Nyerere, mirrored the difficulties, dilemmas, and aspirations facing his country in a series of public statements in the summer of 1966, when he emphasized the costs of an independent nonaligned policy, the necessity for developing national economic and political strength, and the need for African cooperation to this end. As far as political nonalignment was concerned, he stressed the view that its enduring elements were protection of independence, friendship with all countries (or nonengagements with any bloc), and adaptation from any source of institutions which contribute to economic development. At the same time, these efforts could only be successful, in his view, when accompanied by co-operation among Africans to settle disputes and to build toward African unity.[5] Other leaders saw the problem differently, thereby confirming the general impression that there was no single response to the changing African scene.

An increasing emphasis on economic development also occurred in this period of transition, although its themes are difficult to identify, even in a tentative manner. It can be said—if not proved—that, proportionately, there was greater concern with economic problems as of the mid-1960's than earlier in the decade. Political independence had run its course for the time being—with the exception of Botswana and Lesotho in 1966—but political independence had not brought the economic growth that the leaders hoped or that many of the people expected. Hence, there was broader realization of the economic difficulties facing Africa and greater recognition that Africa faced a "long haul" in this field of effort. An eloquent description of Africa's needs and one nation's proposals to meet these problems was given by the Kenyan Chairman, Mr. Tom Mboya, at the biennial United Nations Economic Commission for Africa (ECA) conference in Lagos, February 1967.[6]

The consequences of the greater concern for economic development were numerous, and in their total effect they contributed to reconsideration of views on economic nonalignment which a few years earlier were widely, if not generally, accepted. As African leaders measured the magnitude of problems facing them and felt the continued pressure of their people for improving living conditions, they recognized all the more clearly the fundamental importance of external assistance. Facing a plateau in the over-all amount of assistance available from foreign donors, moreover, some African nations began to reconsider their previous positions and, along with this review, to modify some of their views and tactics of nonalignment.

One of the changes in emphasis took

---

[5] Julius K. Nyerere, "The Cost of Nonalignment," *Africa Report* (October 1966), pp. 61–65. (Memorandum to TANU of June 9, 1966); "Africa Faces a Dilemma," Speech at the University of Zambia, Lusaka, July 13, 1966; Address delivered at Mogadiscio, Somalia, August 23, 1966.

[6] Tom Mboya, "A Development Strategy for Africa: Problems and Proposals," Statement at the Eighth Session of the ECA, Lagos, February 13, 1967.

place in the attitude of African nations with respect to the European Common Market. The eighteen-nation-association agreement had been signed on July 20, 1963. Discussion for admission as associated members were opened by Nigeria, Uganda, Kenya, and Tanzania during 1965–1966, thus adding to the number of African nations which are seeking economic benefits through a formal association with European countries.

Another change was the higher priority given to commodity agreements, particularly those concerning coffee and cocoa. African countries began to take a more active role in implementing the coffee agreement and in seeking the conclusion of a cocoa agreement. Indicating a wider recognition of the importance of co-operative institutions for the regulation of such crops, the nations directly concerned settled down in 1966 to negotiations necessary to reach a workable solution to the cocoa problem.

A third trend has been a decrease in the suspicions directed against private business as agents of neocolonialism. Not only have a number of states enacted legislation to attract business, but, during the period 1964–1967, they signed some thirteen investment guarantee agreements with the United States and gave other indications of their interest in the co-operation of United States and other firms in their development.

These scattered illustrations, however, point to another trend which also suggests a greater pragmatism. This is the recognition of the role of "self-help" in economic development. Such an emphasis, of course, relates to one of the initial elements of nonalignment, that of achieving real independence. One can argue that "self-help" is a new way of dealing with an old desire.

Throughout most of the period of the rise and modification of nonalignment, African nations had welcomed international co-operation in the field of economic development. The United Nations Economic Commission for Africa, established in 1958, had been more active than its counterparts in other regions of the world. This trend continued during the period of transition with respect to nonalignment. The elements abetting the modification of attitudes towards nonalignment appeared, in this instance, to reinforce what had been gradually developing during previous years. The United Nations Development Program, for example, increased its African activities, especially in the direction of regional river basin projects. The World Bank similarly continued to expand its activities in Africa during the mid-1960's. International institutions were particularly attractive to these countries concerned with nonalignment, since they thought that any political conditions would be avoided by virtue of the nature of the lending agency.[7]

Another development in international organization, however, took place during the mid-1960's, which may have considerable effect in reshaping the African views on economic nonalignment. This was the growth within the United Nations of a common effort on the part of underdeveloped countries to devote more of the United Nations efforts to their problems. This feeling had helped stimulate the holding of the United Nations Conference on Trade and Development (UNCTAD) in 1964. At this conference, some seventy-five of the members from the undeveloped parts of the world grouped themselves together to further their common goal of rapid economic growth. Declaring

---

[7] An editorial in the *Ethiopian Herald*, March 29, 1967, is one example of this point of view.

that a division of the world between the affluent and the impoverished was intolerable, they hailed their unity at the conference as the first step toward achieving development.[8] Both the approach and substance of the seventy-five (now seventy-seven) suggest some of the concerns which underlay earlier nonalignment, but they began developing a far different strategy as they sought to secure greater economic benefits and, therefore, economic independence for the developing nations of the world. The proposal made on several occasions in the past year by President Senghor that these nations meet, possibly in Algiers, to prepare for the next UNCTAD conference, presently planned for 1968, may lead to further steps in this direction. In referring to this meeting as an economic nonaligned conference, President Senghor was adapting an old label to a new situation.

CONCLUSION

A description which indicates so many strands of development and so much diversity in the patterns of events cannot fail to lead to highly qualified conclusions. Yet it is clear, at the tactical level at least, that certain of the modalities of nonalignment have been discarded. For example, the large conference producing many resolutions has been abandoned for the time being. Moreover, some of the assumptions which gave rise to nonalignment have been called into question. Thus, the fears which metropoles instinctively incited in many newly independent na-

---

[8] For one assessment, see Sidney Weintraub, "After the UN Trade Conference: Lessons and Portents," *Foreign Affairs* (October 1964), pp. 37–50.

tions are receding into the background as time goes by. In addition, in the balance of attention which every leader must strike on the problems that preoccupy him, those matters closer to home have become proportionately more important than those which stimulated some of the nonaligned pronouncements of previous years. Political stability, relations with nearby nations, and Africa's own tranquility have weighed more importantly than Berlin, Tibet, or Cuba.

That this transformation is not a simple turning within, a sort of African version of isolation, however, is especially clear in the fields of economics. Recognition of the tremendous task of development has accentuated the need for national action, self-reliance, and self-help. But it has also stimulated more relations with the outside world, in particular Europe and the Western Hemisphere. It has brought renewed attention to problems of trade and commodities. And, as a long-term trend, it may well lead to a new community of interest among the underdeveloped nations. While any action in conference will be very different from the meetings between Bandung and Cairo, African leaders will nevertheless be dealing with some of the same issues which stimulated the first wave of non-alignment: national independence, economic development, and relations with non-African powers. In such a situation, it is safe to say that the pragmatism which is a significant characteristic of the transitional period through which nonalignment is now going will help to avoid some of the abstraction and unreality which characterized the African movement during its initial decade.

Bibliography

This bibliography is primarily a selected list of recent periodical literature on contemporary African politics. The material is culled from approximately two hundred articles we considered while compiling selections for this reader. It reflects the variety of topics and methods of analysis that are current in the study of African politics. We have also included a representative sampling of books in the fields as well as a listing of periodicals that are primarily devoted to African topics.

We wish to emphasize, however, that the bibliography is by no means exhaustive. Students seeking comprehensive bibliographies should consult, among other sources, the periodic issues of the *African Section* of the United States Library of Congress and such surveys as appear in *Africa, African Abstracts, International Political Science Abstracts,* the *American Political Science Review* (up to 1967), *Centre d'Analyse et de Recherche documentaires pour l'Afrique Noire, Fiches analytiques* [*et*] *Fiches Signaletiques: Sciences Africanistes,* (issued jointly with the Centre of African Studies, Cambridge, England), and the *International Bibliography of the Social Sciences.*

Periodical Literature

1. Determinants of Political Behavior

Abu-Lughod, Ibrahim, "The Islamic Factor in African Politics." *Orbis,* VIII, No. 2 (Summer 1964) : 425–44.

Albert, Ethel, "Socio-Political Organization and Receptivity to Change: Some Differences Between Ruanda and Urundi." *Southwestern Journal of Anthropology,* XVI (Spring 1960) : 46–74.

Apter, David E., "The Role of Traditionalism in the Political Modernization of Ghana and Uganda." *World Politics,* XIII, No. 1 (October 1960) : 54–68.

Dow, Thomas E., Jr., "The Role of Charisma in Modern African Development." *Social Forces,* XLVI, No. 3 (March 1968) : 328–38.

Eisenstadt, S. N., "Primitive Political Systems: A Preliminary Comparative Analysis." *American Anthropologist,* XLI (April 1959) : 200–220.

Irele, Abiola, "Negritude or Black Cultural Nationalism." *Journal of Modern African Studies,* III, No. 3 (October 1965) : 321–48.

Kilson, Martin L., Jr., "Nationalism and Social Classes in British West Africa." *Journal of Politics,* XX, No. 2 (May 1958) : 368–87.

Koff, David, and George von der Muhll, "Political Socialization in Kenya and Tanzania—A Comparative Analysis." *Journal of Modern African Studies,* V, No. 1 (May 1967) : 13–51.

Mazrui, Ali A., "The English Language and Political Consciousness in British Colonial Africa." *Journal of Modern African Studies,* IV, No. 3 (November 1966) : 295–311.

Mphahlele, Ezekiel, "The Fabric of African Cultures." *Foreign Affairs,* XLII, No. 4 (July 1964) : 614–27.

Rotberg, Robert I., "The Rise of African Nationalism: The Case of East and Central Africa." *World Politics,* XV, No. 1 (October 1962) : 75–90.

Smith, M. G., "Historical and Cultural Conditions of Political Corruption Among the Hausa." *Comparative Studies in Society and History,* VI, No. 2 (January 1964) : 164–94.

Smythe, Hugh H., and Mabel M., "Black Africa's New Power Elite." *South Atlantic Quarterly,* LIX, No. 1 (Winter 1960) : 13–23.

Turnbull, Colin, "Tribalism and Social Evolution in Africa." *The Annals,* CCCLIV (July 1964) : 22–32.

Wallerstein, Immanuel, "Elites in French-Speaking West Africa: The Social Basis of Ideas." *Journal of Modern African Studies,* III, No. 1 (May 1965) : 1–33.

Watt, W. Montgomery, "The Political Relevance of Islam in East Africa." *International Affairs,* XLII, No. 1 (January 1966) : 35–44.

Weingrod, Alex, "Political Sociology, Social Anthropology and the Study of New Nations." *British Journal of Sociology,* XVIII, No. 2 (June 1967) : 121–34.

2. Agencies of Political Mobilization

Drake, St. Clair, "Traditional Authority and Social Action in Former British West Africa." *Human Organization,* XIX, No. 3 (Fall 1960) : 150–58.

Fernandez, James W., "African Religious Movements—Types and Dynamics." *Journal of Modern African Studies,* II, No. 4 (December 1964) : 531–49.

Finlay, David J., "Students and Politics in Ghana." *Daedalus,* XCVII, No. 1 (Winter 1968) : 51–68.

Hazard, John W., "Negritude, Socialism and the Law." *Columbia Law Review,* LXV (May 1965) : 778–809.

Hess, Robert L., and Gerhard Loewenberg, "The Ethiopian No-Party State : A Note on the Functions of Political Parties in Developing States." *American Political Science Review,* LVIII, No. 4 (December 1964) : 947–50.

Kilson, Martin L., "Authoritarian and Single-Party Tendencies in African Politics." *World Politics,* XV, No. 2 (January 1963) : 262–94.

Little, Kenneth, "The Organization of Voluntary Associations in West Africa." *Civilisations,* IX, No. 3 (1959) : 283–300.

Mazrui, Ali A., "Islam, Political Leadership and Economic Radicalism in Africa." *Comparative Studies in Society and History,* IX, No. 3 (April 1967) : 274–91.

Mboya, Tom J., "The Party System and Democracy in Africa." *Foreign Affairs,* XLI, No. 4 (July 1963) : 650–58.

Nicol, Davidson, "Politics, Nationalism and Universities in Africa." *African Affairs,* LXII (January 1963) : 20–27.

Peil, M., "Ghanaian University Students : The Broadening Base." *British Journal of Sociology,* XVI (March 1965) : 19–28.

Schachter, Ruth, "Single-Party Systems in West Africa." *American Political Science Review,* LV, No. 2 (June 1961) : 294–307.

Shils, Edward, "Opposition in the New States of Asia and Africa." *Government and Opposition,* I, No. 2 (February 1966) : 175–204.

Trachtman, Lester, "The Labour Movement of Ghana : A Study in Political Unionism." *Economic Development and Cultural Change,* X, No. 2 (January 1962) : 183–200.

Zolberg, Aristide R., "Mass Parties and National Integration : The Case of the Ivory Coast." *Journal of Politics,* XXV, No. 1 (February 1963) : 36–48.

3. Structures and Processes of Government

Cowan, L. Gray, "The Military and African Politics." *International Journal,* XXI, No. 3 (Summer 1966) : 289–97.

Dryden, Stanley, "Local Government in Tanzania." *Journal of Administration Overseas,* Part 1 : VI, No. 2 (April 1967), 109–20; Part 2 : VI, No. 3 (July 1967), 165–78.

Engholm, G. F., "The Westminster Model in Uganda." *International Journal,* XVIII, No. 4 (Autumn 1963) : 468–87.

Fleming, William G., "Authority, Efficiency, and Role Stress : Problems in the Development of East African Bureaucracies." *Administrative Science Quarterly,* II, No. 3 (December 1966) : 386–404.

Hannigan, A. St. J., "The Role of Rural Local Government in an

Independent Kenya." *Journal of Local Administration Overseas,* IV, No. 3 (July 1965) : 165–72.

Hopkins, Keith, "Civil-Military Relations in Developing Countries." *British Journal of Sociology,* XVII (June 1966) : 165–82.

Idenburg, P. J., "Political Structural Development in Tropical Africa." *Orbis,* XI, No. 1 (Spring 1967) : 256–70.

Mackintosh, John P., "The Nigerian Federal Parliament." *Public Law* (Autumn 1963), 333–61.

Mazrui, Ali A., and Donald Rothchild, "The Soldier and the State in East Africa: Some Theoretical Conclusions on the Army Mutinies of 1964." *Western Political Quarterly,* XX, No. 1 (March 1967): 82–96.

Pratt, R. Cranford, "The Administration of Economic Planning in a Newly Independent State: The Tanzanian Experience, 1963–66." *Journal of Commonwealth Political Studies,* V, No. 1 (March 1967) : 38–59.

Rweyemamu, Anthony H., "Managing Planned Development: Tanzania's Experience." *Journal of Modern African Studies,* IV, No. 1 (May 1966) : 1–16.

Werlin, Herbert H., "The Nairobi City Council: A Study in Comparative Local Government." *Comparative Studies in Society and History,* VIII, No. 2 (January 1966) : 181–98.

4. Political Integration

Ake, Claude, "Charismatic Legitimation and Political Integration." *Comparative Studies in Society and History,* IX, No. 1 (October 1966) : 1–13.

Apter, David E., "Nkrumah, Charisma, and the Coup," *Daedalus* (Summer 1968) : 757–92.

———— and Charles Andrain, "Comparative Government: Developing New Nations." *Journal of Politics,* XXX, No. 2 (May 1968): 372–416.

Ashford, Douglas E., "The Last Revolution: Community and Nation in Africa." *The Annals,* CCCLIV (July 1964) : 33–45.

Austin, Dennis, "The Underlying Problems of the Army Coups d'Etat in Africa." *Optima,* XVI, No. 2 (June 1966) : 65–72.

Grundy, Kenneth W., "The 'Class Struggle' in Africa: An Examination of Conflicting Theories." *Journal of Modern African Studies,* II, No. 3 (September 1964) : 379–93.

Lemarchand, René, "Political Instability in Africa: The Case of Rwanda and Burundi." *Civilisations,* XVI, No. 3 (1966) : 307–37.

O'Connell, James, "The Inevitability of Instability." *Journal of Modern African Studies,* V, No. 2 (September 1967) : 181–91.

Post, K.W.J., "Is There a Case for Biafra?" *International Affairs,* XLIV, No. 1 (January 1968) : 26–39.

Rothchild, Donald, "The Politics of African Separatism." *Journal of International Affairs*, XV, No. 1 (1961) : 18–28.

Whitaker, C.S., Jr., "Three Perspectives on Hierarchy : Political Thought and Leadership in Northern Nigeria." *Journal of Commonwealth Political Studies*, III, No. 1 (March 1965) : 1–19.

Zolberg, Aristide R., "The Structure of Political Conflict in the New States of Tropical Africa." *American Political Science Review*, LXII, No. 1 (March 1968) : 70–87.

5. Development

Ahooja, Krishna, "Development Legislation in Africa." *Journal of Development Studies*, II, No. 3 (April 1966) : 297–322.

Allardt, E., "Reactions to Social and Political Change in a Developing Society." *International Journal of Comparative Sociology*, VII, Nos. 1–2 (March 1966) : 1–11.

Badeau, J. S., "The Clashing Paths to Modernization." *Journal of International Affairs*, XIX, No. 1 (1965) : 1–7.

Bienen, Henry, "What Does Political Development Mean in Africa?" *World Politics*, XX, No. 1 (October 1967) : 128–41.

Cutright, Phillips, "National Political Development: Measurement and Analysis." *American Sociological Review*, XXVIII, No. 2 (April 1963) : 253–64.

Dalton, George, "History, Politics and Economic Development in Liberia." *Journal of Economic History*, XXV, No. 4 (December 1965) : 569–91.

Dalton, John H., "Colony and Metropolis: Some Aspects of British Rule in Gold Coast and Their Implications for an Understanding of Ghana Today." *Journal of Economic History*, XXI, No. 4 (December 1961) : 552–65.

Eisenstadt, S.N., "Transformation of Social, Political, and Cultural Orders in Modernization." *American Sociology Review*, XXX, No. 5 (October 1965) : 659–73.

Friedland, William H., "Four Sociological Trends in African Socialism." *Africa Report*, VIII, No. 5 (May 1963) : 7–10.

Grundy, Kenneth W., "Nkrumah's Theory of Underdevelopment: An Analysis of Recurrent Themes." *World Politics*, XV, No. 3 (April 1963) : 438–54.

Kilson, Martin L., "African Political Change and the Modernisation Process." *Journal of Modern African Studies*, I, No. 4 (December 1963) : 425–40.

Lemarchand, René, "Social Change and Political Modernisation in Burundi." *Journal of Modern African Studies*, IV, No. 4 (December 1966) : 401–33.

Scarritt, James R., "The Adoption of Political Styles by African Politicians in the Rhodesias." *Midwest Journal of Political Science*, X, No. 1 (February 1966) : 1–28.

Skurnik, Walter A. E., "Léopold Sédar Senghor and African Socialism." *Journal of Modern African Studies,* III, No. 3 (October 1965): 349–69.

West, Robert, "Looking At African Development." *Africa Report,* XIII. No. 5 (May 1968): 58–61.

Whitaker, C. S. Jr., "A Dysrhythmic Process of Political Change." *World Politics,* XXIX, No. 2 (January 1967): 190–217.

6. Inter-African and World Affairs

Bowman, Larry, "The Subordinate State System of Southern Africa." *International Studies Quarterly,* XII, No. 3 (September 1968): 231–61.

Drake, St. Clair, "Pan-Africanism, Negritude, and the African Personality." *Boston University Graduate Journal,* X (1960): 38–51.

Elias, T. O., "The Charter of the Organization of African Unity." *American Journal of International Law,* LIX, No. 2 (April 1965): 243–67.

Good, Robert C., "Changing Patterns of African International Relations." *American Political Science Review,* LVIII, No. 3 (September 1964): 632–41.

Hovet, Thomas, Jr., "The Role of Africa in the United Nations." *The Annals,* CCCLIV (July 1964): 122–34.

Karefa-Smart, John, "Africa and the United Nations." *International Organization,* XIX, No. 3 (Summer, 1965): 764–73.

Mazrui, Ali A., "On the Concept 'We are All Africans'." *American Political Science Review,* LVII, No. 1 (March 1963): 88–97.

McGowan, Patrick J., "Africa and Non-Alignment: A Comparative Study of Foreign Policy." *International Studies Quarterly,* XII, No. 3 (September 1968): 262–95.

McKeon, Nora, "The African States and the OAU." *International Affairs,* XLII, No. 3 (July 1966): 390–409.

Meyers, Benjamin D., "African Voting in the United Nations General Assembly." *Journal of Modern African Studies,* IV, No. 2 (October 1966): 213–27.

Padelford, N. J., and Rupert Emerson (eds), "Africa and International Organization." *International Organization,* XVI, No. 2 (Spring 1962): 275–404 and 426–48.

Pauker, Guy, "The Rise and Fall of Afro-Asian Solidarity." *Asian Survey,* V, No. 9 (September 1965): 425–32.

Soper, Tom, "The EEC and Aid to Africa." *International Affairs,* XLI, No. 3 (July 1965): 463–77.

Touval, Saadia, "The Organization of African Unity and African Borders." *International Organization,* XXI, No. 1 (Winter 1967): 102–27.

Wallerstein, Immanuel, "The Early Years of the OAU: The Search for Organizational Pre-Eminence." *International Organization,* XX, No. 4 (Autumn 1966): 774–87.

Books

Apter, David E. *The Politics of Modernization.* Chicago: University of Chicago Press, 1965.

Coleman, James S., and Carl G. Rosberg, Jr., eds. *Political Parties and National Integration in Tropical Africa.* Berkeley and Los Angeles: University of California Press, 1966.

Emerson, Rupert. *From Empire to Nation.* Cambridge: Harvard University Press, 1960.

Fortes, M., and E. E. Evans-Pritchard, eds. *African Political Systems.* London: Oxford University Press, 1964.

Friedland, William H., and Carl G. Rosberg, Jr., eds. *African Socialism.* Stanford: Stanford University Press, 1964.

Geertz, Clifford, ed. *Old Societies and New States.* New York: The Free Press of Glencoe, 1963.

Gutteridge, William. *Military Institutions and Power in the New States.* New York: Frederick A. Praeger, Inc., 1965.

Hazlewood, Arthur, ed. *African Integration and Disintegration: Case Studies in Economic and Political Union.* New York: Oxford University Press, Inc., 1967.

Hodgkin, Thomas. *African Political Parties.* Harmondsworth: Penguin Books, Inc., 1961.

———— *Nationalism in Colonial Africa.* New York: New York University Press, 1957.

Hovet, Thomas, Jr. *Africa in the United Nations.* Evanston, Ill.: Northwestern University Press, 1963.

Legum, Colin. *Pan-Africanism.* New York: Frederick A. Praeger, Inc., 1962.

Mair, Lucy. *Primitive Government.* Harmondsworth: Penguin Books, Inc., 1962.

Morganthau, Ruth Schachter. *Political Parties in French-Speaking West Africa.* Oxford: The Clarendon Press, 1964.

Shils, Edward. *Political Development in the New States.* The Hague: Mouton, 1962.

Wallerstein, Immanuel. *Africa: The Politics of Unity.* New York: Random House, Inc., 1967.

Zartman, I. William. *International Relations in the New Africa.* Englewood Cliffs, N. J.: Prentice-Hall, Inc., 1966.

Zolberg, Aristide R. *Creating Political Order: The Party-States of West Africa.* Chicago: Rand McNally & Co., 1966.

Selected Periodicals Devoted Primarily to African Affairs:

(With date of origin, institutional affiliation, if any, and location)

Africa. (1928) International African Institute. London.

Africa. (1943) Instituto de Estudios Africanos. Madrid.

Africa Diary. (1961) New Delhi, India.

Africa Digest. (1953) Africa Bureau. London.

Africa Quarterly. (1961) Indian Council for Africa. New Delhi, India.

Africa Report. (1956) African-American Institute. Washington, D.C.

Africa Today. (1967) University of Denver, Graduate School of International Studies. Denver, Colorado.

African Affairs Quarterly. (1901) Royal African Society. London.

African Historical Studies. (1968) African Studies Center, Boston University. Boston.

African Notes. (1963) Institute of African Studies, University of Ibadan. Ibadan, Nigeria.

African Studies. (1921) Johannesburg, South Africa.

African Studies Bulletin. (1958) African Studies Association. New York.

Bulletin de l'Institut Fondamental d'Afrique Noire, Series B: Sciences Humaines. (1954) Institut Français d'Afrique Noire. Dakar, Senegal.

Cahiers d'Etudes Africaines. (1960) École Pratique des Hautes Études, Sorbonne. Paris.

Canadian Journal of African Studies. (1967) Committee on African Studies, Loyola College. Montreal, Canada.

East African Economic Review. (1954) University College, University of East Africa. Nairobi, Kenya.

Journal of African History. (1960) London.

Journal of Modern African Studies. (1963) Cambridge, England.

Mawazo. (1968) Makerere University College, University of East Africa. Kampala, Uganda.

Présence Africaine. (1947) Paris.

INDEPENDENT AFRICAN STATES and MAJOR DEPENDENCIES*

Name[1]	Capital	Area (thousands of square miles)	Population[2] (thousands)	GNP per capita	Year of Independence
Algeria	Algiers	920	12,146 (1.9%)	$220	1962
Angola	Luanda	481	5,258 (1.4%)	170	Portuguese possession
Botswana (Bechuanaland)	Gaberones	220	595 (3.0%)	60	1966
Burundi (Urundi in Ruanda-Urundi)	Bujumbura	11	3,274 (2.0%)	50	1962
Cameroon	Yaoundé	187	5,350 (2.2%)	110	1960
Central African Republic (Ubangi-Shari)	Bangui	238	1,437 (2.4%)	110	1960
Chad	Fort-Lamy	496	3,361 (1.5%)	70	1960
Congo, Republic of the (Middle Congo[3])	Brazzaville	132	850 (1.7%)	180	1960
Congo, Democratic Republic of (Belgian Congo)	Kinshasha	906	16,210 (2.3%)	60	1960
Dahomey	Porto Novo	45	2,462 (2.8%)	80	1960
Equatorial Guinea (Spanish Guinea)	Santa Isabel	11	277 (n.a.)	—	1968
Ethiopia	Addis Ababa	455	23,000 (1.8%)	60	c.1040
French Territory of Afars and Issas (French Somaliland)	Djibouti	9	84 (n.a.)	570	French possession
Gabon	Libreville	102	473 (0.7%)	400	1960
Gambia, The	Bathurst	4	343 (2.0%)	90	1965
Ghana (Gold Coast)	Accra	92	8,263 (2.7%)	230	1957
Guinea (French Guinea)	Conakry	95	3,357 (3.0%)	80	1958
Ivory Coast	Abidjan	125	3,920 (2.3%)	220	1960
Kenya	Nairobi	225	9,643 (3.0%)	90	1963
Lesotho (Basutoland)	Maseru	12	1,000 (2.9%)	60	1966
Liberia	Monrovia	43	1,090 (1.7%)	210	1847
Libya	Benghazi/Tripoli	679	1,682 (3.7%)	640	1951
Malagasy Republic (Madagascar)	Tananarive	230	6,615 (3.5%)	90	1960
Malawi (Nyasaland)	Zomba	46	4,042 (2.5%)	50	1964
Mali (Sudan)	Bamako	465	4,745 (2.0%)	60	1960

continued

Name[1]	Capital	Area (thousands of square miles)	Population[2] (thousands)	GNP per capita	Year of Independence
Mauritania	Nouakchott	419	1,100 (1.7%)	130	1960
Morocco	Rabat	174	13,725 (3.1%)	170	1956
Mozambique	Lourenço Marques	303	7,040 (1.3%)	100	Portuguese possession
Niger	Niamey	489	3,433 (3.0%)	80	1960
Nigeria	Lagos	357	59,700 (2.1%)	80	1960
Portuguese Guinea	Bissau	14	528 (n.a.)	—	Portuguese possession
Rwanda (Ruanda in Ruanda-Urundi)	Kigli	10	3,204 (3.1%)	40	1962
Senegal	Dakar	76	3,580 (2.1%)	210	1960
Sierra Leone	Freetown	28	2,403 (1.5%)	150	1961
Somali Republic (Somalia and Br. Somaliland)	Mogadiscio	246	2,580 (2.9%)	50	1960
South Africa, Republic (South West Africa)[5]	Pretoria / Windhoek	472 / 318	18,300 (2.3%) / 574 (1.9%)	560 / —	1926 / Administered by South Africa
Southern Rhodesia	Salisbury	150	4,400 (3.2%)	210	British possession[4]
Spanish Sahara	El Aiún	103	48 (n.a.)	—	Spanish possession
Sudan (Anglo-Egyptian Sudan)	Khartoum	967	13,940 (2.9%)	100	1956
Swaziland	Mbabane	7	375 (2.7%)	290	1968
Tanzania (Tanganyika and Zanzibar)[6]	Dar es Salaam	363	12,231 (1.9%)	70	1961
Togo (French Togoland)	Lomé	22	1,680 (2.6%)	100	1960
Tunisia	Tunis	63	4,548 (2.3%)	200	1956
Uganda	Kampala	91	7,740 (2.5%)	100	1962
Upper Volta	Ouagadougou	106	5,054 (2.0%)	50	1960
United Arab Republic (Egypt)	Cairo	387	30,904 (n.a.)	—	1922
Zambia (Northern Rhodesia)	Lusaka	291	3,827 (2.9%)	180	1964

*Statistics compiled from: (a) "Market Indicators for Africa" *Overseas Business Report*, April, 1968; (b) "Africa: Pattern of Sovereignty," *Geographic Bulletin*, No. 6, United States Department of State, Revised June, 1968; (c) *Africa Report*, XIV, No. 1 (January 1969). Readers should note that economic statistics are subject to variations in reporting and recording.

Footnotes: (1) Former name in parentheses; (2) Annual growth rate in parentheses; (3) Formerly part of French Equatorial Africa; (4) Declared a unilateral declaration of independence in November 1965; no state has announced *de jure* recognition of the government. (5) Since 1968 African Nationalists in the territory and the United Nations General Assembly refer to South West Africa as *Namibia*. (6) Tanganyika became independent in 1961 and Zanzibar in 1963. They merged in April 1964 when the two countries ratified an Act of Union after disturbances in Zanzibar.